How Arbitration Works

By

FRANK ELKOURI
Professor of Law
University of Oklahoma

and

EDNA ASPER ELKOURI, J.D.,
The George Washington University
Law School

REVISED EDITION

BNA Incorporated   Washington , D. C.

Printed in the United States of America
Library of Congress Catalog Card Number: 60-11972

TO OUR PARENTS

PREFACE TO SECOND EDITION

The period since publication of the first edition of *How Arbitration Works* has witnessed a great outpouring of arbitration decisions as well as writings by arbitrators and students of arbitration. Thus, the past few years might well be termed a "classical" period in the history of arbitration. Much new thought has emerged, much previous thinking has been modified, and some of the old has departed. This is convincing evidence of the progressive and dynamic nature of arbitration in our industrial scheme of things today. The words of John Day Larkin, speaking as President of the National Academy of Arbitrators in 1956, effectively tell the story:

> "The work of arbitrators, like that of judges, is in one sense enduring and in another sense ephemeral. That which is erroneous is sure to perish. The good remains, the foundation on which new policies, practices and procedures will be built. That which is bad will be cast off in due time. Little by little, old and outworn doctrines are undermined, both through the process of negotiation by the parties and by the sounder reasoning of those called upon to interpret the language which the parties have hammered out in the heat of economic conflict, and through long hours of patient effort to reach an agreement." *

It is with the above thoughts in mind that the Authors offer the second edition of *How Arbitration Works* to arbitrators, students of arbitration, and especially to employers and employees.

Frank Elkouri
Edna Asper Elkouri

---

* Larkin, "Introduction: The First Decade," Critical Issues in Labor Arbitration viii, xv (BNA Incorporated, 1957).

FOREWORD TO FIRST EDITION

This study is a product of the graduate and research program of the University of Michigan Law School. The subject was selected on the basis of its current and increasing importance in the field of labor-management relations and as one which, partaking of many of the characteristics of a legal institution, is suitable for examination by lawyers as well as others.

Mr. Elkouri has sought from an examination of the reported arbitration cases themselves to throw new light on the procedural and substantive aspects of the arbitration process. He has modestly, and, in my opinion wisely, refrained on the whole from attempting to pass judgment on the wisdom and soundness of particular decisions and of general principles which appear to be emerging in the cases. Perhaps a study which undertakes such a critique will emerge in time, possibly from Mr. Elkouri himself. Meanwhile, what he has done is important enough.

It is still too early to determine the full impact of arbitration on collective bargaining. The next decade should disclose whether the recorded and published decisions of arbitrators have developed some generalized thinking about collective bargaining problems which has become an important part of the utilized knowledge of bargainers and of students of the subject. If experience with other bodies of accumulated knowledge is any criterion—and I can think of no valid reason why the field of labor relations should be set apart as an exception—we are likely to see just such a development. Some may view this prospect with alarm, based on a fear of stereotyped thinking and undue reverence for precedent. This attitude seems to me to show a lack of understanding of the judicial process. It is simply contrary to every canon of progress to refuse in this field or any other to conserve the accumulated wisdom and experience of the problems as sound judgment may dictate.

Russell A. Smith
Professor of Law
University of Michigan
1952

ACKNOWLEDGMENT, FIRST EDITION

I wish to acknowledge my deep indebtedness to Professor Russell A. Smith of the Michigan Law School, who, as my friend and Chairman of my Research Committee, contributed in so many ways to this book. I also wish to acknowledge my special indebtedness to the following persons, each of whom, in his respective way, contributed generously to make this book possible: E. Blythe Stason, Dean of Michigan Law School; Professor Lewis M. Simes, Director of Legal Research at Michigan Law School; Professor John E. Tracy, Professor Edgar N. Durfee, Professor L. Hart Wright and Professor Burke Shartel, all of Michigan Law School; Professor Hobart Coffey, Director of the Michigan Law School Library; Professor Coffey's Staff; Judge Frank P. Douglass and Mr. Leverett Edwards, both of the National Mediation Board; U. S. Senator Mike Monroney; Professor John B. Cheadle, Professor Victor H. Kulp and Professor Maurice H. Merrill, all of Oklahoma Law School; Professor Sylvester Petro of New York University Law School; Professor George Wolbert of Washington and Lee Law School; Ford Motor Company Umpire Harry Shulman; Chrysler Motor Company Umpire David A. Wolff; Arbitrator Francis J. Robertson of Washington, D. C.; John D. Stewart, Executive Editor of The Bureau of National Affairs, Inc.; and, finally, the many arbitrators whose work has provided the basic material for this study.

Frank Elkouri

ACKNOWLEDGMENT, SECOND EDITION

In addition to the persons named above, the Authors wish to thank David Ross Boyd, Professor George B. Fraser and Professor Mortimer Schwartz, both of the University of Oklahoma College of Law, for their valuable suggestions in connection with the second edition.

Frank Elkouri
Edna Asper Elkouri

SUMMARY OF CONTENTS

(See following pages for complete table of contents)

TABLE OF CONTENTS

CHAPTER 1

ARBITRATION AND ITS SETTING

The labor dispute is a natural characteristic of our enterprise system in the context of worker organization and collective bargaining. Such disputes reflect the determination of labor and capital, respectively, to receive what each considers to be its "fair share" of industrial production.

Whether such conflict is an evil, and, if so, a necessary one, is not the concern here. What is important is that society and many disputants themselves recognize that production stoppages resulting from disputes should be minimized, and that an effective means of accomplishing this end is arbitration. Indeed, National Labor Relations Board Member Joseph A. Jenkins has declared: "I call arbitrators 'peacemakers' because they have it within their power to contribute more to the maintenance of good relations between conflicting forces in our society than any other group, whether public or private." [1]

This book deals with the workings of labor-management arbitration and with the numerous questions and problems that have confronted the parties and their arbitrators. The most realistic picture of how arbitration works and the most practical answers to its problems, it is believed, can be obtained through analysis of actual awards. So it is to awards that the Authors turn for their primary source material.

Arbitration Defined—Historical Background

Arbitration, to use the words of one writer, is a "simple proceeding voluntarily chosen by parties who want a dispute

---

[1] Jenkins, "The Peacemakers," 47 Georgetown L. J. 435, 436 (1959).

determined by an impartial judge of their own mutual selection, whose decision, based on the merits of the case, they agree in advance to accept as final and binding." [2]

Submission of disputes to arbitration may be made compulsory by law. However, except as otherwise indicated, the use of the term "arbitration" in this book refers to voluntary arbitration. When parties voluntarily agree to arbitrate their differences, it thereafter becomes "obligatory" upon either party to arbitrate at the request of the other. Although both parties have voluntarily agreed to arbitrate, arbitration will not be resorted to unless at least one of them thereafter so wishes.

Arbitration as an institution is not new, having been in use many centuries before the beginning of the English common law. Indeed, one court has called arbitration "the oldest known method of settlement of disputes between men." [3]

King Solomon was an arbitrator,[4] and it is interesting to note that the procedure used by him was in many respects similar to that used by arbitrators today.

Commercial arbitration has long been used as a substitute for court action in the settlement of disputes between businessmen.[5] International arbitration has been used for the settlement of differences between nations, differences which, if not removed, might lead to war. Development of labor arbitration in the United States began during the latter part of the nineteenth century; its most rapid advance has been made since the United States became involved in World War II.[6]

---

[2] Chappell, "Arbitrate . . . and Avoid Stomach Ulcers," 2 Arb. Mag., Nos. 11-12, pp. 6, 7 (1944). For a similar definition by a court see Gates v. Arizona Brewing Co., 95 P. 2d 49, 50 (1939). Also see 3 Am. Jur., Arbitration and Award, 830, par. 2.

[3] McAmis v. Panhandle Pipe Line Co., 23 LA 570, 574 (Kan. City Ct. of App., 1954).

[4] Bible, 1 Kings, 3, 16-28.

[5] For the historical development of commercial arbitration see Keller, Arbitration and the Legal Profession (Am. Arb. Assn., 1952).

[6] For the historical development of labor arbitration in the United States see Witte, "The Future of Labor Arbitration—A Challenge," The Profession of Labor Arbitration 1, 3-11 (BNA Incorporated 1957); Witte, Historical Survey of Labor Arbitration (U. of Pa. Press, 1952); Keller, Arbitration and the Legal Profession (Am. Arb. Assn., 1952); Oliver, "The Arbitration of Labor Disputes," 83 U. of Pa. L. Rev. 206 (1934).

Commercial arbitration grew up as an alternative to court action, while labor-management arbitration has evolved primarily as a substitute for strikes.

The development of labor-management arbitration generally has followed the development of collective bargaining. It has been most successful where collective bargaining has been successful. In the full-fashioned hosiery industry, for example, where the use of collective bargaining has been highly successful, over 1,500 disputes were decided over a ten-year period by the industry's impartial chairman. There was not a single reported instance of noncompliance with or nonacceptance of an award.[7]

Collective Bargaining, Mediation, Fact-Finding, and Arbitration

The distinction between collective bargaining, mediation, fact-finding, and arbitration can be seen more clearly if one considers each a stage in the relationship between labor and management. Collective bargaining is the first stage in the relationship; arbitration the last. Conciliation or mediation, and fact-finding, occupy intermediate stages.

Conciliation or mediation may be resorted to as an aid to negotiations. Technically, conciliation is carried on without the intervention of a third party, while mediation implies the intervention of an outside person, but the two terms are commonly used interchangeably.[8] The essence of mediation and conciliation is compromise. The mediator does not make a decision. Rather, his aim is to persuade negotiators, by proposals or arguments, to come to voluntary agreement.

"Fact-finding," as the term is most commonly used, refers to a method of handling labor-management disputes which

---

[7] Millis, How Collective Bargaining Works 460 (1942). For a comprehensive summary of the development of collective bargaining and its effect upon arbitration see Millis, id. at 871-907. For general evaluation of arbitration from the union, management and arbitrator's viewpoint see Guthrie, "Arbitration and Industrial Self-Government," The Arbitrator and The Parties vii-xv (BNA Incorporated, 1958); Segal, "Arbitration: A Union Viewpoint," Id. at 47-75; Ahner, "Arbitration: A Management Viewpoint," Id. at 76-92.

[8] Millis & Montgomery, Organized Labor 719, n. 2 (1945).

prohibits strikes and lockouts until an official agency, usually a fact-finding board, has had opportunity to investigate and report. Changes in the status quo, except when made by mutual consent of the parties, are prohibited during the "cooling-off" period, which runs concurrently with the period of investigation and report. The function of fact-finders is to investigate and assemble all facts surrounding disputes. After the investigation, a report is made which, unlike the findings of an arbitrator, the disputants have a choice of accepting or rejecting.

In arbitrating, parties are compelled by their own agreement to accept the decision of an arbitrator as final and binding. The objective of arbitration is adjudication, not compromise. Resort to arbitration usually occurs after the techniques of conciliation or mediation (and possibly fact-finding) have failed to produce agreement.

Arbitration As a Substitute for Work Stoppages

It has been said that the "most important difference between civilization and savagery is the habitual willingness of civilized men and nations to submit their differences of opinion to a factual test," and that "it is a mark of civilization to present reasons rather than arms." [9] Again, "industrial peace is not a God-given product. It must be cultivated and worked for constantly. * * * Conciliation, mediation and voluntary arbitration are the marks of civilization. They are the enemies of distrust and force. They do away with the fang and the claw." [10] Moreover, "if the rules and standards of orderly social behavior accepted for society at large are to be valid also for industrial relations, it would seem that settlement of labor disputes on rights should be sought as far as possible through judicial methods rather than through strikes and lockouts." [11] One method of settling labor-management differences

---

[9] Boland, "Labor Disputes: The Preventive and Cure," Arbitration in Action 6 (Dec. 1943).

[10] McGrady, "Industrial Peace: A Joint Enterprise," 2 Arb. J. 339, 343 (1938).

[11] Spielmans, "Labor Disputes on Rights and on Interests," Am. Ec. Rev. 299 (June, 1939).

without resort to strike or lockout is voluntary arbitration.

In America, the right to strike is looked upon as an essential economic freedom. Like all freedoms, however, it can be abused; it can be used unwisely and without sufficient justification. Many times, for example, strikes or lockouts have occurred not because of a real difference between the parties, but because one of them could not, or would not, of his own volition recede from a position irrevocably taken.[12] Here, of course, there is no social justification for a work stoppage. Even where a real difference exists, possibilities for a peaceful solution may make resort to force uncalled for. A difference that looms large to disputants may be without complexities when viewed by a disinterested observer. A basic tenet of arbitration is that the arbitrator will be able to look at the issue objectively; accordingly, a reasonable decision based upon the true merits of the dispute can be expected.

An agreement to arbitrate effects a complete surrender of the employer's right to determine the controversy by unilateral action and of the right of both parties to support their contentions by a show of economic strength.[13] This surrender has been the basis of considerable distrust of arbitration. One management argument against arbitration is that it substitutes for the experienced, responsible judgment of management the judgment of an outsider who lacks the responsibility for conducting the business. Labor, in turn, sometimes feels that giving up its freedom to strike, in reliance upon the understanding of an outsider who might prove to be not so understanding, involves too great a risk.

The answer to such fears is that the initially uninformed outsider is soon enlightened, for both parties have adequate opportunity to inform him as to their views, and he carries a responsibility for his decision akin to that of a judge. Indeed, some persons would place complete trust in arbitration.

---

[12] For views on use of arbitration for purposes of "face saving," see Warren & Bernstein, "A Profile of Labor Arbitration," 16 LA 970, 979 (1951).
[13] Pan American Airways, Inc., 5 LA 590 (1946).

Consider, for instance, the following view: "When the arbitration clause is made a part of a basic contract both parties know beforehand that any dispute arising will be settled by the simple, speedy, and equitable process of arbitration. Thus, they know beforehand that intelligent, intellectual reaction to disputes is in order; both parties know that, as individuals who believe in self regulation, they have arranged for any dispute that gets out of their personal control to go under the mutual control of arbitration. The party who doesn't want to worry about a dispute will demand arbitration. And then the other fellow can stop worrying too."[14]

Contracts that make arbitration the final step in the grievance procedure generally prohibit, for the life of the agreement or at least until all grievance machinery has been used, strikes or lockouts over arbitrable issues.[15]

Moreover, there is an increasing disposition on the part of labor and management to provide, as the final grievance step, for the arbitration of contract interpretation and application disputes. A study made by The Bureau of National Affairs, Inc., in 1958 indicated that at least 91 percent of the collective bargaining agreements in the nation's important industries provided for arbitration as the terminal point of the grievance machinery. A study made in 1952 by the United States Bureau of Labor Statistics showed a comparable percentage of 89.[16]

It is interesting to note, however, that a much smaller percentage of the agreements studied specifically authorized the arbitration of contract negotiation disputes.[17]

In the light of union liability for violation of collective agreements under the Labor-Management Relations Act of

---

[14] Chappell, "Arbitrate . . . and Avoid Stomach Ulcers," 2 Arb. Mag., Nos. 11-12, p. 6 (1944). Also see Zack, Arbitration of Labor Disputes 21 (1947).
[15] Even where the contract does not specifically prohibit strikes, the existence of an arbitration clause might be held to imply some restriction upon the freedom to strike, as in Mead, Inc. v. Teamsters Union, 23 LA 552, 553-555 (U.S. Dist. Ct., 1954).
[16] Moore & Nix, "Arbitration Provisions in Collective Agreements, 1952," 76 Monthly Lab. Rev. 261 (Bureau of Lab. Stat., 1953).
[17] Id. at 264.

1947, some no-strike clauses have been revised to eliminate liability for stoppages, especially where unauthorized.[18]

Many agreements now provide that the union is not to be held responsible for unauthorized acts of its members, but that it will make reasonable effort to prevent unauthorized stoppages.

Advantages of Arbitration Over Litigation

Arbitration claims among its advantages the saving of time, expense, and trouble. While it is true that the courts of some jurisdictions have recognized that parties to collective agreements have legally enforceable rights thereunder, costly prolonged and technical court procedures are not well adapted to the peculiar needs of labor-management relations. Arbitration, on the other hand, is more adequate "where a speedy decision by men with a practical knowledge of the subject is desired." [19]

The courts themselves often have acknowledged that judicial proceedings are not well adapted to the needs of labor-management relations, and that arbitration is the superior method of resolving disputes under collective agreements.[20]

This superiority of arbitration was emphasized by Professor Harry Shulman when he said that litigation "results in a victory perhaps, results in a decision in any event, which disposes of the particular controversy, but which does not affirmatively act to advance the parties' cooperative effort, which does not affirmatively act to affect their attitudes in their relations with one another. Arbitration can be made to do that." [21]

Parties to an industrial dispute must "live with" the judg-

---

[18] For instance, see West Penn Power Co., 11 LA 166, 176 (Dash, 1948).

[19] Webster v. Van Allen, 216 N.Y.S. 552, 554, 217 App. Div. 219 (1926).

[20] Ibid. For other instances where the court praised arbitration see statements by court in 27 LA 285, 287 (Miss., 1956); 24 LA 573, 576 (Maine, 1955); 23 LA 302, 304-305 (Ore., 1954); 22 LA 62, 63 (Pa., 1954). Also see dissenting opinion in Lincoln Mills v. Textile Workers, 25 LA 810, 820 (C.A. 5th, 1956), which opinion prevailed when the case was reviewed by the United States Supreme Court.

[21] Conference on Training of Law Students in Labor Relations, Vol. III, Transcript of Proceedings, 709 (1947). Also see comments by Loiseaux, "Some Questions About Labor Arbitration," Wash. U.L.Q., 1956 Vol., 51, 55-56.

ment or award rendered by the adjudicator. Courts of general jurisdiction are not often versed in labor relations problems. This recognized, some countries have established labor courts as a part of their judicial system.[22]

Like such labor courts, labor-management arbitrators are presumed to be familiar with the needs and techniques of industrial relations, so parties generally will be able to "live with" their awards.

The parties can make arbitration, as compared to litigation, quick and relatively inexpensive. Sometimes only a few days, and usually no more than a few weeks, are required from the time the arbitrator is selected until his award is rendered.[23]

Since the parties arbitrate voluntarily, quick compliance with the award is obtained in most cases. Only infrequently is court action required for the enforcement or vacation of awards.[24]

Other Important Roles of Arbitration

We have noted that arbitration is a substitute for work stoppages and for litigation. But it is much more than a substitute. Professor Harry Shulman declared:

"To consider * * * arbitration as a substitute for court litigation or as the consideration for a no-strike pledge is to take a foreshortened view of it. In a sense it is a substitute for both—but in the sense in which a transport airplane is a substitute for a stagecoach. The arbitration is an integral part of the system of self-government. And the system is designed to aid management in its quest for efficiency, to assist union leadership in its participation in the enterprise, and to secure justice for the employees. It is a means of making collective bargaining work and thus preserving private enterprise in a free government.[25]

---

[22] See Handsaker, "Labor Courts in Germany," 8 Arb. J. (N.S.) 131 (1953); Lenhoff, "Some Basic Features of American and European Labor Law: A Comparison," 26 Notre Dame Law 389 (1951).

[23] One study indicates that while arbitration is still relatively speedy, the time required has tended to lengthen in recent years. Ross, "The Well-Aged Arbitration Case," 11 Ind. & Lab. Rel. Rev. 262 (1958).

[24] A study by the American Arbitration Association indicates that in only about 1 percent of the cases studied had any type of court action been instituted in connection with any aspect of the arbitration. "Procedural Aspects of Labor-Management Arbitration," 28 LA 933, 939 (1954 statistics).

[25] Shulman, "Reason, Contract, and Law in Labor Relations," 68 Harv. L. Rev. 999, 1024 (1955), reprinted in Management Rights and the Arbitration Process 169, 198 (BNA Incorporated 1956).

Professor George W. Taylor has observed that "In a very real sense, the parties who establish their own labor arbitration machinery create a judicial procedure where none has existed." [26] In the latter connection, not all jurisdictions hold that collective bargaining agreements give rights which are enforceable in the courts. Moreover, the National Labor Relations Board refuses to exercise jurisdiction over contract-interpretation disputes. The Board "has held for many years, with the approval of the courts: [that] '. . . it will not effectuate the statutory policy . . . for the Board to assume the role of policing collective contracts between employers and labor organizations by attempting to decide whether disputes as to the meaning and administration of such contracts constitute unfair labor practices under the Act.' " [27]

Then, too, insofar as contract-negotiation disputes are concerned arbitration provides essentially the only available tribunal for the final and binding resolution of such disputes after negotiations and mediation have failed to produce a settlement. Thus, it is obvious that even aside from any consideration of work stoppages and their avoidance, cases are taken to arbitration simply to obtain an answer to the dispute.

Another role of arbitration has been described by Professor Louis L. Jaffe in such manner as also to protray realistically the spirit of the arbitration hearing:

"Arbitration * * * is a school, an arena, a theater. Everyone both participates and observes. The whole company of actors—arbitrator, union and employer officials, the griever, and the witnesses (mostly employees)—sits at one table. Argument, assertion, testimony, charge and countercharge, even angry abuse—sometimes spontaneous, sometimes 'for the record'—flow freely in quick, continuous intercourse. The arbitrator may let the discussion take its head for a moment, then rein it in; an occasional question, a request for clarification. Because the process is relatively free, it may assume many forms, some quiet and orderly, some volatile and discordant. The form is in fact a function of the general labor relations—of the maturity, the degree of mutual understanding and respect, the intelligence, of the opposing officials. * * *

[26] Statement by Professor Taylor in Preface to Freidin, Labor Arbitration and the Courts (1952).
[27] United Telephone Co. of the West, 112 NLRB 779, 781 (1955), citing Consolidated Aircraft Corp., 47 NLRB 694 (1943), enforced, 141 F. 2d 785 (C.A. 9th, 1944).

"Arbitration takes its stand in the very current of industrial life. The scene, the dramatis personae, the vocabulary, being familiar, raise no barriers to comprehension. The worker sees his case analyzed by his leaders, among whom I include employer as well as union officials. They reveal the clashing propositions at the heart of the grievance. The arbitrator relates his answer to basic industrial premises.* * *" [28]

Finally, it may be noted that a union might arbitrate a dispute because the employees or subordinate union officers directly involved simply could not be convinced that they were wrong; the company might do likewise in regard to its own subordinate officials. In either instance, higher officials may find it preferable to let an arbitrator make it clear to such persons that they were wrong. [29]

Arbitration and National War Labor Board

A great impetus in the use of arbitration was given by the National War Labor Board during World War II. The work of the Board constitutes an extensive experience in the use of arbitration. It was created by executive order in 1942 and was given statutory authority by the War Labor Disputes Act in 1943. Most of the 20,000 labor dispute cases determined by the Board during the war emergency were disputes over the terms of collective agreements. Of special importance was the Board's policy of requiring the use of clauses providing for arbitration of future disputes over the interpretation or application of the agreement. This policy of the Board laid the foundation for the popular practice today of terminating the contract grievance procedure with the final step of arbitration. [30]

Recommendations of the President's National Labor-Management Conference of 1945

The President's National Labor-Management Conference of 1945 was called for the purpose of laying the groundwork

---

[28] Jaffe, "Labor Arbitration and the Individual Worker," The Annals of the American Academy of Political and Social Science, 34, 40-41 (May, 1953).
[29] See Ahner, "Arbitration: A Management Viewpoint," The Arbitrator and The Parties 76, 80 (BNA Incorporated, 1958); Killingsworth, "Arbitration: Its Uses in Industrial Relations," 21 LA 859, 865 (1953).
[30] See Freidin & Ulman, "Arbitration and the War Labor Board," 58 Harv. L. Rev. 309 (1945).

for industrial peace by studying the major causes of industrial strife and possibilities for their elimination. It was attended by delegates representing the American Federation of Labor, the United States Chamber of Commerce, the Congress of Industrial Organizations, the National Association of Manufacturers, the United Mine Workers of America, and the Railway Brotherhoods.

In regard to the setting of new contract terms the Conference recommended that parties first undertake good-faith collective bargaining and thereafter, if necessary, conciliation and consideration of voluntary arbitration. It recommended, however, that, before voluntary arbitration is accepted, the parties should agree upon the precise issues to be decided, the terms of the submission, and principles or factors by which the arbitrator is to be governed.[31]

As to the settlement of grievances or disputes involving the interpretation or application of the agreement, the Conference recommended:

"4. The parties should provide by mutual agreement for the final determination of any unsettled grievances or disputes involving the interpretation or application of the agreement by an impartial chairman, umpire, arbitrator, or board. In this connection the agreement should provide:

"(a) A definite and mutually agreed-upon procedure of selecting the impartial chairman, umpire, arbitrator, or board;

"(b) That the impartial chairman, umpire, arbitrator, or board should have no power to add to, subtract from, change, or modify any provision of the agreement, but should be authorized only to interpret the existing provisions of the agreement and apply them to the specific facts of the grievance or dispute;

"(c) That reference of a grievance or dispute to an impartial chairman, umpire, arbitrator, or board should be reserved as the final step in the procedure and should not be resorted to unless the settlement procedures of the earlier steps have been exhausted;

"(d) That the decision of the impartial chairman, umpire, arbitrator, or board should be accepted by both parties as final and binding;

"(e) That the cost of such impartial chairman, umpire, arbitrator, or board should be shared equally by both parties.

---

[31] The President's National Labor-Management Conference, Nov. 5-30, 1945 (U.S. Dept. of Labor, Div. of Labor Standards, Bull. No. 77, pp. 42-43, 1946).

"5. Any question not involving the application or interpretation of the agreement as then existing but which may properly be raised pursuant to agreement provisions should be subject to negotiation, conciliation, or such other means of settlement as the parties may provide." [32]

Compulsory Arbitration

Many of the considerations involved in the use of compulsory arbitration are helpful in an analysis of voluntary arbitration. They are valuable in helping define the area of desirable use of voluntary arbitration. They also indicate pitfalls that may be faced in the use of arbitration generally. [33]

Compulsory arbitration has been defined by the Department of Labor to mean a "process of settlement of employer-labor disputes by a government agency (or other means provided by government) which has power to investigate and make an award which *must* be accepted by all parties concerned." [34] Stated otherwise, compulsory arbitration "is that required by law." [35]

Thus, even where neither party wishes to arbitrate, both may be required to do so under compulsory arbitration. At times there has been agitation for legislation to subject all types of labor-management disputes to compulsory arbitration where settlement by any but a peaceful procedure would result in loss to third persons or the general public. While there is considerable support for use of compulsory arbitration in such situations, its use otherwise is generally opposed by labor and management alike. [36]

The principal argument in favor of compulsory arbitration is that unions and industries have grown so large and our economy has become so intermeshed that one strike can paralyze a large part of the nation. This consideration is particularly urgent where the strike interferes with national defense.

---

[32] Id. at 46-47.

[33] For a discussion of the development of compulsory arbitration in the United States and abroad, see Williams, "The Compulsory Settlement of Contract Negotiation Labor Disputes," 27 Texas L. Rev. 587 (1949).

[34] "Should the Federal Government Require Arbitration of Labor Disputes in All Basic American Industries?" 26 Cong. Dig. 193, 195 (1947).

[35] C.C.H. Dictionary of Labor Terms.

[36] See statistics and views in Warren & Bernstein, "A Profile of Labor Arbitration," 16 LA 970, 972-973 (1951).

Moreover, local critical disputes, such as those in transportation and other public utility enterprises, severely burden the general public. Proponents of compulsory arbitration contend that in such cases state action is warranted to protect the general welfare; that, when collective bargaining, mediation, and all other steps have failed, the state should step in as a last resort to prevent ruinous strikes, and, as a quid pro quo, provide for the settlement of the issues on their merits.[37]

There is strong argument against compulsory arbitration:

"Compulsory arbitration is the antithesis of free collective bargaining. Labor and representative management are in complete agreement in their opposition to measures compelling arbitration. Both are aware that the existence of compulsory arbitration laws not only eliminates free collective bargaining in situations where the parties are genuinely at odds, but will frequently encourage one or both of the disputants to make only a pretense of bargaining in anticipation of a more favorable award from an arbitrator than would be realizable through their own efforts." [38]

It has also been said that while compulsion can force parties to submit to a procedure and temporarily force an unwilling acceptance of the results, forced obedience generates resistance and is a source of further conflict; [39] that Government arbitration tribunals would be subject to political pressure which would have little or nothing to do with the merits of the dispute; [40] that, if compulsory arbitration is to succeed in eliminating work stoppages, it can do so only by abolishing or restricting the right to strike; [41] and that the freedom to bargain collectively implies freedom to resort to trials of economic strength by strike or lockout if mutually satisfactory terms or settlement cannot otherwise be obtained, the right to strike being the only potent weapon possessed by labor in

---

[37] "Should the Federal Government Require Arbitration of Labor Disputes in All Basic American Industries?" 26 Cong. Dig. 193, 208 (1947). Also see Richberg, "Industrial Disputes and the Public Interest—I," Institute of Ind. Rel., U. of Calif., 59, 60 (1947); Huebner, "Compulsory Arbitration of Labor Disputes," 30 J. Am. Jud. Soc. 123 (1946).

[38] "Should the Federal Government Require Arbitration of Labor Disputes in All Basic American Industries?" 26 Cong. Dig. 193, 203 (1947) [words of Lewis B. Schwellenbach, while Secretary of Labor].

[39] Id. at 207 [statement of Boris Shishkin, Economist for the AFL].

[40] Id. at 219 [statement by Ira Mosher, Chairman of NAM Executive Committee].

[41] Id. at 205 [statement by Lewis B. Schwellenbach].

bargaining.[42] Furthermore, it is said that compulsory arbitration simply means that the Government writes a contract for the parties: [43]

> "Both management and labor oppose such an extension of control for they know that, if a free-enterprise economy is to be preserved, the terms of labor-management agreements should not be dictated by Government. This relationship touches the most vital activity of an overwhelming majority of our adult population. Freedom to contract in the sense that parties are free to refrain from entering into contracts, even where public policy requires the setting of some of the terms, is basic to the preservation of a free society." [44]

The most extensive experience (over 50 years) with compulsory arbitration is that of Australia. Writers who have made extensive studies of the Australian system are by no means in agreement as to its degree of success, but they all agree that it has not eliminated strikes.[45]

In 1920 Kansas enacted a compulsory arbitration act which set up a court of industrial relations for disputes in industries affecting the public interest. Broad interpretation of the Kansas law led to its application to industries other than public utilities. In 1923 the United States Supreme Court declared the wage-fixing provisions of the statute unconstitutional as violating the "due process clause of the Fourteenth Amendment.[46] In light of more recent decisions of the Supreme Court, however, it seems possible that the exercise of similar power by the states at this time would withstand constitutional challenge.[47]

---

[42] Id. at 221 [statement of Joseph A. Beirne, President of Nat. Fed. of Telephone Workers].

[43] Schwellenbach, "Industrial Disputes and the Public Interest—II," Institute of Ind. Rel., U. of Calif., 71 (1947).

[44] Id. at 74.

[45] See Sykes, "Labor Regulation by Courts: The Australian Experience," 52 Northwestern U. L. Rev. 462 (1957); Merrifield, "Wage Determination Under Compulsory Arbitration: Margins For Skill in Australia," 24 Geo. Wash. L. Rev. 267 (1956); Oxnam, "Industrial Arbitration in Australia," 9 Ind. & Lab. Rel. Rev. 610 (1956); Starnes, Survey of the Methods for the Promotion of Industrial Peace 42 (1939). The New Zealand compulsory arbitration system likewise has not eliminated strikes. See Zack, Arbitration of Labor Disputes 22 (1947).

[46] Chas. Wolff Packing Co. v. Court of Industrial Relations of Kansas, 262 U.S. 522, 43 S.Ct. 630 (1923).

[47] For a survey of decisions which bear upon the matter see Fairview Hospitals v. Hospital Employees, 22 LA 279, 282-289 (Minn. Sup. Ct., 1954). Also, Spruck, "Compulsory Arbitration of Labor Disputes," 47 Mich. L. Rev. 242 (1948); Huebner, "Compulsory Arbitration of Labor Disputes," 30 J. Am. Jud. Soc. 123 (1946).

Some states have enacted compulsory arbitration statutes for their public utilities. These statutes prohibit work stoppages. Some of them provide for outright compulsory arbitration; others require the use of settlement procedures which amount to compulsory arbitration. Much of this legislation was adopted about 1947, evidencing the growing public concern over work stoppages which cause hardship to the general consuming public. Such legislation, however, is of doubtful validity in view of a holding by the United States Supreme Court in 1951 that state power in this field must fall where the law conflicts with the Labor-Management Relations Act.[48]

Arbitration Costs

The arbitrator's fee and expenses often constitute the primary cost of arbitration. The parties and the arbitrator should always agree in advance, and usually do, as to his compensation or the basis upon which it is to be determined.

If counsel is retained, then of course counsel fees are involved. Additional costs are also entailed when a transcript of the proceedings is desired.[49] However, there are no court costs.[50]

The total cost of arbitration often is only a fraction of the cost of taking the dispute to court. Arbitration costs, except for counsel fees, generally are shared by the parties. Even where the parties had reached no agreement as to costs, the arbitrator required equal division since such "is common practice in arbitration." [51]

---

[48] See Amalgamated Association etc. v. Wisconsin ERB, 71 S.Ct. 359, 27 LRR Man. 2385 (1951). For a thorough discussion of this public utility legislation see Spruck, "Compulsory Arbitration of Labor Disputes," 47 Mich. L. Rev. 242 (1948); also, "New Jersey Act Providing for Compulsory Arbitration in Public Utility Labor Disputes Held Constitutional," 62 Harv. L. Rev. 516 (1949).

[49] See Chapter 7, topic titled "Transcript of Hearing."

[50] Parties who use the services of the American Arbitration Association pay an administrative fee.

[51] P. P. Williams Co., 24 LA 587, 592 (Reynard, 1955). Occasionally the parties agree that the loser shall pay all, as in 27 LA 611, 613; 22 LA 484, 489; and 16 LA 454, 457—in all of which cases, however, the arbitrator divided the costs equally since neither party lost all aspects of the case. For statistics and discussion regarding the cost of arbitration, see "Procedural Aspects of Labor-Management Arbitration," 28 LA 933, 939-943 (1954 data); Warren & Bernstein, "A Profile of Labor Arbitration," 16 LA 970, 983-984 (1951).

National Academy of Arbitrators

The National Academy of Arbitrators is a nonprofit, professional and honorary association of arbitrators.[52] While many of our most experienced arbitrators are included among the Academy's members, it is not an agency for the selection of arbitrators. Rather, it was founded in 1947 to establish and foster high standards of conduct and competence for labor-management arbitrators and to promote the study and understanding of the arbitration process. The Academy conducts an extensive and highly important educational program through its various committees, study groups, and its annual meetings. The proceedings of the annual meetings, including all important committee reports, have been published by The Bureau of National Affairs, Inc., and thus are easily available to all persons interested in arbitration.[53]

Government Agencies Serving Arbitration

The Federal Mediation and Conciliation Service's "basic arbitration function has come to be the maintenance of a roster" from which the Service can nominate arbitrators to the parties, and "the suggesting of certain procedures and guides that [the Service believes] will enhance the acceptability of arbitration as an alternative to the use of economic force in the industrial arena." [54]

The National Mediation Board performs important functions in the promotion of arbitration and the selection of arbitrators for the railroad and airline industries under the Railway Labor Act. These functions are described in detail in Chapter 4.

---

[52] The Academy's Constitution and By-Laws are published in Critical Issues in Labor Arbitration 205-208 (BNA Incorporated, 1957). For full discussion of the Academy, see Larkin, "Introduction: The First Decade," id. at viii-xvi.

[53] The Profession of Labor Arbitration (selected papers from 1948-1954 proceedings); Arbitration Today (1955 proceedings); Management Rights and the Arbitration Process (1956 proceedings); Critical Issues in Labor Arbitration (1957 proceedings); The Arbitrator and The Parties (1958 proceedings); Arbitration and the Law (1959 proceedings).

[54] Finnegan, "Federal Mediation and Conciliation Service," Management Rights and The Arbitration Process 96 (BNA Incorporated, 1956).

The various state mediation agencies likewise perform services in the furtherance and assistance of arbitration. The New York State Board of Mediation, for instance, maintains a panel of private arbitrators and the Board's members and staff also serve as arbitrators.

American Arbitration Association

The American Arbitration Association is a private non-profit organization which offers services and facilities for voluntary arbitration. It is an administrative agency solely, never acting as arbitrator. It maintains panels from which arbitrators may be selected, and it provides administrative personnel and procedures for cases being arbitrated under its rules.[55]

The Association is "devoted to the development and extension of the use of arbitration for the settlement of disputes in all fields of human endeavor."[56] In this connection, the Association conducts an extensive educational program through its various publications and through its promotion of arbitration conferences at colleges and universities.

---

[55] The Association's Labor Arbitration Rules are published in full in 30 **LA** 1086-1091.
[56] Braden, "Policy and Practice of American Arbitration Association," Management Rights and The Arbitration Process 84, 93 (BNA Incorporated, 1956).

CHAPTER 2

LEGAL STATUS OF ARBITRATION

By and large the law has played only a very limited role in labor-mangement arbitration in the United States. Fundamentally, arbitration is the product of private contract between labor and management.[1]

Thus private contract and custom, rather than court decision or statute, have shaped the principal features of arbitration. Having chosen arbitration as the best means of resolving their differences, the parties in the vast majority of cases have honored their agreement to arbitrate by proceeding faithfully to arbitration, by presenting their case informally but fully to the arbitrator, and by carrying out his award as the final disposition of the dispute—probably giving little or no thought to the legal status of arbitration at any time during the entire process. In any event, in only a very small percentage of cases has court action been instituted in connection with any aspect of the arbitration.[2]

Regarding the arbitration of hundreds of cases at Bethlehem Steel, for instance, Arbitrator Charles C. Killingsworth has observed:

"* * * the record of compliance with arbitration decisions is almost perfect, even though there have been some decisions with which one side or the other has been seriously dissatisfied. The Company has never refused to carry out an award in favor of the Union and has never challenged one

---

[1] Except where expressly stated otherwise, the term "arbitration" wherever used in this book refers to voluntary arbitration.

[2] See statistics in "Procedural Aspects of Labor-Management Arbitration," 28 LA 933, 939 (1954 statistics); Howard, "Labor-Management Arbitration: 'There Ought to be a Law'—Or Ought There?" 21 Mo. L. Rev. 1, 18-20 (1956).

in court. The Union has never authorized a strike against an award, and I know of only one outlaw strike against an award." [3]

In turn, the courts and the legislatures also have honored the "private contract" nature of arbitration by wisely limiting their roles in the process.

Indeed, the role of the law has been largely limited to the preliminaries and the "postliminaries" of the arbitration process. That is, the law has been concerned primarily with the enforceability of agreements to arbitrate, at the outset, and with the review and enforcement of awards at the close. The heart of the arbitration process, from the time the arbitrator is selected until his award has been issued, has been left largely within the exclusive control of and determination by the parties and their arbitrator. The temperance of the law, avoiding undue interference with the arbitration process, has permitted the high degree of flexibility essential to the success of the process.

However, even the limited role of law in the arbitration process involves some complex problems. The present book deals primarily with that part of the arbitration process which falls largely within the exclusive determination of the parties and their arbitrator, and does not deal extensively with either the legal status of arbitration or the problems involved in determining that status precisely in the various jurisdictions. The Authors, however, do offer the following brief view of these matters and they cite numerous detailed studies for the use of persons seeking exhaustive insight into the legal status of arbitration. [4]

Common Law v. Statutory Arbitration

Arbitration law is derived either from the common law or from statute, or from both. In many states the legal status of arbitration is probably governed more by the common law than by statute. While most states have some type

---

[3] Charles C. Killingsworth, "Arbitration: Its Uses in Industrial Relations," 21 LA 859, 861 (1953).
[4] Throughout other parts of the book, also, the Authors refer briefly to relevant decisional and statutory law.

of arbitration statute, many of them do not apply to labor arbitration. Moreover, many of those that do apply are very general in nature, leaving many details to be supplied by court decisions under the common law. Even as to matters covered by statute it has usually been held that the statute does not abrogate the common law—rather, the remedy is cumulative and not exclusive.[5]

Thus, for example, if a purported statutory award fails to comply in some respect with the statute, it may be treated as a common law award for purposes of judicial review.[6] The Washington statute, however, has been held to supersede the common law completely, the court declaring that "Contrary to the practice and procedure in the vast majority of the states, [Washington] does not recognize or permit common law arbitration."[7]

But the Washington court significantly indicated that the parties may elect to establish arbitration procedures of their own in lieu of using the statutory procedure, the court recognizing the contractual nature of arbitration.[8]

The right of election noted by the Washington court serves to emphasize again that arbitration is fundamentally the product of private contract, rarely restricted by positive mandates or prohibitions of the law; indeed, most statutory and common law procedures alike may be disregarded by the parties to the extent that both parties choose to proceed along other lines.

---

[5] See Jones, "Judicial Review of Arbitral Awards—Common-Law Confusion and Statutory Clarification", 31 S. Cal. L. Rev. 1, 2 (1957); Gregory & Orlikoff, "The Enforcement of Labor Arbitration Agreements," 17 U. of Chi. L. Rev. 233, 254-255 (1950); Williston on Contracts § 1927 (Rev. Ed., 1938); Povey v. Midvale Co., 22 LA 662, 664 (Pa. Super. Ct., 1954); Jones v. Johnson & Sons, 22 LA 585 (N.Y. Sup. Ct., 1954).

[6] Jones, "Judicial Review of Arbitral Awards—Common-Law Confusion and Statutory Clarification," 31 S. Cal. L. Rev. 1,2 (1957).

[7] Puget Sound Bridge & Dredging Co. v. Lake Washington Shipyards, 96 P.2d 257, 259 (1939).

[8] Id. at 261. The "Puget Sound" case was reaffirmed in Greyhound Corp. v. Motor Coach Employees, 22 LA 555, 558 (Wash. Sup. Ct., 1954).

The Common Law

While the common law of any given jurisdiction might not always accord in all respects with that of other jurisdictions, a general summary of common law arbitration and its relation to statutory arbitration has been provided by the United States Department of Labor:

"Common law arbitration rests upon the voluntary agreement of the parties to submit their dispute to an outsider. The submission agreement may be oral and may be revoked at any time before the rendering of the award. The tribunal, permanent or temporary, may be composed of any number of arbitrators. They must be free from bias and interest in the subject matter, and may not be related by affinity or consanguinity to either party. The arbitrators need not be sworn. Only existing disputes may be submitted to them. The parties must be given notice of hearings and are entitled to be present when all the evidence is received. The arbitrators have no power to subpoena witnesses or records and need not conform to legal rules of hearing procedure other than to give the parties an opportunity to present all competent evidence. All arbitrators must attend the hearings, consider the evidence jointly and arrive at an award by a unanimous vote. The award may be oral, but if written, all the arbitrators must sign it. It must dispose of every substantial issue submitted to arbitration. An award may be set aside only for fraud, misconduct, gross mistake, or substantial breach of a common law rule. The only method of enforcing the common law award is to file suit upon it and the judgment thus obtained may be enforced as any other judgment. Insofar as a State arbitration statute fails to state a correlative rule and is not in conflict with any of these common law rules, it may be said that an arbitration proceeding under such statute is governed also by these rules." [9]

Arbitration Statutes

State arbitration statutes are of three general types: (1) general statutes designed primarily for commercial disputes, but some of which may be used to a limited extent for labor disputes; (2) special labor arbitration statutes, which contain some detail as to procedure; and (3) statutes which merely "promote" arbitration by charging a state agency to encour-

---

[9] Ziskind, Labor Arbitration Under State Statutes 3 (U.S. Dept. of Labor, 1943). As noted hereinbelow, many jurisdictions hold, both under the common law and under statute, that awards ordinarily may not be set aside for mistake of law.

age its use.[10] One of the most detailed and most utilized statutes is that of New York, which was amended in 1940 for the specific purpose of covering labor cases.[11]

In 1955 a proposed Uniform Arbitration Act was promulgated by the National Conference by Commissioners on Uniform Laws.[12]

As of 1959 approximately one-third of the states had some sort of "modern" arbitration statute. There is no absolute uniformity among these statutes, and a detailed study of their provisions is beyond the scope of this book. However, it may be noted that provisions along the following general lines are frequently found in the "modern" statutes:

1. Agreements to arbitrate existing and future disputes are made valid and enforceable.

2. Courts are given jurisdiction to compel arbitration, or to stay arbitration if no agreement to arbitrate exists.

3. Courts are given jurisdiction to stay litigation when one party to an arbitrable dispute attempts to take it to court instead of arbitrating.

4. Courts are authorized to appoint arbitrators where the parties fail to provide a method for appointment.

5. Majority action by arbitration boards is authorized.

6. Provision is made for oath by the arbitrator and/or witnesses, unless waived by the parties.

7. Default proceedings (in the absence of a party) are authorized under certain circumstances.

8. Provision is made for continuances and adjournments of hearings.

9. Limitation is placed upon the effect of waivers of the right to be represented by counsel.

---

[10] See Ziskind, Labor Arbitration Under State Statutes (U.S. Dept. of Labor, 1943). Also see Howard, "Labor-Management Arbitration: 'There Ought To Be A Law'—Or Ought There?" 21 Mo. L. Rev. 1,5 (1956); Lillard, "State Arbitration Statutes Applicable to Labor Disputes," 19 Mo. L. Rev. 280, 282-286 (1954).

[11] For discussion of this statute and its application, see "Decisions on Arbitration by New York Courts," 16 LA 994-998 (1951); An Outline of Arbitration Procedure (N.Y. City Bar Assn., 1956).

[12] The Act is published in 24 LA 886-889. The Act as amended in 1956 is published in 27 LA 909-912. For extensive discussion of the Act, see "The Proposed Uniform Arbitration Act: A Panel Discussion," Critical Issues in Labor Arbitration 112-143 (BNA Incorporated, 1957); Pirsig, "Some Comments on Arbitration Legislation and the Uniform Act," 10 Vanderbilt L. Rev. 685 (1957); Frey, "The Proposed Uniform Arbitration Act Should Not Be Adopted," Id. at 709; Howard, "Labor-Management Arbitration: 'There Ought To Be A Law'—Or Ought There?" 21 Mo. L. Rev. 1 (1956). The Uniform Act was adopted by Minnesota in 1957 and by Wyoming in 1959.

10. Arbitrators are given the subpoena power.
11. Awards are required to be in writing and signed by the arbitrator, and some limitation is stated regarding the time within which awards must be rendered.
12. Arbitrators are granted limited authority to modify or correct awards.
13. A summary procedure is provided for (1) court confirmation of awards, (2) court vacation of awards on limited grounds stated by the statute, (3) court modification or correction of awards on limited grounds stated by the statute.
14. Courts are authorized to enter judgment upon awards as confirmed, modified or corrected; the judgment is then enforceable as any other judgment.
15. Provision is made for appeals from court orders and judgments under the statute.

To be noted at the federal level are the United States Arbitration Act, the Labor-Management Relations Act, and the Railway Labor Act. The Railway Labor Act deals extensively with arbitration and is discussed elsewhere in this book.[13]

While the United States Arbitration Act provides significant support for arbitration, the courts are in extreme disagreement as to whether the Act applies to collective bargaining agreements.[14]

The Labor-Management Relations Act lends policy support to arbitration by declaring in Section 203 that final adjustment by a method agreed upon by the parties is the most desirable way to settle disputes over the interpretation and application of collective agreements. Moreover, in the celebrated "Lincoln Mills" case, discussed below, the United States Supreme Court held that the Act provides enforceable support for arbitration.

Enforceability of Agreements to Arbitrate

One of the most pronounced concerns of the law with the arbitration process has involved the enforceability of executory agreements to arbitrate (executory in the sense that the

---

[13] See Chapters 3 and 4.
[14] For thorough discussion of the Act and the conflict as to its coverage, see Burnstein, "The United States Arbitration Act—A Reevaluation," 3 Villanova L. Rev. 125; 9 Labor L. J. 511 (1958). Also see Cox, "Grievance Arbitration in the Federal Courts," 67 Harv. L. Rev. 591 (1954).

arbitration has not proceeded as far as issuance of an award).
Under the common law either party may repudiate or withdraw from arbitration at any time prior to issuance of an
award since executory agreements to arbitrate future disputes
have no binding effect and will not be enforced either by way
of damages or specific enforcement, and since executory agreements to arbitrate existing disputes likewise will not be specifically enforced, although in some jurisdictions breach of the
latter agreements may be the basis of suit for damages (usually
nominal only).[15]

This common law rule against enforceability of executory
agreements to arbitrate still prevails in many states.[16] However, it has been modified by statute in some jurisdictions.
Agreements to arbitrate both existing and future disputes
have been made specifically enforceable by statute in about
one-third of the states (but not all of these statutes apply to
arbitration clauses in collective agreements).[17]

Under the statutes of some other states agreements to
arbitrate existing disputes may be specifically enforced but
agreements to arbitrate future disputes may not be.[18]

At the federal level, agreements to arbitrate both existing and future disputes are made specifically enforceable by
the United States Arbitration Act. As noted above, however,
the courts are in extreme disagreement as to whether that
Act applies to collective agreements. No such uncertainty
exists under the Labor-Management Relations Act of 1947.

---

[15] See Freidin, Labor Arbitration and the Courts 2 (1952); Gregory & Orlikoff,
"The Enforcement of Labor Arbitration Agreements," 17 U. of Chi. L. Rev. 233, 236, 241
(1950); Industrial Union v. Dunn Worsted Mills, 25 LA 41, 42-43 (U.S. Dist. Ct.,
1955). Also see American Bar Association Committee on Arbitration, "Report on
Labor Arbitration," 28 LA 913, 929 (1957); Howard, "Labor-Management Arbitration: 'There Ought To Be A Law'—Or Ought There?" 21 Mo. L. Rev. 1 (1956).

[16] American Bar Association Committee on Arbitration, "Report on Labor Arbitration," 28 LA 913, 929 (1957). Also see Gregory & Orlikoff, "The Enforcement
of Labor Arbitration Agreements," 17 U. of Chi. L. Rev. 233, 234, 241 (1950).

[17] The Lawyer and Arbitration (Am. Arb. Assn., 1958). These statutes are
listed and their coverage analysized in Lillard, "State Arbitration Statutes Applicable
to Labor Disputes," 19 Mo. L. Rev. 280, 285 (1954); Freidin, Labor Arbitration
and the Courts (1952).

[18] See Gregory & Orlikoff, "The Enforcement of Labor Arbitration Agreements",
17 U. of Chi. L. Rev. 233, 239-240 (1950).

Section 301 of the latter Act authorizes suits in the federal courts for violation of collective agreements in industries affecting interstate commerce.[19] In the "Lincoln Mills" case the United States Supreme Court held that Section 301 authorizes the federal courts to fashion a body of federal law for the enforcement of collective agreement provisions for arbitration.[20]

The Court declared that it was clear "that Congress adopted a policy which placed sanctions behind agreements to arbitrate grievance disputes, by implication rejecting the common-law rule * * * against enforcement of executory agreements to arbitrate." [21]

However, in another case the Supreme Court held that the enforceability of agreements to arbitrate must be decided on the basis of state law when the federal courts have jurisdiction only by virtue of diversity and not by virtue of any federal statute providing for arbitration.[22]

Review and Enforcement of Awards

While awards are carried out without controversy in the vast majority of cases, in a small percentage of cases the award is taken to court to be enforced, modified, corrected or set aside. Since the arbitrator's authority terminates under the

---

[19] Not all states consider collective agreements to be legally enforceable contracts. See Chamberlain, "Collective Bargaining and the Concept of Contract," 48 Col. L. Rev. 829 (1948); Witmer, "Collective Labor Agreements in the Courts," 48 Yale L. J. 195 (1938). But Professor Archibald Cox has noted that collective agreements do create legal and binding obligations "in almost every State to face the question in recent years." United Drill & Tool Corp., 28 LA 677, 683 (Cox, 1957).

[20] Textile Workers v. Lincoln Mills of Alabama, 77 Sup. Ct. 912, 40 LRRM 2113 (1957).

[21] Id. at 917. For analysis of the "Lincoln Mills" decision, see American Bar Association Committee on Arbitration, "Report on Labor Arbitration," 28 LA 913, 914-922 (1957), where it is observed that complicated questions of conflict between federal and state laws, and the question of outright federal pre-emption, remain unanswered. Also see Jenkins, "The Peacemakers," 47 Georgetown L. J. 435, 449-467 (1959); Jenkins, "The Impact of Lincoln Mills on the National Labor Relations Board," 6 U.C.L.A. L. Rev. 355 (1959); Perk, "Venue and Jurisdiction in Suits to Enforce Labor Arbitration," 35 U. of Detroit L. J. 505 (1958); Pirsig, "The Minnesota Uniform Arbitration Act and the Lincoln Mills Case," 42 Minn. L. Rev. 333 (1958); Arbitration and the Law, BNA Incorporated (1959).

[22] Bernhardt v. Polygraphic Company of America, 76 Sup. Ct. 273, 25 LA 693 (1956).

common law upon issuance of his award, any review and enforcement of his award must be left to the courts, except to
the extent that the parties or applicable statute give him authority to interpret or otherwise deal with the award after its
issuance.[23]

Although executory agreements to arbitrate are not specifically enforceable at common law, once an arbitration proceeding has been conducted and an award issued the courts
will take jurisdiction to enforce or vacate the award. At
common law the issuance of an award generally bars any
subsequent court action on the original claim, but suit may
be filed for enforcement of the award itself to the same extent as any contract.[24]

Some arbitration statutes provide a summary procedure
for court enforcement whereby the award is deposited with
the court for confirmation and entry of judgment thereupon.[25]
These statutes provide, of course, that if the court finds that
the award should be vacated, modified or corrected, the judgment shall be entered in accordance with that finding.[26] In the
latter regard, both at common law and under arbitration
statutes a party who is dissatisfied with an award may initiate
action for court review or may challenge the award when the
satisfied party seeks court enforcement.[27]

Under both the common law and the statutes awards will
not be set aside by the courts except on limited grounds.[28] The

---

[23] Regarding termination of the arbitrator's authority, see Updegraff & McCoy,
Arbitration of Labor Disputes 120-124 (1946), discussing also the question of power
in the arbitrator to correct obvious mistakes and clerical errors in the award.

[24] Williston on Contracts § 1927 (Rev. Ed., 1938). For full discussion, see
Dowell, "Judicial Enforcement of Arbitration Awards in Labor Disputes," 3 Rutgers
L. Rev. 65, 70-72 (1949).

[25] See Lillard, "State Arbitration Statutes Applicable to Labor Disputes," 19 Mo.
L. Rev. 280, 294-295 (1954).

[26] Ibid.

[27] See Justin, "Arbitration: Proving Your Case," 10 LA 955, 967 (1948); Updegraff & McCoy, Arbitration of Labor Disputes 125 (1946); Ziskind, Labor Arbitration Under State Statutes 21 (U. S. Dept. of Labor, 1943).

[28] See, generally, "Judicial Review of Arbitration Awards on the Merits," 63
Harv. L. Rev. 681 (1950).

grounds for attacking awards at common law are generally limited to: [29]

1. Fraud, misconduct or partiality by the arbitrator, or gross unfairness in the conduct of the proceedings.

2. Fraud or misconduct by the parties affecting the result.

3. Complete want of jurisdiction in the arbitrator. Also, failure of the arbitrator to stay within his jurisdiction or to carry it out fully— that is, he decides too much or too little.

4. Violation of public policy as by ordering the commission of an unlawful act.[30]

Under the common law awards generally will not be set aside for mistake of law or fact (and as noted hereinbelow, this is also generally true under the statutes). As one court has stated, "Unless they are restricted by the submission, the arbitrators are the final judges of both law and fact and their award will not be disturbed for a mistake of either." [31]

The limited grounds for setting aside awards under many of the state statutes and under the United States Arbitration Act are along the following general lines (which differ little from the common law grounds): [32]

1. The award was procured by corruption, fraud, or other undue means.

---

[29] See "When May an Arbitrator's Award be Vacated?" 7 DePaul L. Rev. 236 (1958); Rothstein, "Vacation of Awards for Fraud, Bias, Misconduct and Partiality," 10 Vanderbilt L. Rev. 813 (1957); Freidin, Labor Arbitration and the Courts 31 (1952); Updegraff & McCoy, Arbitration of Labor Disputes 117, 120, 126-127 (1946).

[30] Regarding the latter ground, see Sturges, Commercial Arbitrations and Awards § 61, p. 202 (1930). Also see Cox, "The Place of Law in Labor Arbitration," The Profession of Labor Arbitration 76, 78-79 (BNA Incorporated, 1957).

[31] Reading Tube Corp. v. Steel Workers Federation, 20 LA 780, 782 (Pa. Super. Ct., 1953). For large collections of cases to the same general effect, see 6 C.J.S., Arbitration and Award, § 105, p. 251; 3 Am. Jur., Arbitration and Award, § 92, pp. 923-924. Under an exception applied by some states an award will be set aside for mistake of law if the arbitrator clearly intended to decide according to law and was in error as to the law. See Collingswood Mills v. Hosiery Workers, 23 LA 16 (N.J. Super. Ct., 1954); In re Finn, 22 LA 870, 871 (N.Y. Sup. Ct., 1954). One writer has aptly explained, however, that this exception "makes little sense." Freidin, Labor Arbitration and the Courts 34 (1952). Regarding the use of substantive law in arbitration, see Chapter 10.

[32] See Lillard, "State Arbitration Statutes Applicable to Labor Disputes," 19 Mo. L. Rev. 280, 293 (1954); Freidin, Labor Arbitration and the Courts 31-44 (1952); Justin, "Arbitration: Proving Your Case," 10 LA 955, 967 (1948); Uniform Arbitration Act, 27 LA 909, 910-911; United States Arbitration Act, 9 U.S.C. § 10. Also see Jones, "The Nature of the Court's 'Jurisdiction' in Statutory Arbitration Post-Award Motions," 46 Cal. L. Rev. 411 (1958); Dowell, "Judicial Enforcement of Arbitration Awards in Labor Disputes," 3 Rutgers L. Rev. 65, 86 (1944).

2. The arbitrator was guilty of evident partiality, corruption, or misconduct.

3. The arbitrator refused to postpone the hearing upon sufficient cause shown, or refused to hear material evidence; or otherwise so conducted the hearing as to prejudice substantially the rights of a party.

4. The arbitrator exceeded his powers, or so imperfectly executed them that a mutual, final and definite award upon the subject matter submitted was not made.

5. There was no valid agreement to arbitrate and objection to that fact was properly raised.

Some statutes authorize the courts to modify or correct awards on grounds essentially as follows: [33]

1. Where there was an evident miscalculation of figures, or an evident mistake in the description of any person, thing or property referred to in the award.

2. Where the arbitrators have awarded upon a matter not submitted to them, not affecting the merits of the decision upon the matter submitted.

3. Where the award is imperfect in a matter of form not affecting the merits of the controversy.

It is obvious from the above that the statutes generally provide no right of court review for errors of law or errors as to finding of fact.[34]

---

[33] See Lillard, "State Arbitration Statutes Applicable to Labor Disputes," 19 Mo. L. Rev. 280, 294 (1954); Justin, "Arbitration: Proving Your Case," 10 LA 955, 967 (1948); Uniform Arbitration Act, 27 LA 909, 911; United States Arbitration Act, 9 U.S.C. § 11. In absence of statutory authority the courts may not be permitted to modify awards. See Updegraff & McCoy, Arbitration of Labor Disputes 127 (1946).
[34] Also see Justin, "Arbitration: Proving Your Case," 10 LA 955, 967 (1948).

CHAPTER 3

SCOPE OF LABOR ARBITRATION

While many labor disputes are clearly suitable for arbitration, one of the potential hazards of labor arbitration has been said to be an "overoptimistic estimate" of its effective scope, "which tends to consider it an all-purpose tool or panacea for the resolution of any and all disputes which the parties fail to settle privately." [1]

Certainly, not all disputes are equally suitable for arbitration. The most popular use of labor arbitration is with respect to disputes involving the interpretation or application of the collective agreement. There is much less enthusiasm for its use, even on a voluntary basis, as a means of resolving disputes over terms of new or renewal contracts. [2]

There are some matters, too, which are considered to belong so intimately to one or the other of the parties that they are seldom submitted to arbitration. [3] Management naturally hesitates to submit to arbitration issues involving its normal prerogatives in the conduct of the business, such as the determination of methods of operation, operation policies, and finances. Labor usually considers that the settlement of an internal union conflict is "a matter in which management should not be permitted to participate, and it would be undesirable to permit the company to become involved in this question indirectly or in any manner whatsover." [4] Improper

---

[1] Davey, "Hazards in Labor Arbitration," 1 Ind. and Lab. Rel. Rev. 386, 387 (1948). Later Mr. Davey indicated his "impression" that "an increasing number of companies are avoiding excessive arbitration in an intelligent and discriminating fashion." Davey, "Labor Arbitration: A Current Appraisal," 9 Ind. and Lab. Rel. Rev. 85, 90 (1955).

[2] For extent of acceptance of the various uses of arbitration, see survey by Warren & Bernstein, "A Profile of Labor Arbitration," 16 LA 970, 971-973 (1951).

[3] See Moore & Mix, "Arbitration Provisions in Collective Agreements," 76 Monthly Lab. Rev. 261-264 (1953); Lapp, Labor Arbitration, 44 (1942).

[4] Babcock & Wilcox Co., 8 LA 58, 61 (Dworkin, 1947).

activities of union officials in the administration of grievances have been held to be improper subjects for arbitration, since a contrary approach "might well result in a form of policing of internal union affairs by a third party who clearly was not intended nor competent to accomplish such a purpose. * * * The remedy lies with the union membership, which has the ultimate power, through democratic means, to control the selection of their representatives." [5]

Also, the right to strike ordinarily would not be considered by labor to be a proper subject for arbitration. While labor hesitates to submit such matters to arbitration with management as a party, there is a significant trend toward increased use of arbitration to resolve inter-union disputes (especially jurisdictional disputes); in these cases both parties to the arbitration are unions. [6]

While it has been suggested that "Arbitration is most effective when used sparingly," [7] Ford Umpire Harry H. Platt has declared that "it would hardly be right to judge the effectiveness or worth of an arbitration system or the health of a labor-mangement relationship by the number of cases decided each year by the umpire." [8] Umpire Platt asserted that labor relations at Ford are "at least as good as at Chrysler" even though Ford has a much heavier arbitration caseload than Chrysler. [9]

Disputes on 'Rights' and 'Interests'

The distinction between "rights" and "interests" is basic in the classification of labor disputes and in views as to arbi-

---

[5] Spencer Kellogg & Sons, Inc., 1 LA 291, 294 (Miller, 1945). Cf., North American Aviation, Inc., 17 LA 199, 204 (Komaroff, 1951).

[6] See, for example, Upholsterers' Union (AFL) v. Furniture Workers (CIO), 23 LA 827 (Cole, 1955). For a general discussion, see Cole, Feinsinger & Dunlop, "Arbitration of Jurisdictional Disputes," Arbitration Today, 149-165 (BNA Incorporated, 1955).

[7] Davey, "Labor Arbitration: A Current Appraisal," 9 Ind. and Lab. Rel. Rev. 85, 90 (1955).

[8] Comments by Umpire Platt in "The Chrysler-UAW Umpire System," The Arbitrator and The Parties, 111, 142-143 (BNA Incorporated, 1958).

[9] Ibid. Umpire Platt offered numerous explanations and justifications for the heavier caseload at Ford.

trability. Disputes as to "rights" involve the interpretation or application of laws, agreements, or customary practices, whereas disputes as to "interests" involve the question of what shall be the basic terms and conditions of employment. This nomenclature is derived from the Scandinavian countries, which have treated the distinction between rights and interests as basic in their labor legislation. Sweden, for instance, has permanent national labor courts whose jurisdiction is carefully restricted to disputes concerning "rights" under collective agreements.[10]

The United States Supreme Court has explained the fundamental distinction between "interests" and "rights" disputes:

"The first relates to disputes over the formation of collective agreements or efforts to secure them. They arise where there is no such agreement or where it is sought to change the terms of one, and therefore the issue is not whether an existing agreement controls the controversy. They look to the acquisition of rights for the future, not to assertion of rights claimed to have vested in the past.

"The second class, however, contemplates the existence of a collective agreement already concluded or, at any rate, a situation in which no effort is made to bring about a formal change in terms or to create a new one. The dispute relates either to the meaning or proper application of a particular provision with reference to a specific situation or to an omitted case. In the latter event the claim is founded upon some incident of the employment relation, or asserted one, independent of those covered by the collective agreement * * *. In either case the claim is to rights accrued, not merely to have new ones created for the future." [11]

Disputes as to "rights" are adjudicable under the laws or agreements on which the rights are based, and are readily adaptable to settlement by arbitration. Disputes as to "interests," on the other hand, involve questions of policy which, for lack of predetermined standards, are not generally regarded as justiciable or arbitrable. Yet, many "interests" disputes are settled by arbitration, and, as was seen in Chapter 1, some states have concluded that public utility "interests" disputes involve

---

[10] Spielmans, "Labor Disputes on Rights and on Interests," 29 Am. Econ. Rev. 299 (1939).

[11] Elgin, J. & E. Ry. Co. v. Burley, 65 S.Ct. 1282, 1290, 16 LRRM 749 (1945), involving the Railway Labor Act. The Court noted that the two basic types of disputes are traditionally called "major" and "minor" disputes in the railroad industry. Ibid. The Railway Labor Act is discussed hereinbelow.

such serious risk of public harm that a requirement of compulsory arbitration of such disputes is justified. Sometimes laws are passed which settle specific contested economic issues; and in such cases there is, of course, a transfer of the contested matter from the zone of "interests" to that of "rights." [12]

It is highly important that the distinction between these two basic types of disputes be recognized and preserved in considering methods of settlement. This distinction has for many years been recognized in the full-fashioned hosiery industry, which has adopted one method of procedure for "rights" disputes and another for "interests" disputes. This has been explained:

> "The jurisdiction of the Impartial Chairman does not extend to disputes regarding the general level of wages in the industry. Since decisions of this type would involve changing all the rates specified in the Agreement, they are excluded from his jurisdiction by the provision which denies him the right to change any of the terms of the contract. Furthermore, the parties have established in the Agreement a special procedure for handling disputes over general wage-level changes. The 'flexibility clause' permits either party to seek a change in the general wage level at any time during the life of the agreement and provides for the establishment of a special wage tribunal in case the parties cannot agree on the percentage change to be made." [13]

The industry has considered that, because there is no uniformly accepted body of principles for determining wage levels, one or both of the parties will be likely to feel that a given "interests" decision is grossly inequitable. Recognition of this fact gives special point to the use of one set of machinery for the arbitration of "rights" disputes and another for "interests" disputes in permanent umpire or permanent chairman systems. Ill feeling against an arbitrator after an "interests" decision may be so general and so severe that one decision will destroy his usefulness to the industry.

Of the first six arbitrators chosen to determine general wage-level changes under the flexibility clause in the hosiery

---

[12] For a splendid article on this subject see Spielmans, "Labor Disputes on Rights and on Interests," 29 Am. Econ. Rev. 299 (1939).

[13] Kennedy, Effective Labor Arbitration, 37 (1948). This is a comprehensive treatise of the Impartial Chairmanship of the Full-Fashioned Hosiery Industry.

industry, not one was invited to serve a second time. Since it is not easy to find a person who combines the specialized knowledge of the industry and the type of personality which is necessary for success as an Impartial Chairman, the parties have decided not to risk the loss of a good Impartial Chairman by asking him to decide general wage-level cases which can be handled by other arbitrators.[14] The same problem is recognized in respect to other new contract issues.[15]

Railroad labor legislation of the United States has also come to recognize the distinction between "rights" and "interests" disputes. The first three federal acts did not differentiate between them,[16] but the Transportation Act of 1920 provided for special treatment of the two types of disputes. Since then the distinction has been sharpened.

The Railway Labor Act of 1926, as amended in 1934, created the National Railroad Adjustment Board, which, upon submission of a complaint by either party, takes jurisdiction over "disputes" between an employee or group of employees and a carrier or carriers growing out of grievances or out of the interpretation or application of agreements concerning rates of pay, rules, or working conditions * * *" after they have been "handled in the usual manner up to and including the chief operating officer of the carrier designated to handle such disputes." On the other hand, disputes concerning "changes in rates of pay, rules, or working conditions not adjusted by the parties in conference" and "any other dispute not referable to the National Railroad Adjustment Board and not adjusted in conference between the parties or where conferences are refused" are handled by the National Mediation Board.

The function of the Adjustment Board is to interpret and apply collective agreements, not to make or modify them. The Mediation Board, on the other hand, is directed to help the parties, through mediation, to reach agreement on the terms of collective agreements and, upon failure to bring

---

[14] Id. at 38-39.
[15] Id. at 39.
[16] Acts of 1888, 1898, and 1913.

about an agreement, to attempt to induce the parties to submit their dispute to voluntary arbitration.[17]

Recognizing the important distinction between the arbitration of "rights" and "interests" disputes, the various appointing agencies consider the type of dispute when requested by the parties to provide assistance in the selection of an arbitrator.[18]

While most disputes clearly fall into one of the two categories, basically involving "rights" or basically involving "interests," some disputes involve elements of both and cannot be clearly classified as falling exclusively within either of the categories. Arbitrability of the latter cases depends, as in other cases, upon whether the arbitration clause or submission is broad enough to cover the dispute.

Purpose and Subjects of 'Interests' Arbitration

It is generally believed that the best labor-management contracts are those that are negotiated through collective bargaining without outside assistance. There are frequent instances, however, where the parties find it difficult or impossible to reach agreement by direct negotiation. In these instances, they may choose to settle the conflict by a test of strength, making use of the strike or lockout. But this can be costly and injurious to both parties. Moreover, a suspension of operations may bring great hardship upon others, as in the case of a cessation of public utility activities, for which neither labor nor management may wish to risk public censure.

In these situations voluntary arbitration is a way out of the dilemma. One arbitration board, which was itself determining the provisions to be included in a utility renewal contract, stated the case for arbitration as follows: "Arbitration should be a last resort and not an easy pillow on which to fall just because difficulties are encountered. There is some evidence that in the transit industry there has not been the

---

[17] For thorough treatment of this matter see Lecht, Experience Under Railway Labor Legislation (1955); Jones, Handling of R.R. Labor Disputes 1888-1940 (1941).

[18] For instance, see policy statement of the United States Conciliation Service, U. S. Dept. of Lab. Rel. S. 47-152 (1946).

fullest utilization of collective bargaining just because there has existed a ready alternative. But, on the other hand, it cannot be denied that even some minor over-use of arbitration is preferable to long and costly strikes in this vital utility." [19]

Arbitration of "interests" disputes may be viewed more as an instrument of collective bargaining than as a process of adjudication. In this connection it may be noted that this kind of arbitration is most frequently found in industries where collective bargaining is well established. In fact, Professor Charles O. Gregory has suggested that the compulsory arbitration of "interests" should be called "compulsory collective bargaining" rather than arbitration.[20]

An objection commonly urged against the arbitration of "interests" issues is the absence of definite principles or standards to govern the decision. This belief is not entirely justified, however. There are a number of standards which, while not as adequate as may be desired, are available and applied in the arbitration of such disputes. These standards are discussed in Chapter 16. Moreover, it is not uncommon for parties to agree upon general principles to be observed by the arbitrator, leaving to him only the task of applying these principles in the light of evidence.

The subject matter of "interests" arbitration can be as extensive and varied as the parties choose to make it. Any subject comprehended by collective bargaining can be placed in the agreement by arbitration. In determining over 20,000 labor-management disputes, most of which were over the terms of new agreements, the National War Labor Board of World War II traversed practically the entire range of collective bargaining issues.

Wage issues, as would be expected, constitute the most common subject of "interests" arbitration.[21] Among other

---

[19] Reading Street Railway Co., 6 LA 860, 871 (Simkin, 1947).
[20] Gregory, "The Enforcement of Collective Labor Agreements by Arbitration," 13 U. Chi. L. Rev. 445, 469-470 (1946).
[21] For many cases involving the arbitration of wage issues see Chapter 16.

issues frequently submitted to such arbitration or to emergency boards are those involving (the Authors cite only a few of the many reported cases involving the issues listed) : holidays,[22] vacations,[23] sick leave,[24] health and hospitalization benefits.[25] pension and retirement benefits,[26] meal periods,[27] rest periods,[28] work schedules and shifts,[29] length of workday or workweek,[30] life insurance plans,[31] union shop,[32] checkoff,[33] length of contract term.[34]

The problem is to avoid indiscriminate use of "interests" arbitration, for such use may impede healthy development of the labor-management relationship. In particular, parties who abdicate to arbitrators the responsibility of writing the bulk of the collective agreement risk serious disappointment.

Leaving too many "interests" issues to be resolved by neutrals has been severely criticized by the neutrals themselves,[35] and has produced some pronounced disappointments of dispute settlement efforts.[36]

Arbitrator's Function in 'Interests' Disputes

The function of an "interests" arbitrator can be said to be one of dictation, or legislation, of terms of a new or renewal agreement.

---

[22] E.g., 27 LA 728, 25 LA 352, 21 LA 494, 19 LA 361, 18 LA 290, 16 LA 933.
[23] E.g., 28 LA 182, 24 LA 835, 22 LA 688, 21 LA 494, 18 LA 290, 17 LA 353.
[24] E.g., 17 LA 559, 16 LA 749, 16 LA 532, 14 LA 574, 13 LA 103, 11 LA 450.
[25] E.g., 26 LA 303, 25 LA 352, 22 LA 392, 21 LA 356, 16 LA 933, 16 LA 749, 11 LA 450.
[26] E.g., 29 LA 101, 25 LA 54, 19 LA 538, 18 LA 5, 15 LA 496, 14 LA 321, 13 LA 813, 13 LA 702, 13 LA 46, 11 LA 1037.
[27] 17 LA 353, 16 LA 749, 11 LA 166, 9 LA 577, 4 LA 548, 2 LA 663.
[28] 17 LA 353, 7 LA 845, 6 LA 98, 2 LA 227.
[29] E.g., 11 LA 501, 6 LA 860, 5 LA 269, 3 LA 804, 2 LA 10.
[30] E.g., 28 LA 600, 27 LA 343, 25 LA 54, 21 LA 307, 19 LA 538, 18 LA 903.
[31] E.g., 28 LA 600, 22 LA 392, 21 LA 310, 16 LA 749, 13 LA 46.
[32] E.g., 18 LA 112, 16 LA 611, 14 LA 574, 13 LA 620, 11 LA 501.
[33] E.g., 17 LA 833, 14 LA 574, 11 LA 501, 8 LA 149.
[34] E.g., 27 LA 468, 21 LA 356, 19 LA 538, 18 LA 174, 15 LA 871.
[35] See Consumers Power Co., 18 LA 686, 688-689 (Fact-Finding Board, 1952); Pan-American World Airways, Inc., 17 LA 878, 881 (Emergency Board, 1952).
[36] New England Transportation Co., 15 LA 126, 133 (Company Dissent, 1950); Duquesne Light Co., 6 LA 470, 487, 492, 498 (Company and Union Dissents, 1947).

It has been well said:

"[The arbitrator is] not a superior sort of dictator, dispensing justice from on high, but an agent of the two sides to the collective bargain. His job is to reach a solution that will be satisfactory enough to both sides to be workable. He has to take into consideration their relative strength and their relative necessities. He has to remember not to depart so far from a possible compromise, consistent with the respective power and desires of the parties, that one or the other of them will be likely next time to prefer open hostility to peaceful settlement. He has also to remember that a decision is useless if it cannot be enforced and that the power and ability of the respective parties to administer a decision successfully is an integral part of the decision itself.

"A decision which cannot be carried into effect or which will create lasting dissatisfaction is not really a decision at all. On this account a wage arbitration is not an exercise in pure reason, and a summary of merely logical arguments, accompanied by the opinion accompanying the decision, does not tell the whole story. Arbitrators frequently do not, of course, fully understand these limitations, but the more successful ones do so." [37]

While this statement was made in reference to wage issues, it would appear to be equally applicable to other "interests" matters.

Sometimes it is possible for the parties to agree upon the criteria to be observed by an arbitrator in deciding the issues submitted to him. But even with agreed-upon points of reference, the discretion of the arbitrator can be expected to be quite broad. "Interests" arbitration, as a part of the collective bargaining process, is essentially dynamic and fluid. The aggressor seeks to move into a new field, to expand the limits of an old area, or to reduce rights previously granted. It can be expected that something new will come from the arbitrator and that there will be some substitution of his judgment for that of the respective parties. It must be recognized that if the strike is to be relegated to a position of being the "very last resort, reasonable innovations must be possible through the arbitration process. Otherwise either progress would be unduly slowed or strikes invited, or both." [38]

---

[37] Soule, Wage Arbitration, 6-7 (1928).
[38] San Diego Electric Ry. Co., 11 LA 458, 461 (Kerr, 1948).

In one sense the function of the "interests" arbitrator is to supplement the collective bargaining process by doing the bargaining for both parties after they have failed to reach agreement through their own bargaining efforts. Possibly the responsibility of the arbitrator is best understood when viewed in that light. This responsibility and the attitude of humility that so appropriately accompanies it, have been splendidly described by one board of arbitration, speaking through its Chairman, Whitley P. McCoy, as follows:

"* * * Arbitration of contract terms differs radically from arbitration of grievances. The latter calls for a judicial determination of existing contract rights; the former calls for a determination, upon considerations of policy, fairness, and expediency, of what the contract rights ought to be. In submitting this case to arbitration, the parties have merely extended their negotiations—they have left it to this board to determine what they should, by negotiation, have agreed upon. We take it that the fundamental inquiry, as to each issue, is: what should the parties themselves, as reasonable men, have voluntarily agreed to? * * * We believe that an unusual demand, that is, one that has not found substantial acceptance in other properties, casts upon the union the burden of showing that, because of its minor character or its inherent reasonableness, the negotiators should, as reasonable men, have voluntarily agreed to it. We would not deny such a demand merely because it had not found substantial acceptance, but it would take clear evidence to persuade us that the negotiators were unreasonable in rejecting it. We do not conceive it to be our function to impose on the parties contract terms merely because they embody our own individual economic or social theories. To repeat, our endeavor will be to decide the issues as, upon the evidence, we think reasonable negotiators, regardless of their social or economic theories might have decided them in the give and take process of bargaining. We agree with the company that the interests of stockholders and the public must be considered, and consideration of their interests will enter into our conclusions as to what the parties should reasonably have agreed on." [39]

In concluding its opinion, the board said:

"We render this award not with pride but with some humility. The parties have placed upon us a tremendous task. In judging the results reached and deciding whether the award as a whole is fair, we invite the parties to consider whether, if an offer embodying this entire award had been made in bargaining, it would have been accepted as a reasonable

---

[39] Twin City Rapid Transit Co., 7 LA 845, 848 (1947). Similar views have been expressed by other highly respected arbitrators. See North American Aviation, Inc., 19 LA 76, 77 (Cole, Aaron, Wirtz, 1952).

compromise of many demands. If it would have been, we have performed the function we set for ourselves at the outset, namely, to determine what the parties, as reasonable men, should themselves have agreed to at the bargaining table." [40]

'Interests' Arbitration and Contract Clauses

Specific Provision For 'Interests' Arbitration

Occasionally, a collective agreement will provide specifically for arbitration, at its expiration, of unsettled disputes over the terms of a new agreement. A collective agreement clause providing for arbitration of future "interests" disputes may, for example, be as follows:

> "Any differences that may arise between the company and the local union concerning wage reviews at dates specified in the agreement, or concerning amendments to the agreement at any termination date, which the representatives of the company and the local union are unable to settle, shall be submitted at the request of either party, to a Board of Arbitration to be selected in a manner as specified hereinafter. The company and the local union agree that the majority decision of such Board shall be final and binding on both parties." [41]

More often, however, parties do not reach any agreement to arbitrate new contract terms until the old contract has expired and an impasse in negotiations has been reached. [42]

Clauses Equivocal As To 'Interests' Disputes

Some collective agreements contain provisions which on their face indicate a very broad scope of arbitration, without providing a clue as to whether the process was intended to be limited to disputes involving the interpretation of the agreement or was intended to include also disputes not arising under the agreement. Such provisions may state that "any grievance or complaint" or "any difference" or "any dispute over wages,

---

[40] Twin City Rapid Transit Co., 7 LA 845, 858 (1947). Arbitrator McCoy also used "reasonable compromise" terminology in Printing Industries of Indiana, Inc., 29 LA 7, 10 (1957).
[41] Agreement between San Diego Gas & Electric Co. and IBEW-AFL (agreement has expired).
[42] For the type of instrument that may be used in such cases see River Valley Tissue Mills, Inc., 3 LA 245, 246 (Blair, 1946).

hours, or other conditions of employment" may be arbitrated. In some instances such provisions have been held to provide an authoritative basis for the arbitration of "interests" disputes, while in other instances a restrictive interpretation has been placed upon them.

Issues concerning changes and modifications of the agreement were held by a court to be arbitrable under a clause providing that the "Company agrees to meet and treat with" the union on "all questions relating to hours, wages and working conditions" and that, "should any difference arise between them which cannot be mutually adjusted, the same shall be submitted at the request of either party to a Board of Arbitration." [43] Similarly, "interests" type issues have been held arbitrable under *broad* arbitration clauses by other courts,[44] and by some arbitrators.[45]

On the other hand, even under a similarly broad arbitration clause, an arbitrator held that in the absence of a written stipulation for the arbitration of such matters as pay for unworked holidays, they could not be "arbitrated into" the contract; the arbitrator said that a contrary ruling would be in accordance with neither "the spirit or the intent of Labor-Management agreements as they now exist in the United States." [46]

Another arbitrator has held that while a provision for arbitration of "all" unsettled disputes made a demand for amendment of the contract arbitrable in the procedural sense that the arbitrator could rule upon it, the fact that granting the demand would alter the contract was good reason for its denial, since it would be unsound and unwise for him to

[43] Northland Greyhound Lines v. Amalgamated Ass'n., 66 F. Supp. 431, 3 LA 887 (U.S. Dist. Ct., 1946).

[44] Beech Nut Packing Co, 23 LA 125 (N.Y. Sup. Ct., 1954); Textile Workers Union v. Cheney Bros., 22 LA 512 (Conn. Sup. Ct., 1954); In re Dumas, 12 LA 243 (N.Y. Sup. Ct., 1949); Electrical Workers v. Pneumatic Co., 4 LA 836 (N.J. Sup. Ct., 1946).

[45] Velvet Textile Corp., 7 LA 685, 686 (Pope, 1947); Moeller Instrument Co., 6 LA 639, 641 (Brissenden, 1947).

[46] Shook Bronze Co., 9 LA 656, 657 (Lehoczky, 1948). In general accord, Textron, Inc., 12 LA 475, 478 (Wallen, 1949).

impose his judgment where the appropriate course of action is bilateral negotiation and agreement.[47]

Efforts of a party to arbitrate pure "interests" issues under *narrow* arbitration clauses have often failed. For instance, under a clause providing only for arbitration of disputes involving the interpretation or application of the agreement, the fact that the agreement permitted reopening for consideration of general wage adjustments did not oblige the parties to agree on wage increases or, upon failing to agree, to permit an arbitrator to decide for them.[48]

But the fact that a contract excepts general wage increases from arbitration does not prevent arbitration of the question whether the wage reopening clause permits more than one reopening during the contract term, since this issue involves the interpretation of the contract, rather than a general wage increase as such.[49]

Subject Matter of 'Rights' Arbitration

The sources of the subject matter of "rights" disputes are usually agreements, laws, and customary practices. Among the infinite number of matters that may be the subject of "rights" arbitration are questions with respect to seniority rights, vacations, holidays, discharge and discipline, layoffs, job classification, and the like.

But not all issues that are taken to arbitrators fall into such commonly recognized categories. This is illustrated by the "Case of the Lady in Red Slacks" which was decided by Umpire Shulman. A Ford Motor Company employee was reprimanded and docked one half hour because she wore

---

[47] Dictograph Products, Inc., 8 LA 1033, 1038 (Kaplan, 1947). Also see Chapter 7, topic on "Advisory Recommendations by Arbitrator."

[48] In re Berger, 9 LA 1048 (N.Y. Sup. Ct., 1948), aff'd, 10 LA 929 (N.Y. App. Div., 1948). Accord, West Penn Power Co., 24 LA 741, 744 (McCoy, 1955); Air Reduction Sales Co., 10 LA 528 (Livingston, 1948). Also see P. P. Williams Co., 24 LA 587, 589-591 (Reynard, 1955). Cf., Sacramento Wholesale Bakers Assn., 20 LA 106, 107-108 (Kerr, 1952); Lincoln Dairy Co., 14 LA 1055, 1058 (Donnelly, 1950).

[49] F. H. Hill Co., 8 LA 223 (Blair, 1947). To similar effect, Northern Tube Co., 22 LA 261 (Piercey, 1954); Cords, Ltd., 7 LA 748 (Stein, 1947).

slacks described as bright red in color. The objection was to the color, not to the slacks, which female employees were required to wear. The issue was whether a lady's red slacks constituted a production hazard because of a tendency to distract male employees. Umpire Shulman stated that "it is common knowledge that wolves, unlike bulls, may be attracted by colors other than red and by various other enticements in the art and fit of female attire." The reprimand was expunged and the employee was reimbursed for the pay that she had been docked.[50]

Arbitrator's Function in 'Rights' Disputes

Generally the parties provide that the arbitrator shall have no power to add to, subtract from, or modify any provision of the agreement. Such prohibitions restrict the function of the arbitrator to that of contract interpretation and application, and are intended to prohibit him from crossing the boundary line between interpretation and legislation. But this line cannot be established with certainty. One arbitrator has remarked: "The arbitration of this dispute must be confined within the scope of the existing labor agreement, including all modifications, addendums, and supplements thereto. However, its adjudication necessitates some legislating and interpreting to the extent deemed necessary to clarify and remove the uncertainties, obscurities, and ambiguities which now appear to exist." [51] On the whole, however, it may be concluded that the function of the "rights" arbitrator is quite similar to that of a court in construing contracts, and, like a court, an arbitrator may apply either a liberal or a strict construction to the provisions of an agreement, depending upon the question and circumstances involved, the attitude of the parties, and, of course, the general attitude of the arbitrator. (The standards and techniques of interpretation used by arbitrators are discussed in Chapter 9.)

---

[50] Shulman, Opinions of the Umpire, Opinion A-117 (1944). Another dispute about female attire was arbitrated in Lawrence Bros., Inc., 28 LA 83 (Davis, 1957).
[51] Borg-Warner Corp., 3 LA 423, 428-429 (Gilden, 1944).

Helpful insight into "rights" arbitration, and in particular in regard to the function of the arbitrator, is provided by observing one of the nation's most extensive experiences in such arbitration—the National Railroad Adjustment Board. The Railway Labor Act gives the Adjustment Board jurisdiction over "disputes between an employee or group of employees and a carrier or carriers growing out of grievances or out of the interpretation or application of agreements concerning rates of pay, rules, or working conditions * * *." While the word "Adjustment" in the Board's name might suggest that under this grant of jurisdiction the Board was intended to serve as an extension and continuation of the bargaining process,[52] in actual practice the function of the Board is much like true adjudication:

> "In hearing and deciding the cases which come before the Board [the Board members] do not act as negotiators or adjusters. Whatever may have been the intent of the law in setting up an Adjustment Board, there has been no trace in the history of the Board of any view on its part that its function is to iron out differences by taking into account the situation and needs of the parties and the practical effect of their respective demands, and on the basis of such consideration making concessions to one party in return for concessions by it for the good of the industry as a whole. The Board has never taken this view of its function. Instead it has assumed with the strictest legalistic viewpoint that the loosely drawn and often vague terms of the schedules and agreements which come before it have a rigid technical meaning, and that this meaning is to be discovered by a process of purely technical reasoning. The most cursory examination of the nature of the arguments put up to the Board and the grounds of its decisions, where these are given, conclusively demonstrates that it regards its function as one of strict legal interpretation rather than compromise and adjustment."[53]

Probably most persons familiar with the activities of the

---

[52] The labor members of the Board at one time expressed the view that this was the intended function of the Board. See statement of labor members submitted to the Attorney General's Committee on Administrative Procedure, in Railway Labor, 9-10 (1940), reprinted in Jones, Natl. R.R. Adjustment Board, 226 (1941). Those "who were mainly responsible for the statutory creation of the Board in 1934 hoped and doubtless believed that the Board would grow up to live chiefly as a collective bargaining agency * * * rather than as a real arbitration tribunal of last resort. * * * this hope has not been fulfilled for many years * * *" Daugherty, "Arbitration by the National Railroad Adjustment Board," Arbitration Today, 93, 94 (BNA Incorporated, 1955).

[53] Railway Labor, ibid. The quotation is the statement of a carrier spokesman before the Attorney General's Committee.

Adjustment Board would agree that the just-quoted statement is basically accurate and applies with equal force today. Certainly, when a referee is called in to sit as a member of the Board in deadlocked cases, the function of the Board is adjudication. But even in adjudication some rule making is inevitable:

> "Even on the assumption that the Adjustment Board is strictly confined to the interpretation and application of existing rules, it is inescapable, particularly in deadlocked cases, that it will exercise a greater or less influence on the nature and scope of agreements between carriers and labor organizations. The Constitution of the United States is a small compact document; but one can gain no appreciation of its meaning and scope without examining the thousands of decisions in which the Supreme Court, in its interpretation, has molded and modified it. In a similar manner, it is inevitable that the Adjustment Board, subject to judicial review, will mold and modify railway collective agreements." [54]

In industries that use the permanent umpire or chairman device, the function of the umpire or chairman varies. The jurisdiction of the Impartial Umpire for the Ford Motor Company and the UAW has been limited generally to "alleged violations of the terms" of the parties' agreements. By specific provision he has been denied the power to "add to or subtract from or modify any of the terms of any agreement"; or to "substitute his discretion for the company's discretion in cases where the company is given discretion" by any agreement; or to "provide agreement for the parties in those cases where they have in their contract agreed that further negotiations shall or may provide for certain contingencies to cover certain Subjects." [55]

On the other hand, the Impartial Chairman of the full-fashioned hosiery industry has been given authority to determine all disputes except those involving new or renewal contract terms. In this industry, all disputes arising during the

---

[54] Spencer, The National Railroad Adjustment Board, 31 (1938) [reprinted in Jones, National R.R. Adjustment Board, p. 181 of appendix (1941)].
[55] See Ford Motor Co., 6 LA 952, 953 (Shulman, 1944). The quoted provisions were continued in the 1958 agreement between the Ford Motor Company and the UAW-AFL-CIO. The jurisdiction of the Chrysler Appeal Board is somewhat similar to that of the Ford umpire. See Wolff, Crane & Cole, "The Chrysler-UAW Umpire System," The Arbitrator and The Parties, 111, 114 (BNA Incorporated, 1958).

life of the contract "including but not limited to the interpretation, construction or application of the terms of this agreement" are "submitted to the Impartial Chairman for final and binding decision by him." Thus the Impartial Chairman has jurisdiction of extra-contract as well as contract issues. The Impartial Chairman is denied the power to "alter, modify, or change" the "Agreement or any of the terms or provisions thereof," but there is no denial of power to add to the agreement, and the grant of power to decide issues not covered by the agreement can be viewed as giving him authority to add, by decisions, to the agreement.[56]

This subject should not be dismissed without taking note of the view, as expressed by Dr. George W. Taylor, former Chairman of the National War Labor Board and a former Impartial Chairman for the full-fashioned hosiery industry, that grievance settlement often becomes an integral part of agreement-making. In an address before the Second Annual Meeting of the National Academy of Arbitrators, he said:

> "A third important characteristic of grievance arbitration should be mentioned. Contrary to the views of many arbitrators, grievance settlement is not simply a process of contract interpretation. * * * the difficult grievances arise because the labor contract reflects only a partial or an inconclusive meeting of minds. It doesn't give the reasonably clear answer to a dispute. In such cases, grievance settlement becomes an integral part of agreement-making. At any event, the manner in which the grievances are settled provides understandings that are as durable, or more so, than the actual terms of the labor contract themselves. No one need amplify to this audience the weight of 'established practices.' "[57]

Dr. Taylor also said that no sharp line can be drawn "between agreement-making and agreement administration," that "grievance settlement involves not merely the application of clear and unmistakable agreement terms to individual cases but, particularly in the early stages of a relationship or as respects new terms added to an old contract, is also related to a completion of the agreement of the parties." This, he

---

[56] Kennedy, Effective Labor Arbitration, 34-36 (1948).
[57] Taylor, "Effectuating the Labor Contract Through Arbitration," The Profession of Labor Arbitration, 20, 21 (BNA Incorporated, 1957).

added, "applies to the arbitration clause itself, which commonly does not constitute a complete meeting of minds about the kind of arbitration to be employed." [58]

'Rights' Arbitration Contract Clauses

Frequently the arbitration clause of the collective agreement is designed to restrict the arbitrator to the interpretation and application of the agreement. Under these narrow arbitration clauses a dispute ordinarily will be held arbitrable only if it somehow involves "rights" traceable to the agreement. However, disputes are sometimes held arbitrable under such clauses even though the agreement contains no specific provision on the subject of the alleged "right," as where the claimed "right" may be inherent in clauses on other subjects. [59]

Under the narrow "interpretation and application" arbitration clauses, disputes which arise prior to execution of the agreement are not arbitrable, even though the grievance is filed after the agreement is executed. [60] Once vested, however, rights under a collective agreement may be enforced under "interpretation and application" clauses even after the agreement has expired or even though the grievants are no longer employees. [61]

Some arbitration clauses are sufficiently broad to permit the arbitration of a wide variety of "rights" disputes, including those which do not involve the interpretation and application of the agreement (and including some which also involve some "interests" elements). For instance, under such "all disputes" clauses the following disputes were held arbitrable though not involving interpretation or application of

---

[58] Id. at 39.

[59] See Arbitrator Marshall in 23 LA 228; Donnelly in 13 LA 747; Wallen in 9 LA 757; Sklar Mfg. Co. v. Fay, 11 LA 1022 (N.Y. Sup. Ct., 1949). Also see Arbitrator Shister in 25 LA 50; Kaplan in 3 LA 259; Franklin Needle Co. v. Hosiery Workers, 22 LA 509 (N.H. Sup. Ct., 1954).

[60] Arbitrator Wettach in 25 LA 772, 773; Platt in 20 LA 850, 851-852; Millar in 20 LA 207, 210; McCoy in 8 LA 66, 67; Marshall in 6 LA 460, 461.

[61] Arbitrator Kelliher in 23 LA 298, 300; Rosenfarb in 19 LA 365, 368. Also, Jones v. Tide Water Oil Co., 22 LA 562 (Calif. Super. Ct., 1954); In re Commercial Telegraphers' Union, 20 LA 487 (N.Y. Sup. Ct., 1953).

the agreement: compensation for damage to clothing; [62] compulsory retirement; [63] employer's right to institute incentive pay plan; [64] merit increases for individual employees; [65] union request that employer supply job descriptions; [66] and other disputes. [67]

However, under narrow arbitration clauses such disputes have been denied, or remanded, with the suggestion that the matter be negotiated by the parties. [68]

Arbitrability of claims for damages for breach of no-strike clauses depends largely upon the scope of the arbitration clause; such claims have been held arbitrable under clauses of the broad "all disputes" type, [69] but non-arbitrable under narrow "interpretation and application" clauses. [70]

Further regarding no-strike clauses, it has been held that a clause forbidding strikes over unresolved disputes does not imply that all kinds of disputes may be arbitrated where the agreement also contains a provision restricting arbitration to grievances involving its meaning and application. [71]

Finally, breach of the no-strike clause was held not to prevent the union from arbitrating vacation and other rights under the agreement, which provided for arbitration of disputes arising out of or relating to the agreement. [72]

---

[62] Best Mfg. Co., 22 LA 482, 483-484 (Handsaker, 1954).

[63] John Morrell & Co., 17 LA 81, 84 (Gilden, 1951).

[64] Fay v. Farber & Shlevin, Inc., 24 LA 678, 679-680 (N.Y. Sup. Ct., 1955). Cf., Hinson Mfg. Co., 22 LA 657, 661 (Davey, 1954).

[65] F. H. Hill Co., 6 LA 661, 662-663 (Whiting, 1947); Warren City Mfg. Co., 7 LA 202, 217 (Abernethy, 1947).

[66] Kendall Mills, 8 LA 306 (Lane, 1947).

[67] Philadelphia Dress Joint Board v. Rosinsky, 24 LA 707, 709-710 (U. S. Dist. Ct., 1955); Munising Wood Products Co., 22 LA 769, 771 (Ryder, 1954); Rock Hill Printing & Finishing Co., 19 LA 872, 874 (Jaffee, 1953).

[68] See Chapter 7, topic on "Advisory Recommendations by Arbitrator."

[69] Signal-Stat Corp. v. UE, 26 LA 736 (U.S.C.A. 2d, 1956); Reading Street Railway Co., 8 LA 930 Simkin, 1947).

[70] UE v. Miller Metal Products, Inc., 23 LA 18 (U.S. C. A. 4th, 1954); Markel Electric Products, Inc. v. UE, 19 LA 849 (U.S. C.A. 2d, 1953). Contra, Bee Line, Inc., 20 LA 675 (Feinberg, 1953).

[71] Bethlehem Steel Co., 10 LA 748 (Selekman, 1948).

[72] Potoker v. Brooklyn Eagle, 25 LA 577, 579 (N.Y. Sup. Ct., 1955); Stewart Stamping Corp., 24 LA 115 (N.Y. Sup. Ct., 1955).

CHAPTER 4

THE ARBITRATION TRIBUNAL

Several types of tribunals are available for parties who wish to arbitrate. Also available are a variety of methods for selecting the arbitrator. Parties may choose in general between the use of a "temporary" arbitrator or the use of a "permanent" arbitrator. They also have a choice as to the number of arbitrators to be used, either single or multiple. The choice exercised in these matters may be of such importance as to determine the success of the arbitration.

Single Arbitrator v. Arbitration Board

The parties have a choice as to the number of arbitrators to be used for their case. The most common practice is to use a single neutral arbitrator.[1] When an arbitration board is used, it may be composed entirely of neutrals or it may be tripartite in its membership.[2] As between the two types of boards, the tripartite board is used much more frequently than the board of neutrals.

When a board of neutrals is used it will ordinarily have three members. Sometimes an alternate is also designated.[3] Under one variation in the use of neutral boards, only one member hears the case and makes findings of fact, then a decision based upon such findings is made by the full board.[4]

---

[1] See, for instance, statistics in "Procedural Aspects of Labor-Management Arbitration," 28 LA 933, 934-935 (1954 statistics).
[2] See "Tripartite Arbitration Boards," below.
[3] As in Southern Bell Telephone & Telegraph Co., 25 LA 85, 86 (Alexander, McCoy, Schedler & Whiting, 1955).
[4] Ibid.

'Temporary' or 'Ad Hoc' Arbitrators

The "temporary" or *"ad hoc"* arbitrator is selected after the dispute arises. He is named to arbitrate a specific dispute or a specific group of disputes, and there is no commitment to select him again. Most "interests" arbitrations involve temporary arbitrators. In a high percentage of "rights" arbitrations, too, temporary arbitrators are used. Most of the latter arbitrations are conducted pursuant to an arbitration clause in the collective agreement. The details of such clauses vary considerably from agreement to agreement, but it is customary to state at least: (1) what grievances may be submitted to arbitration; (2) the procedure for selecting the arbitrator; and, (3) the scope of the arbitrator's jurisdiction and the binding effect of his award.

(a) Advantages

The possibility of easy change of arbitrators is one of the chief advantages of the use of temporary arbitrators. At the same time, as long as an arbitrator continues to be satisfactory to the parties, he can be selected again and again if available, for cases as they arise. When parties first begin to arbitrate, the use of temporary arbitrators makes experimentation possible. Thus they may become acquainted with arbitration and, at the same time, better determine their particular needs in regard to its use. Later, the parties might graduate to the use of a permanent system.

For those parties who find themselves in the happy situation of having relatively few disputes, the appointment of arbitrators only as needed generally is more satisfactory, and especially so from the standpoint of economy.

Use of temporary arbitrators permits the selection, in each case, of an arbitrator who has special qualifications for deciding that particular dispute. While the use of a specialist, as such, may not be required often, some issues are of such technical nature that it is advisable to select an arbitrator who has special training or knowledge in regard thereto.

Finally, it is probable that a temporary arbitrator, not being personally acquainted with either party, will not be swayed too far by the personalities of the parties. In other words, brief tenure in office make it unlikely that a temporary arbitrator will acquire a bias in favor of either party.

(b) Disadvantages

The selection of an arbitrator after a dispute has arisen may involve as much difficulty as the dispute itself. Much time and effort may be lost because parties who are no longer friendly find themselves unable to agree upon an arbitrator, or even upon a method of selecting one. In the meantime the dispute remains unsettled, which may result in additional damage to the parties' relationship.

The arbitrator who is chosen for only one dispute, or a specific group of disputes, usually will not be familiar with the general circumstances of the parties. He will know little of the background of the dispute or the setting in which the collective agreement operates. At best, the parties may seek to educate him as to these matters, and even if additional hearing time is spent in his enlightenment, the arbitrator's knowledge of the parties' relationship will be shallow. The most successful arbitration is that which sets a smooth course for future operations. Thorough knowledge of the past relationship of the parties is an invaluable aid to one who would pursue this end. Moreover, since temporary arbitrators are selected on something of an emergency basis, the parties often do not have adequate opportunity to check the qualifications of the arbitrator. Thus there is additional hazard that the parties may have to accept a decision which leaves their relationship in a weaker condition than existed prior to the rendition of the award.

Another disadvantage of the use of temporary arbitrators is that when several arbitrators render interpretations of the same contract, there is a real danger that conflicting decisions may create more differences than have been settled. In fact, it is not uncommon for a losing party to take the very same issue again to arbitration if it is thought that there is any possibility of obtaining a different ruling. An award by one temporary arbitrator may have so little precedential force as viewed by a subsequent arbitrator that the latter will decide contra.

Because it is easy to change temporary arbitrators, losing parties frequently will demand a change of arbitrators even though there may be no reasonable cause for a change. Thus the parties may be deprived of future valuable service of the eliminated arbitrator. Moreover, frequent and indiscriminate change of arbitrators permits none to become truly acquainted with the needs of the parties. This means that the parties may deprive themselves of the best possible arbitration services.[5]

'Permanent' Arbitrators

A "permanent" arbitrator is one who is selected to serve for a period of time, rather than for just one case or specific group of cases. He may be selected to serve for the term of the collective agreement, for some other specific period, or even at the pleasure of the parties.[6] His responsibilities and functions are determined by the contract by which his office is created. The terms of permanent umpire contracts vary widely, especially as to the precise jurisdiction of the umpire, since each such contract is carefully tailored to meet the special needs and wishes of the parties. He may be employed on a full-time basis, but more often he is employed on a part-time basis, subject to call when needed. The use of a permanent arbitrator in an industry is evidence that labor-management relations have reached a relatively high degree of maturity.

---

[5] For a splendid discussion of the advantages and disadvantages of using temporary arbitrators, see Simkin & Kennedy, Arbitration of Grievances (U.S. Dept. of Labor, Div. of Labor Standards, Bull. No. 82, 1946). Also see Warren & Bernstein, "A Profile of Labor Arbitration," 16 LA 970 (1951); also, "Labor Arbitration Today: Accomplishments and Problems," 16 LA 987 (1951).

[6] The permanent umpire under the 1958 General Motors-U.A.W. agreement "shall serve for one year from date of appointment provided he continues to be acceptable to both parties." The umpire under the 1958 Ford Motor Company-U.A.W. agreement "shall continue to serve only so long as he continues to be acceptable to both parties."

The permanent arbitrator usually is called either "Impartial Umpire" or "Impartial Chairman." The Impartial Umpire usually sits alone. His function is similar to that of the temporary arbitrator, except that he is appointed to consider all arbitrable disputes which arise during his tenure. The Umpire generally is not commissioned to mediate, his function being quasijudicial in the sense that it is one of contract interpretation and application.[7]

The Impartial Chairman, on the other hand, usually sits as the only impartial member of an arbitration board. Often the Impartial Chairman is commissioned to be something more than an arbitrator, although his functions vary considerably from industry to industry. He may be authorized to mediate, and, where such is the case, he will arbitrate only after other methods fail, making it a last-resort solution. But when the Impartial Chairman does find it necessary to assume the role of an arbitrator, he too may then be restricted to contract interpretation and application.

The type of situation to which use of the permanent arbitrator is especially well adapted is indicated in the recommendation of a fact-finding board appointed by the Secretary of Labor in 1946 to serve in connection with an International Harvester Company dispute:

> "While the Board believes that a permanent umpire system of arbitration would be more desirable here because of the complexity of the issues involved in the numerous grievances which have arisen under the recently expired contract, as witnessed by cases involving these grievances which have come before the National War Labor Board, we hesitate to recommend provision for a permanent umpire system in the contract unless by agreement of the parties. We recommend that the parties give serious consideration to naming an arbitrator in the contract, whose term of office would extend for the life of the agreement unless otherwise changed by mutual agreement. We believe that the value of the services of an arbitrator to the industrial relations welfare of the parties may be considerably enhanced by the experience gained through more frequent

---

[7] An interesting variation utilized by the New York City Transit Authority is the "Impartial Advisor," whose authority is not only restricted to agreement interpretation but is also limited to making findings and recommendations only. New York City Transit Authority, 27 LA 838 (Stark, 1955).

contact with the shop practices prevailing in the various International Harvester plants and the characteristics of the company's wage and incentive system than would be possible under an ad hoc arrangement." [8]

Accepting the above recommendation, the parties established a permanent umpire system at International Harvester and one informed observer has been quoted as saying that it "proved to be the turning point in bringing order out of chaos in the field of contract interpretation." [9]

The use of permanent labor-management arbitrators is not new in the United States. Some industries have had umpire systems since the turn of the century. The anthracite coal industry, for instance, established a permanent system in 1903. Increase in the use of permanent arbitrators was gradual at first, but since 1935 it has been fairly rapid. Permanent-arbitrator provisions occur most frequently in collective agreements within the automobile, aircraft, meat-packing, steel, and rubber industries.[10] Sometimes a permanent arbitrator is selected for an entire industry, as for instance, in the full-fashioned hosiery industry.[11]

The Chrysler Corporation uses an Appeal Board which consists of two representatives of each of the parties and an Impartial Chairman. The partisan members of the Board first attempt to settle all grievances properly referred to the Board. If the partisan members are unable to settle a matter, it is decided by the Impartial Chairman.[12]

---

[8] International Harvester Co., 1 LA 512, 522 (Marshall, Spencer & Holly, 1946).

[9] Reilly, "Arbitration's Impact on Bargaining," 16 LA 987, 990 (1951).

[10] Arbitration Provisions in Union Agreements (U. S. Dept. of Labor, Bureau of Labor Statistics, Bull. No. 780, p. 3, 1944). For extensive discussion of some umpire systems see Davey, "The John Deere-UAW Permanent Arbitration System," Critical Issues in Labor Arbitration 161-192 (BNA, Incorporated, 1957); Arbitration of Labor-Management Grievances (U.S. Dept. of Labor, Bull. 1159, 1954), a study of the Bethlehem Steel system.

[11] See Kennedy, Effective Labor Arbitration 20, 24 (1948).

[12] For a detailed discussion of the Appeal Board, see Wolff, Crane & Cole, "The Chrysler-UAW Umpire System," The Arbitrator and The Parties, 111-136 (BNA Incorporated, 1958), which discussion is followed by comment by Ford Umpire Platt and General Motors Umpire Feinsinger comparing their respective umpire systems with that at Chrysler. Id. at 141-148. Also see "Chrysler Procedure," 29 LA 885 (1958).

Sometimes permanent umpire panels are maintained, as, for instance, in the case of the Bethlehem and United States Steel Companies.[13] Umpires are called in turn from these panels. Sometimes, too, recommended decisions are made by individual members of a panel, subject to approval by another member thereof.[14]

(a) Advantages

Many persons active as arbitrators or as students of arbitration feel that great value is to be realized from the use of the permanent arbitrator. Dr. George W. Taylor, for instance, urges that ad hoc arbitration should be looked upon, at best, as a transitory method and as entailing comparative disadvantages. "As a support for industrial relations stability, a permanent arbitrator is a prime requisite. Out of the continuing relationship, consistent policy and mutually acceptable procedures can gradually be evolved." [15]

Since the permanent arbitrator is appointed in advance, no time need be lost in selecting one after a dispute arises. Moreover, the advance selection of the arbitrator permits time for careful consideration of his qualifications of impartiality, skill, and knowledge of labor-management relations. The permanent arbitrator usually is selected by the highly desirable method of mutual choice of the parties, rather than by some outside person or agency.

The permanent arbitrator becomes familiar with the provisions of the parties' agreement. He comes to know the day-to-day relationships of the parties, their circumstances, their personalities, and their customary practices. The importance of this knowledge has been emphasized by Umpire Harry Shulman:

---

[13] See Killingsworth, "Arbitration: Its Uses in Industrial Relations," 21 LA 859, 860 (1953).

[14] See, for instance, Bethlehem Supply Co., 25 LA 366, 368-369 (recommended decision by Springfield, aproved by Seward, 1955); Bethlehem Steel Co., 24 LA 379 (recommended decision by Alexander, approved by Seward, 1955).

[15] Taylor, "Effectuating the Labor Contract Through Arbitration," The Profession of Labor Arbitration p. 20 (BNA Incorporated, 1957).

"An opportunity should be provided, if possible, for the arbitrator by continuous association with the parties, or at least by repeated association with the parties, to get to know them better. A good many disputes that come to arbitration are deceptive. * * * Some are deceptive even because they don't really portray what the parties are concerned about. They seem to be fighting about one thing, and actually it is something else which is bothering them. That kind of thing happens, at least in my experience, quite frequently. A grievance is filed partly as a sort of pressure technic. It is filed partly in order to lay a foundation for a claim subsequently to be made. An arbitrator who doesn't know and doesn't sense what he is getting into, what a decision one way or the other will lead to in the developing strategy, might find himself regretting subsequently, when he finds out what the parties were really after—regretting he made that kind of determination. And so an arbitrator who is in continuous association with the parties may be in a better position to realize what the parties are really fighting for rather than what they appear to be fighting for." [16]

In respect to the matter of costs, if the parties have a large number of disputes so as to require frequent resort to arbitration, the use of a permanent arbitrator is a definite advantage. Moreover, with increased knowledge of the parties' relationship, the permanent arbitrator is able to shorten hearings; from the outset, many details already will be known to him. He needs less time for making investigations since he is familiar with the parties and the industry in which they operate. For the same reason time is saved in the preparation of opinions. Naturally, the saving of time means a reduction of costs.

Permanent arbitrators make their awards available for the guidance of the parties. Cases which do not involve new issues or new situations are likely to be settled at early stages of the grievance procedure since the parties know how the arbitrator has decided similar disputes. Thus one effect of a decision covering a disputed point may be its application by the parties themselves to other disputes involving the same issue. The awards of a permanent arbitrator generally will be consistent with one another, thus avoiding the confusion that sometimes results from having two or more temporary arbitrators rule on similar issues.

---

[16] Conference on Training of Law Students in Labor Relations, Vol. III, Transcript of Proceedings, 710-711 (1947).

The permanent arbitrator has special reason for concern regarding the ultimate effect of each decision. He expects to continue to serve the parties after each decision is rendered and expects to be confronted time and again by his own decisions. The situation is somewhat different with a temporary arbitrator, who, while in good conscience is eager to render a sound award, serves with the realization that he may never again have contact with the parties.

(b) Disadvantages

The difficulty of finding enough mutually acceptable and available grade "A" men is a problem, at least, if not a disadvantage, to be faced in the use of permanent arbitrators. Any arbitrator given tenure of office should be able to inspire a high degree of confidence in both parties, and he should be experienced. The field of choice is necessarily limited.

There is always a danger that the parties will be too quick to turn to the permanent arbitrator. Once selected, he is easily available. There is temptation to take a short-cut route to dispute settlement. Arbitration should not be substituted for negotiation—harm results when the parties fail to exhaust all possibilities of settlement at the pre-arbitration steps of the grievance procedure. Moreover, there is a danger that some cases will be sent to the arbitrator just to make him earn his salary.

The use of a permanent arbitrator obligates the parties in advance of need to some expense. The arbitrator's retainer fee must be paid regardless of whether his services prove to be needed.[17]

Danger of Favoritism or of 'Splitting' Awards

In deciding whether to use permanent or temporary arbitrators another matter should be considered. Both labor and

---

[17] Sometimes a retainer is provided plus a certain amount per case. For a discussion of the pros and cons of the use of permanent arbitrators, see Simkin & Kennedy, Arbitration of Grievances (U. S. Dept. of Labor, Div. of Labor Standards, Bull. No. 82, 1946).

management should be quick to disown any arbitrator who appears to be playing favorites or appears to have the faintest taint of prejudice in favor of either party. Permanent value can be had from arbitration only if decisions are rendered on the merits. In this regard there are two potential dangers. First, the arbitrator might acquire a bias in favor of one side or the other. Second, the arbitrator might go to the other extreme and, in his desire to please both parties, render approximately the same number of awards for each side. In common parlance this is known as "splitting" awards.

Some persons believe that a temporary arbitrator is less likely to acquire a bias in favor of either side and is in a better position to decide cases impartially on the merits. On the other hand, it is argued that the relative stability of the permanent arbitration relationship is the best insurance for decisions on the merits. It is recognized, however, that each of these conclusions is debatable.[18]

Possibly there has been too much concern over this matter. Faith in the integrity and sound judgment of arbitrators generally and in their ability to "see through" attempts to obtain decisions not based on the merits should be sufficient to eliminate initial concern at least. If adequate evidence is produced showing that an arbitrator is not deciding issues on the merits, the parties need lose no time in terminating his services. This matter has been given special consideration by the late Harry Shulman. His splendid analysis and expression of views leaves little more to be said:

> "Another, and perhaps less lofty thought, should be expressed. There seems to be a feeling on the part of some that a party can win a greater number of cases if it presents a greater number for decision, the assumption being that some purposeful percentage is maintained. There are many reasons why this point of view is wholly unsound. No Umpire should be retained in office if he is really believed to be making decisions on such a basis. An Umpire should be employed only so long as he renders decisions on the basis of his best and honest judgment on the merits of the controversies presented, and only so long as both parties believe that

---

[18] Davey, "Hazards in Labor Arbitration," 1 Ind. & Lab. Rel. Rev. 386, 394, n. 22 (1948).

he does so. If he is believed to be making his decisions on a percentage basis, the remedy is to put him out of office rather than to give him more cases for arbitrary decision.

"Moreover, as anyone concerned with industrial relations thoroughly knows, there is a great deal of room in the relation between a company and its employees for honest and reasonable differences of opinion on important questions of interpretation and application. If only such questions were brought to an Umpire, their normal, honest determination could fairly be expected in proper course to fall on both sides of the line. A purposeful percentage would be as unnecessary as it would be dishonest.

"From the selfish point of view of a party, there is a great advantage in appealing only cases believed to be entirely good rather than appealing indiscriminately many cases for the purpose of winning a percentage. When a party brings only strong cases, it breeds in others a feeling of confidence in its judgment and in its reasonableness which may tip the scales in cases of doubt and give it a considerable advantage at the start. If, on the other hand, a party brings cases carelessly, without substantial evidence and without apparent judgment in selection, it tends to breed in others a lack of confidence in its judgment which starts it off with a considerable disadvantage. This is particularly true in the 'did or didn't he' type of case here mentioned. For in such cases, [speaking of cases in which the evidence is not conclusive] as already stated, there is little to go on except the conflicting testimony of witnesses and the confidence in the parties developed over a period of time as a result of the record of their own selections." [19]

Mediation by Permanent Arbitrators

As we have noted, Impartial Chairmen often are commissioned to try to bring about settlement of differences through mediation. Sometimes an Impartial Umpire, too, exercises this function. The Impartial Chairman for the full-fashioned hosiery industry has acted as a mediator as well as an arbitrator.[20] The Impartial Chairman for the men's clothing industry in New York City has had the duty of continuing negotiations concerning disputes brought to him and of deciding issues only if agreement is not reached through such negotiations.[21] It is understood that the General Motors Umpire does not mediate, but that in the past the Ford Motor

---

[19] Ford Motor Company, 1 ALAA ¶ 67,274, p. 67,620 (1945). Also see comments by Arbitrator D. Emmett Ferguson in Servel, Inc., 1 LA 163, 165 (1945).

[20] Kennedy, Effective Labor Arbitration 57 (1948).

[21] Morgan, Arbitration in the Men's Clothing Industry in New York City 1, 5 (1940).

Company Umpire has performed some mediation functions. Speaking of this matter, Ford Umpire Harry Shulman said:

> "The Umpire's contractual jurisdiction is limited to the interpretation, application or alleged violation of the terms of the parties' written agreements, with few exceptions. But, as the parties and I came to know each other better, my actual functions were greatly expanded. With the full consent of both sides, I conferred with the parties separately and jointly on diverse problems outside that contractual jurisdiction, sat with them as mutual friend and adviser in their negotiations of amendments and supplements, spoke at educational classes and other union meetings, and was generally available for such help as a well-intentioned mutual friend could give in the interest of the total enterprise." [22]

Umpire Shulman also observed that sometimes the parties may press the umpire to decide issues which might be left undecided or at least delayed until time and experience provide greater assurance of wise judgment; in "cases of this character, and others in which the arbitrator conscientiously feels baffled, it may be much wiser to permit him to mediate between the parties for an acceptable solution." [23]

One of the strongest advocates of mediation by permanent arbitrators has been Dr. George W. Taylor. It has been his belief that collective bargaining should be carried on through the arbitration step and that the essential task of most chairmen is to bring about a meeting of minds if possible.[24] His view of the Impartial Chairman's office has been expressed as follows:

> "An impartial chairman, then, is first of all a mediator. But he is a very special kind of mediator. He has a reserve power to decide the case either by effectuating his own judgment or by joining with one of the partisan board members to make a majority decision, depending upon the procedure designated by the agreement. A new reason for labor and management to agree is introduced—to avoid a decision. By bringing in a fresh viewpoint, moreover, the impartial chairman may be able to assist the parties in working out their problem in a mutually satisfactory manner. To me, such a result has always seemed to be highly preferable to a decision that is unacceptable to either of the parties. What's wrong

---

[22] Shulman, Opinions of the Umpire, p. 3 of Preface (1943-1946).
[23] Shulman, "Reason, Contract, and Law in Labor Relations," 68 Harv. L. Rev. 999, 1022-1023 (1955), reprinted in Management Rights and the Arbitration Process 169, 195-197 (BNA Incorporated, 1957).
[24] Taylor, Effectuating the Labor Contract Through Arbitration, op. cit.

per se about an agreement when agreeing is the essence of collective bargaining?" [25]

Dr. Taylor has recognized the widespread belief among industrial relations people that an arbitrator should not mediate, and he has hastened to warn that the Impartial Chairman approach is not universally applicable; "it is only usable when both parties see eye-to-eye on the point." [26] It is interesting to note that over one-third of all problems presented to Dr. Taylor as Impartial Chairman of the full-fashioned hosiery industry were settled by agreement of the parties.[27] A criticism of that office since Dr. Taylor stepped down has been in regard to the decreased number of such voluntary settlements.[28]

Combination of arbitration and mediation functions has been criticized by those who believe that there should be a clear distinction between the two and that the arbitrator's usefulness is reduced when he attempts to mediate.[29]

In some umpire systems neither party wishes the umpire to act as a mediator at any time.[30] It does appear from the experience of some industries, however, that mediation by permanent arbitrators, when the function is properly conceived and executed, can do much to strengthen the parties' relations.[31]

Tripartite Arbitration Board

The tripartite arbitration board, which may be either temporary or permanent, is one made up of one or more members selected by management, an equal number selected by labor, and a neutral member who serves as chairman. The labor

---

[25] Id. at 10.

[26] Id. at 11.

[27] Kennedy, Effective Labor Arbitration 28 (1948).

[28] Id. at 216.

[29] For a collection of views expressed in opposition to Dr. Taylor's, see Braden, "The Function of the Arbitrator in Labor-Management Disputes," 4 Arb. J. (N.S.) 35 (1949).

[30] See, for instance, Davey, "The John Deere-UAW Permanent Arbitration System," Critical Issues in Labor Arbitrattion 161, 162, 185 (BNA Incorporated, 1957).

[31] For a statistical survey of views on the desirability of mediation by arbitrators, see Warren & Bernstein, "A Profile of Labor Arbitration," 16 LA 970, 981-982 (1951). For further discussion of the pros and cons of mediation by arbitrators, see Simkin, Acceptability as a Factor in Arbitration Under an Existing Agreement 61-63 (U. of Pa. Press, 1952); also see "Symposium on Arbitration," 15 LA 966, 967-969 (1950).

and mangement members generally are partisans and act as advocates for their respective sides.[32]

Thus the impartial member, in some respects, is a single arbitrator, and it is something of a misnomer to call the partisan members "arbitrators." Some writers believe that it would be more realistic to call them "representatives in arbitration" or use some other such title to acknowledge that the dispute is to be submitted to the neutral member, and to agree that he is to act as sole arbitrator.[33]

Tripartite boards do not often reach unanimous decisions.[34] In this regard, the collective agreements, statutes, and other instruments under which tripartite boards are established usually provide that a majority award of the board shall be final and binding.[35] The side whose position is favored by the neutral member generally joins him in a majority award.

Some agreements give the impartial member the right and responsibility of making the final decision, regardless of whether it is a majority award.[36] Even where the agreement does not give the neutral this right, the parties may agree at the hearing that he alone shall write the opinion and award and that same shall be final and binding upon the parties;[37] or they may agree that if no majority award is reached, the award of the neutral shall be final and binding.[38] Indeed, when arbitration commences the parties frequently agree to waive the collective agreement provision for use of a tripartite board,

---

[32] Sometimes they even present the evidence and argument for their respective sides, no other representatives being used. As in Pfeiffer Brewing Co., 16 LA 89, 90 (R. Smith, 1951). Sometimes when they thus serve as counsel, they agree to make the neutral the sole arbitrator. As in United Tavern, 16 LA 210, 211 (Slavney, 1951).

[33] Updegraff & McCoy, Arbitration of Labor Disputes 27 (1946). Also see comments in Reynard, "Drafting of Grievance and Arbitration Articles of Collective Bargaining Agreements," 10 Vanderbilt L. Rev. 749, 757 (1957).

[34] See statistics in "Procedural Aspects of Labor-Management Arbitration," 28 LA 933, 935 (1954 statistics).

[35] Thus in most cases the common law rule requiring a unanimous decision does not apply.

[36] For views on this see Warren & Bernstein, "A Profile of Labor Arbitration," 16 LA 970, 977 (1951).

[37] For instance, see 24 LA 116, 117; 20 LA 684 (right to dissent reserved); 16 LA 501; 15 LA 608.

[38] See 23 LA 429, 430; 21 LA 456, 457.

and they agree that the neutral is to act as sole arbitrator from the outset.[39]

When tripartite boards are used without giving the impartial member authority to render a binding award even without a majority vote, he might be faced with the necessity of compromising his own views or even accepting the extreme position of one side or the other in order to have a majority award.[40] Sometimes neither party will vote with him in favor of an award based upon the true merits of the case.

(a) Advantages

One advantage of using a tripartite board is that the neutral member may get valuable advice and assistance from the partisan members.[41] The usual practice is for the parties to select persons from their own ranks who are familiar with the background of the dispute. The technical assistance that such persons may give to the neutral member may be of special value. Moreover, use of the tripartite board gives the parties a better opportunity to keep the neutral arbitrator informed as to their real positions, which may not be exactly the same as their official positions.

The tripartite board has its greatest utility in the arbitration of "interests" disputes.[42] In this regard, the tripartite composition of the National War Labor Board was considered in reality to be a substitute for the lack of completely satisfactory guiding principles and points of reference.[43] In the arbitration of contract-negotiation disputes, it is of the utmost

---

[39] See 19 LA 658, 659; 17 LA 125, 126; 16 LA 210, 211; 16 LA 12, 13. This was likewise done in Food Employers Council, Inc., 20 LA 724, 725, 730 (Van de Water, 1953), but the parties also authorized the neutral to call upon counsel for the parties for a joint discussion of the issues brought out at the hearing.

[40] For instance, see Remington Rand, Inc., 20 LA 799, 800 (Lehoczky, 1953), in which the arbitrator withdrew his first proposed award (reported in 20 LA 271) and issued an amended award which attained a majority vote.

[41] See discussion in Bell Aircraft Corp., 13 LA 813, 820-821 (Day, 1950).

[42] See discussion by Freidin, Labor Arbitration and the Courts 44-46 (U. of Pa. Press, 1952).

[43] See Taylor, "The Arbitration of Labor Disputes," 1 Arb. J. (N.S.) 409, 413 (1946).

importance that clear understanding of the underlying needs and requirements of the parties be obtained. To this end the neutral member of a tripartite board has the assistance of the partisan members, which may serve to prevent serious errors of judgment.[44]

Awards of tripartite boards, when they are unanimous, tend to carry more weight than awards by single arbitrators.

(b) Disadvantages

Tripartite boards often cause delay not only in the initial appointment of the partisan members, but also both at hearings and afterwards.[45] The members selected by the parties may insist upon complete reargument of the case after the hearing is concluded. This tendency of the partisan members to act as advocates instead of arbitrators leads to unduly extended sessions. Also, additional time may be lost in waiting for dissenting opinions to be written. Any additional time required necessarily adds to the costs.

The task of the impartial member often is unhappy and difficult. Too frequently he must act as conciliator for the other members, and, as has been seen, he may be forced to compromise his own best judgment in order to secure a majority vote, where such vote is required.

Because of these disadvantages, many parties prefer not to use tripartite boards for "rights" disputes.[46] Indeed, a definite decline in use of tripartite boards in grievance arbitration has been noted by one observer.[47]

---

[44] See Davey, "Hazards in Labor Arbitration," 1 Ind. & Lab. Rel. Rev. 386, 399 (1948).

[45] Regarding the problem of delay and possibilities of minimizing it, see Bell Aircraft Corp., 13 LA 813, 820-821 (Day, 1950).

[46] For strong criticism of use of tripartite boards for grievance arbitration, see Reynard, "Drafting of Grievance and Arbitration Articles of Collective Bargaining Agreements," 10 Vanderbilt L. Rev. 749, 755-760 (1957); Braden, "Recurring Problems in Grievance Arbitration," Preparing and Presenting Arbitration Cases 28, 33-34 (1954).

[47] See Davey, "Labor Arbitration: A Current Appraisal," 9 Ind. & Lab. Rel. Rev. 85, 87 (1955).

Procedure Following the Hearing

The inherent nature of tripartite boards brings certain procedural matters into special consideration, particularly in regard to the extent of consultation and discussion between the impartial chairman and the partisan members following the arbitration hearing.[48]

The members of tripartite boards in many cases meet in executive session to discuss the case after the hearing has been completed.[49] Customarily the impartial chairman of the board will inquire as to the wishes of the partisan members in regard to meeting in executive session. In some cases it will be specifically agreed that there will be no executive session, and that the neutral member will write the opinion and award with each party reserving the right to file a dissent.[50] When this procedure is followed it may be agreed also that if the award prepared by the neutral does not receive a majority vote, the board will then meet in executive session to discuss the case further.[51]

More often tripartite boards do meet in executive session prior to the preparation of any proposed award. But while the session ordinarily gives the neutral a better insight into the dispute, only infrequently does it produce a unanimous decision. Often when the executive session fails to resolve the dispute, it will be understood that the neutral will prepare a proposed award without further conference or communication with the partisan members other than to submit the award to them for concurrence or dissent.[52]

Usually the neutral prepares an opinion to accompany his proposed award but it is commonly understood that a partisan member in signing an award does not necessarily indicate concurrence with any or all of the statements made by the neutral

---

[48] For discussion of arbitration procedure generally, see Chapter 7.

[49] Sometimes it is agreed that counsel for the parties may attend the session, as in Safeway Stores, Inc., 22 LA 466, 467 (Hildebrand, 1954).

[50] As in Texas Co., 24 LA 240, 241 (White, 1955).

[51] See Kraft Foods Co., 15 LA 38, 39 (Updegraff, 1950).

[52] As in 26 LA 477, 478; 21 LA 367, 369; 17 LA 335, 341.

in his opinion.[53] Even where an executive session produces a unanimous decision, the responsibility for preparing a supporting opinion may be placed solely in the neutral member.[54]

Under some circumstances, at least, the neutral member of a tripartite board might not be compelled to meet in executive session with the partisan members even though the latter members have not expressly waived such session. For instance, in arbitration by a tripartite board under the Railway Labor Act a United States District Court declared that the provisions of said Act "necessarily recognize that the partisan members [of the tripartite board] will champion the position of their respective employers," and where all members of the board attended the arbitration hearing the Court held that the failure of the neutral mmber to call the board together after his proposed findings had been submitted to them should, at most, "be considered as a mere irregularity and not sufficient to vitiate the action of the majority of the Board." There was no showing that the members of the board ever conferred or consulted together as to the findings or as to the award to be made, nor that such consultation was requested by either party. As to this the Court said: "The amenities of the situation might well have suggested to the Chairman that the other two members be advised that he would call the Board together for a conference if it was deemed desirable after the draft of the findings and award had been submitted to them. But, realistically considered, it must be recognized that such gesture would have accomplished nothing." The neutral's findings and award, when submitted to the partisan members, were concurred in by the company member and accordingly became the binding award by a majority of the board.[55]

---

[53] Sometimes the neutral himself emphasizes the latter fact. See Arbitrator Dash in 23 LA 177; R. Smith in 20 LA 625; Pension in 17 LA 152, 153.

[54] As in Shenango Valley Transit Co., 21 LA 356, 357 (Brecht, 1953).

[55] In re Duluth, Missabe and Iron Range Railway Co., 124 F. Supp. 923, 928-929 (D. Minn., 1954). The opposite result was reached under New York law in Simons v. News Syndicate, Inc., 26 LA 281 (N.Y. Sup. Ct., 1956). Failure of the neutral to call an executive session prior to issuance of his proposed award was strongly criticized by one of the parties in Northwest Airlines, Inc., 29 LA 541, 545-546 (1957).

The refusal of a partisan member of a tripartite board to attend the board's executive session, and indeed, the resignation or withdrawl of a partisan member prior to issuance of the award, has in several cases been held not to defeat the proceedings nor prevent the issuance of a binding majority award by the other members of the board.[56]

Even if the common law rule which permits either party to withdraw from arbitration at any time prior to issuance of an award is otherwise applicable, it is said that where an arbitrator orally "announces what his decision will be, it is doubtful whether a party could withdraw between the time of that announcement and the formal written rendition."[57]

Methods of Selecting Arbitrators

Selection of an arbitrator satisfactory to both parties often entails difficulties. No part of the arbitration process is more important than that of selecting the person who is to render the decision. Fortunately, a variety of selection methods are available.

It is generally assumed that selection by mutual agreement of the parties is the most desirable method. This may be true in terms of insuring acceptance of the award, although there is no inherent reason why an equally if not more competent arbitrator might not be selected by a third party. However, there does appear to be more justification for mutual selection of permanent arbitrators since they ordinarily have some tenure of office.

---

[56] See Publishers' Assn. of New York City v. New York Stereotypers' Union No. 1, 181 N.Y.S. 2d 527 (N.Y. Sup. Ct., 1959); Shoeworkers Assn. v. Federal Shoe, Inc., 24 LA 573, 576 (Maine Sup. Ct., 1955); Street Ry. Employees v. Connecticut Co., 24 LA 107, 108-110 (Conn. Sup. Ct., 1955); American Eagle Fire Ins. Co. v. New Jersey Ins. Co., 148 N.E. 562, 565 (N.Y. Ct. App., 1925). cf., Fromer Foods, Inc. v. Edelstein Foods, Inc., 181 N.Y.S. 2d 352 (N.Y. Sup. Ct, 1959), involving death of a partisan member. Also see Consumers Power Co., 24 LA 581, 582 (R. Smith, Howlett & Sorensen, 1955). For a related discussion see Chapter 7, topic titled "Default Awards."

[57] Updegraff & McCoy, Arbitration of Labor Disputes 122 (1946). Regarding the common law and its modification by statute, see Chapter 2, topic titled "Enforceability of Agreements to Arbitrate."

Collective agreements often provide for selection by the parties [58] and, at the same time, alternative methods to be used if they fail to agree within a specified time. Provision for alternative methods of appointment always should be made in the agreement. Otherwise, proposed arbitration may be defeated for want of an effective means of selecting the arbitrator.[59]

The neutral member, or members, of tripartite boards may be selected by the members appointed by the parties. Agreements often provide that each party shall choose one or more arbitrators and that the arbitrators so chosen shall select a neutral chairman. The partisan members, however, may fail to agree upon the neutral, so here too the agreement should provide alternate methods of selection.

Aid from an outside agency, whether requested at the outset or after the parties have failed to agree upon an arbitrator, generally takes one of two forms: (1) A list is submitted from which, often by a process of elimination, the parties select an arbitrator; or (2) direct appointment of the arbitrator by the agency. An agreement may designate the Federal Mediation and Conciliation Service, a state agency, the American Arbitration Association, a judge, some public official, or any other impartial agency.[60]

The type of aid rendered by the Federal Mediation and Conciliation Service depends upon the nature of the dispute and the authority vested in the service by the parties. The service encourage the parties to make their own selection from a list of qualified arbitrators. Only as a last resort, or if the parties insist on it, will the service make a direct appointment.

Under the Rules of the American Arbitration Association, parties may select the arbitrator as they please. However, in order to facilitate selection, the Association sends lists of

---

[58] This step may be waived. See Barbet Mills, Inc., 16 LA 563 (Livengood, 1951).

[59] See discussion by board of inquiry in Rochester Transit Corp., 19 LA 538, 558 (Tolley, McKelvey & Turkus, 1952). Under modern arbitration statutes the arbitrator will be appointed by a court if the parties cannot agree upon one or upon a method of appointment.

[60] Regarding use of appointing agencies, see Warren & Bernstein, "A Profile of Labor Arbitration," 16 LA 970, 974-975 (1951).

names to the parties. They have the privilege of crossing off names objected to. The Association then makes the appointment from the names remaining on the lists, in order of preference. If the parties fail to agree upon any of the names submitted, they may request additional lists. If they still are not able to agree, the Association appoints an arbitrator whose name has not appeared on the lists.[61] It is interesting to note that the Association rarely has to make the final appointments, in some years making final appointments in only about 5 percent of the cases submitted to it for administration.[62]

Under the procedure of the New York State Mediation Board, each party eliminates two of the five names submitted. The New Jersey Board submits a list of names and asks the parties to rank the names in order of acceptability; then appoints in that order.

Some state arbitration statutes provide for court appointment of arbitrators where the parties cannot agree on an arbitrator and one or both of them so requests. Under the New York Civil Practice Act a court may, on its own motion, appoint an arbitrator where the agreement provides for the appointment of an arbitrator by the parties and they fail to agree upon one.[63]

Experience has shown the government agencies or departments which deal with labor relations are especially well qualified to select arbitrators.[64]

Qualifications of Arbitrators

With the rapid expansion of labor-mangement arbitration in recent years, there has emerged a large group of persons experienced and available for arbitration service. Special or

---

[61] Labor Arbitration 14-15 (American Arbitration Association, 1957).

[62] See statistics in "Procedural Aspects of Labor-Management Arbitration," 28 LA 933, 935; also, Murphy, "Free Choice of Arbitrators Is Still the American Way in Labor Arbitrations," 3 Arb. J. (N.S.) 234 (1948). The Association may aid in the selection of the arbitrator even where it is not administering other aspects of the case, as in Celotex Corp., 24 LA 369, 370 (Reynard, 1955).

[63] Feuer Transportation, Inc., 1 LA 318 (N.Y. Ct. App., 1946).

[64] See Lapp, Labor Arbitration 95 (1942).

technical training is not necessary except as specifically required by the parties. It is not surprising, then, that arbitrators come from a wide variety of backgrounds. Indeed, the group includes professors, lawyers, judges, public office holders, ministers, accountants, economists, professional arbitrators, and others.[65]

Qualifications Set Forth in Agreement

The parties may, by agreement, specify qualifications which must be possessed by the arbitrator. The selection of an arbitrator may be hampered seriously, however, by an attempt to fix qualifications rigidly in the agreement. It may be impossible to secure an arbitrator who meets the qualifications so specified. Although the determination of qualifications generally is left to the parties, a few state arbitration statutes do prescribe qualifications designed to insure impartiality.

Impartiality

No qualification is more important than that of impartiality.[66] It may well be that no man can be absolutely free from bias or prejudice of any kind, but it is not too much to expect an arbitrator to be able to divest himself of any personal inclinations, and to be able to stand between the parties with an open mind. This does not mean, however, that an arbitrator should decide contrary to his own best judgment. Indeed, the element of honesty is not satisfied unless the arbitrator fully believes that he is doing what is right. To be an arbitrator worthy of the name, one must always be able and ready to "call 'em as he sees 'em." As long as both parties be-

---

[65] For a general discussion of arbitrators, see Cole, Freidin & Oliver, "The Status and Expendability of The Labor Arbitrator," The Profession of Labor Arbitration 42-65 (BNA Incorporated, 1957). Also see "Survey of the Arbitration Profession," The Profession of Labor Arbitration 176-182 (BNA Incorporated, 1957). For statistics on the occupational status of arbitrators, see "Procedural Aspects of Labor-Management Arbitration," 28 LA 933, 936 (1954 statistics); Warren & Bernstein, "A Profile of Labor Arbitration," 16 LA 970, 973-974 (1951).

[66] Arbitrators have been deemed to be judicial officers, sharing certain immunities from suit by parties, since arbitrators "must be free from the fear of reprisals" and "must of necessity be uninfluenced by any fear of consequences for their acts." Babylon Milk & Cream Co. v. Horvitz, 26 LA 121, 122 (N.Y. Sup. Ct., 1956).

lieve that an arbitrator is doing just that, they will respect him whether or not they "see 'em" the same way he does.

Integrity

The integrity of arbitrators generally can be expected to be of the highest. Appointed judges often are criticized as receiving political "plums." Elected judges often are criticized as being politicians. Arbitrators generally are not open to such criticism, being selected by free choice of the parties or their agent. But how may a prospective arbitrator be tested for integrity and impartiality? Careful consideration of his personal and business background and affiliations is enlightening in this respect. Has the arbitrator any financial or business interest in the affairs of either party? Has there been any such interest in the past? Does the arbitrator have any personal affiliations, either directly or indirectly, with either of the parties? Does he have strong opinions in favor of either labor or management? [67] What has been his past record as an arbitrator? The parties may review some past awards of the arbitrator, but the number of awards rendered in favor of each side should not be used as a test of impartiality. An arbitrator who deliberately tries to please both sides by "splitting" awards is not one who decides cases objectively. It is the arbitrator's fairness and good judgment, as indicated by his past awards and by his general reputation, that the parties should be concerned with.

Ability

Naturally, extensive arbitration experience is one indication of ability. But at the outset a labor-management arbitrator should have a broad background of social and economic study or experience. He should have an analytical mind and should be able to orient himself quickly when dealing with new sub-

---

[67] A New York court was upheld in removing an arbitrator it had appointed but who, the court later learned, was partisan toward labor, although his integrity and honesty were not questioned. Western Union v. Selly, 2 LA 688 (N.Y. Ct. App., 1946). Also see In re Steuben, 14 LA 541 (N.Y. Sup. Ct., 1950); In re Culinary Bar & Grill Employees, 11 LA 1119 (N.Y. Sup. Ct., 1949).

ject matter. Maturity of judgment is indispensable. Diplomacy helps too.

Must an arbitrator be something of a specialist in the subject matter which he is to consider? Generally speaking, no. While neither side cares to appoint persons completely unfamiliar with industrial matters, an arbitrator generally will not be disqualified merely because he is not an expert in the subject of the dispute. An acceptable expert may be difficult or impossible to secure. Moreover, the parties often prefer an arbitrator who has general business or financial experience or who is versed in law. Arbitrators, as judges, generally should be selected for their ability to understand all sorts of problems. But in some disputes a specialist may be considered essential. Thus the parties may seek an industrial engineer, or a doctor, or some other type of specialist, depending upon the technical matter involved.[68]

Legal Training

Persons trained in law often make able arbitrators, although legal training is not indispensable. Many labor-management arbitrators are lawyers. Lawyers are considered especially desirable for the position of neutral chairman of arbitration boards.[69] Legal training helps an arbitrator to be objective. It improves his ability to analyze and evaluate facts. This means that the arbitrator who has had legal training may be less likely to be moved by personal bias or by extraneous evidence. By no means, however, do all lawyers make good arbitrators. Especially ineffective is the lawyer who is so concerned with technical rules of evidence and procedure that the arbitration process is made unduly complicated. Such concern also may result in an award which fails to give sufficient consideration to the real merits of the dispute. Legal training alone is not enough to make an able arbitrator, but if a person possesses the other qualifications, legal training will make him even better.

---

[68] Regarding need for technical expertness of arbitrators, see Warren & Bernstein, "A Profile of Labor Arbitration," 16 LA 970, 975 (1951).

[69] Gotshal, "The Lawyer's Place in Arbitration," 1 Arb. J. (N.S.) 367 (1946).

Data on Arbitrators

Information concerning the qualifications of some of the more active arbitrators may be had by consulting the "Directory of Arbitrators" prepared by The Bureau of National Affairs, Inc., or the "Who's Who" (of arbitrators) prepared by Prentice-Hall, Inc. This information includes the name, age, address, education, occupation, affiliations, experience, articles or books written, awards published, and other miscellaneous information concerning the arbitrator.

The Federal Mediation and Conciliation Service provides biographical data on the arbitrators whose names are supplied to the parties for selection, and most other designating agencies follow the same practice.

Tribunals Under Railway Labor Act

One of the nation's most extensive experiences in labor-management arbitration has resulted from the arbitration provisions of the Railway Labor Act of 1926,[70] as amended in 1934.[71]

Since it has been suggested frequently that arbitration tribunals of the Railway Labor Act variety be used for other industries, consideration is given here to the basic features of those tribunals. As was seen in Chapter 3, the present railroad labor legislation of the United States recognizes the distinction between disputes as to "rights" and those as to "interests." The National Mediation Board is concerned primarily with "interests" disputes, while the National Railroad Adjustment Board is concerned with "rights" disputes.

Railroad 'Interests' Disputes

The National Mediation Board has jurisdiction over any "dispute concerning changes in rates of pay, rules, or working conditions not adjusted by the parties in conference," or any

---

[70] 44 Stat. 577.

[71] 44 Stat. 1185; 1 LRR Man. 843; 45 U.S.C. §§ 151-163, 181-188. See generally, Lecht, Experience Under Railway Labor Legislation (Colum. Univ. Press, 1955).

"other disputes not referable to the National Railroad Adjustment Board and not adjusted in conference between the parties or where conferences are refused." Either party may invoke the services of the Mediation Board, or the Board may proffer its services if a labor emergency is found to exist. The primary function of the Mediation Board is to help the parties, through mediation, to reach agreement. Upon failure to bring about an amicable settlement through mediation, however, the Board seeks to induce the parties to submit the controversy to voluntary arbitration.

Section 7 of the Act provides details for the organization of the arbitration tribunal. It provides that, whenever a controversy is not settled "either in conference between representatives of the parties or by the appropriate adjustment board or through mediation," it may, by agreement of the parties, be submitted "to the arbitration of a board of three (or, if the parties to the controversy to stipulate, of six) persons * * *." If the parties choose a board of three, then each party selects one member and the two so selected choose the neutral member. If a board of six is desired, each side selects two members and the four so selected choose the two neutral members. If the members selected by the parties cannot agree upon the neutral or neutrals, they are appointed by the Mediation Board. The board of arbitration selects one of its members to serve as chairman and makes such rules as are necessary for conducting hearings. The members selected by the parties do not need to be impartial. Each party compensates its appointees and the Mediation Board compensates neutrals.

The award of the board, when signed by a majority of the members, may be filed with the clerk of the district court of the United States for the district in which the controversy arose or the arbitration is entered into. When so filed, it is conclusive on the parties as to the merits and facts of the controversy, and, unless within ten days a petition to impeach it on grounds specifically set out in the Act is filed with the court, judgment will be entered on the award.

National Railroad Adjustment Board

Upon submission of a petition by either side, the National Railroad Adjustment Board takes jurisdiction over "disputes between an employee or group of employees and a carrier or carriers growing out of grievances or out of the interpretation or application of agreements concerning rates of pay, rules, or working conditions," after they have been "handled in the usual manner up to and including the chief operating officer of the carrier designated to handle such disputes." Thus it is seen that the Adjustment Board handles "rights" disputes. It assumes jurisdiction only if at least one of the parties wishes it to do so.

The Adjustment Board is strictly bipartisan. It is composed of thirty-six members, eighteen of whom are selected and compensated by the carriers and eighteen by the railroad labor organizations. The Board is organized into four Divisions, each Division having jurisdiction over specified classes of railroad employees. The Adjustment Board functions almost entirely through the individual Divisions, and each Division for all practical purposes is independent of the others. Each Division really amounts to a distinct arbitration tribunal, bipartisan in nature, with equal representation from the carriers and the labor organizations. The First, Second, and Third Divisions have ten permanent members each, the Fourth Division has six.

When a dispute is referred to one of the Divisions a hearing is held, unless waived. At the hearing the parties may be heard either in person, by counsel, or by other representatives. After the hearing, the Division proceeds to decide the case. As a matter of practice the Divisions frequently hold successive hearings on a group of cases, then hold sessions for deliberation and decision of the cases. Since each Division is equally represented by labor and management and since the representatives of each side tend almost always to vote the same way, a unanimous vote generally is necessary to decide a case. While many cases do receive the required vote, numerous others do not.

Deadlocks are inevitable and frequent. The Act provides for the selection of referees in such cases. The referee sits with the Division as a temporary member and decides the cases for which he is appointed. Usually a referee's appointment will be for a group of cases. Deadlocked cases are set aside until a sufficient number have accumulated to warrant calling in a referee.

Initial responsibility for the selection of referees is upon the Divisions. If a Division, however, is unable to agree upon a neutral person to serve as referee, one is selected by the National Mediation Board. Within ten days after a Division certifies to the Mediation Board the fact of inability to agree upon a referee, the Mediation Board makes the appointment. The Divisions, generally speaking, have not been able to agree upon referees, so the primary responsibility for appointment of referees has been with the Mediation Board. All referees are compensated by the Mediation Board.

Cases assigned to a referee are presented to him by Division members. Occasionally, if request is made, some Divisions permit oral argument by the parties before the referee. Generally, however, the referee's knowledge of a case comes from the parties' written submissions and from briefs and arguments of Division members.[72] Each Division has both labor and management members highly skilled in presenting cases to the referees. The referee is given opportunity to study case records prior to meeting with Division members. Division members often present written briefs to the referee and always give him opportunity to ask questions.

The referee then takes the cases under advisement, makes his findings, and writes the proposed opinions and awards. Practice varies as to the length of opinions. The Third Division, for instance, expects its referees to write relatively long opinions. The First Division prefers brevity. The referee discusses proposed awards with the Division and voting follows. The side in whose favor an award is rendered generally will

---

[72] The Adjustment Board is essentially an appellate tribunal. The Chrysler Corporation Appeal Board, too, is an appellate tribunal, the grievant never appearing in person before the Board.

vote with the referee to provide the required majority vote.[73]

If an award is in favor of the employees, the Division is directed by the Act to issue an order requiring the carrier to make the award effective. After such order is issued, the Division has nothing to do with its enforcement. If the award is not complied with, the party in whose favor it stands may sue upon it in the appropriate federal district court. In such suit the findings and order of the Adjustment Board Division are prima facie evidence of the facts stated therein.[74]

The party against whom an award is directed has no right to take it to the courts. Essentially the only way an award may be tested in court is for it to be in favor of the employees, for the carrier to refuse to comply with the award, and for the employees then to take it to court for enforcement. Theoretically, the carrier needs no right to go to court on its own initiative since it can refuse to comply with an award in favor of employees and let them take it to court. The weakness of this approach, however, is that employees have at times chosen to strike instead of suing to force carrier compliance. This means that in such instances the carrier has no effective right of court review.

Finally, it should be noted that sometimes neither party to a dispute will submit it to the Adjustment Board even though the dispute is a "rights" or "minor" dispute of the type for which the Board was established. While the United States Supreme Court has held that railroad employees have no freedom to strike over such disputes if they are actually pending before the Adjustment Board and that the federal

---

[73] For other studies and discussions of the Adjustment Board, see Kaufman, "Grievance Arbitration in the Railroad Industry," 9 Labor L. J. 244 (1958); Daugherty, Whiting & Guthrie, "Arbitration by the National Railroad Adjustment Board," Arbitration Today 93-127 (BNA Incorporated, 1955); Lecht, Experience Under Railway Labor Legislation 10-11, 83, 163, 171, 191-192 (1955); Jones, National Railroad Adjustment Board (1941); Spencer, The National Railroad Adjustment Board (1938); Garrison, "The National Railroad Adjustment Board; A Unique Administrative Agency," 46 Yale L. J. 567 (1937).

[74] The burden of seeking court enforcement of awards is somewhat reduced by a provision of the Act which relieves the petitioner from some of the court costs and which allows a petitioner who prevails in his action a reasonable attorney's fee.

courts may enjoin strikes in such instances,[75] strikes over such disputes apparently may not be enjoined if the dispute is not actually pending before the Adjustment Board.[76]

Existing differences which neither party will submit to the Board may plague the parties year after year until finally a sufficient number will have accumulated to cause a strike. At this point the National Mediation Board sometimes induces the parties to accept arbitration by a three-man or six-man board, or to establish a special board of adjustment for the cases in question.

Statutory Tribunals for Critical Industrial Disputes

Both the Railway Labor Act and the Labor Management Relations Act of 1947 contain provisions for special tribunals for critical industrial disputes, and both Acts contain provisions for requiring the parties to maintain the *status quo* without work stoppages pending investigation and report by the special tribunal. These tribunals should be noted briefly in passing even though, technically speaking, they are not arbitration tribunals.

Section 10 of the Railway Labor Act provides that if a dispute between a carrier and its employees is not settled by use of the Act's other machinery, and if the National Mediation Board finds that the dispute threatens a substantial interruption of interstate commerce, the President may in his discretion create an Emergency Board to investigate and report the facts and circumstances of the dispute and make recommendations as to its settlement.[77]

---

[75] Brotherhood of Railroad Trainmen v. Chicago R. & I. R. Co., 77 Sup. Ct. 635, 39 LRRM 2578 (1957). The carriers sometimes submit disputes to the Board as a means of avoiding strikes.

[76] A state court injunction against one such strike was vacated by the United States Supreme Court where the dispute was not pending before the Adjustment Board. Manion v. Kansas City Terminal Railway Company, 77 Sup. Ct. 706, 39 LRRM 2641 (1957).

[77] For detailed discussion of these boards, see Railroads v. Nonoperating Unions, 17 LA 833, 841, 843 (Cole, Horvitz & Osborne, 1952); Kaufman, "Emergency Boards Under the Railway Labor Act," 9 Labor Law J. 910 (1958); Lecht, Experience Under Railway Labor Legislation 6, 11-12, 53-54, 176, 190-191 (1955).

Section 206 of the Labor Management-Relations Act of 1947 provides that in national emergency disputes, imperiling the national health or safety, the President may appoint a Board of Inquiry to inquire into the issues involved in the dispute and to make a written report which "shall include a statement of the facts with respect to the dispute, including each party's statement of its position but shall not contain any recommendations." [78]

Boards of Inquiry may also be established under state statute. The function of one such board, which had authority to make recommendations, was deemed by its members to "contain elements both of mediation and arbitration," since:

"Like a mediator, the Board must think about the acceptability of its proposals. Like an arbitrator, it is concerned with the weight of the evidence and with the merits of the questions before it. As a statutory Board appointed by the State of New York, the Board has the additional function of serving a public interest which is not necessarily present in private proceedings." [79]

While the parties are not legally compelled to accept the findings of emergency boards and boards of inquiry, public pressure may strongly motivate them to do so, especially where the board has authority to make recommendations and actually does so.

---

[78] For the reports of some of these Boards of Inquiry, see Maritime Industry, 21 LA 489, and 21 LA 189 (Cole, Carman & Comey, 1953); American Locomotive Co., 19 LA 839, and 19 LA 532 (Harris, Cheney & Levy, 1953). For general discussion see Cole, "Major Labor Disputes—Reexamination and Recommendations," The Profession of Labor Arbitration 90 (BNA Incorporated, 1957).

[79] Rochester Transit Corp., 19 LA 538, 542 (Tolley, McKelvey & Turkus, 1952).

CHAPTER 5

GRIEVANCES—PRELUDE TO ARBITRATION

Arbitration generally is the last step or terminal point of dispute settlement under union contracts. A happy situation exists when the preliminary steps of dispute-settlement machinery function effectively, resulting in settlement of a high percentage of disputes prior to the arbitration stage. If the preliminary steps do not function smoothly, the arbitration tribunal may be swamped with cases, which, in turn, may lead to a breakdown of the system. It is generally agreed that no dispute should be taken to arbitration until all possibilities of settlement at the negotiation stages of the grievance procedure have been exhausted. Once, however, the preliminary steps have been exhausted without success, resort to arbitration should be prompt.

The Grievance Procedure

It is said that collective bargaining is not confined to the making of an agreement once a year but is a day-to-day process, one in which the grievance procedure has a very important role.[1] Some writers declare the grievance procedure to be the core of the collective bargaining agreement.[2] Professor Harry Shulman expressed a similar view:

"In labor negotiations there are factors peculiar to them which affirmatively press for almost deliberate incompleteness and uncertainty in the agreement; but, even if it were otherwise, it surely is true that no collective agreement has been or can be written which covers in detail all the exigencies with which the parties may be confronted in the contract period, or which makes crystal-clear its meaning with respect to the matters that it does cover. * * * It is this that makes collective bargaining an unending process

---
[1] Chrysler Corp., 10 War Lab. Rep. 551, 554 (1943).
[2] Hill & Hook, Mangement at the Bargaining Table 199 (1945).

79

in labor relations, and it is this that makes the grievance procedure the heart of the collective agreement." [3]

The extreme importance of a good grievance procedure in large companies has been emphasized by Arbitrator Michael I. Komaroff, who called the grievance machinery the "life-blood of a collective bargaining relationship." [4] In the coal mining industry the grievance procedure "is seen to be the 'safety-valve' in industrial relations, the procedure which gives a vital flexibility to the whole system of collective bargaining." [5]

The President's National Labor-Management Conference of 1945 recommended that every collective bargaining agreement contain provision for an effective grievance procedure. The Conference outlined some of the standards which a grievance procedure, to be "effective," should meet:

"1. Collective bargaining agreements should contain provisions that grievances and disputes involving the interpretation or application of the terms of the agreement are to be settled without resort to strikes, lockouts, or other interruptions to normal operations by an effective grievance procedure with arbitration as its final step.

"2. To be effective, the procedure established for the settlement of such grievances and disputes should meet at least the following standards:

"(a) The successive steps in the procedure, the method of presenting grievances or disputes, and the method of taking an appeal from one step to another should be so clearly stated in the agreement as to be readily understood by all employees, union officials, and management representatives.

"(b) The procedure should be adaptable to the handling of the various types of grievances and disputes which come under the terms of the agreement.

"(c) The procedure should be designed to facilitate the settlement of grievances and disputes as soon as possible after they arise. To this end:

"(1) The agreement should provide adequate stated time limits for the presentation of grievances and disputes, the rendering of decisions, and the taking of appeals.

"(2) Issues should be clearly formulated at the earliest possible moment. In all cases which cannot be settled in the first informal discussions, the positions of both sides should be reduced to writing.

---

[3] Conference on Training of Law Students in Labor Relations. Vol. III, Transcript of Proceedings 669 (1947).

[4] North American Aviation, Inc., 16 LA 744, 747 (1951).

[5] Somers, Grievance Settlement in Coal Mining 43 (W. Va. Univ. Bull. Series 56, No. 12-2, 1956).

"(3)   Management and union should encourage their representatives to settle at the lower steps grievances which do not involve broad questions of policy or of contract interpretation and should delegate sufficient authority to them to accomplish this end.

"(4)   The agreement should provide adequate opportunity for both parties to investigate grievances under discussion.

"(5)   Provision should be made for priority handling of grievances involving discharge, suspension, or other disciplinary action.

"(d)   The procedure should be open to the submission of grievances by all parties to the agreement.

"3.   Managements and unions should inform and train their representatives in the proper functioning of the grievance procedure and in their responsibilities under it. In such a program it should be emphasized:

"(a)   That the basic objective of the grievance procedure is the achievement of sound and fair settlements and not the "winning" of cases;

"(b)   That the filing of grievances should be considered by foremen or supervisors as aids in discovering and removing causes of discontent in their departments;

"(c)   That any tendency by either party to support the earlier decisions of its representatives when such decisions are wrong should be discouraged;

"(d)   That the willingness of management and union officials to give adequate time and attention to the handling and disposition of grievances and disputes is necessary to the effective functioning of the procedure;

"(e)   That for the sound handling of grievances and disputes both management and union representatives should be thoroughly familiar with the entire collective bargaining agreement." [6]

Most collective bargaining agreements give recognition to some, at least, of these standards, and arbitrators of "interests" disputes have been known to direct the parties to "spell out" the details of their grievance procedures in accordance with the recommendations of the National Labor Management Conference.[7]

---

[6] The President's National Labor-Management Conference, Nov. 5-30, 1945 (U. S. Dept. of Labor, Div. of Labor Standards, Bull. No. 77, pp. 45-46, 1946).

[7] See N. Y. Shipping Assn., 1 LA 80, 84, 87-88 (Davis, 1945). Also see comments of Arbitrator Maurice H. Merrill in 20 LA 211, 212. For general discussion of grievance procedures, see The Grievance Process (Mich. State Univ. Lab. & Ind. Rel. Center, 1956); Reynard, "Drafting of Grievance and Arbitration Articles of Collective Bargaining Agreements," 10 Vanderbilt L. Rev. 749 (1957).

Grievances Defined

What is a "grievance"? Comprehensively, it is that which the parties to a particular collective agreement say it is. Such a definition, of course, does no more than apprise one of the fact that labor relations authorities disagree widely as to the precise meaning of the term and that collective agreements reflect this lack of accord. The term connotes conflict and irritation, and thus could be defined as any "gripe" or any type of complaint by an employee or a union against the employer or by an employer against his employee or the union. It is generally understood, however, that disputes involving demands for changes in the terms of a collective bargaining agreement ("interests" disputes) and disputes arising out of representation issues are not grievances.

Grievances may arise from an infinite number of causes, which may be either real or imaginary. This suggests inquiry as to what determines when a person has a grievance. Must there have been a wrong done? One employer has urged that a grievance does not come into existence so as to be subject to the grievance procedure until some harmful or disciplinary action has been taken against the complainant. The arbitrator who considered this view rejected it as being too narrow. He said: "Whether a man has a grievance or not is primarily his own feeling about the matter. Generally speaking, if a man thinks he has a grievance, he has a grievance." [8]

From a more technical standpoint, however, Arbitrator Charles O. Gregory has stated that the term "grievance" as it appears in the average contract refers to "a formal complaint" by persons who believe they have been wronged. [9]

Attitude of Parties to the Grievance Procedure

The parties' attitude in handling grievances, probably more than in any other aspect of the labor-management rela-

---

[8] Cudahy Packing Co., 7 LA 645, 646 (Fisher, 1947).
[9] E. I. Du Pont De Nemours & Co., 29 LA 646, 650 (1957). But Cf., Braniff Airways, Inc., 27 LA 892 (J. Williams, 1957).

tionship, indicates their good faith. Nowhere in that relationship is mutual good faith more important. The attitude of the parties is even more important than the type of grievance provisions contained in the agreement.[10] This view has been shared by unions and management alike in most cases in which the grievance procedure has been considered successful and in the majority of cases in which the procedure has broken down.[11] Good grievance machinery is important, but such machinery alone will not insure success. The attitude, judgment, experience, and training of the individual involved are of prime importance. Moreover, a desire to settle grievances, rather than to win them, is essential.

No grievance should be presented unless there is a real basis for complaint or need for decision. Much responsibility belongs directly to the union stewards, and indirectly to the union, to screen out complaints that have no real merit. The United States Department of Labor has suggested that persons responsible for the preparation of stewards' manuals give serious thought to the inclusion of the following instructions to stewards:

" * * * *Use your best judgment in deciding whether or not a grievance is justified.*—If you are convinced that the worker does not have a real case it is better to tell him so right from the beginning. Taking up a lot of poor cases will cost you the respect of all concerned. On the other hand, don't forget that you are the worker's representative. If the case is a borderline one but you feel that the worker has considerable justice on his side, tell him frankly that you are not sure what is the correct answer. Then take the case up and get a definite ruling through the grievance procedure." [12]

Both parties should make every effort to settle grievances at the lowest step. Grievances become magnified in importance and increasingly more difficult to settle as they progress toward the top. Good will at the outset breeds more good will. Where good will exists, grievances can be adjusted more readily, thus

[10] "Grievance Procedure Under Collective Bargaining," 63 Monthly Labor Review 175 (U. S. Dept. of Labor, Bureau of Labor Statistics, 1946).

[11] Ibid.

[12] Preparing a Steward's Manual (U. S. Dept. of Labor, Div. of Labor Standards, Bull. No. 59, p. 7, 1943).

leading to constant improvement of the labor-management relationship.

When approached with the proper attitude, grievance machinery serves the mutual advantage of employer, employees, and the union. It helps management discover and correct sore spots in plant operations before they cause serious trouble. Grievances constitute a channel of communication, informing top management of things concerning which employees or the union feel strongly.[13] It is to the employer's advantage to make it as easy as possible to present grievances, and employees should be encouraged, not only to present their complaints, but also to present them while they are still "warm." Grievance machinery provides the union a mechanism for enforcing the rules which it has worked for and achieved through collective bargaining.

Moreover, through use of grievance machinery the union performs a service to the employees, which will increase their loyalty to the union. "To the individual worker, grievance procedure provides the means of enforcing the terms of the contract and * * * a democratic method of appeal against any one person's arbitrary decision affecting his wages or working conditions. It protects the democratic rights of the individual in industry in the same way that our judicial system protects his democratic rights in civil life."[14]

Should Grievance Machinery Be Open to All Complaints?

There is no strong reason why parties should place limitations upon the subject matter that may be taken to the grievance procedure, even though a complaint is ultimately rejected as constituting an attempt to amend the agreement. Complaints often shrink in importance and are easily disposed of once they are brought into the open, while employees who have no outlet for their complaints tend to magnify them far beyond

---

[13] Hill & Hook, Management at the Bargaining Table 199 (1945).

[14] Settling Plant Grievances (U. S. Dept. of Labor, Div. of Labor Standards, Bull. No. 60, p. 1, 1943).

their true importance. Harry Shulman urged that every griev-ance should be received, heard, and considered seriously and sympathetically and that, to the extent possible, every griev-ance should be made the occasion for additional education of the parties and for a little more smoothing out of the wrinkles in their relationship.[15]

Some agreements do open the door of the grievance machinery to any complaint. The clause to this effect may take the following form:

"In the event of any complaints, grievances, difficulties, disagreements or disputes arising between the Company, its employees within the collective bargaining unit hereinabove defined, or the Union, there shall be no suspension of plant operations but an earnest effort shall be made to settle such difference, complaints, grievances, difficulties, disagreements, or disputes forthwith in the following manner [grievance procedure then described]." [16]

Many agreements, however, limit the grievance procedure to complaints involving the "interpretation or application" of the agreement. Agreements which limit the subject matter that may be taken to the grievance procedure are most commonly found in newly organized industries, where the parties have not acquired sufficient mutual confidence to open the door to any and all complaints. Some of these agreements define "grievance" in a restrictive way, limiting the types of complaints that will be considered. Or the types of complaints that will be heard may be listed specifically, thus excluding those not listed. Some agreements spell out specific types of complaints which may *not* be taken to the grievance procedure, as, for instance, "matters clearly within the field of exclusive management functions."

The right of former employees to utilize the grievance procedure for grievances based upon their previous employ-ment status has sometimes been at issue. In one such instance,

---

[15] Conference on Training of Law Students in Labor Relations, Vol. III, Transcript of Proceedings 702-703 (1947).

[16] From an agreement between Windsor Mfg. Co. and Textile Workers Union—CIO.

Arbitrator Mark L. Kahn declared that the union not only has a right but also a duty to utilize the grievance procedure in behalf of the former employee.[17] But the right of former employees to use the grievance procedure has not always been upheld.[18]

Company Grievances

Provision is sometimes made for the initiation of management grievances at some stage of the grievance procedure. In the absence of language clearly permitting the company to initiate grievances, however, the grievance clause might be construed not to open the grievance procedure to company grievances.[19]

Some management spokesmen urge that every contract which provides for arbitration as the final step of the grievance procedure should include machinery available to management for presenting grievances against the union.[20]

Identification and Signature of Individual Grievants; Group Grievances

Sometimes an agreement will require, either specifically or by implication, that employee grievances be signed or otherwise presented by the aggrieved employee. Umpire Harry Shulman held that under such an agreement no employee grievance can be considered to exist unless a specific employee feels himself aggrieved and requests that a grievance be filed—

---

[17] Hudson Tool & Machine Co., 21 LA 431, 433-434 (1953).

[18] See Kelly v. Adler, Inc., 25 LA 214 (N.Y. Sup. Ct., 1955). For a case involving the right of the union to use the grievance procedure in behalf of a supervisor who was discharged instead of being returned to the bargaining unit, see Tin Processing Corp., 16 LA 48, 51 (Emery, 1951).

[19] As in Bassick Co. v. Bassick Local 229, IUE, 24 LA 59 (U.S. D.C., 1954). Also see Hinson Mfg. Co., 20 LA 688, 690 (Davey, 1953). By discussing a company grievance through the grievance procedure up to arbitration the union waived any right to object that the contract made no provision for company grievances, in Whitlock Mfg. Co., 19 LA 234, 236 (Stutz, 1952).

[20] Hill & Hook, Management at the Bargaining Table 216 (1945).

a complaint signed only by a committeeman would not qualify as a grievance.[21]

Arbitrator Clarence M. Updegraff has explained that: "Such provisions are * * * designed to prevent the filing of grievances anonymously, or by union officers only, in circumstances in which the employer will be handicapped in meeting a grievance by not knowing exactly in respect to whom it is accused of some impropriety." [22] In that case the agreement required that all grievances other than those "of a general character" be signed by the aggrieved employee, and Arbitrator Updegraff disallowed that part of the back-pay claim which pertained to employees who did not sign the grievance but who also may have been adversely affected by the employer's misinterpretation of the agreement; the grievance was held not to fall within the exception to the signature requirement since its subject matter affected only a very limited number of employees.[23]

On the other hand, some contracts have been construed to permit the union to file "group," "class," and/or "policy" grievances without signatures by (and in some cases without identification of) all specific individuals covered by the grievance.[24] Moreover, though signed by only one employee, grievances have been treated as group grievances at the arbitration stage where they were so treated at the earlier steps of the grievance procedure.[25]

Even where the contract language implied that the grievance procedure applied only to individually authorized griev-

---

[21] Ford Motor Co., 3 LA 840, 841 (1946). Also see International Harvester Co., 23 LA 64, 65 (Cole, 1954).

[22] John Deere Harvester Works, 10 LA 778, 782 (1948).

[23] Ibid. Cf., Republic Steel Corp., 11 LA 691, 694-695 (McCoy, 1948).

[24] See Arbitrator S. Wolff in 27 LA 448, 452; Stutz in 27 LA 386, 388-389; R. Williams in 25 LA 748, 749-750; Lennard in 25 LA 644, 648-649; Dworkin in 23 LA 481, 482; Kelliher in 14 LA 1049, 1053. Also see Duff in 30 LA 441, 444; Thompson in 29 LA 518, 520. Arbitrator Howlett interpreted a contract not to permit group grievances in 28 LA 633, 634.

[25] See Arbitrator Updegraff in 20 LA 243, 245; Davey in 17 LA 330, 333; Grant in 11 LA 312, 314.

ances, Arbitrator Philip E. Marshall held that grievances not personal in nature and those involving the whole of the bargaining unit could be filed by the union without specific authorizations. Arbitrator Marshall asserted that "industrial practice generally recognizes the fact that certain types of grievances involving conflicting interpretations of contractual provisions are frequently brought by union representatives in behalf of the entire membership." [26]

Somewhat conversely, under a clause permitting the union to file grievances which apply to "employees as a group," Arbitrator Maurice H. Merrill held that the union could file the grievance of an individual employee since the situation was one which could occur to any employee and therefore the grievance did affect the employees as a group.[27]

Steps in Grievance Procedure

Grievance machinery usually consists of a series of procedural steps to be taken within specified time limits. The nature of the procedure will depend upon the structure of the company and on the needs and desires of the parties, but there is a tendency to follow a fairly definite pattern. Grievances ordinarily are taken by the aggrieved employee, either with or without a union representative, to the foreman, and, if no settlement is reached, may be appealed through successive steps of the management hierarchy and, in most cases, to arbitration. The aggrieved may be represented successively by the shop steward, the business agent, the union shop committee, and international union representatives.

Small companies can be expected to have short, simple grievance procedures, sometimes with only one or two steps. Larger companies usually have multi-step procedures. Three-step and four-step procedures probably are most common, but procedures with five or six steps are sometimes used, especially

---

[26] Timken-Detroit Axle Co., 6 LA 926, 934 (1947). Also see McCoy in 11 LA 691, 694-695.
[27] Jonco Aircraft Corp., 22 LA 887 (1954).

in plants which are units of a multi-plant company.[28] The employee often is represented by the union grievance committee at the intermediate steps and by an international union representative at the next to last step and also at the last step.[29] The more steps in a grievance procedure, the more formal it can be expected to be. There is such variation in multi-step procedures that no one plan may be said to be really typical. An indication, however, of what might be found in a multi-step procedure is provided by the following illustration:

"Should any employee, subject to this agreement, believe he has been unjustly dealt with, or that any of the provisions of this agreement have been violated, he shall present his alleged grievance to the Foreman of his department within five (5) days of the occurrence of such grievance.

"In case the grievance is not adjusted by the foreman it shall be reduced to writing upon forms provided by the Company and signed and dated by the aggrieved employee and his department committeeman and three copies furnished the foreman. The foreman will have inserted in the proper place on the form his disposition of the matter and will sign and date the same returning one (1) copy to the aggrieved employee and one (1) copy to the department committeeman representing the employee within five (5) days.

"If satisfactory adjustment is not made the department committeeman or his representative shall then take up the grievance with the General Foreman and General Superintendent in their respective order, within ten (10) days.

"If no satisfactory adjustment is then reached it shall be submitted for consideration and handling to the Manager of Works, or his representative, by the duly authorized General Committee or their representative, within ten (10) days.

"If after such consideration by the General Committee and the management, the grievance shall be unsettled, then the question shall be jointly submitted to the Chief Executive of the Company and the Chief Executive of the Brotherhood of Railway Carmen of America (or their representative) for joint conference within ten (10) days." [30]

---

[28] "Grievance Procedure Under Collective Bargaining," 63 Monthly Labor Review 175, 179 (U.S. Dept. of Labor, Bureau of Labor Statistics, 1946).

[29] Id. at 180.

[30] From an agreement between the Pullman-Standard Car Mfg. Co. and Brotherhood of Railway Carmen.

Advanced Step Filing

There are certain issues which by nature are not capable of being settled at the preliminary stages of the procedure. Fundamental issues concerning company policies, for instance, are of this type. Provision sometimes is made for filing such grievances at an advanced step of the procedure.

The question might be raised whether, in the absence of such provision, it should be permissible to file grievances at an advanced step where it is obvious that they cannot be settled at preliminary steps. The view has been expressed that there should be strict conformity with the agreement lest the exception be used to short-circuit the first steps in all cases.[31]

But Arbitrator Robert J. Wagner expressed a different view, holding that a grievance concerning veterans' vacation rights was properly initiated at the third step of the grievance procedure without presentation to the foreman at an earlier step. While he denied the union's contention that it had the right to enter an advanced step "at any time they choose," nevertheless he held that it could do so in proper cases. He stated that it is well recognized in the practice of industrial relations that certain disputes of a general nature can only be resolved at a high union-management level. "Then, again, particular circumstances may make it impractical to begin processing a grievance at the first step." Arbitrator Wagner concluded: "It would seem to be quite proper for this grievance to be processed at the third-step level, for only at this level are all negotiators of the contract, those officers of company and union who knew the meaning and intent of the language of the contractual provision controlling, required to appear." [32]

---

[31] Lapp, How to Handle Labor Grievances 95-96 (1945).

[32] Manion Steel Barrel Co., 6 LA 164, 168 (1947). Advanced step filing under proper circumstances was also permitted by Arbitrator Prasow in 27 LA 153, 155-156; Kelliher in 14 LA 1049, 1053.

In any event, the right to object to the lack of discussion of a grievance at a preliminary step may be held waived by failure to make a timely objection.[33]

Grievance Mediation

Some parties add a "grievance mediation" step to the grievance procedure. When this is done, a neutral is called in to discuss the case with the parties immediately prior to the arbitration stage. This process can dispose of some cases that otherwise must be arbitrated and it may well deserve more experimentation in the future.[34]

Time for Holding Hearings

Agreements vary as to the time prescribed for holding hearings on grievances. Some agreements provide that differences are to be taken up "as soon as possible"; others simply provide that "grievances shall be first taken up by the grievant and the foreman," without specifying a time; still others provide that grievances may be adjusted with the foreman "at the end of the working day." Reason should be exercised in determining when to present grievances. It has been held, for instance, that when the number of employees involved in a grievance is so great that their absence from the job would interfere with production and upset morale and discipline, the shop steward has a clear duty to give management an opportunity to adjust the grievance without an interruption of work. Accordingly, a shop steward who took six or seven men off the job to discuss a grievance, without having made advance arrangements with management, was held to have been properly admonished not to do so again.[35]

---

[33] See Arbitrator Callaghan in 28 LA 659, 663; Donnely in 28 LA 621, 622; Kelliher in 20 LA 618, 619; Jaffe in 17 LA 187, 189-190.

[34] For informative discussion of grievance mediation see McPherson, Grievance Mediation Under Collective Bargaining (Univ. of Ill. Institute of Lab. & Ind. Relations Reprint Series No. 44, 1956); "Grievance Mediation," The Grievance Process 53-54, 59 (Mich. State Univ. Lab. & Ind. Relations Center, 1956).

[35] Dwight Mfg. Co., 10 LA 786, 792 (McCoy, 1948).

Similar results have been reached in other such cases where employees or their representative interfered with production and disregarded the need for orderly presentation of grievances in seeking to rush the hearing of their complaint.[36]

Advanced-step hearings generally are scheduled more definitely. Many plants hold regularly scheduled meetings at specified intervals to negotiate appealed grievances.[37] Such meetings are usually held weekly during working hours, but may be held monthly or at other intervals.

Sometimes, however, these meetings are not regularly scheduled, but are made subject to "call," to be held whenever necessary. "Call" meetings may be preferred because they provide the necessary flexibility for more prompt disposition of complaints, and the number of meetings can be adjusted to the number of cases. On the other hand, some parties prefer regularly scheduled meetings because of the assurance that grievances will be considered within a definite period. Moreover, regular meetings provide better opportunity for the discussion of mutual problems of policy and for the anticipation of difficulties, thus preventing future grievances.[38] When the agreement provides for regularly scheduled meetings, it might also provide for emergency meetings when either party feels that consideration of a grievance should not be delayed.[39]

Grievance Representatives

Unless restricted by the agreement, both the union and the company are free to determine the kind and number of representatives it wishes to use.[40] Limitation as to the number of representatives who may appear at various hearings or negotiations is a common feature of collective agreements.

---

[36] See Arbitrator Platt in 21 LA 220, 221-222; Komaroff in 21 LA 67, 70-71; Shister in 17 LA 230, 232. Cf., NLRB v. Kennametal, Inc., 182 F.2d 817 (C. A. 3, 1950), where there was no grievance procedure for the employees to turn to.

[37] "Grievance Procedure Under Collective Bargaining," 63 Monthly Labor Review 175, 183 (U.S. Dept. of Labor, Bureau of Labor Statistics, 1946).

[38] Ibid.

[39] Cudahy Packing Co., 7 LA 645, 646 (Fisher, 1947).

[40] Ford Motor Co., 1 ALAA par. 67,045 (Shulman, 1944).

Such limitation is said to be both legitimate and proper, and to be a proper subject for negotiation between the parties.[41]

Unions most often use "shop stewards" and grievance "committeemen." The steward represents the employee at the initial stages of the grievance procedure. The steward who performs successfully the responsibilities with which he is entrusted is an asset to management as well as to the employees whom he represents. As an employee spokesman he has the responsibility of policing the collective agreement, but he also has the responsibility of dissuading employees from pursuing complaints that are without merit. In dealing with management he seeks to effectuate general union policies. Union grievance committeemen usually represent employees in the intermediate stages of the grievance procedure. The grievance committee frequently has the responsibility of determining union policy in connection with grievances.

The management representative closest to the employees and their work is the foreman. The foreman's effectiveness in grievance settlement is determined largely by his own capability and the amount of authority given him; if he is able and sufficient authority is given him, better settlements as a rule will be obtained at the foreman level than at later steps, since the foreman often understands shop problems better than those above him.[42] "Foremen trained by experience, observation, and study of labor and industrial psychology are able to prevent and to rectify most of the ordinary grievances of the workers." [43] Of course, to state this is to state the ideal only. Unfortunately, in numerous plants foremen lack authority, or fail to use it, and "pass the buck" to higher management officials.[44]

---

[41] Ibid.

[42] "Grievance Procedure Under Collective Bargaining," 63 Monthly Labor Review 175, 179 (U.S. Dept. of Labor, Bureau of Labor Statistics, 1946).

[43] Lapp, How to Handle Labor Grievances 109-110 (1945).

[44] "Grievance Procedure Under Collective Bargaining," 63 Monthly Labor Review 175, 179 (U.S. Dept. of Labor, Bureau of Labor Statistics). Some reasons why the "ideal" of foreman-steward settlement often is not attained include personality clashes between foreman and steward, fear by both management and unions that such settlements may establish undesirable precedents, and fear by both the foreman and the steward that they will be reversed by their superiors. The Grievance Process 57-58 (Mich. State Univ. Lab. & Ind. Rel. Center, 1956).

Many employers, however, conduct training courses for foremen for the purpose of enabling them better to deal with grievances and acquaint them with the applicable company policies.

Many unions and companies conduct training programs for their representatives. Such training usually covers the provisions of the collective agreement and basic union or company policy. Proper training should develop a feeling of mutual respect and confidence between stewards and foremen; one of its primary purposes should be to foster the attitude that grievances are problems to be solved, not arguments to be won. Training, too, increases employee understanding of the use and objectives of the grievance procedure.[45]

Many plants have industrial relations departments to handle labor relations. Generally it is the function of this department to centralize and unify the company's policy and dealings with the union. Some industrial relations departments handle grievances. Opinion differs as to whether this is desirable. While some feel that it is an aid to grievance processing, others feel that it forces more grievances to the higher stages of the procedure because it cuts into the authority of the foreman.[46]

Right to Union Representation at First Step

Unions and management frequently disagree as to whether, in the interest of better relationships, employee grievances should be taken directly to the foreman or first to the union steward and then by the steward to the foreman.

Management often insists that the aggrieved employee should go to his foreman alone before going to his steward and that the union should not enter the picture until after the first step of the grievance procedure. It is argued that better relationships are fostered if the individual employee and the foreman discuss the grievance alone. The presence of the steward,

---

[45] These points regarding training programs are stated and discussed in "Grievance Procedure Under Collective Bargaining," 63 Monthly Labor Review 175, 177-183 (U.S. Dept. of Labor, Bureau of Labor Statistics, 1946).

[46] Id. at 184.

it is thought, tends to make the grievance appear more serious than it really is.

On the other hand, unions often take the position that the steward should handle grievances from the start. The employee is believed to need the assistance and moral support of the steward to insure recognition of all of his rights. Unions wish to be able to "push" grievances of employees who are too timid to approach the foreman alone. Moreover, unions say that management benefits by the union's screening of grievances, a process which eliminates complaints that have no merit. Finally, unions feel that settlements by individuals make it possible for foremen to play favorites and that uniform settlements can be had only if the union is present from the outset.

Arbitrators, in turn, have sometimes been directly confronted with the question of when an employee is first entitled to demand union representation in the handling of his grievance. In discipline cases some arbitrators have held in effect that unless the contract provides otherwise an employee has no absolute right to have a union representative present during the investigation stage prior to the actual filing of charges or assessment of discipline against the employee.[47]

However, where a grievance questioned management's distribution of overtime the grievant was held to have the right to union representation during a formative stage of the grievance in which the foreman participated; the arbitrator reversed management's action in discharging the grievant for refusing to discuss his "overtime" grievance with the foreman in the absence of a union representative.[48]

In any event, it appears clear that arbitrators recognize a right to union representation at least commencing with the first step of the grievance procedure.

---

[47] See Arbitrator Gregory in 29 LA 646, 650-651; Wenke in 28 LA 179, 180. But Cf., Cahn in 28 LA 570, 571-572; Shister in 20 LA 448, 449-450, and in 18 LA 374; Reynolds in 19 LA 344, 346-347.

[48] Braniff Airways, Inc., 27 LA 892, 896-898 (J. Williams, 1957). Also see statement by Arbitrator Platt in 21 LA 344, 347.

Grievance Adjustment by Individual Employees

While the Labor-Management Relations Act of 1947 provides in Section 8 (d) that the duty of the employer and union
to bargain includes the duty to confer in good faith with respect
to questions arising under the collective agreement, it also provides in Section 9 (a) that "any individual employee or a group
of employees shall have the right at any time to present grievances to their employer and to have such grievances adjusted,
without the intervention of the bargaining representative, as
long as the adjustment is not inconsistent with the terms of a
collective-bargaining contract or agreement then in effect",
and as long as "the bargaining representative has been given
opportunity to be present at such adjustment." Thus employees
covered by the Act appear to have some choice as to union
assistance in grievance processing.[49]

Even aside from any legal right of individual employees to
choose whether to have union assistance in grievance processing,
such choice is recognized in many agreements.

When a collective agreement is interpreted to give individual employees the right to resort to the grievance procedure
and/or arbitration, the right may receive strong support from
arbitrators. For instance, under a contract giving employees
believed to have been unjustly discharged the right to seek re-

---

[49] One writer concluded that under Section 9 (a) individual employees have a
substantive right to settle their grievances directly with the employer and that no
agreement between the union and the employer can deprive them of this right. See
Lenhoff, "The Effect of Labor Arbitration Clauses Upon the Individual," 9 Arb. J. 3,
14-16 (1954). Also see General Cable Corp., 20 LA 443, 444-445 (Hays, 1953).
But the opposite conclusion appears to have been reached by another writer. See
Cox, "Rights Under a Labor Agreement," 69 Harv. L. Rev. 601, 621-624 (1956).
Insofar as the Railway Labor Act is concerned, the United States Supreme Court indicated in the "Burley" cases that in order for a union to bind individual employees in
grievance settlements before the National Railroad Adjustment Board it must appear
that the employees authorized the union in some "legally sufficient manner," which
may be by custom, by union rules in the case of union members, or by the failure of
an individual employee with notice of proceedings to assert his rights. See Elgin,
Joliet & Eastern Ry. Co. v. Burley cases in 325 U.S. 711, 16 LRR Man. 749 (1945);
327 U.S. 661, 17 LRR Man. 241 (1946). For discussion of the "Burley" cases see
59 Harv. L. Rev. 992; 46 Col. L. Rev. 678; 31 Iowa L. Rev. 436. It has been
suggested that the "Burley" decisions probably have application only to cases under
the Railway Labor Act. See, Isaacson, "Labor Arbitration in State Courts," 12 Arb. J.
179, 188 (1957).

dress through the grievance procedure, Arbitrator Harry H. Platt held that alleged union acquiescence in a discharge did not have the effect of depriving the discharged employee of the right to protest through the grievance procedure.[50]

However, with particular regard to the arbitration stage many court cases have construed the collective agreement to give the individual employee no right to use the arbitration machinery of the agreement without being represented by the union or against the wishes of the union, although some of these cases have recognized certain collateral remedies sometimes available to the individual employee against the union or the employer for failure to arbitrate his grievance.[51]

Privileges and Protection of Grievance Representatives

In order to facilitate the operation of the grievance machinery, collective agreements frequently give special privileges and protection to union grievance representatives. The agreement may provide superseniority for them to assure their continued employment as long as they hold office. Some agreements require union consent for the transfer of grievance representatives from one shift to another, and some give the union the right to demand a transfer where grievance handling requires such.[52]

---

[50] Riley Stoker Corp., 7 LA 764, 768 (1947). To similar effect, Arbitrator Platt in 6 LA 678, 680. Also see Arbitrator Hays in 20 LA 443, 444-445; Myers in 8 LA 483, 485-486. An individual employee was held to have the right to arbitrate without union backing in Gilden v. Singer Mfg. Co., 30 LA 113 (Conn. Sup. Ct., 1958).

[51] See cases and discussion in "American Bar Association Report on Labor Arbitration," 28 LA 913, 925-928 (1957); Isaacson, "Labor Arbitration in State Courts," 12 Arb. J. 179, 184-190 (1957); Cox, "Rights Under A Labor Agreement," 69 Harv. L. Rev. 601 (1956); Lenhoff, "The Effect of Labor Arbitration Clauses Upon the Individual," 9 Arb. J. 3 (1954); Freidin, Labor Arbitration and the Courts 25-30 (1952). Where the union wanted to arbitrate but the employees did not the union prevailed in New York Times v. Newspaper Guild, 26 LA 607 (N. Y. Sup. Ct., 1956). It is said that arbitrators have generally refused to permit the grievant to be represented by counsel of his own choosing rather than by the union that is a party to the contract. See Wirtz, "Due Process of Arbitration," The Arbitrator and The Parties 1, 25 (BNA Incorporated, 1958). But see Soto v. Lenscraft Optical Corp., 28 LA 278 (N.Y. Sup. Ct., 1957). For cases involving attempts of third parties or minority groups of employees to intervene in cases being processed by the union, see In re Iroquois Beverage Corp., 28 LA 906 (N.Y. Sup. Ct., 1955), permitting intervention; Ball Brothers Co., 27 LA 353, 354-355 (Sembower, 1956), not permitting intervention.

[52] See BNA's Collective Bargaining Negotiations and Contracts, pp. 51:181-183.

Investigation of Grievances

Many agreements give representatives access to the plant for the purpose of investigating grievances.[53] Thus, non-employee union representatives, such as the union business agent, may be given reasonable access to the plant. It is essential that union representatives be given opportunity, as management is, to examine all circumstances surrounding grievances.[54]

In one case, under an agreement permitting union officers to enter the plant for the purpose of assisting in the adjustment of grievances, the word "plant" was interpreted to mean the "entire working area where employee grievances may arise." [55] Under another agreement giving union representatives the right to investigate grievances in the plant the company had no right to determine unilaterally that a grievance was not bona fide and use that determination to deny access to the plant.[56]

But certain limitations must be observed. In one of the cases just considered, for instance, Arbitrator James C. Hill held that under this type of provision the employer is entitled to know the subject of the grievance for which the union representative seeks entry to the plant.[57] Speaking of the right of entrance, Arbitrator Hill said:

> "There should be a legitimate reason for entering a specific area of the plant. It does not give the Union representative the right to roam the plant at will, and it would be a clear violation of the agreement for the Union to use this opportunity to engage in organizational activities." [58]

Special Immunity

It has been held as a general rule incidents taking place and words spoken at grievance meetings may not be used as a

---

[53] In the absence of such contractual right, union representatives might not have the right of free access to the plant to investigate grievances. See Westinghouse Electric Corp., 113 NLRB 954 (1955).

[54] For a discussion of the respective obligations of the parties in the investigation of grievances, see Jonco Aircraft Corp., 20 LA 211, 212 (Merrill, 1953).

[55] Standard Motor Products, Inc., 11 LA 1147, 1153 (Hill, 1949).

[56] Aluminum Co. of America, 23 LA 317, 320-321 (Prasow, 1954).

[57] Standard Motor Products, Inc., 11 LA 1147, 1152 (Hill, 1949).

[58] Id. at 1153. Regarding the scope of the company's obligation to make records available to union representatives under plant access "investigation" clauses, see North American Aviation, Inc., 19 LA 385, 389-390 (Komaroff, 1952).

basis for disciplinary action; in that case the employer was held not to be entitled to discharge an employee for threatening physical violence and using abusive language in an argument with a foreman during a grievance committee meeting.[59]

Moreover, arbitrators have recognized an even broader, though not unlimited, immunity of union representatives against punishment by the employer for their actions in performing their duties as such.[60] But the suspension of a shop committeeman was upheld where he was found guilty, in processing grievances, of conduct jeopardizing morale and production efficiency; the committeeman, previously warned and reprimanded, insulted and abused a foreman in the presence of other employees, at least one of whom was the foreman's subordinate.[61]

Pay for Grievance Time

Commonly, management compensates union representatives and other employees for time spent in handling grievances during working hours.[62] In some large plants it is the practice of management to pay for full-time union stewards.[63]

---

[59] Federal Mining & Smelting Co., 3 LA 497, 498 (Dwyer, 1946).

[60] See Arbitrator Bothwell in 28 LA 543, 547-548; Reynolds in 18 LA 772, 773; Komaroff in 17 LA 199, 204. Cf., Jaffee in 21 LA 53, 54-55.

[61] American Hoist & Derrick Co., 1 ALAA par. 67,428 (1946). Also see Arbitrator Doyle in 19 LA 111, 121.

[62] "Grievance Procedure Under Collective Bargaining," 63 Monthly Labor Review 175, 184 (U.S. Dept. of Labor, Bureau of Labor Statistics, 1946).

[63] Under the Labor-Management Relations Act of 1947 the practice of paying for time spent by union representatives in discussing grievances with management is legal, but the Act is ambiguous as to whether payment may be made for grievance activities other than those of "conferring" with management. In Borg-Warner Corp., 10 LA 471 (1948), Arbitrator Charles O. Gregory ruled that the provision making it unlawful for an employer to make payments to union representatives except for services rendered does not relieve the employer from the obligation, contractually assumed, of paying union stewards and committeemen for time spent during working hours in negotiating grievances with company representatives. In so holding, Gregory queried: "And then, is it not highly unlikely that Congress would want to interfere with a fairly well-established practice against which employers as a rule do not complain but have frequently agreed to recognize in collective bargaining agreements?" Id. at 473. He did, however, state a realization that a court might disagree with him on the matter. Id. at 474. Also see Arbitrator Kelliher in 16 LA 734, 735-736. In Douglas & Lomanson Co., 23 LA 812, 814 (Willcox, 1954), the contract was interpreted to require the employer to pay union representatives for time spent in negotiating grievances but Arbitrator Willcox stated that his award was "subject to any applicable ruling by the National Labor Relations Board or a court of law as to legality of any such payments."

Unions take the position that the activity of union grievance representatives benefits management as much as employees.
Of course, both parties will agree that it is to the advantage of
both if only persons of responsibility act as grievance representatives. Payment for time spent in handling grievances is one
way to secure the services of such persons. Grievance pay also
facilitates prompt settlement, thereby improving morale and
plant efficiency.

Even where the agreement did not specifically require pay
for time spent by employees in discussing their conduct with
management prior to possible assessment of discipline, they were
held entitled to pay for all time lost from work (but not for
time spent after working hours).[64]

Some arbitrators have held that past practice should determine whether grievance time is to be compensated where the
agreement is silent or ambiguous on the matter.[65]

In some cases the employer has not been required to pay
union representatives for time spent at arbitration hearings in
the absence of a clear and specific contractual requirement for
such pay,[66] but so definite a provision for such pay has not been
required in all cases.[67]

Under an agreement providing that union representatives
shall be paid for time spent "conferring with management",
time spent researching company records (relevant to grievances) in the absence of management was held to be compen-
sable if the amount of time is "relatively slight and of an incidental nature."[68]

Payment for grievance work is generally made on a
straight-time basis.[69] Some agreements, however, provide that

---

[64] Bethlehem Steel Co., 19 LA 261, 262-264 (Shipman, 1952).
[65] See Arbitrator Lehoczky in 27 LA 187, 188; McCoy in 16 LA 240, 241-242;
Hepburn in 13 LA 418, 422. Cf., Gorder in 8 LA 945, 947-948.
[66] See Arbitrator Fulda in 14 LA 775, 780; Gorder in 8 LA 945, 946-948. Also see
Ensinger in 6 LA 136, 139.
[67] See Modine Mfg. Co., 23 LA 243, 245 (Porter, 1954).
[68] Standard Oil Co., 16 LA 734, 735-736 (Kelliher, 1951).
[69] "Grievance Procedure Under Collective Bargaining," 63 Monthly Labor Review
175, 184 (U.S. Dept. of Labor, Bureau of Labor Statistics, 1946). But see International
Harvester Co., 22 LA 196, 197-198 (Cole, 1954).

grievance representatives "shall not lose pay for time spent" in grievance meetings with management. Under such a provision it was held in one case that representatives had to be paid a special differential which they would have received had they not been called from work for grievance meetings, even though another provision of the agreement stated that the differential was to be paid only in case of actual performance of differential work.[70] But under a similar provision in an agreement which provided that grievance conferences should be held during working hours, a minimum of four hours' pay at straight time, in accordance with call-in pay provisions, was held to be sufficient for less than four hours of grievance work performed after working hours; the arbitrator rejected the union demand for payment at the overtime rate.[71]

Various means of control have been used to prevent abuse of grievance-pay practices. Some agreements limit the amount of time that may be spent in such activity; others contain no specific limit, but say that a "reasonable amount" of time will be paid for. Management has been held to be entitled to require the union to fill out forms, giving a general account of grievance services performed and the time involved. This right is said to accompany management's contractual obligation to pay for such services.[72] Use of such report forms is not considered to be espionage or interference with union activity.[73] Many companies require union representatives to report to their foremen before leaving work to handle grievances. Under agreements which contain provisions to this effect, management may be allowed to require stewards to clock in and out when leaving work to process grievances.[74] But such action by management may be shortsighted in view of the dissatisfaction which it may cause.[75] Another means of protecting grievance-pay practices from abuse is to provide, in the agreement, that management

---

[70] Bethlehem Steel Co., 10 LA 284, 287-288 (Dodd, 1948).
[71] Ford Roofing Products Co., 5 LA 182, 184 (Wardlaw, 1946).
[72] Bell Aircraft Corp., 11 LA 729, 730-731 (Jaffe, 1948).
[73] Ford Motor Co., 2 LA 382, 383 (Shulman, 1944).
[74] Jenkins Bros., 11 LA 432, 434-435 (Donnelly, 1948).
[75] Ibid.

may inaugurate a grievance at an advanced step of the grievance procedure if abuse is believed to exist.[76]

Written Statement of Grievance

There are numerous reasons why grievances should be presented in writing at an early stage of the grievance procedure, and to do so is the general practice. The written complaint establishes a record of the grievance. By putting the grievance in writing it is less likely to become distorted as it is processed through the grievance procedure.[77] Then, too, if grievances must be stated in writing those that lack merit often are dropped.

Some persons consider it important to have a written grievance filed at the beginning, or "first step", of the grievance procedure in view of the value of a complete written record.[78] However, many parties prefer informal oral discussion at the first step, considering written grievances to be best suited to the later steps of the procedure. These parties may oppose written presentation of grievances at the first step on the ground that it makes the procedure too inflexible and cumbersome, discourages employees from voicing their complaints, and impedes prompt settlement.

One "interests" arbitrator, recognizing that the presentation of grievances in writing is a well established practice in industry, granted an employer's request for a provision requiring grievances carried beyond the employee's immediate superior to be presented in writing on simple forms provided by the company.[79] In this connection, a clause requiring that grievances be "filed" at the second step within a specified time was interpreted to require that grievances be stated "in writing" at that step.[80]

---

[76] See Fact-Finders Van Fossen, Humphrey & Prifrel in 2 LA 227, 241; Marshall, Spencer & Holly in 1 LA 512, 521-522.

[77] For a related discussion see Chapter 7, topic entitled "Extent of Permissible Deviation From Pre-Arbitral Discussion Of Case."

[78] Updegraff & McCoy, Arbitration of Labor Disputes 53 (1946).

[79] New York City Omnibus Corp., 7 LA 794, 820-821 (Cole, 1947).

[80] Jones & Laughlin Steel Corp., 16 LA 788, 789 (Cahn, 1951).

In some instances the discussion of grievances not filed in writing as required by the agreement has been held to waive the "written grievance" requirement.[81] One arbitrator, in placing the burden upon management to raise the issue promptly, stated that if management desires to insist upon strict compliance with "written grievance" requirements, it should express its disapproval of oral grievances at the time when they first become a subject of discussion between the parties. "The company's failure to raise the objection at that time constitutes a waiver of that requirement."[82] But another arbitrator ruled otherwise, declaring that "if there is any place in the interpretation of collective bargaining agreements where strict or technical construction is necessary it is in that which provides for the grievance machinery and procedure."[83]

Time Limitations

Promptness is one of the most important aspects of grievance settlement. Failure to settle grievances with dispatch is sure to lead to labor unrest. All parties agree that promptness in the settlement of grievances leads to better labor-management relationships; opinion differs, however, as to the best means of insuring such promptness. While many agreements provide time limits for taking complaints to the grievance procedure as well as time limits for processing grievances through the various steps of the procedure, other agreements contain no such provisions. Some parties feel that time limits provide a safeguard against stalling, and against the accumulation of cases and pressing of stale claims. On the other hand, others believe that the setting of specific time allowances permits uncooperative parties to stall to the maximum allowable time and operates to bar some grievances which should be settled for the sake of improving the relations of the parties.

In the final analysis, prompt settlement of grievances depends, not upon the presence of contractual time limits, but

---

[81] See Arbitrator Greene in 10 LA 567, 568; Gilden in 3 LA 327, 332-333.
[82] Lapham-Hickey Co., 3 LA 327, 333 (Gilden, 1946).
[83] Firestone Tire & Rubber Co., 9 LA 518, 522 (Rader, 1948).

upon a sincere desire of the parties to settle differences. But that time limits do have definite value may be presumed from the fact that numerous agreements contain them. Without question, such limits provide an additional element of order to the grievance procedure.[84]

No set formula is available for the establishment of time limits. Rather, the special circumstances of the parties should determine, in each instance, the nature of the time-limit provisions of their agreement. Some agreements fix time limits for each step of the procedure. Others fix an over-all time limit for the complete processing of a grievance. Another form of time limitation is that which simply forbids delay. Any of these forms might be coupled with a time limit for the initial submission of grievances. Different limits may be prescribed for the submission of different types of grievances. This was done, for instance, by a fact-finding board recommendation of a five-day limit for filing discharge and pay adjustment disputes, and a thirty-day limit for all other grievances.[85]

Under contracts which contain no time limits for filing grievances, it has been held that grievances which do not antedate the contract may be filed at any time during its term.[86] But it has been held also that where the contract states no time limit for filing grievances but does state specific time limits for taking grievances to the various steps of the procedure once they have been filed, the evident intent of the contract is that grievances must be filed with reasonable promptness.[87]

Grievances which antedate the current contract might be rejected for that reason unless the current contract expressly

---

[84] For general discussion of advantages of using time limits, see The Grievance Process 60 (Mich. State Univ. Lab. & Ind. Rel. Center, 1956).

[85] Minneapolis-Moline Power Implement Co., 2 LA 227, 241 (Van Fossen, Humphrey & Prifrel, 1946).

[86] See Arbitrator Gilden in 6 LA 238, 260, and in 3 LA 327, 333; Whiting in 5 LA 477, 478. Also see Havighurst in 26 LA 688, 692; Copelof in 21 LA 788, 792. But even where a contract stated no time limit for filing, the arbitrator imposed a limit of one year in Bell Aircraft Corp., 24 LA 324, 330 (Somers, 1955).

[87] See Arbitrator R. Williams in 26 LA 505, 507; Maggs in 19 LA 677, 681, and in 12 LA 311, 316.

reserves the right to file such grievances,[88] or unless delayed filing is justified by the circumstances.[89]

Once instituted, however, grievances ordinarily do not die merely because not settled or arbitrated before the expiration of the contract under which they arose.[90]

While the absence of strict time limitations often results in the acceptance of grievances notwithstanding delayed filing, in such cases arbitrators will ordinarily make grievance adjustments retroactive only to the date on which the grievance was filed.[91]

In particular, arbitrators can be expected to deny that part of a claim which, if allowed, would result in a loss to one party caused by the negligent delay of the other party in asserting the claim. Whether the arbitrator calls such delay laches, acquiescence, or sleeping on one's rights, the principle involved appears to be generally recognized and applied.[92]

If the agreement does contain clear time limits for filing and prosecuting grievances, failure to observe them generally will result in a dismissal of the grievance if the failure is protested.[93] But this will not be the result if circumstances are such that it would be unreasonable to require filing of the grievance strictly within the time specified by the contract.[94] Also, the time requirement will not be enforced by arbitrators if both

---

[88] A grievance was so rejected in Aluminum Co. of America, 5 LA 148, 150 (Cheney, 1946). For a similar view see The Grievance Process 60 (1956).

[89] As in Ross-Meeham Foundries, 5 LA 175, 177 (Ingle, 1946), where grievants had been inducted into the armed services, thus making it unreasonable to have expected earlier presentation of claims.

[90] See Jones v. Tide Water Oil Co., 22 LA 562, 563 (Calif. Super. Ct., 1954), and cases cited therein; Whitlock Mfg. Co., 19 LA 234, 236 (Stutz, 1952).

[91] See Arbitrator Lockhart in 16 LA 156, 160-161; Davey in 9 LA 139, 140; Bandschain in 7 LA 785, 787; Gilden in 2 LA 655, 659-660. Also see cases cited in next footnote. But see Appleby in 20 LA 183, 188-189.

[92] See extensive statement by Arbitrator William B. Lockhart in Lavoris Co., 16 LA 156, 160-161 (1951). Also see Arbitrator Cornsweet in 12 LA 482, 483-484; S. Wolff in 10 LA 288, 293-294; Lehoczky in 9 LA 659, 660; Brandschain in 7 LA 785, 787; Gilden in 2 LA 608, 612.

[93] See Arbitrator Livengood in 27 LA 157, 159; Morvant in 26 LA 732, 735-736; Prasow in 25 LA 225, 228-230; Maggs in 19 LA 677, 680; Cahn in 17 LA 277, 280; Handsaker in 16 LA 369, 372; Holden in 13 LA 387, 390; McCoy in 11 LA 98, 100; Kelliher in 10 LA 525, 527; Rader in 7 LA 595, 597-598.

[94] See Arbitrator Reid in 23 LA 135, 136; Sturges in 16 LA 794, 800; Maggs in 15 LA 934, 935. Also see Pierson in 13 LA 782, 786.

parties have been guilty of contract violation in respect to the grievance procedure.[95] This principle has been expressed elaborately by Arbitrator Alvin B. Biscoe as follows:

> "Time limits are set in contracts by agreement of the parties. Both sides must abide by the contract or utter confusion will result. When one party violates the contract and one party is in compliance, the innocent party must not be made to suffer. However, when both parties are in violation of the time limits, the grievance can be heard on its merits. Violation by both sides, unless by mutual agreement, provides the only circumstance that justifies an arbitration board in ignoring the time limits. If this exception is not recognized, one party can impose intolerable conditions upon the other party by deliberate delays. In brief, the complainant must appear before the Board with 'clean hands' when it desires to enforce time limits." [96]

In any event, time limits may be held waived by a party in recognizing and negotiating a grievance without making clear and timely objection.[97] It has been suggested that upon making timely objection to delayed filing, the objecting party ordinarily should then discuss the grievance on the merits so that all issues will be ready for presentation to an arbitrator if the case reaches that stage.[98] Under a less expeditious procedure the objecting party may refuse to entertain the grievance on the ground that it is null and void, leaving the grievant free to file a second grievance involving the time issue alone; discussion of the original dispute on the merits would thus be delayed pending final resolution of the time issue.[99]

The particular contractual provision would appear to determine whether Saturdays, Sundays, holidays and the day of the occurrence are to be counted in computing time.[100]

---

[95] See Arbitrator Biscoe in 9 LA 595, 596; Cornsweet in 9 LA 625, 626; Rauch in 4 LA 170, 173. Also see Killingsworth in 19 LA 186, 187.

[96] Anchor Rome Mills, Inc., 9 LA 595, 596 (1947).

[97] See Arbitrator Whiting in 28 LA 398; Platt in 27 LA 685, 687; Klamon in 24 LA 869, 873; Ross in 24 LA 857, 859; Slavney in 24 LA 593, 596; Howlett in 24 LA 232, 237; Day in 22 LA 775, 778. Also see Anderson in 20 LA 715, 717. Cf., Davey in 18 LA 497, 504.

[98] North American Aviation, Inc., 17 LA 715, 719 (Komaroff, 1951).

[99] Square D Co., 25 LA 225, 230 (Prasow, 1955).

[100] See Arbitrator Ralston in 15 LA 640, 642-643; Ebeling in 11 LA 732, 737; Shulman in 1 ALAA par. 67,040.

Grievances are not always discovered at the time they occur. Some agreements provide specifically that grievances are to be filed within a certain number of days after they "occur or are discovered." [101] Even without such specific provision, arbitrators have held that one cannot be expected to file a grievance until he is aware or should be aware of the action upon which the grievance is based.[102]

A party sometimes announces its intention to do a given act but does not do or culminate the act until several days later. In some such situations arbitrators have held that the act occurred, for purposes of applying time limits, not when it was announced but when it was culminated.[103]

In this general connection, too, it was held that a grievance protesting a layoff, which was filed seven days after the employer signed the layoff notice, was timely although the contract placed a five-day limit on filing grievances; it was said to be reasonable to assume that two days were required for the notice to reach the grievant.[104]

Under some circumstances a party may be permitted to toll the running of time limits by giving notice to the other party of reasonable basis for delaying the filing of a grievance.[105]

Numerous arbitrators have held that "continuing" violations of the agreement (as opposed to a single, isolated and completed transaction) give rise to "continuing" grievances in the sense that the act complained of may be said to be repeated from day to day—each day there is a new "occurrence"; these arbitrators have permitted the filing of such grievances at any time, this not being deemed a violation of the specific time limits

---

[101] As in International Minerals and Chemical Co., 3 LA 405, 406 (Dwyer, 1946).

[102] See Arbitrator Donahue in 26 LA 501, 502-503; Holly in 24 LA 268, 271; Platt in 24 LA 141, 143; Willcox in 23 LA 21, 23; Maggs in 19 LA 647, 649; Komaroff in 17 LA 715, 718, and in 16 LA 303, 305. Also see McCoy in 20 LA 416, 419.

[103] See Arbitrator Komaroff in 26 LA 622, 626, and in 20 LA 789, 792-793; Warren in 18 LA 662, 663-664. Cf., Komaroff in 19 LA 385, 387. Arbitrator Prasow held that an act occurred on the day it was announced in 25 LA 225, 228-229, but there the union itself had clearly recognized the existence of a grievance as of that day.

[104] Torrington Co., 13 LA 323, 325 (Stutz, Mottram & Sviridoff, 1949).

[105] See American Smelting & Refining Co., 29 LA 262, 265 (Ross, 1957). Also see Monogram Productions, Inc., 13 LA 782, 786 (Pierson, 1949).

stated in the agreement (although any back pay ordinarily runs only from the date of filing).[106] For example, where the agreement provided for filing "within ten working days of the occurrence," it was held that where employees were erroneously denied work each day lost was to be considered a new "occurrence" and that a grievance presented within ten working days of any such day lost would be timely.[107]

Sometimes an agreement will provide that any grievance not appealed from one step to the next within a specified time shall be considered settled on the basis of the last answer. On one occasion this type of provision was applied strictly with the result that a grievance which, by error, had been left unappealed until the time limit had expired was held to have been settled.[108]

If the foreman does not answer within the prescribed time, the grievant may take the complaint to the next step of the procedure. The failure of the foreman to answer will not be interpreted as an admission of the grievance by default, since the burden is on the grievant to carry the complaint to the next step following the lapse of the specified time.[109] But it has been emphasized that the foreman should make a decision or comment on each grievance.[110]

Observance of Grievance Procedure

Arbitrators recognize that the grievance procedure, when adhered to, advances peaceful and constructive industrial relations, with resultant benefits alike to labor, management, and the public. Moreover, arbitrators realize that the success of

---

[106] See Arbitrator Warns in 28 LA 424, 428; Platt in 27 LA 262, 264-265; Cahn in 26 LA 649, 650-651; Kates in 26 LA 172, 174-175; Seward in 23 LA 538, 540, and in 20 LA 87, 92; Justin in 17 LA 303, 309; Gregory in 15 LA 147, 149; Hepburn in 14 LA 387, 388. Cf., Livengood in 27 LA 157, 159; Feinberg in 26 LA 550, 551-552; Aaron in 12 LA 786, 793-794.

[107] Pacific Mills, 14 LA 387, 388 (Hepburn, 1950).

[108] Chrysler Corporation, 1 ALAA par. 67,017 (1945). Also see Arbitrator Duff in 25 LA 534, 537-538; Platt in 25 LA 437, 438.

[109] See Arbitrator Seligson in 26 LA 393, 394; Boles in 24 LA 295, 299; Updegraff in 3 LA 737, 742-743. The "authority" to refer a grievance to the next step is said to rest with the grievant, not with the foreman. Ford Motor Co., 3 LA 840 (Shulman, 1946).

[110] Ford Motor Co., 3 LA 840, 841 (Shulman, 1946). Also see Bethlehem Steel Co., 19 LA 521, 522 (Feinberg, 1952).

arbitration itself may be jeopardized if the grievance procedure is not carefully followed.

Arbitration awards show that arbitrators expect the parties to pay due respect to the grievance procedure, not only by using it, but also by observing its formal requirements. Such respect is something of a "condition precedent." In some cases it is a condition precedent to an award of requested relief. In these cases the arbitrator takes jurisdiction but, upon learning of the grievant's failure to fulfill the condition precedent, denies relief, in whole or in part. In other cases it is a condition precedent to the assumption of jurisdiction by the arbitrator. The requirement that these conditions precedent be met is somewhat analogous to the requirement by the courts that the administrative remedy, if any, be exhausted before the court will give relief.

Use of Grievance Procedure v. Self-Help

Arbitrators often deny or limit requested relief, notwithstanding the merits of the original complaint, where the grievant has resorted to self-help rather than to the grievance procedure. Many arbitrators have taken the position that employees must not take matters into their own hands but must obey orders and carry out their assignments, even if believed to violate the agreement, then turn to the grievance procedure for relief.[111]

---

[111] See Arbitrator Boles in 29 LA 693, 696-697; Gregory in 29 LA 646, 649; Howlett in 29 LA 404, 407; Warns in 29 LA 412, 413; Duff in 29 LA 267, 270-271; Donnelly in 29 LA 74, 76-77; Sembower in 28 LA 486, 490; Haughton in 28 LA 394, 397; J. Williams in 27 LA 892, 900; Reynard in 27 LA 400, 403-404; Dworkin in 27 LA 148, 152; Begley in 25 LA 802, 804; Lyons in 25 LA 727, 729-730; Klamon in 24 LA 839, 845; Boyer in 21 LA 736, 740; Shipman in 21 LA 335, 337; Young in 21 LA 145, 150; Ralston in 20 LA 875, 877; Anrod in 20 LA 653, 656-657; Komaroff in 19 LA 712, 715-716; Rosenfarb in 18 LA 418, 428; Maggs in 17 LA 606, 610; Stein in 17 LA 256, 257; McCoy in 16 LA 307, 310; Feinberg in 15 LA 749, 752; Kerr in 11 LA 219, 221-222;·Blair in 8 LA 68, 70-71; Scheiber in 7 LA 3, 4-7; Updegraff in 5 LA 561, 563; Kharas in 2 LA 274, 276. Contra in part, R. R. Williams in 29 LA 80, 81-82. In most of the above cases the grievant's action in taking matters into his own hands was a significant factor in the arbitrator's decision to deny the grievance or to grant relief in part only.

An important exception exists where obedience would involve an unusual health hazard or similar sacrifice.[112] But this exception has been held inapplicable where the hazard is inherent in the employee's job.[113] Moreover, mere uncomfortable coldness in the plant may not justify a refusal to work.[114]

Some arbitrators have recognized other possible exceptions to the duty to obey orders, as where the order commands the performance of an immoral or criminal act;[115] or where the order violates the rights or domain of the union itself as by interfering with the union's contractual right to investigate and process grievances;[116] or where an order interferes with the employee's proper use of the grievance procedure;[117] or where the order commands a skilled craftsman to perform work wholly unrelated to his craft;[118] or where the order "is *quite clearly and indisputably* beyond the authority of" the company.[119]

Union representatives should not instruct employees to disobey management's orders.[120] Indeed, numerous arbitrators have recognized a special responsibility on the part of union leaders to take affirmative action to persuade employees to use the grievance procedure for matters subject thereto in lieu of taking

---

[112] Most of the arbitrators cited in the previous footnote specifically recognized this exception. Also see Arbitrator Barrett in 27 LA 523, 526-530; Parker in 22 LA 624, 626, and in 21 LA 410; Shipman in 21 LA 335, 337-338; Elson in 8 LA 826, 831; McCoy in 8 LA 647, 651-652.

[113] American Radiator & Standard Sanitary Corp., 26 LA 915, 917 (Duff, 1956). Cf., Arbitrator Gilden in 5 LA 300, 302-304.

[114] See Arbitrator Stutz in 22 LA 841; R. Smith in 22 LA 835, 837.

[115] This possible exception was recognized but did not apply in Temco Aircraft Corp., 29 LA 693, 696 (Boles, 1957).

[116] See Arbitrator McCoy in 16 LA 307, 310-311; Shulman in 10 LA 213, 214.

[117] See Arbitrator J. Williams in 27 LA 892, 900; Rosenfarb in 18 LA 418, 428.

[118] See Arbitrator Haughton in 28 LA 394, 397; Shulman in 3 LA 782, 783 (but Shulman declared that this exception would apply in rare cases only, in 19 LA 237, 238-239, and this limitation was again emphasized by Arbitrator Platt in 30 LA 46, 55).

[119] Dwight Mfg. Co., 12 LA 990, 996 (McCoy, 1949). Possibly thinking in terms of such exception, some arbitrators have held that employees need not obey orders to work overtime where the contract permits them to refuse such work. See Arbitrator Begley in 27 LA 458, 461-463; Maggs in 17 LA 606, 609-610. Cf., Young in 21 LA 145, 150; Fuchs in 15 LA 645, 651.

[120] See Arbitrator Feinberg in 19 LA 43, 46-47; Kerr in 11 LA 219, 221-222; Scheiber in 7 LA 3, 4-7; Shulman in 3 LA 779, 780. An exception has been recognized, however, as to "action falling primarily within the Union's domain." Ford Motor Co., 10 LA 213, 214 (Shulman, 1948).

matters into their own hands (as by refusing to obey orders or by striking in violation of a no-strike clause).[121]

The over-all necessity for observing the grievance procedure is effectively explained in the following statement of Umpire Harry Shulman:

> "Some men apparently think that, when a violation of contract seems clear, the employee may refuse to obey and thus resort to self-help rather than the grievance procedure. That is an erroneous point of view. In the first place, what appears to one party to be a clear violation may not seem so at all to the other party. Neither party can be the final judge as to whether the contract has been violated. The determination of that issue rests in collective negotiation through the grievance procedure. But, in the second place, and more important, the grievance procedure is prescribed in the contract precisely because the parties anticipated that there would be claims of violations which would require adjustment. That procedure is prescribed for all grievances, not merely for doubtful ones. Nothing in the contract even suggests the idea that only doubtful violations need be processed through the grievance procedure and that clear violations can be resisted through individual self-help. The only difference between a 'clear' violation and a 'doubtful' one is that the former makes a clear grievance and the latter a doubtful one. But both must be handled in the regular prescribed manner." [122]

Umpire Shulman observed further that:

> "When a controversy arises, production cannot wait for exhaustion of the grievance procedure. While that procedure is being pursued, production must go on. And someone must have the authority to direct the manner in which it is to go on until the controversy is settled. That authority is vested in supervision. It must be vested there because the responsibility for production is also vested there; and responsibility must be accompanied by authority. It is fairly vested there because the grievance procedure is capable of adequately recompensing employees for abuse of authority by supervision." [123]

---

[121] Ibid. Also, Arbitrator Kelliher in 29 LA 622, 623-624; Howlett in 19 LA 495, 497; Burr in 29 LA 142, 145-146; Davis in 28 LA 782, 791; Sembower in 25 LA 774, 777; Larkin in 22 LA 589, 597; Feinberg in 21 LA 421, 424; Platt in 21 LA 239, 241-242; Laskin in 18 LA 919-923, 924; Seward in 14 LA 986, 988-989; Gilden in 8 LA 758, 769-770; McCoy in 4 LA 744, 745 (also see McCoy in 16 LA 307, 310); Shipman in 2 LA 194, 198-199. While all these arbitrators recognize the existence of the special responsibility, they are by no means agreed as to what punishment, if any, may be assessed for failure to fulfill that special responsibility. In the latter regard, also see Arbitrator McCoy in 29 LA 644, 645-646; Howlett in 29 LA 495, 497; Seward in 29 LA 635, 643.

[122] Ford Motor Co., 3 LA 779, 780-781 (1944).

[123] Id. at 781. However, Umpire Shulman recognized the "unusual health hazard or similar sacrifice" exception to the duty to obey orders. Id. at 782.

The offense of disobeying orders has sometimes been considered to have been mitigated somewhat where the initial refusal to obey was followed by obedience.[124]

Company Obligation to Honor Grievance Procedure

In several cases arbitrators have considered management's obligation to preserve the integrity of the grievance procedure. In view of its obligation to utilize fully the possibilities of settlement inherent in the grievance procedure, an employer was held to have acted improperly in by-passing the union committee which represented certain grievants and communicating an offer of settlement directly to the grievants themselves.[125]

In another case the company was held to have an obligation to furnish information to the union, upon request, as to how the company had complied with a grievance settlement reached in the grievance procedure so the union could determine if the settlement was carried out.[126]

Where an arbitrator found a contractual obligation of management to exhaust the negotiation machinery before resorting to disciplinary action, its failure to do so was held to be sufficient basis for reinstating discharged employees, although the discharges were otherwise justified.[127] In a "slowdown" case the arbitrator condemned the company for taking "the law into its own hands" by assessing a wage cut for the slowdown instead of utilizing the "adequate grievance provisions" or other remedies available under the contract (including the right to discipline or lockout employees engaged in the slowdown).[128]

Exhaustion of Grievance Procedure as
Condition Precedent for Arbitration

A limitation by arbitrators of their jurisdiction to cases which the parties have made bona fide efforts to settle can be

---

[124] See Arbitrator Stutz in 28 LA 255, 257; Reynard in 24 LA 66, 71.
[125] Central Franklin Process Co., 17 LA 142, 145 (Marshall, 1951).
[126] North American Aviation, Inc., 17 LA 121, 124-125 (Komaroff, 1951).
[127] Gloucester, Mass. Fisheries, 1 ALAA par. 67,340 (1946).
[128] Jacobs Mfg. Co., 29 LA 512, 517-518 (Scheiber, 1957).

expected to result in improved handling of grievances at the lower levels. The National War Labor Board learned from experience that settlements through negotiations are encouraged when arbitrators refuse to take jurisdiction over grievance issues until the parties show that they have exhausted all chances of settlement through negotiations.[129] Arbitrators can do this unless the agreement permits direct resort to arbitration.[130] A New York court, in granting an employer's motion for a stay of arbitration, spoke of the requirement that conditions precedent be performed prior to arbitration:

> "One of the preliminary steps, viz. submission to the grievance committee of the association, was omitted entirely as were other steps in connection with some of the issues tendered for arbitration. No explanation is here given for such omission or neglect. It was incumbent upon the union, under the terms of the contract, to exhaust all other methods of conciliation as provided for therein before it could invoke the remedy of arbitration. Until it complies with the conditions of the contract in respect to all the essential acts on its part to be performed or offers a reasonable and just excuse for non-performance, the union will be enjoined from proceeding with the arbitration." [131]

The critical nature of some disputes leads the parties to stipulate that all pre-arbitral steps are waived and that the dispute is to be taken directly to arbitration.[132] The agreement itself may make provision for the direct appeal of such disputes to arbitration, but this type of provision has been held inapplicable to ordinary employee grievances.[133]

A party who refuses to comply with the negotiation steps of the grievance procedure will not be permitted to prevent arbitration on the ground that the grievance procedure has not

---

[129] Aluminum Co. of America, 12 War Lab. Rep. 446, 455 (1943).

[130] For instance, where the grievance procedure had not been exhausted the dispute was held to be non-arbitrable by Arbitrator Feinberg in 20 LA 675, 678; Komaroff in 19 LA 729, 731-733.

[131] In re Picture Frame Workers Union, 8 LA 1063, 1064 (N.Y. Sup. Ct., 1947). Some courts have held that the question whether conditions precedent for arbitration have been complied with is for the arbitrator rather than the court. See Jones v. Tide Water Oil Co., 22 LA 562, 563 (Calif. Super. Ct., 1954), and cases cited therein; United Cement, Lime & Gypsum Workers Union, Local 55 v. Allentown-Portland Cement Co., 163 F. Supp. 816 (D.C. Pa., 1958). For related discussions see Chapter 6, Determining Arbitrability.

[132] As in Calumet & Hecla, Inc., 25 LA 663, 664 (R. Smith, 1955).

[133] Ford Motor Co., 1 ALAA par. 67,030 (1944).

been exhausted.[134] Nor must the grievance procedure be exhausted where to do so would be "futile",[135] or a "useless and idle gesture".[136]

Then, too, if an agreement provides only an informal type of grievance procedure, the arbitrator may not be exacting as to the preliminaries necessary to give him jurisdiction. Arbitrator William E. Simkin has said, for instance, that to give an arbitrator jurisdiction in such a case it is necessary only that the issue be one on which the parties have had some prior discussion and on which the "realistic possibilities" of settlement at the lower grievance steps have been exhausted.[137] Finally, the right to object that the grievance procedure has not been exhausted may be held waived by agreeing to arbitrate the dispute.[138]

Grievance Settlements As Binding Precedents

It seems obvious that where a grievance has been settled by mutual agreement of the parties, the same issue that is involved in such "settled" grievance, though appearing in the guise of another grievance, should not ordinarily be subject to arbitration at the request of only one party. "It is essential to good labor-management relations * * * that grievance settlements not be disturbed in the absence of a conclusive showing of changed conditions."[139] One arbitrator would add that settlements are open to investigation on substantial charge of fraud or grievous error.[140]

Aside from any effect of mutual settlements as binding precedents, such settlements may be accepted by an arbitrator as indicating the proper interpretation of ambiguous contract

---

[134] Brynmore Press, Inc., 8 LA 511, 512-514 (Rains, 1947).
[135] Barbet Mills, Inc., 16 LA 563, 565 (Livengood, 1951). Also, In re Roto Supply Sales Co., 28 LA 657, 658 (N.Y. Sup. Ct., 1957).
[136] In re Greenstone, 29 LA 161, 162 (N.Y. Sup. Ct., 1957).
[137] Reading Street Railway Co., 8 LA 930, 933 (1947).
[138] United Tavern, 16 LA 210, 214 (Slavney, 1951).
[139] Standard Oil. Co. (Indiana), 13 LA 799, 800 (Kelliher, 1949). Accord, International Harvester Co., 19 LA 812, 814 (Emery, 1953); Tennessee Coal, Iron & Railroad Co., 7 LA 378, 380 (Blumer, 1947). Also see Arbitrator Wallen in 17 LA 36, 38-39. Cf., Brandschain in 15 LA 672, 673.
[140] Tennessee Coal, Iron & Railroad Co., 7 LA 378, 380 (Blumer, 1947).

language. It has been observed, in this regard, that "Where the parties themselves settle a grievance the evidence of intent as to the meaning of a provision carries special weight." [141]

Somewhat different considerations are involved, however, where a grievance has not been mutually settled, but simply has been denied by management at some pre-arbitral step of the grievance procedure and, for various possible reasons, has not been appealed further. If management's denial of a grievance is "accepted" by the union so as to provide the elements of a "settlement" an arbitrator might consider it a binding precedent.[142] But several arbitrators have held that the mere failure to appeal a grievance is not per se acquiescence in the disposition of the issue on the basis of management's final answer so as to bar the issue from arbitration in a subsequent case.[143] This is particularly so where withdrawal of a case from the grievance procedure is done "without prejudice",[144] or where the withdrawing party indicates that it intends ultimately to seek an arbitral ruling on the issue.[145]

In deciding not to appeal the grievance further, a party apparently should state some such condition to protect its interests; otherwise, a binding precedent might result.[146]

Sometimes the collective agreement deals specifically with this matter. For example, under a clause providing that grievances not appealed to arbitration were "to be considered settled on the basis of the decision last made," Arbitrator Harry H. Platt refused to decide an issue which had been involved in two prior grievances which had been withdrawn:

"The present grievance appears plainly to be an attempt to reinstate the former grievances which had already been withdrawn by the Union. To permit this, in the absence of proof that the earlier withdrawal was

---

[141] Bendix-Westinghouse Automotive Air Brake Co., 23 LA 706, 710 (Mathews, 1954).

[142] See U.S. Steel Corp., 21 LA 26, 30 (Garrett 1953).

[143] National Fireworks Ordnance Corp., 23 LA 289, 291 (L. Smith, 1954); Union Carbide & Carbon Corp., 16 LA 811, 816 (Gilden, 1951); Tennessee Coal, Iron & Railroad Co., 6 LA 426, 429 (Blumer, 1945).

[144] Greer Hydraulics, Inc., 29 LA 706, 708 (Friedman, 1957).

[145] Lion Oil Co., 25 LA 549, 552 (Reynard, 1955).

[146] Kaiser Aluminum & Chemical Corp., 28 LA 439, 440 (McCoy, 1957).

induced by the Company through fraud, misrepresentation, intentional concealment of facts, overreaching or through mutual mistake, would encourage the relitigation of grievances after they had been disposed of by the parties in the proper exercise of their discretion. This would indeed undermine the grievance procedure and the Umpire system. Here, there is no claim or proof that the Company had anything to do with the Union's decision to withdraw the earlier grievances from the procedure and from arbitration. It was a voluntary action presumably taken with full knowledge of all the facts, and must be held binding on the Union." [147]

Reaching a similar result, Arbitrator Harry J. Dworkin stated that the only exception "would be a situation in which the 'new' grievance would embrace factors and changed conditions which would clearly distinguish the latter grievance from the former." [148]

Notice of Intent to Arbitrate

Collective agreements frequently provide that parties who wish to arbitrate disputes not settled by the negotiation steps of the grievance procedure must give notice of desire and intent to arbitrate within a specified period of time. Arbitrators often have held that failure to give the required notice, unless waived by the other party or otherwise excused, renders the dispute nonarbitrable. [149]

Under an agreement requiring written notice of appeal to arbitration, a New York court ruled that failure to give notice within the specified time barred a demand for arbitration. The court said that the provision for notice was, in effect, a statute of limitations—a contractual right, not a mere technicality. [150] But under an agreement which did not require that notice be in writing, the same court held that "substantial compliance" with

---

[147] Republic Steel Corp., 25 LA 437, 438 (1955). Apparently contra, Pittsburgh Steel Co., 25 LA 157, 162 (May, 1955).
[148] Babcock & Wilcox Co., 24 LA 541, 547-548 (1955).
[149] See Arbitrator McCoy in 20 LA 34, 34-35; Emery in 20 LA 865, 866; Handsaker in 16 LA 369, 371; Abersold in 13 LA 266, 267-269; Levy in 6 LA 397, 399-403; Dodd in 5 LA 742, 744-746; Updegraff in 4 LA 458, 461. Courts have ruled both ways on the question whether the sufficiency and timeliness of notices for arbitration are matters for determination by the court or by the arbitrator. See Inspection Unit v. Bell Aircraft Corp., 21 LA 727 (N.Y. Sup. Ct., 1954); Boston Mutual Life Ins. Co. v. Insurance Agents, 258 F.2d 516 (C.A. 1, 1958). Also see Kyne v. Molfetas, 28 LA 208 (N.Y. Sup. Ct., 1957). For related discussion see Chapter 6, Determining Arbitrability.
[150] In re Ketchum & Co., 7 LA 954 (N.Y. Sup. Ct., 1947).

the provision was sufficient in absence of any other provision making time of the essence. The court further held that institution of the proceeding to compel arbitration constituted the required "substantial compliance." [151]

A timely oral announcement of intent to arbitrate has been held sufficient where the agreement does not specifically require written notice.[152] But under an agreement which required such notice to be in writing, a timely oral announcement of intention to submit a grievance to arbitration was held not to be sufficient.[153]

Some agreements provide that within a specified time after notice of intent to arbitrate has been given, a joint request is to be submitted asking that an arbitrator act on the dispute. Failure to notify the arbitrator within the specified time may be held to render the dispute nonarbitrable.[154] But if one party fails to meet its obligation in respect to the joint request, that party cannot prevent arbitration on the ground that the other party alone referred the case to arbitration.[155]

Although arbitrators are compelled to apply contractual limitations, they often do so with apparent displeasure. Witness, for example, the statement of Arbitrator Bert W. Levy:

"It should be frankly noted that the umpire reaches his conclusion with real regret. 'A time limitation is a summary bar. Its imposition precludes application of principles of equity, of fairness, and of justice, regardless of merit * * *.' But the company in these cases has carefully refrained from any conduct which could properly be deemed a waiver of the strict procedural requirements * * *. There is nothing here to buttress the liberal interpretation which the umpire would much prefer to adopt, no peg upon which he can 'hang his hat.' These grievances must be choked off at this point. It is ruled that they have all been appealed too late * * *." [156]

As might be expected, reasonable excuse for failure to meet notice requirements or the presence of other justification

[151] In re Rabinowitz, 8 LA 1062 (N.Y. Sup. Ct., 1947).
[152] See Arbitrator Whiting in 28 LA 398, 400; Barrett in 19 LA 489, 491.
[153] Bethlehem Steel Co., 5 LA 742, 746 (Dodd, 1946).
[154] John Deere Harvester Works, 10 LA 778, 781-782 (Updegraff, 1948).
[155] Malone & Hyde, Inc., 5 LA 443, 445-446 (Wardlaw, 1946).
[156] Bethlehem Steel Co., 6 LA 397, 402 (1947).

for the arbitrator not to enforce such requirements strictly, may prevent a forfeiture of the right of arbitration. In such cases jurisdiction will be assumed and the dispute will be decided on the merits.[157] This was true where the parties in the past had mutually accepted loose interpretation of their contractual time limits.[158] A reasonable excuse may be a good-faith mistake or difference of opinion,[159] or it may be the unavoidable absence of an essential party, so as to make the observance of time limits impracticable.[160] Furthermore, a reasonable excuse may be said to exist if it would be futile to request arbitration within the time limit.[161]

In an estoppel situation, a commitment made but later repudiated by one party was held to be a reasonable excuse for the failure of the other party to comply literally with the notice requirement.[162] Finally, the right to enforce time limits may be waived, as by signing a submission agreement to arbitrate and failing to raise the time issue until the arbitration hearing.[163]

---

[157] See Arbitrator Lehoczcky in 26 LA 633, 634; Stutz in 19 LA 234, 236; Abruzzi in 18 LA 193, 195-196; Prasow in 17 LA 205, 206; Selekman in 17 LA 7, 8; McCoy in 8 LA 883, 884; Trotta in 8 LA 844, 845; Simkin in 7 LA 276, 278; Brandschain in 4 LA 509, 510-513; Wardlaw in 3 LA 500, 503-504. Also see court cases in 28 LA 29 (Mass.); 23 LA 672 (N.Y.).

[158] Standard-Thompson Corp., 26 LA 633, 634 (Lehozcky, 1956). Also see Arbitrator Abruzzi in 18 LA 193, 195-196.

[159] See Arbitrator Simkin in 7 LA 276, 278; Wardlaw in 3 LA 500, 503-504.

[160] Ohmer Corp., 5 LA 278, 280 (Lehoczcky, 1946).

[161] Manhattan Transit Co., 8 LA 844, 845 (Trotta, 1947).

[162] B. F. Goodrich Co., 8 LA 883, 884 (McCoy, 1947).

[163] See Arbitrator L. Smith in 23 LA 289, 291; Marshall in 14 LA 310, 311.

CHAPTER 6

DETERMINING ARBITRABILITY

When an existing dispute is taken to arbitration by a joint submission of the parties there ordinarily is no problem of arbitrability since by the submission the parties identify the dispute and agree to its arbitration. A different situation may be presented, however, when one party invokes the arbitration clause of a collective agreement by a demand or notice of intent to arbitrate a dispute which has arisen during the term of the agreement. Here arbitration may be resisted by the other party on the ground that the dispute is not arbitrable. It may be asserted, for instance, that the case does not involve any of the types of disputes that are covered by the arbitration clause,[1] or that while covered by the arbitration clause the dispute is not arbitrable because some condition precedent to arbitration, such as exhaustion of the grievance procedure or timely notice of intent to arbitrate, has not been met.[2]

Challenges to arbitrability are presented either to the arbitrator or to the courts. If an appointing agency is named in the arbitration clause, the challenge may be filed with it. There is no uniformity of policy of the various agencies in regard to processing cases and appointing an arbitrator where one party files a challenge to arbitrability. Some of the agencies do appoint an arbitrator in such instances, at least where a minimal showing of an arbitration clause is made, and the

---

[1] For important related discussion see Chapter 3, topics titled " 'Interests' Arbitration Contract Clauses"; " 'Rights' Arbitration Contract Clauses."

[2] See Chapter 5 for discussion of these conditions precedent.

party protesting arbitrability is permitted to raise that issue before the arbitrator or the courts.[3]

In deciding where to lodge the challenge to arbitrability, the challenger may be influenced in varying degree by the particular language of the arbitration clause, by the state or federal law that governs the case, and, possibly most important, by the challenger's general attitude toward the arbitration process. Then, too, he might take a passive attitude, forcing the other party to seek enforcement of the arbitration clause by a court or arbitrator, at which stage the challenger will raise the issue of arbitrability.

Determination by the Arbitrator

The determination of arbitrability is most often left to the arbitrator.[4] There are sound reasons for this. The delay and expense of court proceedings are avoided. Moreover, the arbitrator can be expected to exercise the industrial relations expertise which the parties contemplated when they provided for arbitration.

The collective agreement itself may specifically provide that the arbitrator is to rule on questions of arbitrability as well as upon the merits of the dispute. This provides the surest method for parties to minimize court participation or "interference" in the arbitration process.[5] Even if the collective agreement does not state specifically who is to determine arbitrability, the plain implication is that the arbitrator should have exclusive authority to do so if the arbitration clause is broad enough to cover all disputes, differences, and grievances of the parties.

---

[3] For a discussion of the policy and procedures of the various appointing agencies where arbitrability is questioned, see Justin, "Arbitrability and the Arbitrator's Jurisdiction," Management Rights and the Arbitration Process, 1, 11-15 (BNA, Incorporated 1956). Also see "Arbitrability," 18 LA 942, 951 (1951).

[4] For an extensive study of arbitrators' awards on arbitrability issues, see the Committee Report of the American Bar Association Section of Labor Law, "Arbitrability," 18 LA 942-955 (1951). Also see materials in Chapter 3, Scope of Labor Arbitration.

[5] This right of the parties to remove the question of arbitrability from the courts to the arbitrator was emphasized in UAW v. Benton Harbor Malleable Industries, 242 F.2d 536, 39 LRRM 2689 (6th Cir., 1957).

Further, the parties by special submission or stipulation may authorize the arbitrator, either specifically or impliedly, to rule both on questions or arbitrability and on the merits of the dispute. Here again, the question obviously is whether the language used is sufficient to vest the exclusive and final right of determination in the arbitrator.

Most significant, however, is the fact that even where the parties have not clearly authorized the arbitrator to determine arbitrability, he often does so (as an inherent part of his duty) and they generally accept his conclusions without resort to litigation. One group of arbitrators has suggested that the arbitrator's "right to rule upon arbitrability is related to his duty to the parties to interpret any part of the contract, including the arbitration clause itself." [6] To like effect, Arbitrator Douglass B. Maggs has urged that "an agreement to arbitrate future disputes of a specified kind vests in a duly appointed arbitrator power to determine whether a particular dispute, with respect to which one party invokes arbitration, is a dispute of that kind." [7]

An American Bar Association Committee has stated that "the function of the arbitrator to decide whether or not an allegation of non-arbitrability is sound could be compared to that of a trial judge who is asked to dismiss a complaint on motion for a directed verdict or for failure to state a cause of action. This analogy indicates that a preliminary decision relating to arbitrability by the arbitrator *is an inherent part of his duty*." [8] The Committee suggested that: "Where the contract calls for the arbitration of grievances relating to the application, interpretation or alleged violations of any provision of a collective bargaining agreement, an assertion that a particular dispute is not subject to arbitration should not

---

[6] Guides For Labor Arbitration, 5 (Univ. of Pa. Press, 1953). Also see comments of Arbitrator Whitley P. McCoy in West Penn Power Co., 24 LA 741, 742 (1955).

[7] Barbet Mills, Inc., 19 LA 737, 738 (1952).

[8] "Arbitrability," 18 LA 942, 950 (1951), Report of the Committee on Administration of Union-Employer Contracts, Section of Labor Law, A.B.A. (Emphasis added)

prevent the arbitrator from deciding whether the dispute is arbitrable." [9]

That arbitrators are capable of self-restraint is evidenced by the Committee's conclusion, based upon examination of many awards, that "arbitrators generally are well aware of the limitations of their authority and scrupulously try to avoid any transgression of those limitations." [10] Then, too, as the Committee noted, arbitrators often have denied grievances which they found arbitrable—"A finding of arbitrability thus means only that the arbitrator believes the grievance has sufficient color to warrant consideration and disposition on the merits instead of rejection on jurisdictional grounds." [11]

Procedural Techniques for Ruling on Arbitrability

Sometimes arbitrability is the sole question before the arbitrator, but probably more often he is called upon to rule both on the preliminary issue of arbitrability and, if he finds the dispute arbitrable, also on the merits.[12]

Where the arbitrator is to rule on both arbitrability and the merits, evidence and argument on the question of arbitrability will be *heard* before the presentation on the merits. But the procedural question remains as to whether the arbitrator should *rule* on arbitrability before any presentation is made on the merits, or whether he should reserve his ruling on arbitrability until the full case has been presented.

One school of thought holds that a ruling on arbitrability should be made before the presentation on the merits. This view is elaborated by Arbitrator Harry J. Dworkin:

"The Chairman is of the opinion that when a party raises the issue of arbitrability, it is better practice to pass upon this issue at the time it is presented, and before hearing the dispute on the merits, for the reason that

---

[9] Id. at 951-952.
[10] Id. at 951.
[11] Id. at 949.
[12] See statistics in "Substantive Aspects of Labor-Management Arbitration," 28 LA 943, 944 (1957).

whenever possible parties should have the right to an interim decision or ruling on any question presented during the course of the hearing, and that this procedure is preferable to the reservation of the ruling until after the conclusion of the hearing." [13]

Another view holds that the ruling on arbitrability may be reserved until the full case has been heard. As elaborated by Arbitrator Douglass B. Maggs:

"The arbitrator may properly reserve his ruling upon. arbitrability until after he has heard evidence and argument upon the merits. A contrary rule would cause needless delay and expense, necessitating two hearings whenever the arbitrator needed time to consider the question of arbitrability. Furthermore, in many cases, it is only after a hearing on the merits has informed the arbitrator of the nature of the dispute that he is in a position to determine whether it is of the kind covered by the agreement to arbitrate.

"* * * This procedure does not, of course, preclude the party who loses from obtaining any judicial review of the arbitrator's decision to which it is entitled by law; to reassure the Company about this I explicitly ruled that its participation in the hearing upon the merits would not constitute a waiver of its objections to arbitrability." [14]

It would seem that the choice between these two procedures should be dictated by consideration of all the circumstances of the particular case. Such a flexible procedure is used by the Connecticut State Board of Mediation:

"The Board will inform the party protesting arbitrability that it will be permitted to raise that issue at the hearing. The Board will then first hear arguments on arbitrability before it proceeds to the merits of the dispute. The Board makes clear that at the hearing both parties must be prepared to proceed on the merits after the Board has heard them on arbitrability.

"After the issue on arbitrability has been presented, 'the Board will assess the circumstances then obtaining to determine if it will proceed directly to the merits.'

"Under its policy, the Board reserves the right either to require the parties 'to go forward directly on the merits' at the same hearing or to determine that 'the decision on arbitrability should be made first before proceeding on the merits.' " [15]

---

[13] Babcock & Wilcox Co., 22 LA 456, 460 (1954).

[14] Barbet Mills, Inc., 19 LA 737, 738 (1952). Arbitrator Maggs explained his view in greater detail in Caledonia Mills, Inc., 15 LA 474, 476-477 (1950). This approach is suggested also in "Arbitrability," 18 LA 941, 950-951 (1951).

[15] Justin, "Arbitrability and the Arbitrator's Jurisdiction," Management Rights and the Arbitration Process, 1, 12 (BNA Incorporated, 1956)

Regardless of *when* the ruling on arbitrability is made, it will often be placed in the arbitrator's written decision of the case at a point prior to his discussion of the merits.[16]

Determination by the Courts

Arbitrability questions are not always left entirely in the hands of the arbitrator, but are sometimes involved when the courts are drawn into the arbitration process. The nature and extent of court participation may depend largely upon the prevailing law and the language of the arbitration clause. The courts may become concerned with arbitrability questions in several ways:[17]

(1) The party challenging arbitrability may seek a temporary injunction or "stay of arbitration" pending determination of arbitrability.

(2) The party demanding arbitration may seek a court order compelling the other party to arbitrate where the prevailing law upholds agreements to arbitrate future disputes; the latter party then raises the issue of arbitrability.

(3) The issue of arbitrability may be considered when an award is taken to court for review or enforcement, unless the parties have clearly vested the arbitrator with the exclusive and final right of determining arbitrability, or unless the right to challenge arbitrability is held by the court to have been otherwise waived under the circumstances of the case.[18]

When a court is asked to enjoin or compel arbitration the question of arbitrability ordinarily becomes involved.

---

[16] As Arbitrator Dworkin did in Babcock & Wilcox Co., 22 LA 456, 460 (1954), and Arbitrator Maggs in Barbet Mills, Inc., 19 LA 737, 739 (1952).

[17] For collection and discussion of court cases involving arbitrability, see Kharas & Koretz, "Judicial Determination of the Arbitrable Issue," 11 Arb. J. (n.s.) 135-149 (1956); Justin, "Arbitrability and the Arbitrator's Jurisdiction," Management Rights and the Arbitration Process, 1-40 (BNA Incorporated, 1956); "ABA Report on Labor Arbitration," 28 LA 913, 924-925 (1957); Freidin, Labor Arbitration and the Courts, 4-24 (Univ. of Pa. Press, 1952); Hillman, "Determination of Arbitrability in Collective Bargaining Contracts," 46 Calif. L. Rev. 462-467 (1958); Arbitration and the Law, 1-89 (BNA Incorporated, 1959). Also see materials in Chapter 3, Scope of Labor Arbitration.

[18] Regarding waiver of right to court review of arbitrability see this Chapter, Delay In Contesting Arbitrability, below.

Occasionally the court will leave determination of arbitrability, initially, at least, to the arbitrator.[19] Moreover, the court might find that the exclusive and final right of determination has been vested in the arbitrator by the parties. However, given any opportunity to rule on arbitrability, many courts have been quick to assume this function. These courts have generally taken the position that arbitrability involves a question of law for decision by the court, unless the parties have specifically authorized the arbitrator to make the determination.[20]

An American Bar Association Committee study of court decisions on arbitrability has revealed "diverse and conflicting rulings on basically similar questions." [21] This Committee suggested that "These conflicts may be traced to the general application of the Cutler-Hammer doctrine that 'If the meaning of the provision of the contract sought to be arbitrated is beyond dispute, there cannot be anything to arbitrate and the contract cannot be said to provide for arbitration.' " [22]

A weakness of this "no dispute" doctrine is that in many cases the clarity or the ambiguity of contract language as applied to a given set of facts can be fairly determined only after a thorough hearing on those facts. Indeed, the determination of whether there is any ambiguity often determines the grievance itself, and the existence of ambiguity is often a matter upon which reasonable men may disagree. A similarly close situation, requiring a thorough hearing and possibly resulting in a judicial expression on the merits, may be involved where arbitrability is contested on the grounds that a condi-

---

[19] For a strong argument in favor of leaving initial determination to the arbitrator, preserving the right of court review of arbitrability when the award is reviewed, see Hillman, "Determination of Arbitrability in Collective Bargaining Contracts," 46 Calif. L. Rev. 462-467 (1958).

[20] See In re N.Y. Mirror, 29 LA 278, 279 (N.Y. Sup. Ct., 1957); UAW v. Benton Harbor Malleable Industries, 242 F.2d 536, 39 LRRM 2689 (6th Cir., 1957); Southside Theatres v. Projectionists, 23 LA 824 (Calif. Super. Ct., 1954).

[21] "ABA Report on Labor Arbitration," 28 LA 913, 924 (1957).

[22] Ibid. See Cutler-Hammer, Inc., 6 LA 1031, aff'd. 7 LA 959 (N.Y. Ct. App., 1947). For a collection of later cases applying this doctrine, see Standard Oil Union v. Esso Co., 25 LA 868 (N.J. Super. Ct., 1955); Marceau, "Are All Interpretations 'Admissible'?" 12 Arb. J. 150 (1957).

tion precedent to arbitration has not been met, or that the dispute simply is not one of the types covered by the arbitration clause. Thus, it is not surprising that some critics believe the courts have tended to usurp the function of the arbitrator by actually making determinations of the merits while ostensibly ruling only on arbitrability." [23]

In adopting an arbitration clause the parties obviously intend that the merits of their disputes be resolved by an arbitrator. This recognized, it is encouraging that one court has noted that "The trend of decisions of appellate courts has been towards a very liberal interpretation favoring arbitration, once a contract to arbitrate has been found to exist." [24]

Further, it has been "surmised" that "the pleas for [judicial] self-restraint have been widely honored," and that the trend may be toward decreasing judicial intervention in the arbitration process.[25]

Delay in Contesting Arbitrability

The right to contest arbitrability before the arbitrator is not waived merely by failing to raise the issue of arbitrability until the arbitration hearing.[26]

Whether participation in an arbitration hearing on the merits constitutes a waiver of the right to court review of arbitrability may depend upon the terms of an applicable statute or upon the view of the particular court.[27] As a pre-

---

[23] E.g., Summers, "Judicial Review of Labor Arbitration or Alice Through the Looking Glass," 2 Buff. L. Rev. 1, 10-11 (1952); Rosenfarb, "The Courts and Arbitration," N.Y.U. Sixth Annual Conference of Labor, 161, 162 (1953).
[24] Carey v. General Electric Co., 28 LA 614, 615 (N.Y. Sup. Ct., 1957). One court has more recently declared, for instance, that "Issues do not lose their quality of arbitrability because they can be correctly decided only one way." New Bedford Defense Products Div. v. Local No. 1113, 160 F.Supp. 103, 112 (D. Mass., 1958), aff'd. 258 F.2d 522, 42 LRRM 2518 (1st Cir., 1958).
[25] Kharas & Koretz, "Judicial Determination of the Arbitrable Issue," 11 Arb. J. (n.s.) 135, 143, 149 (1956).
[26] E.g., Arbitrator Young in 20 LA 289, 292; Kerr in 11 LA 219, 220; Rader in 7 LA 595, 598. Also see Prasow in 12 LA 1131, 1135.
[27] For example, see Towns & James, Inc. v. Barasch, 14 LA 293, 295 (N.Y. Sup. Ct., 1950); Brampton Woolen Co. v. Local Union, 11 LA 487 (N.H. Sup. Ct., 1948). Also see Overseas Distributors Exchange v. Benedict & Brothers, 173 N.Y.S. 2d 110 (N.Y. Sup. Ct., 1958).

caution against such waiver, a participant in an arbitration hearing on the merits may expressly reserve the right to court review of arbitrability. Likewise, an arbitrator who calls for argument on the merits of a dispute before he rules on a challenge to arbitrability may emphasize that "participation in the hearing upon the merits would not constitute a waiver of objections to arbitrability." [28]

---

[28] Barbet Mills, Inc., 19 LA 737, 738 (Maggs, 1952).

CHAPTER 7

ARBITRATION PROCEDURES AND TECHNIQUES
Source of Procedural Rules

it is difficult to generalize concerning arbitration procedures since rarely do the procedures followed in any given case spring from a single source. Indeed, it frequently happens that in a given case some of the procedure utilized is based upon statutory requirements, some upon agreement of the parties, and some upon directive of the arbitrator. Then, too, if the parties have agreed to arbitrate under the rules of some administrative agency, such as the American Arbitration Association, many procedural matters will be governed by the rules of the agency. Accordingly, the readers should bear in mind that the procedures outlined in this chapter do not necessarily apply in all cases, but may be varied significantly as to some cases by the prevailing law, administrative agency rules, or special agreement of the parties.

It is highly desirable that arbitration procedures be based, to the extent reasonably possible, upon the wishes of the parties and the judgment of their arbitrator. In this regard, it is significant that most arbitration statutes contain very little detail regarding that part of the arbitration process from the time the arbitrator is selected until his award has been issued.[1] Then, too, even where statutes deal with this part of the process, the parties may be permitted to waive statutory requirements.[2] Likewise, the procedural rules of administrative agencies ordinarily may be waived by the parties by pro-

---

[1] The limited role of the law in the arbitration process is discussed in Chapter 2.
[2] For instance, see In re Aranson, 6 LA 1033 (N.Y. Sup. Ct., 1946). Also see Chapter 2.

ceeding without objection when the rules are not observed.[3]

It is the function and responsibility of the arbitrator to determine procedural matters which are not covered by any applicable statute or administrative agency rule and upon which the parties have not reached agreement. In actual practice arbitrators frequently determine what procedure shall be followed in regard to many aspects of the arbitration process.[4] It must be emphasized, however, that the arbitrator will endeavor to comply with the wishes of the parties whenever they agree on procedural matters.[5]

Initiating Arbitration: Submission v. Arbitration Clause

Arbitration may be initiated either (1) by a "submission," or (2) by a demand or notice invoking a collective agreement arbitration clause. Sometimes both instruments are used in a case.

A submission (sometimes called a "stipulation" or an "agreement to arbitrate") is used where there is no previous agreement to arbitrate. The submission, which must be signed by both parties, describes an existing dispute; it often also names the arbitrator (or the method of appointment) and it sometimes contains considerable detail regarding the arbitrator's authority, the procedure to be used at the hearing, and other matters which the parties wish to control.[6]

Since collective agreements generally do not provide for the arbitration of "interests" disputes that might arise in the future, the agreement to arbitrate such disputes most often is entered into after the dispute has materialized and at a time when the issues can be defined. In such cases the parties

---

[3] Such waiver is permitted, for instance, by American Arbitration Association Rule 33, 30 LA 1089.

[4] The cases and materials throughout this Chapter illustrate this function of the arbitrator. In this regard, too, American Arbitration Association Rule 47 empowers the arbitrator to interpret its rules "insofar as they relate to his powers and duties." 30 LA 1091.

[5] See "Code of Ethics and Procedural Standards for Labor-Management Arbitration," 15 LA 961, 964 (1951).

[6] For example, see the submission in Goodyear Engineering Corp., 24 LA 360, 361-362 (Warns, 1955).

will use one instrument only, which will contain full provision for the arbitration.[7]

However, most collective agreements do provide for arbitration of "rights" disputes involving the application or interpretation of the agreement. Thus there is an "agreement to arbitrate" future disputes that may arise under and during the term of the collective agreement. If a dispute is covered by such an arbitration clause, arbitration may be initiated unilaterally by one party by serving upon the other a written demand or notice of intent to arbitrate; the latter party may reply with a statement covering its position, but the arbitration proceeds regardless of whether any such reply is made. Use of a demand only, with no joint submission, is common practice where the collective agreement contains an arbitration clause.[8] Moreover, in such cases no submission may be required even to make arbitration enforceable by the courts if the case is covered by a state or federal law making agreements to arbitrate future disputes specifically enforceable.[9]

However, even where the collective agreement contains an arbitration clause covering a dispute, the parties sometimes choose also to execute a submission after the dispute has materialized. Some reasons for doing this are:

1. To expand or diminish the authority of the arbitrator more than provided by the collective agreement.[10]
2. To state precisely the issue to be decided by the arbitrator, and thus to indicate the scope of his jurisdiction more precisely.[11]
3. To state procedural details where the parties desire to control them and the collective agreement contains little or no detail in regard thereto.

---

[7] For such an instrument see River Valley Tissue Mills, Inc., 3 La 245, 246 (Blair, 1946). Also see submission instruments in 28 LA 477, 478-479; 26 LA 904, 904-905; 25 LA 54, 55.

[8] See "Procedural Aspects of Labor-Management Arbitration," 28 LA 933, 934 (1954 statistics). "Many arbitrational hearings and awards proceed to final performance without a formal submission to the contract to arbitrate and grievance statement." Updegraff & McCoy, Arbitration of Labor Disputes, 53 (1946).

[9] See In re Publishers' Assn., 18 LA 1, 2-3 (N.Y. Sup. Ct., 1952).

[10] For example, see International Shoe Co., 21 LA 550, 550-551 (Rader, 1953).

[11] See North American Cement Corp., 28 LA 414, 417-418 (Callaghan, 1957).

4. In arbitration under a statute, to complete any statutory requirements not met by the arbitration clause of the collective agreement.

5. In cases not covered by any state or federal law making agreements
to arbitrate future disputes specifically enforceable, to provide a
contract after the dispute has materialized, contracts to arbitrate
existing disputes being the basis of damage actions under the common law of some jurisdictions and sometimes being made specifically
enforceable by statute even where agreements to arbitrate future
disputes are not.[12]

6. To confirm the arbitrability of the particular dispute.[13]

It is obvious from the above discussion that any use of a
submission depends upon the particular case, and that the
particular contents and form of submissions which are used
will vary greatly from case to case. Some submissions are very
brief, while others are quite detailed.

The arbitration clause of the collective agreement and/or
the submission define the limits of the arbitrator's jurisdiction.
An award may be vulnerable to successful court challenge if
it decides any issue or matter not submitted to the arbitrator
by at least one of these instruments, and also if it fails to
decide all issues and matters so submitted.[14] Obviously, great
care should be exercised in drafting these instruments.

Stating the Issue

Arbitration does not utilize formal pleadings similar to
those used by courts to determine the precise issue or issues to
be resolved. Such formal pleadings would destroy at least
some of the simplicity and utility of arbitration. But somewhere in the course of an arbitration proceeding the issue to
be resolved by the arbitrator must be specifically stated or
pin-pointed.

If the parties jointly initiate the arbitration by a submission agreement the issue will ordinarily be stated clearly

---

[12] See Chapter 2, topic titled "Enforcement of Agreements to Arbitrate." Also
see Updegraff & McCoy, Arbitration of Labor Disputes 56-58 (1946).
[13] As in Kraft Foods Co., 15 LA 336 (Elson, 1950).
[14] See Sloan v. Journal Publishing Co., 23 LA 302, 304-305 (Ore. Cir. Ct., 1954);
In re MacMahon, 4 LA 830, 831 (N.Y. Sup. Ct., 1946). Also see Chapter 2, topic
titled "Enforcement and Review of Awards."

in that instrument. However, as noted above, frequent practice is to use only a demand for arbitration where the collective agreement contains an arbitration clause covering the dispute.

Although no submission is used, the arbitrator will have jurisdiction of a dispute if it is covered by an arbitration clause in the collective agreement. To illustrate, if the arbitration clause covers disputes over the application or interpretation of the collective agreement, then any such dispute becomes arbitrable when either party serves the other with a demand or notice of intent to arbitrate. This demand or notice will identify the case in general terms at least, but often it does not state the precise issue in dispute.[15]

The arbitrator selected for the case has jurisdiction to decide the dispute since it involves the application or interpretation of the collective agreement; but the question remains, what is the precise issue to be resolved by him? The issue, or issues, must be identified or pin-pointed. This may be achieved in any of several ways where the parties have not done so sometime prior to the hearing.

Use of Original Grievance

The grievance statement as processed through the grievance procedure often serves as the statement of the issue, especially if the grievance statement is carefully worded.[16] The parties sometimes specifically stipulate that the written grievance is to be the statement of the issue,[17] particularly after they have tried but failed to agree on a specific statement of the issue.[18] The arbitrator himself might turn to the original griev-

---

[15] For instance, one Bethlehem Steel arbitrator noted that it had "not been the practice under the Bethlehem Agreement for the parties to formulate 'submissions' defining precisely and exclusively the issues to be resolved." Bethlehem Steel Co., 17 LA 295, 300 (Selekman, 1951). Also see Davey, "The John Deere-UAW Permanent Arbitration System," Critical Issues in Labor Arbitration, 161, 190 (BNA Incorporated, 1957).

[16] As in Borden Mfg. Co., 25 LA 629, 630 (Wettach, 1955); Lukens Steel Co., 15 LA 408, 409 (D'Andrade, 1950).

[17] As in Texas Gas Transmission Corp., 27 LA 413 (Hebert, 1956).

[18] As in New Haven Clock & Watch Co., 18 LA 203 (Stutz, 1952).

ance when the parties have not agreed upon a specific statement of the issue.[19]

Too often, however, the original grievance is too poorly worded to provide a key to the precise issue in dispute. Also, the discussion at the pre-arbitral grievance steps sometimes develops the issue in different or modified channels. To a limited extent this may happen also at the arbitration stage, as in the case wherein Arbitrator Meredith Reid noted that "at the hearing the broad issue suggested by the grievance was narrowed very substantially as a result of testimony and argument." [20]

Parties Stipulate Issue at the Hearing

At the commencement of the arbitration hearing the parties may execute a stipulation or submission precisely stating the issue.[21] The arbitrator has the privilege of asking, at the hearing, for statements clarifying the issue.[22]

Unfortunately, the parties frequently are unable to agree upon any specific statement of the issue, and sometimes even attempts to do so tend to generate more dispute. Indeed, the parties themselves do not always know precisely what the issue is at the outset of the hearing.[23] Moreover, even when the parties have signed a submission stating the issue it may be ambiguous and in need of clarification.[24]

Likewise, the issue as stated by the parties may be too narrow to dispose of the entire dispute; in such instances the arbitrator may so inform the parties in order that they might authorize him to resolve the dispute fully.[25]

---

[19] As in Bridgeport Brass Co., 19 LA 690, 691 (Donnelly, 1952).

[20] Heppenstall Co., 22 LA 84, 85 (1954).

[21] As in Jos. Schlitz Brewing Co., 23 LA 126, 127 (Whelan, 1954); Kroger Co., 15 LA 363, 364 (Kelliher, 1950). The parties orally stipulated the issue in Pacific Hard Rubber Co., 16 LA 165, 166 (Aaron, 1950).

[22] American Arbitration Rule 26, for example, specifically recognizes such authority in the arbitrator.

[23] See Mundet Cork Corp., 18 LA 254, 255 (Reynolds, 1952).

[24] See McKinney Mfg. Co., 19 LA 291, 292 (Reid, 1952), where the arbitrator had implied authority to restate the issue contained in the submission.

[25] American Smelting & Refining Co., 29 LA 262, 264 (Ross, 1957).

Sometimes the parties agree to a statement of the issue during the course of the hearing.[26] After some testimony has been received the dispute often appears in sharper focus. At an opportune moment the arbitrator may call for a discussion to clarify the issue. Such discussion may produce an agreed statement of the issue—perhaps one worded by the arbitrator and accepted by the parties. However, it has been suggested that arbitrators should not press the parties unduly to arrive at an exact statement of the issue.[27]

Issue Pin-Pointed by Arbitrator

In many cases the burden of clarifying or pin-pointing the issue settles upon the arbitrator. Ordinarily the general nature of the issue or issues underlying the dispute becomes apparent to the arbitrator before the hearing has progressed very far, and he usually has no difficulty in discerning the precise issue or issues after he has studied the entire case.

The parties may specifically request that the arbitrator determine what the issue is.[28] A similar result may be produced by the collective agreement itself, as where the agreement provided that if the parties "fail to agree on a joint submission each shall submit a separate submission and the arbitrator shall determine the issue or issues to be heard." [29]

Sometimes the burden of pin-pointing the issue falls to the arbitrator after the parties have attempted without success to agree upon a statement thereof at the hearing; in these instances the parties' discussion may aid the arbitrator in stating the issue.[30]

---

[26] As in Republic Oil Co., 15 LA 895 (Klamon, 1951).

[27] Sembower, "Halting the Trend Toward Technicalities in Arbitration," Critical Issues in Labor Arbitration, 98, 101 (BNA Incorporated, 1957).

[28] As in Hillbro Newspaper Printing Co., 28 LA 769, 775 (Hildebrand, 1957). Also see Colonial Bakery Co., 22 LA 163 (Bauder, 1953).

[29] Lockheed Aircraft Corp., 23 LA 815, 815-816 (Marshall, 1955). Also see National Seal Co., 29 LA 29, 31, 35 (Dworkin, 1957).

[30] See Vickers, Inc., 27 LA 251, 253 (R. Smith, 1956); Joerns Bros. Furniture Co., 20 LA 715, 716 (Anderson, 1953).

In many cases there is no discussion by either the arbitrator or the parties at the hearing specifically directed toward pin-pointing the issue, even where it has not been previously defined clearly. In these cases the arbitrator arrives at a precise statement of the issue or issues after he has studied the entire record of the case, including, if available to him, such matters as the original grievance statement and the grievance procedure minutes, the demand for arbitration and any reply of the other party, correspondence of the parties, the transcript of the hearing (or the arbitrator's notes), the parties' exhibits, and the parties' briefs.[31]

Frequently the arbitrator finds that the issue is clearly and accurately stated in a single one of these sources. Again, the arbitrator may conclude that one party's wording of the issue is an accurate statement thereof.[32]

Simultaneous Arbitration of Several Grievances

The question sometimes arises whether one party may be compelled by the other to arbitrate several grievances before the same arbitrator in one proceeding. Numerous arbitrators have held that such simultaneous arbitration of all grievances which reach the arbitration stage at the same time can be compelled by either party unless the arbitration clause of the collective agreement clearly and unambiguously provides otherwise.[33] Simultaneous arbitration of grievances is said to reflect "the best ideals of the whole arbitration process, which are devoted to efficiency, expeditious disposition and economy."[34]

---

[31] For cases in which the arbitrator pin-pointed the issue, see Arbitrator Hildebrand in 28 LA 769, 775; Marshall in 25 LA 480, 481; Dworkin in 24 LA 73, 74; Bauder in 22 LA 163; Cole in 22 LA 868, 869; Merrill in 20 LA 527, 531; Bailer in 19 LA 257, 259; Piper in 18 LA 801, 804; Prasow in 17 LA 25, 26; Healy in 15 LA 764, 765; Gregory in 15 LA 420, 424.

[32] See Gisholt Machine Co., 23 LA 105, 108 (Kelliher, 1954).

[33] See Arbitrator Warns in 28 LA 586, 588-589; Luskin in 25 LA 171, 172-173; Feinberg in 23 LA 588, 589-590; Williams in 23 LA 13, 14-15; Rader in 20 LA 441, 442-443; Trotta in 13 LA 878, 879; Gregory in 12 LA 305, 306-307. A court ruled likewise in Electrical Workers v. Kidde Mfg. Co., 12 LA 446, 448 (N.J. Super. Ct., 1949). Apparently contra, Arbitrator Morvant in 24 LA 186, 187-188; Taylor in 7 LA 112

[34] Stewart-Warner Corp., 12 LA 305, 306 (Gregory, 1949). For statistics on frequency of multiple grievance cases see "Substantive Aspects of Labor-Management Arbitration," 28 LA 943, 944 (1954 statistics).

Once an arbitrator has been selected, however, a party has very little basis for submitting additional grievances to the arbitrator without his consent and agreement by the other party.[35] In this regard, for instance, American Arbitration Association Rule 7 provides that "After the Arbitrator is appointed no new or different claim may be submitted to him except with the consent of the Arbitrator and all other parties." [36]

Advisory Opinions

Arbitrators generally are reluctant to issue advisory opinions or "declaratory judgments." Arbitrator D. Emmett Ferguson has ruled, for example, that it was premature to submit to arbitration "a hypothetical question" and that "each case must be judged on its own merits when, and if, it arises." [37] Arbitrator August G. Eckhardt has elaborated:

> "There are many vague clauses in any collective bargaining agreement; clauses which may lead to arbitrable disputes. However, it is not contemplated that one party to the agreement can insist upon arbitration to settle hypothetical questions which are based on such clauses. Until an actual dispute arises together with the related, specific facts, neither party has a right to demand arbitration." [38]

An arbitrator may be more inclined to issue an advisory opinion if the requesting party demonstrates that it is necessary to protect the party's interests under the contract,[39] or if the arbitrator is convinced that both parties desire one.[40]

---

[35] See discussion by Arbitrator Bert L. Luskin in Maremont Automotive Products, Inc., 25 LA 171, 172-173 (1955).

[36] 30 LA 1086. But see Sylvania Electric Products, Inc., 24 LA 199, 201-205, 210 (Brecht, 1954), where under Rule 7 grievances filed at the start of the arbitration hearing were accepted by an arbitrator against the objection of one party where they added no new issue, arose from the same action as the grievance specifically identified in the demand for arbitration, and were fully anticipated in that demand.

[37] Monarch Machine Tool Co., 27 LA 640, 642 (1956).

[38] Inland Container Corp., 29 LA 861, 862 (1957). Also see Aurora Gasoline Co., 29 LA 495, 501 (Howlett, 1957); Carbide & Carbon Chemicals Co., 26 LA 74, 78 (Marshall, 1956). For a related discussion see Shulman, "Reason, Contract, and Law in Labor Relations," 68 Harv. L. Rev. 999, 1022-1023 (1955), reprinted in Management Rights and the Arbitration Process, 169 (BNA Incorporated, 1956).

[39] See Bell Aircraft Corp., 25 LA 755, 758 (Kharas, 1955).

[40] See Rexall Drug Co., 25 LA 830, 835 (Klamon, 1956).

The parties may specifically provide by contract for advisory opinions. The Chrysler Corporation, for instance, has "an Agreement-provided 'declaratory judgment' procedure for securing determinations of basic issues in advance of actual grievance situations." [41] A disadvantage of such provisions is said to be that "an actual grievance may present an issue of contract interpretation in sharper focus than a claim stated in general terms." [42]

Extent of Permissible Deviation from Pre-Arbitral Discussion of Case

Occasionally one party to an arbitration objects to an alleged attempt by the other party to enlarge the scope of the case by unilaterally injecting new issues, arguments, or claims for the first time at the arbitration stage. In disposing of these objections arbitrators tend to emphasize substance over form in seeking to uncover the real merits of the case.

An arbitrator may refuse to confine the parties rigidly to what occurred prior to the arbitration if the deviation from the pre-arbitral stage does not amount to the addition of new issues, but merely involves a modified line of argument, or an additional element closely related to the original issue, or the refinement or correction of an ineptly stated grievance, or the introduction of new evidence.[43]

To this extent, new aspects of the dispute may be aired initially at the arbitration stage, unless the arbitration tribunal is serving purely in an "appellate" capacity. For example, in overruling a party's objection to the consideration of an element which was relevant to the dispute but which had not been discussed by the parties prior to arbitration, Arbitrator

[41] Wolff, Crane, & Cole, "The Chrysler-UAW Umpire System," The Arbitrator and the Parties, 111, 118 (BNA Incorporated, 1958).

[42] Id. at 147 (discussion by General Motors Umpire Nathan P. Feinsinger).

[43] For discussion of use of new evidence at the arbitration stage, see Chapter 8, topic titled " 'New' Evidence at Arbitration Hearing." Also see Chapter 15, topic titled "Post-Discharge Conduct or Charges." Permitting a reasonable amount of deviation at the arbitration stage also enhances the possibility of settlement. See "Settlements at Arbitration Stage," below.

Benton Gillingham stated that the objection was "based upon an unreasonably and unjustifiably limited and restrictive concept of arbitration" as it is "generally conceived and currently applied in the field of labor relations." [44] Arbitrator Gillingham explained further:

> "* * * arbitration is not strictly comparable to the appeal process in the courts, or in any system of judicial or quasi-judicial agencies, where the appeal process involves a review by a higher authority of a judgment already rendered by a subordinate or inferior agency. To the contrary, arbitration is a process involving the use of a third party to resolve a dispute where the primary parties have been unable to resolve the disagreement. Thus it would appear that arbitration is much more nearly analogous to the litigation of a controversy in a judicial or quasi-judicial agency of *initial jurisdiction* * * *" [45]

Arbitrator Robert Feinberg has stated that contentions which do not change the issue should always be available to the parties, although he indicated that he would reject attempts to broaden the scope of the grievance for the first time in arbitration.[46] In turn, Arbitrator Walter Boles has declared that "any arbitrator would be derelict in his duty if, in considering whether or not a given section of a contract was applicable to a matter before him, he limited his inquiry only to points of argument raised before the matter came on to hearing." [47]

Nor will an ineptly worded grievance statement, or one which gives an incorrect basis for the claim, ordinarily bind the grievant rigidly at the arbitration stage.[48] This has been emphasized by Arbitrator Langley Coffey:

> "Neither is it acceptable as a valid objection, that, because the Union in its written protest, and in claiming that the aggrieved employee has been discriminated against, cites provisions of the contract other than the one upon which jurisdiction rests, it has foreclosed its right to enlarge upon its claim that the discharge was in violation of the contract. Such objec-

---

[44] Washington Motor Transport Assn., 28 LA 6, 9 (1956).

[45] Ibid. Emphasis added.

[46] Mergenthaler Linotype Co., 15 LA 707, 708 (1950).

[47] Temco Aircraft Corp., 22 LA 826, 828 (1954), wherein Arbitrator Boles distinguished a prior case in which he refused to hear "an entirely new issue."

[48] See Arbitrator Jaffee in 27 LA 844, 854; Gorder in 20 LA 880, 882; Coffey in 17 LA 125, 129; McCoy in 16 LA 775, 776.

tions admittedly have standing in places where the record means more than it does in arbitrations. However, where there is no requirement by contract, or otherwise, that either party submit or stand on any formal written protest or answer, formalities are dispensed with in hearings of this kind, and technical objections are brushed aside in an endeavor to get at the facts of a given case, and to do equity and complete justice to the rights of all parties, without let or hindrance, or the entanglements of formal pleadings, procedures or techniques." [49]

If a party materially changes its position from the grievance procedure to the arbitration stage in such a way that the other party is taken by surprise and finds it difficult or impossible to present its case adequately, the arbitrator may take some appropriate action (such as granting a continuance or remanding the case to the parties for further negotiations). [50]

However, if a deviation from what occurred at the pre-arbitral stage actually constitutes the addition of a new issue or dispute that has not been previously discussed by the parties, or the addition of a claim that has not been filed as required by the collective agreement, and if this by-passing of the grievance procedure is objected to by one of the parties, the arbitrator will ordinarily refuse to dispose of the new matter in his award. [51] In this regard, a General Motors Umpire has stated:

> "It is the function of the Umpire to decide questions which the parties themselves have tried to settle without success. New contentions presented for the first time at the Fourth Step are untimely, for their late presentation defeats the avowed aim of the grievance procedure—to settle disputes by collective bargaining whenever possible and to refer to the Umpire only those cases in which collective bargaining has been tried and has failed." [52]

Preparing Cases for Arbitration

Thorough preparation of cases for arbitration is of para-

---

[49] Charles Eneu Johnson Co., 17 LA 125, 129 (1950).
[50] See comments of Arbitrator Cahn in 23 LA 397, 398; Emery in 17 LA 90, 93.
[51] See comments of Arbitrator Meltzer in 27 LA 580, 584; Wolff in 27 LA 448, 453; Rosenfarb in 21 LA 22, 23; Davey in 20 LA 844, 849; Piper in 18 LA 801, 806; Seward in 17 LA 537, 540; Selekman in 17 LA 295, 300. Cf., view of Brecht in 24 LA 199, 204-206. Also see American Arbitration Association Rule 7(b) which appears to touch upon this matter.
[52] Umpire Decision No. E-276 (1949). Also, Decision No. E-295 (1949).

mount importance. Ordinarily most or all of the arbitrator's knowledge and understanding of the case is based upon the evidence and arguments presented at the arbitration hearing. Moreover, a party must fully understand its own case in order to communicate it effectively to the arbitrator, and full understanding depends upon thorough preparation.

What is necessary for thorough preparation of any given case will depend largely upon the nature of the case. For instance, in some cases the facts are especially important and each party will concentrate upon proving, largely through testimony of witnesses, that the facts are as that party sees them. In other cases the facts may be less important or not disputed, the controversy being centered upon some other matter, for instance, the proper interpretation of the collective agreement. Here each party's case will be devoted largely to arguments about how the agreement should be interpreted. In still other cases, economic and statistical data may be especially important.

Thus, the nature of the case should be considered in determining which items of the following "preparation" check list should be emphasized in any particular case. Since not all items are pertinent to every case, no significance lies in the order in which they are listed.

a) Review the history of the case as developed at the pre-arbitral steps of the grievance procedure.

b) Study the entire collective agreement to ascertain all clauses bearing directly or indirectly on the dispute.

c) So as to determine the general authority of the arbitrator, and accordingly the scope of the arbitration, examine the instruments used to initiate the arbitration. (See "Initiating Arbitration: Submission v. Arbitration Clause"; and "Stating the Issue" above.)

d) Talk to all persons (even those the other party might use as witnesses) who might be able to aid development of a full picture of the case, including different viewpoints. You will thus better understand not only your own case but your opponent's as well; if you can anticipate your opponent's case you can better prepare to rebut it.

e) Interview each of your own witnesses (1) to determine what they know about the case; (2) to make certain they understand the relation of their testimony to the whole case; and (3) to cross-examine them to check their testimony and to acquaint them with the process of cross-examination. Make a written summary of the expected testimony of each witness; this can be reviewed when the witness testifies to insure that no important points are overlooked. Some parties outline in advance the questions to be asked each witness.

f) Examine all records and documents that might be relevant to the case. Organize those you expect to use and make copies for use by the arbitrator and the other party at the hearing. If needed documents are in the exclusive possession of the other party, ask that they be made available before or at the hearing. (For other possible means of obtaining such evidence, and for the significance of the other party's refusal to produce it, see Chapter 8.)

g) Visit the physical premises involved in the dispute to better visualize what occurred and what the dispute is about. Also, consider the advisability of asking at the hearing that the arbitrator (accompanied by both parties) also visit the site of the dispute.

h) Consider the utility of pictorial or statistical exhibits. One exhibit can be more effective than many words, if the matter is suited to the exhibit form of portrayal. However, exhibits which do not "fit" the case, and those which are inaccurate or misleading, are almost certain to be ineffective or to be damaging to their proponent.

i) Consider what the parties' past practice has been in comparable situations. (For the significance of past practice, see Chapter 12.)

j) Attempt to determine whether there is some "key" point upon which the case might turn. If so, it may be to your advantage to concentrate upon that point.

k) In "interpretation" cases prepare a written argument to support your view as to the proper interpretation of the disputed language. (For the standards or rules used by arbitrators in interpreting contract language, see Chapter 9.)

l) In "interests" or "contract writing" cases collect and prepare economic and statistical data to aid evaluation of the dispute. (For the standards or guides used by arbitrators in "interests" disputes, see Chapter 16.)

m) Research the parties' prior arbitration awards and the published awards of other parties on the subject of the dispute for an indication of how similar issues have been approached in other cases. (Regarding the use of prior awards, see Chapter 11.)

n) Prepare an outline of your case and discuss it with other persons in your group. This insures better understanding of the case, and will strengthen it by uncovering matters that need further attention. Then, too, it will tend to underscore policy and strategy considerations that may be very important in the ultimate handling of the case. Use of the outline at the hearing will facilitate an organized and systematic presentation of the case.

Thorough preparation involves the use of ingenuity to illuminate all the possibilities of the case. Certainly, the arbitrator needs a full picture of the case and he will be interested in all its possibilities to aid him in reaching a sound decision.

Fact Stipulations

An agreed statement of facts can serve well to expedite the arbitration hearing by reducing the number of necessary witnesses and by permitting concentration upon the disputed aspects of the case. This recognized, the parties may come to the hearing with a fact stipulation, or they may enter into one at the hearing.[53]

Sometimes fact stipulations are entered into at the suggestion of the arbitrator, who may recess the hearing to permit the parties to determine whether any facts can be stipulated.[54]

Need for Hearing

A hearing in the presence of the arbitrator is deemed imperative in virtually all cases. In giving each party full and fair opportunity to be heard, the arbitration hearing simultaneously serves to inform the arbitrator fully regarding all material aspects of the dispute. However, in some cases the parties believe that the arbitrator can be adequately informed without a hearing in his presence, so they submit the dispute for decision entirely on the basis of stipulated facts, written briefs, and sometimes affidavits.[55]

Representatives in Arbitration

It is generally agreed that each party has the right to be represented in arbitration proceedings by persons of its own choosing. As Arbitrator Morton Singer has declared, neither side "may compel the other side to retain or consult with any

---

[53] As in Campbell Soup Co., 17 LA 800 (Ryan, 1951).
[54] As in Inland Container Corp., 28 LA 312 (Ferguson, 1957).
[55] For instances where the dispute was submitted to the arbitrator for decision without a hearing, see Kent of Grand Rapids, Inc., 18 LA 160 (Platt, 1952); North American Aviation, Inc., 16 LA 489, 494 (Komaroff, 1951); C. O. Porter Machinery Co., 16 LA 379 (Platt, 1951).

person other than one of their own free will and choice." [56]

Some parties prefer to be represented in arbitration by the person who served as their spokesman in the pre-arbitral stages of the grievance procedure, since he is thoroughly familiar with the dispute. That person, however, may lack the skill needed to present the case clearly to an outsider who has no background knowledge of the parties or their dispute. This recognized, other representatives such as higher union or company officials may be used to present the case at the arbitration stage. Then, too, attorneys often are used by one or both parties.[57]

Regarding use of attorneys, Arbitrator Benjamin Aaron has aptly observed that an attorney, if he is well-trained and if he understands the nature of collective bargaining and the purposes of arbitration, will have the ability to outline the dispute clearly and simply, to come directly to the point at issue, to present his evidence in an orderly fashion, and to sum up his arguments and relate them to the record made at the hearing.[58] Legal training may be especially important in still other respects if the case is governed by any detailed arbitration statute.

Of course, some laymen possess the ability and experience to present cases very skillfully and effectively. Indeed, as one union consultant has been quoted, "a good union representative" may be "more than an even match for a company attorney." [59]

Some arbitration statutes expressly state that either party has a right to be represented by an attorney and that waivers of this right are subject to limitations stated in the statute.

---

[56] Bronx County Pharmaceutical Assn., 16 LA 835, 838 (1951), where Arbitrator Singer proceeded without one of the parties, who refused to appear in the same room with counsel for the opposition.

[57] See statistics in "Procedural Aspects of Labor-Management Arbitration," 28 LA 933, 936-937 (1954 statistics); Warren & Bernstein, "A Profile of Labor Arbitration," 16 LA 970, 980-981 (1951).

[58] Aaron, "Some Procedural Problems in Arbitration," 10 Vanderbilt L. Rev. 733, 748 (1957)). Also see Feinsinger, "Collective Bargaining, Labor Arbitration and the Lawyer," id. at 761; Merrill, "A Labor Arbitrator Views His Work," id. at 789, 794.

[59] Warren & Bernstein, "A Profile of Labor Arbitration," 16 LA 970, 981 (1951).

However, it would seem that in all cases if either party plans to be represented by an attorney the other party, at least as a courtesy, should ordinarily be so informed.[60]

Privilege to Attend Hearing

Arbitration is a private proceeding and the hearing is not, as a rule, open to the public. However, all persons having a direct interest in the case ordinarily are entitled to attend the hearing. Other persons may be permitted to attend with permission of the arbitrator,[61] or the parties. It would seem that the arbitrator would hesitate to grant such permission against the wishes of the parties.

Limiting Attendance by Witnesses

The arbitrator customarily has authority to require witnesses (except those who are direct parties) to leave the hearing room during the testimony of other witnesses.[62] This is explained by Arbitrator Maurice H. Merrill:

> "One of the traditional methods for preserving the purity of testimony, 'the rule' that witnesses be excluded from the hearing chamber during the reception of others' testimony, frequently is invoked in arbitration. Whenever it is sought, I grant it, except, of course, as to the parties. On several occasions, I have observed the effectiveness of this safeguard against the possibility that one witness may be influenced in his testimony by what he has heard some one else say." [63]

Time, Place, and Notice of Hearing

No fixed rule exists for setting the date and locale of arbitration hearings. Ordinarily the arbitrator will meet at any time and place agreed to by the parties, if he can be available. If the parties cannot agree upon these matters, the arbitrator or the administering agency must set them. In this regard, it is generally accepted that the "arbitrator [or agency]

---

[60] Advance notice of intent to use an attorney is specified by American Arbitration Association Rule 20. 30 LA 1088.

[61] See American Arbitration Association Rule 22, in 30 LA 1088.

[62] See American Arbitration Rule 22, ibid. Also see Douglas Aircraft Co., 28 LA 198, 203-204 (E. Jones, 1957).

[63] Merrill, "A Labor Arbitrator Views His Work," 10 Vanderbilt L. Rev. 789, 795 (1957). Also see Updegraff & McCoy, Arbitration of Labor Disputes 97-98 (1946).

should consult the convenience of the parties in fixing the time and place for the hearing but should not allow one party to delay unduly the fixing of a date for the hearing. Written and timely notice of the date, time and place of the hearing should be given." [64]

Under some arbitration statutes the time and place for the hearing are fixed by the arbitrator, who may also be responsible for giving timely notice thereof. In any case, the arbitrator should always take action to insure adequate notice to the parties.

The hearing room itself is ordinarily selected by the parties or by an administering agency. Frequently some "neutral ground" such as a hotel suite is used; this may minimize interruptions that sometimes occur when the hearing is held at the plant. However, some parties prefer to use a conference room at the company since this may reduce costs, will make records and witnesses more quickly available, and will require less time for any visit by the arbitrator to the site of the dispute.

A conference table arrangement (with the arbitrator at the head of the table) is most satisfactory if there are not too many participants. A "courtroom" arrangement tends to be more formal, but it may be best if there are numerous participants.

Default Awards

Arbitrators sometimes feel compelled to render default awards, akin to the "default judgments" of courts. Arbitrator Liston Pope has pointedly observed, "A general arbitration clause in a contract would be rendered meaningless if its implementation depended on the willingness of each party to the contract to present its case, as the party desiring no change in relationships could nullify arbitration simply by refusing to make an appearance." [65]

---

[64] "Code of Ethics and Procedural Standards for Labor-Management Arbitration." 15 I.A 961, 964 (1951).
[65] Velvet Textile Corp., 7 LA 685, 691 (1947).

However, it has also been observed by Arbitrator Joseph Rosenfarb that "our judicial system looks askance at the finality of decisions based on default appearances. The Arbitration process is no exception. Only an unexplained failure to appear, not a delay in appearance, can justify an ex parte proceeding." [66] In this case one party was tardy and the other party requested that the hearing proceed without the tardy party under American Arbitration Association Rule 27 (discussed below); this request was refused by the arbitrator, who rescheduled the hearing for a later date at which time both parties participated.

In cases of willful or deliberate default by one party after due notice, arbitrators have heard testimony and rendered awards as if both parties had participated.[67] Generally these cases have involved state arbitration statutes providing for default judgments, or collective bargaining agreements which specifically provided for default awards in the event of willful or deliberate default by one of the parties, or application of American Arbitration Association Rule 27. Rule 27 provides:

> "*Arbitration in the Absence of a Party*—Unless the law provides to the contrary, the arbitration may proceed in the absence of any party, who, after due notice, fails to be present or fails to obtain an adjournment. An award shall not be made solely on the default of a party. The Arbitrator shall require the other party to submit such evidence as he may require for the making of an award." [68]

An indication of how an arbitrator might proceed in the absence of one party is provided by Arbitrator Samuel H. Jaffee's approach under said Rule 27:

> "The hearing then proceeded in the absence of * * * any Company representative or of any Company observer. Counsel for the Union re-

[66] Busch's Jewelry Co., 19 LA 365, 367 (1952).

[67] E.g., Arbitrator Cole in 24 LA 529, 531; Singer in 16 LA 835, 838; Jaffee in 15 LA 715, 720-721; Pope in 7 LA 685, 691; Baskind in 4 LA 719, 720. Also, Simons v. New York Herald Tribune, 26 LA 282 (N.Y. Sup. Ct., 1956); Teamsters Union v. Purity Food Co., 14 LA 934 (Conn. Super. Ct., 1950).

[68] For statistics regarding the number of ex parte proceedings under Rule 27, see "Procedural Aspects of Labor-Management Arbitration," 28 LA 933, 937 (1954 statistics)

mained with his clients and witnesses. These witnesses were sworn in normal course and testified in the usual way, but without the benefit of any cross-examination and in response only to questions of Union counsel, though the arbitrator took it upon himself to ask a substantial number of questions of some of them.

"The findings which follow, and the conclusions based on such findings, of necessity, then, are based upon the evidence received pursuant to the procedure described above. Because of the absence of Company counsel I have examined the evidence with extreme care. The fact that such evidence was uncontradicted did not necessarily mean that it was accepted. Some has been rejected. In evaluating such evidence I have done all I could, within the limitations of the procedure described, to apply such tests and criteria as are applied in courts generally. But the evaluation was of necessity handicapped by the absence of Company counsel, especially, of course, since I had no knowledge of the facts in these cases until evidence was received concerning them." [69]

As Arbitrator Jaffee stated, evaluation of one party's testimony is "of necessity handicapped" by the absence of the other party. A potential means of diminishing this handicap is to make the evidence and argument submitted at the hearing subsequently available to the other party (unless some other procedure is required by statute or the collective agreement) for its comments thereon within a reasonable time.[70]

Any court enforcement of default awards will depend in part upon due process considerations and possibly upon statutory requirements. For instance, it is unlikely that any default award will be upheld by a court if the absent party was not given notice of the exact nature of the claim asserted against it.[71] Court enforcement will also be affected by the extent that the case is covered by the common law rule of unenforceability of executory agreements to arbitrate (under which rule either party may withdraw from arbitration prior to issuance of an award).[72] However, in an increasingly large number of cases that rule will have been displaced by state

---

[69] Aleo Mfg. Co., 15 LA 715, 721 (1950)

[70] A similar approach has been suggested, for instance, by a group of arbitrators in the Philadelphia area. See Guides For Labor Arbitration 5-6 (U. of Pa. Press, 1953).

[71] For example, see Goldman Bros., 28 LA 589 (N.Y. Sup. Ct., 1957).

[72] See Chapter 2, topic titled "Enforceability Of Agreements To Arbitrate." Also regarding the right to withdraw, see Updegraff & McCoy, Arbitration of Labor Disputes 121-122 (1946).

statute or court decision, or by federal law such as under Section 301 of the Labor-Management Relations Act.[73]

Regardless of whether a given default award is legally enforceable, a probably more important consideration lies in the fact that default awards impose a moral obligation on the losing party at the least, and the party favored by such award obviously achieves a moral and psychological victory which may be very significant.

Withdrawal of Case from Arbitration

Related to the matter of default awards is the withdrawal of the case from arbitration. While the parties may withdraw a case through agreement, we have observed the rendition of default awards in some cases wherein the charged party refused to participate in the hearing. But it is not always the charged party who avoids the case. Sometimes the aggrieved party seeks to withdraw it from arbitration.

It has been suggested that the complainant usually may withdraw the case at any point prior to the arbitration hearing, but that after the hearing has commenced he may not withdraw the case over the objection of the other party unless permitted by arbitrator.[74]

From a strictly legal standpoint, either party may withdraw from arbitration at any time prior to issuance of an award if the common law rule permitting such withdrawal has not been modified by the jurisdiction in question. Aside from legal considerations, the right of the aggrieved to withdraw the case from arbitration may depend upon the peculiar circumstances. For example, a union which submitted an issue to arbitration but then learned that the company had not taken the action complained of was held under such cir-

---

[73] See B. Z. Wesche Electric Co., 20 LA 216 (Sembower, 1956); Simons v. New York Herald Tribune, 26 LA 282 (N.Y. Sup. Ct., 1956).
[74] See Guides For Labor Arbitration 6 (U. of Pa. Press, 1953).

cumstances to be entitled to withdraw the issue "without prejudice" prior to its consideration by the arbitrator.[75]

However, a less flexible approach sometimes holds, as in the Chrysler-UAW Umpire System, where "Cases which have been referred to the appeal board, and on which the board is empowered to rule, may not be withdrawn at all, except by mutual consent." [76]

Continuances

Arbitrators may grant continuances or adjourn the hearing from time to time upon their own motion or upon joint request of the parties. Moreover, arbitrators do not hesitate to do so upon the application of only one party for good cause shown. Indeed, failure to grant a continuance for good cause may make the proceedings vulnerable to court challenge.[77]

The "good cause" showing is essential since, as Arbitrator David L. Cole has declared, if arbitration proceedings "are to have dignity and command respect, then no party to a dispute can be allowed to decide when, where and how the hearings are to be conducted." [78] Arbitrator Cole emphasized, however, that for "good cause" he would "always try to accommodate the parties and meet their convenience within reason." [79] In that case one continuance had been granted the absent party, whose request for another continuance was denied as not being for "good cause"; that party's absence from the hearing resulted in a default award.

Not infrequently continuances are requested because of the absence of witnesses. In such instances a continuance ordinarily will be granted, though opposed by the other party, if the arbitrator is convinced that the request for a continuance

---

[75] Princeton Worsted Mills, 25 LA 587, 588 (Hill, 1955).

[76] Wolff, Crane & Cole, "The Chrysler-UAW Umpire System," The Arbitrator and The Parties, 111, 121 (BNA Incorporated, 1958).

[77] See Chapter 2, topic titled "Enforcement And Review Of Awards."

[78] Textile Workers (CIO) v. Upholsterers' Union (AFL), 24 LA 529, 531 (1955).

[79] Ibid.

was made in good faith and that the absence of the witness was without fault on the part of the requesting party.[80]

If a continuance on the ground of absence of witnesses or evidence is requested after the hearing has commenced, in particular where the participants are numerous and have traveled long distances to attend the hearing or where it would otherwise be difficult to arrange a satisfactory time for reconvening the hearing, arbitrators sometimes use a procedure akin to that commonly used by courts. That is, no continuance will be granted upon the ground of absence of evidence (either documentary, witnesses, or otherwise) except upon a statement or affidavit showing the materiality of the evidence and also showing: (1) that due diligence has been exercised and the evidence still has been unavailable; (2) where the evidence is; (3) the probability of securing it within a reasonable time; and (4) that the party making the statement or affidavit believes the evidence to be true. After this is submitted, the opposing party still may avoid a continuance by agreeing to accept the evidentiary facts alleged in the statement or affidavit as having been proved for purposes of the case. Then, too, in arbitration it is sometimes simply agreed that absent evidence may be submitted within a stated time after the hearing (if testimony, in the form of an affidavit or deposition). The opposing party is then given a reasonable opportunity to reply.

In the event the submission or other agreement specifies time limits within which action must be taken, no continuance should be granted which would overreach any applicable time limit (unless extended by agreement of the parties).

Split Hearings

In some cases the parties and the arbitrator agree that the hearing should be divided into two parts, the arbitrator to hear and rule upon some aspects of the case before completing the

---

[80] For example, see Bethlehem Steel Co., 17 LA 676, 677 (Shipman, 1951).

hearing as to other aspects. For instance, where an alleged contract violation, if established, would have involved possible losses by numerous employees whose individual factual situations were not identical, it was agreed that a decision on the proper interpretation of the contract would be reached "before taking further testimony upon the detailed rights and possible losses of each individual employee * * * because of the length of time which seemed likely to be consumed in testimony upon the individual situations, which time would prove to be wasted if the Board should hold that the Company had not breached the Agreement." [81]

Then, too, the arbitrator may rule upon some aspects of the case and refer other aspects back to the parties for further negotiations, to be heard and ruled upon ultimately by him only if negotiations fail.[82] Similarly, if an arbitrator concludes after the hearing that additional information is necessary to enable him to reach a decision he might return the case to the parties for additional fact-finding.[83]

Use of Interim Award

Where the case is divided into phases, as in some of the above situations, the arbitrator may use what he calls an "Interim Award" in disposing of the first phase and a "Supplemental Award" or "Final Award" in disposing of the later phase.[84] From the legal standpoint, use of "interim" or "partial" awards may be subject to challenge unless authorized by the parties.[85] It would seem, however, that any requirement of authorization might be waived by the parties if they proceed to the issuance of a final award without objection.[86]

---

[81] Fruehauf Trailer Co., 19 LA 159, 160 (Spaulding, 1952). Also, Color Corp. of America, 25 LA 644, 651, 657 (Lennard, 1955).

[82] As in Veeder-Root, Inc., 21 LA 387, 391 (Shipman, 1953).

[83] As in National Carbide Co., 27 LA 290, 293 (Warns, 1956). Or he might deny the grievance without prejudice, as in Jones & Laughlin Steel Corp., 23 LA 33, 37 (Cahn, 1954). Also see "Reopening The Hearing", below.

[84] See Arbitrator Warns in 27 LA 290, 293; Lennard in 25 LA 644, 651, 657; Shipman in 21 LA 387, 391. Also see Dworkin in 24 LA 541, 549.

[85] See discussion in Updegraff & McCoy, Arbitration of Labor Disputes 122 (1946).

[86] See Updegraff & McCoy, Ibid.

Transcript of Hearing

A formal written record of the hearing is not always necessary. Use of a reporter is the exception rather than the general practice.[87]

In simple cases the arbitrator can take adequate notes. Likewise, in cases involving contract interpretation only, there being no disputed facts, the arbitrator's notes and the parties' exhibits and/or briefs ordinarily make a transcript unnecessary. However, in complicated or lengthy cases stenographic records may be very helpful, if not indispensable; the transcript will aid not only the arbitrator in studying the case, but also the parties in preparing briefs. The transcript may be invaluable in any court review of the arbitration proceedings.[88] It is said that the palest ink is more accurate than the most retentive memory.

Whether the expense and additional time involved in use of a transcript are justified depends upon the case. Only the parties singly or together can decide. Ordinarily, a reporter will be used if either party so desires.[89]

The parties may have the hearing recorded, with the understanding that if the arbitrator finds need for all or portions of the record it shall be transcribed.[90] The sharing of the cost of any transcript is a matter for the parties to determine. The cost frequently is shared equally.[91] Each party pays for extra copies it orders. Ordinarily a party not agreeing to use of a transcript and not ordering a copy is not

---

[87] See discussion in Braden, "Problems in Labor Arbitration," 13 Missouri L. Rev. 143, 162 (1948). For statistics on extent of use see, American Arbitration Association Survey, 28 LA 937-938.

[88] See In re Ruppert, 26 LA 283, 284 (N.Y. Sup. Ct., 1956).

[89] As under American Arbitration Association Rule 21. 30 LA 1088.

[90] American Potash & Chemical Corp., 17 LA 364, 370 (Grant, 1951).

[91] E.g., Building Owners & Managers Assn. of San Francisco, 22 LA 226, 227 (Ross, 1954); Food Employers Council, 20 LA 724, 725 (Van de Water, 1953). Arbitrator Clarence Updegraff advocates equal sharing for most cases. "Preparing For Arbitration", 22 LA 889, 890. Also see American Arbitration Association Rule 44. 30 LA 1090.

required to share its cost.[92] It has been suggested that otherwise, if sharing of cost is mandatory, "one side may be obliged to curtail its testimony in the interests of economy, while the other might be inclined to prolong the case in order to discourage future arbitration proceedings." [93] One means of mitigating expenses is for one party to provide stenographic services or a tape recorder, in lieu of a formal transcript, to record substantially what transpires.[94]

Obviously, the bulk of the transcript will be composed of the opening statements, if any, the testimony of the witnesses, and closing arguments, if any. Certain other matters, however, should be included in the record so the transcript will reflect a complete picture of the case. Thus, the arbitrator or tribunal clerk will open the hearing by putting such information as the following into the record:

a) Names of the parties;

b) If there is a special agreement, submission, or stipulation for arbitration, identify it by date and read it into the record (the latter may be done by handing a copy to the reporter with instructions that it be written into the record at that point);

c) The date, hour, and place of the hearing;

d) The name of the arbitrator or arbitrators, and how selected (as by agreement of the parties, appointment by a neutral agency, etc.);

e) Name of the Chairman, if it is an arbitration board (the Chairman is ordinarily selected by the board in executive session immediately prior to opening the hearing—the manner in which the Chairman was designated should be indicated in the record);

f) Announcement of appearances for the parties, that is, the attorneys or other representatives who are to present the case for the parties (state the name, title, and address of each person and state the party for whom he appears—all of this information may be written on a sheet of paper to be handed to the reporter for inclusion in the record, or it may be stated orally by the parties);

---

[92] Stenzor v. Leon, 24 LA 306, 309 (Calif. D. Ct. of App., 1955); Mutual Telephone Co., 19 LA 270, 271 (Roberts, 1952), where the parties specifically requested a ruling on the issue under a clause specifying equal division of all "fees" of arbitration; they agreed that the ruling was not to be used as a precedent between them for any future case. Also see American Arbitration Association Rule 21, 30 LA 1088.

[93] Guides For Labor Arbitration, 2 (U. of Pa. Press, 1953), authored by a group of Philadelphia area arbitrators.

[94] Moog Industries, Inc., 15 LA 676, 677 (Klamon, 1950).

g) Name of the reporter;

h) Hours for the hearing, if it is likely to require several days;

i) Any other material information, especially such items as fact stipulations.

After the above information has been read into the record the hearing generally proceeds to the opening statements and on to the introduction of evidence.

In order to avoid cluttering the record, the arbitrator or parties may go "off the record" for comment or discussion which promises to be not material to the record, or for matter on which the spokesman desires not to be committed. It may be then decided that any such matter or any understanding growing out of the discussion should be placed in the record; the hearing would then go "on the record" for this purpose and for continuing with the introduction of evidence.

Both delay and errors in preparation of the transcript can be avoided if parties who intend to read or quote lengthy passages at the hearing furnish extra copies of the material for use by the reporter.

Where witnesses are to be sworn, each witness may be sworn individually immediately prior to his initial testimony, or all persons scheduled to testify may be sworn (if present) when the hearing is opened. Under the latter procedure the reporter should indicate, at the outset of the testimony of each witness, that the witness has been sworn.

Exhibits

Even where no reporter is used, a portion of the evidence will ordinarily be presented and preserved in written form as exhibits. Each party may submit its own exhibits and the parties may also submit exhibits jointly.[95]

Exhibits customarily are introduced into evidence at the point of the hearing where the data in the exhibit is most

---

[95] As in Republic Steel Corp., 16 LA 618 (Selekman, 1951), where 19 exhibits were submitted—10 mutually, 1 by the union, and 8 by the company.

relevant. While the parties may number their exhibits in advance, the more common practice is to number them when introduced into evidence since the parties do not always know in advance the order in which their exhibits will be submitted. Thus, exhibits generally are numbered in numerical or alphabetical order of introduction. A separate series is used for each party, as well as for joint exhibits. The first exhibit submitted by the company would be identified as Company Ex. # 1, the next as Company Ex. # 2, and so on. The union's exhibits would be identified as Union Ex. # 1, and so on. To avoid confusion parties often choose to use alphabetical designations, A, B, C, etc., to identify one party's exhibits, and to use numbers 1, 2, 3, etc., to identify the other party's exhibits.

Several copies of each exhibit should be prepared in advance to insure a copy for each party, one for personal use by the arbitrator during the hearing, and a copy to be handed to the reporter, if one is used, to be incorporated by reference into the record.

Oath by Arbitrator and Witnesses

Acceptable practice regarding the arbitrator's oath of office and the swearing of witnesses is effectively summarized by American Arbitration Association Rule 24, which provides:

"Oaths—Before proceeding with the first hearing, each Arbitrator may take an Oath of Office, and if required by law, shall do so. The Arbitrator may, in his discretion, require witnesses to testify under oath administered by any duly qualified person, or if required by law or demanded by either party, shall do so."

Even where the arbitrator's oath is required by statute (it is not required under the common law) it ordinarily may be waived by the parties, and very often is.[96] When the oath of office is taken, the arbitrator swears that he will faithfully and fairly hear and examine the matters in controversy and

---

[96] For statistics on extent of use of arbitrator's oath, see "Procedural Aspects of Labor-Management Arbitration," 28 LA 933, 936 (1954 statistics).

make a just award according to the best of his understanding.[97] Under practice of some appointing agencies the oath of office is written into the instrument of appointment and is affirmed by the arbitrator by signing the instrument in accepting the case.[98]

In adversary proceedings such as arbitration the swearing of witnesses is often preferred, whether required by statute or not (it is not required under the common law). In swearing witnesses, the arbitrator or hearing clerk asks the witness if he solemnly swears that the testimony he is about to give in the case is the truth, the whole truth, and nothing but the truth, so help him God. The witness, with right hand raised, answers "I do." [99]

Participation by Arbitrator in Hearing

Arbitrators should be informed as fully as possible about the disputes they are to resolve. Accordingly, the arbitrator must feel free to participate personally in the hearing by asking questions, seeking information and exploring all angles to the extent reasonably necessary to satisfy himself that he has in fact been informed as fully as possible. Arbitrator Harry Shulman emphasized, in this regard, that the arbitrator "should be satisfied that he knows enough to be able to decide the case" and that he "cannot simply sit back and judge a debate. He must seek to inform himself as fully as possible and encourage the parties to provide him with the information." [100]

Similarly, it has been emphasized that while the arbitrator obviously should not take sides, he must be free to ask questions and to explore all angles which he deems necessary to a full

---

[97] Ibid. Also, "Code of Ethics and Procedural Standards for Labor-Management Arbitration," 15 LA 961, 964 (1951).

[98] See "Procedural Aspects of Labor-Management Arbitration," 28 LA 933, 936 (1957).

[99] Regarding the procedural point at which witnesses are sworn see this Chapter, topic on "Transcript Of Hearings".

[100] Shulman, "Reason, Contract, and Law in Labor Relations," 68 Harv. L. Rev. 999, 1017-1018 (1955), also reported in Management Rights and the Arbitration Process, 169, 190-191 (BNA Incorporated, 1957).

understanding of the case "even if they have not occurred to either one or both of the parties." [101]

It has been observed that:

> "Where testimony is controverted, it is quite proper for the Arbitrator to take the initiative, if necessaary, in reconciling apparent contradictions, or in seeking insight into the motives of those whose testimony is at odds. It is the parties' primary responsibility to present facts and to rebut contrary testimony, but the Arbitrator may also use his office to elicit information or to secure insights where, in his opinion, such procedure is made necessary by the critical nature of the controverted testimony." [102]

Likewise, arbitrators are justified in making an independent study of the entire collective agreement to insure consideration of all provisions that might be relevant to the disposition of the case.[103]

Order of Presenting Case

There is no rigid order in which the parties must present their case in arbitration.[104] The party asserting a claim usually presents its case first, or at least a preliminary or introductory case, but this practice may not be followed where the nature of the issue makes a different procedure preferable. A somewhat typical approach in regard to the presentation of proof is that under American Arbitration Association Rule 26:

> "The party initiating the arbitration, or his counsel, shall [first] present his claim and proofs, and his witnesses, who shall submit to questions or other examination. The answering party or his counsel shall then present his proofs, and his witnesses, who shall submit to questions or other examination. *The Arbitrator may, in his discretion, vary this procedure* but shall afford full and equal opportunity to all parties and witnesses for presentation of any material or relevant proofs." [105]

---

[101] Guides For Labor Arbitration 11-12 (U. of Pa. Press, 1953). For similar views see "Code of Ethics and Procedural Standards for Labor-Management Arbitration," 15 LA 961, 964. Also see Aaron, "Some Procedural Problems in Arbitration," 10 Vanderbilt L. Rev. 733, 745 (1957).

[102] Guides For Labor Arbitration 8 (1953).

[103] Arbitrator Maxwell Copelof vigorously defended this practice against the charge that it helped the other party make out its case in West Virginia Pulp & Paper Co., 20 LA 385, 391-393 (1953). Also see comments of Arbitrator Walter E. Boles in Temco Aircraft Corp., 22 LA 826, 828 (1954).

[104] For a related discussion see Chapter 8, topic titled "Burden of Proof".

[105] 30 LA 1088-1089, emphasis added.

Logically, "the determination of the order of presentation in an arbitration case should depend exclusively on how the facts can best be developed in an orderly way." [106] If the arbitrator can see at the outset of a hearing that one of the parties possesses the basic facts of the case and that the case of the other party will consist primarily of a rebuttal, the arbitrator upon his own initiative or at the request of a party may suggest or require that the party in possession of the basic facts present its case first.[107]

After both parties have presented their basic case, each party in turn will be given full opportunity to present its rebuttal case. Indeed, the hearing will not be adjourned until each party has nothing further to add.

Opening Statements and Closing Arguments

Opening statements are brief, generalized statements in clear language designed to acquaint the arbitrator with each party's view of what the dispute is about and what the party expects to prove by its evidence. Use of opening statements is ordinarily optional with the parties, but sometimes the arbitrator specifically requests that each party make one.[108]

Sometimes both parties make opening statements at the outset of the hearing, before any evidence is introduced by either party. This is especially helpful to the arbitrator as it enables him to grasp more quickly what the dispute is about. Another possibility is that each party will make its opening statement immediately prior to presenting its initial evidence; thus one party will have made its opening statement and presented its evidence before the other party makes its opening statement. Ordinarily the arbitrator will follow whatever pro-

---

[106] Aaron, "Some Procedural Problems in Arbitration," 10 Vanderbilt L. Rev. 733, 739 (1957).

[107] This is not uncommon, for instance, in discharge and discipline cases. See Aaron, id. at 739-740; Douglas Aircraft Co., 28 LA 198, 202-203 (E. Jones, 1957); Armstrong Cork Co., 18 LA 651 (Pigors, 1952).

[108] As requested in Inland Container Corp., 28 LA 312 (Ferguson, 1957).

cedure the parties desire, unless he is convinced that some particular procedure is essential for proper presentation of the case.

By making closing arguments after all the evidence of both parties has been presented, the parties "can render a real service to the arbitrator as well as to themselves by carefully analyzing and synthesizing the important aspects of the case, emphasizing the facts they feel they have proved and placing them in proper relation to the ultimate fact sought to be established or to the ultimate conclusion at which they seek to persuade the arbitrator to arrive." [109]

The arbitrator will always permit the parties to make closing arguments (though he may limit the amount of time), and he sometimes requests specifically that they do so. Closing arguments and post-hearing briefs sometimes serve much the same purpose, and while the parties sometimes choose to use both they more frequently choose only to use either one or the other.[110]

Examining Witnesses

The manner in which witnesses are used, both in direct and cross-examination, may either promote or impede a party's case and it will also affect the character of the arbitration proceeding generally. In this regard, an excellent guide has been offered by Arbitrator Clarence M. Updegraff:

"Prove your case by your own witnesses. Do not try to establish it by evidence gleaned from people put on the stand by your opponent. They are there to oppose you, not to help you.

"If you cross-examine the other parties' witnesses, *make it short.* Do not unduly prolong cross-examination in attempts to get damaging admissions. The more questions you ask on cross-examination, the more opportunity you give a hostile witness to repeat the adverse testimony he came to give. Choose most carefully the inquiries you make of such parties. Make them as few as possible.

"Each party has the right to ask leading questions [so worded as to suggest an answer] when cross-examining hostile witnesses. Each party

---

[109] Howard, "Informing the Arbitrator," 10 Vanderbilt L. Rev. 771, 786-787 (1957).
[110] As in William Brooks Shoe Co., 19 LA 65, 67 (Dworkin, 1952).

should save time by asking its own witnesses leading questions, excepting at points where disputed facts are involved. Testimony on controverted matters should be brought out by questions which do not suggest the answer, if possible." [111]

In contrast to the question-answer method of examining witnesses, it is sometimes best to request that one's own witness tell his story in his own way. Obviously, the latter method is not advisable for the examination or cross-examination of adverse witnesses.

Objections to Evidence

Each party is entitled to object when it believes the other party is seeking to introduce improper evidence or argument at the arbitration hearing. Such objections, when based upon some plausible grounds, can serve a useful function even if overruled, for the arbitrator will have been cautioned to examine the challenged evidence or argument more closely before giving it weight.

However, objections which have no plausible basis, and those which are repetitious, should be avoided, as advised by Arbitrator Clarence M. Updegraff:

"Do not make captious, whimsical or unnecessary objections to testimony or arguments of the other party. Such interruptions are likely to waste time and confuse issues. The arbitrator, no doubt, will realize without having the matter expressly mentioned more than once, when he is hearing weak testimony such as hearsay and immaterial statements." [112]

Plant Visits by Arbitrator

Sometimes the arbitrator's understanding of the case can be greatly improved if he personally visits the physical site directly involved in the dispute. The values of a plant visit have been elaborated by Arbitrator William E. Simkin:

"The eye is better than the ear in many aspects of disputes, or at least is a valuable supplement to oral or written evidence. A plant visit is a simple device by which the arbitrator can secure a better understanding of the background of a case. In some instances a plant visit either before or

---

[111] Updegraff, "Preparation For Arbitration," 22 LA 889, 890 (1954).
[112] Updegraff, "Preparation For Arbitration," 22 LA 889, 890 (1954).

during the hearing will serve to avoid voluminous testimony. The award may be more realistic and therefore acceptable because the plant visit fills part of the gap in the arbitrator's knowledge." [113]

Frequently the parties suggest a plant visit by the arbitrator. However, the arbitrator may suggest one if he feels it essential. For instance, Arbitrator Paul Prasow sought and obtained permission from the parties to make first-hand observations where evidence submitted at the hearing failed to reveal clearly the distinction betweeen two job classifications involved in the dispute; as a result of the plant visit much of the confusion caused by the apparently conflicting contentions of the parties was eliminated. [114]

The arbitrator has discretionary authority to make plant visits in cases governed by American Arbitration Association Rule 30, which provides: "Whenever the Arbitrator deems it necessary, he may make an inspection in connection with the subject matter of the dispute after written notice to the parties, who may if they so desire be present at such inspection." [115] Unless the parties are arbitrating under a provision such as Rule 30, or unless the case is governed by an arbitration statute which gives the arbitrator similar authority, plant visits by the arbitrator may be deemed improper unless consented to by both parties. [116]

Settlements at Arbitration Stage

Sometimes disputes are settled by the parties after arbitration has been initiated. Some settlements occur prior to the arbitration hearing, and possibilities of settlement may be even stronger after the hearing is commenced. [117] The parties sometimes see the dispute in new light during arbitration, especially

---

[113] Simkin, Acceptability as a Factor in Arbitration Under an Existing Agreement, 24 (U. of Pa. Press, 1952). Also see American Steel & Wire Co., 16 LA 264, 266 (Forrester, 1951).

[114] Procter & Gamble Mfg. Co., 1 LA 313, 314 (1945).

[115] 30 LA 1089.

[116] See Justin, "Arbitration: Proving Your Case," 10 LA 955, 964 (1948); Berizzi Co. v. Krausz, 146 N.E. 436, 239 N.Y. 315, 319-320 (N.Y. Ct. App., 1925).

[117] For related material see "Extent Of Permissible Deviation From Pre-Arbitral Discussion Of Case", above.

upon participating at the hearing. Ford Umpire Harry H. Platt has observed in this regard:

> "Under a system in which grievances are heard by the umpire *de novo* and in the presence of all interested parties to the controversy, it is not unusual for the hearing to disclose an underlying misunderstanding that may have blocked an earlier settlement or uncover new thoughts, new facts, and occasionally new areas of agreement that provide real opportunities for constructive settlements. At Ford, these opportunities are usually not ignored, even though it may be thought that this tends to encourage appeals to the umpire." [118]

Likewise, other parties and arbitrators do not ignore real possibilities for constructive settlements. Some of the available procedures for accommodating further negotiations between the parties include the following:

a) The hearing may be recessed for direct negotiations at the request of the parties or at the arbitrator's suggestion, if accepted by the parties.[119]

b) The hearing may be closed with the understanding that the award will be delayed pending negotiations by the parties for a specified time, an award to be issued thereafter only if no settlement is reached.[120]

c) It may be agreed that the arbitrator will rule or comment by an interim decision upon some aspects of the case, referring the unresolved matters back to the parties for further negotiations, to be ruled upon ultimately in a supplemental award by the arbitrator only if the negotiations fail.[121]

Whatever procedure is used, it should be undertaken only by sanction of the parties. If they show no interest in an arbitrator's suggestion for further negotiations he should not attempt to force acceptance.[122] Concededly, an arbitrator "should not undertake to induce a settlement of the dispute against the

---

[118] Comments of Umpire Platt in The Arbitrator and The Parties, 141, 144 (BNA Incorporated, 1958), in response to statement by the Chairman of the Chrysler Appeal Board, which has a basically appellate jurisdiction, that cases are not often referred back to the parties for settlement efforts after the case once reaches the Impartial Chairman, but that many cases are settled by the pre-arbitral meetings of the Appeal Board. See "The Chrysler-UAW Umpire System," id. at 111, 124, 133.

[119] For full discussion of this and other settlement procedures, see Simkin, Acceptability as a Factor in Arbitration Under an Existing Agreement, 57-65 (U. of Pa. Press, 1952).

[120] See Victor Chemical Works, 22 LA 71, 72 (Dworet, 1953), where the parties requested this procedure.

[121] This general procedure was used in Color Corp. of America, 25 LA 644, 651, 657 (Lennard, 1955); Veeder-Root, Inc., 21 LA 387, 391 (Shipman, 1953); Pittsburgh Steel Co., 18 LA 17, 20 (Seward, 1952).

[122] See Instant Milk Co., 24 LA 756, 758 (Anderson, 1955).

wishes of either party. If, however, an atmosphere is created or the issues are so simplified or reduced as to lead to a voluntary settlement by the parties, a function of his office has been fulfilled." [123]

Ordinarily the settlement negotiations themselves are carried on only by the parties, without participation by the arbitrator. However, in limited situations the arbitrator may perform some mediation role. Only rarely do ad hoc arbitrators mediate,[124] but mediation by permanent arbitrators is not uncommon.[125]

Putting Settlement in Form of Award

When parties settle their dispute during the course of arbitration they often request that the arbitrator set forth the terms of the settlement in an award. In making such request, they "should give the arbitrator a full explanation of the reasons therefor in order that he may judge whether he desires to make or join in such an award." [126] Unless there is some aspect of the settlement to which the arbitrator cannot subscribe, he will carry out their request.

Briefs

Practice varies considerably regarding use of briefs in arbitration. In many cases no briefs of any type are used. However, use of post-hearing briefs is fairly common,[127] and sometimes pre-hearing (or hearing) briefs or statements are submitted.[128] Then, too, in some cases both pre-hearing (or hear-

---

[123] "Code of Ethics and Procedural Standards For Labor-Management Arbitration," 15 LA 961, 963 (1951).

[124] For an instance where an ad hoc arbitrator "suggested several alternative solutions to the parties" see Southern California Edison Co., 15 LA 162, 168 (Aaron, 1950).

[125] For discussion of mediation by permanent arbitrators see Chapter 4.

[126] "Code of Ethics and Procedural Standards For Labor-Management Arbitration," 15 LA 961, 966 (1951); also id. at 965. Also see American Arbitration Association Rule 39, in 30 LA 1090.

[127] For statistics on use of post-hearing briefs, and for American Arbitration Association procedures in regard thereto, see "Procedural Aspects of Labor-Management Arbitration," 28 LA 933, 938 (1954 statistics).

[128] Pre-hearing briefs were used in 29 LA 635, 638; 17 LA 412; 15 LA 792.

ing) and post-hearing briefs are used,[129] and still other possibilities include use of rebuttal and supplemental briefs.[130]

Hearing or pre-hearing briefs outline the party's view of the case as it stands before the hearing; one of their chief advantages is that the hearing may be shortened by their use.[131] The purpose of post-hearing briefs is "summarization of the evidence presented at the hearing, together with the arguments of the parties and their comments on the evidence." [132]

No new evidence should be included in post-hearing briefs.[133] However, expanded discussion regarding the proper interpretation of the agreement, and citation and discussion of precedents, articles, and the like for the first time in post-hearing briefs is not unusual. Occasionally arbitrators find it necessary to confer with the parties or to call them together again for additional hearing when some point of critical importance develops as a result of filing briefs.

Briefs can be of valuable assistance to the arbitrator.[134] Sometimes the arbitrator deems briefs sufficiently advisable that he specifically requests them.[135]

From the standpoint of the parties, the privilege of submitting briefs may be considered essential to a "fair hearing." [136] However, an arbitrator's refusal to accept post-hearing briefs was declared by a Pennsylvania court not to warrant vacating the award either at common law or under the statutes of that state.[137]

---

[129] As in 22 LA 251, 252; 18 LA 20, 21; 16 LA 955.

[130] See 23 LA 706, 707; 16 LA 149; 16 LA 274, 275.

[131] For discussion of the advantages and disadvantages of using pre-hearing and post-hearing briefs, see Simkin, Acceptability as a Factor in Arbitration Under an Existing Agreement, 21-23 (U. of Pa. Press, 1952).

[132] "Code of Ethics and Procedural Standards for Labor-Management Arbitration," 15 LA 961, 966 (1951).

[133] Ibid. Also, Continental Can Co., 29 LA 67, 73 (Sembower, 1956).

[134] See comments of Arbitrator Mathews in 23 LA 706, 707; McCoy in 16 LA 1, 2.

[135] See Merrill, "A Labor Arbitrator Views His Work," 10 Vanderbilt L. Rev. 789, 796-797 (1957).

[136] See Updegraff, "Preparation for Arbitration," 22 LA 889, 890 (1954).

[137] Technical Employees v. U.S. Steel Co., 22 LA 62, 64-65 (Pa. Com. Pleas Ct., 1954). The court observed that it "is not at all unusual" for judges to "decline to accept post-hearing briefs and make an immediate decision." Id. at 65.

Sometimes the question of what briefs, if any, may be submitted is handled by stipulation of the parties.[138] Such stipulations will be enforced by the arbitrator unless modified by mutual agreement.[139] Where there is no agreement regarding briefs, the arbitrator ordinarily will accept and consider the brief of either party desiring to submit one, and the other party may be allowed time to submit a reply brief.[140] Either party desiring to file a post-hearing brief should give notice at the hearing; if notice is first given after the hearing is closed the arbitrator may be more reluctant to accept a brief filed over the opposition of the other party.

An arbitrator may take unusual steps to permit consideration of briefs. For instance, where one party requested permission to file a brief but, because of a misunderstanding by the arbitrator the award was issued prior to receipt of the brief, the arbitrator secured agreement by the parties to permit issuance of a supplement to the award to allow consideration of the brief.[141]

When briefs are to be used, a time limit within which they can be filed will be set by stipulation of the parties or by the arbitrator. If either party fails to submit a brief within the specified time the arbitrator will proceed to decide the case without waiting for the brief,[142] especially if no request is made for more time.[143] However, for reasonable cause the arbitrator may grant a request for more time, especially if the other party after due notice does not object.[144]

Copies of all briefs submitted to the arbitrator should always be submitted simultaneously to the other party.

---

[138] As in 20 LA 642, 643; 15 LA 573, 574.

[139] See Sayles Biltmore Bleacheries, Inc., 24 LA 408 (Livengood, 1955).

[140] See Steinway & Sons, 17 LA 31 (Justin, 1951).

[141] Crook Paper Box Co., 27 LA 836 (Compton, 1957); the supplement to the award did not change the result.

[142] See Beech-Nut Packing Co., 20 LA 575, 576 (Davis, 1953).

[143] See Pan American Refining Corp., 15 LA 464, 465 (Klamon, 1950).

[144] As in Great Lakes Carbon Corp., 16 LA 918, 919 (Livengood, 1951).

Closing the Hearing and Time Limit for Rendering Award

Customarily arbitration hearings are deemed "closed" when all evidence and arguments of the parties has been received and the hearing is ready for adjournment with no additional days of hearing being contemplated. However, where briefs or other documents are to be filed after final adjournment of the hearing, it appears clear that the hearing will be deemed "closed" as of the final date for receipt of these items.[145]

The point at which an arbitration hearing is deemed "closed" is significant in determining the time within which the award must be rendered since ordinarily the time commences to run at the point where the hearing is deemed "closed".

In the absence of a mandatory time limit, the award may be made within a reasonable time.[146] However, if by agreement of the parties or by the prevailing law an award must be rendered within a specific time limit, the award will be invalid if not made within that time,[147] unless the parties agree to an extension.[148] Under some statutes the right to object to a tardy award is waived by failure to object prior to its issuance.

Reopening the Hearing

Under accepted practice the arbitrator on his own motion, or upon request of a party for good cause shown, may reopen the hearing at any time before the award is rendered. If there is some mandatory time within which the award must be made and reopening would prevent issuance of the award within that time, however, the hearing may not be reopened unless the parties agree to extend the time limit.[149]

---

[145] See Danbury Rubber Co. v. Rubber Workers, 29 LA 815, 817 (Conn. Sup. Ct., 1958); American Arbitration Association Rule 31, in 30 LA 1089. Also see Public Service Co. v. Utility Workers, 23 LA 326 (N.J. Super. Ct., 1954).

[146] See Danbury Rubber Co. v. Rubber Workers, 29 LA 815, 817-818 (Conn. Sup. Ct., 1958), and authorities there cited.

[147] See Public Service Co. v. Utility Workers, 23 LA 326 (N.J. Super. Ct., 1954).

[148] As in Pfeiffer Brewing Co., 26 LA 570, 571 (Ryder, 1956).

[149] See American Arbitration Association Rule 32, in 30 LA 1089; also, Guides For Labor Arbitration, 15 (U. of Pa. Press, 1953), by a group of prominent arbitrators.

One type of situation in which reopening may be justified was discussed by Arbitrator Edward A. Levy in reopening a hearing for introduction of new evidence:

> "Ordinarily where a hearing has been had in which all parties have participated, and have presented all evidence, and have stated on the record that they have nothing further to offer, the matter is deemed to be officially closed for the taking of evidence. However, where certain evidence is evidentiary and of material import and the admission thereof will probably affect the outcome of a cause, is unavailable at the time of the hearing, and if the same is produced subsequently without seriously affecting any substantial right, and it is shown that reasonable grounds existed for its non-production at the time of the hearing, the arbitrator may, in his discretion, reopen the arbitration for the introduction of such evidence only. The reason for this rule is to afford to each of the parties full opportunity to present such material evidence as will assist the arbitrator in ascertaining the truth of all matters in controversy." [150]

In one case, Arbitrator George H. Hildebrand refused to reopen the hearing to receive new evidence where the party requesting reopening could not show that the new evidence could be clearly established.[151]

Sometimes the arbitrator, without reopening the hearing, will simply call "upon each party for clarifying data and information",[152] or he might invite further written argument regarding some aspect of the case.[153]

The Award and Opinion

The award is the arbitrator's decision of the case. Awards usually are short, and they should be definite, certain and final, disposing conclusively of all matters submitted to the arbitrator. Awards may be oral unless a written award is required by the submission or by statute.[154]

---

[150] Madison Institute, 18 LA 78, 81 (1952), an arbitration administered by the New Jersey State Board of Mediation. For a related discussion, see Chapter 8, topic titled "Evidence Submitted After Hearing".

[151] Safeway Stores, Inc., 22 LA 466, 467 (1954).

[152] As did Arbitrator George W. Taylor in Full-Fashioned Hosiery Mfrs., 15 LA 452, 454 (1954). Also see Chapter 8, topic titled "Evidence Submitted After Hearing".

[153] As did Arbitrator David Louisell in Donaldson Co., 21 LA 254, 255 (1953).

[154] Oral awards are sufficient under the common law, but if in writing they must be signed. See Chapter 2, topic titled "Common Law vs. Statutory Arbitration".

Except in rare instances awards are issued in writing. Even where an oral award is rendered the arbitrator usually later reduces it to writing.[155] The written award must be signed by the arbitrator. Awards of arbitration boards must be signed by all members where a unanimous decision is required, otherwise they must be signed by at least a majority.[156]

Often the arbitrator accompanies his award with a written opinion stating the reasons for his decision. The award should be stated separately from the opinion to indicate clearly where the opinion ends and the award begins; in agreeing in advance to accept the arbitrator's award the parties do not necessarily promise to agree with all of his reasoning.

Attitudes vary as to the desirability of reasoned opinions, but a large majority of parties and of arbitrators favor their use.[157]

A well reasoned opinion can contribute greatly to the acceptance of the award by the parties by persuading them that the arbitrator understands the case and that his award is basically sound. Then, too, such opinions can have significant educational value to the parties and can aid them in adjusting future related problems. In the latter regard Arbitrator Whitley P. McCoy explained in one case:

> "In explanation of my having discussed issues and contentions upon which the ultimate decision is not to be based, I may say that parties do not spend many days of preparation, three days of hearings, and thousands of dollars worth of the time of important officers and attorneys, for the purpose of finding out whether one girl should or should not have got a trivial promotion. They are interested in principles. They are entitled, for their future guidance in various respects, to the arbitrator's findings upon the evidence and the various contentions." [158]

Some parties, however, prefer not to have an opinion for

---

[155] See discussion of oral awards in Guides For Labor Arbitration 14 (U. of Pa. Press, 1953).

[156] The common law requirement of a unanimous decision has been modified by many arbitration statutes and is frequently modified by the parties themselves.

[157] For statistics, see Warren & Bernstein, "A Profile of Labor Arbitration," 16 LA 970, 983 (1951). For an excellent discussion of the role of reasoned opinions, see Syme, "Opinions and Awards," 15 LA 953, 956-958 (1950).

[158] Southern Bell Telephone & Telegraph Co., 16 LA 1, 9 (1951).

fear that the arbitrator might make comments not germane to the issue and thus possibly stimulate future disputes. Also, reasoned opinions require more of the arbitrator's time, increasing the cost of arbitration. In view of the cost factor the arbitrator may ask the parties to indicate specifically whether they want an opinion.[159]

Interpretation of Award

Except where the common law has been changed by statute the power of the arbitrator ends when the award is issued,[160] and he should not issue an interpretation of the award unless empowered to do so by agreement of both parties. In this regard, it has been suggested that "if one party requests that the Arbitrator issue an interpretation or clarification of his award, he should refuse to comply, but should indicate that he will give consideration to the request if made by both parties." [161]

Labor, management, and arbitrators alike appear generally to favor giving the arbitrator power to interpret his award when differences arise as to its meaning.[162]

Recommendations by Arbitrator

Many "rights" arbitrators are authorized only to interpret and apply the collective agreement and are denied the power to add to or modify the agreement. In these instances the award must be based upon what is or is not required by the agreement and there is only limited room, if any at all, for application of "equity." For instance, in refusing to follow a prior award based upon equitable grounds Arbitrator Whitley P. McCoy declared:

"I cannot agree with that decision, which was based on so-called 'equitable' grounds. When it becomes customary and legitimate for arbitrators to

---

[159] See Trailmobile, Inc., 28 LA 710, 711 (Coffey, 1957).

[160] For further discussion regarding termination of the arbitrator's jurisdiction, see Updegraff & McCoy, Arbitration of Labor. Disputes 120-124 (1946).

[161] Guides For Labor Arbitration, 15 (U. of Pa. Press, 1953).

[162] See statistics in Warren & Bernstein, "A Profile of Labor Arbitration," 16 LA 970, 979 (1951).

amend and add to contracts according to their sense of equity, i.e., what the contract *ought* to provide, then I shall fall in line." [163]

However, arbitrators occasionally do make purely advisory recommendations based upon equitable considerations. In some such cases where the grievance could be sustained only by adding to or modifying the agreement or by otherwise exceeding the arbitrator's authority, but where the arbitrator is convinced that the grievance has merit from the standpoint of equity, he will deny the grievance (or he might dismiss it) and at the same time make an advisory recommendation as to how he thinks it should be disposed of for the best interests of both parties. [164]

In doing this Arbitrator Joseph Shister explained:

"Since the Arbitration Board must rule according to the so-called 'contractual approach' to the issue, it has no alternative but to deny the grievance. But while the Board's authority to *rule* is so circumscribed, its powers of *recommendation* are considerably broader. For in making such recommendations it can avail itself of the guideposts afforded by what one might term, 'Industrial relations equity'." [165]

Similarly, where an arbitrator concludes that the dispute essentially involves "interests", rather than "rights" under the existing agreement, so that a sustaining award would in effect be legislating for the parties, he may deny the claim, or remand it, with the suggestion that the matter be negotiated by the parties. [166] But the arbitrator may undertake to decide the dispute by "legislating" for the parties if he believes both parties want and have authorized him to do so. [167]

---

[163] Esso Standard Oil Co., 16 LA 73, 75 (1951). Also see Arbitrator Hebert in 29 LA, 469, 473; Dworkin in 21 LA 133, 139; Barrett in 16 LA 466, 472. Cf., Handsaker in 15 LA 209, 210.

[164] This approach was taken by Arbitrator Hebert in 29 LA 469, 476; Roberts in 28 LA 470, 477; Davey in 25 LA 394, 397; Kelliher in 21 LA 444, 446; Anrod in 20 LA 653, 658; Aaron in 15 LA 162, 168. Also see Arbitrator Copelof in 15 LA 229, 233.

[165] General Aniline & Film Corp., 25 LA 50, 54 (1955). In this case Arbitrator Shister apparently departed from his earlier view, expressed in National Carbon Co., 23 LA 263, 264 (1954), that where the contract is silent on the matter in dispute the award itself may be based upon "logic and equity".

[166] This approach was taken by Arbitrator Seward in 26 LA 646, 648; Klamon in 26 LA 48, 54; Copelof in 18 LA 486, 489; Kelliher in 16 LA 394, 396; Komaroff in 16 LA 303, 307. Also see Chapter 9, topic titled "Ambiguity"; Chapter 10, topic titled "Contract Principles".

[167] See Colonial Provision Co., 16 LA 176, 178-179 (Copelof, 1951). For related discussion and cases see Chapter 3, topic on " 'Rights' Arbitration Contract Clauses".

'Injunctions' by Arbitrators

In giving relief through their awards arbitrators have rarely spoken literally in terms of "injunction". Certainly, an unusual type of relief to be included in arbitration awards is an injunction ordering a party not to do (or to cease doing) some specified act which the arbitrator has ruled violative of the collective agreement. However, the New York Court of Appeals has recognized significant authority in arbitrators to grant such injunctive relief in proper circumstances, the court observing that "Traditionally, arbitrators have been licensed to direct such conduct of the parties as is necessary to the settlement of the matters in dispute." [168]

In the latter case the court upheld an award containing an injunction where the collective agreement did not directly affirm or deny power in the arbitrator to use such remedy, and where nothing short of an injunction would have accomplished the intent of the parties for speedy relief against the prohibited activity.[169] Moreover, the court also held that the New York Anti-Injunction Act did not forbid injunctions by arbitrators even though that Act severely limited the jurisdiction of the courts to issue injunctions in labor disputes.[170]

In contrast to the infrequency of awards which prohibit a party from carrying out some specified future act, awards in the nature of "mandatory injunctions" which command a party to take some affirmative action, such as an award ordering the employer to reinstate an employee, are common in arbitration.

Common Errors in Arbitration

On the basis of its extensive experience in administering arbitration proceedings the American Arbitration Association

---

[168] In re Ruppert, 29 LA 775, 776-777 (1958).

[169] Ibid. Also see Centra Leather Goods Corp., 25 LA 804 (Kheel, 1956), reviewed in Pocketbook Workers Union, 25 LA 807 (N.Y. Sup. Ct. 1956). The New York arbitration statute (Article 84, Civil Practice Act) does not deal specifically with injunctions by the arbitrator.

[170] In re Ruppert, 29 LA 775, 777 (N.Y. Ct. App., 1958).

has concluded that a party may harm its case by the following practices:

" 1. Over-emphasis and exaggeration of the grievance.

" 2. Reliance on a minimum of facts and a maximum of arguments.

" 3. Using arguments where witnesses or exhibits would better establish the facts.

" 4. Concealing essential facts; distorting the truth.

" 5. Holding back books, records and other supporting documents.

" 6. Tying up proceedings with legal technicalities.

" 7. Introducing witnesses who have not been properly instructed on demeanor and on the place of their testimony in the entire case.

" 8. Withholding full cooperation from the arbitrator.

" 9. Disregarding the ordinary rules of courtesy and decorum.

"10. Becoming involved in arguments with the other side. The time to try to convince the other party was before arbitration, during grievance processing. At the arbitration hearing, all efforts should be concentrated on convincing the arbitrator." [171]

Tripartite Board Procedures

Tripartite arbitration boards are made up of one or more members selected by management, an equal number selected by labor, and a neutral who serves as chairman. While most of the material in this Chapter applies equally to tripartite boards and to arbitration tribunals composed only of one or more neutrals, the tripartite composition of the former tribunals raises certain other procedural questions. Both tripartite boards and the procedural questions which are particularly applicable to such boards are discussed in detail in Chapter 4.

Procedure of Boards Under Railway Labor Act

Under the Railway Labor Act boards exist or may be established for both "rights" and "interests" disputes. The procedures of these boards, which are of tripartite composition, are likewise discussed in detail in Chapter 4.

---

[171] Labor Arbitration Procedures and Techniques 19 (A.A.A., 1957).

CHAPTER 8

EVIDENCE

Strict Observance of Legal Rules of Evidence
Usually Not Required

It is well established under common law that unless expressly required by the parties in submitting their case to an arbitrator, strict observance of legal rules of evidence is not necessary.[1] While the parties may expressly require the arbitrator to observe legal rules of evidence, they seldom do so. In fact, they sometimes specifically provide that strict observance of such rules shall not be required.[2] Adherence to legal rules of evidence is necessary under a few arbitration statutes, but not under most.[3] Many of the statutes are either silent or not specific on the point, and where either is true the common law ordinarily applies.[4]

Parties arbitrating under the rules of the American Arbitration Association are subject to its Rule 28, which provides, in part: "The Arbitrator shall be the judge of the relevancy and materiality of the evidence offered and conformity to legal rules of evidence shall not be necessary."[5] Likewise, the National Railroad Adjustment Board does not require strict adherence to the rules of evidence used by judicial tribunals.[6]

The net result is that in a majority of cases, "any evidence, information, or testimony is acceptable which is pertinent to

---

[1] See cases cited in 6 C.J.S. 203, n. 52.
[2] As in Goodyear Engineering Corp., 24 LA 360, 361 (Warns, 1955).
[3] See Justin, "Arbitration: Proving Your Case," 10 LA 955, 962-963 (1948).
[4] See Chapter 2, topic titled "Common Law vs. Statutory Arbitration".
[5] 30 LA 1086, 1089.
[6] Jones, National Railroad Adjustment Board, 24 (1941). This is a finding of the Attorney General's Committee on Administrative Procedure.

the case and which helps the arbitrator to understand and decide the problem before him." [7]

In regard to the flexible application of legal rules of evidence in arbitration proceedings, Arbitrator Willard W. Wirtz has concluded that:

> "[Arbitrators] have established the pattern of ordered informality; performing major surgery on the legal rules of evidence and procedure but retaining the good sense of those rules; greatly simplifying but not eliminating the hearsay and parole evidence rules; taking the rules for the admissibility of evidence and remolding them into rules for weighing it; striking the fat but saving the heart of the practices of cross-examination, presumptions, burden of proof, and the like." [8]

Flexible arbitral application of formal rules of evidence is particularly justified in regard to those rules of proof which come from the criminal law. The application of these principles of proof in the field of arbitration, which deals with intraplant employer-employee relations, probably should not be accepted in all cases without some consideration of the appropriateness of their use in the determination of rights under collective agreements by means of a special tribunal.

Liberal Admission of Evidence

Although strict observance of legal rules of evidence usually is not required, the parties in all cases must be given adequate opportunity to present all of their evidence and argument. Arbitrators are usually extremely liberal in the reception of evidence, giving the parties a free hand in presenting any type of evidence thought to strengthen and clarify their case. Indeed, Arbitrator Harry Shulman has observed that "the more serious danger is not that the arbitrator will hear too much irrelevancy, but rather that he will not hear enough of the relevant." [9]

---

[7] Simkin & Kennedy, Arbitration of Grievances, (U.S. Dept. of Labor, Div. of Labor Standards, Bull. No. 82, p. 25, 1946).

[8] Wirtz, "Due Process of Arbitration," The Arbitrator and The Parties 1, 13 BNA, Incorporated, 1958).

[9] Shulman, "Reason, Contract, and Law in Labor Relations," 68 Harv. L. Rev. 999, 1017 (1955).

An interesting view has been expressed by Arbitrator William E. Simkin in justification of the free reception of evidence:

> "One of the fundamental purposes of an arbitration hearing is to let people get things off their chest, regardless of the decision. The arbitration proceeding is the opportunity for a third party, an outside party, to come in and act as a sort of father confessor to the parties, to let them get rid of their troubles, get them out in the open, and have a feeling of someone hearing their troubles. Because I believe so strongly that that is one of the fundamental purposes of arbitration, I don't think you ought to use any rules of evidence. You have to make up your own mind as to what is pertinent or not in the case. Lots of times I have let people talk for five minutes, when I knew all the time that they were talking it had absolutely nothing to do with the case—just completely foreign to it. But there was a fellow testifying, either as a worker or a company representative, who had something that was important for him to get rid of. It was a good time for him to get rid of it." [10]

It might be noted that the liberal reception of evidence is not as extreme a departure from traditional judicial practice as many persons might believe; it is not unusual for judges who are trying cases without a jury to receive evidence very freely, on the basis that they can determine its weight and relevancy after all the case is in.

Some excursions into extraneous matter may help the arbitrator get the background of the case or may help him understand the viewpoints of the parties. Moreover, the relevance of evidence offered in arbitration, though it may appear at first glance not to be germane to the case, cannot always be determined accurately until the entire case has been unfolded. Accordingly, from a procedural standpoint arbitrators sometimes accept evidence while reserving their response thereto until the challenged evidence can be evaluated in the light of the whole record.[11] The objection to the evidence, even if overruled, will serve to caution the arbitrator to examine the challenged evidence more closely before giving it weight.[12]

---

[10] Conference on Training of Law Students in Labor Relations, Vol. III, Transcript of Proceedings 636-637 (1947).

[11] As in Potash Co. of America, 16 LA 32 (Garrett, 1951).

[12] For further discussion, see Chapter 7, topic titled "Objections to Evidence."

Actually, the liberal admission of evidence is much less likely to render the proceedings vulnerable to court challenge than is the rejection of competent evidence. Under some statutes, for instance, an arbitrator's refusal to hear all relevant evidence is a ground for vacating the award.[13]

But an arbitrator may properly refuse to admit evidence that lacks revelance or probative value, for if no limitation is placed upon the reception of evidence the hearing can too easily go far afield. Moreover, under some circumstances an award may be properly rendered even though certain relevant evidence has not been formally received by the arbitrator. For instance, where data requested by an arbitrator was not submitted within the specified time, the issuance of the award prior to receipt of the requested data was held not to be ground for vacating the award where the court found that the arbitrator had in fact been fully informed as to the facts and issues of the case.[14]

Evidence to Be Heard by Entire Board

It is a general requirement that, where there is a board of arbitration, all evidence must be taken in the presence of all of the arbitrators. This requirement prevails in common-law arbitration,[15] and in arbitration under state statutes.[16] It is also a general requirement under American Arbitration Association Rule 28.[17]

It has been held under the New York statute, for instance, that an agreement to arbitrate entitles the parties to the considered judgment of arbitrators based upon evidence submitted in the presence of all the arbitrators, and that participation at

---

[13] As under the New York Civil Practice Act, Sec. 1462, applied in Excell Pharmacal Co., 21 LA 831 (N.Y. Sup. Ct., 1954); Industrial Marine Workers, 7 LA 951 (N.Y. Sup. Ct., 1947).

[14] In re Aranson, 6 LA 1033 (N.Y. Sup. Ct., 1946). But cf., Excel Pharmacal Co., 21 LA 831 (N.Y. Sup. Ct., 1954). For a related discussion see Chapter 7, topic titled "Default Awards"

[15] Ziskind, Labor Arbitration Under State Statutes 3 (U.S. Dept. of Labor, 1943).

[16] Id. at 15. While still providing that the hearing shall be conducted by all the arbitrators, some statutes provide that a majority may determine any question and render a final award. As, for instance, under the Uniform Arbitration Act, 27 LA 909, 910.

[17] 30 LA 1086, 1089

proceedings at which only three of six arbitrators were present did not constitute a waiver of the requirement that all arbitrators be present for a binding award.[18]

It should be noted, however, that the deliberate refusal by a party and its representatives on a tripartite board to attend the hearing may result in the issuance of a default award.[19]

What Type of Evidence Should Be Used

Of course the specific evidence introduced in individual cases will vary greatly from case to case according to the question involved. It is likewise obvious, however, that each general type of case requires a more or less specific type of evidence. In disputes over the setting of general wage rates, for instance, the most important type of evidence is documented statistical and economic data on such matters as prevailing practice, cost of living, ability to pay, and the like.

In discharge or discipline cases the most important evidence generally comes in the form of testimony of witnesses, the facts which led to the disciplinary action being of great importance. If, however, there is no disagreement as to these facts and if the primary issue is one concerning proper punishment, then the past record of the employee and evidence of past disciplinary action taken in similar cases enter the picture in a major capacity.

In contract interpretation cases the history of precontract negotiations and the past practice of the parties in applying the disputed provision may be of great importance.

In some cases visual or pictorial evidence is useful. The arbitrator's understanding of the dispute may be greatly improved, for instance, by his visiting the physical site directly involved in the case.[20] Pictorial evidence may also be provided at the hearing room, as where photographs of employees oper-

---

[18] Buitoni Products, Inc. v. Nappi, 12 LA 667 (N.Y. Sup. Ct., 1949).

[19] See Chapter 7, topic titled "Default Awards". Also, Uniform Arbitration Act, 27 LA 909, 910.

[20] For full discussion, see Chapter 7, topic titled "Plant Visits By Arbitrator".

ating machines were submitted to the arbitrator in a job-rating dispute.[21]

Indeed, as long as evidence "fits" and is relevant to the case the unusual nature of the evidence should not bar its admission and consideration. Thus, in one case a significant type of evidence was sound and time recordings of the movements of a diesel locomotive to indicate the extent to which it was being utilized in a certain operation and to compare its efficiency with that of a steam locomotive.[22]

'New' Evidence at Arbitration Hearing

Evidence is sometimes presented at the arbitration hearing which was not disclosed at the pre-arbitral grievance steps.[23] Some of the considerations involved in an arbitrator's decision to accept or reject such evidence include his great need for all the facts relevant to the case, the need to protect the integrity of the pre-arbitral grievance machinery, and general concepts of fairness. Thus it is not surprising that, in balancing these considerations, such evidence has been accepted in some cases but rejected in others.

It should be emphasized that whatever element of unfairness may be involved in the use of new evidence, it is largely mitigated or eliminated by the fact that arbitrators who accept newly submitted evidence will take any reasonable steps necessary to insure the opposite party adequate opportunity to respond thereto, regardless of whether the evidence had been withheld in good or bad faith. If the arbitrator deems it necessary, for instance, he may return the case to the parties for further consideration in the light of the new evidence or he may recess the hearing for whatever time necessary to give the surprised party opportunity to prepare or revise its defense.[24]

---

[21] Brown & Sharpe Mfg. Co., 21 LA 461, 464-469 (Waite, 1953). See also Westinghouse Electric Corp., 26 LA 836, 842 (Simkin, 1956).

[22] Republic Steel Corp., 24 LA 336, 339 (Platt, 1955).

[23] For a related discussion see Chapter 7, topic titled "Extent of Permissible Deviation from Pre-Arbitral Discussion of Case"; Chapter 15, topic titled "Post-Discharge Conduct or Charges".

[24] See Wirtz, "Due Process of Arbitration," The Arbitrator and The Parties 1, 16 (BNA Incorporated, 1958)

Such interruptions of the arbitration hearing can be avoided if parties using new evidence will submit it to the other party prior to the hearing whenever the nature of the evidence makes it reasonably foreseeable that the other party will need time to prepare a response.[25]

A survey conducted by Arbitrator W. Willard Wirtz indicated that "unless some deliberate attempt to mislead the other party is disclosed, and particularly if the 'new' evidence or argument appears substantially material, most arbitrators will be disinclined to rule the matter out of the proceedings." [26] In this regard, Arbitrator Ralph Seward has explained that many pre-arbitral grievance meetings "are informal and deal with the surface of a problem without in any sense taking real evidence," [27] and Arbitrator Wirtz has observed that the "company, for its part, may very reasonably not have made the thorough investigation it will properly consider warranted if the union ultimately decides to take the case seriously enough to go to arbitration." [28]

The absence of any contract provision restricting acceptance of new evidence has sometimes been emphasized by arbitrators in receiving evidence presented for the first time at the arbitration hearing.[29] But even where an agreement provided that "the facts concerning the case shall be made available to both parties" at an early stage, facts acquired later could be introduced at subsequent steps of the grievance procedure or at the arbitration hearing.[30]

Also, under a contract requiring the employer to furnish all available evidence to the union "and/or" the arbitrator, the

---

[25] See suggestions of Arbitrator Maurice H. Merrill in Jonco Aircraft Corp., 22 LA 819, 823 (1954).

[26] Wirtz, "Due Process of Arbitration," The Arbitrator and The Parties 1, 15 (BNA Incorporated, 1958). Also see North American Aviation, Inc., 17 LA 183, 185-186 (Komaroff, 1951); Carbon Fuel Company, 1 ALAA ¶ 67,327 (1946).

[27] Wirtz, "Due Process of Arbitration," The Arbitrator and The Parties 1, 15 (BNA Incorporated, 1958).

[28] Ibid.

[29] See North American Aviation, Inc., 17 LA 183, 185-186 (Komaroff, 1951); Carbon Fuel Company, 1 ALAA ¶ 67,327 (1946).

[30] American Steel & Wire Co., 5 LA 193, 206-207 (Blumer, 1946).

withholding of evidence until the arbitration hearing was held not to be improper where the union was granted ten days to consider the evidence; sufficient time for consideration of evidence was deemed the basic purpose of the provision.[31]

While stating that "it is understandable that the evidence which comes out at the arbitration hearing is more detailed and more complete than that which is produced in the preliminary steps of the grievance machinery," Umpire I. Robert Feinberg considers that delay in presenting evidence "mitigates its relative importance".[32] Moreover, he has refused to accept evidence offered by a party for the first time at the arbitration stage where the evidence was known to the party at the earlier grievance stages and would have expanded the party's claim if admitted at the arbitration stage.[33]

It is the intentional, calculated, withholding of evidence that arbitrators criticize most severely. In this regard, the view of Umpire Gabriel N. Alexander is no doubt shared by many arbitrators:

"[S]ound collective bargaining requires frank and candid disclosure at the earliest opportunity of all the facts known to each party. There will undoubtedly be times when facts are not discovered, and therefore not disclosed, until after the grievance has been partially processed, and problem enough is created by those instances. There is not a scintilla of justification for the withholding of information by either party from and after the time it is discovered." [34]

But the calculated withholding of evidence did not result in its rejection by the arbitrator where, from the outset, the attitude of the party from whom it was withheld was such as to put all pre-arbitral steps on an adversary basis, "with both sides primarily pointed at an ultimate arbitration instead of mutual ascertainment of fact, compromise, or some other solution based upon general collective bargaining considerations." [35]

---

[31] Texas Co., 7 LA 735, 739 (Carmichael, 1947).
[32] Bethlehem Steel Co., 21 LA 655, 656 (1953).
[33] Bethlehem Steel Co., 18 LA 366, 367 (1951).
[34] General Motors Umpire Decision No. F-97 (1950). It has been suggested that the intentional withholding of evidence "is likely to boomerang." Davey, "The John Deere-UAW Permanent Arbitration System," Critical Issues in Labor Arbitration 161, 170 (BNA Incorporated, 1957).
[35] Bethlehem Steel Co., 6 LA 617, 619 (Wyckoff, 1947).

If the arbitration tribunal is serving essentially in an appellate capacity there is obviously strong reason to confine the evidence to what was considered below. In this regard, the rules of the National Railroad Adjustment Board require that "all data submitted in support" of the party's position "must affirmatively show the same to have been presented to the [other party] and made a part of the particular question in dispute." [36]

Requiring the Production of Evidence

Apart from statute the arbitrator has no power of subpoena. Since many arbitrations are carried out under common-law rules only, or under statutes which do not give the arbitrator subpoena power, it frequently is not available to him. The absence of this power, however, is not very important, since the parties are usually willing to provide any data or evidence requested by the arbitrator.[37]

Arbitrators do not hesitate to request the production of data or information if they have reasonable basis to believe that it will be germane to the case.[38] Indeed, the arbitrator himself often initiates the request for the production of evidence.[39] In other instances the arbitrator may make the request on the motion of the party who otherwise does not have access to the evidence in question.[40] In one such case Arbitrator I. Robert Feinberg issued "an interim award", during the course of the hearing, "directing the Company to submit certain payroll information to the Union for its use in connection with" the case.[41]

---

[36] National Railroad Adjustment Board, Organization and Certain Rules of Procedure, Circular No. 1 issued Oct. 10, 1934.

[37] As in Clay City Pipe Co., 20 LA 538, 542 (Young, 1952).

[38] See discussion by Arbitrator Harry J. Dworkin in Chesapeake & Potomac Telephone Co. of West Virginia, 21 LA 367, 369-371 (1953).

[39] As in Resistoflex Corp., 19 LA 761, 762 (Levy, 1952).

[40] See Arbitrator E. Jones in 29 LA 372, 373; Justin in 24 LA 44, 47; Dworkin in 21 LA 367, 369-371; Feinberg in 18 LA 55, 56. Cf., D. Wolff in 22 LA 128, 138.

[41] News Syndicate Co., 18 LA 55, 56 (1952). For the pros and cons of arbitral use of "discovery" procedures similar to those used by some courts, see Sembower, "Halting the Trend Toward Technicalities in Arbitration," Critical Issues in Labor Arbitration 98, 102 (BNA Incorporated, 1957). Also see Arbitrator Merrill in 20 LA 211, 212; Komaroff in 19 LA 385, 390.

While the National Railroad Adjustment Board does not have the subpoena power,[42] its rules of procedure provide that the parties are "charged with the duty and responsibility of including in their original written submission all known relevant, argumentative facts and documentary evidence."[43]

Significance of Failure to Provide Evidence

The significance of a refusal or failure to provide requested data or evidence is indicated by a statement of Arbitrator Saul Wallen:

> "An arbitrator has no right to compel the production of documents [it might be otherwise if the arbitration is carried out under an arbitration statute] by either side. He may, however, give such weight as he deems appropriate to the failure of a party to produce documents on demand. The degree of weight to be attached to such failure will depend upon the relevancy of the documents requested to the issues at hand. If the information withheld appears to be strongly pertinent, the withholding of it may be vital in the making of a decision. If it is of doubtful relevancy and merely represents an attempt by one party to probe through the files of another on the mere chance that its position may be generally strengthened thereby, then the failure to produce such records should be disregarded."[44]

The failure of a party to use a person as a witness who should be in a position to contribute informed testimony may create some sort of inference against the party or at least cause the arbitrator to wonder why the person was not called to testify.[45]

Failure of Grievant to Testify

The failure of a grievant to appear and testify at the hearing of his grievance may be one of the factors leading to the arbitrator's conclusion that the grievance is without merit.[46]

---

[42] Jones, National Railroad Adjustment Board 25 (1941).

[43] National Railroad Adjustment Board, Organization and Certain Rules of Procedure, Circular No. 1 issued Oct. 10, 1934.

[44] American Telephone & Telegraph Co., 6 LA 31, 43 (1947). Cf., view of Arbitrator Dworkin in 21 LA 367, 371.

[45] See, for instance, Standard Oil Co. (Indiana), 25 LA 32, 36 (Burris, 1955). For a related discussion, see this Chapter, topic titled "Failure of Grievant to Testify."

[46] See Arbitrator McCoy in 26 LA 742, 745-746; Maggs in 22 LA 761, 764; Klamon in 16 LA 461, 465-466. Also see Cole in 23 LA 64, 65. For a related discussion see this Chapter, topic titled "Requiring the Production of Evidence."

To prevent this, the parties may stipulate that the non-appearance of the grievant shall not be prejudicial to his interests.[47]

A related consideration concerns the question whether there is any privilege against self incrimination in arbitration. One survey has indicated that "there is a fairly clear consensus in the arbitration opinions" that the privilege against self incrimination, "established in the criminal law, has no place, at least as such, in the arbitration of grievance cases (invariably discharge or disciplinary cases)."[48] However, Arbitrator Nathan P. Feinsinger spoke in that survey as follows: "My evaluation of a discharged employee's not testifying has depended on the circumstances. * * * I don't think one can generalize here."

Right of Cross-Examination

Arbitrators uphold the right of cross-examination, but probably not so strongly as do courts of law. An arbitrator ordinarily will not accept an offer of evidence if it is conditioned upon nondisclosure to the other party. Thus, for instance disciplinary action based solely on the charge of an employee whose identity the employer was unwilling to reveal was set aside by Arbitrator David A. Wolff, who stated that no matter how meritorious the reasons for nondisclosure may be, it results in a lack of competent proof.[49]

In certain limited situations, however, nondisclosure has not resulted in rejection of evidence. For example, Arbitrator George H. Hildebrand accepted reports of professional "spotters", although the bus driver against whom the reports were used was not permitted to confront the spotters or otherwise know their identity, considering that (1) control over bus

---

[47] As in U.S. Rubber Co., 25 LA 417, 418 (Hall, 1955).

[48] Wirtz, "Due Process of Arbitration," The Arbitrator and the Parties 1, 19-20 (BNA Incorporated, 1958), where several unreported arbitration decisions are noted. Also see comments of Arbitrator Maggs in 27 LA 709, 712-713; Klamon in 16 LA 461, 465-466.

[49] Murray Corporation of America, 8 LA 713, 714 (1947). To similar effect, Arbitrator Scheiber in 24 LA 538, 540-541; Bowles in 22 LA 320, 323; Aaron in 13 LA 433, 434. Also see discussion of "absentee evidence" in Wirtz, "Due Process of Arbitration," The Arbitrator and the Parties 1, 16-17 (BNA Incorporated, 1958).

drivers is essential for the safety of the public and protection of company property, and the spotter system provides the only practical means by which supervision can exert its responsibility in the transit industry; (2) open identification of the spotters would destroy the effectiveness of the system; (3) the spotters, unlike ordinary employees, were trained observers taught to be accurate and objective, having no personal contacts with the employees and having no incentive to falsify facts; (4) the spotters' reports were prepared before the decision to discharge was made; and (5) there was no tangible basis for believing that the company was biased against the grievant.[50]

Sometimes the collective agreement itself will indicate the extent that the testimony or proof by professional investigators may be used and the extent to which it must be subjected to cross-examination.[51]

The admission of hearsay evidence denies the opposing party opportunity for complete cross-examination. Courts of law ordinarily refuse hearsay testimony for this reason. While arbitrators admit hearsay evidence, they seek to offset the effects of incomplete cross-examination by admitting it only "for what it is worth".[52]

Since the arbitrator has a paramount interest in securing all of the facts, he may refuse to restrict cross-examination to matters brought out in the examination-in-chief, and he can be expected not to place strict limitation upon the number of re-cross or re-direct examinations.

While the parties are allowed considerable latitude in cross-examining adverse witnesses, to reveal conflicts in their testimony and to challenge credibility, arbitrators will not condone use of personal invectives against witnesses.[53]

---

[50] Los Angeles Transit Lines, 25 LA 740, 744-746 (1955). In general accord are the views of Arbitrator Brecht in 23 LA 362, 365. Also see Arbitrator Oppenheim in 29 LA 291, 292; Seward in 19 LA 210, 211.
[51] As in Bee Line, Inc., 20 LA 675, 676 (Feinberg, 1953).
[52] See this Chapter, topic titled "Hearsay Evidence."
[53] See Friden Calculating Machine Co., 27 LA 496, 500-501 (Justin, 1956).

Evidence Submitted After Hearing

While ordinarily no new data or evidence may be presented after the hearing, in briefs or otherwise, there are exceptions.[54] Sometimes discussion at the hearing indicates need for additional data which are not quickly available, and if the parties desire not to recess or otherwise delay the hearing they may agree to the submission of the data to the arbitrator after the hearing has been completed. Likewise, the arbitrator during or after the hearing has been completed may request post-hearing data or information.[55]

Then, too, important evidence sometimes is discovered or first becomes available after the hearing.[56]

Such post-hearing data often will be jointly prepared and submitted by the parties. If the data are individually prepared each party ordinarily must be furnished a copy of the other party's data so that comment may be made thereon or so that a further hearing can be requested in case of gross discrepancies.[57]

Weight and Credibility of Evidence

It is within the province of the arbitrator to determine the weight, relevancy, and authenticity of evidence. The general approach of arbitrators in giving weight and credibility to evidence is effectively illustrated by a statement made by Arbitrator George Cheney in reviewing the discharge of an employee. He noted that the case was illustrative of the type of situation in which the facts are to a large extent determined by the weight and credibility accorded to the testimony of the witnesses and to the documentary evidence offered by the parties. He pointed out that, in arriving at the truth in such a

---

[54] See Chapter 7, topic titled "Briefs" and topic titled "Reopening the Hearing."
[55] For instance, after receiving post-hearing briefs Arbitrator Russell A. Smith requested additional data in McInerney Spring & Wire Co., 20 LA 642, 643 (1953).
[56] See discussion in Chapter 7, topic titled "Reopening the Hearing."
[57] See McInerney Spring & Wire Co., 20 LA 642, 643 (R. Smith, 1953); Simkin, Acceptability as a Factor in Arbitration Under an Existing Agreement 59-60 (U. of Pa. Press, 1952); Updegraff & McCoy, Arbitration of Labor Disputes 103 (1946). For related considerations see this Chapter, topic titled "Right of Cross-Examination."

case, an arbitrator must consider whether conflicting statements ring true or false; that he will note the witnesses' demeanor while on the stand; and that he will credit or discredit testimony according to his impressions of the witnesses' veracity. Arbitrator Cheney also pointed out that, in determining where the preponderance of the evidence lies with respect to any material point, the arbitrator will take into consideration whether the witness speaks from first-hand information or whether his testimony is largely based on hearsay or gossip. In summarizing, Arbitrator Cheney stated that the duty of the arbitrator is simply to determine the truth respecting material matters in controversy, as he believes it to be, based upon a full and fair consideration of the entire evidence and after he has accorded each witness and each piece of documentary evidence, the weight, if any, to which he honestly believes it to be entitled.[58]

Arbitrator Clair V. Duff, in turn, has offered some considerations relevant in evaluating testimony:

"Any attempt to sort credible testimony from that which is not worthy of belief is very difficult for at least four basic reasons. They may be briefly stated:

"INTEREST. While having an interest or stake in the outcome does not disqualify a witness, it renders his testimony subject to most careful scrutiny. * * * Few witnesses will deliberately falsify but there is a common tendency to 'put your best foot forward.' This tendency, either consciously or subconsciously, leads many witnesses to remember and express testimony in a way favorable to the result which they hope the Hearing will produce.

"PERCEPTION. Frequently the initial observation is faulty or incomplete because the observer has no prior knowledge that a dispute will develop concerning what he has seen or heard and his casual sensory impression is not sharp and keen.

"MEMORY. The remembrance of an event weeks or months after it occurred is frequently dim and inaccurate and a witness may be confused as to facts which initially he correctly perceived. By lapse of time precise details may elude his memory.

---

[58] Andrew Williams Meat Co., 8 LA 518, 519 (1947). Also see Arbitrator Coffey in 28 LA 710, 715.

"COMMUNICATION. The manner in which a witness expresses what he saw and heard may fail to communicate exactly his initial perception of the occurrence, so that after listening to the testimony and the cross-examination of the witnesses, the fact-finder may not have had transmitted to him a completely accurate impression of the facts, even though they were initially observed carefully and well remembered by the witness." [59]

Arbitrator Joseph Rosenfarb cautioned that while "both sides might be subject to the unconscious influences of self-interest, personal predilection or antipathy," it is the duty of the arbitrator "to examine the testimony of each witness on its own merits"—Arbitrator Rosenfarb considered that union members are not necessarily prejudiced witnesses any more than are supervisors. [60]

Widely differing versions of the facts are too frequently presented by the parties. Where the testimony is highly contradictory it ordinarily "becomes incumbent upon the Arbitrator to sift and evaluate the testimony to the best of his ability, and reach the best conclusion he can as to the actual fact situation." [61] However, sometimes "It is unnecessary to resolve the substantial conflict in the evidence to obtain an unobstructed view of the scene. By piecing together the parts, the broad outlines of the whole picture emerges." [62] Arbitrator Sidney L. Cahn has observed that, in discipline cases, the truth often "lies somewhere between" the widely conflicting versions of the facts. [63]

In any event, as Arbitrator R. W. Fleming has aptly observed:

"Arbitrators are not equipped with any special divining rod which enables them to know who is telling the truth and who is not where a conflict in testimony develops. They can only do what the courts have done in similar circumstances for centuries. A judgment must finally be

---

[59] South Penn Oil Co., 29 LA 718, 720 (1957). Also see discussion by Arbitrator Edgar Jones in 28 LA 198, 204-205.

[60] Poloron Products of Pa., Inc., 23 LA 789, 793 (1955).

[61] Texas Electric Steel Casting Co., 28 LA 757, 758 (Abernethy, 1957).

[62] Sampsel Time Control, Inc., 18 LA 453, 456 (Gilden, 1951).

[63] Republic Aviation Corp., 17 LA 577, 579 (1951).

made, and there is a possibility that that judgment when made is wrong." [64]

It seems clear that inconsistencies in the testimony of any witness will ordinarily detract much from its credibility.[65]

Special Considerations in Discipline Cases

Special considerations are involved in weighing testimony in discharge and discipline cases. Thus Umpire Harry Shulman has recognized that an accused employee has an incentive for denying the charge against him, in that he stands immediately to gain or lose in the case, and that normally there is no reason to suppose that a plant protection man, for example, would unjustifiably pick one employee out of hundreds and accuse him of an offense, although in particular cases the plant protection man may be mistaken or in some cases even malicious. Umpire Shulman declared that, if there is no evidence of ill-will toward the accused on the part of the accuser and if there are no circumstances upon which to base a conclusion that the accuser is mistaken, the conclusion that the charge is true can hardly be deemed improper.[66]

Similarly, the testimony of a foreman was accepted over that of the employee whom he accused where the foreman had many years of satisfactory service as against seven months' service by the accused and the foreman had never discharged an employee before.[67] Obviously, however, the testimony of the accuser will be subject to doubt and careful scrutiny if there is evidence of ill-will on his part against the accused.[68]

Another factor which might be considered by an arbitrator in weighing testimony in discharge and discipline cases is the so-called "code" which inhibits one member of an organ-

---

[64] General Cable Co., 28 LA 97, 99 (1957).
[65] As in Walter Butler Shipbuilders, Inc., 2 LA 633, 635-636 (Gorder, 1944).
[66] Ford Motor Co., 1 ALAA ¶ 67,274, p. 67,620 (1945). In general accord, Pennsylvania Greyhound Lines, Inc., 19 LA 210, 211 (Seward, 1952); Sun Shipbuilding & Dry Dock Co., 1 ALAA ¶ 67,648 (1947).
[67] Jenkins Bros., 11 LA 432, 434 (Donnelly, 1948). For similar results see Arbitrator Abernethy in 28 LA 757, 758-759; Coffey in 28 LA 710, 715.
[68] As in Bethlehem Steel Co., 2 LA 187, 190-191 (Dodd, 1945).

ization and frequently one member of an unorganized working force from testifying against another.[69]

Formal v. Informal Records

Business records are a frequent source of proof in arbitration. Complete data taken directly from original business records will ordinarily be given more weight than estimates or
informal records.[70] However, even informal records kept by
the union or by the employees themselves may be given significant weight if the company has kept no formal records of the
activity in question.[71]

Burden of Proof

It is very difficult to generalize on the application of the
doctrine of "burden of proof" in the field of arbitration. The
burden of proof may depend upon the nature of the issue, the
specific contract provision, or a usage established by the parties.
In many cases the arbitrator simply gets the facts and decides
the issue without any express indication that he is thinking in
terms of burden of proof.

Arbitrators have talked specifically in terms of burden of
proof much more frequently in some types of cases than in
other types. For instance, burden of proof considerations have
been stressed fairly often in discharge and discipline cases, as
well as in cases involving seniority clauses which require consideration of the fitness and ability of employees.[72] In contrast,
for example, Arbitrator Harry Shulman has emphasized that

---

[69] General Motors Corp., 2 LA 491, 502 (Hotchkiss, 1938).

[70] See Jonco Aircraft Corp., 22 LA 819, 823 (Merrill, 1954).

[71] See Bethlehem Steel Co., 16 LA 926, 927-928, 931-932 (Feinberg, 1951).

[72] See Chapter 15, topic titled "Burden and Quantum of Proof"; Chapter 14, topic
titled "Review of Management's Determination: Evidence and Burden of Proof." For
some other types of issues in which an arbitrator has spoken specifically in terms of
burden of proof see Arbitrator Duff in 24 LA 715, 717; Reynard in 24 LA 369, 372-
373; Holly in 24 LA 268, 273; Loucks in 24 LA 81, 84; Reid in 19 LA 291, 294;
Livengood in 19 LA 205, 207; Cheney in 8 LA 187, 188; Cole in 3 LA 723, 724. For
a related discussion see this Chapter, topic titled "Unsupported Allegations."

"notions of burden of proof are hardly applicable to issues of interpretation." [73]

It is probable that in arbitration the "burden of proof" concept is usually more important in its substantive than in its procedural significance. There is, for instance, no required order of presenting evidence in arbitration cases. While the party asserting a claim usually presents his proof first, or at least a preliminary or introductory case, this practice may not be followed where the nature of the issue makes a different procedure preferable. [74]

Unsupported Allegations

Too often a party goes to arbitration with nothing but allegations to support some of its contentions or even its basic position. But allegations or assertions are not proof, and mere allegations unsupported by evidence are ordinarily given no weight by arbitrators. [75]

Sometimes, too, a party will present no direct case at all, but will rely entirely upon cross-examination of the other party's witnesses, or will simply contend that the other party has the burden of proof and has not proved its case. This practice has been severely criticized by arbitrators. [76]

Hearsay Evidence

Evidence of a hearsay character is often presented at arbitration hearings. Arbitrators generally admit such evidence, but qualify its reception by informing the parties that it is

---

[73] Shulman, "Reason, Contract, and Law in Labor Relations," 68 Harv. L. Rev. 999, 1018 (1955). Arbitrator Benjamin Aaron has spoken vigorously against use of "burden of proof" concepts in arbitration (except in certain types of discharge cases), and in this regard has declared: "To insist that the complaining party carries the burden of proof is manifestly absurd. Neither side has a burden of proof or disproof, but both have an obligation to cooperate in an effort to give the arbitrator as much guidance as possible." Aaron, "Some Procedural Problems in Arbitration," 10 Vanderbilt Law Rev. 733, 740-742 (1957).

[74] For For full discussion see Chapter 7, topic titled "Order of Presenting Case."

[75] See Arbitrator Crawford in 29 LA 837, 841; Justin in 24 LA 45, 47; DiLeone in 16 LA 613, 615; Barrett in 16 LA 466, 468.

[76] See John Deere Waterloo Tractor Works, 20 LA 583, 584-585 (Davey, 1953); Felsway Shoe Corp., 17 LA 505, 509-510 (Justin, 1951). For a related discussion see Chapter 7, topic titled "Default Awards."

admitted only "for what it is worth".[77] It is impossible to say just what the arbitrator in an individual case will consider hearsay evidence to be "worth". Arbitrator Arthur R. Lewis has observed that "the reasons calling for the existence of a hearsay rule in common law jury actions should at least guide the judgment of the arbitrator in the evaluation of the weight, if any, to be attributed to such evidence in an arbitration proceeding." [78]

In many cases very little weight is given to hearsay evidence, and it is exceedingly unlikely that an arbitrator will render a decision supported by hearsay evidence alone.[79] Then, too, hearsay evidence will be given little weight if contradicted by evidence which has been subjected to cross-examination.[80]

A pertinent observation concerning the weight of hearsay evidence has been offered by Arbitrator Benjamin Aaron:

"[A] competent arbitrator may be depended upon substantially to discount some kinds of hearsay evidence that he has admitted over objection. He will do so selectively, however, and not on the assumption that hearsay evidence, as such, is not to be credited. If, for example, a newly appointed personnel manager, or a recently elected business agent, offers a letter to his predecessor from a third party, the arbitrator is likely to ignore the fact that the evidence is hearsay; if satisfied that the document is genuine, he will give it such weight as its relevancy dictates. On the other hand, hearsay testimony about statements allegedly made by 'the boys in the shop' or by executives in the 'front office,' though perhaps not excluded from the record by the arbitrator, probably will have no effect on his decision." [81]

Affidavits

Affidavits are sometimes used in arbitration but are subject to the same limitations as other forms of hearsay evidence.[82]

---

[77] For a related discussion see this Chapter, topic titled "Right of Cross-Examination."

[78] Continental Paper Co., 16 LA 727, 728 (1951).

[79] In the latter regard, see Arbitrator Gorder in 20 LA 880, 885-886; Klamon in 19 LA 571, 574; Cheney in 8 LA 518, 522.

[80] See, for instance, Howell Refining Co., 27 LA 486, 492 (Hale, 1956). Also see Arbitrator Rubin in 20 LA 483, 484.

[81] Aaron, "Some Procedural Problems in Arbitration," 10 Vanderbilt L. Rev. 733, 744 (1957).

[82] See, for instance, Borden Co., 20 LA 483, 484 (Rubin, 1953).

In this connection, the Rules of the American Arbitration Association provide that arbitrators serving thereunder may receive and consider the evidence of witnesses by affidavit but should give it only such weight as they deem it entitled to after consideration of any objections made to its admission.[83]

Circumstantial Evidence

Arbitrators sometimes decide cases on the basis of circumstantial evidence. For instance, such evidence was used to sustain the discharge of an employee charged with violation of a no-smoking rule; Arbitrator Jean McKelvey noted that the evidence was purely circumstantial but said that the proof, circumstantial as it was, indicated beyond a reasonable doubt that no person other than the accused could have been responsible for the smoke in the men's room.[84]

In another case the circumstances did not point so definitely to guilt, but a web of circumstances did exist to support the discharge of several employees for instigating an unauthorized strike; the reasoning of Arbitrator Whitley P. McCoy indicates how circumstantial evidence may be found sufficient to support a finding of guilt:

> "Because of the secret nature of the offense of these men, proof is extremely difficult. It does not follow from this that proof may be dispensed with or that mere suspicious circumstances may take the place of proof, as I have indicated in sustaining the grievances of four men. But I think it does follow that something less than the most direct and the most positive proof is sufficient; in other words, that, just as in cases of fraud and conspiracy, legitimate inferences may be drawn from such circumstances as a prior knowledge of the time set for the strike. Unusual actions in circulating among the employees just prior to 9:30, communication of the time set to employees, and signals, however sureptitious, given at that hour. Mere prior guilty knowledge of the time set would not alone be sufficient since presumably many of the employees must have been told the time a half hour, an hour, or several hours in advance. Nor would merely being the first in a department to quit at the stroke of 9:30, standing alone, be sufficient. A wave of the hand, which might as reasonably be inter-

---

[83] American Arbitration Association Rule 29, 30 LA 1086, 1089.

[84] Columbian Rope Co., 7 LA 450, 455 (1947). Circumstantial evidence was also given significant weight by Arbitrator Larkin in 22 LA 589, 600; Marshall in 22 LA 573, 575; Klamon in 16 LA 461, 466.

preted as a signal of good-bye as a signal to the others to go out, as in the case of Hollingsworth, would of itself be insufficient. But these or other suspicious circumstances, in combination, and especially in case of known leaders in the union's affairs, may be sufficient to convince the reasonable mind of guilt." [85]

As Arbitrator Clair V. Duff has emphasized, an arbitrator in using circumstantial evidence "must exercise extreme care so that by due deliberation and careful judgment he may avoid making hasty or false deductions. If the evidence producing the chain of circumstances pointing to [guilt] is weak and inconclusive, no probability of fact may be inferred from the combined circumstances." [86]

Or, as Arbitrator Paul M. Herbert has stated, use of circumstantial evidence "does not eliminate in any sense the requirement that there must be clear and convincing proof to establish that the offense charged was committed." [87] Certainly, mere suspicion is not enough to establish wrongdoing.[88]

Improperly Obtained Evidence

Arbitrators may refuse to admit or act upon evidence obtained through illegal or other improper means, as by disregard of the personal or property rights of employees. For instance, in a case involving the discharge of a female employee for violating a rule against possession of dangerous knives on company premises, Arbitrator Joseph D. Lohman emphasized that the company guard had obtained knowledge of the employee's possession of the knife through unilateral entry and search of her locker and purse, that she was escorted to the guard office and asked to empty her purse without being told the reason for the inquiry, and that the guard had been instructed not to disclose the reason for the inquiry. Arbitrator Lohman said this tactic bordered on entrapment, and that the

---

[85] Stockham Pipe Fittings Co., 4 LA 744, 746-747 (1946). Also see Arbitrator Harter in 7 LA 239.

[86] South Penn Oil Co., 29 LA 718, 721 (1957).

[87] Reed Roller Bit Co., 29 LA 604, 606 (1957). Also see Arbitrator Bowles in 24 LA 761, 764; Kadish in 24 LA 102, 104-105; Platt in 21 LA 428, 429.

[88] See Enterprise & Century Undergarment Co., 24 LA 63, 64 (Donnelly, 1955). Also see comments of Arbitrator Prasow in 23 LA 317, 321; Updegraff in 19 LA 413, 416.

employee's locker and purse continued inviolate as the private realm of the individual even though the entire episode was confined to the premises of the company.[89]

Arbitrator Lohman concluded that "Knowledge, even though incriminating, if acquired through such illegitimate procedures, is of questionable validity in bringing action against the individual." The evidence obtained through such procedures was held inadmissible, and consequently the discharge was held unjustified.[90]

In another case employees complained of entrapment where a night foreman, being reasonably suspicious that a poker game was in progress, returned to the plant after he had previously driven away. Arbitrator Harold M. Gilden rejected the contention of entrapment, stating that the foreman's action must be deemed within his general line of duty, and that the situation was to be distinguished from one where a carefully devised plan is formulated and bait is set or invitations extended for the express purpose of capturing persons in the commission of a wrongful act.[91]

In some industries use of unidentified "spotters" and admission of their reports and testimony as evidence of rule violations by employees has been held justified.[92]

Confessions

An arbitrator may be expected to refuse to give weight to a signed "confession" if the signature was obtained through inducements, commitments, or threats.[93] "Such methods of obtaining confessions of guilt are patently wrong. A confession, to be valid in prosecuting a case must be statements given by the suspected person of his own free will and choice.

---

[80] Campbell Soup Co., 2 LA 27, 31 (1946).

[90] Ibid. But see Lockheed Aircraft Corp., 27 LA 709, 712-713 (Maggs, 1956).

[91] Borg-Warner Corp., 3 LA 423, 432 (1944). Regarding entrapment, also see Arbitrator Hampton in 3 LA 789; Courshon in 1 LA 350; Wirtz, "Due Process of Arbitration," The Arbitrator and the Parties 1, 17 (BNA Incorporated, 1958).

[92] See this Chapter, topic titled "Right of Cross-Examination."

[93] See Arbitrator Babb in 29 LA 272, 277; Blair in 12 LA 1065, 1067.

Inducements and threats invalidate such documents as evidence." [94]

Offers of Compromise and Admissions

Offers of compromise and admissions made in attempting settlement of "rights" disputes prior to submission to arbitration may be received but probably will be given very little, if any, weight by arbitrators.[95] It is recognized that a party to a dispute may make an offer with the hope that a compromise can be reached and the dispute ended.[96] Even the mere introduction of such evidence may impair future attempts at dispute settlements.

While admissions and statements against interest other than those made in settlement attempts may be considered by an arbitrator, he can be expected to recognize that as a matter of law they are not conclusive.[97]

Admissions which have been acted on by others, however, and those that appear in the record of prior proceedings so as to partake of the nature of judicial admissions may be held by arbitrators to be weighty evidence against the party making them.[98] Thus, where a party assumed a position in an arbitration case which was inconsistent with the position of that party in a prior arbitration case involving the same contract clause, the position taken in the prior case was one of the reasons for a decision against the party in the subsequent case.[99]

Testimony from other proceedings must be evaluated with special care and in the full setting of the prior proceeding. Moreover, Arbitrator Bertram F. Willcox has observed that

---

[94] Kroger Co., 12 LA 1065, 1067 (Blair, 1949).
[95] See Arbitrator Prasow in 25 LA 398, 403-404; Marshall in 24 LA 430, 436; Cornsweet in 14 LA 494, 497. Also see Chapter 9, topic titled "No consideration to Compromise Offers."
[96] Universal Milking Machine Co., 2 LA 399, 402 (Elson, 1946).
[97] Harley-Davidson Co., 6 LA 395, 397 (Lappin, 1947).
[98] For instance, see Arbitrator Komaroff in 21 LA 248, 251; McCoy in 6 LA 681, 684. Also see Meltzer in 28 LA 303, 308.
[99] Goodyear Tire & Rubber Co. of Ala., 6 LA 681, 684 (McCoy, 1947). The prior case was Goodyear Tire & Rubber Co., 4 LA 231 (McCoy, 1946).

sometimes even in the same case an apparently damaging admission by a witness will have resulted from a momentary confusion and that the arbitrator should exercise care not to over-emphasize any single item of testimony, especially if it is inconsistent with other testimony of the witness and with the rest of the party's case.[100]

Testimony by Persons from Outside

The nature of some cases makes the use of impartial technicians helpful. In such cases, arbitrators sometimes request permission to bring in specialists for impartial study of the disputed matter. This was done, for example, by Arbitrator David Wolff who consulted an electrical engineer, in the presence of both parties, as to whether a power failure was a cause beyond the employer's control (so as to relieve him of any obligation for call-in pay).[101] It has also been done in the determination of proper incentive rates for new operations.[102] Likewise, Arbitrator Peter M. Kelliher was authorized to secure the services of a handwriting expert in fixing responsibility for errors in shipping orders.[103]

A limitation upon the use of outside testimony has been defined by Arbitrator Willard E. Hotchkiss, who has accepted but refused to consider testimony of outsiders to the effect that a discharged employee had admitted his guilt to them; Arbitrator Hotchkiss urged that testimony of outsiders, whether or not relevant, should not generally be admitted since the frequent admission of such testimony would tend to retard the growth of healthy industrial relations and would encourage the calling of character witnesses to refute or support the testimony of the outsiders, the building of technical alibis, and other legalistic practices which would prolong hearings at great expense but to no useful purpose.[104]

---

[100] General Electric Corp., 16 LA 554, 559 (1951).
[101] Chrysler Corp., 21 LA 573, 577 (1953).
[102] Container Co., 6 LA 218, 220 (Whiting, 1946).
[103] Hiram Walker & Sons, Inc., 18 LA 447, 448 (1952).
[104] General Motors Corp., 2 LA 491, 497, 503 (1938). Cf., Continental Paper Co., 16 LA 727, 728-729 (Lewis, 1951).

Medical Evidence

A frequent use of medical evidence in arbitration concerns the physical fitness or qualifications of employees for some given type of work or, indeed, for any continued employment at all with the company. While doctors sometimes testify in person, their testimony is frequently offered in the form of written statements or affidavits. In the latter connection, the parties may stipulate that written statements of doctors (though not subject to cross-examination) shall be given the same effect as if the doctors had testified.[105] Even without such stipulation the arbitrator might give the statements "full weight" in the absence of other evidence minimizing their significance.[106]

Often both parties submit medical evidence concerning the grievant's physical qualifications, and it is not surprising that the opinion of the grievant's doctor and that of the employer's medical adviser do not always agree. Arbitrators appear reluctant to attempt to resolve such conflicts in medical evidence, but are inclined to uphold the employer if he acted in good faith pursuant to good-faith medical advice from his doctor.[107] Arbitrator W. Willard Wirtz, for instance, has stated that the arbitrator can only decide "whether the medical determination was made in a manner and by * * * a procedure indicating that it was fairly and reasonably made." [108]

Although Arbitrator Maurice H. Merrill apparently would to some extent weigh conflicting medical testimony, he has held that where there is "direct conflict in the medical testimony, with nothing to swing the balance preponderantly on one side or the other," the company "is entitled to rely on the

---

[105] As in Southern Cotton Oil Co., 26 LA 353, 356 (Kelliher, 1956).

[106] As in White Motor Co., 28 LA 823, 829 (Lazarus, 1957). The weight of written statements was greatly reduced by other evidence in American Iron & Machine Works Co., 19 LA 417, 420 (Merill, 1952).

[107] See Arbitrator Prasow in 24 LA 732, 738 (quoting Arbitrator Gregory); Abernethy in 24 LA 290, 298; Wirtz in 24 LA 274, 275. But an employee receiving postoperative medical care from a personal physician has a right to rely upon that doctor's advice respecting date of return to work. International Harvester Co., 22 LA 138, 139 (Platt, 1954).

[108] International Harvester Co., 24 LA 274, 275 (1955).

views of its own medical advisers, if it has given" the grievant "fair notice and opportunity to overcome those views before reaching a final decision." [109]

Another frequent use of medical evidence concerns written certificates from doctors stating that employees named in the certificates were examined on a stated date and were found to be ailing. Arbitrators have held that these certificates, although not conclusive, should be given significant weight in determining whether the absence from work is to be excused due to illness.[110] Such certificates, however, may be impeached if shown to have been given as a favor, to have been obtained through misrepresentation, or to have been based upon mistake.[111]

Protecting Witnesses

In some situations giving testimony in arbitration proceedings may subject the witness to varied risks of retaliation. For instance, employees and supervisors alike may incur the displeasure of the employer as a result of their testimony. Likewise, employees may jeopardize their relations with fellow workers for testifying at the employer's request. When he feels the need, the arbitrator may seek to protect the interests of persons facing this predicament by reminding the parties of the risks involved.[112]

Although the arbitrator cannot insure definite protection if the person does testify, there may be firm basis for a valid grievance or unfair labor practice charges in some situations of retaliation for giving testimony.

---

[109] Ideal Cement Co., 20 LA 480, 482 (1953). Also see Arbitrator Merrill in 19 LA 417, 420; Kelliher in 26 LA 353, 356.

[110] See Arbitrator Oppenheim in 29 LA 291, 292; Livengood in 20 LA 451, 453; Seward in 11 LA 909, 912; Griffin in 1 LA 281, 282.

[111] See Arbitrator Oppenheim in 29 LA 291, 292; Livengood in 20 LA 451, 453; Courshon in 2 LA 509, 513.

[112] See Guides for Labor Arbitration 9 (U. of Pa. Press, 1953).

Chapter 9

STANDARDS FOR INTERPRETING CONTRACT LANGUAGE

Ambiguity

Probably no function of the labor-management arbitrator is more important than that of interpreting the collective bargaining agreement. The great bulk of arbitration cases involve disputes over "rights" under such agreements. In these cases the agreement itself is the point of concentration, and the function of the arbitrator is to interpret and apply its provisions.

There is no need for interpretation unless the agreement is ambiguous. If the words are plain and clear, conveying a distinct idea, there is no occasion to resort to technical rules of interpretation and the clear meaning will ordinarily be applied by arbitrators.[1]

An agreement is not ambiguous if the arbitrator can determine its meaning without any other guide than a knowledge of the simple facts on which, from the nature of language in general, its meaning depends.[2] But an agreement is ambiguous if "plausible contentions may be made for conflicting interpretations" thereof.[3] Moreover, it is recognized that whether a document is or is not ambiguous is a matter of impression rather than of definition; and this is obviously so, because

---

[1] See, for instance, Arbitrator Klamon in 15 LA 676, 682; Kelliher in 15 LA 46, 49. Where the arbitration is subject to court review on matters of law the court may apply this principle. See cases discussed in Marceau, "Are All Interpretations 'Admissible'?" 12 Arb. J. 150 (1957).
[2] 13 Corpus Juris, Sec. 481, p. 520.
[3] Armstrong Rubber Co., 17 LA 741, 744 (Gorder, 1952).

each provision may be as clear and definite as language can make it, yet the result of the whole be doubtful from lack of harmony in its various parts.[4]

Most persons experienced in collective bargaining recognize the collective agreement as a comprehensive, but necessarily flexible, instrument which governs the relations between the parties. The very fact that almost all such agreements provide for the arbitration of grievances concerning agreement interpretation suggests that the parties recognize the impossibility of foreseeing and providing for all questions which may arise during the life of the agreement.[5]

As Arbitrator Martin Raphael has pointed out, language cannot be tailored to fit precisely the variant meanings which parties to an agreement may have in their minds; language is frequently used which is general in nature and flexible enough to include those meanings which future experience necessitates being filled in. This arbitrator quoted Mr. Justice Holmes: "A word is not a crystal, transparent and unchanged; it is the skin of a living thought and may vary greatly in color and content according to the circumstances and the time in which it is used." [6]

The primary goal of the "rights" arbitrator is to determine and carry out the mutual intent of the parties. An ambiguity in a contract usually means that the parties have failed to express that intent with clarity. Sometimes, however, an ambiguity may mean more. It may mean that there never was any meeting of the minds. When this is found to be the case, the matter should ordinarily be returned to the parties for negotiations,[7] unless the parties expressly or impliedly authorize the arbitrator to decide the issue.[8]

---

[4] Butte Water Co. v. Butte, 138 P. 195, 197 (Mont., 1914).
[5] Loew's Inc., 10 LA 227, 232 (Aaron, 1948).
[6] Yale & Towne Mfg. Co., 5 LA 753 (1946).
[7] As did Arbitrator Sweeney in 29 LA 188, 191; Killingsworth in 12 LA 709, 714, and in 7 LA 70, 74; Copelof in 7 LA 507, 510, and in 6 LA 667, 669. Cf. Arbitrator Lehoczky in 19 LA 766, 767. For related discussion see Chapter 7, topic titled "Recommendations by Arbitrator"; Chapter 10, topic titled "Contract Principles."
[8] See Arbitrator Beatty in 24 LA 424, 425; Ryder in 22 LA 769, 771.

Accepting, then, that the basic function of the "rights" arbitrator is agreement interpretation, an inquiry should be made concerning the techniques, standards, or rules used by arbitrators in executing this function. An analysis of these techniques and standards should be of much value to contract negotiators as well as to parties preparing cases for arbitration. Such analysis will provide guides which, if observed in the drafting of collective agreements, will tend to protect the parties against pitfalls in the use of language.

This study may suggest the desirability of the use by negotiators of skilled counsel in rephrasing the agreement after mutual understanding is reached. While the agreement should be stated in simple language, understandable by the employees, negotiators are not always capable of expressing their true intent, either in simple language or otherwise. Moreover, negotiators are inclined to read into that which they have written, however ambiguous its face, the meaning which they have agreed upon, and to lose sight of the problem which may exist for a third party who must read the contract.

It should be emphasized that the courts, when called upon to construe collective agreements, use accepted standards of interpretation of general application.[9]

Arbitrators likewise use these standards of construction. In other words, it should be recognized that all written instruments, constitutions, statutes, and contracts are interpreted by the same general principles, although the specific subject matter may call for strictness or liberality.[10] Accordingly, collective agreements should be drafted with the same care and precision exercised in drafting commercial contracts.

[9] See Smith v. Bowen, 121 N.E. 814 (Mass., 1919); Mueller v. Chicago & N.W. Ry. Co., 259 N.W. 798 (Minn., 1935); Reichert v. Quindazzi, 6 N.Y.S, 2d 284 (N.Y., 1938).

[10] See Moran Towing and Transportation Co., 1 ALAA ¶ 67,012, p. 67,015 (Kidd, 1944). This view is practiced by many arbitrators, but there have been occasional expressions of doubt, as in Crescent Warehouse Co., 10 LA 168, 171 (Aaron, 1948). Some parties specifically provide that in making his decision the arbitrator shall be bound by the principles of interpretation used by courts.

On the other hand, the standards of construction as used by arbitrators are not inflexible. They are but "aids to the finding of intent, not hard and fast rules to be used to defeat intent." [11] Parties probably expect arbitrators to be less circumscribed by rigid rules of construction than the courts, and this helps to protect against harsh and unworkable results.

Sometimes two or more of the rules of interpretation conflict in a given case. Where this is so, the arbitrator is free to apply that rule which he believes will produce the better result. Sometimes, however, a combination of two or more of the standards may be consistently applied in construing an ambiguous word or clause. The statement of Mr. Justice Holmes, that "it is not an adequate discharge of duty for courts to say: We see what you are driving at, but you have not said it, and therefore we shall go on as before," [12] would appear to express the attitude of the many arbitrators who strive to determine what the parties were driving at and to effectuate their intent.

It is recognized that there are dangers to collective bargaining both in a mere literal, mechanical approach to agreement interpretation and, at the other extreme, in the indirect rewriting of the agreement by the substitution of the arbitrator's views under the guise of interpretation.[13] It is to be expected, however, that something of the arbitrator's personality will creep into his decision. The award of the arbitrator is based upon *his interpretation,* not that of somebody else.[14]

The line between interpretation and "legislation" cannot be drawn absolutely and it is inevitable that this line will be crossed frequently. One arbitrator has openly declared that although the arbitration of a dispute must be confined within the scope of the existing agreement, its adjudication necessitates some *legislating* and interpreting to clarify and remove

---

[11] Republic Steel Corp., 5 LA 609, 614 (McCoy, 1946).
[12] Johnson v. United States, 163 Fed. 30, 32 (1st Cir., 1908).
[13] National Tube Co., 11 LA 378, 380 (Seward, 1948).
[14] Kendall Mills, 8 LA 306, 309 (Lane, 1947).

the uncertainties, obscurities, and ambiguities which exist in the agreement.[15]

Some gap-filling is a natural part of the interpretative process. Situations unforeseen when the agreement was written, but falling within its general framework, often arise. Arbitrators considering these situations must decide, insofar as possible, what the parties would have agreed upon, within the general framework of the agreement, had the matter been specifically before them.[16]

At least, as long as gap-filling is primarily a matter of interpretation or application of what does appear in the contract, it should not be deemed prohibited.[17] Gap-filling, however, is improper (unless authorized) when it results in a basic addition to, subtraction from, or modification of the agreement.[18]

There are, at the extremes, arbitrators who take a strict legalistic view of interpretation and those who recognize few limitations; but it may be safely said that most arbitrators take an intermediate approach, refusing to pay slavish deference to legalisms but also seeking to give effect to the contract which the parties themselves have made.

Intent of the Parties

The rule primarily to be observed in the construction of written agreements is that the interpreter must, if possible, ascertain and give effect to the mutual intent of the parties. The collective agreement should be construed, not narrowly and technically, but broadly and so as to accomplish its evident aims.[19]

---

[15] Borg-Warner Corp., 3 LA 423, 428-429 (Gilden, 1944). Also see Arbitrator Rice in 8 LA 586, 588-589.

[16] See Arbitrator McKelvey in 25 LA 94, 99; Hampton in 18 LA 581, 583. Also see Killingsworth, "Arbitration: Its Uses in Industrial Relations," 21 LA 859, 861-862 (1953).

[17] See Pacific American Shipowners Assn., 3 LA 383, 389 (Handsaker, 1946). Also see Arbitrator Abernethy in 21 LA 129, 131.

[18] See Pacific American Shipowners Assn., 3 LA 383, 392 (Handsaker, 1946). Also see Arbitrator Sweeney in 29 LA 188, 191.

[19] Rentschler v. Missouri Pacific R.R., 253 N.W. 694 (Neb., 1934).

In determining the intent of the parties, inquiry is made as to what the language meant to the parties when the agreement was written.[20] It is this meaning that governs, not the meaning that can be possibly read into the language.[21]

The "intent of the parties" rule has been elaborated as follows:

> "Whatever may be the inaccuracy of expression or the inaptness of words used in an instrument in a legal view, if the intention of the parties can be clearly discovered, the court will give effect to it and construe the words accordingly. It must not be supposed, however, that an attempt is made to ascertain the actual mental processes of the parties to a particular contract. The law presumes that the parties understood the import of their contract and that they had the intention which its terms manifest. It is not within the function of the judiciary to look outside of the instrument to get at the intention of the parties and then carry out that intention regardless of whether the instrument contains language sufficient to express it; but their sole duty is to find out what was meant by the language of the instrument. This language must be sufficient, when looked at in the light of such facts as the court is entitled to consider, to sustain whatever effect is given to the instrument." [22]

Language Which Is Clear and Unambiguous

If the language of an agreement is clear and unequivocal, an arbitrator generally will not give it a meaning other than that expressed. Even though the parties to an agreement disagree as to its meaning, an arbitrator who finds the language to be unambiguous will enforce the clear meaning.[23]

An arbitrator, as a neutral person, is less likely than the parties to commit the error of seeing what one would like to find in written language rather than what is actually there. Even when both parties declare a provision to be ambiguous the arbitrator may find it not so.[24] On the other hand, lan-

---

[20] Brampton Woolen Co. v. Local Union 112 et al., 61 A. 2d 796 (N.H., 1948). Also see Arbitrator Platt in 13 LA 126, 131. Cf., Arbitrator Boles in 20 LA 227, 231.

[21] Autocar Co., 10 LA 61, 63 (Brecht, 1948). Also see Arbitrator Davey in 21 LA 139, 144.

[22] 12 American Jurisprudence, § 227, pp. 746-748 (citations omitted).

[23] See, for example, Arbitrator Shipman in 9 LA 716, 718; Blumer in 5 LA 378, 382; Rader in 4 LA 497, 502; Epstein in 3 LA 412, 414; Updegraff in 2 LA 469, 472; Peifer in 2 LA 66, 67.

[24] As in Andrew Williams Meat Co., 8 LA 518, 524 (Cheney, 1947).

guage which appears on the surface to be clear sometimes will prove to have a latent or hidden ambiguity.[25]

Because arbitrators apply the principle that parties to a contract are charged with full knowledge of its provisions and of the significance of its language,[26] the clear meaning of language may be enforced even though the results are harsh or contrary to the original expectations of one of the parties.[27] The arbitrator may say that his award must be based upon the logical interpretation of the contract, although, if the decision were based upon the equities involved, it might be possible to reach a different conclusion.[28]

If, however, an arbitrator finds that as a result of mutual mistake or typographical error the parties used language or punctuation which does not express their true intent, a reformation may be granted so as to effectuate the true intent of the parties.[29] Also, where very broad language has been used an arbitrator might refuse to apply it literally, but apply it restrictively so as to produce the intended result.[30]

Interpretation in Light of the Law

Arbitrators strive to give effect to the collective agreement rather than to dismember it, and, whenever two interpretations are possible, one making the agreement valid and lawful and the other making it unlawful, the former will be used. The parties are presumed to have intended a valid contract.[31]

---

[25] As in Carlile & Doughty, Inc., 9 LA 239, 241 (Brandschain, 1947).

[26] See Arbitrator Platt in 7 LA 708, 711; Updegraff in 3 LA 229, 232 (citing law cases), and 2 LA 469, 472.

[27] See Arbitrator Ross in 28 LA 557, 558; Shipman in 20 LA 756, 758-759; Copelof in 13 LA 110, 114; Potter in 7 LA 724, 729; Cheney in 6 LA 962, 965; Marshall in 6 LA 838, 843; Prasow in 6 LA 540, 543; Carmichael in 1 ALAA ¶ 67,096. Also see Arbitrator Duff in 24 LA 715, 716; Garrett in 15 LA 834, 838.

[28] As in Merrill Stevens Dry Dock & Repair Co., 6 LA 838, 843 (Marshall, 1947).

[29] See Arbitrator Compton in 27 LA 829, 831; Willcox in 23 LA 21, 24. Also see Emery in 20 LA 865, 867; McCoy in 3 LA 257, 259. For further development of this matter see Chapter 10, topic titled "Remedies for Mistake".

[30] As in Shook Bronze Co., 9 LA 656, 657 (Lehoczky, 1948).

[31] See Arbitrator Gorder in 20 LA 880, 889; Horvitz in 9 LA 702, 703; Tischler in 5 LA 282, 283; Shake in 2 LA 445, 452.

When parties use language in their agreement which is the same as language of a statute, the meaning given to that language by courts and administrative tribunals may be persuasive upon arbitrators as indicating the proper interpretation of the language.[82]

Normal and Technical Usage

Arbitrators give words their ordinary and popularly accepted meaning in the absence of anything indicating that they were used in a different sense or that the parties intended some special colloquial meaning.[33] For instance, the word "may" has been given its ordinary "permissive" meaning in absence of strong evidence that the parties intended a mandatory meaning.[84]

Trade or technical terms will be interpreted in a trade or technical sense unless clearly used otherwise. For instance, the term "union shop" was applied in the sense commonly used in labor circles instead of in a special sense (which would not have required maintenance of membership) urged by management; the arbitrator declared that if the employer did not intend that which was meant by the term in the parlance of organized labor or did not understand the term, he should not have let it be used in the contract.[85]

Any term not characteristically a trade or technical term will be construed in its natural, usual sense unless the context or evidence indicates that a technical meaning was intended by the parties.[86]

It is said to be "a well recognized rule of construction that a word used by parties in one sense is to be interpreted,

---

[33] See Arbitrator Reeves in 20 LA 564, 566; Horvitz in 20 LA 318, 320; Platt in 19 LA 457, 458. For extensive discussion of use by arbitrators of substantive rules of law, see Chapter 10.

[83] See Arbitrator Slavney in 28 LA 532, 534; Prasow in 27 LA 40, 45; Feinberg in 18 LA 227, 231; Shulman in 12 LA 949, 954; McCoy in 12 LA 650, 652; Lewis in 6 LA 202, 203; Kelliher in 5 LA 409, 410; Rader in 3 LA 605, 607. Also see Boles in 20 LA 227, 231.

[84] See Arbitrator Hogan in 25 LA 243, 246; Reynard in 22 LA 880, 881.

[85] Safeway Stores, Inc., 1 ALAA ¶ 67,096, p. 67,169 (Carmichael, 1944).

[86] Great Lakes Dredge & Dock Co., 5 LA 409, 410 (Kelliher, 1946).

in the absence of countervailing reasons, as employed in the same sense throughout the writing." [37]

It is also stated that when parties have changed the language of their agreement there is a presumption that they intended a changed meaning." [38]

Use of Dictionary Definitions

Arbitrators have often ruled that in the absence of a showing of mutual understanding of the parties to the contrary, the usual and ordinary definition of terms as defined by a reliable dictionary should govern.[39] However, an examination of the entire agreement and its application to the subject matter being considered by the arbitrator may result in the interpretation of words not in the general dictionary sense but in a mutually agreed sense.[40]

Furthermore, it sometimes happens that dictionary definitions can be found to cover opposing contentions.[41] In such situations (and indeed ordinarily) it is desirable that interpretations not rest upon dictionary definitions alone but be additionally supported by other considerations, especially where the persons drafting the agreement were laymen untrained in the precise use of words.[42]

Agreement to Be Construed as a Whole

It is said that the "primary rule in construing a written instrument is to determine, not alone from a single word or phrase, but from the instrument as a whole, the true intent of the parties and to interpret the meaning of a questioned word or part with regard to the connection in which it is

[37] Vickers, Inc., 15 LA 353, 356 (Platt, 1950).
[38] Deep Rock Oil Corp., 20 LA 865, 867 (Emery, 1953).
[39] E.g., Arbitrator Cahn in 29 LA 597, 603; Hebert in 23 LA 497, 500; Gorder in 20 LA 880, 888; Luskin in 18 LA 459, 461; Abrahams in 17 LA 50, 53; Merrill in 11 LA 25, 29; Rogers in 3 LA 815, 817.
[40] See Moran Towing and Transportation Co., 1 ALAA ¶ 67,012 (Kidd, 1944).
[41] As in Atlanta Newspapers, Inc., 20 LA 809, 817 (Dworet, 1953).
[42] See Comments of Arbitrator Lockhart in 16 LA 173, 175; McCoy in 12 LA 650, 652, and 5 LA 492, 494.

used, the subject matter and its relation to all other parts or provisions." [43]

Similarly, "Sections or portions cannot be isolated from the rest of the agreement and given construction independently of the purpose and agreement of the parties as evidenced by the entire document. * * * The meaning of each paragraph and each sentence must be determined in relation to the contract as a whole." [44] This standard requiring the agreement to be construed as a whole is applied very frequently.[45]

Giving Effect to All Clauses and Words

If an arbitrator finds that alternative interpretations of a clause are possible, one of which would give meaning and effect to another provision of the contract, while the other would render the other provision meaningless or ineffective, he will be inclined to use the interpretation which would give effect to all provisions.[46] In the words of one arbitrator:

> "It is axiomatic in contract construction that an interpretation which tends to nullify or render meaningless any part of the contract should be avoided because of the general presumption that the parties do not carefully write into a solemnly negotiated agreement words intended to have no effect." [47]

Ordinarily all words used in an agreement should be given effect. The fact that a word is used indicates that the parties intended it to have some meaning, and it will not be declared surplusage if a reasonable meaning can be given to it consistent with the rest of the agreement.[48] However, if no reasonable meaning can be given to a word or clause, either from the context in which it is used or by examining the whole agree-

---

[43] Riley Stoker Corp., 7 LA 764, 767 (Platt, 1947).
[44] Great Lakes Dredge & Dock Co., 5 LA 409, 410 (Kelliher, 1946).
[45] E.g., Arbitrator Merrill in 29 LA 334, 339-342; Scheiber in 26 LA 117, 120; Ryder in 20 LA 337, 340; Maggs in 11 LA 992, 993; Hampton in 10 LA 487, 493; McCoy in 5 LA 609, 613; Gilden in 1 ALAA ¶ 67,315.
[46] E.g., Arbitrator Hebert in 29 LA 469, 473; Kelliher in 27 LA 798, 800; Coffey in 12 LA 1117, 1120; Gilden in 12 LA 624, 628; Merrill in 11 LA 25, 30; Aaron in 10 LA 227, 233; Potter in 8 LA 634, 639; Updegraff in 5 LA 631, 632; McCoy in 4 LA 310, 313; Blair in 3 LA 753, 756. Cf., Platt in 9 LA 91, 94.
[47] John Deere Tractor Co., 5 LA 631, 632 (Updegraff, 1946).
[48] Borden's Farm Products, Inc., 3 LA 401, 402 (Burke, 1945).

ment, it may be treated as surplusage and declared to be inoperative.[49]

Words may be implied into an agreement with as much force and effect as if expressed therein if, from a consideration of the agreement as a whole, such inclusion by implication is called for.[50] Thus, in one instance the arbitrator decided that the words "job classification" were impliedly meant to precede the phrase "hourly rates of pay." [51]

Avoidance of Harsh, Absurd, or Nonsensical Results

When one interpretation of an ambiguous contract would lead to harsh, absurd, or nonsensical results, while an alternative interpretation, equally consistent, would lead to just and reasonable results, the latter interpretation will be used.[52]

Thus, for instance, a provision for paid vacations for employees in the "active employ" of the company on a specified date, provided they met other requirements, would not be interpreted so as to produce the "absurd" result of disqualifying employees absent on such date due to illness or any other valid reason.[53] Likewise, an interpretation was rejected which, if applied, would have placed a premium on contract violation by encouraging unauthorized strikes.[54]

To Express One Thing Is to Exclude Another

Sometimes arbitrators apply the principle that to expressly include one or more of a class in a written instrument must be taken as an exclusion of all others.[55] The hazards of this

---

[49] American Shearer Mfg. Co., 6 LA 984, 985-986 (Myers, 1947).

[50] J. M. Huber, Inc., 5 LA 100, 103 (Shipman, 1946). Also see Arbitrator Platt in 15 LA 352, 356.

[51] J. M. Huber, Inc., 5 LA 100, 103 (Shipman, 1946).

[52] See Arbitrator Dworkin in 23 LA 481, 486; Shipman in 21 LA 35, 37-38; Hays in 20 LA 443, 446; Platt in 15 LA 353, 355; Merrill in 11 LA 25, 29; Raphael in 5 LA 753, 757; Blair in LA 446, 448; McCoy in 2 LA 367, 370; Gilden in 1 LA 417, 419.

[53] Rockwell Spring & Axle Co., 23 LA 481, 486 (Dworkin, 1954).

[54] A. D. Julliard & Co., 2 LA 140, 141 (Copelof, 1946).

[55] See Arbitrator Rosenfarb in 18 LA 418, 423; Copelof in 16 LA 685, 688; Hobbs in 10 LA 541, 549; Hampton in 10 LA 487, 494; Potter in 7 LA 81, 84; McCoy in 3 LA 257, 259. Cf., Arbitrator Holly in 24 LA 268, 271; Maggs in 22 LA 761, 762; Gilden in 15 LA 345, 349.

rule of construction, known as *"expressio unius est exclusio alterius,"* in some instances leads parties to use general rather than specific language,[56] or to follow a specific enumeration with the statement that the clause is not to be restricted necessarily to the things specifically listed.

Doctrine of *Ejusdem Generis*

It is axiomatic under the doctrine of *ejusdem generis* that where general words follow an enumeration of specific terms the general words will be interpreted to include or cover only things of the same general nature or class as those enumerated, unless it is shown that a wider sense was intended.[57]

Under this doctrine, for instance, it was held that a clause providing that seniority shall govern in all cases of layoff, transfer "or other adjustment of personnel," should not be construed to require allocation of overtime work on the basis of seniority.[58] The doctrine has been held inapplicable, however, where the specific words preceding the general words embrace all objects of their class since, except for this qualification, the general words that follow the specific enumeration would be meaningless.[59]

Specific v. General Language

Where there is conflict between specific language and general language in an agreement, the specific language will govern.[60]

For example, where a contract contained a general provision stating that the Company should "continue to make reasonable provisions for the safety and health of its employees" and another provision stating that "wearing apparel and other equipment necessary properly to protect employees from in-

---

[56] Loew's Inc., 10 LA 227, 232 (Aaron, 1948).
[57] See 12 Am. Jur. 799-780 (Contracts § 244).
[58] Canadian Industries Limited, 19 LA 170, 172 (Hanrahan, 1951).
[59] St. Louis Terminal Warehouse Co., 19 LA 807, 808-809 (Treiman, 1952).
[60] See Arbitrator McKelvey in 29 LA 376, 380; Fleming in 28 LA 554, 556; McCoy in 12 LA 530, 531; Wyckoff in 12 LA 462, 469.

jury shall be provided by the Company in accordance with practices now prevailing * * * or as such practices may be improved from time to time by the Company," it was held that the employer was not obligated to furnish rain clothes to employees where such had not been furnished or required in the past; the arbitrator said that had the general clause stood alone he would have been required to determine whether the furnishing of rain clothes was reasonably necessary for the safety and health of the employees.[61]

Arbitrators also may be expected to rule that, when an exception is stated to a general principle, the exception should prevail where it is applicable.[62]

Construction in Light of Context

Definite meaning may be given to ambiguous or doubtful words by construing them in the light of the context.[63] "*Noscitur a sociis* is an old maxim which summarizes the rule both of language and of law that the meaning of words may be controlled by those with which they are associated."[64]

Avoidance of a Forfeiture

If an agreement is susceptible of two constructions, one of which would work a forfeiture and one of which would not, the arbitrator will be inclined to adopt the interpretation that will prevent the forfeiture. This principle has been elaborated by Arbitrator George Cheney:

"A party claiming a forfeiture or penalty under a written instrument has the burden of proving that such is the unmistakable intention of the parties to the document. In addition, the courts have ruled that a contract is not to be construed to provide a forfeiture or penalty unless no other construction or interpretation is reasonably possible. Since forfeitures are not favored either in law or in equity, courts are reluctant to

---

[61] Tennessee Coal, Iron and R.R. Co., 12 LA 530, 531 (McCoy, 1949).

[62] Fulton-Sylphon Co., 8 LA 983, 984 (Greene, 1947).

[63] See Arbitrator Gorder in 20 LA 880, 888; Merrill in 11 LA 25, 31; Wallen in 6 LA 179, 182.

[64] Williston, Contracts, § 618.

declare and enforce a forfeiture if by reasonable interpretation it can be avoided." [65]

In that case a clause requiring retroactive pay for employees unjustly discharged was interpreted as an indemnity (rather than forfeiture) clause not requiring retroactive pay where employees suffer no loss of earnings while off the company payroll.[66]

Precontract Negotiations

Precontract negotiations frequently provide a valuable aid in the interpretation of ambiguous provisions. Where the meaning of a term is not clear, it will be deemed, if there is no evidence to the contrary, that the parties intended it to have the same meaning as that given it during the negotiations leading up to the agreement.[67] In such case, consideration will be given to all of the circumstances leading up to the making of the contract.[68]

The arbitrator must place himself, to the extent possible, in the situation of the parties at the time of the negotiations so as to view the circumstances as the parties viewed them and to judge the meaning of the agreement accordingly. The history of the negotiations, as evidenced by recordings or minutes of bargaining meetings, is very important.[69] Even where no stenographic record is kept and no notes are taken, the history of negotiations may be relied upon by the arbitrator if he is satisfied as to the accuracy of the oral testimony of persons who attended the negotiations.[70]

If, however, an agreement is not ambiguous, it is improper

---

[65] Mode O'Day Corp., 1 LA 490, 494 (1946), wherein numerous court cases were cited. Accord, Alpha Cellulose Corp., 27 LA 798, 800 (Kelliher, 1956).

[66] Mode O'Day Corp., 1 LA 490, 494 (Cheney, 1946).

[67] Bell Aircraft Corporation, 1 ALAA ¶ 67,025, p. 67,041 (Bouwhuis, 1945).

[68] Kohlenberger Engineering Corp., 12 LA 380, 384 (Prasow, 1949).

[69] See Arbitrator Grant in 21 LA 704, 706; Komaroff in 19 LA 138, 143; Blumer in 7 LA 512, 514; Blair in 5 LA 446, 448.

[70] Borden's Farm Products, Inc., 3 LA 401, 402-403 (Burke, 1945).

to modify its meaning by invoking the record of prior negotiations.[71]

The intent manifested by the parties during negotiations, rather than any undisclosed intent, is considered by arbitrators to be most important. If one party to negotiations is negligent or unreasonable in permitting the use of a term which does not clearly express the meaning intended by that party and if the other party is thus reasonably misled as to the first party's intentions, a contract may be held to exist in accordance with the second party's understanding.[72]

If a party attempts but fails, in contract negotiations, to include a specific provision in the agreement, an arbitrator will hesitate to read such provision into the agreement through the process of interpretation.[73] However, the withdrawal during contract negotiations of a proposed clause spelling out a right was held not to be an admission that the right did not exist without the clause, where the party had stated in withdrawing the proposal that it would stand firm on the position that the right existed even without the proposed clause.[74]

No Consideration to Compromise Offers

In the interpretation of an ambiguous agreement no consideration will be given to compromise offers or to concessions offered by one party and rejected by the other during negotiations which precede arbitration.[75] "[It] is clear that any offer made by either party during the course of conciliation cannot prejudice that party's case when the case comes to arbitration. It is the very essence of conciliation that compromise pro-

---

[71] See Arbitrator Cole in 18 LA 916, 918; Blair in 3 LA 753, 756; Whiting in 3 LA 482, 486. For further discussion see Chapter 10, topic titled "Parol Evidence".

[72] See Arbitrator Emery in 17 LA 632, 635; Merrill in 11 LA 25, 31; D. Wolff in 8 LA 452; Blair in 4 LA 110, 111; McCoy in 1 LA 165, 167. Also see Garrett in 15 LA 834, 838. Cf., Brandschain in 5 LA 164, 166; McCoy in 1 LA 556, 560.

[73] See Arbitrator Jaffee in 27 LA 126, 128; Reynard in 24 LA 224, 228; Reid in 21 LA 699, 702-703.

[74] Robertshaw-Fulton Controls Co., 21 LA 436, 439 (S. Wolff, 1953).

[75] See Arbitrator Garrett in 26 LA 812, 824; Prasow in 25 LA 398, 403-404; Gorder in 25 LA 202, 205; Davey in 20 LA 737, 742; O'Rourke in 10 LA 417, 419; Greene in 8 LA 993, 996; Elson in 2 LA 399, 402.

posals will go further than a party may consider itself bound to go on a strict interpretation of its rights." [76]

Experience and Training of Negotiators

Whether or not an arbitrator will apply a strict interpretation to an ambiguous agreement may to some extent depend upon the training and experience of the negotiators. If the arbitrator finds that the negotiators were laymen untrained in the precise use of words and if the contract on its face bears evidence of a lack of precision, he may refuse to apply a strict construction.[77] Under such circumstances the arbitrator might conclude that the writing "should be considered as a somewhat imperfect attempt to embody rules which were better understood than it was possible to express in words." [78]

A less liberal approach is likely to be taken if the arbitrator knows that the negotiators for both parties were experts in drafting collective agreements.[79] or, to state it another way, if the arbitrator believes that the negotiators were "capable and shrewd." [80]

In applying a strict interpretation to a contested provision, Umpire Harry Shulman emphasized that: "The negotiators were not tyros in the art. They were skilled hands who worked hard, intelligently, and alertly. The agreement was not negotiated in a hurry or under pressure. Careful scrutiny was given to the language after agreement was reached on the substance." [81]

Custom and Past Practice of the Parties

One of the most important standards used by arbitrators in the interpretation of ambiguous contract language is that

---

[76] Fulton-Sylphon Co., 8 LA 993, 996 (Greene, 1947).
[77] As in U. S. Pipe & Foundry Co., 5 LA 492, 494 (McCoy, 1946). Also see Arbitrator McCoy in 11 LA 556, 560.
[78] Moran Towing and Transportation Co., 1 ALAA ¶ 67,012, p. 67,015 (Kidd, 1944).
[79] See Arbitrator Morvant in 26 LA 526, 528; Anderson in 20 LA 910, 911; Margulies in 19 LA 683, 686; Lane in 8 LA 306, 308.
[80] Carnation Co., 3 LA 229, 232 (Updegraff, 1946). Also see Arbitrator Updegraff in 2 LA 469, 472.
[81] Ford Motor Company, 1 ALAA ¶ 67,126, p. 67,265 (1945).

of custom or past practice of the parties. For extensive discussion of this standard of interpretation the reader is directed to Chapter 12, topic titled "Role of Custom and Practice in Interpretation of Ambiguous Language".

Industry Practice

Reference to custom and practice of the industry in which the parties operate may shed light upon the intended meaning of an ambiguous provision.[82] An even stronger guide is supplied when the same agreement has been entered into by one employer with several unions or by one union with several employers. In this situation practice of any of the pairs of parties operating under the agreement may be taken as some indication of the intended meaning of the language used.[83]

Where past practice of the parties in the plant and industry practice differ, the plant practice will ordinarily govern.[84] However, if the industry practice is well established, while the plant practice is not adequately established, the arbitrator may follow the industry practice as the better guide.[85]

Custom and practice of an industry other than that in which the parties operate may be accorded little if any weight. A practice which may be necessary and reasonable in one industry might be meaningless or foolish in another industry.[86] Moreover, while evidence of industry custom will be permitted for the purpose of clarifying the meaning of an ambiguous contract, it must not be given weight where the contract is clear and unambiguous.[87]

Prior Settlements as Aid to Interpretation

Sometimes light is shed upon ambiguous provisions by prior settlements by the parties of grievances involving those

---

[82] See Arbitrator Hill in 11 LA 1081, 1082; Wallen in 6 LA 1017, 1022; Wagner in 6 LA 292, 293. See also Young in 21 LA 278, 282.
[83] See Arbitrator Marshall in 20 LA 297, 299; Sherbow in 17 LA 524, 526; McCoy in 1 ALAA ¶ 67,186. Also see Emery in 20 LA 458, 459-460.
[84] As in New York Seven Up Bottling Co., 24 LA 601, 603 (Cahn, 1955).
[85] As did Arbitrator Loucks in 24 LA 81, 84, 87-88; Maggs in 17 LA 451, 454.
[86] Certain-Teed Products Corp., 1 LA 354, 358 (Gorder, 1946).
[87] Western Union Tel. Co. v. American Communications Ass'n. C.I.O., 79 N.Y.S. 2d 545 (N.Y., 1949).

provisions. It has been suggested, in this regard, that "Where the parties themselves settle a grievance the evidence of intent as to the meaning of a provision carries special weight."[88] In effect, mutual settlements often constitute binding precedents for the parties.[89]

Similarly, even oral agreements of the parties as to the application of ambiguous language may subsequently be given significant weight by an arbitrator in interpreting that language if such oral agreements are clearly proven.[90]

If the agreement is not ambiguous, however, a past settlement which is inconsistent with the clear language of the agreement may be disregarded by an arbitrator in subsequent cases involving that language.[91]

Interpretation Against Party Selecting the Language

It is incumbent upon the proponent of a contract provision either to explain what is contemplated or to use language which does not leave the matter in doubt.[92] Where doubt exists, any ambiguity not removed by any other rule of interpretation may be removed by construing the ambiguous language against the party who proposed it.[93] It is reasoned that the draftsman, by exactness of expression, can more easily prevent doubts as to meaning.[94]

Courts of law, however, apply this rule only if a satisfactory result cannot be reached by any other rule of construction,[95] and it would seem that arbitrators should observe the same limitation.[96] Moreover, the rule will not be applied if

---

[88] Bendix-Westinghouse Automotive Air Brake Co., 23 LA 706, 710 (Mathews, 1954). Also see Arbitrator Emery in 19 LA 812, 814-815; Wallen in 17 LA 36, 39.
[89] For discussion of this role of grievance settlements, see Chapter 5, topic titled "Grievance Settlements as Binding Precedents".
[90] See Autocar Co., 19 LA 89, 92 (Jaffee, 1952).
[91] International Harvester Co., 19 LA 812, 815 (Emery, 1953).
[92] Timken-Detroit Axle Co., 21 LA 196, 198 (R. Smith, 1953). Also see Arbitrator Emery in 17 LA 632, 635.
[93] See Arbitrator R. Smith in 21 LA 196, 198; Healy in 11 LA 228, 233; Merrill in 11 LA 25, 32; D. Wolff in 8 LA 452, 458; Elson in 2 LA 399, 403.
[94] Brown & Sharpe Mfg. Co., 11 LA 228, 233 (Healy, 1948).
[95] For cases see 13 Corpus Juris 545, n. 44.
[96] The limitation was stated in Deep Rock Oil Corp., 11 LA 25, 32 (Merrill, 1948).

there is no ambiguity,[97] or if there are special reasons for refusal to apply it, as where the clause finally used differed substantially from the one originally prepared unilaterally and both parties approved the final draft.[98]

Further, it has been held that ambiguous language need not be interpreted against the party who proposed it where there is no showing that the other party was misled.[99]

Reason and Equity

It is widely recognized that if a contract "is clear and unambiguous it must be applied in accordance with its terms despite the equities that may be present on either side." [100] Arbitrators strive where possible, however, to give *ambiguous* language a construction which is reasonable and equitable to both parties rather than one which would give one party an unfair and unreasonable advantage.[101]

The arbitrator, it has been said, should "look at the language in the light of experience and choose that course which does the least violence to the judgment of a reasonable man." [102]

---

[97] John Deere Tractor Co., 2 LA 469, 472 (Updegraff, 1945).
[98] Crescent Warehouse Co., 10 LA 168, 171 (Aaron, 1948).
[99] International Harvester Co., 13 LA 133, 135 (McCoy, 1949).
[100] Firestone Tire & Rubber Co., 29 LA 469, 473 (Hebert, 1957). For other cases and discussion of this principle see Chapter 7, topic titled "Recommendations by Arbitrator".
[101] See Arbitrator Maggs in 17 LA 606, 609; Broadwin in 12 LA 478, 481; Stein in 11 LA 1019, 1020.
[102] Clifton Paper Board Co., 11 LA 1019, 1020 (Stein, 1949).

CHAPTER 10

USE OF SUBSTANTIVE RULES OF LAW

Extent of Use and Reasons Therefor

In agreeing to resolve disputes by arbitration, parties choose to substitute a private solution for litigation in courts of law. Unless the parties specifically limit the powers of the arbitrator in deciding various aspects of the issue submitted to him, it is presumed that they intend to make him the final judge on any questions which arise in the disposition of the case, including not only questions of fact but also questions of contract interpretation, rules of interpretation, and issues, if any, with respect to substantive law. In this connection, under the common law "it is ordinarily held that an award is not vitiated or rendered subject to impeachment merely because it is based upon, or has resulted from, a mistaken or erroneous view of the arbitrators as to the law or facts, or both." [1]

Since the appointment and authority of the arbitrator are under the control of the parties, however, they can provide in the submission agreement the extent to which his decision is to be final. Thus, for instance, they may provide that the award is to be final only with respect to limited areas, such as questions of fact,[2] or they may provide that it is to be final except in case of "gross mistake of law or fact." [3]

If the arbitration is carried out under a statute providing for judicial review, the award will have finality only to the

---

[1] 6 Corpus Juris Secundum, Arbitration And Award, § 105, p. 251, where many cases are cited. For related discussion, see Chapter 2, topic titled "Enforcement and Review of Awards".

[2] See submission in Food Employers Council Inc., 20 LA 724, 725 (Van de Water, 1953), which specifically made the award reviewable as to law by the courts.

[3] As in Goodyear Engineering Corp., 24 LA 360, 362 (Warns, 1955).

extent provided by the statute. Very few statutes, however, grant any right of review for mistake of law.[4] Such omission leaves more to the judgment of the arbitrator, but it does not mean that courts under the statute, or under the common law for that matter, are likely to honor any award which directs a party to commit an act or engage in conduct clearly prohibited by state or federal law.[5]

On the whole, relatively wide discretion is left to arbitrators to deal with the law according to their best judgment. The inquiry in this Chapter touches upon the extent to which arbitrators do in fact have recourse to substantive law and to decisions of courts and administrative agencies on questions similar to the one before the arbitrator.

The reader will observe that arbitrators do give consideration to "the law", but the extent of adherence thereto may vary considerably from case to case depending largely upon the source, form, and status of the legal rule or principle before the arbitrator. Thus, firm prohibitions contained in codified law will obviously be given greater weight by an arbitrator than general substantive law principles of agency, contracts, damages, and the like (although these will not be slighted). Clearly defined law will be given more consideration than unsettled and uncertain law. Decisions by courts of final jurisdiction normally carry more weight than those of lower courts. Then, too, the extent to which an arbitrator will consider any factor outside the collective agreement may depend upon the degree to which the parties have restricted his authority to the interpretation and application of the agreement.[6]

Frequently in arbitration cases, just as in litigated matters, there is one primary legal basis for the decision, such as a rule of agency, or a principle of waiver or estoppel, or some other

---

[4] See Chapter 2, topic titled "Enforcement and Review of Awards". Also see Justin, "Arbitration: Proving Your Case," 10 LA 955, 967 (1948).

[5] See Sturges, Commercial Arbitrations and Awards § 61, p. 202 (1930). Also see Cox, "The Place of Law in Labor Arbitration," The Profession of Labor Arbitration 76, 78-79 (BNA Incorporated, 1957).

[6] See discussion by Cox, "The Place of Law in Labor Arbitration," The Profession of Labor Arbitration 76, 80-83 (BNA Incorporated, 1957).

rule of law. It is true that arbitrators do not often cite legal decisions, but they do take cognizance—in essence judicial notice—of the legal principle concerning the issue under consideration. In the informality of arbitration it seems natural for arbitrators to state such principles without deeming it necessary to cite specific authority in support thereof.

It should be apparent from the materials contained in the remainder of this Chapter that parties preparing cases for arbitration, and indeed parties concerned with the initial negotiation of collective agreements, should take into consideration pertinent laws, legal principles, and court and administrative rulings.

The authors do not propose to show in this Chapter every situation in which arbitrators have observed or deviated from "the law". Rather, the objective will be to examine the views and practice of arbitrators in sufficient instances to indicate generally what may be expected.

Sometimes the arbitrator will expressly state a determination to adhere to legal principles. For instance, Arbitrator George Cheney has stated that: "If the arbitration process is to serve a just and useful purpose, it cannot exist outside of the framework of the law." [7]

Arbitrator Arvid Anderson has declared: "I do not have authority to knowingly make a decision which is in direct conflict with statutes and court decisions dealing with the same subject." [8] And Arbitrator Harry H. Platt has emphasized: "This Arbitrator is bound by the law as much as any court * * *". [9]

A statement which is believed to be somewhat typical of the outlook of many arbitrators is that of Arbitrator Albert K. Whitton:

"The collective bargaining process implies a system of industrial jurisprudence operating within a framework of substantive and procedural

---

[7] Andrew Williams Meat Co., 8 LA 518, 525-526 (1947).
[8] Hillside Transit Co., 22 LA 470, 473 (1954).
[9] Bond Clothes, Inc., 7 LA 708, 712 (1947).

rules of law. The parties are bound to observe the sanctity of contracts, to deal fairly and frankly with one another, and are subject to all applicable statutes and principles of common law. The arbitrator is the court of last resort in the process and should follow generally accepted procedural rules in arriving at his decision." [10]

On the other hand, arbitrators sometimes have refused to be bound by judicial decisions involving similar or related questions arising at law. In one case, for instance, Arbitrator William E. Simkin noted the employer's argument that employees participating in an illegal strike could be lawfully discharged; he also noted that the employer had cited a substantial number of N.L.R.B. and court decisions arising under the National Labor Relations Act. In refusing to be bound by such decisions, Arbitrator Simkin explained:

"It would be possible to uphold this position if I should take the narrow view that I have been retained to arbitrate this case solely as a substitute for legal proceedings under the National Labor Relations Act. But to my knowledge there was never any thought by either party of proceeding in this case under the National Labor Relations Act. This is a case arising not under the law but out of the relationship between the parties under a collective bargaining agreement. * * * Furthermore, the parties had foreknowledge that I am not a lawyer and in fact have had no legal training as such. It is not likely that the parties would knowingly choose a non-lawyer to handle a case solely on the legal issues involved and primarily to apply N.L.R.B. and Court decisions." [11]

Even where the parties had provided, in submitting discharges to arbitration, that the arbitrators "shall consider the standards of strike misconduct as contained in adjudications under the National Labor Relations Act", Arbitrators Alexander, McCoy, Schedler, and Whiting declared that while the word "shall" required them to give decisions under said Act

---

[10] American Optical Co., 4 LA 288, 292 (1946). For a similar statement see Arbitrator Abernethy in 8 LA 62, 65. The National War Labor Board of World War II invoked established legal doctrine even though its orders were not reviewable. Freidin & Ulman, "Arbitration and The National War Labor Board," 58 Harv. L. Rev. 309, 319 (1945).

[11] Blue Swan Mills (Allentown, Pa.), 3 ALAA ¶ 68,192, at p. 70,162 (1949). Also see Arbitrator Jaffee in 27 LA 844, 850; Warns in 27 LA 179, 181; Bowles in 24 LA 761, 764; Cole in 24 LA 332, 335; Smith v. Hillerich & Bradsby Co., 19 LA 745, 746 (Ky. Ct. App., 1952).

"considerable weight" it did not require them "to follow any of such decisions blindly." [12]

Statutory Law

Sometimes the arbitrator is specifically authorized by the submission to determine the validity of a contract provision under statutory law.[13] Even without such specific direction, however, it is highly unlikely that an award will be rendered which would result in the violation of a pertinent statute. Illegality of claims is reason for their rejection.[14] Arbitrator Hyman Parker has declared in this regard that "all agreements are made subject to the applicable provisions of Federal or State laws, and the parties must be presumed to have intended an agreement which is not in violation of any law." [15]

Arbitrator Thomas P. Whelan has held that regulations under the National Security Act are as a matter of public policy superimposed upon the collective agreement when the employer enters into a "security agreement" with the Department of Defense, and they take precedence over any provisions of the collective agreement that conflict with them.[16] In a similar note, Arbitrator David L. Cole has explained that "in any conflict between a collective bargain agreement and the law with reference to the rights of a returning veteran, it has repeatedly been held that the law must prevail." [17]

Arbitrator Byron R. Abernethy has emphasized that if compliance with a contractual provision would place one party in violation of the National Labor Relations Act, then compliance may neither be expected by the other party nor directed

---

[12] Southern Bell Telephone & Telegraph Co., 25 LA 85, 86-87 (1955).

[13] As in Morton Salt Co., 21 LA 797, 805 (Hale, 1953).

[14] For a related discussion, see Chapter 9, topic titled "Interpretation in Light of the Law".

[15] Hancock Steel Co., 23 LA 44, 47 (1954). Also see Arbitrator Anderson in 22 LA 470, 473; Emery in 17 LA 349, 351.

[16] Wisconsin Telephone Co., 26 LA 792, 806 (1956). Also see Arbitrator Warns in 24 LA 360, 364.

[17] International Harvester Co., 22 LA 583, 585 (1954).

by an arbitrator.[18] Similarly, a past practice of the parties was not enforced by an arbitrator since the practice had been "rendered impracticable and legally unworkable" by the Fair Labor Standards Act and the Walsh-Healey Act.[19]

In another case the claim of a union as to overtime was disallowed because its allowance would have resulted in a clear violation of the Wage Stabilization Act.[20] Indeed, in times of wage stabilization arbitrators have generally taken steps to avoid transgression upon wage stabilization legislation.[21] Arbitrator Joseph Rosenfarb, however, emphasized that while wage stabilization regulations should be taken into account in determining wage adjustments, the influence of wage stabilization on an arbitrator's decision should vary "in direct ratio to the certainty, clarity and stage of its evolution." [22]

Where an employer alleged that the performance of a contractual obligation to serve beer to employees would result in a violation of state law, the parties were ordered to make inquiry of the state alcoholic beverage commission as to the legality of the contractual provision. The arbitrator was of the opinion that the employer had an obligation to perform the requirement only if it could be done without violating the law.[23]

In another case, the seniority rights of women who were taken off jobs requiring eight hours' continous work were held not to have been violated although men with less seniority continued to work on continuous operation jobs, where state law prohibited the working of women for more than five hours without a rest period and the employer had good

---

[18] F. H. Hill Co., 8 LA 62, 64 (1947). Also see Arbitrator Anderson in 22 LA 470, 472-473; Copelof in 21 LA 535, 546; Appleby in 21 LA 646, 648-650; Davis in 20 LA 575, 578-579; McCoy in 2 LA 545, 548.

[19] Youngstown Sheet and Tube Co., 14 LA 752, 756 (Updegraff, 1950). Cf., Seward in 17 LA 29, 30; Marshall in 16 LA 335, 337.

[20] Monsanto Chemical Company, 1 ALAA ¶ 67,089 (1944).

[21] See, for instance, Arbitrator Donnelly in 17 LA 748, 750-751; Warren in 17 LA 353, 354, 361; Lesser in 16 LA 881, 882; Justin in 16 LA 399, 404. Also see Rose in 19 LA 303, 306. For related discussion see Chapter 16, topic titled "Governmental Wage Stabilization."

[22] Merchants Bank of New York, 16 LA 901, 904 (1951).

[23] Terre Haute Brewing Co., 10 LA 487, 489-490 (Hampton, 1948).

reasons for placing the jobs in question on continuous operation. [24]

In general, the courts can be expected to hold any award invalid which the court believes would, if carried out, result in the violation of a penal law. For instance, an award holding that employees of a telegraph company had the right to refuse to handle messages going to or coming from international companies whose employees were on strike was held to be invalid because it sanctioned the violation of a New York penal law making it a crime for employees of a telegraph company to wilfully delay or refuse to transmit or deliver messages.[25]

An arbitrator may be inclined to apply this principle in spite of any contention that the statute in question is unconstitutional. Note, for instance, the view of Arbitrator Clarence M. Updegraff:

> "No award of this board can give validity to any contract which contravenes the law of any state. If it is indeed true that the Kansas law is ineffective because unconstitutional, that result has not yet been authoritatively declared by a court of last resort. The act must be assumed effective until otherwise determined." [26]

Arbitrator Updegraff accordingly assumed the statute and the city ordinance involved in that case to be valid and constitutional.

It has been held that if a collective agreement specifically adopts one of two alternative courses of action permitted by a statute, the agreement does not conflict with the statute but simply limits the parties to one of two possibilities under the law.[27]

Even where a given statute does not cover the parties, or where it permits variations through the collective agreement,

---

[24] Republic Steel Corp., 24 LA 288, 289 (Platt, 1955).

[25] In re Western Union Telegraph Co., 10 LA 923, 924 (N.Y. Sup. Ct., 1948), affirmed, 86 N.E. 2d 162 (N.Y. Ct. App., 1949), 12 LA 516, 519-520. See discussion of this case in Cox, "The Place of Law in Labor Arbitration," The Profession of Labor Arbitration 76, 87-89 (BNA Incorporated, 1957).

[26] Kansas City Public Service Co., 8 LA 149, 159 (1947).

[27] Wilson and Company, Inc., 1 LA 367, 378 (Lohman, date not given).

the statute may be used as a guide if the parties' agreement contains no method of determining the issue.[28]

In some cases arbitrators, especially where restricted in authority to application of the collective agreement, have been unwilling to rule upon claims based upon law rather than the agreement.[29] Thus, Arbitrator Ralph T. Seward considered it "clearly beyond his jurisdiction to decide" claims for voting-time pay to the extent that they were based upon state law rather than upon the collective agreement.[30]

Then, too, where a claim was based upon the collective agreement but the opposing party contended that the claim should be decided on the basis of a statute, Arbitrator Seward considered that he was authorized only to "interpret and apply the Agreement and the Agreement alone," and he refused "to base his decisions on federal or state laws, on governmental rulings or court judgments."[31]

However, if the arbitrator acknowledges or finds no such restriction upon his authority, or if he takes the view that all agreements are made subject to applicable federal and state laws, he will likely make an extensive study of legal rulings on the question before him if it directly involves the application of statutory law and the scope of rights thereunder.[32]

Indeed, Arbitrator Aaron Horvitz has observed that if the case directly involves the application of a statute, the role of the arbitrator is somewhat different:

"What we are concerned with, therefore, is the application of a statute. To this extent then, my role is not strictly the normal arbitral one of interpreting and applying the provisions of a voluntary agreement between the parties, the determination of which is conclusive. Here a statute is

[28] See, for example, Arbitrator Aaron in 22 LA 249, 250-251; Ralston in 21 LA 381, 385; Myers in 7 LA 1, 2. Also see Broach in 15 LA 861, 862.

[29] For instance, see Arbitrator Shister in 24 LA 786, 787; Donnelly in 23 LA 655, 656; Seward in 23 LA 606, 607.

[30] Allegheny Ludlum Steel Corp., 23 LA 606, 607 (1954).

[31] International Harvester Co., 17 LA 29, 30 (1951). Also see Marshall in 16 LA 335, 337.

[32] See, for instance, Arbitrator Garrett in 25 LA 778, 782-785; Justin in 23 LA 113, 119-124; J. K. Mann in 22 LA 738, 744-750; Hale in 21 LA 797, 811-813; Doyle in 19 LA 111, 112, 120-122.

controlling and I must interpret and apply the provisions of a legislative enactment. While therefore acutely aware of my inherent powers to decide this case on the facts before me and not be bound to follow precedents, if they exist, I feel that prior rulings, if sound and if applicable, are entitled to serious consideration." [33]

In this case Arbitrator Horvitz, in construing and applying a Railway Labor Act provision, discussed and relied upon decisions construing a similar provision in the Taft-Hartley Act.

The fact that the legality of a contract clause was at issue in a proceeding before the National Labor Relations Board did not deter the Connecticut State Board of Mediation and Arbitration from deciding a dispute involving the same clause:

"While the Board recognizes that the validity of the union security clause in this contract must be determined by the NLRB, it can not agree with the Company's suggestion that this matter is not arbitrable because a related case is pending before the NLRB. This arbitration Board's responsibility is to decide a dispute over the proper application of a clause in an existing labor contract. That decision can not properly be withheld pending outcome of the NLRB proceedings, for to so hold would be to set the stage for a possible frustration of the entire collective bargaining relationship. Obviously, an arbitration board would render an extremely vulnerable award if it ordered either party to act contrary to law, but this clause has not been declared illegal, nor can we know whether such might be the outcome of the NLRB cases. Meanwhile, we have a duly processed dispute before this Board over contract interpretation, and the Board sees no basis for declaring the matter non-arbitrable." [34]

In another situation Arbitrator George E. Bowles confined his attention to contract interpretation in ruling upon the obligation of the company to pay union representatives for time spent in negotiations, but he emphasized that his award did not constitute a ruling on any question of law and that it was "subject to any applicable ruling by the National Labor

---

[33] New York Central Railroad, 20 LA 318, 320 (1953). Also see Leary in 23 LA 234, 241; Justin in 23 LA 113, 119-124; Horvitz in 20 LA 312, 313; Barrett in 17 LA 53, 54-56.

[34] Marlin Rockwell Corp., 22 LA 651, 652 (Stutz, Mottram & Curry, 1954). In general accord, Kaplan in 22 LA 201, 207; Updegraff, Klamon & Raymond in 19 LA 609, 611-612. Also see Gamser in 26 LA 428, 430; Pierson in 24 LA 314, 316-317.

Relations Board or a court of law as to legality of any such payments."[35]

Arbitrator E. E. Hale likewise confined his attention to the interpretation of the contract provision before him where he believed the submission did not authorize him to determine whether the provision conflicted with state or federal law. The parties thereupon executed an additional submission specifically authorizing him to determine whether the provision was "null and void as being in conflict with any law of the State of Texas or of the United States," and, if so, "to determine what remedy" should be awarded. Arbitrator Hale thereupon conducted a second hearing centering upon the legality of the provision; he concluded that it was illegal both under state law and under the National Labor Relations Act and he ordered the provision stricken from the agreement.[36]

It may be noted that even when a dispute involves some unfair labor practice aspect, the National Labor Relations Board may refuse jurisdiction if an arbitrator has issued an award thereon. The Board has refused jurisdiction, for instance, where the prior arbitration proceedings appeared to have been fair and regular, all parties had agreed to be bound, and the award was not clearly repugnant to the purposes and policies of the Act; the Board stated that in these circumstances the desirable objective of encouraging the voluntary settlement of labor disputes would best be served by the Board's recognition of the award.[37]

Court Decisions

An arbitrator's willingness to follow judicial precedents on a question will depend to a large extent upon the level of the court rendering the decision and upon the unanimity of other decisions on the point. Arbitrators naturally feel con-

---

[35] Douglas & Lomason Co., 23 LA 812, 814 (1954). Also see Arbitrator Willcox in 23 LA 21, 26.

[36] Morton Salt Co., 21 LA 797, 804-805, 813-814 (1953).

[37] Spielberg Mfg Co., 112 NLRB 1080, 1082 (1955), which cites several instances, however, in which the Board has disregarded arbitration awards.

strained to follow decisions of courts of last resort. When the
United States Supreme Court or the highest tribunal of the
state in which the parties operate has ruled on a point, it is
unlikely that an arbitrator will accept any view which conflicts with such ruling.[38]

On the other hand, if an arbitrator does not agree with a
decision handed down by a court other than one of last resort
he may refuse to follow it. Where one arbitrator, for instance,
felt that an opinion by a federal district court was contrary
to all accepted rules of statutory construction, he refused to
follow it, declaring that since it was not a decision of a court
of last resort he was not bound thereby.[39]

Moreover, arbitrators are less likely to honor conflicting
lower court decisions. Thus, where two federal district courts
had ruled one way and two others had ruled otherwise, an
arbitrator declared that the parties were without the benefit
of authoritative judicial decisions, and he decided the issue
without reliance upon any of the precedents.[40]

Administrative Rulings

The weight to be given by arbitrators to rulings of administrative and executive agencies of the government may be
determined by a variety of factors, the most important of
which is the authority of the agency making the ruling. For
instance, rulings and regulations of wage stabilization agencies
are likely to be given serious consideration, prevailing over a
conflicting collective agreement provision[41] and over bulletins
of other government agencies or officials.[42]

---

[38] See Arbitrator Cole in 22 LA 583, 584; Anderson in 22 LA 470, 472; Seward
in 16 LA 376; Kallenbach in 6 LA 736, 741.
[39] Dow Chemical Co., 1 LA 70, 74-75 (Whiting, 1945). Also see Seering in 22
LA 108, 110.
[40] Bell Aircraft Corp., 2 LA 22, 24 (Sharkey, 1946). Later one of the conflicting
views was adopted by the Court of Appeals, so that view was subsequently followed by
Arbitrator McCoy in 2 LA 217, 220. Regarding conflicting court decisions, also see
Arbitrator Sanders in 21 LA 180, 181.
[41] As in Libby, McNeill & Libby, 5 LA 564, 569 (Prasow, 1946). See also
Chapter 16, topic titled "Governmental Wage Stabilization".
[42] As in Peabody Coal Co., 5 LA 18, 23 (Fries, 1946).

While administrative opinions by the Bureau of Veterans Reemployment Rights have been given weight by some arbitrators,[43] another arbitrator gave no weight to advice from the Bureau to an employer, the arbitrator emphasizing that the Bureau's only function is to "render aid" to former servicemen.[44]

Official interpretations by executive departments of the government are given significant weight where relevant. Thus, arbitrators have respected rulings by the Assistant United States Attorney General regarding the scope of provisions of the Taft-Hartley Act,[45] and an interpretation by the United States Department of Labor of an executive order.[46]

Indeed, executive and administrative rulings or interpretations in cases similar to the one being considered by the arbitrator may be relied upon as persuasive, though not controlling, even though the Act to which the ruling applies does not cover the parties before the arbitrator. For instance, the interpretation that had been given the word "day" by officials enforcing the Walsh-Healey Act was persuasive upon an arbitrator in a subsequent case not covered by that Act.[47]

An interesting view regarding the weight to be given to administrative rulings was expressed by Arbitrator L. F. Sharkey in considering an interpretation of the Selective Service Act made by the Director of Selective Service:

"The interpretation of an administrative agency is entitled to weight, but it is not decisive especially when it is a newly formulated one and one not long in effect, one on which the actions of men have not been based over a long period of time. In this instance, the opinion of the Director is one man's opinion entitled to respect. It may be persuasive, but it is not con-

---

[43] See Arbitrator Parker in 23 LA 44, 45; Sanders in 21 LA 180, 181-182. Also see Garrett in 25 LA 778, 781-782.

[44] Archer-Daniels-Midland Co., 26 LA 561, 564 (Lindquist, 1955).

[45] See Arbitrator Boles in 23 LA 93, 97-98; Barrett in 17 LA 53, 55; Komaroff in 11 LA 395, 397.

[46] Warren Foundry & Pipe Corp., 5 LA 282, 283 (Tischler, 1946).

[47] Corn Products Refining Co., 7 LA 125, 131-132 (Updegraff, 1947). Also see Gager Lime Mfg. Co., 1 ALAA ¶ 67,181 (1942).

trolling. It has not the authority of law. It has not the power to change the provisions of a statute or a contract." [48]

Arbitrator Sharkey thereupon declared that the interpretation of the Director had raised doubts in the minds of honest men and he refused to rely upon it.

Agency Principles

Arbitrators place strong reliance upon the generally recognized principles of agency. Thus, parties are held responsible for the acts of their authorized agents.[49] For instance, the employer has been required to compensate an employee for lost earnings due to the erroneous diagnosis by the employer's doctor of the employee's condition.[50]

A union which authorized its Vice-President to settle a grievance was held bound by the settlement even though it was rejected by the union membership when submitted for their approval.[51] Commitments made by past union officials have bound their successors.[52]

Moreover, while an arbitrator will not hold a party bound by an act of another unless the act was antecedently authorized or subsequently ratified by the former, ratification may be implied by silence after knowledge of the unauthorized act[53] or by actual operation under an unauthorized agreement.[54]

Arbitrators have often been strict in requiring a showing of authorization or ratification by the union membership of any action of a union committee which changes the terms of the collective agreement. "To hold otherwise would mean that a local Union committee meeting with management could dis-

---

[48] Bell Aircraft Corp., 2 LA 22, 24 (1946). Also see Arbitrator Lindquist in 26 LA 561, 564.

[49] See Bethlehem Steel Co., 26 LA 646, 647 (Seward, 1956).

[50] Arbitrator Bothwell in 27 LA 404, 406-407; Bowles in 26 LA 370, 373; Anderson in 24 LA 756, 758-759.

[51] Kendall Cotton Mills, 24 LA 684, 687-688 (Dworet, 1955).

[52] General Aniline & Film Corp., 25 LA 50, 53 (Shister, 1955).

[53] Pacific American Shipowners Assn., 10 LA 736, 746 (Miller, 1948). Also see Cox in 28 LA 677, 690.

[54] Lafe Pharmacy, 1 ALAA ¶ 67,469 (1946).

sipate the contractual benefits of its membership without its approval." [55]

The Connecticut State Board of Mediation and Arbitration has held that, in view of the customary procedure of collective bargaining by which all matters of high importance, such as annual wage increases, must be submitted to the membership for final approval, a presumption exists against the validity of action taken by a union committee in respect to these matters until proof of authority or ratification is shown.[56]

Likewise, a shop steward has no authority to bind the union by an agreement altering or creating an exception to the collective agreement, nor has he authority to waive strict performance of the agreement.[57] Nor does a union field representative have authority to change the collective agreement unless such authority is clearly vested in him by the membership.[58]

Such a strict rule, however, would not apply to an action taken in grievance settlements which does not have the effect of changing the terms of the agreement.[59] Moreover, an oral agreement between the company and a union President was held binding though it involved deviation from the seniority provisions of the collective agreement since he had made numerous such agreements in the past without objection from the union.[60]

The basic rule of required authorization likewise applies to management representatives, who accordingly can act only within their authority.[61] Thus, an employer was held not bound by an agreement reached between the plant superin-

[55] Flintkote Co., 9 LA 976, 977 (Naggi, 1948). In accord with the general proposition, Arbitrator Thompson in 23 LA 89, 91; Platt in 12 LA 161, 164, and in 11 LA 805, 808; Donnelly, Curry & Clark in 10 LA 55. Cf., Anrod in 29 LA 848, 852-854; Warns in 28 LA 424, 427-428 (dealing particularly with the authority of the union to change "individual" rights).

[56] Russell Mfg. Co., 10 LA 55 (Donnelly, Curry & Clark, 1948).

[57] Pacific Mills, 2 LA 545, 548 (McCoy, 1946). Also, Ryder in 25 LA 83, 84.

[58] McLouth Steel Corp., 11 LA 805, 808 (Platt, 1948).

[59] Jarecki Machine & Tool Co., 12 LA 161, 164 (Platt, 1949).

[60] Lockheed Aircraft Corp., 23 LA 815, 820-821 (Marshall, 1955).

[61] See, for instance, Simmons Co., 25 LA 426, 429 (Daugherty, 1955).

tendent and the union committee where both the committee and the superintendent knew that it was subject to the approval—never received—of company officials.[62]

An arbitrator will hold a party bound by the act of its agent, though unauthorized, if the party is found to have clothed the agent with "apparent" or "ostensible" authority to act.[63] For instance, a company was so bound where it held out an employers association as its agent by permitting one of its officers to sit on the association's bargaining committee without disclosing an intent not to be bound by the agreement being negotiated on behalf of the association's members.[64]

The rule that knowledge of an agent is imputed to the principal has been applied by arbitrators. Knowledge held by a union regarding the existence and nature of a grievance settlement may be charged to the employee affected, and the employer relieved from making good any loss suffered by the employee as a result of the union's failure to notify him of the settlement.[65]

Knowledge held by a management representative may be imputed to the employer.[66] Knowledge of a union agent may be charged to the union, but that of individual union members generally will not be charged to the union, for the members of a union are not necessarily its agents.[67]

Contract Principles

Arbitrators may be expected to recognize fundamental principles of contract law, such as those concerning the need for consideration to produce a binding contract,[68] those con-

---

[62] Kempsmith Machine Co., 5 LA 520, 530 (Marshall, 1946).

[63] See Arbitrator Anrod in 29 LA 848, 852-853; Cox in 28 LA 677, 690; Marshall in 23 LA 815, 820-821; Myers in 16 LA 584, 585.

[64] Pope and Talbot, Inc., 1 ALAA ¶ 67,157, p. 67,324 (1942).

[65] Ford Motor Co., 1 LA 409, 410 (Shulman, 1945). Also see Warns in 27 LA 179, 182.

[66] Pope and Talbot, Inc., 1 ALAA ¶ 67,157 (1942).

[67] Boys & Mens' Shop, 8 LA 214, 217-218 (Rosenfarb, 1947).

[68] See United Drill & Tool Corp., 28 LA 677, 685-686 (Cox, 1957).

cerning offer and acceptance,[69] and those concerning the obligation to perform contractual commitments, in spite of hardship.[70]

The principle that there can be no binding contract without a meeting of the minds has been applied by arbitrators.[71] Where the arbitrator finds that there has been no meeting of the minds on a matter he will often recommend further negotiations by the parties,[72] unless the parties have not prohibited him from adding to the collective agreement and his authority is broad enough to empower him to decide the dispute on the merits.[73]

Remedies for Mistake

The remedy of reformation to correct a mutual mistake in a contract is well established at law, and has been recognized by arbitrators.[74] In fact, a reformation may be granted even where the evidence falls short of what a court of equity would require for contractual reformation if upon consideration of all the evidence the arbitrator is persuaded that fairness and justice, even though not strictly "equity" as it is administered in the courts, requires this kind of relief.[75]

However, arbitrators, like courts, will grant relief only in case of *mutual* mistake; unilateral errors are not sufficient.[76]

The common prohibition against adding to, subtracting from, or modifying the terms of the agreement by the arbi-

---

[69] See General Cable Corp., 20 LA 406, 408 (Hays, 1953).

[70] See American Iron & Machine Works Co., 18 LA 285, 287 (Horton, 1952).

[71] See Arbitrator Johannes in 20 LA 362, 363; Garman in 20 LA 199, 201-202; Brandschain in 9 LA 239, 241; Copelof in 8 LA 475, 478, and 7 LA 507, 510; McCoy in 1 LA 556, 560.

[72] As in some of the cases cited in the previous note. Also, Arbitrator Brandschain in 4 LA 759, 765. For related discussion and other cases see Chapter 9, topic titled "Ambiguity"; Chapter 7, topic titled "Recommendations by Arbitrator".

[73] See Arbitrator Beatty in 24 LA 424, 425; Ryder in 22 LA 769, 771; Wallen in 6 LA 286, 288; Rice in 8 LA 586, 589.

[74] For instance, see Patterson-Sargent Co., 23 LA 21, 24 (Willcox, 1954). Also see statements by Arbitrator Compton in 27 LA 829, 830-831; Duff in 25 LA 534, 536; Tilford in 20 LA 446, 447; Emery in 17 LA 632, 635; Forrester in 17 LA 592, 594.

[75] See Huntsville Mfg. Co., 6 LA 515, 516-517 (McCoy, 1947).

[76] See Arbitrator Howlett in 29 LA 495, 500; Bowles in 23 LA 746, 749; Platt in 7 LA 708, 711-712; McCoy in 3 LA 257, 259.

trator would seem to provide special justification for the refusal to grant a reformation solely on the basis of unilateral mistake. Moreover, this same prohibition dictates against the setting aside of the terms of an agreement merely because its operation has not been up to the expectations of one of the parties or because, at the time of signing the agreement, the full implications of its provisions may not have been realized by one of the parties.[77]

Like reformation of contract, the remedy of rescission for mistake is ordinarily available only under limited circumstances. In particular, a unilateral mistake is not sufficient basis for rescission unless the mistake was basic and the other party knew and took advantage of it.[78]

Another type of "mistake" situation that has arisen in arbitration has involved the payment of money. In one case, for instance, employees recovered sums which their employer owed them but had mistakenly failed to pay.[79] But in another case the employer was denied recovery of payments to his employees which were not required by the collective agreement but which were made as a result of his "mistake of law" with full knowledge of all the facts.[80]

Waiver and Estoppel

Frequently one party to a collective agreement will charge that the other party has waived or is estopped from asserting a right under the agreement. Arbitrators do not appear to be concerned with all of the fine legal distinctions between the term "waiver" and the term "estoppel," but they have frequently applied the underlying principle.

---

[77] For cases see Chapter 9, topic titled "Language Which Is Clear and Unambiguous".

[78] For a thorough discussion of mistake as a basis for rescission see Arbitrator Archibald Cox in United Drill & Tool Corp., 28 LA 677, 687-689 (1957), and Arbitrator Douglas B. Maggs in Glendale Mfg. Co., 28 LA 298, 300-301 (1957). Also see Forrester in 17 LA 592, 594; Townsend in 17 LA 472, 478.

[79] A. D. Julliard & Co., 20 LA 579, 582-583 (Maggs, 1953).

[80] Milwaukee Linen Supply Co., 23 LA 392, 394 (Anderson, 1954), containing a general discussion of the law concerning the right to recover money paid by mistake.

Especially common in arbitration is that species of waiver known in law as "acquiescence." This term denotes a waiver which arises by tacit consent or by failure of a person for an unreasonable length of time to act upon rights of which he has full knowledge.

Arbitrators have frequently held that where one party, with actual or constructive knowledge of his rights, stands by and offers no protest with respect to the conduct of the other, thereby reasonably inducing the latter to believe that his conduct is fully concurred in, the matter will be treated as closed insofar as it relates to past transactions. But repeated violations of an express rule by one party or acquiescence on the part of the other ordinarily will not affect application of the rule in future operations.[81]

One arbitrator has held that the failure to enforce a right does not constitute a waiver unless the other party is misled to his prejudice, damage, or injury, or unless other elements of estoppel are present.[82] While many arbitrators do not appear to require such a strong showing, most do adhere to fairly strict minimum standards: Clear evidence will be required;[83] only one with authority to waive provisions of an agreement may do so;[84] the waiver of one provision, standing alone, will not be held to constitute the waiver of another.[85]

Sometimes arbitrators decide issues specifically on the basis of estoppel.[86] For instance, where a company gave an oral

---

[81] See Arbitrator Emery in 17 LA 90, 91; Maggs in 12 LA 311, 316; Douglas in 10 LA 562, 563; Courshon in 9 LA 484, 490-491; D. Wolff in 5 LA 333, 336; McCoy in 4 LA 231, 233. Also see Morvant in 24 LA 750, 752, and cases cited in Chapter 12, topic titled "Custom and Practice vs. Clear Contract Language". Very strong proof is required to establish amendment of the contract by custom. See Chapter 12, subtopic titled "Amendment of Contract".

[82] Allis-Chalmers Mfg. Co., 8 LA 945, 947 (Gorder, 1947). Accord, Somers in 24 LA 324, 327.

[83] Mosaic Tile Co., 13 LA 949, 950 (Cornsweet, 1950); Super-Cold Corp., 8 LA 187, 188 (Cheney, 1947).

[84] Republic Steel Corp., 5 LA 609, 618 (McCoy, 1946), and McCoy in 2 LA 545, 548.

[85] Stearms Coal and Lumber Co., 1 LA 274, 276 (Dwyer, 1946).

[86] See Arbitrator Reid in 21 LA 199, 203; Cahn in 20 LA 130, 136; Forrester in 18 LA 306, 307; Klamon in 17 LA 654, 661; Emery in 17 LA 632, 635; McCoy in 17 LA 101, 103, and in 16 LA 240, 241.

assurance on a matter during contract negotiations to induce the union to agree on a contract and end a strike, Arbitrator Whitley P. McCoy held that an estoppel had been created against the company since the union had changed its position, suffering detriment, in reliance upon the assurance. Accordingly, the company was held bound by the oral assurance, which limited the number of employees the company could reclassify under a provision of the contract.[87]

Sometimes, too, arbitrators decide issues essentially on the basis of estoppel without so stating specifically and without requiring as clear a showing of the elements of estoppel as might be required by a court of law.[88] In the latter type of cases emphasis is often placed upon equity, something like a "fair and just result" standard being applied.

An approach similar to the "election" principle of equity courts, limiting a party to the exercise of only one of two inconsistent or alternate rights, has been followed by Arbitrator David A. Wolff in not permitting a party to assume the position of "having his cake and eating it too."[89]

Principles of Damages

In empowering the arbitrator to resolve their dispute, the parties generally are considered to have clothed him with authority to grant adequate relief where he finds that the grievance has merit. In this regard, Arbitrator W. Willard Wirtz has emphasized that arbitrators have authority to award money damages for contract violations even though the contract does not specifically provide such remedy. To restrict arbitrators to remedies specifically set forth in the contract would negate arbitration as a method of dispute settlement or would result in cluttering contracts with numerous liquidated

---

[87] International Harvester Co., 17 LA 101, 103 (1951). To similar effect, Forrester in 18 LA 306, 307.

[88] See Arbitrator Klamon in 21 LA 300, 305; Hays in 20 LA 406, 408; Luskin in 16 LA 237, 238; Miller in 10 LA 736, 746; Rosenfarb in 8 LA 214, 217; Blair in 4 LA 110, 111.

[89] Chrysler Corp., 6 LA 369, 372 (1947). Also see Arbitrator Cahn in 22 LA 270, 272-273.

damages provisions which would invite more trouble than they could prevent.[90]

Monetary damages in arbitration should "normally correspond to specific monetary losses suffered." [91] Arbitrator Ralph T. Seward has explained: "The ordinary rule at common law and in the developing law of labor relations is that an award of damages should be limited to the amount necessary to make the injured party 'whole.' Unless the agreement provides that some other rule should be followed, this rule must apply." [92] Thus, Arbitrator Maurice S. Trotta has required a showing of injury to justify damages and where the existence of any such injury was too speculative Arbitrator Trotta refused to award damages.[93]

Even though a party is found to have violated the agreement, the arbitrator may be expected to refuse to award any penalty which would in essence be an award of punitive damages, unless, under the circumstances of the case, punitive damages are clearly justified. For instance, where the company violated the agreement but no employee suffered any financial loss from the violation the arbitrator refused the union's demand that a penalty of $500 payable to a charity be imposed against the company.[94]

An employer who violated the agreement by effecting a brief shutdown without consulting the union was not required to grant back pay for the shutdown period, since he acted in the belief that the clause did not apply and the clause merely required him to discuss his plans with the union. Arbitrator Philip E. Marshall said that a back-pay award under these circumstances would be punitive and out of line with the nature

---

[90] International Harvester Co., 9 LA 894, 896 (1947). In accord, see Arbitrator Reynard in 27 LA 625, 628; Willcox in 23 LA 21, 23; Louisell in 21 LA 254, 259; Emery in 17 LA 721, 722-723, and in 17 LA 349, 352. Also see Laskin in 18 LA 925, 926; S. Wolff in 15 LA 822, 827.

[91] Patterson-Sargent Co., 23 LA 21, 23 (Willcox, 1954). Also see Laskin in 18 LA 925, 926; Emery in 17 LA 721, 723.

[92] International Harvester Co., 15 LA 1 (1950).

[93] Permutit Co., 19 LA 599, 600 (1952).

[94] A. C. And C. Co., 24 LA 538, 541 (Scheiber, 1955).

of the employer's offense.[95] Even where a collective agreement authorized the arbitrator to assess punitive damages, a court held an award of such damages unenforceable as contrary to judicial policy.[96]

The question of interest on the principal sum awarded has sometimes arisen. Arbitrator Sanford H. Kadish has refused to order payment of interest on his award of holiday pay since neither the collective agreement nor the submission expressly authorized him to order the payment of interest and "it is not customary in arbitrations for the arbitrator to grant interest on claims which he finds owing."[97]

Damages will not be denied merely because the amount is difficult to determine. When difficulty is encountered, the simplest fair method available for determining the amount will be used.[98] One possible solution in this type of situation is for the arbitrator to make a finding as to liability and provide that, in the light of the difficulty of determining the exact amount of damages, the liability may be discharged by a lump-sum settlement if the parties can reach one. This was done, for instance, where a time-consuming and expensive process of review of records covering a five-year period would have been necessary to determine the exact amount due.[99]

Where no other solution is available, the arbitrator "is bound to resort to his own good sense and judgment, and after considering all the pertinent facts and circumstances make a reasonable approximation."[100]

---

[95] Timken-Detroit Axle Co., 6 LA 926, 935 (1947). For other instances where the "good faith" element contributed to the denial or reduction of back pay, see Arbitrator Reid in 29 LA 743, 747; Gray in 26 LA 723, 726; Duff in 24 LA 623, 625; Horvitz in 22 LA 390, 392. Also see Shister in 17 LA 254, 256. Cf., Young in 29 LA 137, 142.

[96] Publishers' Assn. v. Newspaper Union, 18 LA 855, 858-860 (N.Y. Sup. Ct., 1952).

[97] Intermountain Operators League, 26 LA 149, 154 (1956).

[98] Eagle-Picher Mining & Smelting Co., 6 LA 544, 549 (Elson, 1947).

[99] Corn Products Refining Co., 7 LA 125, 132-133 (Updegraff, 1947). Also see Arbitrator Feinberg in 16 LA 926, 931-932. Some collective agreements provide for liquidated damages for violation thereof. As in Capital Decorating Co., 25 LA 424, 426 (Slavney, 1955).

[100] American Machine & Foundry Co., 15 LA 822, 827-828 (S. Wolff, 1950).

Arbitrators sometimes apply the rule of *de minimis non curat lex,* under which trifling or immaterial matters will not be taken into account, in denying grievances.[101] But application of the *de minimis* rule has been rejected where "the amount has been small but the principle large." [102] In any event, Arbitrator Harold W. Davey has explained that no hard and fast mathematical line should be drawn between minimal on the one hand and substantial on the other, but that each case should be decided in terms of its own circumstances.[103]

Employees who have been wronged by the employer may be obligated to take reasonable steps to mitigate the damages. Thus back pay, either in whole or in part, may be denied where the employee fails to take advantage of reasonable employment opportunities.[104] But this view has not always been accepted, as where an arbitrator stated that "while it may be proper to deduct from a back pay award sums actually earned by an employee before reinstatement, or sums received indirectly from his employer, as through unemployment compensation, no authority exists in an Arbitrator to penalize an employee financially for failing to have earnings." [105]

Even the arbitrators who recognize a duty to mitigate damages may apply some limitations, such as requiring the employer to introduce affirmative evidence to show the inexcusable failure of the employee to minimize damages,[106] and not requiring the employee to accept unsuitable or lower rated work during the pendency of his appeal.[107]

---

[101] As did Arbitrator Cahn in 28 LA 458, 460-461; Swanson in 27 LA 553, 556; Donnelly in 21 LA 681, 682; Shipman in 17 LA 76, 79; Aaron in 15 LA 168, 172; Cheney in 12 LA 422, 426-427.

[102] Bethlehem-Sparrows Point Shipyard, Inc., 26 LA 483, 490 (Feinberg, 1956).

[103] John Deere Planter Works, 29 LA 328, 331 (1957).

[104] See Arbitrator Parker in 23 LA 640, 642; McCoy in 12 LA 990, 997; Healy in 11 LA 827, 831-832; S. Wolff in 10 LA 288, 294; Lappin in 5 LA 161, 164; Vokum in 2 LA 283, 286. Also see Livengood in 17 LA 419, 423.

[105] Shakespeare & Shakespeare Products Co., 9 LA 813, 817-818 (Platt, 1948). Regarding deduction of unemployment compensation, see Arbitrator Seward in 16 LA 376

[106] As in Armour & Co., 11 LA 600, 605 (Gilden, 1948).

[107] See Airequipment Co., 10 LA 162, 164 (Aaron, 1948). Also, Parker in 23 LA 640, 642.

Judicial Notice and Presumptions

The subjects of judicial notice and presumptions could have been considered in the Evidence chapter. The authors, however, recognize the view of those who believe that these subjects belong to the general topic of legal or judicial reasoning, and they are accordingly considered here.

Judges take judicial notice of notorious facts of commerce, industry, history, and natural science, and of ordinary meanings of words. Similarly, in arbitration many matters are assumed or accepted without discussion or citation of authority. Thus it may be said that arbitrators also take judicial notice.[108]

Of special significance is the practice of arbitrators of taking judicial notice of industry practice affecting some disputed matters.[109] Thus, judicial notice has been taken of the "general understanding that tips, unless guaranteed by the employer, cannot and should not be used in making a 'wage adjustment'." [110] Another arbitrator took judicial notice of the fact that it is not common industrial practice to use the rate received by the highest paid experimental employees as the base rate on new jobs when production begins.[111]

Arbitrators also may use presumptions as aids in deciding issues. Presumptions, which are related to the matter of judicial notice, result in the prima facie assumption of the truth of a matter. Thus they take the place of evidence on the part of the party in whose favor they operate, and they require the other party to produce evidence or argument to show that which is presumed is not true.

To illustrate, Arbitrator Mitchell M. Shipman has held that in determining the right to benefits under an employee

---

[108] For instance, see Arbitrator Lockhart in 20 LA 658, 662-663; Ryder in 20 LA 337, 340; Komaroff in 19 LA 10, 13; Maggs in 17 LA 451, 454; Donnelly in 16 LA 914, 915; Platt in 16 LA 317, 319; Cahn in 7 LA 355, 357; Shipman in 7 LA 121, 122; Wagner in 6 LA 575, 578, and 6 LA 292, 294.

[109] See Arbitrators Komaroff, Maggs, Donnelly, Platt, Cahn, Shipman, and Wagner in preceding footnote. Also see In re Hopkins, 13 LA 716, 717 (N.Y. Sup. Ct., 1949).

[110] Christ Cella's Restaurant, 7 LA 355, 357 (Cahn, 1947).

[111] Pittsburgh Steel Co., 6 LA 575, 578 (Wagner, 1947).

group insurance plan a wife's dependency upon her husband for support is so basic that it will be presumed in the absence of proof to the contrary.[112] Presumptions are used frequently in the interpretation of contract provisions. For instance, parties are presumed to have intended a valid contract,[113] to have intended all words used in an agreement to have effect,[114] and to have intended language to have its commonly accepted meaning.[115]

Presumptions may also be used in "interests" matters. Thus, Arbitrator David L. Cole, in determining the amount of wage increase necessary to offset a rise in living costs, ruled that it was "presumptively proper" to consider only the change in living costs occurring after the parties' last wage negotiation, there being a presumption that all pertinent factors were considered in previous bargaining.[116]

Parol Evidence

Under the parol-evidence rule a written agreement may not be changed or modified by any oral statements or arguments made by the parties in connection with the negotiation of the agreement. A written contract consummating previous oral and written negotiations is deemed, under the rule, to embrace the entire agreement, and, if the writing is clear and unambiguous, parol evidence will not be allowed to vary the contract.[117] This is said to be a rule of substantive law which when applicable defines the limits of a contract.[118]

The parol-evidence rule is very frequently advanced and generally applied in arbitration cases.[119] Sometimes the collec-

---

[112] Rock Hill Printing & Finishing Co., 21 LA 335, 340 (1953).
[113] Warren Foundry & Pipe Corp., 5 LA 282, 283 (Tischler, 1946).
[114] John Deere Tractor Co., 5 LA 631, 632 (Updegraff, 1946).
[115] Goodyear Tire & Rubber Co., 2 LA 367, 370-371 (McCoy, 1946).
[116] New York City Omnibus Corp., 7 LA 794, 802 (1947).
[117] See Wigmore, Evidence, § 2400 (2d Ed.); Cohn v. Dunn, 149 Atl. 851, 70 A.L.R. 740 (Conn., 1930). For full discussion of this rule, see United Drill & Tool Co, 28 LA 677, 679-683 (Cox, 1957).
[118] 2 Williston, Contracts, § 631 (1920 Ed.).
[119] E.g., Arbitrator Hebert in 29 LA 667, 671; Beatty in 26 LA 100, 102; Feinberg in 25 LA 385, 390; Margulies in 19 LA 683, 685; Cahn in 10 LA 577, 578; Cornsweet

tive agreement will provide specifically against verbal agreements that conflict with it.[120]

While some might argue that arbitrators should consider any evidence showing the true intention of the parties and that this intention should be given effect whether expressed by the language used or not, the general denial of power to add to, subtract from, or modify the agreement provides special justification for the observance of the parol-evidence rule by arbitrators.

There are exceptions to the parol-evidence rule, however. Thus, a collateral agreement not intended to be reduced to writing or an entirely distinct contemporaneous agreement may be held valid.[121]   Moreover, an arbitrator may permit the use of parol evidence to show fraud or mutual mistake at the time of negotiations.[122]   Then, too, if the contract is ambiguous, evidence of the precontract negotiations is admissible to aid in the interpretation of the ambiguous language.[123]

---

in 9 LA 598, 599; Leonard in 9 LA 501, 502; Brandschain in 6 LA 603, 609; Lappin in 6 LA 395, 396; Updegraff in 5 LA 747, 749; Whiting in 3 LA 482, 486; McCoy in 3 LA 257, 258. The rule might be held waived if not advanced at the hearing. See American Can Co., 1 ALAA ¶ 67,165 (1943).

[120] As in Pillsbury Mills, Inc., 14 LA 1045, 1047-1048 (Kelliher, 1950).

[121] See Arbitrator Cox in 28 LA 677, 680-681; Spillane in 23 LA 574, 580; Gregory in 8 LA 428, 429.

[122] Terre Haute Water Works Corp., 5 LA 747, 749 (Updegraff, 1946). Also see Arbitrator Forrester in 17 LA 592, 594. Also see this Chapter, topic titled "Remedies for Mistake".

[123] See Chapter 9, topic titled "Precontract Negotiations".

CHAPTER 11

PRECEDENT VALUE OF AWARDS

Diverse views exist concerning the use of prior awards as precedents in the arbitration of labor-management controversies. The authors propose to develop some of these views and to consider the degrees of precedential force actually exerted by arbitration awards. In order to obtain a more accurate and realistic picture of the use of awards, some consideration will be given to the force of legal decisions under the doctrine of stare decisis. A comparison of arbitration awards and legal decisions, it is believed, will lead to helpful conclusions in regard to the percise effect of arbitration awards as precedent. It is believed also that the views expressed by individual arbitrators will be especially enlightening.

The reporting of labor arbitration awards is said to represent a necessary means of making available one of the most hopeful factors in lessening the economic and social cost of industrial disputes.[1] It is also said that arbitrators are producing a tremendous mass of hard, practical experience in the field of labor relations and that the welfare of the country demands that their expressions of experience be made available to labor and management.[2]

It is obvious, however, that the most logical reason for reporting awards is to make them available for some type of precedential or guidance use in other cases. Publication of

---

[1] Statement of John W. Taylor, "Reporting of Labor Arbitration: Pro and Con," 1 Arb. J. (N.S.) 420 (1946). Publication of awards is strongly favored by unions, management, and arbitrators alike according to statistics in Warren & Bernstein, "A Profile of Labor Arbitration," 16 LA 970, 983 (1951).

[2] Statement of Theodore Kheel, Id., at 424.

awards also is an effective way to help insure accountability of arbitrators. No doubt, an arbitrator will take greater care to make his award clear and his reasoning logical if he knows that the award will be subject to public inspection. The old Holmesian adage that the best test of truth is in the open market would appear to be applicable here. If the product of labor arbitration is worthy, it can survive open-market inspection.

Arbitrator Carl A. Warns has stated that "it is obvious that in arbitration as in other fields, respect must be paid to accumulated wisdom and experience." [3] Arbitrator Jules Justin has spoken of reported awards as being "live tools, to be used in shaping and applying the collective bargaining agreement." [4] Arbitrator Arthur Ross has observed that "published awards are not binding on another arbitrator, but the thinking of experienced men is often helpful to him." [5] Arbitrator Raymond Roberts, in turn, has stated that prior awards "may be referred to for advice and for statements of the prevailing rule and standards." [6] Numerous other arbitrators have made similar statements.[7] These statements are consistent with the undoubted wisdom of seeking to profit by past experience. Published awards on a matter will, in any event, provide the setting for evaluating related cases.[8]

A highly practical need for the reasoned opinions of prior awards was made clear in the report of an emergency board created under the Railway Labor Act. One conclusion of the board was that the principal cause of the large number of undisposed claims before the First Division of the National Railroad Adjustment Board was that the First Division did not write fully reasoned opinions or encourage such opinions by

---

[3] Cochran Foil Co., 26 LA 155, 157 (1956).

[4] Justin, "Arbitration: Precedent Value of Reported Awards," 21 LRRM 8 (1947).

[5] S. H. Kress & Co., 25 LA 77, 79 (1955).

[6] National Lead Co., 28 LA 470, 474 (1957).

[7] E.g., Arbitrator Thompson in 29 LA 518, 523; Boles in 26 LA 84, 87; Scheiber in 25 LA 379, 381-382; Reid in 25 LA 146, 149; Livengood in 21 LA 456, 460; Wettach in 19 LA 797, 799; Schmidt in 19 LA 432, 434.

[8] See statement of Arbitrator John Dunlop in Pratt & Whitney Co., 28 LA 668, 672 (1957).

referees assigned to it. The result of such practice was the accumulation of a vast number of awards of no precedential value and of no assistance in the application of rules interpreted by the awards.[9]

A cogent statement regarding use of prior awards is that of Arbitrator Maurice H. Merrill:

> "As to arbitral decisions rendered under other contracts between parties not related to those in the case at hand, usefulness depends upon similarity of the terms and of the situations to which they are to be applied. They must be weighed and appraised, not only in respect to these characteristics, but also with regard to the soundness of the principles upon which they proceed. Certainly, an arbitrator may be aided in formulating his own conclusions by knowledge of how other men have solved similar problems. He ought not to arrogate as his own special virtues the wisdom and justice essential to sound decision. In at least two instances in recent months I have found by investigation that a strong current of arbitral decision had overborne my first impression of the implications of particular language. To yield to this "common sense of most," especially as, on examination, the reasoning on which it was based carried plausibility, was neither to evade my responsibility nor to sacrifice my intellectual integrity. Contrariwise, it reduced discriminatory application of similar provisions. It enabled me to make use of the wisdom of others at work in the same field." [10]

Prior awards can be of value to parties engaged in the negotiation of collective bargaining agreements. Knowledge of how specific clauses have been interpreted by arbitrators will help negotiators avoid pitfalls in the use of agreement language. That awards have such value has been recognized, and is one of the important reasons for writing fully reasoned opinions.[11]

The opponents of the precedential use of awards often voice the same type of criticism sometimes directed toward the

---

[9] Report to the President by the Emergency Board created July 18, 1947, under Section 10 of the Railway Labor Act, as amended (Report dated July 30, 1947). In contrast to the practice of Division I, Divisions II, III, and IV do prepare fully reasoned opinions. Sometimes arguments before a referee sitting with one of these Divisions will consist largely of debates about the meaning and applicability of particular precedents. See Garrison, "The National Railroad Adjustment Board: A Unique Administrative Agency," 46 Yale L.J. 567, 581-582 (1937); Miller, "The Railroad Adjustment Board," 3 Arb. J. (N.S.) 181 (1948). Also see Daugherty, Whiting & Guthrie, "Arbitration by the National Railroad Adjustment Board," Arbitration Today, 93-127 (BNA Incorporated, 1955).

[10] Merrill, "A Labor Arbitrator Views His Work," 10 Vanderbilt L. Rev. 789, 797-798 (1957).

[11] Deep Rock Oil Corp., 11 LA 25, 26 (Merrill, 1948).

doctrine of precedent in law; i.e., the binding force of prior decisions ties the present to the past in such a degree as to stultify progress, and the observance of precedent becomes an end in itself, with the result that justice sometimes is forced to give way to the symmetrical majesty of the decisions. These antagonists assert that the arbitrator should search for a rule of reason which will render justice and at the same time permit the parties to continue "living together"; they say that the desirable rule is determined in part by the character of the disputants—by their economic position, their strength or weakness, their importance to the community, the history of their past relationships, and their objectives in taking their present stand. These factors require each case to be decided on its own and explain why two arbitrators dealing with different parties but similar facts will arrive at seemingly opposing decisions.[12]

Another argument is that arbitration proceedings are private business matters, involving the presentation of confidential data which should be kept secret from competitors. It is also said that one of the great advantages of arbitration, namely, its high degree of informality, would be lost should the arbitration tribunal be bound by precedent and legalism. One of the strongest and most bitter statements against giving precedential force to awards was by Leo Cherne:

> "The effects of publishing domestic arbitration awards are inevitable and inevitably undesirable. The fact of publication itself creates the atmosphere of precedent. The arbitrators in each subsequent dispute are submitted to the continuous and frequently unconscious pressure to conform. A bad award—and there are such in both the courtroom and the arbitration tribunal—will have the effect of stimulating other bad ones; a good one, by the weight of precedent, may be applied where the subtleties of fact should urge a different award." [13]

Despite the opposition of such critics, it is now recognized widely that prior awards do have great value. Many employers and unions acknowledge arbitration awards to be a rapidly ex-

---

[12] See views of Levenstein in "Reporting of Labor Arbitration: Pro and Con," 1 Arb. J. (N.S.) 420, 426 (1946).
[13] Cherne, "Should Arbitration Awards Be Published?" 1 Arb. J. (N.S.) 75 (1946). For other arguments against use of awards as precedent see McPherson, "Should Labor Arbitrators Play Follow-The-Leader?" 4 Arb. J. (N.S.) 163 (1949).

panding body of labor-management rules. Parties in arbitration cases very frequently cite and discuss many prior awards of other parties as well as their own.[14] Indeed, parties sometimes even direct or specifically authorize their arbitrator to consider awards of other arbitrators.[15] Parties thus appreciate the great utility of using tested experience, and even where collective agreements expressly provide that no decision is to establish a precedent for other cases, actual practice under such provisions may disclose the parties themselves applying decisions to other disputes involving the same point.[16]

Also from the standpoint of the parties, recognition that "the body of recorded decisional precedent in arbitration proceedings is constantly growing" was one reason for preparation of a dissenting opinion by a partisan member of a tripartite board "to guide those who may have occasion in the future to refer to the decision and award as a precedent." [17]

Of great practical significance is the attitude of arbitrators themselves. An extensive survey of labor arbitration disclosed that 77% of the 238 responding arbitrators believed that precedents, even under *other* contracts, should be given "some weight." [18]

Arbitrators are often unwilling to rely solely upon the parties for making precedents available, and such arbitrators "search out" relevant awards on their own.[19] Where one party has cited precedents, the arbitrator may allow the other party time to consider and answer them.[20] Where neither party has

---

[14] For example, see Dow Chemical Co., 22 LA 336, 341-345 (Klamon, 1954). For many other such instances the reader need merely scan volumes of reported awards.

[15] Burris Mills, Inc., 26 LA 250 (Whittaker, 1956); Southern Bell Telephone & Telegraph Co., 25 LA 85 (Alexander, et al., 1955).

[16] Rosenblatt, 'The Impartial Machinery of the Coat and Suit Industry," 3 Arb. J. 224, 226 (1939).

[17] Journal Publishing Co., 22 LA 108, 113 (1954).

[18] Warren & Bernstein, "A Profile of Labor Arbitration," 16 LA 970, 982 (1951).

[19] E.g., Arbitrator Reid in 26 LA 258, 262-263; Merrill in 24 LA 191, 192-195; Hebert in 24 LA 178, 181; Thompson in 23 LA 39, 42; Marshall in 22 LA 181, 182-183; Gross in 20 LA 749, 750; Emery in 19 LA 812, 815; Klamon in 19 LA 639, 646; Dworkin in 19 LA 65, 70.

[20] Simmons Co., 15 LA 921, 922 (Elson, 1950).

cited precedents, the arbitrator may invite both parties to submit any that are considered relevant.[21]

While it might be expected that persons trained in law would be more inclined to adhere to the doctrine of precedent, it is important to note that many of the arbitrators who give precedential force to prior awards are not lawyers. The authors, like another observer, have received the "distinct impression that laymen in a judicial position are quite as eager as lawyers in pursuing, and quite as contentious in dissecting, the available precedents * * *"[22]

Accepting, then, that prior awards are of some precedential value and realizing that they do have and will continue to have some force as precedent, the authors turn to inquire into the quantum of force given them and to the probable course of future development. In seeking an answer it is helpful to consider the force given legal decisions under the doctrine of precedent.

Precedent Value of Legal Decisions

Confusion results when one has in mind the inflexible English rule of stare decisis because even in England the force actually given to prior decisions is not absolute or inflexible. Therefore, for the purpose of this discussion, the authors speak of the doctrine of precedent as meaning *the force which is given to prior decisions.*

A basic difference between the Anglo-American systems of law and the civil law systems is the official nonacceptance of the doctrine of precedent by the civil law systems. But Professors Shartel and Wolff have pointed out that the difference between the common law and civil law systems on this point is more apparent than real in that our own courts do not follow precedents as slavishly as many of their utterances would suggest, while the civil law courts do not ignore precedents to the

---

[21] A. D. Juilliard & Co., 15 LA 934, 938 (Maggs, 1951).
[22] Garrison, "The National Railroad Adjustment Board: A Unique Administrative Agency," 46 Yale L.J. 567, 583 (1937).

extent that their general theories might indicate. Further, they have pointed out that in all of the civil law countries the binding force of precedents is recognized definitely in practice in one situation, termed a settled course of decision. Thus, although a single prior decision is not regarded as binding, a settled course of decision on a point is regarded as controlling.[23] As will appear presently, the precedential operation of labor arbitration awards seems to be something of a hybrid of the civil law and common law approaches.

But how does the doctrine of precedent under the common law system operate? As was indicated above, it does not operate as inexorably as many persons carelessly assume. Salmond, in his *Jurisprudence*, considered the English doctrine of precedent.[24] He divided decisions into two classes, authoritative and persuasive. These were said to differ in the kind of influence exercised by each upon the future course of the administration of justice.

The authoritative precedent was defined as one which judges must follow whether they approve of it or not; the persuasive precedent one which judges are under no obligation to follow, but which is to be taken into consideration and given such weight as its intrinsic merit seems to demand.

Salmond specified as authoritative the decisions of the superior courts of justice in England.[25] A great body of decisions were designated as persuasive, including (1) foreign judgments, and more especially those of American courts, (2) decisions of superior courts in other parts of the British Empire, (3) the judgments of the Privy Council when sitting as the final court of appeal from the colonies, and (4) judicial dicta.

---

[23] Shartel and Wolff, "Civil Justice in Germany," 42 Mich. L. Rev. 863, 866-867 (1944).

[24] Salmond, Jurisprudence, § 58 (10th ed., 1947).

[25] Salmond also divided authoritative precedents into two kinds, absolute and conditional. Absolute decisions must be followed without question, however unreasonable or erroneous they may be considered to be. On the other hand, courts possess a certain limited power to disregard decisions having merely conditional authority. See Salmond, Jurisprudence § 59 (10th Ed., 1947).

Thus we see that even in England, where the most extreme adherence to the doctrine of precedent is found, a large body of decisions have persuasive force only.

In America, the doctrine is even more flexible than in England. That the degree of control to be allowed a prior decision varies with the particular case has been emphasized by von Moschzisker, who, after referring to the tenet that stare decisis is based on the premise that certainty in law is preferable to reason and correct legal principles, made the following statement:

> "If the rule demanded absolute rigid adherence to precedents (as in the English House of Lords), then there might be good ground for the persistence among the uninformed of the erroneous idea just referred to, but the proper American conception comprehends *stare decisis* as a flexible doctrine, under which the degree of control to be allowed a prior judicial determination depends largely on the nature of the question at issue, the circumstances attending its decision, and, perhaps, somewhat on the attitude of individual participating judges." [26]

Von Moschzisker also spoke of the situation in which the precedent should be departed from:

> "Therefore, except in the classes of cases which demand strict adherence to precedent, when a court is faced with an ancient decision, rendered under conditions of society radically differenct from those of today, and when it is sought to have this ancient decision control present-day conditions even though the attending facts in the two controversies be alike, still there is nothing in the doctrine of *stare decisis* to prevent a departure from the earlier decision and (in the absence of a legislative enactment covering the matter) the restatement of th governing rule there laid down, or acted on, to meet the change in the life of the people to serve whose best interests it was originally invoked." [27]

Professor Shartel has stated that precedents are not self-effectuating; rather, that they control only to the extent that they are accepted as binding by judges in later cases, and that

---

[26] Moschzisker, "Stare Decisis in Courts of Last Resort," 37 Harv. L. Rev. 409, 414 (1924).

[27] Id. at 418.

varying force is attached to different kinds of precedents.[28] An effective summary of the American doctrine of stare decisis is contained in Chamberlain's classic statement:

> "A deliberate or solemn decision of a court or judge, made after argument on a question of law fairly arising in a case, and necessary to its determination, is an authority, or binding precedent, in the same court or in other courts of equal or lower rank, in subsequent cases, where 'the very point' is again in controversy; but the degree of authority belonging to such precedent depends, of necessity, on its agreement with the spirit of the times or the judgment of subsequent tribunals upon its correctness as a statement of the existing, or actual law, and the compulsion or exigency of the doctrine is, in the last analysis, more and intellectual, rather than arbitrary or inflexible." [29]

The essence of the above discussion of the doctrine of precedent at common law supports the foregoing definition of precedent as meaning *the force which is given to prior decisions.* Confusion naturally results when one seeks to limit the doctrine to one of inflexibility, since, in fact, the weight given to any prior decision is entirely a question of degree.

Authoritative Prior Awards

Although prior labor arbitration awards are not binding in exactly the same sense that authoritative legal decisions are, yet they may have a force which can be characterized as authoritative. This is true of arbitration both by permanent umpires and by temporary or ad hoc arbitrators.

Permanent Umpires

The most pronounced situation in which prior arbitration awards have "authoritative" type force is that of arbitration by

---

[28] Shartel, Our Legal System And How It Operates, c. 7 (1947). This is a litho-printed book published by The Overbeck Company, Ann Arbor, Michigan. Professor Shartel indicated the several respects in which the variation in weight of precedents is apparent: (1) As regards the place and court in which the precedent is cited—a decision of the supreme court of state X has a different weight when cited in state X than when cited in state Y; (2) as regards the character of the judicial statement—a unanimous opinion will have more weight than a divided opinion; (3) as regards the scope of acceptance of the view—one supported by general authority will be more forceful; (4) as regards age and confirmation in later cases; (5) as regards the subject matter involved in the previous decision. Ibid.

[29] Chamberlain, The Doctrine of Stare Decisis, 19 (1885). Also see Catlett, "The Development of the Doctrine of Stare Decisis and the Extent to Which it Should be Applied," 21 Wash. L. Rev. 159 (1946).

permanent umpires or chairmen. One of the ablest arbitrators, Harry Shulman, who served for many years as umpire for the Ford Motor Company and the United Automobile Workers, spoke of precedent in such systems as follows:

> "[I]n this system a form of precedent and stare decisis is inevitable and desirable. I am not referring to the use in one enterprise, say United States Steel, of awards made by another arbitrator in another enterprise, say General Motors. * * *

> "But the precedent of which I am now speaking refers to the successive decisions within the same enterprise. Even in the absence of arbitration, the parties themselves seek to establish a form of stare decisis or precedent for their own guidance—by statements of policy, instructions, manuals of procedure, and the like. This is but a means of avoiding the pain of rethinking every recurring case from scratch, of securing uniformity of action. * * *

> "When the parties submit to arbitration in the system of which I speak, they seek not merely resolution of the particular stalemate, but guidance for the future, at least for similar cases. They could hardly have a high opinion of the arbitrator's mind if it were a constantly changing mind. Adherence to prior decisions, except when departure is adequately explained, is one sign that the determinations are based on reason and are not merely random judgments." [30]

In the full-fashioned hosiery industry prior awards have become a part of the "common law" of the industry. "The Impartial Chairman will hesitate, therefore, to write any decision contrary to the precedents already established." [31] In that industry the principles enunciated in the decisions, not the personage of the Impartial Chairman, are all-important; the mere fact that the person of the Impartial Chairman changes from time to time does not lead to the voiding of past decisions.[32]

---

[30] Shulman, "Reason, Contract, and Law in Labor Relations," 68 Harv. L. Rev. 999, 1020 (1955), reprinted in Management Rights and the Arbitration Process, 169, 193-194 (BNA Incorporated, 1956). For more on the important role of precedent in umpireships, see Killingsworth, "Arbitration: Its Uses in Industrial Relations," 21 LA 859, 861-863 (1953); Reilly, "Arbitration's Impact on Bargaining," 16 LA 987, 990-991 (1951); Davey, "The John Deere-UAW Permanent Arbitration System, Critical Issues in Labor Arbitration, 161, 174 (BNA, Incorporated, 1957). Wolff, Crane & Cole, "The Chrysler-UAW Umpire System," The Arbitrator and the Parties, 111, 115, 128 (BNA Incorporated, 1958).

[31] Kennedy, Effective Labor Arbitration, 63 (1948). "In fact each decision becomes a part of the National Labor Agreement which provides 'all decisions and rulings of the Impartial Chairman * * * not in conflict with the terms of this Agreement are hereby adopted and shall be binding upon the parties hereto'." Id. at 62.

[32] Full-Fashioned Hosiery Industry, 2 ALAA par. 67,542 (1946).

One permanent board of arbitration, Arbitrator Herbert Blumer serving as Chairman, was called upon to render an opinion as to the binding effect of decisions made at grievance meetings or arbitration hearings. After defining "grievance" as referring to a particular complaint and "issue" as referring to the general contractual question that is raised, the arbitrators made the following statement of position:

"(1) A grievance which has been settled in grievance meetings or in arbitration or which has not been appropriately appealed if the proposed settlement has not been accepted, remains settled. This grievance cannot be reinstituted.

"(2) An issue that is settled by the parties in grievance meetings remains settled. Such a settlement, if accepted by both parties, is equivalent to a separate, local agreement. [For full discussion of the precedential effect of grievance settlements, see Chapter 5.]

"(3) Either party may bring an issue to this Board (by the appropriate procedure) even though the party has not appealed the decision on a grievance incorporating the issue. While the given grievance may not be reinstated, another grievance may be processed to the Board in order that the party may secure a final ruling on the issue.

"(4) A grievance even though generally similar to a grievance which has been settled may be processed if it raises an issue which is anyway different from an issue that has been settled.

"(5) An issue which has been ruled on by an umpire prior to the constitution of this Board remains settled unless the ruling is in conflict with the ruling of other umpires entrusted with the same issue. In such a situation, either party is entitled to a ruling from this Board (by following the procedure prescribed in the Agreement) which will dissipate the conflicting arbitration decisions. Further, if the ruling by the umpire is not clear, either party is privileged to process a grievance to this Board so as to secure a clear ruling on the issue. Also, if the ruling of the umpire on an issue appears not to be in line with the rulings of this Board, a grievance dealing with that issue may be processed to this Board. Rulings by this Board on issues have precedence over the rulings made by other umpires. Issues ruled on by this Board shall remain settled and no grievance clearly confined to such issues may be processed to this Board." [33]

Bethlehem Steel Company Umpire Ralph T. Seward has stated that "though he does not consider that he is necessarily bound by the decisions of prior umpires, he does believe that a

---

[33] Tennessee Coal, Iron & Railroad Co., 6 LA 426, 429 (1945). It was decided that the issue presently involved had been ruled on previously, so the grievance was denied. Also see American Steel and Wire Co., 11 LA 945 (1948).

heavy burden of persuasion rests on the party who urges that such prior decisions should be reversed.[34] When this heavy burden is met and a later umpire is convinced that a prior decision is erroneous, it will be reversed.[35]

Then, too, umpires sometimes reverse themselves, as Umpire Seward has.[36] Finally, Umpire Seward has observed that mere dictum statements of other Bethlehem system umpires "are entitled to respect", but are not binding.[37]

In implementing such views as those noted hereinabove, the awards of many permanent umpires are published for the guidance of both unions and management and to discourage the appeal of cases which do not present issues or involve situations different from those previously considered.

Temporary Arbitrators

Prior awards also may have authoritative force where temporary arbitrators are used. An award interpreting a collective agreement usually becomes a binding part of the agreement and will be applied by arbitrators thereafter.[38]

This has been emphasized by Arbitrator Whitley P. Mc-Coy, who has said that where a "prior decision involves the interpretation of the identical contract provision, between the same company and union, every principle of common sense,

---

[34] Bethlehem Cornwall Corp., 25 LA 894, 897 (1956). For more of Umpire Seward's views on this, see Bethlehem Steel Co., 20 LA 87, 90-91 (1953).

[35] Bethlehem Steel Co., 24 LA 379, 380-381 (Recommended decision by Alexander, approved by Seward, 1955).

[36] See comments of Permanent Arbitrator David L. Cole in International Harvester Co., 21 LA 214, 215 (1953).

[37] Bethlehem Steel Co., 28 LA 351, 352 (1957).

[38] E.g., Arbitrator Moore in 29 LA 83, 85; Roberts in 28 LA 470, 476-477; Daugherty in 25 LA 426, 428; Kelliher in 16 LA 816, 818; R. Smith in 12 LA 132, 135; Abernethy in 7 LA 202, 213; McCoy in 6 LA 85, 87; Blumer in 1 ALAA par. 67,121, p. 67,248; Kirsh in 1 ALAA par. 67,331. For the opposing view, see Baab in 23 LA 562, 567; Wallen in 9 LA 757, 763 (but Wallen did hold a prior award binding in 16 LA 365, 368). Arbitrator Ryder, in 22 LA 605, 606, would give such awards "serious and weighty consideration though not binding." For court decisions holding awards to be res judicata, see Hall v. Sperry Gyroscope Co., 21 LA 758, 762 (N.Y. Sup. Ct., 1954), where numerous other court cases are collected.

policy, and labor relations demands that it stand until the parties annul it by a newly worded contract provision." [39]

Arbitrator Russell A. Smith has urged that a proper regard for the arbitration process and for stability in collective bargaining relations requires acceptance by an arbitrator, even though he is not technically bound, of any interpretation of the parties' contractual relations rendered by a previous arbitrator, if in point and if based on the same agreement. [40]

It seems obvious that the binding force of any award ordinarily should not continue after the provision upon which it is based is materially changed or is eliminated entirely from the parties' agreement. [41] However, if the agreement is renegotiated without materially changing a provision that has been interpreted by arbitration, the parties may be held to have adopted the award as a part of the contract. [42] Indeed, the binding force of an award may even be strengthened by such renegotiation without change. For instance, while Arbitrator Jules J. Justin apparently would ordinarily give an award of the same parties only "a 'persuasive' force which compels consideration", still, where the parties did not disturb an award in renegotiating their agreement, he found "no basis or warrant to disturb it." [43] Similarly, Arbitrator Saul Wallen apparently would give a prior award increased precedential weight after the parties have renegotiated the agreement without disturbing the provision covered by the award. [44]

---

[39] Pan American Refining Corp., 2 ALAA par. 67,937, p. 69,464 (1948).

[40] O & S Bearing Co., 12 LA 132, 135 (1949). But in that case the prior award was not followed since it involved a temporary special agreement rather than the agreement before Arbitrator Smith.

[41] An award may cease to be binding even before the contract expires if the parties follow a practice inconsistent with the award. Waterfront Employers Assn. of the Pacific Coast, 2 ALAA par. 67,949 (1948).

[42] E.g., Arbitrator Justin in 22 LA 721, 725-727; Kelliher in 16 LA 816, 818; Wallen in 16 LA 365, 368; McCoy in 16 LA 217, 218-219. Also see Kaplan, 18 LA 777, 779-780. Cf., Komaroff in 15 LA 626, 630-631.

[43] Federal Bearings Co., 22 LA 721, 725-727 (1954).

[44] Compare statement of Arbitrator Wallen in 9 LA 757, 763, with his statement in 16 LA 365, 368. Also see Reilly, "Arbitration's Impact on Bargaining," 987, 991 (1951), regarding the difficulty of changing decisions which only one party deems erroneous.

The parties are free in any case to stipulate as to what precedential role a forthcoming award shall play.[45]

While Arbitrator Herbert Blumer has declared that "it is only fair and reasonable to expect an arbitrator's decision to apply to subsequent cases of the same nature" and that "the refusal to apply the arbitrator's decision to similar cases leaves unsolved and unsettled the general problem covered by the decision", still, he would justify the refusal to apply an award to cases of the same nature where it is shown that any one of the following elements is present: (1) The previous decision of the arbitrator clearly was an instance of bad judgment; (2) the arbitration decision was made without the benefit of some important and relevant facts or considerations; or (3) new conditions have arisen questioning the reasonableness of the continued application of the decision.[46]

Arbitrator Clark Kerr would add obvious and substantial errors of fact or law and the lack of fair and full hearing as justification for refusal to apply the prior award (however, he would place the burden of proof upon the party alleging any of these grounds).[47] Arbitrator Joseph M. Klamon refused to follow a prior award, of the same parties, which he considered erroneous and which was "entirely unsupported by any precedents or practice" in the industry.[48]

Frequently when prior awards are cited as being authoritative, the arbitrator will avoid such effect by distinguishing them.[49] Often the distinction will be clear, but there are cases where the drawing of a distinction can prove to be troublesome. For instance, in one case the company cited an award rendered two years earlier in a case involving the same company but a

---

[45] Milwaukee Cartage Exchange, 19 LA 106 (Anderson, 1952).

[46] Inland Steel Company, 1 ALAA par. 67,121, p. 67,248 (1944). Also see Librascope, Inc., 19 LA 424, 427 (Van de Water, 1952); North American Aviation, Inc., 15 LA 626, 630-631 (Komaroff, 1950).

[47] Waterfront Employers Assn. of Pacific Coast, 7 LA 757, 758 (1947).

[48] American Steel Foundries, 19 LA 779, 787 (1952).

[49] E.g., Arbitrator Davey in 23 LA 343, 347-348; Abruzzi in 18 LA 193, 195; Barrett in 16 LA 466, 470; Kirsh in 6 LA 124, 126; Carmichael in 3 LA 798, 800-801. Also see Standard Oil Company, 1 ALAA par. 67,182 (1946).

different union. The arbitrator, James J. Healy, said that the similarity of the two cases made the prior award germane; moreover, the question itself was not one of peculiar relevancy to a particular bargaining unit. But then he stated that, while the prior decision carried weight in appraising the merits of the present case, its mere existence did not foreclose the arbitrator from reaching a different conclusion. Apparently realizing the inconsistency, he qualified the latter statement by saying that there was no adequate opinion in the earlier award and that it was on a slightly different issue. The arbitrator expressed the dilemma in the following words:

> "Placing the Company in the position of having two arbitrators make different rulings on the same question is repugnant to all parties; the very dignity of arbitration is endangered, and, on the surface, it would appear that arbitration is dangerously subjective. Therefore, it is only after sincere and prolonged deliberation that the undersigned makes the following ruling. * * *" [50]

It appears that the fact situations of the cases were enough alike that he did not feel entirely free to deviate from the prior award because to do so would make it appear that arbitration is "dangerously subjective." He concluded, however, that there was sufficient distinction between the cases to justify a refusal to be bound by the prior award.[51]

Persuasive Prior Awards

While prior awards have authoritative force in some situations, the great mass of awards are considered to have persuasive force only.[52] Nothing is settled by saying that prior awards do or do not have the force of precedent. Rather, it is essential that one recognize that the precedential force of prior awards

---

[50] Brown & Sharpe Mfg. Co., 7 LA 134, 138-139 (1947).

[51] Sometimes an arbitrator will enforce the prior award of another arbitrator, as was the case where an award included an unpaid amount due an employee under an earlier award. Hertz Pharmacy, 6 LA 463 (1947). Also see Industrial Council of Cloak, Suit & Skirt Manufacturers, Inc., 1 ALAA par. 67,524 (1946).

[52] Salmond defined the persuasive precedent as one which depends for its influence upon its own merits and upon that alone. Salmond, Jurisprudence, § 58 (10th ed., 1947). He also included judicial dicta with the persuasive precedents. Thus it might be said that dicta in prior awards differ from decisions in prior awards primarily in regard to the degree of force exerted by each.

always is a question of degree. The range is broad, covering prior awards that have absolutely no persuasive force as well as those which are binding in future like cases. The dividing line cannot be drawn with finality, just as the line between authoritative force and persuasive force cannot be established absolutely. Confusion is avoided by remembering that it is only a question of degree in each particular case. The following analysis is made with these thoughts in mind.

There are many cases where, in varying degree, the arbitrator was persuaded by prior awards; in some of these cases the arbitrator spoke in terms of finding "support" in prior awards, but in either case the effect is the same—the arbitrator relied upon or otherwise made use of prior awards.[53]

It is easy for an arbitrator to be persuaded by or to rely upon a prior award that is in near agreement with his own views. Moreover, most *careful* awards rely upon principles which will command respect by reason of their logic and the fair result which they yield under the facts. In law we speak of the "reasonably prudent man." Most good awards can be said to incorporate the view of the reasonably prudent man, and it is reasonable to expect other men, in similar cases, to be persuaded to some extent by the awards and their supporting reasoning. In particular, the considered judgment of any widely known and respected arbitrator cannot be dismissed lightly or ignored.[54]

The attitude of one eminent arbitrator confronted by an award of another eminent arbitrator is possibly typified by

---

[53] E.g., Arbitrator Livengood in 28 LA 844, 847; Parkman in 28 LA 1, 4-5; Welch in 28 LA 51, 55-56; Carroll in 27 LA 867, 868-869; Merrill in 26 LA 114, 116; Reid in 26 LA 258, 262-263; Larkin in 25 LA 308, 312; Spaulding in 25 LA 181, 185; Graff in 24 LA 299, 305; Hebert in 24 LA 178, 181; Kleinsorge in 23 LA 733, 740 ("interests" dispute); Singletary in 23 LA 456, 458-459; Vining in 23 LA 86, 88; Reynard in 22 LA 880, 882-883; Baab in 22 LA 709, 719-720; Kelly in 22 LA 266, 268; Hanrahan in 19 LA 170, 173-174; Fulda in 18 LA 315, 317-319; Kelliher in 18 LA 216, 218; Rosenfarb in 18 LA 184, 188; Forrester in 18 LA 69, 70; Handsaker in 15 LA 209, 213-214; McCreary in 12 LA 1044, 1049-1053; Ingle in 9 LA 515, 517; Aaron in 8 LA 261, 271; Potter in 7 LA 724, 729; Whiting in 7 LA 79, 80; Wallen in 6 LA 1017, 1019.

[54] E.g., see statement of Arbitrator Spaulding in 25 LA 181, 185; Reynard in 22 LA 880, 882-883; Gorder in 20 LA 880, 888; Fulda in 18 LA 315, 319; Aaron in 8 LA 261, 272; Levy in 6 LA 397, 402.

Chrysler Umpire David A. Wolff in considering an award of Ford Umpire Harry Shulman:

"The Chairman realizes that, despite the great similarity of contract provisions and their apparent common origin and despite the fact of similarity of parties, location and type of business, there are distinctions which exist and must be observed. The parties are not the same parties. Their practices are not identical. Even their application of the considered contract provisions has varied. Further, while Dr. Shulman and the Chairman both act as umpires they were not selected, nor do they act for, the same parties. The parties making the selections undoubtedly had in mind the known general thinking of each at the time of selections and made the selections on an individual basis. On the other hand, points of similarity may not be disregarded. In addition the Chairman has high regard for Dr. Shulman's sincerity, clarity of thought, and reasoning processes. The Chairman does not propose to unthinkingly adopt Dr. Shulman's determination in another case as his own in the instant case. However, to the extent to which he believes it here applicable, he makes use of it with appreciation." [55]

In any event, it would seem that when either party cites an award, the arbitrator cannot disregard it lightly. Good faith and respect for the citing party require the arbitrator at least to consider the contentions of the party.

An interesting case illustrating the extreme to which arbitrators might go in order at least to give consideration to a prior award involved an arbitration board, with Saul Wallen as Chairman.[56] At the arbitration hearing the union presented oral testimony in regard to the existence of an award rendered more than a quarter of a century earlier, which was alleged to support the union's contention. After the hearing was adjourned, the union was able to secure the documents involved in the prior case and requested that the arbitration board be reconvened for the purpose of considering the prior award and the data involved therein. The employers first argued that the earlier decision was irrelevant but later consented to a second hearing (on the condition that it not be a precedent with respect to the submission of evidence after a hearing is closed). At the second hearing the prior award was considered but found not to involve an analogous situation, so it was given no weight.

---

[55] Chrysler Appeal Board Case No. 573 (1948).
[56] Boston Daily Newspapers, 6 LA 179 (1946).

While precedential use of awards occurs primarily in "rights" arbitration, such use is by no means unknown to "interests" arbitration as well. Prior awards are considered fairly frequently in "interests" cases.[57] In some circumstances a prior "interests" award may have special persuasive significance to other parties "similarly facing the same inquiry."[58]

In all civil law countries, as we have noted, the binding force of precedents is recognized definitely in practice in one situation, which is called a settled course of decision. An analogous situation is found in labor arbitration awards. Where there is a settled course of arbitral decision on a point, the principle stated in the decisions is often very presuasive, or at least highly comforting support for a later ruling.[59] It is unlikely that any such course of decision will be achieved upon faulty reasoning. Thus, in a sense, it can be correctly said that "it is not the long line of previous decisions that is determinative," but "the validity of the reasoning behind the principle."[60]

By no means are arbitrators always swayed by cited awards, even awards which are reasonably in point. Arbitrators are alert to distinction between cases.[61] Moreover, when arbitrators cannot agree with the conclusion of cited precedents, they do not hesitate so to state.[62] Sometimes an arbitrator will dismiss cited awards with the statement that he has examined them carefully and has found nothing to alter his thinking

---

[57] For example, in Patriot News Co., 15 LA 871, 874 (Egan, 1950), the arbitrator spoke of studying "dozens of arbitration decisions."

[58] Union Railroad Co., 20 LA 219, 224 (Gilden, 1953).

[59] E.g., see Arbitrator Updegraff in 29 LA 559, 562; Kadish in 29 LA 424, 427; Whitton in 25 LA 687, 690-691; Ross in 24 LA 857, 860-861; Howard in 24 LA 667, 672; Howlett in 24 LA 232, 237; Larson in 23 LA 349, 352-353; R. Smith in 23 LA 338, 340; Livengood in 17 LA 419, 423; McCoy in 16 LA 307, 311; Killingsworth in 16 LA 111, 113; Kelliher in 12 LA 779, 783; Hill in 11 LA 1081, 1083; Whiting in 7 LA 79, 80; Wallen in 6 LA 1017, 1019; Levy in 6 LA 397, 402.

[60] Bachmann Uxbridge Worsted Corp., 23 LA 596, 602 (Hogan, 1954).

[61] E.g., Arbitrator Townsend in 28 LA 664, 668; Phelps in 28 LA 88, 91; Hebert in 23 LA 497, 502; Abernethy in 23 LA 379, 382; Scheiber in 15 LA 111, 114; Updegraff in 12 LA 865, 869; Killingsworth in 12 LA 709, 713.

[62] E.g., Arbitrator McCoy in 20 LA 34, 36; Handsaker in 16 LA 964, 966; Whitton in 6 LA 714, 716.

on the matter.[63] Then, too, an arbitrator might acknowledge cited awards but give no indication as to their persuasive force upon him.[64]

On the other hand, an arbitrator may reject prior awards which are unconvincing or which fail to set forth with clarity the reasons therefor and he may accept clearly reasoned opinions with the statement that the "reasoning applies with persuasive force to the instant case." [65]

Because arbitrators recognize that use of their awards may be sought in similar cases, they sometimes caution against the precedential use of a particular award, especially if there are features peculiar to that case which make the award inappropriate as a guide for any other case.[66]

Finally, in the event of court review an award may be strengthened in the eyes of the court if supported by prior awards.[67]

Precedent and Development of Substantive Principles

The controversy over use of awards as precedents is accompanied by a related and integrated controversy regarding development of substantive principles through arbitration. The authors offer in the following discussion their own evaluation of these matters.

The authors are convinced that considerable use of precedents in arbitration is inevitable. They are convinced also that development of substantive principles through arbitration is likewise inevitable—and desirable. Most arbitrators, able though they be, do not possess enough of Solomon's wisdom to justify rule by man instead of rule by principle. Not all cases can best be decided in a vacuum.

---

[63] E.g., Arbitrator Cheney in 8 LA 518, 525; Prasow in 7 LA 67, 69.

[64] E.g., Arbitrator Scheiber in 10 LA 20, 24; Brandschain in 6 LA 633, 634.

[65] Arbitrator Whitton in 6 LA 714, 716-717. Similarly, Merrill in 19 LA 854, 855-856.

[66] E.g., Arbitrator Seitz in 29 LA 322, 324; Ralston in 20 LA 465, 467; Wolff in 19 LA 430, 431; Prasow in 6 LA 323, 326. Also see International Railway Company, 1 ALAA par. 67,211 (1946).

[67] See Bakery Workers Union v. Hall Baking Co., 69 N.E. 2d 111 (Mass. 1946).

The authors agree that the question is "not *whether* principles are being evolved, but *what* they are and *how far* they should carry." [68]

As to "how far" substantive principles should carry, it is obvious that no principle should be promiscuously applied.[69] In any event, general principles should be applied to cases only after careful thought and thorough consideration.

Precedent, the Siamese twin of substantive principles,[70] is totally out of place in some arbitration cases. In other cases only a *little* use of precedent is justified. In a sense, each collective bargaining relationship is a world of its own—a world which may be given features of infinite variety under the virtually unlimited right of contract enjoyed by Americans. The phrase "each case must be decided on its own" does have a definite place in arbitration.

Still, issues being arbitrated do frequently have counterparts in reported awards. In arbitration as in other important areas of human activity, growth and refinement through use of tested experience is inevitable and desirable. Then, too, from the arbitrator's viewpoint, it is comforting to know that his decision finds support in other awards, or to know at least that it does not vary drastically from what others have decided.

No arbitrator can serve long without becoming aware of the existence of certain more or less generally recognized principles and penetrating propositions. It is questionable whether any arbitrator, and especially the experienced, can always eliminate the influence of what he knows others have done.

It is difficult to determine precisely the extent to which substantive principles are being evolved and applied since, for

---

[68] Petshek, "Discussion of Principles Emerging From Grievance Arbitration," 1953 Proceedings of Industrial Relations Research Association, 154, 156.

[69] See words of Arbitrator Joseph Shister in Electro Metallurgical Co., 22 LA 684, 686 (1954).

[70] "The appearance of precedent in labor arbitration probably results less from a conscious effort to develop a case law, and more from general recognition of the validity of certain principles for the treatment of similar cases." Holman, "The Back-Pay Issue in Arbitration," I. L. Research, Vol. II, No. 1, pp. 6-8 (1955).

a variety of reasons, many awards are never published. Frequently where an arbitrator might be inclined to consider precedent, there simply is no reported case similar to that under consideration.[71]

Moreover, many of the awards which are published have little utility as guides for other parties. However, as one spokesman has stated, some decisions, "due to the logic of their problem-solving persuasiveness, are potential candidates for wide application beyond the parties." [72] And, as another observer has begrudgingly admitted, "From the published awards, it is evident that standards have been turned by the lathe of arbitration for a wide range of problems." [73]

The authors readily agree with those who believe that the term "principle" is "abused when it is employed as a synonym for *binding* precedent." [74] However, it should be recognized that regarding the development of principles for *widespread* application there is not too much concern with the "authoritative" or "binding" force which awards often exert in subsequent cases involving the same parties and the same contract language. Rather, the emphasis falls much more on the "persuasive" or "guiding" force that awards under *other* contracts often exert. Arbitration awards under other contracts *are* important as precedents. A glance through recent volumes of reported arbitration decisions reveals the very frequent citation, discussion and use of such precedents.

The persuasive or guidance force of prior awards varies widely. Many awards exert little or no force, but some awards are quite useful in other cases, especially where there is a settled course of arbitral decision on a point.

---

[71] E.g., see comment of Arbitrator Singletary in 29 LA 504, 507; Dworkin in 28 LA 362, 369; Marshall in 23 LA 228, 233; Merrill in 22 LA 706, 707; Treiman in 19 LA 807, 808; Schmidt in 19 LA 432, 434.

[72] Petshek, "Discussion of Principles Emerging From Grievance Arbitration," 1953 Proceedings of Industrial Relations Research Association, 154, 157.

[73] Manson, "Substantive Principles Emerging From Grievance Arbitration: Some Observations," 1953 Proceedings of Industrial Relations Research Association, 136, 137.

[74] Id. at 147 (emphasis added).

Furthermore, a substantive principle might be revealed through a single well-reasoned decision, which becomes the "leading case" on the point.[75] Then, too, arbitrators sometimes discern substantive principles through a process which might be called "negative inference." For instance, in one case Arbitrator Whitley P. McCoy stated: "I have been unable to find any authority among the thousands of arbitration decisions for a holding that disloyalty [to the employer], in and of itself, is an offense, much less a dischargeable offense." [76]

In actual practice it is not at all uncommon for an arbitrator to preface the assertion of an established rule or principle with some statement such as "it has become a well-accepted principle," or "it is a general rule that," or "the consensus is," or "the weight of authority is." In doing this arbitrators freqeuntly cite precedents,[77] but just as frequently they cite few or no specific cases to support their assertion that the principle does in fact exist.[78] Possibly the true significance of such statements lies in the fact that the arbitrator was willing to accept arbitration awards as a source of fundamental substantive principles.

---

[75] For example, see Struthers-Wells Corp., 17 LA 483, 485 (Strashower, 1951), recognizing the leading case status of a decision of Umpire Harry Shulman; Grand Sheet Metal Products Co., 17 LA 388, 390 (Kelliher, 1951), noting the leading case status of a decision by Arbitrator Irving Bernstein.

[76] U. S. Pipe & Foundry Co., 20 LA 513, 516 (1953). A similar approach was taken by Arbitrator Howard in 23 LA 440, 446; Cheit in 21 LA 293, 298; Williams in 20 LA 784, 787.

[77] E.g., see Arbitrator Larson in 29 LA 795, 802; Piercey in 29 LA 220, 224; Spaulding in 29 LA 182, 185-186; Parkman in 27 LA 107, 109-110; Howlett in 26 LA 713, 716; Kharas in 25 LA 755, 757-758; Kelliher in 25 LA 736, 737; Ebeling in 24 LA 874, 876; Nagle in 24 LA 770, 774; Kotin in 23 LA 663, 670; Healy in 23 LA 504, 510; Parker in 23 LA 44, 47; Louisell in 21 LA 254, 259; Oppenheimer in 20 LA 399, 401-402; Updegraff in 19 LA 601, 602; Maggs in 18 LA 896, 897-898; Horton in 18 LA 285, 289-290; Whitton in 18 LA 174, 178; Shister in 17 LA 230, 234.

[78] E.g., Arbitrator Kelliher in 29 LA 615, 617; Cheit in 28 LA 390, 393; Seward in 28 LA 351, 352; Fleming in 28 LA 97, 100; Prasow in 27 LA 153, 156; Thompson in 26 LA 575, 577; Holly in 26 LA 325, 327; Kadish in 26 LA 149, 154; Klamon in 25 LA 841, 844; Shister in 25 LA 618, 622; Shapiro in 25 LA 341, 343; Alexander in 24 LA 353, 355; Crawford in 23 LA 548, 551; Platt in 23 LA 137, 141; Williams in 23 LA 13, 14; Witte in 21 LA 774, 776; Feinberg in 21 LA 614, 616; McCoy in 19 LA 569, 571; Sachs in 18 LA 616, 620; Luskin in 18 LA 459, 461; Blair in 17 LA 570, 571. However, if the parties themselves allege existence of established principle they should be prepared to prove it. See comments of Arbitrator Fisher in 27 LA 812, 814; Hill in 25 LA 587, 591.

Finally, it must be emphasized that a great contribution to industrial stability lies in the probability that many disputes are settled by the parties themselves before reaching arbitration because they are aware of prior awards on the issue involved which point out the objective merits of contentions and which are indicative of results likely to be had through arbitration.

CHAPTER 12

CUSTOM AND PAST PRACTICE

Unquestionably custom and past practice constitute one of the most significant factors in labor-management arbitration. Evidence of custom and past practice may be introduced for any of the following major purposes: (1) to provide the basis of rules governing matters not included in the written contract; (2) to indicate the proper interpretation of ambiguous contract language; or (3) to support allegations that clear language of the written contract has been amended by mutual action or agreement. In the present Chapter use of custom and past practice for each of these purposes will be discussed.[1]

Custom and Practice as Part of the Contract

Under certain circumstances custom and past practice may be held enforceable through arbitration as being in essence a part of the parties' "whole" agreement. Some of the general reasoning of arbitrators in this regard should be noted:

Arbitrator Dudley E. Whiting: "Collective labor agreements are not negotiated in a vacuum but in a setting of past practices and prior agreements. Such an agreement has the effect of eliminating prior practices which are in conflict with the terms of the agreement but, unless the agreement specifically provides otherwise, practices consistent with the agreement remain in effect."[2]

Arbitrator Arthur T. Jacobs: "A union-management contract is far more than words on paper. It is also all the oral understandings, interpretations and mutually acceptable habits of action which have grown up around it over the course of time. Stable and peaceful relations between

---

[1] For an interesting and useful discussion of custom and practice see Aaron, Davis and Bailer, "The Uses of the Past," Arbitration Today, 1-24 (BNA Incorporated, 1955).
[2] American Seating Co., 16 LA 115, 117 (1951).

the parties depend upon the development of a mutually satisfactory super-structure of understanding which gives operating significance and prac-ticality to the purely legal wording of the written contract. Peaceful relations depend, further, upon both parties faithfully living up to their mutual commitments as embodied not only in the actual contract itself but also in the modes of action which have become an integral part of it." [3]

Arbitrator Whitley P. McCoy: "Custom can, under some circumstances, form an implied term of a contract. Where the Company has always done a certain thing, and the matter is so well understood and taken for granted that it may be said that the contract was entered into upon the assumption that that customary action would continue to be taken, such customary action may be an implied term." [4]

Arbitrator Maurice H. Merrill: "In the light of the [arbitration] deci-sions, * * * it seems to me that the current of opinion has set strongly in favor of the position that existing practices, in respect to major condi-tions of employment, are to be regarded as included within a collective bargaining contract, negotiated after the practice has become established and not repudiated or limited by it. This also seems to me the reasonable view, since the negotiators work within the frame of existent practice and must be taken to be conscious of it." [5]

Numerous other arbitrators have expressed similar views. [6]

Statement of such views, however, does not always decide specific cases. The problem remains: Under what circumstances shall custom be binding for the future? Are all types of matters to be treated as "custom" for this purpose? What of the clash between two legitimate objectives: (1) the need for industrial stability, which is served by custom, and (2) the need for managerial freedom of action to operate the business efficiently?

Examination of many reported decisions suggests that as yet there are no unanimously accepted standards for determin-ing precisely under what circumstances unwritten practices and custom will be held binding. Certainly the result reached in any given case may depend much upon the thinking of the

---

[3] Coca-Cola Bottling Co., 9 LA 197, 198 (1947).
[4] Esso Standard Oil Co., 16 LA 73, 74 (1951).
[5] Phillips Petroleum Co., 24 LA 191, 194-195 (1955).
[6] E.g., Edgar Jones in 29 LA 372, 375; Prasow in 27 LA 6, 10; Dworkin in 24 LA 614, 618-619; Levinson in 23 LA 277, 280; Gorder in 20 LA 880, 883; Hale in 20 LA 818, 823; Wirtz in 20 LA 276, 280; Updegraff in 20 LA 243, 244; Talbott in 19 LA 628, 629; Marshall in 17 LA 105, 108; Gilden in 17 LA 81, 85; Hampton in 16 LA 59, 62. Also see Barrett in 30 LA 100, 103; Maggs in 27 LA 858, 862; Kheel in 26 LA 627, 629; Myers in 23 LA 776, 779.

particular person who has been authorized by the parties to decide the case. However, it may be noted that in some of the cases cited above, and in other cases, certain considerations have been stressed.

First of all, to be given binding effect, custom must be well established—strong proof of its existence may be required.[7]

"The existence of the alleged custom and its limitations present a question of fact for the determination of the arbitrators * * *"[8]

The continued binding effect of custom has often been based upon "implied mutual agreement."[9] But the "mutuality" aspect may also be approached on the basis of how the custom commenced; whether it was instituted by bilateral action as opposed to unilateral action by only one of the parties is a factor often considered,[10] but it would seem that the fact of unilateral establishment should not necessarily be given controlling weight.

One arbitrator has suggested that an established practice may be unilaterally discontinued if it involves a "gratuity," but that it is binding if it concerns a "working condition."[11] But another arbitrator has doubted the validity of this test and has suggested that perhaps the best test, though admittedly inexact, is that the usage, to achieve contractual status, must concern a "major condition of employment."[12]

Professors Archibald Cox and John T. Dunlop have urged that "A collective bargaining agreement should be deemed,

---

[7] Natvar Corp., 24 LA 753, 754 (Justin, 1955); Sioux City Battery Co., 20 LA 243, 244 (Updegraff, 1953).

[8] In re Publishers' Assn., 25 LA 900, 901 (N.Y. Sup. Ct., 1956), and cases cited therein.

[9] Continental Baking Co., 20 LA 309, 311 (Updegraff, 1953).

[10] See statement of Umpire Shulman quoted above. Also see, Cortland Baking Co., 25 LA 853, 855-856 (Kharas, 1955); International Harvester Co., 20 LA 276, 280 (Wirtz, 1953); General Cable Corp., 17 LA 780, 783 (Cahn, 1952). For discussion of what a party should do to avoid being bound by a practice unilaterally established by the other party, see Donaldson Co., 20 LA 826, 830-831 (Louisell, 1953).

[11] Fawick Airflex Co., 11 LA 666, 668-669 (Cornsweet, 1948).

[12] Phillips Petroleum Co., 24 LA 191, 194 (Merrill, 1955). Other arbitrators have utilized some type of major-minor test: Reynard in 25 LA 611, 613 (1955); Updegraff in 20 LA 309, 311 (1953); Talbott in 19 LA 628, 629 (1952).

unless a contrary intention is manifest, to carry forward for its term the major terms and conditions of employment, not covered by the agreement, which prevailed when the agreement was executed." [13] As noted above, the "major condition of employment" test is inexact. From whose standpoint is something "major"? Where is the line to be drawn? Cox and Dunlop include as "major" such things as "basic wages, seniority, and pensions," but they are apparently willing to exclude such matters as job content, work loads, and incentive systems.[14]

The line between practices which are binding and those which are not may well be drawn on the basis of whether the matter involves methods of operation or direction of the working force, or whether it involves a "benefit" of peculiar personal value to the employees (though also involving the employer's purse).

Arbitrators are often hesitant to permit unwritten past practice or methods of doing things to restrict the exercise of legitimate functions of management. For example, such hesitance is evidenced by Arbitrator Whitley P. McCoy:

> "But caution must be exercised in reading into contracts implied terms, lest arbitrators start re-making the contracts which the parties have themselves made. The mere failure of the Company, over a long period of time, to exercise a legitimate function of management, is not a surrender of the right to start exercising such right. If a Company had never, in 15 years and under 15 contracts, disciplined an employee for tardiness, could it thereby be contended that the Company could not decide to institute a reasonable system of penalties for tardiness? Mere non use of a right does not entail a loss of it." [15]

One of the most cogent and provocative statements published regarding the binding force of custom is that of Umpire Harry Shulman, in a case involving operating methods and direction of the working force (assignment of work), wherein

---

[13] Cox and Dunlop, "The Duty to Bargain Collectively During the Term of an Existing Agreement," 63 Harv. L. Rev. 1097, 1116-1117 (1950). For further discussion of this view in relation to the duty to bargain collectively under the LMRA of 1947, see Chapter 13, subtopic titled "The Duty To Bargain: Right Of Unilateral Action."

[14] Id. at 1118.

[15] Esso Standard Oil Co., 16 LA 73, 74 (1951).

he urged that past practice not be "enshrined without carefully thought out and articulated limitations":

"A practice, whether or not fully stated in writing, may be the result of an agreement or mutual understanding. And in some industries there are contractual provisions requiring the continuance of unnamed practices in existence at the execution of the collective agreement. (There are no such provisions in the Ford Agreement or in those of the automobile industry generally.) A practice thus based on mutual agreement may be subject to change only by mutual agreement. Its binding quality is due, however, not to the fact that it is past practice but rather to the agreement in which it is based.

"But there are other practices which are not the result of joint determination at all. They may be mere happenstance, that is, methods that developed without design or deliberation. Or they may be choices by Management in the exercise of managerial discretion as to the convenient methods at the time. In such cases there is no thought of obligation or commitment for the future. Such practices are merely present ways, not prescribed ways, of doing things. The relevant item of significance is not the nature of the particular method but the managerial freedom with respect to it. Being the product of managerial determination in its permitted discretion such practices are, in the absence of contractual provision to the contrary, subject to change in the same discretion. The law and the policy of collective bargaining may well require that the employer inform the Union and that he be ready to discuss the matter with it on request. But there is no requirement of mutual agreement as a condition precedent to a change of practice of this character.

"A contrary holding would place past practice on a par with written agreement and create the anomaly that, while the parties expend great energy and time in negotiating the details of the Agreement, they unknowingly and unintentionally commit themselves to unstated and perhaps more important matters which in the future may be found to have been past practice. The contrary holding would also raise other questions very difficult to answer. For example, what is properly a subject of a practice? Would the long time use of a wheelbarrow become a practice not to be changed by the substitution of four-wheeled buggies drawn by a tractor? Or would the long time use of single drill presses be a practice prohibiting the introduction of multiple drill presses? Such restraints on technological change are alien to the automobile industry. Yet such might be the restraints, if past practice were enshrined without carefully thought out and articulated limitations. Again, when is a practice? How frequently and over how long a period must something be done before it is to be called a practice with the consequences claimed? And how is the existence of the past practice to be determined in the light of the very conflicting testimony that is common in such cases? The Union's witnesses remember only the occasions on which the work was done in the manner they urge.

Supervision remembers the occasions on which the work was done otherwise. Each remembers details the other does not; each is surprised at the other's perversity; and both forget or omit important circumstances. Rarely is alleged past practice clear, detailed and undisputed; commonly, inquiry into past practice of the type that is not the result of joint determination or agreement produces immersion in a bog of contradictions, fragments, doubts, and one-sided views. All this is not to say that past practice may not be important and even decisive in applying provisions of the Agreement. The discussion is addressed to the different claim that, apart from any basis in the Agreement, a method of operation or assignment employed in the past may not be changed except by mutual agreement." [16]

Arbitrators frequently (but not always) have recognized wide authority in management to control methods of operation and to direct the working forces, which authority includes the right without penalty to make changes *if these do not violate some right of the employees under the written contract.* If a given change or the method of putting it into effect does result in the violation of some contractual right of identified employees, then the arbitrator can be expected to award compensation to the employees for the loss sustained, even if he does not take the further step of ordering management to revert to the prior practice.

Numerous cases involving the authority of management to control methods of operation and to direct the working forces are collected in Chapter 13, topics on Control of Quality Standards, Control of Operation Methods (some changes in operation methods may require new rates of pay for jobs affected by the change), Job and Classification Control, Scheduling Work, Determination of Size of Crews, and other such topics. At this point, however, a few specific examples may be noted.

For instance, in some cases past practice has not been permitted to prevent management from changing work sched-

---

[16] Ford Motor Co., 19 LA 237, 241-242 (1952). For additional discussion of this subject, see Shulman, "Reason, Contract, and Law in Labor Relations," 68 Harv. L. Rev. 999, 1011-1013 (1955), reprinted in Management Rights and the Arbitration Process 169, 184-188 (BNA, Incorporated, 1956).

ules,[17] from reassigning work,[18] from determining the number of workers needed on a job,[19] from adding or eliminating job duties within reasonable limits,[20] from eliminating a job,[21] from discontinuing collateral information on seniority lists,[22] from using a formal instead of informal method of determining skill and ability of employees,[23] or from rotating certain employees between two operating units to familiarize them with both operations.[24] But if past practice *supports* management's actions in such matters, it will provide additional reason for upholding management.[25]

In permitting unilateral change by management, arbitrators sometimes have emphasized that the matter may be subject to negotiations if requested by the union, but, if any such negotiations fail to produce agreement management may exercise its unilateral judgment in making or continuing the change.[26] It has been suggested also that even as to changes concerning which management may not be strictly required to discuss, discussion may be "the better practice." [27]

Then, too, consider the following view of Professor Neil W. Chamberlain:

"To me, the fact of recognition of the union as bargaining agent carries with it the obligation by management to seek agreement with the

---

[17] See Arbitrator Reid in 27 LA 123, 125; Ryder in 24 LA 496, 499-500; McCoy in 16 LA 73, 74-75.

[18] See Arbitrator Blair in 22 LA 701, 703; Shulman in 19 LA 237, 240-242. Cf., Myers in 23 LA 776, 778-779.

[19] See Arbitrator Updegraff in 30 LA 115, 117, and in 18 LA 827, 830-831; Marshall in 29 LA 687, 692-693.

[20] See Arbitrator Reynard in 25 LA 611, 613-614; Klamon in 22 LA 336, 342-343, 351; Updegraff in 20 LA 890, 891, and in 18 LA 320, 322-323.

[21] See Arbitrator Warns in 29 LA 324, 326-328, and in 26 LA 155, 160; E. Warren in 19 LA 283, 286-287.

[22] See International Harvester Co., 22 LA 191, 192 (Platt, 1954).

[23] Lockheed Aircraft Corp., 25 LA 748, 751-752 (R. Williams, 1956). Also see Arbitrator Garrett in 15 LA 840, 841-842.

[24] Mathieson Chemical Corp., 18 LA 620, 624-625 (L. Smith, 1952).

[25] Pan-Am Southern Corp., 25 LA 611 (Reynard, 1955); American Seating Co., 16 LA 115 (Whiting, 1951).

[26] For instance, see Arbitrator Hepburn in 28 LA 467, 467-468; R. Williams in 25 LA 748, 751-752; Updegraff in 7 LA 943, 945; Whiting in 7 LA 183, 187. Regarding the duty to bargain during the term of the agreement see Chapter 13, subtopic titled "The Duty To Bargain; Right Of Unilateral Action."

[27] Bethlehem Steel Co., 16 LA 68, 70 (Feinberg, 1950).

union on matters relevant to the union-management relationship before taking action. But by no means does this interpretation carry with it the corollary that the functions of management are thereby being shared. * * * I would argue that the union has no injunctive authority, no veto power, to prevent management from acting, nor is there any obligation on management's part to accept the union viewpoint. Failing agreement, management remains free to act. It has not lost its powers of managing. It has simply undertaken to negotiate in good faith with that group whose interests it has recognized." [28]

Arbitrators have often ruled custom to be binding where it involved a "benefit" of peculiar personal value to the employees. These cases generally did not involve methods of operation or control of the working force (except perhaps indirectly). Thus, where the benefit was supported by established custom, management was not permitted to change or discontinue the following "benefits" or "working conditions": wash-up periods,[29] lunch period arrangements,[30] company-supplied electricity for employee homes,[31] maternity leaves of absence,[32] vacation pay,[33] bonuses,[34] right to higher rate when substituting on higher-rated work,[35] pay for time lost from work while receiving reprimand,[36] notice to union before discharge for dishonesty is effected,[37] right of senior employee to receive test before being rejected for job vacancy,[38] and change

---

[28] "Management's Reserved Rights," Management Rights and the Arbitration Process 118, 145-146 (BNA, Incorporated, 1956). Regarding the binding effect of practice, Professor Chamberlain observed: "* * * I suspect that there are *some* kinds of practices which do create obligations on management, though I would find it difficult to spell out the nature of such practices or the criteria by which they may be identified, or even the nature of management's obligation under them. Certainly I cannot agree * * * that the union has a stake in all existing practices such as to preclude management initiative." Id. at 147.

[29] International Harvester Co., 20 LA 276 (Wirtz, 1953); John Deere Waterloo Tractor Workers, 18 LA 276 (Davey, 1952).

[30] See Arbitrator Wagner in 30 LA 35; Dworkin in 24 LA 614; McCoy in 3 LA 137. Cf., Shister in 21 LA 476.

[31] Phillips Petroleum Co., 24 LA 191 (Merrill, 1955).

[32] Northland Greyhound Lines, Inc., 23 LA 277, 280 (Levinson, 1954).

[33] Franklin Assn. of Chicago, 7 LA 614, 620 (Gilden, 1947).

[34] See cases cited in Chapter 13, topic titled "Bonuses," where cases permitting the discontinuance of bonuses are also cited.

[35] Mt. Carmel Public Utility Co., 16 LA 59, 62 (Hampton, 1951).

[36] Firestone Tire & Rubber Co., 20 LA 880, 882-883 (Gorder, 1953).

[37] Coca-Cola Bottling Co., 9 LA 197 (Jacobs, 1947).

[38] Fruehauf Trailer Co., 29 LA 372 (E. Jones, 1957).

in job evaluation plan resulting in lower rate for employee.[39]

In some cases, however, management has been upheld in discontinuing customary employee benefits.[40] In some of these cases the company in giving the benefit had emphasized that it was to be a gratuity only and not a part of the wage structure, or there was some special justification for discontinuing the benefit. Another possibility is that the arbitrator will permit management to discontinue customary employee benefits, but only after negotiations; if negotiations fail to produce agreement, the employer may then take unilateral action even prior to the end of the contract term.[41]

We have noted that where custom has been enforced the element of "mutuality" has usually been supplied by implication—that is, there has been "implied mutual agreement." In this regard, existing employee benefits usually affect all or at least sizeable groups of employees, and thus are likely to be in the thoughts of union and company negotiators. It may reasonably be assumed that the parties in shaping bargaining demands as to wages and other employee benefits do so with silent recognition of existing unwritten benefits and favorable working conditions. This accepted, such matters may well be called "major" (for those who would apply a "major-minor" test).

It may be less plausible to assume that such bargaining demands are shaped with any comparable silent thought as to existing practices regarding methods of operation and direction of the working force—matters legitimately falling within the fundamental areas of basic management responsibility.

In the final analysis, management in most cases is not really oppressed when it is required to continue customary benefits for the remainder of the contract term. Management itself,

---

[39] General Aniline & Film Corp., 19 LA 628 (Talbott, 1952).

[40] See Arbitrator Schmidt in 30 LA 593, 595-598; Morris in 24 LA 745, 747-748; Louisell in 20 LA 826, 829-831; Giardino in 19 LA 421, 422; Naggi in 10 LA 804, 805. For cases in which management has been permitted to discontinue bonuses see Chapter 13, topic titled "Bonuses."

[41] See Ryan Aeronautical Co., 17 LA 395, 398-399 (Komaroff, 1951). Cf., Arbitrator Cahn in 17 LA 780, 783. Also see McCoy in 1 LA 556.

either unilaterally or by mutual decision, initially agreed to grant the benefits in most cases. In negotiating the collective bargaining agreement management, because of existing benefits, may very well have been faced with tempered wage demands by the employees. On the other hand, in most instances, it does not oppress the employees to deny continuance of established methods of operation or established practice regarding direction of the working force. Management freedom of action in the latter matters, though sometimes considered unjustified by the frequently few workers directly affected, is essential for efficient and progressive operation of the enterprise, and this serves the long-run interests of all the employees as well as management.

The above discussion suggests a test of "employee benefits" vs. "basic management functions," with which test many reported arbitration awards are compatible. Moreover, some of the awards which appear at first glance to be contrary to this test may conform to it upon closer analysis, the award being based in fact upon some clause of the written contract. The test gives the employees the benefit of the doubt as to certain matters and management is given the benefit of the doubt as to others. From this standpoint, too, the test may be deemed "fair" or "just."

While the above discussion provides some general guides for predicting the extent that unwritten practice and custom will be enforced by arbitrators, variations will often result from the peculiar facts and circumstances of the individual cases as well as from the thinking of the particular arbitrator making the ruling. It is entirely possible that under very similar circumstances one arbitrator might hold established practice subject to change or discontinuance during the term of the contract only by mutual agreement, but a second arbitrator might hold it subject to unilateral change or discontinuance at any time even without negotiations. Taking an intermediate approach, a third arbitrator might hold the practice subject to unilateral change or discontinuance during the term of the contract, but only after negotiations have failed to produce agreement.

In any event, if management does not choose to continue a customary benefit, negotiations can always be requested at the end of the contract term, and possibly sooner under federal legislation (if it covers the parties). Such request will no doubt affect the union's demands, however, and whether the benefit is then continued or ultimately eliminated by management after bargaining has run its course may depend, as in the case of other bargaining items, upon the parties' "trading" and the resulting "package" of terms ultimately included in the new written agreement. For treatment of the relevant federal legislation and for further consideration of managerial right to take unilateral action, the reader is directed to Chapter 13, subtopic titled "The Duty to Bargain; Right of Unilateral Action."

Contract Clauses Regarding Custom

The status of unwritten practice and custom may be dealt with specifically in the written agreement. All binding force of customary practices may be eliminated *if* the contract language is quite strong. Thus, even where a bonus practice was the product of negotiations between company and union and had been paid for several years, but where it was not written into the contract, it could be unilaterally discontinued by the employer since the written contract provided:

> "This contract represents complete collective bargaining and full agreement by the parties in respect to rates of pay, wages, hours of employment or other conditions of employment which shall prevail during the term hereof and any matters or subjects not herein covered have been satisfactorily adjusted, compromised or waived by the parties for the life of this agreement." [42]

But a weaker clause, stating that "this contract expresses the entire agreement between the parties," was held to eliminate

---

[42] Bassick Co., 26 LA 627, 630 (Kheel, 1956). Also see clause in Illinois Brick Co., 21 LA 398, 400 (Edes, 1953).

automatically only those practices which conflicted with the contract's terms, since practices, the arbitrator said, are not necessarily matters for agreement.[43]

Though a contract provided that it "cancels all previous Agreements, both written and oral, and constitutes the entire Agreement between the parties," an arbitrator declared that the provision "has no magical dissolving effect upon practices or customs which are continued in fact unabated and which span successive contract periods." [44]

Some collective agreements contain clauses designed to insure continuance of certain established practices.[45] Where a letter of local practices agreement specifically listed certain practices to be continued, an arbitrator ruled that the omission of other practices from the list did not imply that they could be unilaterally eliminated; rather, the effect of the list was to eliminate need for proof as to the existence of the practices listed. Other usages were not annulled without explicit language supporting their termination.[46]

"A general 'catch-all' provision, designed to freeze general working conditions, cannot be construed to nullify an express provision of the contract." [47] Thus, such a clause was held not to require the employer to continue a customary paid holiday the day before Christmas since the contract specifically listed paid holidays and Christmas Eve was not on the list. The general "custom" clause could not "expand and broaden an already specific provision." [48]

The agreement may provide that if the employer changes or eliminates established practices he shall, upon challenge through the grievance procedure, bear the burden to "justify"

[43] American Seating Co., 16 LA 115, 116-117 (Whiting, 1951).
[44] Fruehauf Trailer Co., 29 LA 372, 374-375 (E. Jones, 1957). Cf., New York Trap Rock Corp., 19 LA 421 (Giardino, 1952).
[45] As in Armco Steel Corp., 29 LA 737 (Cahn, 1957).
[46] Bakelite Co., 29 LA 555, 558-559 (Updegraff, 1957).
[47] Valley Dolomite Corp., 11 LA 98, 100 (McCoy, 1948).
[48] Machlett Laboratories, Inc., 26 LA 117, 120 (Scheiber, 1956).

his action.[49] A similar result might be reached even without a specific contract clause.[50]

Question of Arbitrability

The question of arbitrability in disputes concerning the binding status of custom was not raised in many of the cases cited above. Ordinarily there is little basis for raising the question where the collective agreement contains a broad arbitration clause or where the dispute is taken to arbitration by a joint submission. However, the question of arbitrability of custom disputes has sometimes been raised where the arbitration clause was limited to disputes concerning the interpretation or application of the "agreement." The question was answered in the affirmative in some cases,[51] but not in others.[52]

Role of Custom and Practice in Interpretation of Ambiguous Language

One of the most important standards used by arbitrators in the interpretation of ambiguous contract language is the custom or past practice of the parties. Indeed, use of past practice to give meaning to ambiguous contract language is so common that no citation of authority is necessary. The general attitude of arbitrators is illustrated by Arbitrator Charles C. Killingsworth, who, in noting that the parties had operated under a provision for nearly three years before requesting an arbitrator to interpret it, stated that he had "a context of practices, usages, and rule-of-thumb interpretations by which the parties themselves" had gradually given substance to the disputed term.[53]

---

[49] Bethlehem Steel Co., cases in 29 LA 418 (1957), and 17 LA 382 (1951). Also see Haddon Craftsmen, Inc., 23 LA 210, 212 (Gill, 1954).

[50] John Deere Waterloo Tractor Works, 18 LA 276, 278 (Davey, 1952).

[51] Garment Workers' Union v. Nazareth Mills Co., 22 LA 862, 867 (Pa. Comm. Pleas, 1954); Franklin Assn. of Chicago, 7 LA 614, 620-621 (Gilden, 1947). Also see General Cable Corp., 17 LA 780, 783 (Cahn, 1952).

[52] U. S. Industrial Chemicals Co., 28 LA 401, 402 (Alexander, 1957); M. T. Stevens & Sons Co., 7 LA 585, 587 (Copelof, 1947). Also see Chambersburg Engineering Co, 3 LA 254 (Brandschain, 1946); Uprichard v. Otis Elevator Co., 24 LA 58, 59 (N.Y. Sup. Ct., 1955).

[53] Eastern Stainless Steel Corp., 12 LA 709, 713 (1949).

Where past practice has established a meaning for language that is subsequently used by the parties in a new agreement, the language will be presumed to have the meaning given it by past practice.[54] "There would have to be very strong and compelling reasons for an arbitrator to change the practice by which a contract provision has been interpreted in a plant over a period of several years and several contracts. There would have to be a clear and unambiguous direction in the language used to effect such a change * * * "[55]

The weight to be accorded past practice as an interpretation guide may vary greatly from case to case. In this regard, the degree of mutuality is an important factor. Unilateral interpretations might not bind the other party.[56] However, continued failure of one party to object to the other party's interpretation is sometimes held to constitute acceptance of such interpretation so as to make it mutual.[57]

While arbitrators sometimes refuse to charge a party with knowledge of what is going on in the plant,[58] claims of lack of knowledge often carry relatively little weight. Thus, a party may be "assumed" to know what is transpiring,[59] or it might be held that a party "knew or should have reasonably known" of the asserted practice.[60] Even successor unions sometimes are charged with knowledge of practice under the same contract language as administered by the company and the predecessor union.[61]

Another important factor to be considered in determining the weight to be given to past practice is how well it is estab-

---

[54] E.g., Arbitrator Prasow in 23 LA 27, 32; Updegraff in 20 LA 243, 247; McCoy in 16 LA 240, 241; Kelliher in 15 LA 85, 87; Copelof in 7 LA 461, 466.

[55] Webster Tobacco Co., 5 LA 164, 166 (Brandschain, 1946).

[56] See statement of Arbitrator Hebert in 27 LA 762, 766-767; Baab in 23 LA 562, 569; Updegraff in 11 LA 825, 826; Potter in 7 LA 81, 84.

[57] See Arbitrator Allen in 22 LA 289, 291; Kirsh in 4 LA 584, 586; Prasow in 1 LA 313, 316. Also see Arbitrator Klamon in 29 LA 256, 258.

[58] Weber Aircraft Corp., 24 LA 821, 826-827 (E. Jones, 1955).

[59] Baer Bros., 16 LA 822, 824 (Donnelly, 1951).

[60] Owens-Corning Fiberglas Corp., 19 LA 57, 63 (Justin, 1952). Also see Devoe & Raynolds, 22 LA 608, 609 (Porter, 1954).

[61] Wagner Electric Corp., 21 LA 524, 527 (Brown, 1953). Also see Arbitrator Anderson in 29 LA 45, 49-50; Updegraff in 20 LA 243, 247.

lished. Arbitrator Robert E. Mathews has stated that to be given significant weight in contract interpretation, "the practice must be of sufficient generality and duration to imply acceptance of it as an authentic construction of the contract."[62] A "single incident" has been held not to establish a "practice,"[63] and two incidents likewise did not suffice.[64]

It seems reasonable that fewer instances would be required to establish a "practice" where the situation arises only infrequently than would be required where the situation arises often.[65]

Past practice, to be given significant weight, need not be absolutely uniform. Arbitrator Dale Yoder, for instance, held the "predominant pattern of practice" to be controlling even though there had been scattered exceptions to the "clearly established pattern."[66]

However, it is obvious that past practice provides no guide where evidence regarding its nature and duration is "highly contradictory."[67] Where such conflict exists the arbitrator will be inclined to rely entirely upon other standards of interpretation.

Custom and Practice v. Clear Contract Language

While custom and past practice are used very frequently to establish the intent of contract provisions which are so ambiguous or so general as to be capable of different interpretations, they ordinarily will not be used to give meaning to a provision which is clear and unambiguous. For instance, note the following statements:

Arbitrator Jules J. Justin: "Plain and unambiguous words are undisputed facts. The conduct of Parties may be used to fix a meaning to words and

---

[62] Sheller Mfg. Corp., 10 LA 617, 620 (1948). Also see Columbia Carbon Co., 27 LA 762, 766-767 (Hebert, 1956).

[63] Ottawa River Paper Co., 22 LA 835, 837 (R. Smith, 1954).

[64] York Bus Co., 24 LA 81, 87 (Loucks, 1955).

[65] North American Cement Corp., 28 LA 414, 417 (Callaghan, 1957).

[66] Curtis Companies, Inc., 29 LA 434, 439 (1957).

[67] Reliance Steel Products Co., 24 LA 30, 32 (Lehoczky, 1954). Also, Texas-U.S, Chemical Co., 27 LA 793, 795 (Reynard, 1956).

phrases of uncertain meaning. Prior acts cannot be used to change the explicit terms of a contract. An arbitrator's function is not to rewrite the Parties' contract. His function is limited to finding out what the Parties intended under a particular clause. The intent of the Parties is to be found in the words which they, themselves, employed to express their intent. When the language used is clear and explicit, the arbitrator is constrained to give effect to the thought expressed by the words used." [68]

Arbitrator Hubert Wyckoff: "[Established practice] is a useful means of ascertaining intention in case of ambiguity or indefiniteness; but no matter how well established a practice may be, it is unavailing to modify a clear promise." [69]

Many other arbitrators have expressed similar views.[70]

A related rule is that a party's failure to file grievances or to protest past violations of a clear contract rule does not bar that party, after notice to the violator, from insisting upon compliance with the clear contract requirement in future cases.[71]

The clear language of the contract has been enforced even where the arbitrator believed that, on the basis of equity, past practice should have governed:

"In the opinion of the Impartial Tribunal the practice would not have grown up in the first place and would not have been tolerated by the parties if the situation did not justify it. The sudden refusal of the union to continue with a practice that has apparently proved satisfactory for many years, thus precipitating the present dispute, may well be severely criticized as an unreasonable stand not necessary to protect any substantial right of the workers. * * * If it were at all possible the decision should be that the position of the workers is in violation of the contract." [72]

---

[68] Phelps Dodge Copper Products Corp., 16 LA 229, 233 (1951).

[69] Tide Water Oil Co., 17 LA 829, 833 (1952).

[70] E.g., Arbitrator Dworkin in 28 LA 362, 368; Reynard in 27 LA 793, 795; Stutz in 27 LA 662, 665; Duff in 26 LA 105, 107; Donnelly in 25 LA 472, 474; Prasow in 25 LA 398, 404; Morvant in 24 LA 750, 752; Parker in 22 LA 883, 886; Stutz in 21 LA 650, 652; Seward in 21 LA 579, 582; Shister in 21 LA 515, 516; Warren in 21 LA 228, 230; Hale in 20 LA 818, 823; Blair in 20 LA 372, 374-375; Ryder in 20 LA 337, 340-341; Platt in 17 LA 313, 317, and in 15 LA 713, 715; Luskin in 15 LA 918, 921; Cheney in 8 LA 518, 525; Peifer in 2 LA 66, 67. Also in apparent accord, McKelvey in 27 LA 229, 232; Davey in 22 LA 628, 631; Reid in 21 LA 699, 702; Allen in 15 LA 370, 372.

[71] E.g., Arbitrator L. Smith in 23 LA 289, 295; Lockhart in 17 LA 497, 503; Feinberg in 15 LA 688, 689; Luskin in 15 LA 918, 921; Maggs in 12 LA 311, 315; Courshon in 9 LA 484, 491 Wolff in 5 LA 333, 336. Also see McCoy in 24 LA 151. For discussion of related points see Chapter 10, topic titled "Waiver and Estoppel."

[72] Chicago Association of Dress Manufacturers, 1 ALAA par. 67,234, p. 67,521 (1945).

Amendment of Contract

While Arbitrator Harry H. Platt has emphasized that evidence of past practice "is wholly inadmissible where the contract language is plain and unambiguous," [73] he has also recognized that, on the basis of very strong proof, the clear language of the contract may be amended, thus:

> "While, to be sure, parties to a contract may modify it by a later *agreement*, the existence of which is to be deduced from their course of conduct, the conduct relied upon to show such modification must be unequivocal and the terms of modification must be definite, certain, and intentional." [74]

Arbitrator Hamilton Douglas has declared that a party contending that clear language has been modified must "show the assent of the other party and the minds of the parties must be shown to have met on a definite modification." [75] Arbitrator Charles C. Killingsworth would require a showing that "both parties * * * have evinced a positive acceptance or endorsement" of the practice.[76] Other arbitrators, too, have required a showing equivalent to mutual agreement upon contract amendment.[77]

Of course, the parties to a contract may amend it by a subsequent agreement. This result, for instance, was produced by a special "interpretation agreement" of the parties.[78]

Gap-Filling

Arbitrators have sometimes recognized that contract language may cover a matter generally but fail to cover all of its aspects—that is, "gaps" sometimes exist. It has been recognized that established practice may be used, not to set aside contract

---

[73] Penberthy Injector Co., 15 LA 713, 715 (1950).
[74] Gibson Refrigerator Co., 17 LA 313, 318 (1951), emphasis added. Also see comments of Arbitrator Platt in 22 LA 65, 68.
[75] Merrill-Stevens Dry Dock & Repair Co., 10 LA 562, 563 (1948).
[76] Bethlehem Steel Co., 13 LA 556, 560 (1949).
[77] E.g., Arbitrator Roberts in 28 LA 470, 474; Hoban in 27 LA 605, 607; Emery in 17 LA 90, 91. But long, unchallenged, practice was deemed sufficient by Arbitrator Lennard in 27 LA 376, 383; Gifford in 25 LA 826, 827; Sherbow in 17 LA 524, 526.
[78] Borg-Warner Corp., 29 LA 629, 633-634 (Marshall, 1957).

language, but to fill in the contract's gaps.[79] Similarly, past practice might indicate an exception to the general application of a contract clause.[80]

---

[79] E.g., Arbitrator Roberts in 28 LA 470, 474; Hogan in 25 LA 216, 225; Emery in 17 LA 90, 91; Killingsworth in 17 LA 65, 67.
[80] Standard Brands, Inc., 25 LA 851, 853 (Justin, 1955).

CHAPTER 13

MANAGEMENT RIGHTS

Views Regarding Management Rights

Under the common law, owners of business establishments possess certain freedoms of action, incidental to their legal status, which are commonly called "management rights" or "management prerogatives." The word "right" is defined by Webster's New International Dictionary to mean "any power, privilege, or immunity, vested in one by authority, social custom * * * or * * * by the law * * *." The same reference defines the word "prerogative" to mean the "right to exercise a power or privilege in priority to, or to the exclusion of, others * * * for the exercise of which in theory there is no responsibility or accountability as to the fact and the manner of its exercise."

Two management spokesmen, noting that the term "management prerogative" is as distasteful to union representatives as the term "closed shop" is to many management representatives, have denied that "management prerogative" refers to a divine right to manage. These spokesmen would define the term to refer to "those rights, or that authority, which management must have in order successfully to carry out its function of managing the enterprise." [1]

Management spokesmen generally adhere rigidly to the position that "residual" powers are in management. These spokesmen declare that under the common law an employer, as property owner, may operate his business as he chooses, except

---

[1] Hill & Hook, Management at the Bargaining Table 56 (1945). Also see Phelps, "Management's Reserved Rights: an Industry View," Management Rights and the Arbitration Process 102 (BNA Incorporated, 1956).

where his common-law rights have been limited by constitutional legislation or by collective bargaining agreements.[2] Thus management takes the position that it need not look to the collective bargaining agreement to determine what rights it has reserved to itself, but should look to the agreement only to determine what rights it has ceded away or agreed to share with employees. Spokesmen for management may be expected to caution management representatives "that, in drafting a collective bargaining agreement, the principle should be kept in mind that, except for statutory enactments, the employer today has retained the legal right to manage his business as he sees fit and that only through the instrumentality of a collective bargaining agreement can an employer legally lessen or lose this invaluable proprietary right."[3]

As might be expected, spokesmen for labor are not in complete accord with this position. The labor view is well illustrated by the statement of one labor spokesman who, in speaking of the approach taken by employers, said:

> "By this approach employers assert that industrial management is possessed of all wisdom and good judgment in the matters affecting its employees, except in those instances where it has confessed that its judgment is subject to review in a collective bargaining agreement. This approach belies the affirmative role aspired to by virtually all of the American labor movement for the maintenance of a system of private enterprise which affords industrial democracy to its employees. The trade unions of America wish to cooperate with industrial management in demonstrating to the world that an industrial society can achieve an equitable distribution of its goods and services without resort to totalitarian methods. The subordinate role to which the trade union is relegated by this extreme concept of management prerogatives suggests, not that the workers and their organizations are partners of industrial management, but rather that they are merely an incidental nuisance in our economic order, entitled to consideration only to the extent to which their nuisance value has been fixed by their contract."[4]

---

[2] See Hill "Using Management's Rights in Day-to-Day Labor Relations," American Management Association Personnel Series, No. 82, p. 11 (1944); Story, Arbitration as a Part of the Collective Bargaining Agreement (1948).

[3] Story, Arbitration as a Part of the Collective Bargaining Agreement 9 (1948).

[4] Kamin, The Collective Bargaining Agreement and Arbitral Jurisdiction 4-5 (1948). Also see Goldberg, "Management's Reserved Rights: A Labor View," Management Rights and the Arbitration Process 118 (BNA Incorporated, 1956).

This spokesman did state, however, that the American labor movement recognizes that there are legitimate management functions, that decisions concerning such functions are best made by management, and that it is only "when a moat is dug around the castle of 'management prerogatives' that the trade unions become concerned." [5]

In the past some attempt has been made to draw a line separating matters of interest to the union from those of sole concern to management. Such attempt was made at the President's Labor-Management Conference in 1945, but with no success. There, management members of the Committee on Management's Right to Manage did agree upon a specific classification of management functions. The labor members, however, were unable to accept any such clear-cut classification. They submitted a separate report explaining their position:

"The extensive exploratory discussions of the committee have brought forth the wide variety of traditions, customs, and practices that have grown out of relationships between unions and management in various industries over a long period of time.

"Because of the complexities of these relationships, the labor members of the committee think it unwise to specify and classify the functions and responsibilities of management. Because of the insistence by management for such specification, the committee was unable to agree upon a joint report. To do so might well restrict the flexibility so necessary to efficient operation.

"It would be extremely unwise to build a fence around the rights and responsibilities of management on the one hand and the unions on the other. The experience of many years shows that with the growth of mutual understanding the responsibilities of one of the parties today may well become the joint responsibility of both parties tomorrow.

"We cannot have one sharply delimited area designated as management prerogatives and another equally sharply defined area of union prerogatives without either side constantly attempting to invade the forbidden territory, thus creating much unnecessary strife." [6]

---

[5] Kamin, The Collective Bargaining Agreement and Arbitral Jurisdiction 4-5 (1948). "Some unions appear constantly to seek a larger share in the governance of the industry while others believe that they should avoid responsibility for the conduct of the business." Cox & Dunlop, "Regulation of Collective Bargaining by the National Labor Relations Board," 63 Harv. L. Rev. 389, 431 (1950).

[6] The President's National Labor-Management Conference, Nov. 5-30, 1945 (U. S. Dept. of Labor, Div. of Labor Standards, Bull. No. 77, pp. 57-59, 61, 1946).

Objective observers appear to share, in part at least, the views expressed by the labor members of the Committee. Some have declared: "Collective bargaining is too dynamic to permit drawing a statutory line between management's prerogatives and the areas of joint responsibility." [7] The conclusion reached by a group active in the Labor and Management Center at Yale University evidences strong conviction of the futility of attempting any absolute classification of management prerogatives. This group, speaking through Neil W. Chamberlain, Research Director of the Labor and Management Center, reached the following conclusion:

> "Our industrial relations department feels the futility of attempting to draw a separating line. Issues and relationships are evolutionary, and no such line would hold for longer than from one contract period to the next. * * * The Labor-Management Conference approach of attempting to spell out management prerogatives is not only inappropriate but impossible. It is impossible ever to draw up a complete list of management responsibilities and functions. They can't all be put down because they are so numerous and complex and because they are subject to change. The only feasible approach is to leave the settlement of such questions up to collective bargaining itself." [8]

The group recognized, too, that unions are ever penetrating deeper into areas of management control. "There is no consciousness of invading managerial prerogatives. By the same token there is no area of management which most of them would hesitate to put on 'next year's list' if they felt the interests of the union were involved."

Of great importance is the view taken by arbitrators in regard to management rights. Many arbitrators have expressly recognized that the residual powers are in management. [9]

---

[7] Cox & Dunlop, "Regulation of Collective Bargaining by the National Labor Relations Board," 63 Harv. L. Rev. 389, 430 (1950).

[8] Chamberlain, The Union Challenge to Management Control 156-157 (1948) [Quoted with consent of the publisher, Harper & Brothers].

[9] E.g., Arbitrator Larson in 29 LA 795, 800; Howlett in 29 LA 495, 500; Hepburn in 28 LA 467, 467-468; Stouffer in 28 LA 429, 431; Prasow in 27 LA 6, 9-10; R. R. Williams in 27 LA 520, 522; Whelan in 26 LA 792, 806; Beatty in 25 LA 838, 840; Reynard in 24 LA 369, 371-372; Graff in 24 LA 304; McGoldrick in 24 LA 1, 6; Wersing in 23 LA 797, 798; Platt in 22 LA 464, 465-466; Cahn in 22 LA 13, 16; Van de Water in 21 LA 76, 79; L. Smith in 20 LA 710, 712; Hawley in 19 LA 393, 395; Cheney in 16 LA 83, 85; Hampton in 16 LA 59, 64; Klamon in 15 LA 733,

Arbitrator Clarence M. Updegraff, for instance, has said: "It is now a well-established generalization that every employer continues to have all powers previously had or exercised by employers unless such powers have been curtailed or eliminated by statute or by contract with a union." [10]

Arbitrator Whitley P. McCoy has accepted as unassailable the contention of an employer that in the absence of contract, management has the unrestricted right to manage, make rules, set working hours, and fix all other conditions of employment; that, when the employer enters into contractual relations with a union, it gives up such rights only to the extent set forth in the contract.[11]

Arbitrator Dudley E. Whiting has declared that a collective bargaining agreement operates as a limitation upon the previous absolute right of the employer to establish working conditions, but only to the extent that conditions of employment are thereby established. "The pre-existing right of the employer still continues as to all matters not covered by the agreement." [12]

Limitations on Management Rights

In recent decades there has been progressive invasion of once unchallenged areas of exclusive managerial decision. Many things which were once regarded as the "rights" or "prerogatives" of management have ceased to be so characterized. Inroads into management areas have been made by legislation, collective bargaining, and arbitration.

Inroads Made by Legislation

Beginning about 1890 and continuing through the years, the enactment of state and federal legislation has restricted, to

---

139; Davis in 15 LA 274, 280; Kelliher in 12 LA 779, 783; McCreary in 9 LA 834, 839-841; Potter in 8 LA 634, 637; Updegraff in 7 LA 943, 945; Brandschain in 4 LA 52, 54; Whiting in 3 LA 482, 485; McCoy in 1 LA 556, 559; Korey in 1 LA 430, 432. Also see Warns in 29 LA 324, 326; Cheit in 21 LA 98, 104; Emery in 19 LA 663, 665; Feinberg in 16 LA 68, 70; Gregory in 15 LA 420, 424. Cf., Jaffee in 19 LA 467, 469-470.

[10] Blackhawk Mfg. Co., 7 LA 943, 945 (1947).
[11] Goodyear Tire & Rubber Co., 1 LA 556, 559 (1946).
[12] New York Car Wheel Co., 7 LA 183, 187 (1947)

some extent, the right of management to offer employment upon its own terms. Restrictions are found in laws relating to minimum wages and maximum hours, child labor, health and safety, workmen's compensation, unemployment insurance, yellow-dog contracts, fair employment practices, and the like. Such legislation as the Sherman Act, the Clayton Act, the Robinson-Patman Act, and the Securities Exchange Act, each in its own way, has drained the reservoir of management rights. Much of this legislation was enacted largely and directly in the interest of the public. More direct restriction upon management rights came about through the Railway Labor Act of 1926, the National Labor Relations Act of 1935, and the Labor-Management Relations Act of 1947.

The Duty to Bargain: Right of Unilateral Action

The labor relations acts, by stimulating collective bargaining, set the stage for over-all restriction of management rights through the provisions of collective bargaining agreements. The original National Labor Relations Act placed on employers a legally enforceable duty to bargain with duly authorized employee representatives on subjects falling within the terms "rates of pay, wages, hours of employment, or other conditions of employment." The same obligation is continued in the Labor-Management Relations Act.

Cases decided by the National Labor Relations Board and by the courts have established that, in addition to wages and hours, the area of mandatory bargaining covers such subjects as holiday and vacation pay,[13] subcontracting,[14] discharges,[15] work loads and work standards,[16] bonuses,[17] pensions,[18] profit

[13] Singer Mfg. Co., 24 NLRB 444, 6 LRRM 405 (1940), enforced, 119 F. 2d 131, 8 LRRM 740 (C.A. 7th, 1941); Athens Mfg. Co., 69 NLRB 605, 18 LRRM 1235 (1946); Union Mfg. Co., 76 NLRB 322, 21 LRRM 1187 (1948).
[14] Timken Roller Bearing Co., 70 NLRB 500, 18 LRRM 1370 (1946), set aside on other grounds, 161 F. 2d 949, 20 LRRM 2204 (C.A. 6th, 1947).
[15] NLRB v. Bachelder, 120 F. 2d 574, 8 LRRM 723 (C.A. 7th, 1941).
[16] Woodside Cotton Mills Co., 21 NLRB 42, 6 LRRM 68 (1940).
[17] NLRB v. Niles-Bement-Pond Co., 199 F. 2d 713, 31 LRRM 2057 (C.A. 2d, 1952); Union Mfg. Co., 76 NLRB 322, 21 LRRM 1187 (1948).
[18] Inland Steel Co., 77 NLRB 1, 21 LRRM 1310 (1948), enforced, 170 F. 2d 247, 22 LRRM 2506 (C.A. 7th, 1948), cert. den., 336 U.S. 960, 24 LRRM 2019 (1949).

sharing,[19] insurance benefits,[20] merit increases,[21] closed or union shop,[22] work schedules,[23] plant rules,[24] rest periods,[25] placing existing practices in the contract,[26] checkoff of union dues,[27] management rights,[28] incentive pay plans,[29] company owned houses,[30] stock purchase plans,[31] production work by supervisors,[32] paid coffee break,[33] and transfer of employees upon move of plant.[34]

The above enumeration of bargaining subjects is neither exhaustive nor final. It does not include seniority, for instance, which is a most common subject of bargaining and unquestionably falls within the area of mandatory bargaining, although the latter result appears not to have been directly litigated. Then, too, some of the subjects that have been directly held to fall within or without the area of mandatory bargaining might be held otherwise by future decision.

---

[19] NLRB v. Black-Clawson Co., 33 LRRM 2567 (C.A. 6th, 1954); Union Mfg. Co., 76 NLRB 322, 21 LRRM 1187 (1948).
[20] W. W. Cross & Co., 77 NLRB 1162, 22 LRMM 1131 (1948), enforced, 174 F. 2d 875, 24 LRRM 2068 (C.A. 1st, 1949); General Motors Corp., 81 NLRB 779, 23 LRRM 1422 (1949).
[21] NLRB v. J. H. Allison & Co., 70 NLRB 377, 18 LRRM 1369 (1946) enforced, 165 F. 2d 766, 21 LRRM 2238 (C.A. 6th, 1948), cert. den., 335 U.S. 814, 22 LRRM 2564 (1948).
[22] NLRB v. Winona Textile Mills, Inc., 160 F. 2d 201, 19 LRRM 2417 (C.A. 8th, 1947); Andrew Jergens Co., 76 NLRB 363, 21 LRRM 1192 (1948); Alexander Milburn Co., 62 NLRB 482, 16 LRRM 202 (1945). The Labor-Management Relations Act bans closed shops and restricts other forms of union security.
[23] Inter-City Advertising Co., 61 NLRB 1377, 16 LRRM 153 (1945), enforcement den. on other grounds, 154 F. 2d 244, 17 LRRM 916 (C.A. 4th, 1946); Wilson & Co., 19 NLRB 990, 5 LRRM 560 (1940), enforced, 115 F 2d 759, 7 LRRM 575 (C.A. 8th, 1940).
[24] Timken Roller Bearing Co., 70 NLRB 500, 18 LRRM 1370 (1946), enforcement den. on other grounds, 161 F. 2d 949, 20 LRRM 2204 (C.A. 6th, 1947.
[25] National Grinding Wheel Co., 75 NLRB 905, 21 LRRM 1095 (1948).
[26] Nat'l Carbon Div., Union Carbide and Carbon Co., 30 LRRM 1338 (1952), amended without affecting this point, 32 LRRM 1276 (1953).
[27] U.S. Gypsum Co., 94 NLRB 112, 29 LRRM 1015, 1171 (1951).
[28] NLRB v. American National Insurance Co., 343 U.S. 395, 30 LRRM 2147 (1952).
[29] East Texas Steel Castings Co., 99 NLRB 1339 (1952), 33 LRRM 2793 (C.A. 5th, 1954); John W. Bolton & Sons, 91 NLRB 989, 26 LRRM 1598 (1950).
[30] NLRB v. Lehigh Portland Cement Co., 205 F. 2d 821, 32 LRRM 2463 (C.A. 4th, 1953). Cf., NLRB v Bemis Bros. Bag Co., 206 F. 2d 33, 32 LRRM 2535 (C.A. 5th, 1953).
[31] Richfield Oil Corp v. NLRB, 231 F. 2d 717, 37 LRRM 2327 (C.A.D.C., 1956).
[32] Globe-Union, Inc., 97 NLRB 1026, 29 LRRM 1198 (1952).
[33] Fleming Manufacturing Co., 119 NLRB No. 55, 41 LRRM 1115 (1957).
[34] Mount Hope Finishing Co., 106 NLRB 480, 32 LRRM 1492 (1953) (enforcement denied, 211 F. 2d 365, 33 LRRM 2742; 1954).

Section 8 (d) of the Labor-Management Relations Act provides, in part, that "* * * to bargain collectively is the performance of the mutual obligation of the employer and the representative of the employees to meet at reasonable times and confer in good faith with respect to wages, hours, and other terms and conditions of employment, or the negotiation of an agreement, or any question arising thereunder and the execution of a written contract incorporating any agreement reached if requested by either party, but such obligation does not compel either party to agree to a proposal or require the making of a concession * * *." The duty is to bargain upon request.[35]

Section 8 (d) also provides that there is no duty to bargain about proposals to make changes in the collective agreement that would take effect during its term. Nor is the employer required to bargain during the term of the contract upon any subject which was discussed in pre-contract negotiations but not included in the contract.[36]

But in the "Jacobs" case the National Labor Relations Board held, and was affirmed by the Court of Appeals, that "those bargainable issues which have never been discussed by the parties, and which are in no way treated in the contract, remain matters which both the union and the employer are obliged to discuss at any time."[37]

---

[35] NLRB v. Columbian Enameling and Stamping Co., Inc., 306 U.S. 292, 4 LRR Man. 524 (1939); Atlas Life Ins. Co., 29 LRRM 2499 (C.A. 10th, 1952). Where negotiations had resulted in a deadlock and no further conferences had been planned, an employer was not obligated to negotiate further without a request therefor by the employees. NLRB v. Sands Mfg. Co., 306 U.S. 332, 4 LRR Man. 530 (1939). As long as the impasse in negotiations is genuine, there is no refusal to bargain. Mexia Textile Mills, 11 NLRB 1167, 4 LRR Man. 73 (1939); Kentucky Tennessee Clay Co., 49 NLRB 252, 12 LRR Man. 167 (1943).

[36] Union Carbide & Carbon Corp., 100 NLRB 689, 690-691, 30 LRRM 1338 (1952); 104 NLRB 416, 32 LRRM 1276 (1953). Also see The Borden Company, 110 NLRB 802, 804 (1954).

[37] In re Jacobs Manufacturing Company, 94 NLRB 1214 (1951), affirmed in NLRB v. Jacobs Manufacturing Company, 196 F. 2d 680 (C.A. 2d, 1952), which was followed in Local Union No. 9735, U.M.W. v. NLRB, 258 F. 2d 146, 149 (C.A. D.C., 1958). The Board had taken a similar position in Allied Mills, Inc., 82 NLRB 854, 862, 23 LRRM 1632 (1949); Tide Water Ass'd Oil Co., 85 NLRB 1096, 24 LRRM 1518 (1949). In an article written prior to the Board's "Jacobs" decision Professors Archibald Cox and John T. Dunlop had disagreed with the Board. They suggested that "a collective bargaining agreement should be deemed, unless a contrary intention is manifest, to carry forward for its term the major terms and conditions of

The duty to bargain in good faith does not mean that agreement must be reached. Moreover, where bargaining fails to produce agreement upon a matter, management is privileged to take unilateral action. This was emphasized by the United States Court of Appeals, Sixth Circuit, in the "Nichols" case, wherein the court spoke in terms of certain of management's residual "common law" rights:

> "The Labor Management Relations Act in defining the phrase 'to bargain collectively' expressly provides * * * 'but such obligation does not compel either party to agree to a proposal or require the making of a concession.' * * * It would seem to logically follow that the common law right on the part of the employer to select his employees and to terminate their employment at will continues to exist except to the extent that it may be modified by the bargaining contract with the Union. Instead of making this right dependent upon a provision to that effect in the contract, it is a right which an employer normally has unless it has been eliminated or modified by the contract. * * *

> "* * * a collective bargaining agreement does not necessarily express the full coverage of employment rights. It covers such matters only as the parties may have been able to agree upon and leaves unresolved such issues as the parties may not have been able to agree upon and with respect to which the law does not require a concession by either party. As hereinafter pointed out, the evidence in this case shows that compulsory retirement was one of the issues between the Company and the Union upon which no agreement could be reached. * * * A failure to reach an agreement on this subject would not prevent the execution of a collective bargaining agreement covering most of the standard issues usually included in such agreements. N.L.R.B. v. Nash-Finch Co., 8 Cir., 211 F. 2d 622, 626-627. The Union was within its rights in refusing to agree to a compulsory retirement policy, which the evidence shows was presented by the Company in collective bargaining sessions, without it being linked to an adequate and satisfactory pension plan. But such failure to reach an agreement did not deprive the Company of its common law right to hire and fire at will until such an agreement was reached. Williams v. Jacksonville Terminal Co., 315 U.S. 386, 402, 62 S. Ct. 659, 86 L. Ed. 914. Accordingly, instead of searching for a provision in the contract authorizing

---

employment, not covered by the agreement, which prevailed when the agreement was executed", and that it should be an unfair labor practice for either party to make a unilateral change in a major condition of employment during the term of an existing agreement even though the contract does not deal with the subject matter. Cox & Dunlop, "The Duty to Bargain During the Term of an Existing Agreement," 63 Harv. L. Rev. 1097, 1116-1117, 1125 et seq. (1950). The Cox-Dunlop article induced a vigorous defense of the Board's position. See Findling & Colby, "Regulation of Collective Bargaining by the National Labor Relations Board—Another View," 51 Col. L. Rev. 170 (1951).

termination of employment by reason of age, we think it is necessary to determine from a consideration of the terms of the contract whether termination of employment by reason of age was prohibited by the contract." [38]

As previously noted, many arbitrators have recognized that management retains all common law managerial rights except as restricted by statute or collective agreement. Management's freedom to take unilateral action has been elaborated by Arbitrator Dudley E. Whiting:

"[collective] agreement operates as a limitation upon the previous absolute right of the employer to establish working conditions but only to the extent that conditions of employment are thereby established. The pre-existing right of the employer still continues as to all matters not covered by the agreement. The employer thus has an absolute right to establish or change working conditions for which the collective agreement makes no provision.

"Right to Appeal Employer's Actions

"When the employer so acts, during the term of the agreement, the representative of the employee has a right to demand bargaining upon such new or changed condition of employment, provided it was not a subject matter which was 'traded away' in the negotiation of the contract, because collective bargaining is a continuing right and duty. Alternatively, of course, such action may be challenged and tested through the grievance procedures of the contract. But there is no legal requirement that the consent of the employees' bargaining agent be obtained before initiation of the change under such circumstances." [39]

Arbitrator Charles O. Gregory has also observed:

"What if an agreement is completely silent about a certain matter, such as whether or not separate operations may be coordinated and put on assem-

---

[38] United States Steel Corporation v. Nichols, 229 F. 2d 396, 399-400, 37 LRRM 2420 (C.A. 6th, 1956), cert. den. 351 U.S. 950. In the "Nash-Finch" case cited in the above quotation an employer's unilateral discontinuance of bonus benefits, which had been discussed in negotiations but upon which no agreement had been reached, was held not to be unlawful. Also see Steelworkers v. Warrior & Gulf Navigation Co., 43 LRRM 2328 (U.S.D.C., 1958); The Borden Company, 110 NLRB 802, 35 LRRM 1133 (1954). In NLRB v. Crompton-Highland Mills, Inc., 69 S. Ct. 960, 961, 24 LRRM 2088 (1949), the employer unilaterally granted a wage increase, after a bargaining impasse had been reached but before negotiations had been completely terminated, substantially greater than he had proposed in bargaining; the U.S. Supreme Court concluded that "under the circumstances" this was an unfair labor practice. The Court indicated that it would have been proper for the employer to unilaterally grant the increase proposed by him but rejected by the union in bargaining. Id. at 963.

[39] New York Car Wheel Co., 7 LA 183, 187 (1947). Also see statements by Arbitrator Hepburn in 28 LA 467, 467-468; Bowles in 26 LA 931, 933; R. Williams in 25 LA 748, 751-752; Platt in 22 LA 191, 192; Feinberg in 16 LA 68, 70; Cahn in 15 LA 343, 345; Updegraff in 7 LA 943, 945.

bly-line production, and whether or not the various jobs in a certain department may be changed from an individual to a group-incentive basis? If these matters are not covered at all, does this mean that management has the right during the life of the contract unilaterally to make these changes as part of its function to manage? I have always supposed that it did mean just that. Naturally, the union may interpose bargaining demands concerning these changes, with a view to modifying them in the next contract. But I should think management would have to have this unilateral right, as long as its acts are not inconsistent with provisions of the current agreement. * * * Nowadays, this unilateral right is always subject to curtailment if the union insists upon bargaining over the subject matter involved. Whether or not management's unilateral innovations become modified depends entirely upon the course of the bargaining itself." [40]

However, it must be emphasized that numerous arbitrators (including Whiting, Updegraff and some of the other arbitrators cited immediately hereinabove) have accepted the view that under some circumstances unwritten practices and custom, as to some matters, shoud be held binding upon both parties as being in essence a part of their "whole" agreement.[41] Under an arbitration award which applies this view to any given matter, management may not make changes as to that matter during the term of the written agreement without the consent of the union.

The significance of collective agreement arbitration clauses (and awards issued thereunder) in relation to the legal duty to bargain collectively is indicated by the decision of the U. S. Court of Appeals, Sixth Circuit, in the "Timken" case.[42] The agreement involved in that case provided that "any grievance or dispute involving the interpretation or application of the contract not thereby adjusted should be submitted to arbitration." The agreement also provided:

"The management of the works and the direction of the working forces, including the right to hire, suspend or discharge for proper cause,

---

[40] Gregory, "The Collective Bargaining Agreement: Its Nature and Scope," Wash. U.L.Q. 3, 20-21 (Fall, 1949), reprinted in 1 Lab. L.J. 451, 459-460.
[41] For full discussion see Chapter 12, topic titled "Custom And Practice As Part Of The Contract".
[42] Timken Roller Bearing Co. v. National Labor Relations Board, 161 F. 2d 949, 20 LRRM 2204 (C.A. 6th, 1947), denying enforcement to 70 NLRB 500, 18 LRRM 1370 (1946).

or transfer, and the right to relieve employees from duty because of lack of work, or for other legitimate reasons, is vested exclusively in the Company, provided that this will not be used for purposes of discrimination against any member of the Union."

When the union demanded that it be consulted on the subject of subcontracting, the company refused to comply, stating that the matter was essentially a function of management and that it had been made so by the parties' contract. The court held that the employer's refusal to confer with the union on the matter of subcontracting was not, on the facts of the case, a refusal to bargain such as to constitute an unfair labor practice. The court noted that the company for many years had engaged in subcontracting, that it was engaged in subcontracting when the collective agreement was signed, and that no grievances had been filed in respect to the matter except one which had been abandoned before being taken completely through the grievance procedure. The court stated that the practical construction put upon the management clause by both parties was that subcontracting was a function of management. Moreover, the court said: "Be that as it may— the dispute, as it finally developed, was a dispute as to the interpretation of the management clause, and the contract specifically provided that such disputes were to be settled within the grievance procedures and, if they failed, by arbitration." [43] Thus, the court held that the company could lawfully insist on the use of the grievance procedure and ultimately on arbitration to determine whether the management rights clause was broad enough in scope to include subcontracting.

Professors Archibald Cox and John T. Dunlop have stated that this ruling "implies that [the company] could lawfully stand on a favorable arbitration award until the expiration of the contract." [44]

---

[43] Id. at 955. Also see The Borden Company, 110 NLRB 802, 35 LRRM 1133 (1954).

[44] Cox & Dunlop, "Regulation of Collective Bargaining by the National Labor Relations Board," 63 Harv. L. Rev. 389, 424 (1950). In Tide Water Ass'd Oil Co., 85 NLRB 1096, 24 LRRM 1518 (1949), the NLRB ruled that, under a management clause providing that "the management of the Refinery and the direction of

Their conclusion in regard to the significance of collective agreement dispute settlement procedures in relation to the legal duty to bargain collectively is as follows:

> "During the term of a collective bargaining agreement, an offer to follow the contract grievance procedure satisfies any duty to bargain collectively with respect to a matter to which the contract grievance procedure may apply. A refusal either to follow the contract procedure or to discuss the issue at large is a violation of Sections 8(a)(5) and 8(b)(3) [of the Labor-Management Relations Act]." [45]

Inroads Through Collective Bargaining

Collective bargaining is said to be "the very mechanism by which organized workers may achieve control and exercise it jointly with management." "The primary mechanism by which unions may share managerial authority in the corporation is collective bargaining, including both contract neegotiations and grievance procedures, supported by the power of the strike. Management's concern with what it considers an encroachment on its prerogatives arises in the main from demands made, and sometimes won, at the bargaining table." [46]

Restrictions made by collective bargaining agreements upon management prerogatives are not always confined to the area of wages, hours, and conditions of employment. In fact, it is conceivable that such restrictions might invade the entire field of management functions. There is nothing to prevent weaker employers from bargaining, and making concessions, with respect to practically any matter in the area of management functions concerning which stronger unions wish to have a voice. Also, the invasion of management prerogatives through collective bargaining may be more far-reaching than appears on the surface. Concern regarding this possibility was expressed by the economist Summer H. Slichter:

---

the working forces and operations at the Refinery * * * are the exclusive functions of management," the determination of retirement and pension policies was not the exclusive right of management. It would seem that, if an arbitrator had interpreted the management clause to be broad enough in scope to cover these subjects, the award, under the "Timken" decision, would have been binding upon the parties.

[45] Cox & Dunlop, "The Duty to Bargain Collectively During the Term of an Existing Agreement," 63 Harv. L. Rev. 1097, 1101 (1950), italics omitted.

[46] Chamberlain, The Union Challenge to Management Control 105 (1948).

"Protecting the status of management and preserving its essential prerogatives have not been a sufficiently definite objective of either union or employer policy in building up our system of industrial jurisprudence. In actual bargaining, the working rules of trade unions are built up gradually one or two at a time. This leads to an atomistic consideration of their effects, which may cause their effects as a whole to be overlooked." [47]

Management spokesmen declare that, where frontal attacks on management prerogatives have not met with success, union negotiators have developed flanking maneuvers which have been more effective. The success of such maneuvers is said to be due to the fact that they are methods of approach which appear on the surface to be reasonable and that their danger to management often is not perceived until too late. These indirect methods of invasion are considered to include (1) mutual-consent clauses, (2) joint committees of labor and management, (3) clauses for the application of strict length-of-service seniority, and (4) unlimited arbitration clauses.[48]

Inroads Through Arbitration

Sometimes belief is expressed that arbitration is a device by which a union may broaden its authority within an industrial enterprise.[49] It is said that management rights may be lost through the use of "wide open" arbitration clauses under which the arbitrator is given authority to decide questions raised by the union concerning any matter, whether within or without the scope of the collective bargaining agreement. Moreover, warning is given that management rights also may be lost through "the creation of contract ambiguities due to inept use of the English language, which enable an arbitrator to interpret a clause in a manner not intended by the employer." [50] This spokesman also added, however, that management rights may

---

[47] Slichter, Union Policies and Industrial Management 578 (1941).
[48] Hill & Hook, Management at the Bargaining Table 61 (1945); Dunn, Management Rights in Labor Relations 111, 112 (1946).
[49] Ibid. Also, Chamberlain, The Union Challenge to Management Control 107 (1948).
[50] Story, Arbitration as a Part of the Collective Bargaining Agreement 4 (1948).

be protected, too, through the arbitration provisions of an agreement.[51]

When an "interests" dispute is submitted to arbitration, there is some substitution of the judgment of the arbitrator for that of the parties. "To the extent that his decision finds in favor of the union, whether in whole or in part, he becomes the instrument by which union power has been extended." [52] One board of arbitration has explained the surrender of management prerogatives in "interests" arbitration as follows:

"Each collective bargaining contract that is executed necessarily entails a reduction in management's prerogatives and a corresponding reduction in its freedom of absolute action. Thus when management agrees with a union to pay a stipulated wage, it, in effect, surrenders its 'prerogative' to determine its employees' wages by unilateral action.

"Such surrender of 'prerogative' is even more pronounced when management agrees to arbitrate a dispute. An agreement to arbitrate constitutes a complete surrender of a company's right to determine the controversy by unilateral action or voluntary agreement or by a test of economic strength. It likewise constitutes a complete surrender of the union's right to test its contentions by a show of economic strength." [53]

Management spokesmen have recommended, in connection with arbitration clauses in collective agreements, the use of certain "protective" clauses designed to prevent the invasion of management rights through arbitration. The following clauses, for instance, have been suggested:

"Every decision of the impartial referee made within the scope of his jurisdictional authority shall be binding upon the company, the employees, and the union. The jurisdictional authority of the impartial referee is defined as, and limited to, the determination of any allegation of violation of a specific provision of this agreement, submitted to him and considered by him in accordance with the provisions of this agreement." [54]

"In making his decision, the impartial referee shall be bound by the principles of law relating to the interpretation of contracts followed by courts of record of the State of _____." [55]

"Provided, however, that if such a grievance is carried to arbitration, the Arbitrator shall not substitute his judgment for that of Management

---

[51] Id. at 1.
[52] Chamberlain, The Union Challenge to Management Control 107 (1948).
[53] Pan American Airways, Inc., 5 LA 590, 595 (Cahn, Snyder & Forge, 1946).
[54] Story Arbitration as a Part of the Collective Bargaining Agreement 10 (1948).
[55] Ibid.

and shall reverse the decision of Management only if he finds that it has acted arbitrarily and without reason, or for the purpose of escaping or defeating any of the other articles of this Agreement." [56]

Management Rights Clauses

While some difference of opinion exists among management representatives regarding the advisability of having a management rights clause, such provisions, which vary widely in form and content, are common in collective agreements.

A management clause may provide simply:

"Management has the right to manage the plants of the company except insofar as that right is limited by other provisions of this agreement."

This clause is favored because it contains a clear-cut statement of the rule that the employer has all the proprietary rights of management except as restricted by the terms of the collective agreement.[57] Some employers, however, considering that management retains all rights not contracted away by the agreement, might ask: "Why insert such a clause in the contract and run the risk of a possible misinterpretation of the clause itself?" [58]

Another point of view is that management rights clauses serve to remind arbitrators not to substitute their judgment for that of management, and also serve to aid union officials in explaining to the membership what the agreement does and does not give them.[59] In this regard, some employers may consider it "desirable to specify certain powers of management, so that both the representatives of the employees and the employees themselves may thoroughly understand what they are and that they cannot whittle them away during the contract term,

---

[56] Clifton, "Management Functions," N.Y.U. First Ann. Conf. on Labor 89, 97 (1948). A similar clause was involved in De Laval Separator Co., 18 LA 900, 901-903, Finnegan, 1952).

[57] See Story, Arbitration as a Part of the Collective Bargaining Agreement 11 (1948); Dunn, Management Rights in Labor Relations 109 (1946). Also see Hill & Hook, Management at the Bargaining Table 58 (1945); Clifton, "Management Functions," N.Y.U. First Ann. Conf. on Labor 89, 93 (1948).

[58] See Story, Arbitration as a Part of the Collective Bargaining Agreement 11 (1948).

[59] See Phelps, "Management's Reserved Rights: an Industry View," Management Rights and the Arbitration Process 102, 113-114 (BNA Incorporated, 1956).

but only by way of collective bargaining across the table." [60]
Some management clauses do state specific powers to be exercised by management. The following are illustrative of this
type of provision:

"It is mutually agreed that the Company shall have the sole right to
determine the extent to which the plant shall be operated, production or
employment increased or reduced, including the right to plan, direct, and
control plant operations, hire, suspend, or discharge for proper cause and
the right to introduce new or improved methods or facilities * * *." [61]

"Section 1. It is expressly agreed that all rights which ordinarily
vest in and are exercised by employers such as COMPANY, except such
as are clearly relinquished herein by COMPANY, are reserved to and shall
continue to vest in COMPANY. This shall include, this enumeration
being merely by way of illustration and not by way of limitation, the
right to:

"(a) Manage the plant and direct the working forces, including the
right to hire and to suspend, discipline or discharge employees for proper
cause.

"(b) Transfer employees from one department and/or classification
to another.

"(c) Lay off or relieve employees from duty because of lack of work
or for other legitimate reasons.

"(d) Promote and/or transfer employees to positions and classifications not covered by this agreement, it being understood employees in
the bargaining unit cannot be forced to take a position outside the bargaining unit.

"(e) Make such operating changes as are deemed necessary by it for
the efficient and economical operation of the plant, including the right to
change the normal work-week, the number of hours normally worked
during the work-week, the length of the normal work-day, the hours of
work, the beginning and ending time of each shift or assignment, and the
number of shifts to be operated.

"(f) Transfer persons from positions and classifications not covered
by this agreement to positions and/or classifications covered hereby.

"(g) Maintain discipline and efficiency.

"(h) Hire, promote, demote, transfer, discharge or discipline all
levels of supervision or other persons not covered by this agreement.

"(i) Determine the type of products to be manufactured, the location of work within the plant, the schedules of production, the schedules

---

[60] Clifton, "Management Functions," N.Y.U First Ann. Conf. on Labor 89, 93
(1948).
[61] Schick, Inc., 2 LA 552, 553 (1945).

of work within work periods, and the methods, processes, and means of manufacture and the conduct of other plant operations." [62]

Finally, it should be noted that during the term of a collective agreement which contains a broad management rights clause the employer might not be required to bargain about some changes upon which, in the absence of such clause and upon request by the union, he might otherwise be compelled to bargain.[63]

Impact of Arbitration Upon Management Rights

The extensive use of labor-management arbitration is resulting in the evolution of a private system of industrial jurisprudence. Included within the growing body of industrial rulings are many involving management rights issues. While legal principles, as well as court and administrative board decisions, loom in the background, there is, generally speaking, no absolute requirement that these be observed by arbitrators. It shoud be recognized, therefore, that industrial case law is in itself a separate and distinct institution. It should be recognized, also, that the industrial jurisprudence of arbitrators will not always be in absolute harmony with the course of decisions under the National Labor Relations Act. In fact, it might be said that the industrial jurisprudence of arbitrators is closely akin to "the law in action", which, as is well known, is not always the same as "the law in the books".[64]

The primary objective of the remainder of this Chapter will be to consider the effective scope of management prerogatives as evidenced and outlined by arbitration awards.

---

[62] Southern Aircraft Corp. and Int'l. Union of United Automobile, Aircraft, and Agricultural Implement Workers of America, UAW-CIO.

[63] See The Borden Company, 110 NLRB 802, 35 LRRM 1133 (1954).

[64] This, it would appear, was recognized by Professors Archibald Cox and John T. Dunlop when, in emphasizing one gap which seemed to be developing between the needs and practices of voluntary collective bargaining and certain doctrines being developed by the NLRB, they concluded: "Fortunately, management and unions have thus far shaped their own relationships during the term of collective bargaining agreements without too much regard for the NLRB." Cox & Dunlop, "The Duty to Bargain Collectively During the Term of an Existing Agreement," 63 Harv. L. Rev. 1097, 1132-1133 (1950).

Awards of one type involve the interpretation and application of management rights clauses which specify in detail the reserved rights. When certain powers are specified in a management clause, the parties have bargained and reached agreement. But what is their bargain? What is the scope of management's prerogatives under the adopted provision?

Management clauses frequently give the employer "power to direct the working forces." Does "power to direct the working forces" include the power to schedule working hours and shifts? To assign work and job duties? To transfer duties out of the bargaining unit? Parties have turned to arbitrators for answers to these and related questions, and through their awards the scope of employer rights under management clauses is best indicated.

Awards of another type involve agreements which contain no management rights clause or which contain a general clause reserving to management all rights not contracted away. The responsibility of the arbitrator in this type of case is to rule as to what management can do and how far it can go under the so-called "residual" powers.

Control of Operation Methods

Only rarely do collective agreements restrict management in the determination of methods of operation, and for most purposes arbitrators appear to take the view that it is the exclusive right of management to make such determination. Unless restricted by contract, as Arbitrator Jacob E. Courshon has stated, it is management's "prerogative to determine what is to be produced, when it is to be produced, and how it is to be produced." [65] Management must have some discretion as to the method of carrying on its operations. It "should not be put in

---

[65] Torrington Co., 1 LA 35, 42 (1945). Also see Colonial Bakery Co., 22 LA 163, 165 (Bauder, 1953). Unless restricted by the agreement it is the right of management to determine what work shall be done. See Arbitrator McCoy in 9 LA 236, 238; Carmichael in 3 LA 798, 800. Th employer is not required to "create" jobs for employees displaced by other employees. Ibid.

a straight jacket." [66] It is said that it is the primary function of management to operate on the most efficient basis.[67] "In the operation of any plant, management has a fixed obligation to see that unnecessary costs are dispensed with and that production programs are changed to meet changing production demands. This right is an inherent right and is recognized by all unions as such." [68]

An excellent statement regarding the prerogative of management to determine methods of operation was made by Arbitrator Whitley P. McCoy, who, in considering an employer's unilateral change in a method of operation, said:

> "The decision as to whether or not to run a particular operation as continuous is a function of management—just as much so as the decision whether or not to replace an old machine involving simple operations requiring ten men with a new labor-saving and more complicated machine requiring only five men. Such changes are not the sort of changes in working conditions as require negotiation. As long as such decisions are made in good faith, in the interest of efficiency of operation, and do not involve the imposing on employees of conditions different from those already existing with respect to other employees on similar machines or operations, no injustice is done the employees. No employee has a vested right in the use of a particular old machine that would preclude the company from installing a new one nor a vested right that would preclude the company from changing the method. If the new machine or the new method on the old results in too heavy a work load, too low pay, or any other hardship, the employee has his remedy in the grievance machinery. But he does not have the right to delay the exercise of managerial functions by insisting on prior negotiations." [69]

The line of demarcation between "operation methods" and "working conditions" often must of necessity be determined. Arbitrator McCoy noted the difficulty which such determination may entail. The agreement of the parties recognized the

---

[66] Thompson Mahogany Co., 5 LA 397, 399 (Brandschain, 1946).

[67] See Arbitrator Dworkin in 29 LA 782, 792; Marshall in 29 LA 687, 692; Kesselman in 28 LA 441, 445; Ridge in 26 LA 422, 426-427; Myers in 10 LA 261, 265. Regarding the right of management to move the plant and its obligations to employees when it does so, see John B. Stetson Co., 28 LA 514, 517-518 (McGoldrick, 1957).

[68] Youngstown Sheet & Tube Co., 4 LA 514, 517 (Miller, 1946). Also see Arbitrator Gross in 20 LA 749, 750; Klamon in 15 LA 782, 789.

[69] Goodyear Tire & Rubber Co., of Ala., 6 LA 681, 687 (1947). Also see Arbitrator Fleming in 30 LA 147, 149; Dworkin in 29 LA 787, 792; Kesselman in 28 LA 441, 444-445; Roberts in 27 LA 736, 742-743; Klamon in 22 LA 336, 351; Gilden in 18 LA 346, 349. For related discussion see Chapter 12, topic titled "Custom and Practice as Part of the Contract"

exclusive right of management to determine methods of operation, but it also restricted the right of management to change working conditions by requiring negotiations with the union before such changes could be made. The employer changed the operations of some employees from a noncontinuous to a continuous basis in the interest of plant efficiency, with the result that the employees were ordered to work through a period previously allowed for washing up. Arbitrator McCoy ruled that the order requiring the employees to work through the wash-up period was proper as an incidental result of the employer's good-faith exercise of the exclusive right to determine methods of operation. He stated the general considerations involved:

"The distinction between a change in working conditions, which by the terms of the contract must be the subject of negotiation prior to its institution, and a change in methods of operation, which by the terms of the contract is a sole function of management, is not easy to define or even to make clear by example. Abolition or sharp curtailment of an existing practice concerning rest time, wash-up time, paid lunch period, furnishing of shower baths and lockers, matters pertaining to sanitation, safety and health, or such like matter are clearly changes in working conditions. On the other hand, a change from the use of pot heaters to McNeill presses or from noncontinuous to continuous operation is just as clearly a change primarily in methods of operation. The latter changes usually cause, with respect to the individuals affected, some change of their working habits, but they are primarily and essentially changes in methods, not in conditions, and as such are exclusively a management function, subject only to the right of affected employees to resort to the grievance procedure to correct abuses or hardships such as decreased earnings or stretchout. Of course a change that was merely in form one of method, used as a pretext to institute a change of working conditions, would not be justifiable." [70]

The right of management to determine the types of machinery and equipment to be used and to determine the processes of manufacture may be stated specifically in the agreement. This right also might be ruled to be included in a clause reserving the right of general management of the plant

---

[70] Goodyear Tire & Rubber Co., of Ala., 6 LA 681, 687 (1947). Also see Arbitrator Dworkin in 29 LA 787, 792-793; Marshall in 29 LA 687, 692-693; Kesselman in 28 LA 441, 444; Roberts in 27 LA 736, 742-743; Updegraff in 20 LA 890, 891. Cf., Hampton in 15 LA 603, 607-608.

to the employer.[71] It has been held that, even if such right is not specified in the agreement, it can be exercised as a residual management power except as it has been restricted by the agreement.[72]

As a corollary it follows that the employer has the right to have the employees operate improved machines and perform changed operation methods in good faith up to the level of their productive capacity.[73] Employees may, of course, be inclined to resist technological change, for workers who have spent years in a skilled trade are reluctant to risk its disappearance. "The need of the manufacturer to improve production methods is matched by the concern of the employees that they may be thrown out on the streets." [74]

In this general regard, it has been observed that:

"Whenever a job is abolished, a machine discontinued, or work in a department is discontinued, men lose jobs and their seniority rights to jobs are affected. But this involves no wrong of itself; it is merely one of the forms of injury or damage flowing from an act. The primary question is whether the act was wrongful. If it was not, then no question can properly arise as to damage." [75]

It has been suggested, too, that the exercise of this management function serves to protect the interests of the employees as well as of the employer, for if the employer is permitted to operate new machinery "his competitive position will be enhanced, improving his chance to win new business and thereby to provide greater employment." [76]

[71] See Arbitrator Myers in 10 LA 535, 537-539, and 10 LA 261, 264-265. Also see Healy in 11 LA 703, 705-706.

[72] See Arbitrator Updegraff in 30 LA 115, 117, and in 7 LA 943, 945; Beatty in 26 LA 1, 3. Also see Larson in 29 LA 59, 66-67; Townsend in 17 LA 472, 475; Myers in 10 LA 535, 539.

[73] Associated Shoe Industries of Southeastern Mass., Inc., 10 LA 535, 539 (Myers, 1948). To similar effect, Hershey Chocolate Corp., 17 LA 268, 270 (Brecht, 1951).

[74] Associated Shoe Industries of Southeastern Mass., 10 LA 535, 538 (Myers, 1948).

[75] Allegheny Ludlum Steel Corp., 20 LA 455, 457 (McCoy, 1953). Also see Arbitrator Fleming in 30 LA 147, 149; Updegraff in 28 LA 135, 136-137; Roberts in 27 LA 736, 742-744; Beatty in 26 LA 1, 3.

[76] Associated Shoe Industries of Southeastern Mass., Inc., 10 LA 535, 539 (Myers, 1948).

Wage Adjustments Following Changes in Operation Methods

Changes in operation methods, which are largely left within the discretion of management, often necessitate adjustments in wage rates. While the employer has wide discretion in determining operation methods, he is closely restricted in the determination of wage rates for new or changed processes.

The right initially to determine the job rate for a new or altered job may be given to management by the agreement. The following clause is illustrative:

"* * * rates on all new or changed operations shall be temporarily established by the employer * * *. If a grievance arises therefrom, the price shall be negotiated * * *. If unable to agree the matter shall be arbitrated in accordance with this contract." [77]

If the agreement does not give the employer the right initially to set the new rate, an arbitrator may require him to bargain before setting a rate. Arbitrator Harry H. Platt, for instance, speaking as chairman of an arbitration board, ruled that, under an agreement recognizing the union "as the sole collective bargaining agency for the employees of the company" and in the light of the continuing legal duty of the employer to bargain during the entire life of the contract, the employer could not unilaterally establish the rate for a new job.[78]

Another arbitrator, on the other hand, considering a contract which reserved the direction of the working forces to management and which provided that the company could re-timestudy and adjust piece rates after changes in material, tools, or methods, expressed the view that management had and should have the right initially to determine job duties and job rates for new or altered jobs, because the "exigencies of production do not permit the problems arising from improved pro-

---

[77] Associated Shoe Industries of Southeastern Mass., Inc., 10 LA 535, 537 (Myers, 1948). Also see Arbitrator Marshall in 23 LA 228, 233; Shipman in 21 LA 387, 389-390; Gilden in 9 LA 931, 937.

[78] Copco Steel & Engineering Co., 6 LA 156, 164 (1947). To similar effect, Arbitrator Carmichael in 14 LA 544, 546; Justin in 13 LA 177, 180. But see Sizelove in 24 LA 726, 728; Klamon in 15 LA 782, 791. Also see Gregory in 14 LA 802, 805, where past practice of the parties strongly influenced the result reached.

duction methods to be settled in advance." This arbitrator noted that in the steel industry, which he used as an example, these matters are left initially to management determination, subject to the grievance procedure. He did recognize, however, that this "requires the union to have the patience to endure management's determinations until the grievance procedure produces a remedy." [79]

Even where an agreement provided that existing rates should be continued without change, this was held not to preclude management from establishing new piece rates after introducing new equipment which materially changed job duties; Arbitrator Wayne L. Townsend reasoned that the requirement that rates be continued was based upon the assumption that equipment and methods would remain the same and, since that assumption was not borne out by subsequent events, the requirement did not apply.[80]

Many disputes concerning rates for new or changed operating methods have reached arbitration. Arbitrators have recognized certain principles or standards to be considered in determining rates for new or changed operations (these standards are sometimes stated in the agreement). The standards generally observed by arbitrators should be noted because of their obvious practical importance.

Production Standards; Time Studies

"Whether wages are computed on a time or incentive basis, there is usually some formal or informal determination of the output expected of employees on each operation. This expected production is commonly called the work load or production standard and represents the amount of work required or expected to be done in a given time by the average, qualified

---

[79] Diemolding Corp., 2 LA 274, 276 (Kharas, 1945). Also see Thor Corp., 16 LA 770, 772-774 (Baab, 1951). But the view has been expressed that to consider a unilateral action taken by management as a grievance is not a substitute for negotiation prior to the action. General Motors Corp., 7 LA 368, 371 (Griffin, 1947).

[80] A. C. L. Haase Co., 17 LA 472, 477-479 (1951).

operator under normal conditions * * *." [81] Production standards are commonly determined through time study, but they
also may be based on past experience or production records or
on "rule of thumb" determination.[82]

Arbitrators use time study in reviewing rates after operation changes if the parties agree.[83] Moreover, they may order
or sustain its use if it has been used by the parties in past rate
setting.[84]

The purpose of time study is to measure the work content
of an operation. "Each element of the operation is studied and
a determination is made of the time required for its performance by a normal experienced operator working with normal
effort and without undue fatigue." [85] Concerning the use of
time study in incentive rate setting, Arbitrator Paul N. Lehoczky has explained:

> "* * * in conjunction with job evaluation (which determines relative
> base rates) it actually evaluates each incentive job in like terms and makes
> the ideal of 'equal pay for equal work' possible. When properly carried
> out, all jobs in the plant pay relatively equally well, and an expenditure
> of extra effort or skill applied to any job pays off equally well." [86]

The use of time study in setting new rates may be favored
over comparison with rates for similar operations since the
establishment of new rates on the basis of existing rates tends
to perpetuate existing intraplant inequities.[87]

Hourly-Rated Employees

The rule generally applied in the case of employees who
work for hourly rather than incentive rates is that an increase

---

[81] Incentive Wage Provisions; Time Studies and Standards of Production (U.S.
Dept. of Labor, Bureau of Labor Statistics, Bull. No. 908-3, p. 37, 1948).

[82] Ibid. Also see Singer Mfg. Co., 29 LA 828, 832-833 (Cahn, 1958). Regarding
the type of evidence that may be required for the employer to prove substandard productivity by an employee, see Jonco Aircraft Corp., 22 LA 819 (Merrill, 1954).

[83] Container Co., 6 LA 218, 220 (Whiting, 1946).

[84] See Arbitrator Lehoczky in 6 LA 979, 983-984; Gilden in 4 LA 189, 194. But
see Hilpert in 10 LA 295, 296.

[85] Ford Motor Co., 12 LA 949-951 (Shulman, 1949).

[86] Timken Roller Bearing Co., 6 LA 979, 983 (1947).

[87] Id. at 984.

in hourly rates should accompany any *material* increase in the workload. Arbitrator Whitley P. McCoy has ruled, for instance, where the matter was not specifically covered by the contract that, when a change is made in job content, the job should be restudied to determine whether the original workload has been changed sufficiently to necessitate an adjustment in the wage rate. Arbitrator McCoy stated that it does not follow that simply because work has been added to a job there must necessarily be an increase of pay, though presumptively there should be; he stated that whether there should be an increase in pay "depends upon whether the workload was too light and the increase does not make it too heavy or whether the workload was proper and the increase is material and makes it too heavy." [88]

A similar ruling has been made by Arbitrator A. Howard Myers under a contract containing provision for rate revision following workload changes. Arbitrator Myers ruled that not all changes in workload necessitate a revision of wages.

> "The theoretical issue arises as to whether every change in workload or equipment, irrespective of competitive conditions and original workload, justifies a rate increase. I think that the answer must be in the negative where, as here, the change results in raising an abnormally slow job rate to a still slow rate, with pay that is not inequitable in terms of comparable rates in this plant or in other plants * * *." [89]

Arbitrator Clarence M. Updegraff, however, would appear to be unwilling to give so much weight to the factor of a previously light workload where the agreement provides that consideration shall be given to the adjustment of rates when the workload is materially increased. He has ruled that such a provision does not permit the employer to discount entirely a material increase in the workload on the ground that the previous workload was too light, but that this is one of the factors which, without having a decisive effect, may be taken into consideration as limiting the increase to be granted. [90]

---

[88] Goodyear Tire & Rubber Co. of Ala., 6 LA 924, 925 (1947). Also see Arbitrator Marshall in 29 LA 687, 692-693; Valtin in 28 LA 530, 531-532.

[89] Verney Corp., 7 LA 27, 29 (1946). To similar effect, Aleo Mfg. Co., 19 LA 647, 649-650 (Maggs, 1952). Also see Arbitrator Seward in 27 LA 906, 907.

[90] Continental Can Co., 5 LA 247, 250 (1946).

A slight increase in workload does not call for a higher rate. [91] It has been held that changes to new machines which produce more but which require less skill and effort do not constitute such changes in the workload as require revision of rates. [92] Where, however, a new machine or operation involves more than a slight increase in duties, skill, responsibility, or hazards, rate revision may be required. [93]

Incentive Employees

"An incentive wage plan is a method of wage payment by which workers receive extra pay for extra production. In establishing wage incentive plans, consideration must be given to (1) the base rate for the job; (2) the amount of work required to earn the base rate; and (3) the relationship between extra work above the base and extra pay for the extra performance." [94]

A standard sometimes applied by arbitrators in reviewing the rates of incentive employees whose workload has been changed is the maintenance of prior earnings. [95]

The theory underlying this standard is that incentive em-

---

[91] Pan American Refining Corp., 4 LA 773 (Abernethy, 1946). As to what might be considered more than slight see Arbitrator Kelliher in 13 LA 220, 222; Copelof in 5 LA 115, 118.

[92] Central Screw Co., 11 LA 108, 111 (Edes, 1948); E. F. Houghton & Co., 4 LA 716, 717-718 (Cahn, 1946). Also see Arbitrator White in 13 LA 223, 225.

[93] See Arbitrator Justin in 28 LA 548, 553; Harbison in 21 LA 609, 611-612; Jaffee in 19 LA 452, 454; Reid in 19 LA 358, 361; Copelof in 16 LA 76, 78-79; Gilden in 9 LA 931, 937; Blair in 2 LA 572, 576. Also see Seward in 27 LA 906, 907; Donnelly in 23 LA 782, 783-784; Lehoczky in 17 LA 293, 295; Cahn in 17 LA 277, 278-280; Brecht in 17 LA 268, 271-272; Healy in 8 LA 88, 91.

[94] Incentive Wage Provisions; Time Studies and Standards of Production (U.S. Dept. of Labor, Bureau of Labor Statistics, Bull. No. 908-3, p. 1, 1948). For labor, management and neutral views on arbitration of incentive disputes see "Arbitration of Disputes Involving Incentive Problems," Critical Issues in Labor Arbitration 61-97 (BNA Incorporated, 1957). For other general discussions see Davis, "Incentive Problems," Management Rights and the Arbitration Process 50-53 (BNA Incorporated, 1956); Morrison, "Arbitration of Wage Incentives," 11 Arb. J. (n.s.) 199 (1956); Waite, Seybold & Unterberger, "Problems in the Arbitration of Wage Incentives," Arbitration Today 25-44 (BNA Incorporated, 1955).

[95] See Arbitrator Stouffer in 28 LA 259, 264-265; Copelof in 10 LA 933, 940; Keister in 4 LA 386, 389; Dwyer in 4 LA 355, 358. Also see Townsend in 17 LA 472, 479; Garrett in 26 LA 812, 822.

ployees should be able to earn as much under the new operation as under the old. [96]

Another standard, much less concrete, requires the maintenance of the ratio of earnings to effort expended. [97] Under the "ratio of earnings to effort" standard no change in incentive rates is in order unless there is a change in the amount of incentive effort required per unit of incentive production. [98] Application of this standard means that employees receive increased earnings on that part of increased production that is due to increased work effort, and that management receives the benefit from that part of increased production that is due to mechanical improvements as such. [99]

Use of this standard is illustrated by a case in which the employer ordered an increase in the speed at which a machine was to be operated and simultaneously decreased the incentive rate. Although the decreased rate yielded higher earnings than the employees had received before the increase in machine speed, they demanded that the prior incentive rate be reestablished since, even at the higher prior rate, earnings would be increased by a smaller percentage than the increase in effort required to control the machine at the higher speed. The arbitrator found that the increase in machine speed was 19 per cent, that the increase in work effort was 16 per cent, and that, even if the prior higher rate were used, the increase in earnings would amount only to 11.6 per cent. Accordingly, he held the demand of the

---

[96] In this regard, too, where the agreement calls for use of incentive rates management may not be permitted to avoid this requirement and institute hourly rates by claiming a change in method of operation when, in fact, the work elements remain essentially the same. See Arbitrator Warns in 27 LA 758, 760-761; Davey in 23 LA 490, 493-494. Cf., Seward in 17 LA 918, 920-921. Nor would Arbitrator McCoy permit a change in incentive rates where the job was changed only "on paper", in 13 LA 414, 416-417.

[97] This standard was used by Arbitrator Lehoczky in 22 LA 450, 452; Scheiber in 10 LA 20, 23-24; Blumer in 8 LA 846, 849; Hampton in 6 LA 579, 582; Whiting in 6 LA 218, 219-220; Dwyer in 4 LA 482, 483.

[98] American Steel & Wire Co., 8 LA 846, 849 (Blumer, 1947).

[99] Carnegie Illinois Steel Corp., 5 LA 712, 720 (Blumer, 1946), where Arbitrator Blumer also explained that the change in incentive effort is not necessarily the same as the change in work required for the operation. Also see Arbitrator McCoy in 28 LA 129, 131; Shipman in 21 LA 386, 390.

employees to be reasonable and ordered that the prior rate be re-established. [100]

Reduction of incentive rates has been allowed where the introduction of new machinery has resulted in increased production without requiring an increase in effort. [101] Moreover, reduction of incentive rates has been ordered where employees controlled production on new machines at a very low level. [102]

It can be expected that no adjustment in incentive rates will be required as long as the change in the workload is slight. [103]

Control of Quality Standards

Management has been held to have the right at all times to exercise control over the standards of quality of its products since "a lowering in the degree of quality under a competitive market may have serious and disastrous results. [104] Thus, it has been ruled that management had the right to determine what work was faulty and whether it should be reworked or scrapped where the determination was made by men well qualified and experienced in all departments and where it was the employer's policy to resolve all doubts in favor of the employees. [105]

The "competitive market" has been stressed by Arbitrator Clair V. Duff in sustaining the demotion of an employee for faulty work:

> "In managing the Plant and directing the working forces Management has the right and the duty to insure the highest quality standards so that its product can be sold in a competitive market with the resultant benefits to the employer and employees, each of whom has a stake in the

---

[100] Anaconda Wire & Cable Co., 10 LA 20, 24 (Scheiber, 1948).

[101] Jenkins Bros., 11 LA 432, 435 (Donnelly, 1948); Reliance Mfg. Co., 3 LA 677, 679 (Whiting, 1946). Cf., Arbitrator Shipman in 17 LA 650, 653-654.

[102] Associated Shoe Industries of Southeastern Mass., Inc., 10 LA 535, 538-539 (Myers, 1948); Wolverine Shoe & Tanning Corp., 15 LA 195, 196-197 (Platt, 1950).

[103] Schlueter Mfg. Co., 10 LA 295, 296-297 (Hilpert, 1948), where, however it was ruled that the over-all effect of a succession of minor additions to an operation could be considered; Goodyear Tire & Rubber Co. of Ala., 5 LA 30, 35 (McCoy, 1946). Some agreements expressly provide for change in incentive rates when there is a "substantial" change in operations. For cases involving the application of such provisions see 28 LA 129, 21 LA 387, 21 LA 84, 20 LA 455, 18 LA 375.

[104] Torrington Co., 1 LA 20, 26 (Courshon, 1945).

[105] Ibid.

success of the enterprise. How this quality-control is to be attained is also the responsibility of Management.

"* * * We are aware that most industries are becoming more competitive as their respective sales forces contest for a place in the market. Unless quality standards are maintained and unless a Company is in a position where it can provide a high quality product it cannot successfully exist in a competitive economy. Failure to achieve quality in a product not only reduces the benefit to the ultimate consumer but also places the Company in jeopardy with, at least potentially, a resultant disadvantage to itself and to its employees. In not a few industries the competition in quality of final product is as important as price competition." [106]

The company may have a legitimate concern not only with respect to the sale of its product, but also with regard to its reputation and the safety of persons who use its product. In this connection, the grievance of an employee who was discharged for faulty work was denied by Arbitrator Robert G. Howlett, who stated:

"* * * In such situations the manufacturing concern must be in a position to protect its reputation and the quality of its product. A company's failure to do so would redound to the detriment of all persons connected with the enterprise—owners, management and employees." [107]

He stated further:

"The Company necessarily is concerned with the production of good castings and the safety of persons who use its products. If faulty castings are produced by the * * * Company it will not only lose customers but property may be damaged and persons who come in contact with equipment in which its castings are placed may be injured, or even death may result." [108]

While management has wide freedom to control quality standards, the fairness of penalties imposed for faulty work may be closely scrutinized by arbitrators. [109]

Job and Classification Control

It is difficult to formulate neat or precise categories in the discussion of cases involving the right of management to estab-

---

[106] American Radiator & Standard Sanitary Corp., 29 LA 167, 170 (1957).

[107] Valley Steel Casting Co., 22 LA 520, 525 (1954).

[108] Id. at 526.

[109] See Arbitrator Duff in 29 LA 167, 169-170; Graff in 27 LA 656, 659-662; Howlett in 22 LA 520, 524-527; Noel in 19 LA 650, 652.

lish, eliminate, or combine jobs or job classifications, or cases involving its right to transfer duties between jobs or between job classifications. This is likewise true of cases involving the right of management to assign duties and tasks to workers.

This difficulty springs in part from the fact that the words "job" and "classification" at times are used synonymously and at other times are intended to carry different meanings. [110] In addition, different terminology utilized in the decision of cases involving similar issues, different meanings apparently intended in the use of similar terminology, failure of cases to define clearly the terminology that is used, and other such practices, make it virtually impossible to arrange the cases into clearly outlined compartments. The many borderline situations, too, have produced many shadings of arbitral opinion touching upon otherwise basic issues.

For these reasons the authors urge the reader to keep in mind the close relationship between (and frequent overlapping of) the materials in the subtopics which make up the remainder of this topic. [111]

Establishing, Eliminating, and Combining Jobs and Classifications

The right of managements to establish new jobs or job classifications is sometimes specifically stated in the agreement, along with some provision for union challenge of management's actions via the grievance procedure and arbitration. The right also has been recognized as being inherently vested in management where not expressly limited by the agreement, and it like-

---

[110] "There is no question that the word 'job' may have a different meaning from the word 'classification.' Two men may have the same classification, for example, 'painter,' but one may have the job of keeping certain rooms painted while the other has the job of keeping certain equipment painted. On the other hand, the two words are sometimes used synonymously. The question is in what sense did the parties use the word [in their agreement]." Fulton-Sylphon Co., 2 LA 116, 117-118 (McCoy, 1946). Also see Arbitrator Hebert in 27 LA 762, 764-765; Livengood in 20 LA 19, 21; McCoy in 1 LA 121, 124.

[111] Fc ther important related material see Chapter 12, topic titled "Custom and Practice as Part of the Contract".

wise might be included within the scope of a general management clause. [112]

In one case before the National War Labor Board, the employer argued that to grant the union an "equal voice on new classification would be to surrender one of the essential functions of management." [113] In this case the Board refused a union request for joint negotiation of job classifications and ordered the use of a clause to the effect that any dispute arising as to job classifications should be submitted to grievance machinery. [114]

Where job classifications are specifically set up by the agreement, however, and especially if the agreement is rigid as to classifications, management may not be permitted unilaterally to establish new classifications. [115]

Arbitrators often have held that unless restricted by the agreement it is the right of management to eliminate jobs (and where a few duties remain to reallocate them) where production justification exists, as long as they are not eliminated for purpose of discrimination. [116]

Some cases have also recognized management's right, where not restricted by the agreement, to eliminate job classifications when done in good faith. [117] Similar results have been reached where arbitrators have spoken in terms of combining jobs or job classifications. Thus, it has been held that management has

---

[112] See Arbitrator Prasow in 30 LA 444, 448; Platt in 17 LA 697, 700-701; Bowles in 16 LA 955, 957; Reynolds in 8 LA 1041, 1042-1043. Also see Sembower in 25 LA 188, 191; Marshall in 23 LA 228, 233-234; Wallen in 22 LA 831, 833; Gaffey in 18 LA 462, 468; Coffey in 12 LA 676, 679-680. Contra as to job classifications (requiring bargaining before their establishment), Donnelly in 18 LA 90, 92; Griffin in 7 LA 368, 371.

[113] Gray Mfg. Co., 7 War Lab. Rep. 401, 405 (1943).

[114] Id. at 403.

[115] See Arbitrator Gilden in 13 LA 369, 371; Howard in 13 LA 3, 8. Also see McCoy in 2 LA 319, 321.

[116] See Arbitrator Fleming in 30 LA 147, 149-150; Warns in 29 LA 324, 326-328; Seward in 26 LA 146, 147; Wettach in 19 LA 797, 799; Sachs in 18 LA 616, 619-620; Gilden in 16 LA 252, 255-256; Klamon in 15 LA 782, 790-791; Copelof in 15 LA 754, 761; R. Smith in 12 LA 719, 721-722; Pollard in 10 LA 498, 510; Willcox in 10 LA 371, 378; Abernethy in 6 LA 314, 318-319.

[117] See Arbitrator Ridge in 26 LA 422, 427; Prasow in 25 LA 44, 49; Ryder in 20 LA 764, 767. Also see Hays in 32 LA 249.

the right, where not restricted by the agreement, to combine
jobs or job classifications in determining methods of operation. [118]

Several arbitrators have held that management has the
right, unless restricted by the agreement, to combine jobs where
there is insufficient work in one (or in each) of separate classi-
cations for a normal day's work and where excessive workloads
do not result from the combination.[119] Likewise, in the absence of contractual restriction management has been permitted
to abolish two job classifications and establish a new classification
following technological change in equipment, [120] or following
a change in products. [121]

But under the facts and agreement involved in the case,
some arbitrators have recognized a distinction between "jobs"
and "classifications" such as to prevent management from eliminating or combining classifications while not preventing it from
eliminating or combining jobs within classifications. [122] In one
such case, Arbitrator Whitley P. McCoy stated that "Combining the duties of classifications recognized in the contract is
a different thing from combining the duties or job content of
various jobs, or abolishing those jobs"; he interpreted the contract to freeze classifications and he held that management
could not combine the duties of the "Burner" classification and
those of the "Welder" classification. [123]

Inter-Job and Inter-Classification Transfer of Duties

Short of eliminating or combining jobs or job classifica-

---

[118] See Arbitrator Wersing in 23 LA 797, 798-799 (combining jobs); Bowles in
16 LA 955, 957-958 (combining job classifications). Also see Bothwell in 32 LA 260.

[119] See Arbitrator Kesselman in 28 LA 441, 443-445; Somers in 27 LA 466, 467-
468; Kelliher in 18 LA 216, 217-218; Gilden in 16 LA 252, 255-256. Also see Pollick
in 27 LA 689; Hampton in 17 LA 666, 668; Gilden in 16 LA 252, 255-256; Klamon in
15 LA 782, 789-790. Cf., Sembower in 25 LA 188, 190-191.

[120] Great Lakes Carbon Corp., 19 LA 797, 799 (Wettach, 1953). Also see Arbitrator Copelof in 15 LA 754, 761.

[121] Hewitt-Robins, Inc., 30 LA 81, 83-86 (Kates, 1958).

[122] See Arbitrator Doyle in 29 LA 242, 244-245; McCoy in 19 LA 569, 570-571.
Also see Beatty in 25 LA 838, 840-841; Reynard in 22 LA 880, 882.

[123] Esso Standard Oil Co., 19 LA 569, 571 (1952). For related discussion see this
Chapter, topic titled "Assigning Work Out of Bargaining Unit".

tions, some of the duties of one job or job classification are
sometimes transferred to another job or job classification. The
right of management to require workers in the "receiving" job
or classification to perform the work is discussed hereinbelow in
the sub-topic on "Assignment of Duties and Tasks". At this
point, however, the matter is considered primarily from the
standpoint of the effect of the transfer upon workers in the
"giving" job or classification.

Under a contract giving management the right to manage
the works and direct the working force and containing no provision expressly prohibiting unilateral changes in job content,
Arbitrator Benjamin Aaron held that management could remove from the oiler's job the relatively minor tasks of lubricat-
ing and cleaning cranes and assign these duties to crane men,
even though said duties were mentioned in the oiler's job description and not in the craneman's; the union could request
reevaluation of the craneman's job if it believed that the added
duties justified a higher rate, but it could not prevent management from making the changes in job content. [124]   In this case
Arbitrator Aaron noted that the transfer in no way impaired
job security. [125]

Arbitrator Joseph M. Klamon has reconized an "inherent
right of management to take a job which initially or orginally
may require a considerable degree of skill and then to establish
a production line in which a fairly complex job becomes essentially routine and repetitive." [126]   In that case management was
permitted to discontinue the assignment of certain work, after
it had become simplified, to skilled workers (who claimed a
"proprietary interest in the work") and to assign it exclusively
to employees in a lower classification.   To hold otherwise, Arbitrator Klamon declared, would deny the company the right
to operate with the greatest degree of skill and efficiency; he
noted that nothing in the contract prevented the company

---

[124] National Supply Co., 26 LA 666, 668 (1956).
[125] National Supply Co., 26 LA 666, 668 (1956).
[126] McConnell Aircraft Corp., 21 LA 424, 427-428 (1953).

"from using lesser grades of skill on a job if higher grades of skill are wholly unnecessary to perform such jobs." [127]

Where workers in one classification must suffer layoff or other such consequence as a result of management's transfer of substantial work from their classification to another, arbitrators have sometimes deemed such transfer a violation of the workers' seniority rights where the transfer was not justified by emergency or other such reason. [128]

But some arbitrators are unwilling to accept seniority as a guarantee that the job or classification will remain unchanged. For instance, in upholding the right of management to transfer work from one classification to another where not expressly restricted by the agreement, Arbitrator Paul Prasow reasoned:

"* * * Seniority protects and secures an employee's rights in relation to the rights of other employees in his seniority group; it does not protect him in relation to the existence of the job itself. By the use of an objective measure, length of service, the rights of one employee are balanced against the other employees' rights.

"The rights inherent in seniority do not themselves guarantee the continued existence of the job, or that it shall be maintained without change in content. Seniority can only stand as a bar to changes in job content if the contract so expressly provides, or if it can be shown that the changes are motivated on the part of management by a desire to evade the seniority clause. * * *

"While it is certainly true that changes in job content of a classification may adversely affect the job opportunities of the employees involved by reducing the amount of work available to them, the problem is still essentially one of jurisdiction, rather than of seniority. It is a well-established principle in industrial arbitration that management has the right, if exercised in good faith, to transfer duties from one classification to another, to change, eliminate or establish new classifications, unless the Agreement specifically restricts this right." [129]

Speaking in terms of the right of management to transfer work from one seniority unit to another, one arbitrator held that

---

[127] Ibid.

[128] See Arbitrator Livengood in 23 LA 196, 199-202; Gregory in 15 LA 147, 150-151; Ebeling in 14 LA 163, 164-165.

[129] Reynolds Metals Co., 25 LA 44, 48-49 (1955). Also see statement by Arbitrator Updegraff in 29 LA 555, 557; Thompson in 28 LA 374, 376-377; Uible in 25 LA 897, 899; Platt in 17 LA 697, 700-701. For important related discussion see this Chapter, topics titled "Right to Subcontract" and "Assigning Work Out of Bargaining Unit".

management may not do so even though there is no express prohibition in the agreement. [130] But in another case management was permitted to transfer work from one seniority unit to another where there was no specific restriction in the agreement and the transfer was made in good faith in the interest of efficiency. [131]

Assignment of Duties and Tasks

In general management is permitted to exercise much more discretion in assigning individual duties and tasks to workers than it is permitted to exercise in assigning workers to regular jobs. While the assignment of workers to regular jobs often requires the observance of contractual "seniority" and "fitness and ability" considerations, [132] collective agreements much less frequently contain direct restrictions upon the right of management to assign duties and tasks to workers.

Arbitrator Clarence M. Updegraff has observed (speaking of hourly-rated employees) that "it is assumed throughout industry that the employer has the general right to make reasonable changes from time to time in the job duties of every individual. The employer may decrease or increase the duties as long as the total work load remains in reasonable bounds." [133]

Certainly, where jobs are classified by titles (if formally classified at all) but the parties have not negotiated a detailed description of job content, management will be permitted wide authority to assign any work which is of the same general type as, or is reasonably related to, or is incidental to the regular

---

[130] Lukens Steel Co., 15 LA 408, 411-412 (D'Andrade, 1950). Also see R. Wallace & Sons Mfg. Co., 23 LA 776, 778-779 (Myers, 1954).
[131] Douglas & Lomason Co., 23 LA 691, 695 (Bowles, 1954). Also see Bethlehem Supply Co., 25 LA 366, 368 (Springfield & Seward, 1955).
[132] See Chapter 14, Seniority.
[133] St. Joseph Lead Co., 20 LA 890, 891 (1953). Also see Arbitrator Ryder in 29 LA 677, 679; Ridge in 26 LA 422, 426-427; Uible in 25 LA 897, 899; Prasow in 25 LA 44, 48-49; Wallen in 22 LA 831, 833; Klamon in 22 LA 336, 351; Marshall in 20 LA 800, 802; L. Smith in 18 LA 620, 624; Ryan in 17 LA 800, 803. Cf., Dworkin in 29 LA 787, 792. Regarding the duty of employees to do the work assigned to them and to utilize the grievance procedure rather than self-help if they think an assignment is improper see Chapter 5, topic titled "Observance Of Grievance Procedure".

duties of the job. [134]   However, a change in job duties by adding work which is not so related to the regular duties may be held improper. [135]

In two decisions Umpire Harry Shulman recognized a significant limitation upon the right of management to assign work to skilled tradesmen (as opposed to production workers); he did not permit the assignment of work which is of a different trade.[136] Some years later Umpire Harry H. Platt "reaffirmed" these decisions, but in doing so he pointed out important exceptions:

> "(a) Umpire Opinions A-223 and A-278 are reaffirmed. It is ruled that a skilled tradesman may not be required to do work wholly different from and unrelated to the central skill of his trade. If such bald assignment is attempted because of a shortage of work in his trade or a desire to get the other work done, he may refuse it and take a layoff instead.

> "(b) In emergencies, the Company may make assignments across trade lines.

> "(c) In cases where the capabilities of tradesmen overlap, work which is within the scope of two or more trades may be assigned to any of the trades within whose normal and proper scope it falls. In determining whether a task falls within the normal scope of more than one trade, due regard must be had for accepted standards in the trades generally and for clearly established in-plant assignment practices which are based on agreement or mutual understanding or which are characterized by acquiescence for a long time, with the consequences that the parties may be assumed to have agreed with reference to them and for their continuance.

> "(d) Relatively minor tasks which are complementary to a principal job but which do not require a long period of reasonably continuous work and which are within the capabilities of the principal tradesman on the

---

[134] See Arbitrator Ryder in 29 LA 677, 679, and in 26 LA 780, 783; Thompson in 28 LA 374, 376; Uible in 25 LA 897, 899; Reynard in 25 LA 611, 613; Berkowitz in 25 LA 422, 424; Prasow in 25 LA 44, 48-49; Bowles in 23 LA 691, 695; Blair in 22 LA 701, 703; Hawley in 22 LA 157, 161; Dworet in 20 LA 803, 806; Marshall in 20 LA 800, 802; Shulman in 19 LA 237, 238-242; Gaffey in 18 LA 462, 468; Gilden in 17 LA 408, 409; Lesser in 16 LA 505, 507; Kharas in 2 LA 274, 276-277. Also see Feinberg in 28 LA 832. In some of these cases the agreement contained a management rights clause, in others it did not.

[135] American Zinc Co., 18 LA 827, 830-831 (Updegraff, 1952). The right of management to assign workers to tasks outside the plant has sometimes been arbitrated, the right being denied in Schick, Inc., 2 LA 552, 553 (Stone, 1945), but being held to exist on the basis of past practice in Morris Paper Mills, 20 LA 653, 656-657 (Anrod, 1953).

[136] The first case was Ford Motor Co., 3 LA 782, 783 (1946). In the second case, Ford Motor Co., 19 LA 237, 238-239 (1952), Umpire Shulman repeated the restriction but emphasized that it was to be narrowly applied.

job and can be performed by him with safety, are incidental work which can properly be assigned to the principal tradesman." [137]

Regarding the assignment of unskilled work to skilled workers, Arbitrator Edgar L. Warren observed that: "While workers in skilled classifications obviously should not be required to do a large amount of unskilled work, some measure of this is a part of every job. The most practical restraint on the amount of unskilled work that a company will assign to highly skilled workers is the cost involved. Few employers would feel that they could afford to have highly paid hourly employees doing chores which could be performed by unskilled laborers." [138] Arbitrator Warren upheld the right of management to assign clean-up work to craftsmen for a short time every few weeks despite the fact that their job descriptions did not mention such work. [139]

In the absence of contractual restrictions on the right of management to assign new duties or reallocate old duties as reasonably required by technological changes, management may be permitted considerable leeway to do so. [140]

Even when there are detailed job descriptions, Arbitrator J. Fred Holly has held that they do not prohibit minor changes in job content, Arbitrator Holly stating that any ban on such changes must be stated in the agreement "in unmistable language", and that the "purpose of job evaluation and job descriptions is to provide for equitable wage rates, not to provide a control over job content." [141] But the existence of detailed job descriptions, especially if negotiated, may deprive manage-

---

[137] Ford Motor Co., 30 LA 46, 55 (1958).

[138] Lockheed Aircraft Service, Inc., 21 LA 292, 293 (1953).

[139] Ibid. But in another case management was held to have no right to require clean-up work by incentive workers, who were distinguished from hourly-rated workers on the basis that additional duties do not reduce the earnings of the latter. Mosaic Tile Co., 21 LA 278, 282-283 (Young, 1953).

[140] See Arbitrator Seward in 26 LA 146, 147; Beatty in 26 LA 1, 2; Updegraff in 20 LA 890, 891. Also see Larson in 29 LA 59, 66-67; Roberts in 27 LA 736, 741-743; Shister in 26 LA 212, 213; Gilden in 23 LA 164, 166-167. But see Doyle in 22 LA 785, 788-790; Hampton in 12 LA 631, 634.

[141] United States Steel Corp., 26 LA 325, 326 (1956). Also see Arbitrator Klamon in 27 LA 784, 786-787; Davey in 23 LA 206, 209; Whiting in 5 LA 304, 306-307.

ment of the right to make substantial changes in job duties.[142] One arbitrator has gone a step further, holding that even where there is no written job description management may not make a substantial change in "the traditional job content" of classified occupations during the life of the contract. [143]

Some cases speak more in terms of job classifications. In one such case, Arbitrator Marion Beatty upheld the right of management to assign an employee small amounts of work outside his classification, observing that work jurisdictional lines can be very crippling to efficient operations and should not be read into an agreement by inference.[144] While recognizing that management may require employees to perform duties outside their classification for temporary periods, Arbitrator Joseph Shister held that management may not require the performance of such duties as a regular and continual part of their jobs. [145]

It is not unusual, of course, to find duties and tasks which may properly fall within two or more separate job classifications. In this regard, Arbitrator Robert S. Thompson has expressed the following opinion:

> "* * * management may assign tasks which involve minor and occasional variation from job descriptions to employees in different classifications when what is required falls within the skills and other factors which are common to the several classifications. The arbitrator believes that this principle is well established except where there are specific contract provisions otherwise." [146]

In reaching this conclusion Arbitrator Thompson spoke at length of the natural overlapping of duties between classifications:

---

[142] See Arbitrator Bowles in 26 LA 415, 421; Ryder in 23 LA 829, 832-834. Also see Livengood in 23 LA 520, 521; Donnelly in 20 LA 586, 588.

[143] Nebraska Consolidated Mills Co., 22 LA 785, 789-790 (Doyle, 1954). For a similar result see Arbitrator S. Wolff in 18 LA 853, 854.

[144] Phillips Petroleum Co., 29 LA 226, 228 (1957). Also see Arbitrator Thompson in 28 LA 374, 376-377; Uible in 25 LA 897, 899; Prasow in 25 LA 44, 48-49; Wallen in 22 LA 831, 833.

[145] Linde Air Products Co., 20 LA 861, 864 (1953). Also see Arbitrator Donnelly in 20 LA 586, 588; Hampton in 17 LA 666, 668; Feinberg in 17 LA 926, 928-930; Simkin in 8 LA 113, 115-116.

[146] Goodyear Tire & Rubber Co., 28 LA 374, 377 (1957).

"It is understandable that in the interests of job security, unions press for inviolability of job classifications. Certainly, practices which permitted more or less discriminate transfer of duties from one classification to another, or the assignment of tasks now to one classification and now to another, would lead to anxieties about the kind and amount of work that might be available to particular employees at different times.

"However, the reality is that there is much overlapping in jobs and their classifications. It would take an almost completely rationalized industry to provide for each worker absolutely distinct jobs. In highly specialized production work, operations are split off from general operations, and there may in consequence be an approach to fairly exclusive jobs one from another. However, in maintenance work duties are by the nature of the needs necessarily more general.

"It is reassuring to be able to place things in neat categories. Is aspirin a drug and therefore to be sold only under a physician's prescription? How about the new tranquillizers? Is there a sharp line between intelligence and stupidity, or a gradually changing quality ranging from genius to idiot?" [147]

Arbitrator David L. Cole has ruled that when work falls within the job descriptions of two classifications management has the right to decide which classification shall do it if there is insufficient work to keep both classifications busy. [148]

Management generally has been held to have considerable discretion in unusual situations to make temporary or emergency assignments of tasks across job or classification lines. For instance, Arbitrator James P. Miller has ruled that in case of emergency or breakdown it is reasonable for an employer to require maintenance employees with certain occupational titles to assist employees with other occupational titles:

"Many years of experience have proven to me that a plant maintenance crew is somewhat similar to the crew of a ship or a football team. Each member has a designated position or title and spends most of his team time attending to the duties and tasks associated with his designated position. However, when an emergency arises, they all respond as a crew and assist in getting the ship back on an even keel, weathering the storm, or, as in the case of the football team, advancing the ball to the opposing team's goal line." [149]

---

[147] Id. at 376.

[148] International Harvester Co., 21 LA 814, 815 (1953). Also see Arbitrator Prasow in 30 LA 444, 447-448; Klamon in 22 LA 336, 350-351.

[149] Youngstown Sheet & Tube Co., 4 LA 514, 520 (1946).

What Arbitrator Miller thus said in regard to maintenance employees would appear to apply to plant employees generally. For instance, an employer was held to be within his rights in assigning an emergency job which arose on a non-workday to the only two employees scheduled to work on that day, despite the fact that the work did not fall within the duties of their job classifications. The arbitrator stated that management should have the right to meet unusual situations in this manner unless restricted from doing so by the agreement. [150]

Finally, it should be remembered that while management often has wide authority to assign duties and tasks to employees, they in turn may challenge the fairness of the rate paid for the job after its change. [151] Moreover, employees temporarily performing work which is rated higher than their regular work may be entitled to the higher rate for performing the higher-rated work. [152]

Hiring of Employees

Except as restricted by the collective agreement, or by statutes prohibiting employer anti-union or other discriminatory practices, management retains the unqualified right to hire or not to hire. Contractual restrictions upon this right exist most often in seniority or union security provisions.

Specific restrictions on hiring contained in the seniority provisions of the collective agreement may be to the effect, for example, that the employer may not hire new employees to fill vacancies until the rehiring list of laid-off employees is ex-

---

[150] Thompson Mahogany Co., 5 LA 397, 399 (Brandschain, 1946). For other cases permitting such temporary and/or emergency assignments see Arbitrator Sembower in 29 LA 704, 706; Reid in 22 LA 358, 361; R. Williams in 27 LA 790, 792; Klamon in 22 LA 336, 351; Hawley in 22 LA 157, 161; Gilden in 19 LA 802, 805; Kelliher in 18 LA 216, 217-218; Hampton in 17 LA 666, 668; Elson in 8 LA 129, 132.

[151] See Dow Chemical Co., 22 LA 336, 351 (Klamon, 1954). For full discussion see this Chapter, topic titled "Wage Adjustments Following Changes in Operation Methods".

[152] See Arbitrator Kelliher in 25 LA 64, 65-66; Platt in 16 LA 215, 216; Hepburn in 11 LA 145, 147; Elson in 8 LA 389, 393-394. Cf., McCoy in 8 LA 883, 890-891.

hausted,[153] or that the employer must consider present employees for vacancies before hiring new workers.[154]

Where the contract neither explicitly nor by strong implication restricted the right of management to hire new employees, one arbitration board refused to read a restriction into the contract. That board distinguished between the right to hire and the right to promote under a contract which did not specifically restrict management's right to hire but did require the observance of seniority in the event a promotion was made, the arbitrators stating that this "agreement to promote by seniority does not, as such, exclude either explicitly or implicitly the right of the Company not to promote but to hire."[155] Other arbitrators, however, while not speaking in terms of the right to hire, did find a violation of the seniority provisions requiring preferential consideration of senior employees when the company failed to consider its employees for a vacancy and hired an outsider.[156] In another situation where the company conceded that its right to hire was qualified by the seniority clause, the company was nevertheless held not required to fill a job opening from present employees when none of them could perform the job without intensive training. It was permitted to hire an already qualified person.[157]

The employer's discretion in hiring may also be restricted by a union security clause to the extent that any such clause is legal under applicable state and federal statutes. Where the union security provision is lawful, arbitrators appear to frown upon hiring practices which accomplish by indirection the precise condition which such provison was designed to prevent, or which prevent the very condition which such provision was in-

---

[153] As in San Francisco Chronicle, 21 LA 253 (Kerr, 1953).

[154] As in Electric Auto-Lite Co., 24 LA 765, 766 (Kahn, 1955).

[155] Travelers Insurance Co., 18 LA 534, 535 (Donnelly & Mottram, dissent by Sviridoff, 1952). Also see Arbitrators Donnelly, Mannino & Mottram in 24 LA 631, 632.

[156] See Arbitrator Gilden in 27 LA 544, 546-547; Dworkin in 21 LA 589, 595. Also see Arbitrator Feinberg in 13 LA 991, 999.

[157] Wagner Electric Corp., 20 LA 768, 775 (Klamon, 1953). Also see Arbitrator McCoy in 16 LA 28, 29.

tended to accomplish. [158]   For instance, one employer was ordered to discharge again an employee previously discharged pursuant to a membership-maintenance provision while employed as a production worker and subsequently rehired as an assistant foreman.   The arbitrator declared that the rehiring of the worker under these circumstances was a cause of dissention and violated the intent of the membership-maintenance provision. [159]

Under contracts providing for union referrals in hiring but containing the requirement that referrals be satisfactory to management, arbitrators have allowed employers considerable discretion in rejecting union-referred candidates.[160]   But it has been held that the employer must exercise good faith in reaching his decision. [161]

Arbitrators have held that it is the prerogative of management to grant or deny reemployment to employees who have resigned voluntarily. [162]   Also, where employees terminate their employment relationship by an unauthorized strike or are discharged by reason of such participation, it has been held that their reemployment is entirely within the discretion of management. [163]   Management's right not to hire may be upheld in other situations, too.   Thus, it has been held that the employer is not required to hire a new employee to fill a vacancy when he has had no bids from his employees and there is no contractual requirement for maintaining a certain number of employees within the classification. [164]

---

[158] See Arbitrator Aaron in 10 LA 227, 232-233; Updegraff in 1 LA 331, 333; Fabinski in 1 LA 15, 19-20.
[159] Merrill-Stevens Co., 1 LA 15, 19-20 (Fabinski, 1944).
[160] See Arbitrator Feinberg in LA 593, 595; Reynolds in 3 LA 367, 369. Also see Arbitrator Bennett in 18 LA 764, 766, and Wyckoff in 5 LA 38, 40, both involving "interests" disputes.
[161] Matson Navigation Co., 29 LA 209, 213 (Cobb, 1957).
[162] See Arbitrator Dworkin in 29 LA 700, 703; Anderson in 20 LA 715, 718; Stein in 17 LA 256, 257; Cahn in 16 LA 890, 891; Kaplan in 3 LA 239, 241; Gorder in 2 LA 292, 294.
[163] See Arbitrator Pfaus in 19 LA 763, 765, upholding the company's reinstatement of all strikers except the two instigators; Hauser in 7 LA 583, 585. Cf. Lehoczky in 27 LA 131, 133.
[164] Connecticut Coke Co., 28 LA 360, 361-362 (Stutz & Mottram, dissent by Curry, (1957).

Determination of Size of Crews

It has been held that management has the right unilaterally to determine the size of crews necessary for the operation of the plant, either under a general management rights clause,[165] or as a matter of management prerogative,[166] so long as no other provision of the agreement is violated by the employer's determination.

This right may be limited by contract provision, as, for example, a clause providing that "no less than three men shall be employed in a crew",[167] or one stating that "adequate help will be provided,"[168] or one requiring the employer to schedule the "normal number" of employees on a shift.[169] However, even where the contract required continuance of all local working conditions, an employer was not required to assign the same number of employees to a new "line" as were working on the old lines, where the new line was not substantially similar to the old ones.[170]

Management's right to determine the size of work crews has sometimes been challenged on the ground that a reduction in the size of the crew results in a safety or health hazard,[171] or that it results in a work load that is too heavy for the remaining employees.[172] Sometimes management's right to determine the size of the crew is involved indirectly when the union charges that a contract provision (such as seniority or lay-off clauses,

---

[165] Electro Metallurgical Co., 28 LA 252, 254 (Marshall, 1957); Youngstown Sheet & Tube Co., 12 LA 865, 869 (Updegraff, 1949).

[166] National Container Corp., 29 LA 687, 692-693 (Marshall, 1957); Pacific American Shipowners Assn., 10 LA 736, 745 (Miller, 1948). Also see Arbitrator Updegraff in 30 LA 115, 117. The National War Labor Board recognized this to be a management function. American Smelting & Refining Co., 21 War Lab. Rep. 163 (1945).

[167] Weston Biscuit Co., Inc., 21 LA 653, 654 (Flink, 1953).

[168] Pabst Brewing Co., 29 LA 617, 621 (Fleming, 1957).

[169] Sherwin-Williams Co., 25 LA 879, 881 (Kelliher, 1956).

[170] Pierce Governor Co., Inc., 25 LA 162, 165 (Uible, 1955). Also see similar reasoning by Arbitrator Updegraff in 30 LA 115, 117.

[171] Jones & Laughlin Steel Corp., 30 LA 395, 396 (S. Cahn, 1958); Bethlehem Steel Co., 28 LA 651 (Seward, 1957). In neither case, however, did the arbitrator find that a safety or health hazard existed.

[172] National Container Co., 29 LA 687, 692 (Marshall, 1957). The arbitrator found that the work load was not too heavy.

or clauses concerned with filling vacancies) has been violated by some action of management. [173]

Vacancies

It is generally recognized that in the absence of a contract provision limiting management's rights in regard to filling vacancies, as, for example, a requirement to maintain a certain number of employees on a particular job, it is management's right to determine whether a vacancy exists and whether and when it shall be filled. [174]

Scheduling Work

Arbitrators have often ruled that, except as restricted by the agreement, the right to schedule work remains in management. [175] Arbitrator Dudley E. Whiting has declared the general rule to be that "a company is free to operate its plant and direct the work of its employees in any manner not prohibited by law or by the employment or collective bargaining agreement." [176] The agreement there considered by Arbitrator Whiting contained no restrictions upon the right of the company to schedule work, and he stated that the agreement in fact con-

---

[173] See Arbitrator Dworkin in 29 LA 787, 789; Stutz in 28 LA 360, 361; Feinberg in 19 LA 523, 525; S. Wolff in 19 LA 487, 488. For related material see Chapter 14, Seniority; Chapter 12, topic titled "Custom and Practice as Part of the Contract"; this Chapter, topics titled "Layoff of Employees", "Vacancies", "Control of Operation Methods", "Right to Subcontract."

[174] See Arbitrator Abernethy in 29 LA 467, 468; Livengood in 28 LA 844, 847; Hebert in 28 LA 538, 541-542; Marshall in 28 LA 252, 254; Donnelly in 28 LA 162, 166; Roberts in 25 885, 888; Seligson in 25 LA 360, 364; Kelliher in 22 LA 676, 577; Hawley in 22 LA 157, 159; Dworet in 22 LA 71, 74; Klamon in 16 LA 352, 356. Also see Arbitrator Cahn in 22 LA 385, 387; Reid in 22 LA 84, 87-88; Livengood in 17 LA 810, 812; Hampton in 16 LA 59, 63. But see Arbitrator Davey in 29 LA 13, 16-17, where the contract made it mandatory to fill vacancies.

[175] See Arbitrator Shister in 32 LA 77; Kelliher in 29 LA 615, 617; Dworkin in 29 LA 236, 239; Townsend in 28 LA 664, 666-667; Duff in 28 LA 37, 40; Warns in 24 LA 619, 622; Davey in 22 LA 657, 660; Uible in 19 LA 213, 214-215; Rule in 16 LA 328, 330; McCoy in 16 LA 73, 75; Schedler in 13 LA 192, 199; McCreary in 9 LA 834, 839-840 Whiting in 3 LA 482, 485; Korey in 1 LA 430, 432-433. Also see Arbitrator Coffey in 20 LA 432, 433; Guild in 19 LA 891, 892; Klamon in 15 LA 733, 739; McCreary in 12 LA 1044, 1052; Tischler in 13 LA 396, 398. The contract may explicitly provide that scheduling is an exclusive management function, as in 30 LA 797, 30 LA 55, 26 LA 133, 26 LA 43; or it may expressly limit the employer's right to schedule work as in 29 LA 236, 26 LA 761, 24 LA 565, 21 LA 416, 19 LA 891, 19 LA 138, 16 LA 379, 16 LA 277, 16 LA 165.

[176] Ingram-Richardson Mfg. Co. of Indiana, Inc., 3 LA 482, 485 (1946).

firmed that right by providing that "the management of the plant and the direction of the working forces etc. is vested exclusively in the company." [177]   Accordingly, he ruled that the company was within its rights in establishing staggered work schedules. [178]   Under a similar management rights clause, Arbitrator Prasow has held that in the absence of a limiting contract provision management may unilaterally change from fixed to rotating shifts. [179]

Arbitrator Joseph D. Lohman, too, has ruled that the scheduling of work is an aspect of the direction of the working forces:

> "The union contention that the company does not enjoy the right to unilaterally establish work schedules is without merit, except as this prerogative is qualified by other aspects of the agreement. The arranging of work schedules is properly an aspect of the direction of the working force." [180]

Arbitrator Lohman held, however, that while management might be privileged unilaterally to schedule working hours insofar as scheduling operations might prove helpful in regularizing production, it was not privileged to schedule shifts in such a way as to deprive employees of certain rest periods to which they were entitled under the contract. [181]

One arbitrator was asked to decide whether, in the absence of a contractual provision, an employer had the right to reschedule hours of work for operations at night and, if so, on what basis of compensation.   The arbitrator ruled that there was no question as to the company's right to assign employees night work, but that it must pay a night-work differential that had been paid in the past. [182]

---

[177] Ibid.

[178] A similar award on staggered shifts was rendered in Intl. Minerals & Chemical Corp., 13 LA 192, 199 (Schedler, 1949). Also see Sinclair Refining Co., 15 LA 142, 146-147 (Abrahams, 1950).

[179] Morris P. Kirk & Son, Inc., 27 LA 6, 10 (1956).

[180] Wilson & Co., Inc., 1 LA 342, 347 (1946).

[181] Ibid.   Also see Bakelite Co., 29 LA 555, 559 (Updegraff, 1957), involving a change in scheduled lunch periods.

[182] Everett Dyers & Cleaners, 11 LA 462, 466 (Myers, 1948). Also see Arbitrator Jaffee in 30 LA 797, 802.

Arbitrator Charles G. Hampton has stated that the "right" of management to scheule work carries with it the "duty" to do so. He ruled that an employer who abdicates such right by permitting employees to determine their own overtime schedules must be held partly responsible for trouble caused by such schedules. [183]

It has been held that, where an agreement is silent as to the workweek insofar as its commencement and end are concerned, the employer may change the day on which the workweek begins if the change is not made arbitrarily and is made in conformance with industry practice in the area. [184] Similarly, where the contract contained no express restriction on the employer's right to determine the starting time for work shifts, the employer has been permitted unilaterally to change the starting and stopping time. [185]

Also, it has been held that the fact that a work schedule has been traditionally on a "normal" workweek basis of five consecutive days does not in itself establish a vested interest in employees in the continuation of the schedule. The union had argued to the contrary despite the fact that the agreement contained a clause permitting the employer to change schedules in the interest of plant efficiency if not done indiscriminately. [186]

The National War Labor Board also held the residual power to be in management: "Conceding that an hour schedule for a workweek is a proper subject for negotiation in a new contract, the fact remains that, until such matter has been regulated by agreement after negotiation, its disposition falls properly in the realm of managerial policy * * *." [187] In that case the Board

---

[183] Fulton Glass Co., 10 LA 75, 78 (1948).
[184] Schulze's Bakery et al., 5 LA 255, 257 (Wardlaw, 1946).
[185] United States Pipe & Foundry Co., 28 LA 467 (Hepburn, 1957); Federal Rice Drug Co., 27 LA 123, 125 (Reid, 1956).
[186] Columbia Steel Co., 7 LA 881, 883 (Blumer, 1947). Also see Arbitrator Boles in 30 LA 465, 469-470; Kelliher in 29 LA 615, 617; Ryder in 24 LA 496, 500. But see Arbitrator Carmichael in 28 LA 20, 23; Reynard in 27 LA 625, 627; Donnelly, Mottram & Curry in 17 LA 463, 465-466.
[187] Screw Machine Products Co., 3 War Lab. Rep. 553, 556 (1942).

ruled that since the agreement did not limit the employer's right to change hours of work, it was his prerogative to change scheduled hours of work from 9½ hours a day, five days a week, to 8 hours a day six days a week.

In the absence of a specific contract provision regarding the right of management to reduce the workweek, arbitrators have gone both ways on the issue. [188] Thus, one arbitrator has held that management has the right to reduce hours of work in the absence of anything in the agreement restricting such right. [189] There the contract defined the normal workweek as five days of eight hours each and set forth the procedure for layoffs in case of reduction. The board, speaking through its Chairman, Herbert Blumer, held that the employer was not prohibited from reducing hours per day to seven in lieu of making layoffs. The board declared that the clauses defining the normal workday and normay workweek were standard contract clauses serving ostensibly as a basis for the calculation of overtime, that the working of the hours specified was not made mandatory, and that the agreement said nothing in regard to the necessity of making layoffs in lieu of reducing hours of work. [190]

An apparently contrary result was reached by another board of arbitration, which held that an employer who reduced the workweek of some employees from five to four days was required to apply the "layoff" provisions of the agreement in doing so. The agreement provided for a basic workweek of five days and made seniority govern in cases of layoff.[191] A similar ruling was made by Arbitrator Joseph Brandschain in jected the employer's contention that "layoffs believed at their ployees not to report to work because of a shortage of materials should be considered a "scheduling of work" rather than a "layoff":

---

[188] For a collection of cases, see this Chapter topic titled 'Layoff of Employees."
[189] Geuder, Paeschke & Frey Co., 12 LA 1163, 1165 (Blumer, 1949). Also see Arbitrator Shister in 20 LA 861, 862.
[190] Geuder, Paeschke & Frey Co., 12 LA 1163, 1164 (1949).
[191] United Smelting & Aluminum Co., Inc., 13 LA 684, 685-686 (Donnelly & Sviridoff, Mottram dissenting, 1949).

"The umpire finds difficulty with the concept that a direction to an employee not to report to work because of lack of materials is not a 'layoff' but a 'scheduling of work.' Is there any difference between a 'layoff' and a 'scheduling of work' which results in workers being told there is no work for them? Aren't all the indicia and surrounding circumstances of a 'layoff' the same as those of a 'scheduling of work' that results in the enforced idleness of workers? Is the worker who is idle because management has told him he is scheduled not to work in any different state or condition than one who has been told that he is laid off? Is the former any less laid off than the latter?" [192]

Arbitrator Brandschain noted that the agreement made no distinction between temporary and permanent layoffs, and he rejected the employer's contention that "layoffs believed at their inception to be but of brief duration are not layoffs but are matters of scheduling work * * *." [193]

Management may be denied the right to make temporary changes in the work schedule where the purpose of doing so is to avoid overtime payments. Even under a contract providing that nothing therein should "be interpreted as interfering in any way with the Company's right to alter, re-arrange or change, extend, limit or curtail its operations * * * whatever may be the effect upon employment, when, in its sole judgment and discretion, it may deem it advisable to do all or any of said things," it was held that the employer could not change the work schedule for one week where the sole purpose in doing so was to avoid contractual overtime payments. [194] Some arbitrators, however, have held otherwise where the change is made prior to the commencement of the workweek [195] or is made with a full week's notice. [196] Such cases were regarded as not analogous to changes made on short notice.

In the absence of limiting contract language, other arbitrators have permitted management to change work schedules

[192] Bethlehem Steel Co., 5 LA 578, 587 (1946).
[193] Id. at 588.
[194] Kennecott Copper Corp., 6 LA 820, 822 (Kleinsorge, 1947). For other awards denying management the right in question, see Arbitrator Beatty in 21 LA 416, 419; Platt in 17 LA 313, 315; Gilden in 12 LA 624, 627; Blumer in 5 LA 402, 406; Trotta in 5 LA 69, 71.
[195] National Zinc Co., Inc., 4 LA 768, 772 (Wardlaw, 1946).
[196] Wilson & Co., 7 LA 601 (Lohman, 1947).

to avoid the payment of overtime, holding that the company is not obligated to provide overtime work. [197]

Emergency Changes in Work Schedule

Arbitrators appear to be generally inclined to allow management a great deal of flexibility, where it is possible to do so under the agreement, in making unscheduled and emergency changes in the work schedule if made in good faith and for reasonable cause. [198] For instance, under an agreement giving management exclusive authority to schedule production and determine shifts,[199] and under an agreement giving it the right to direct and assign the working force,[200] management has been held not required to pay employees for scheduled hours not worked when, because of severe weather, employees were dismissed early to permit them to reach their homes safely—despite the fact that sufficient work was available. Moreover, it has been held that "The decision as to the suitability of weather conditions for certain types of work must be made by Management; this decision should be made on the basis of its best judgment in the light of the immediate circumstances and must be respected provided there is no abuse by Management of its authority." [201]

One arbitrator has ruled that a clause giving management the exclusive right to schedule working hours permits it to make temporary changes in the work schedule without consulting the union. In that case the arbitrator held that the employer was not obligated to pay employees for a half hour waiting period on a day when they were scheduled to work at 10 a.m. but were unable to begin work until 10:30. The call-in

---

[197] See Arbitrators Stutz & Williams, Cury dissenting, in 27 LA 92, 93; D. Wolff in 21 LA 210, 214; Uible in 19 LA 213, 214-215. Also see Arbitrator Warns in 24 LA 619, 622; Coffey in 20 LA 432, 433; Sturges in 16 LA 517.

[198] See, for example, Arbitrator Thompson in 28 LA 494, 503; Graff in 26 LA 43, 46-47; Platt in 17 LA 313, 315.

[199] Sealed Power Cop., 7 LA 485, 489 (Platt, 1947).

[200] Pan American Airways, Inc., 13 LA 326, 327-328 (Reynolds, 1949). Similarly, American Can Co., 10 LA 579, 581 (Stein, 1948).

[201] Bethlehem Steel Co., 27 LA 482, 485 (Feinberg, 1956), quoting Umpire Stowe in a previous case between the parties.

pay clause was held not to cover the situation because the employees actually worked and received pay for more hours than were guaranteed by the clause. In sustaining the right of the employer to make temporary changes in the work schedule, the arbitrator, R. W. Fleming, said:

> "This is the usual 'management prerogative' type of clause [speaking of the clause giving the employer the right to schedule working hours]. Experience shows that this clause is inserted in the contract at the instance of management to make clear that it has freedom to do certain things without having to consult the unions. So, in this case, the Company retained the exclusive right to schedule working hours, without consultation with the union. In the opinion of the arbiter the clause cannot fairly be read to mean in addition that the Company, once it has set the working hours, must pay for hours not worked unless failure to work was for reasons beyond the Company's control. * * *" [202]

Under an agreement containing a minimum pay guarantee of four hours for employees who report to work and are not put to work and also for employees who, after having been put to work, are laid off before completing four hours of work, but providing that the guarantee should not apply in case of strike, breakdown of equipment, or act of God, Arbitrator Joseph Brandschain ruled that the employer's decision to send employees home when the machine to which they were assigned broke down, rather than to provide them with other work, represented the exercise of a management prerogative which the union was not entitled to challenge in the absence of a contractual requirement that the employer provide alternative work. As to the wisdom of the employer's decision, however, he said:

> "However, in most instances, it might be much wiser from both the point of view of economy of operation and employee morale if a determined effort were made to find other work in these situations, particularly if it is true that preceding foremen used to concern themselves more with this problem. As the union points out, the men suffer the inconvenience and expense of coming to work, packing lunch, and paying for transportation so that management should make every effort to find work for the men to do wherever possible. Still, this is entirely a matter of manage-

---

[202] Libby, McNeill & Libby, 11 LA 872, 874 (Fleming, 1948).

ment policy and not something that management would have to do because of any contract obligation." [203]

Even where the collective agreement limits management's right in regard to scheduling work, arbitrators have held that management may change the work schedule if there is an emergency,[204] or a condition beyond the company's control.[205]

Under an agreement providing for notice when employees are laid off due to a reduction in force except in emergencies, it was held that a strike of some of the employees is an emergency.[206] It has also been held that an emergency existed when a deliberate slowdown by the employees resulted in an accumulation of stock in one department making continued production impossible.[207] Under a contract not providing for emergencies but stating that employees shall be given one week's advance notice in case of "arbitrary layoff," the employer was not required to give advance notice of layoff when a shipment of materials failed to arrive on time, the arbitrator stating that the situation was an emergency.[208]

However, when the occurrence is actually not beyond the control of management, the arbitrator will not find that an emergency exists, as, for example, where there was a power failure in the plant and the company had known of the potential danger and did not take steps to correct it.[209]

Under some contracts, management is relieved certain obligations in the event of a "cause beyond the control of management." Speaking of a contract provision relieving the employer of the obligation for call-in pay if the failure to provide

---

[203] Bethlehem Steel Co., 4 LA 450, 454-455 (1946). For a similar ruling, see Terre Haute Water Works Corp., 5 LA 747, 749 (Updegraff, 1946).

[204] Supermatic Products Corp., 25 LA 794, 797-799 (Prasow, 1956). Cf. Arbitrator Maggs in 28 LA 379, 382.

[205] Inland Steel, 16 LA 277, 279 (Cornsweet, 1950).

[206] American Airlines, Inc., 27 LA 448, 450 (S. Wolff, 1956); Owens-Corning Fiberglas Corp., 23 LA 603, 605-606 (Uible 1954).

[207] Lone Star Steel Co., 28 LA 465, 466 (McCoy, 1957).

[208] Lavoris Co., 16 LA 173, 175 (Lockhart, 1951). In National Airlines, Inc., 16 LA 532, 534 (1951), an "interests" case, Arbitrator Payne recommended that the new contract provide that no notice be required in emergencies.

[209] Chrysler Corp., 21 LA 573, 579 (D. Wolff, 1953).

work is due to a cause beyond his control, Arbitrator David A. Wolff stated:

> "Considered in context 'cause beyond the control of the management' cannot mean all causes over which, regardless of reason, the Company exercises no control. Rather, and at most, it must mean either a cause not falling within the general area of the Company's responsibilities or, if falling within this area, a cause which could not be anticipated or, if anticipated, could not have been guarded against at all or except by unreasonably burdensome or unrealistic measures. However, if a cause does fall within this area and could have been anticipated and reasonably guarded against, failure to provide such necessary safeguards, either unintentially or as a calculated risk, would not place the cause beyond the control of the management." [210]

Right to Require Overtime

It has generally been held by arbitrators that if the collective agreement is silent on the subject of hours of employment or fails explicitly to limit the length of the workday or workweek beyond which no further work may be required, management has the right to demand overtime work from employees.[211] It has also been held that management may require overtime work in the absence of contract prohibition as long as it is of "reasonable duration, commensurate with employee health, safety and endurance, and the direction is issued under reasonable circumstances." [212]

On the other hand, an agreement definitely establishing the length of the workweek may call for a different conclusion. This was the case, for instance, where the agreement provided that the "eight (8) hour day and forty (40) hour week * * * shall be in effect without revision, during the term of this contract." [213] It has been held, however, that the fact that an agreement specifies a "normal" workday as one of a certain

---

[210] Chrysler Corp., 21 LA 573, 579 (1953).

[211] See Arbitrator Fleming in 24 LA 526, 528; Copelof in 13 LA 211, 214; Seward in 12 LA 810, 811; Kelliher in 12 LA 779, 783; S. Wolff in 10 LA 98, 100; McCreary in 9 LA 834, 840; Platt in 9 LA 735, 740.

[212] Texas Co., 14 LA 146, 149 (Gilden, 1949). Also applying the "rule of reason": Arbitrator Howlett in 29 LA 495, 502; Kharas in 25 LA 755, 757; Douglas in 21 LA 513, 515; Reeves in 20 LA 564, 566; Copelof in 13 LA 211, 214; Seward in 12 LA 810, 811.

[213] Connecticut River Mills, Inc., 6 LA 1017, 1019 (Wallen, 1947). To similar effect, Baker & Taylor Co., 1 ALAA par. 67,318 (1944).

number of hours or a "normal" workweek as one of a certain number of days does not prohibit management from requiring employees to work overtime since the use of the word "normal" implies occasional resort to "abnormal." [214] This is said to be especially so where the agreement provides for time and one-half for hours over a certain number a week, since such provision "clearly recognizes an obligation on the company to pay for overtime, and surely by implication, that workers are obliged to work reasonably necessary overtime unless specifically excused." [215]

If the agreement does not expressly state whether overtime work is optional or compulsory, the arbitrator may rule that the determination of whether it is optional must depend upon past practice in the plant, practice in the industry, and the general circumstances of the case. [216] An agreement may specifically or by implication provide that the employee has an option and that he may ask to be excused from doing overtime work. [217] Under such a provision, it has been held that the employee is obligated to indicate whether he will work overtime. [218] Moreover, under a clause giving the employees an option, management has been held not to have the right to force employees who have rightfully rejected an overtime assignment to perform prearranged weekend work by calling such work a work assignment which must be protested under the grievance procedure. [219]

Sometimes the agreement will contain a provision specifically giving management the right to require overtime work of

[214] Carnegie-Illinois Steel Corp., 12 LA 810, 811 (Seward, 1949). Also see Jones & Laughlin Steel Corp., 29 LA 708, 709-710 (Cahn, 1957).

[215] Nebraska Consolidated Mills Co., 13 LA 211, 214 (Copelof, 1949). Also see McDonnell Aircaft Corp., 21 LA 91, 94 (Klamon, 1953). Contra, Arbitrator Maggs in 17 LA 606, 608-609; Lehoczky in 1 LA 468, 470.

[216] Dortch Stove Works, Inc., 9 LA 374 (McCoy, Waller & Graham, 1948). Also see Arbitrator Rock in 29 LA 482, 484-485; Hampton in 6 LA 918, 921.

[217] Lear, Inc., 28 LA 242, 245-246 (Bradley, 1957); West Penn Power Co., 27 LA 458, 462 (Begley, 1956).

[218] Lear, Inc., 28 LA 242, 245-246 (Bradley, 1957).

[219] West Penn Power Co., 27 LA 458, 463 (Begley, 1956).

employees.[220] Even so, the right of the employer to punish for refusal to work overtime may be held to depend upon the facts of the case. There may be extenuating circumstances. Thus, Umpire Harry Shulman stated that, while "an employee's refusal to work overtime may be a breach of duty for which he may properly be disciplined, his refusal may be justified and, if justified, is not ground for disciplinary penalty." [221] In that case, it was found that the employee's refusal was justified since the request for overtime work was made shortly before quitting time, and the reason for the refusal was that the employee would miss his usual ride and the use of public transportation would require additional time far out of proportion to the overtime he was asked to work.[222]

It has been held by another arbitrator that, under a contract which gave management the right to schedule any necessary overtime work and to excuse employees from such work in its discretion, the employer was not justified in discharging an employee who, as a Seventh Day Adventist, refused to work on Saturday since the clause requiring overtime work was negotiated three years after the employee was first hired and the employer had never required him to work on Saturday in the past.[223]

In the absence of contract or statutory restriction, the allocation of overtime has been held to be an exclusive right of management.[224]

Scheduling Vacations

It is said that "one of the prerogatives of management [is] to schedule vacations at such time as best meets the needs of the

---

[220] See Arbitrator Copelof in 13 LA 269, 272; Shulman in 11 LA 1158, 1160; Updegraff in 11 LA 561, 565; Klamon in 2 LA 201, 202.

[221] Ford Motor Co., 11 LA 1158, 1160 (1948). Similarly, Arbitrator Fleming in 24 LA 526, 528; Douglas in 21 LA 513, 515, in both of which there was no express contract provision giving management the right to require overtime.

[222] Ford Motor Co., 11 LA 1158, 1160 (Shulman), 1948.

[223] International Shoe Co., 2 LA 201, 205-206 (Klamon, 1946). Cf., International Shoe Co., 15 LA 121, 123 (Kelliher, 1950). Also on the matter of the propriety of the penalty see Arbitrator Updegraff in 11 LA 561, 565; Platt in 9 LA 735, 742.

[224] Graham Brothers, Inc., 16 LA 83, 85 (Cheney, 1951), citing a War Labor Board case. Also see Arbitrator Marshall in 20 LA 212, 216.

business," and that "in doing so the employer will very often and perhaps wherever possible also try to do his utmost to meet the wishes of employees." [225] Arbitrator Harold W. Davey has elaborated:

"Absent specific contract language, it is generally understood in industrial relations practice that a vacation is an earned equity and is generally to be taken in terms of the employee's preference, subject to the exigencies of the Company's production and maintenance requirements. Where the contract is silent on the specific policy or procedure to be followed, it must be assumed that the employee will request his vacation at a time suitable to his own preferences and that his preferences will be honored to the degree that Company requirements will permit. However, where the contract is silent, it must also be assumed that managerial discretion is greater than in those cases where contract language puts the burden on management to show need for the employee to take his vacation at a particular time, or not to take vacation at a particular time." [226]

Whether management is given the right by the agreement or possesses it as a residual power, the right to schedule vacations should be exercised with certain considerations in mind. The effect of vacation scheduling on operations is an important consideration. For instance, under an agreement permitting employees to select their vacation dates whenever practicable, management was permitted to schedule vacations at such times as would not interfere with its operations or cost it additional money. [227]

Umpire Harry Shulman pointed out that some correlation between vacations and what otherwise would be layoffs is not only permissible but also desirable. [228] Under an agreement giving management the right to schedule vacations, the scheduling of vacations to coincide with temporary shutdowns was permitted. [229] There are limitations, however. For instance, under an agreement giving management the right to schedule vaca-

---

[225] Sinclair Refining Co., 12 LA 183, 189 (Klamon, 1949).

[226] Hubinger Co., 29 LA 459, 461 (1957).

[227] Sinclair Refining Co., 12 LA 183, 190 (Klamon, 1949); National Tube Co., 19 LA 330. 331 (Garrett, 1952). Also see Arbitrator Livengood in 30 LA 225, 229; McKelvey in 25 LA 94, 98, Cf. Arbitrator Emory in 17 LA 461, 462.

[228] Ford Motor Co., 3 LA 829, 831 (1946).

[229] Sefton Fibre Can Co., 12 LA 101, 105 (Townsend, 1948). Also see Aro, Inc., 30 LA 225, 231 (Livengood, 1958).

tions, subject to the requirement that "due consideration" be given to employees' wishes, Umpire Shulman ruled that management could not require employees to take their vacations during a period of indefinite layoff where to do so would destroy the substantive features of a vacation. Umpire Shulman reasoned:

> "A vacation is a period of rest between periods of work. A layoff is a period of anxiety and hardship between periods of work. The tremendous difference lies in the assurance of the vacationer that he will return to work at the end of his vacation and the equal assurance of the employee on layoff that he does not know when he will return to work. The basic difference, with its financial, emotional, and psychological implications, is not obliterated by a form of words or by the receipt of income for a part of the indefinite period of layoff." [230]

Other arbitrators have held that, where the contract provides that the employer is to consider the requests of individual employees for particular vacation times, the company may not close the plant during reduced operations for a vacation period, since to schedule such a vacation would be to fail to take into account the desires of individual employees as required by the contract.[231]

Where the agreement fixes the period for taking vacations, the employer has been held not entitled to designate in addition any other period as vacation.[232] Employees, too, have been confined to the fixed vacation period. Thus, under a contract which entitled employees with a year's service to a paid vacation, the employee who completed his year's service after the end of the vacation period fixed by contract was required to wait until the following vacation season to take his vacation.[233]

Under a contract providing for both vacation and sickness benefits, employees who were on sick leave when the employer

---

[230] Ford Motor Co., 3 LA 829, 831 (1946).
[231] See Arbitrator Seward in 30 LA 992, 994; McKelvey in 25 LA 94, 99-100; Ferguson in 20 LA 684, 686; Kelliher in 18 LA 934, 935; Uible in 10 LA 477, 479. Cf. Arbitrator L. Smith in 15 LA 568, 572-573. But see Arbitrator Garrett in 19 LA 330, 331; Hampton in 13 LA 928, 932.
[232] Cone Mills, 29 LA 346, 350 (McCoy, 1957). Cf. General American Transportation Co., 15 LA 481, 484 (Kelliher, 1950).
[233] Kent of Grand Rapids, Inc. 18 LA 160, 162-163 (Platt, 1952); General Cable Corp., 18 LA 44, 45-46 (Cahn, 1952).

closed the plant for a vacation period were held entitled to
receive the sickness benefits and to select a different time for
their vacations.[234]

Right to Subcontract

The right of management to subcontract, in the absence
of specific contract restriction, has been the subject of numerous arbitration cases. The basic and difficult problem is that of
maintaining a proper balance between the employer's legitimate
interest in efficient operation and effectuating economies on the
one hand, and the union's legitimate interest in protecting the
job security of its members and the stability of the bargaining
unit on the other.[235]

In earlier cases, arbitrators generally held that management has the right, if exercised in good faith, to subcontract
work to independent contractors (the work thus to be done
by non-employees of the employer) unless the agreement specifically restricts the right.[236] This view is also stated in some
of the later cases.[237] The basic reasoning is indicated by the
following statement of Arbitrator I. Robert Feinberg:

> "It is true, of course, that job security, and an opportunity to per-
> form available work, is of concern to a union and that the letting of work
> to outsiders by an employer may in some instances be said to be a deroga-
> tion of the basic purposes of their collective bargaining agreement. Never-
> theless, it is also true that where the subject has assumed importance in
> the relations between the parties a provision is generally inserted in the
> agreement defining their respective rights. It has almost been universally
> recognized that in the absence of such a provision an employer may, under
> his customary right to conduct his business efficiently, let work to outside
> contractors if such letting is done in good faith and without deliberate
> intent to injure his employees." [238]

[234] Toledo Scale Co., 25 LA 94, 99-100 (McKelvey, 1955); Derby Gas & Electric
Co., 21 LA 745 (Donnelly, Mannino & Mottram, 1953).
[235] See Arbitrator Larson in 27 LA 233, 235; Lennard in 25 LA 118, 120; Aaron
in 16 LA 644, 648.
[236] See Arbitrator Feinberg in 13 LA 991; McCoy in 12 LA 707; Kelliher in 11
LA 197; Healy in 10 LA 842; Hill in 10 LA 396; Copelof in 8 LA 990; Kaplan in
7 LA 474.
[237] See Arbitrator Warns in 30 LA 493, 495-496; Dworkin in 27 LA 704, 709;
Marshall in 26 LA 74, 78; Klamon in 20 LA 690, 698.
[238] National Sugar Refining Co., 13 LA 991, 1001 (1949).

Most of the later cases have somewhat modified the above view. Where the agreement does not deal specifically with subcontracting, most of the more recent cases fall into either of two categories: (1) The essence of some cases appears to be that the recognition, seniority, wage and other such clauses of the agreement limit management's right to subcontract, and certain standards of reasonableness and good faith are applied in determining whether these clauses have been violated.[239] (2) The essence of other cases is that management can subcontract if it does so reasonably and in good faith.[240]

It appears obvious, however, that the end result ordinarily would be the same regardless of which of these approaches is taken—that is, the right to subcontract depends upon "reasonableness" and "good faith". To illustrate, Arbitrator Hogan has emphasized that the recognition, seniority, and wage clauses restrict subcontracting:

> "After a thoughtful consideration of this question the Arbitrator concludes that the Recognition Clause when considered together with the Wage Clause, the Seniority Clauses, and other clauses establishing standards for covered jobs and employees limits the Company's right to subcontract during the term of the Contract. The Contract sets forth standards of wages and working conditions applicable to those employees and those jobs covered by the Recognition Clause. When the contract was signed the employees in the mending room were on the covered jobs, and the Contract contemplated that work normally performed by them would continue to be so performed as long as the work was available. To allow the Company, after signing an agreement covering standards of wages and conditions for mending room jobs and employees, to lay off the employees

---

[239] For arbitrators holding that such clauses limit management's right to subcontract, but listing standards or citeria pointing to the test of good faith and reasonableness, see Larson in 27 LA 233, 235; Lennard in 25 LA 118, 120; Hogan in 21 LA 713, 724-725. Other arbitrators not listing such standards, but recognizing a general test of reasonableness and good faith, are: Hill in 30 LA 379, 380; Hebert in 27 LA 413, 419; Aaron in 26 LA 870, 873; Reid in 22 LA 124, 128; Garrett in 17 LA 790, 792-794. Cf. Marshall in 30 LA 449, 454-455.

[240] Arbitrators holding that the recognition, seniority, wage and other such clauses do not restrict management's right to subcontract and basing their awards upon factors pointing to the reasonableness and good faith test are: Wolff in 29 LA 594, 594-595; Wallen in 28 LA 491, 493-494; Kornblum in 28 LA 270, 273; Wolff in 27 LA 174, 178-179; Gray in 26 LA 723, 725; Kates in 25 LA 281, 290; Kelliher in 24 LA 158, 159-160; Kagel in 24 LA 33, 34-37 (see in particular the basis for finding "good faith" at 37); Coffey in 20 LA 432, 433-434; Maggs in 19 LA 503, 506; Grant in 19 LA 219, 220; Maggs in 16 LA 829, 831.

and transfer the work to employees not covered by the agreed standards would subvert the Contract and destroy the meaning of the collective bargaining relation. . . ." [241]

But in this same case, Arbitrator Hogan stated some "conditions crucial to the decision" that subcontracting violated the recognition, wage and seniority clauses of the contract, which "conditions" are similar to some of the standards (outlined below) for determining reasonableness and good faith used by other arbitrators, including those who do not rely upon such clauses.

Standards for Evaluating Propriety of Subcontracting

It should be emphasized that the standards used by arbitrators in evaluating subcontracting cases are merely guides and are not necessarily conclusive. True, sometimes one factor has been considered decisive of the case. More frequently, however, several factors have been considered and applied in combination. The standards most frequently used are:

1. *Past Practice.* Whether the company has subcontracted work in the past.[242]

2. *Justification.* Whether subcontracting is done for reasons such as economy,[243] maintenance of secondary sources for production and manpower aid,[244]

---

[241] A. D. Juilliard Co., Inc., 21 LA 713, 724 (1953).

[242] Past practice was given great weight in American Airlines, Inc., 29 LA 594, 594-595 (Wolff, 1957). Past practice was one of the factors considered by arbitrators: Seward in 30 LA 678, 683; Wallen in 28 LA 491, 493-494; Larson in 27 LA 233, 236; Klamon in 27 LA 57, 70; Gray in 26 LA 723, 725; Haughton in 26 LA 432, 454; Lennard in 25 LA 118, 121; Kelliher in 24 LA 158, 159; Haughton in 24 LA 121, 128-129; Kagel in 24 LA 33, 35; Blair in 23 LA 171, 173; Cummins in 20 LA 60, 61; Grant in 19 LA 219; Copelof in 13 LA 652, 659-660. In one case, past practice could not be relied upon by the company where the union had no knowledge of it and could not be charged with knowledge. Weber Aircraft Corp., 24 LA 821, 826-827 (E. Jones, 1955). The union, however, is sometimes charged with knowledge. Devoe & Raynolds, 22 LA 608, 609 (Porter, 1954). The union was held to have acquiesced in the company's practice of subcontracting by failing to object, in Tungsten Mining Corp., 19 LA 503, 505-506 (Maggs, 1952). For full discussion of custom and practice generally, see Chapter 12, Custom and Past Practice, supra.

[243] Amoskeag Mills, Inc., 8 LA 990, 992 (Copelof, 1947). Also see opinions by arbitrators: Wallen in 28 LA 491, 492-493; Kornblum in 28 LA 270, 273; Wolff in 27 LA 174, 178; Aaron in 26 LA 870, 873; Reid in 22 LA 124, 126; Williams in 21 LA 330, 334; in all of which cases economy was considered along with other factors, and the employer was upheld in subcontracting. But economy may not always be sufficient jusitification. See Thompson Grinder Co., 27 LA 671, 674 (McCoy, 1956); Stockholders Publishing Co., 16 LA 644, 648-650 (Aaron, 1951).

[244] Dalmo Victor Co., 24 LA 33, 37 (Kagel, 1954).

augmenting the regular work force,[245] plant security measures,[246] or other sound business reasons.[247]

3. *Effect on the union.* Whether subcontracting is being used as a method of discriminating against the union and substantially preju- dicing the status and integrity of the bargaining unit.[248]

4. *Effect on unit employees.* Whether members of the union are dis- criminated against,[249] displaced,[250] laid off,[251] or deprived of jobs previously available to them,[252] or lose regular or overtime earn- ings,[253] by reason of the subcontract.

5. *Type of work involved.* Whether it is work which is normally done by unit employees,[254] or work which is frequently the subject of subcontracting in the particular industry,[255] or work which is of a "marginal" or "incidental" nature.[256]

6. *Availability of properly qualified employees.* Whether the skills possessed by available members of the bargaining unit are sufficient to perform the work.[257]

---

[245] Phillips Pipe Line Co., 20 LA 432 (Coffey, 1953); Carborundum Co., 20 LA 60, 61 (Cummins, 1952).

[246] A. D. Juilliard & Co., 22 LA 266, 270 (Kelly, 1954). Cf., Lorraine Mfg. Co., 22 LA 390, 391 (Horovitz, 1954).

[247] Bethlehem Steel Co., 30 LA 678, 683 (Seward, 1958); Babcock Printing Press Corp., 10 LA 396, 405 (Hill, 1948).

[248] See Arbitrator Hebert in 27 LA 413, 420; Aaron in 26 LA 870, 874; Kates in 25 LA 281, 290; Lennard in 25 LA 118, 121; Kelliher in 24 LA 158, 160; Kagel in 24 LA 33, 37; Porter in 22 LA 608, 610; Maggs in 16 LA 829, 831.

[249] See Arbitrator Hebert in 27 LA 413, 420; Williams in 21 LA 330, 334; Holly in 19 LA 815, 818.

[250] See Arbitrator Gray in 26 LA 723, 725-726; Blair in 23 LA 171, 173-174. Arbitrator Wolff found that the number of employees had increased rather than de- creased in 29 LA 594.

[251] See Arbitrator Kornblum in 28 LA 270, 273; Haughton in 28 LA 158, 162; Klamon in 27 LA 57, 70-71; Aaron in 26 LA 870, 874; E. Jones in 24 LA 821, 827; Kelliher in 24 LA 158, 160; Kagel in 24 LA 33, 37; Porter in 22 LA 608, 610; Gilden in 22 LA 68, 70.

[252] Bethlehem Steel Co., 30 LA 678, 679, 683 (Seward, 1958); General Motors Corp., 25 LA 118, 121 (Lennard, 1955).

[253] Arbitrator Reid found no financial loss to any employee in 22 LA 124, 126-127. Arbitrator Hebert found loss of overtime to the employee, but was unable to find any contractual obligation on the employer to call him in for overtime, 27 LA 413, 419- 420. Accord, Coffey in 20 LA 432, 433. Contra, Larson in 21 LA 267, 270.

[254] See A. D. Juilliard Co., Inc., 21 LA 713, 725 (Hogan, 1953).

[255] See Bethlehem Steel Co., 30 LA 678, 683 (Seward, 1958); Tungsten Mining Corp., 19 LA 503, 506 (Maggs, 1952).

[256] See Hershey Chocolate Corp., 28 LA 491, 494 (Wallen, 1957), involving print- ing of labels for the company's product; Kollsman Instrument Corp., 28 LA 270, 273 (Kornblum, 1957), involving cleaning chores at a new plant.

[257] See Arbitrator Duff in 29 LA 609, 612-613 (employees were not qualified to do the work in the time necessary in the emergency which existed); Shister in 28 LA 461, 463 (all employees were working); Larson in 27 LA 233, 235 (only one employee was available to perform only a small part of sub-contracted work); Wolff in 27 LA

7. *Availability of equipment and facilities.* Whether necessary equipment and facilities are presently available or can be economically purchased.[258]

6. *Regularity of subcontracting.* Whether the particular work is frequently or only intermittently subcontracted.[259]

9. *Duration of subcontracted work.* Whether the work is subcontracted for a temporary or limited period, [260] or for a permanent or indefinite period.[261]

10. *Unusual circumstances involved.* Whether an emergency,[262] "special" job,[263] strike,[264] or other unusual situation exists necessitating the action.[265]

11. *History of negotiations on the right to subcontract.* Whether management's right to subcontract has been the subject of contract negotiations.[266]

Another possible standard bears comment. In some cases, an ostensible standard for disapproving subcontracting is the

---

174, 178 (shortage of trained personnel); Seward in 30 LA 678, 683, and Klamon in 27 LA 57, 70 (special skills and training were necessary); Lennard in 25 LA 118, 121 (employees had necessary skills); Hogan in 21 LA 713, 725 (employees were available).

[258] See Arbitrator Wallen in 28 LA 491, 492; Haughton in 26 LA 438, 454; Blair in 23 LA 171, 174; in all of which cases the purchase of expensive machinery would have been necessary. See also Wolff in 27 LA 174, 178 (necessary equipment could only be leased); Seward in 30 LA 678, 683, and Holly in 19 LA 815, 818 (equipment was inadequate to meet the needs); Grant in 19 LA 219, 220 (present machinery was outmoded and employee was physically unable to operate new machine); Lennard in 25 LA 118, 121, and Hogan in 21 LA 713, 725 (in both of which cases the company had the necessary equipment).

[259] See Arbitrator Hebert in 27 LA 413, 419 (first time the job had been necessary); Larson in 27 LA 233, 236 (subcontracting had not been so regular in amount or type of work that additional places could have been made available to permanent employees within the unit); Lennard in 25 LA 118, 121 (subcontracted work was to be done continuously, not intermittently).

[260] See Temco Aircraft Corp., 27 LA 233, 235 (Larson, 1956); Cone Finishing Co., 16 LA 829, 831 (Maggs, 1951).

[261] See General Metals Corp., 25 LA 118, 121 (Lennard, 1955).

[262] See Arbitrator Duff in 29 LA 609, 612; Lennard in 25 LA 118, 121; Kelly in 22 LA 266, 270.

[263] See Texas Gas Transmission Corp., 27 LA 413, 419 (Hebert, 1956).

[264] Cone Finishing Co., 16 LA 829, 831 (Maggs, 1951).

[265] In Owens-Corning Fiberglass Corp., 23 LA 603, 605-606 (Uible, 1954), the company's employees refused to cross the picket line of another union.

[266] See Arbitrator Wolff in 27 LA 174, 177-179; Klamon in 27 LA 57, 71-74; Haughton in 26 LA 438, 453-454; Kates in 25 LA 281, 289; in all of which cases the union had attempted unsuccessfully during negotiations to obtain a ban on subcontracting. See also Kelliher in 24 LA 158, 159; Haughton in 24 LA 121, 128-129; Kagel in 24 LA 33, 35-37; Blair in 23 LA 171, 174; Williams in 21 LA 330, 333; in all of which cases the union was aware of a practice of subcontracting and did not attempt to negotiate a change in the practice. Also see Hogan in 21 LA 713, 725, 726.

fact of performance of the work on the company's premises. However, review of such cases indicates that the arbitrator was primarily concerned about layoff [267] or displacement of employees,[268] loss of regular or overtime pay,[269] or the elimination of a bargaining unit job.[270] Thus, the "premises" standard may be of doubtful significance or value.

Although the test of reasonableness and good faith may appear nebulous and uncertain, nevertheless we have observed the emergence of a set of standards or guides by which the arbitrator may determine whether, under all the circumstances of the case, the action of management in subcontracting was reasonable and in good faith. Indeed, the use of flexible guides has an important and time-honored counterpart in the development and use by courts of general guides under the law of of agency for determining whether a given relationship is that of "independent contractor." [271] The latter guides do not produce automatic results, but it does not follow that they are useless. If they were, they would long since have been discarded. Likewise it does not suffice to say that each subcontracting case must be decided on the basis of its own facts—there must be guides or standards against which to measure those facts, and reported arbitration decisions are providing guides of great utility.

Some other aspects also have been considered by arbitrators. For instance, controversy has sometimes arisen as to whether the relationship involved is in fact that of independent contractor.[272] Similarly, in some cases the arbitrability of disputes involving the right to subcontract has been challenged.[273]

---

[267] Weber Aircraft Corp., 24 LA 821, 827-828 (E. Jones, 1955).

[268] Hearst Consolidated Publications, Inc., 26 LA 723, 725-726 (Gray, 1956).

[269] Magnolia Petroleum Co., 21 LA 267, 269-273 (Larson, 1953).

[270] New Haven Gas Co., 24 LA 882, 884 (Stutz, 1955).

[271] See, Restatement of Law of Agency, §220.

[272] See Arbitrator Sembower in 29 LA 67; Wolff in 27 LA 174; Vokoun in 26 LA 79; Feinberg in 23 LA 685; Wolff in 14 LA 31, 34.

[273] See Arbitrator Marshall in 26 LA 74, 78; R. Smith in 25 LA 1, 4-5; Haughton in 24 LA 121, 128; Larson in 21 LA 267, 271; Boles in 20 LA 227, 230; Simmons in 13 LA 189; Copelof in 8 LA 990. See also in In re Mandel Laces, Inc., 27 LA 440 (N. Y. Sup. Ct., 1956).

Also, arbitrators have treated the question of whether contractual provisions denying management the right to assign work of bargaining unit employees to employees outside the unit prohibit the subcontracting of such work to persons not in the employ of the company at all.[274] Finally, it has been held that the employer is obliged to recover improperly subcontracted work for his employees if possible, but is not obliged to do so if its recovery is not possible.[275] On the other hand, if the subcontracting is found to have been proper, the union might be found to have violated the no-strike clause by refusing to handle the subcontracted material.[276]

In the railroad industry the freedom of management to subcontract is definitely limited. This fact is made clear by the following statement of the Third Division of the National Railroad Adjustment Board:

> "It is well settled, by many decisions of this and the First Division of this Board and predecessor Boards, that as an abstract principle a carrier may not let out to others the performance of work of a type embraced within one of its collective agreements with the employees. See awards of this Division, 180, 232, 521 and 615; of the First Division, 351 and 1237. This conclusion is reached not because of anything stated in the schedule but as a basic legal principle that the contract with the employees covers all the work of the kind involved, except such as may be specifically excepted; ordinarily such exception appears in the Scope Rule, but the decisions likewise recognize that there may be other exceptions, very definite proof of which, however, is necessary. Mere practice alone is not sufficient for, as often held, repeated violations of a contract do not modify it." [277]

---

[274] See Arbitrator Klamon in 27 LA 57, 73; Aaron in 26 LA 870, 873; Porter in 22 LA 608; Cahn in 19 LA 882; McCoy in 12 LA 707, 709

[275] Mullite Refractories, Inc., 13 LA 690 (Donnelly, 1949). In Electric Auto-Lite Co., 30 LA 449, 455 (1958), Arbitrator Marshall stated that the company should terminate the subcontract and return the work to its employees; the company was allowed a reasonable time to comply with the award.

[276] Dalmo Victor Co., 24 LA 33, 37-38 (Kagel, 1954).

[277] Award 757, Third Division, N.R.A.B. Among the recognized exceptions are instances where the carrier can show that it does not have the needed equipment or trained employees to perform a specializd type of work, Award 2338, Third Division, N.R.A.B.; also, where the questioned work is an integral part of a whole project which is a proper subject for subcontracting. Award 7841, Third Division, N.R.A.B., 28 LA 559 (Referee Lynch, 1957).

Assigning Work Out of Bargaining Unit

Arbitrators have ruled both ways on the question of whether, in the absence of contract provisions to the contrary, management has the right to assign bargaining unit work to employees outside the unit. Most of the awards have involved the assignment of such work to supervisory employees; others involve professional, clerical, or other salaried workers, or non-unit production or maintenance employees. The cases in which such action has been permitted occasionally, but not always, conflict with those in which the right has been denied. We will consider herein the factors that have been significant in the thinking of arbitrators.

In holding that management has such right, some arbitrators have emphasized the absence of a specific restriction in the contract. For example, Arbitrator Robert K. Burns has stated:

> "* * * A careful examination of the contract fails to reveal any provision that specifically prohibits the Company from making a bona fide transfer, allocation or assignment of work out of the bargaining unit—which is the issue posed in this particular case. In the absence of a specific prohibition or limitation to the contrary it must be assumed that these are reserved and retained powers of management * * *." [278]

Also noting the lack of contract restriction, other arbitrators have emphasized in varying degrees the existence of justifying circumstances for assigning work out of the unit. Justifying circumstances exist where the quantity of work or the effect on the bargaining unit is minor in nature; [279] where the work is supervisory or managerial in nature,[280] tempo-

---

[278] Stewart-Warner Corp., 22 LA 547, 551 (1954). Other arbitrators emphasizing this factor are: Klamon in 19 LA 264, 267; Hampton in 16 LA 59, 65; Lane in 13 LA 135, 136; Cheney in 7 LA 412, 413-414 [the right had been contracted away in part in this case however]. See also Feinberg in 14 LA 159. In Trailmobile Co., 8 LA 560, 562 (Wardlaw, 1947), the right was held to be included under a general management rights clause.

[279] See Arbitrator Marshall in 30 LA 710, 713; Mann in 28 LA 728, 731; Burns in 22 LA 547, 550; Donnelly in 21 LA 681, 682; Klamon in 20 LA 690, 703; Donnelly in 20 LA 607, 609; Shipman in 17 LA 76, 79; Gilden in 16 LA 252, 258; Blumer in 5 LA 237, 240. Also see McCoy in 19 LA 372, 374.

[280] See Arbitrator Ridge in 26 LA 422, 427; Healy in 23 LA 504, 510-511; Wolff in 23 LA 247, 251; Shipman in 17 LA 76, 778; Kerr in 13 LA 390, 390-391; Uible in 12 LA 893, 895-896. Also see Blumer in 5 LA 237, 240.

rary,[281] not covered by the contract,[282] or experimental;[283] or if there is a change in the character of the work,[284] a technological change,[285] an emergency,[286] or some special situation.[287]

Other arbitrators have ruled against the right of management to assign work out of the bargaining unit, even in some cases in which there might have been justification, on the basis that it is not included within the various types of general management rights clauses.[288] Similarly, arbitrators have so ruled on the basis that the recognition,[289] seniority,[290] or job security clause [291] is violated by such action; or that the job, being listed in the contract, is a part of the contract, the action thus violating the contract.[292]

The reasoning underlying this view has been elaborated by Arbitrator Saul Wallen, who rejected the management rights clause and applied the seniority provisions of the contract:

---

[281] See Arbitrator Fulda in 13 LA 456, 459; Kerr in 13 LA 390, 390-391; D'Andrade in 12 LA 584, 585.

[282] See Arbitrator E. Jones in 30 LA 358, 364; Barrett in 26 LA 853, 854; Klamon in 19 LA 264, 267; Hildebrand in 16 LA 950, 953-954.

[283] See American Steel & Wire Co., 18 LA 219, 225-227 (Sturges, 1952).

[284] See Arbitrator Stutz in 30 LA 282, 288; Pigors in 28 LA 791, 796-197; Reynard in 24 LA 369, 374.

[285] See Van Norman Machine Co., 28 LA 791, 796-797 (Pigors, 1957); Monsanto Chemical Co., 27 LA 736, 743 (Roberts, 1956). But see Hamm Brewing Co., 28 LA 46, 49 (Lockhart, 1956), where the new machine did not change the job, but only made it more efficient.

[286] Intermountain Chemical Co., 26 LA 58, 61 (Kadish, 1956). Also see American Bemberg, 19 LA 372, 374 (McCoy, 1952).

[287] See Arbitrator Merrill in 27 LA 748, 754 (need for supervisor's presence); Aaron in 27 LA 332, 334-335 (plant security problem); Aaron in 25 LA 263, 266 safety problem); Klamon in 20 LA 690, 703 (minor preparations for reopening plant after shutdown due to strike).

[288] See Arbitrator Selekman in 17 LA 295, 299 (supervosry duties); Copelof in 12 LA 1074, 1080; Coffey in 10 LA 254, 256-257; Wallen in 8 LA 720, 722-723.

[289] See Arbitrator Lockhart in 28 LA 46, 48-49; Kelliher in 27 LA 631, 633; Feinberg in 21 LA 283, 284; Boyce in 20 LA 681, 683-684; Komaroff in 13 LA 545, 550 (training a supervisory employee in order to have more accurate supervision).

[290] See Arbitrator Kelliher in 27 LA 631, 633; McCoy in 19 LA 372, 374 (but the arbitrator also stated that in case of emergency or a "de minimus" situation, management could assign work out of the unit); Gilden in 18 LA 346, 351; Killingsworth in 16 LA 111, 113; Copelof in 12 LA 1074, 1080; Wallen in 8 LA 720, 722-723.

[291] See Hamm Brewing Co., 28 LA 46, 48-49 (Lockhart, 1956).

[292] See Arbitrator Kelliher in 27 LA 631, 633; Reynard in 22 LA 880, 882 (economy was not sufficient justification); Shipman in 21 LA 35, 40-41; Lehoczky in 20 LA 603, 604; Levy in 19 LA 761, 763 (supervisory duties); Selekman in 17 LA 295, 300 (supervisory duties); Pollard in 10 LA 498, 502 (supervisory duties).

"* * * Job security is an inherent element of the labor contract, a part of its very being. If wages is the heart of the labor agreement, job security may be considered its soul. Those eligible to share in the degree of job security the contract affords are those to whom the contract applies. * * *

"The transfer of work customarily performed by employees in the bargaining unit must therefore be regarded as an attack on the job security of the employees whom the agreement covers and therefore on one of the contract's basic purposes." [293]

Sometimes the agreement will specifically prohibit management from assigning work of unit employees to non-unit employees. Where such prohibition exists, absent some justifying circumstance, arbitrators generally hold that such action is not permitted under the contract.[294] Where there is some justifying circumstance, some arbitrators, even in the face of a contract ban, permit assignment of work out of the unit,[295] while other arbitrators adhere strictly to the letter of the contract and refuse to permit such action.[296]

Plant Rules

Arbitrator Clarence M. Updegraff has stated that the employer, according to usual authoritative opinion, is fully authorized to make and to post any plant rules not contrary to law and not inconsistent with the provisions of the collective agree-

---

[293] New Britain Machine Co., 8 LA 720, 722 (1947).

[294] See Arbitrator Gamser in 28 LA 70, 71-72; Klamon in 27 LA 692, 696; Emery in 26 LA 397, 398-399; Cole in 24 LA 332, 333; Ralston in 17 LA 669, 670; Hawley in 17 LA 516, 520; Gilden in 16 LA 162, 165; Wardlaw in 10 LA 143, 147.

[295] See Arbitrator Clements in 30 LA 43, 45 (supervisory duties duplicated by unit employee); Luskin in 28 LA 288, 293 (incidental duties which had been performed by supervisors in the past); Schedler in 28 LA 349, 350 (change in job content due to security measures); Luskin in 26 LA 856, 859-860 (supervisory duties); Crawford in 26 LA 399, 400 (amount of work was "de minimus"); Fulda in 24 LA 696. 699 (supervisory duties); Warren in 19 LA 283, 286-287 (supervisory duties); Ralston in 16 LA 321, 323-324 (unit employees refused to do the job); Gilden in 1 LA 417, 419 (supervisory duties).

[296] See Arbitrator Hawley in 28 LA 321, 323 ("de minimus" rejected); Davis in 27 LA 144, 147 (supervisory duties); Kelliher in 21 LA 657, 658 (supervisory duties); Jaffee in 19 LA 467, 469-471 (supervisory duties); Handsaker in 18 LA 476, 477-478 ("de minimus" rejected); King in 18 LA 156, 158-160 (supervisory duties).

ment.[297] Thus, when the agreement is silent upon the subject, management is said to have the right to formulate and enforce plant rules as an ordinary and proper means of maintaining discipline and efficiency and of directing the conduct of the working force.[298] Management also may establish and enforce plant rules to insure the health and safety of employees or others.[299]

This unilateral right of management to establish plant rules also exists under the various types of management rights clauses.[300] Even where an agreement required management to discuss plant rules with the union before being put into effect, Arbitrator Harold M. Gilden observed: "The purpose of the discussion is to ascertain whether the rule itself contains any loopholes, or whether its enforcement will give rise to unexpected problems. After a discussion, the company, at its option, may put the rule into effect, even though union approval is not obtained." [301]

Under an agreement which vested in management the right "to establish reasonable rules for the management of the plant and to maintain discipline among its employees", Arbitrator Maurice H. Merrill held that rules so established must be considered a part of the agreement and that a clause prohibiting the arbitrator from adding to the terms of the agreement did not preclude him from considering established plant rules

[297] Standard Oil Co. (Indiana), 11 LA 689, 690 (1948). To similar effect, Arbitrator Whiting in 7 LA 150, 153, and in 5 LA 60, 69. Also see McCoy in 27 LA 905. The National War Labor Board recognized this right in management. Rueben H. Donnelley Corporation, 15 War Lab. Rep. 551 (1944). For a general discussion of plant rules and their enforcement, see Stessin, "Management Prerogatives and Plant Rule Violations," 14 Arb. J. 3 (1959).

[298] Federal Machine & Welder Co., 5 LA 60, 69 (Whiting, 1946). In accord, Arbitrator Friedman in 28 LA 328, 329; Lynch in 27 LA 653, 655-656; Keller in 26 LA 401, 403.

[299] See Arbitrator Logan in 30 LA 252, 253; Yeager in 29 LA 487, 489; Kelliher in 29 LA 367, 368; Morvant in 24 LA 453, 457; Brecht in 24 LA 199, 209; Seward in 19 LA 210, 211-212; Short in 18 LA 671, 673-675; Shipman in 10 LA 113, 116.

[300] See Arbitrator Stouffer in 26 LA 638, 640; Shister in 20 LA 448, 450-451; Baab in 16 LA 118, 120, 123; McCoy in 12 LA 73, 74-75; Gilden in 9 LA 931, 934; Healy in 6 LA 430, 432.

[301] Borg-Warner Corp., 16 LA 446, 453 (1951).

in determining whether an employee had been properly disciplined. In this case Arbitrator Merrill stated:

> "As a practical matter, it is not possible to embody in a collective bargaining contract a complete code of plant rules. Such a code would make the contract too long and cumbersome. It would introduce into collective bargaining new sources of delay and dispute. It would prevent the necessary adjustments and modifications of rules between periods of negotiation." [302]

After plant rules are promulgated, they may be challenged through the grievance procedure (including arbitration) on the ground that they violate the agreement or that they are unfair, arbitrary, or discriminatory. [303]

While it has been held that management's right to supervise employees does not extend to their personal lives after they leave the plant, [304] the employees' personal lives may be governed by plant rules where the conduct or situation in question affects plant operations. [305]

Management should be permitted to change plant rules, if not restricted by the agreement, to meet changed circumstances. [306] However, it has been emphasized that "Sound industrial relations policy dictates that abrupt changes in rules should be accompanied by a gradual educational process." [307] Moreover, new or changed plant rules which curtail employee

---

[302] American Zinc Co. of Illinois, 20 LA 527, 530 (1953).

[303] Most of the arbitrators previously cited in this topic expressly recognized this right of employees to challenge plant rules. In addition, see Arbitrator Thompson in 30 LA 231, 235; Crawford in 29 LA 731, 733; Crane in 27 LA 717, 720-722; R. Smith in 27 LA 99, 104-105; Donaldson in 13 LA 943, 945; Platt in 7 LA 764, 767. Management has been denied the right to make or change plant rules which would result in a change of established wages. Pullman-Standard Car Mfg. Co., 2 LA 509, 514 (Courshon, 1945).

[304] Pioneer Gen-E-Motors Corp., 3 LA 486, 488 (Blair, 1946). For related material see Chapter 15, topic entitled "Conduct Away From Plant".

[305] See Arbitrator Platt in 28 LA 583, 585-586, and in 18 LA 809, 811; Willingham in 28 LA 411, 413-414; Friedman in 28 LA 328, 330; Kates in 27 LA 540, 542; Keller in 26 LA 401, 402-404; Holden in 24 LA 810, 812-813; Bowles in 22 LA 765, 768-769; Cole in 21 LA 709, 710; Short in 18 LA 671, 673 (but cf. Dash in 18 LA 400, 403-404).

[306] See Florence Stove Co., 19 LA 650, 651 (Noel, 1952).

[307] Joy Mfg. Co., 6 LA 430, 434 (Healy, 1946). Also see The Maccabees, 27 LA 99, 105 (R. Smith, 1956).

privileges supported by long established past practice may be subject to challenge.[308]

Upon demand, management must bargain with respect to such rules as affect conditions of employment, and the filing of a grievance challenging a rule might be construed by an arbitrator "as a demand to negotiate on the subject." [309] Even where the agreement gave management a general right to make and modify rules "for purposes of discipline and efficiency", it was held that "after they have once become a subject of mutual agreements, very specific bargaining and agreement are required to make their modification again exclusively a matter of company decisions and announcements." [310]

Posting of Rules

The decision as to whether plant rules are to be posted is a part of the managerial function, and the posting of rules ordinarily is not a condition precedent to management's right to discipline employees for their violation. [311] However, except where the nature of the prohibited activity is such that employees should know it is improper, [312] rules must be communicated to employees in some manner. [313]

Thus, in the absence of posted rules management's freedom of action may be more restricted than it would be if they were posted, [314] and management is under a somewhat greater re-

[308] See Standard Oil Co. (Indiana), 11 LA 689, 690 (Updegraff, 1948). Also see Goodyear Tire & Rubber Co. of Ala., 4 LA 775, 777-779 (McCoy, 1946). For related discussion see Chapter 12, topic titled "Custom And Practice As Part Of The Contract".

[309] Federal Machine & Welder Co., 5 LA 60, 68-69 (Whiting, 1946). Also see Borg-Warner Corp., 3 LA 423, 433-434 (Gilden, 1944). For full discussion see this Chapter, subtopic titled "The Duty To Bargain: Right Of Unilateral Action".

[310] Ampco Metal, Inc., 3 LA 374, 378-379 (Updegraff, 1946). Also see Arbitrator Hampton in 5 LA 391, 396.

[311] Bethlehem Steel Co., 7 LA 334, 335 (Killingsworth, 1946); Watt Car & Wheel Co., 4 LA 67, 69 (Blair, 1946).

[312] As in Ashland Oil Refining Co., 28 LA 874, 877-878 (Bradley, 1957); Omar, Inc., 26 LA 641, 642 (Beatty, 1956). But Cf. Arbitrator Harkins in 18 LA 336, 339.

[313] See Lawrence Bros., Inc., 28 LA 83, 87 (Davis, 1957); D. M. Watkins Co., 14 LA 787, 790 (Healy, 1950).

[314] Ibid.

sponsibility to show the absence of discrimination in the discipline of an employee. [315] Especially when management chooses to apply a rule rigidly to the point of meeting its violation with discharge, there should be no doubt in the minds of employees as to the existence and nature of the rule. [316]

Seniority

Management's right of action is very often restricted by requirements of seniority recognition. Chapter 14 is devoted to discussion of seniority concepts and to an examination of the standards utilized by arbitrators in evaluating management actions in the setting of seniority requirements.

Layoff of Employees

In the absence of contractual restriction, it is the right of management to determine the number of employees to be used at any given time and to lay off employees, giving any required recognition to seniority, in excess of that number. [317] Recognition of seniority is the only type of restriction placed by most agreements upon the layoff right.

The meaning of the term "layoff" is frequently an issue in arbitration. [318] Arbitrators have ruled that the term must be interpreted to include any suspension from employment arising out of a reduction in the work force, and that the scheduling of employees not to work or the use of the term "not scheduled" by management does not make the occurrence any the less a "layoff." [319] One arbitrator defined "layoff," in the

---

[315] Bethlehem Steel Co. 7 LA 334, 335 (Killingsworth, 1946); Watt Car & Wheel Co., 4 LA 67, 69 (Blair, 1946).

[316] Joy Mfc. Co., 6 LA 430, 434 (Healy, 1946).

[317] See Arbitrator Thompson in 23 LA 89, 91-92; Emery in 22 LA 484, 487, and 19 LA 231, 234; Feinberg in 19 LA 523, 525, and 10 LA 883, 885. Also see Arbitrator Nagle in 24 LA 770, 774; S. Wolff in 19 LA 487, 488. For a discussion of the rights of laid off employees see Arbitrator Whelan in 25 LA 443, 449-451.

[318] See for example, Arbitrator Prasow in 27 LA 40, 45; Campbell in 26 LA 924, 929-930; Platt in 23 LA 137, 141; McCormick in 22 LA 695, 696-698; Marshall in 22 LA 181, 183; Emery in 19 LA 231, 232-233; Piper in 18 LA 801, 808; Feinberg in 16 LA 71, 72.

[319] See Arbitrator Feinberg in 14 LA 191, 195; Donnelly in 13 LA 684, 686; Brandschain in 5 LA 578, 587.

context of a particular clause, as an "actual severance from the Company's payroll, and a break in continuous service." [320]

Downgrading is often tied to layoffs. Some arbitrators have held that downgrading "is such an intimate concomitant of layoff" that layoff seniority provisions must be applied in downgrading. [321] Many contracts contain provisions permitting employees to accept layoff in lieu of downgrading. [322] Where the contract was silent regarding the right of employees to choose layoff rather than downgrading, one arbitrator held that they are deemed to have such a right if downgrading involves a significant reduction in pay. [323]

Numerous cases have arisen involving the observance of seniority in temporary layoffs. Contracts sometimes expressly allow management to disregard seniority in making temporary layoffs.[324] Such agreements generally indicate the maximum period that may be considered temporary, such period varying in different contracts from a specified number of hours up to as many as thirty days.[325]

An interesting situation was presented under a contract which required observance of seniority only in case of layoffs for "indefinite" periods. There the employer was permitted to provide one week's work for all employees and then to lay off all employees for one week, rather than to lay off junior employees indefinitely, the arbitrator ruling that the layoffs were for definite, temporary periods. [326]

---

[320] Bethlehem Steel Co., 16 LA 71, 72 (Feinberg, 1950). Also see Arbitrator Campbell in 26 LA 924, 929.

[321] Kenworth Motor Truck Corp., 8 LA 867, 869 (Seering, 1947). A similar result was reached in Ford Motor Co., Opinions of the Umpire, Opinion A-30 (1943). But this result was not reached where downgrading was not tied to layoffs. Lockheed Aircraft Corp., 10 LA 222, 226 (Aaron, 1948). Also see Arbitrator Mathews in 1 LA 298.

[322] As in 31 LA 891; 20 LA 205, 206.

[323] Caterpillar Tractor Co., 23 LA 313, 315-316 (Fleming, 1954). Also see Arbitrator Shipman in 15 LA 698, 703. Cf. Garrett in 31 LA 988.

[324] As in 28 LA 494, 497; 24 LA 88, 89; 15 LA 910, 913; 10 LA 653; 8 LA 792, 794; 1 LA 544. Also see 15 LA 282, 284.

[325] Ibid. In 18 LA 785, 786, and 12 LA 826, 828, no period was stated.

[326] Whitlock Mfg. Co., 13 LA 253, 254 (Stutz, Mottram & Curry, 1949).

In cases where the agreement contains no specific exception from the requirement of observing seniority in making "temporary" or "emergency" layoffs, arbitrators have ruled both ways as to the right of management to disregard seniority in making such layoffs. [327] Some of these cases can be reconciled on the basis of differing contract language, including contractual requirement for notice of layoff, or by distinguishing between "temporary" and "emergency" layoffs. [328]

Issues concerning "temporary" or "emergency" layoffs may be approached, as has been done by Arbitrator Russell A. Smith, "in the light of the well known fact that the common purpose of seniority layoff provisions is to give protection as between classes of employees on the assumption that some of them may properly be suspended under conditions of lack of work, and not to guarantee work." He construed the contract in question as being broadly applicable to temporary as well as permanent suspensions of work (those where there is no immediate prospective need of the services involved), but not as requiring the employer to follow seniority "when the emergency is such that, due to time limitations, it would be either impossible or unreasonably burdensome to give effect to these rules." [329]

---

[327] Cases requiring observance of seniority: Arbitrator Duff in 3 LA 441, 443; Howlett in 29 LA 724, 726-727; Platt in 23 LA 137, 141; Thompson in 23 LA 89, 92; McCormick in 22 LA 695, 698; Marshall in 22 LA 181, 184; Stutz, Curry & Clark in 21 LA 400, 401; Spaulding in 19 LA 159, 163-164; Feinberg in 14 LA 413, 416; Gorder in 13 LA 529, 531; Uible in 12 LA 893, 895; Stutz, Mottram & Cury in 10 LA 88, 91; Brandschain in 5 LA 578, 587-588; Whiting in 5 LA 24, 25; Gilden in 1 LA 530, 537. Cases not requiring the observance of seniority: Arbitrator Abernethy in 32 LA 345; Hebert in 23 LA 497, 500; Garrett in 21 LA 71, 74-75; Prasow in 20 LA 345, 347-348; Marshall in 20 LA 297, 299; Morgan in 18 LA 517, 518; Horton in 18 LA 285, 289; Lockhart in 16 LA 173, 175; Bauder in 14 LA 681, 685; Feinberg in 14 LA 191, 196; Stein in 10 LA 579, 581; Dwyer in 8 LA 506, 509; Elson in 8 LA 129, 134. Also see Arbitrator Howlett in 24 LA 232, 237-238; Healy in 15 LA 192, 194; Reynolds in 13 LA 326, 327. Observance of seniority in emergency recalls was not required by Arbitrator Platt in 14 LA 970, 976, and 14 LA 552, 562. Cf. Arbitrator Dworkin in 22 LA 875, 880.

[328] In at least one instance, however, opposite results were reached within the same month by two different arbitrators applying the same contractual provision to similar fact situations. See International Harvester Co., 9 LA 399, 401 (Hays, 1947), and International Harvester Co., 8 LA 129, 134 (Elson, 1947).

[329] Dow Chemical Co., 12 LA 763, 767 (1949).

Arbitrator Harry H. Platt has stated that, in the absence of contract prohibition, "it is almost universally recognized that senior employees, under a plant-wide seniority system, have the right to bump junior employees from their jobs in order to avoid their own layoff, provided they can perform the work of the juniors." [330] While it is generally accepted that an employee facing layoff may exercise his bumping right laterally or downward, i. e., in a job equal to his own or a lower classification, arbitrators have ruled both ways on the issue of "upward" bumping. Where arbitrators have denied the right of an employee to bump into a higher-rated classification, they have based their decisions upon one or more of the following reasons:

(1) A layoff may not be used as a means of achieving a promotion; the rationale of these cases seems to be that a promotion can be sought only when a vacancy exists, promotions must be governed by the promotion clause of the collective agreement, and since upward bumping would result in a promotion in violation of the promotion requirements of the contract, it cannot be permitted. [331]

(2) A showing was made that past practice prohibits upward bumping, or there was no showing of past practice of allowing it. [332]

(3) The history of contract negotiations indicates an intent to preclude upward bumping. [333]

(4) While the contract would permit upward bumping, it does not require that it be permitted, and in the absence of

---

[330] Darin & Armstrong, 13 LA 843, 847 (1950). Also see Arbitrator Larson in 26 LA 532, 535-536; Parker in 22 LA 883, 885; Cornsweet in 14 LA 494, 498; Healy in 11 LA 827, 831. But see Arbitrator Fuchs in 15 LA 172, 179, denying the right to bump in a short-term temporary layoff situation. Also see Blair in 30 LA 962, 963. Cf. Seibel in 22 LA 306, 310.

[331] See Arbitrator Larson in 26 LA 532, 536; Hall in 25 LA 417, 420-421; Seward in 24 LA 261, 266-267, and 15 LA 891, 892; Rosenfarb in 23 LA 789, 795-796; Horvitz in 22 LA 736, 737; Abernethy in 14 LA 938, 941. Also see Shulman in 3 LA 863, 865.

[332] See Arbitrator Seward in 30 LA 815, 819; Hebert in 30 LA 1, 8; Warns in 23 LA 220, 222.

[333] See Bethlehem Steel Co., 24 LA 261, 266-267 (Seward, 1955).

a showing of practice by the parties, the arbitrator cannot enforce such a rule. [334]

Some of the arbitrators who have permitted upward bumping have done so upon the basis of one or more if the following reasons:

(1) The contract does not specifically prohibit it.[335]

(2) The layoff provisions of the agreement are broad. [336]

(3) Upward bumping does not conflict with the promotion provisions of the agreement. [337]

(4) Past practice of the parties either supports or does not prohibit upward bumping. [338]

In regard to exercising the bumping right, it has been ruled that senior employees have an obligation to notify management of their desire to exercise bumping privileges, whereupon management has a duty to disclose the jobs that may be bumped into and to inform junor employees of their layoff under the seniority provisions of the agreement. [339] In recalls, however, management has been held to have the duty of taking the initiative in ascertaining from employees whether they are available for jobs to which their seniority entitles them. [340]

The question sometimes arises regarding management's right to reduce the workweek of all its employees in lieu of laying off junior employees. In the absence of a specfic con-

---

[334] See Bethlehem Steel Co., 30 LA 815, 819 (Seward, 1958).

[335] See Arbitrator Burris in 30 LA 886, 892; Marshall in 29 LA 629, 633-634; Cole in 21 LA 214, 216; Low in 20 LA 394, 396. Cf. Arbitrator Seward in 15 LA 891, 892. Arbitrator Shipman in 16 LA 478, 483, recognized that downward bumping is the general rule, but held that there should be some exceptions.

[336] See Arbitrator Burris in 30 LA 886, 892; Low in 20 LA 394, 396; Seward in 14 LA 502, 503-504.

[337] See Arbitrator Warns in 29 LA 439, 441-442. Also see Ebeling in 12 LA 738, 740.

[338] See International Harvester Co., in 21 LA 214, 216 (Cole, 1953).

[339] Union Electric Steel Corp., 13 LA 464, 467 (Blair, 1949). But see Arbitrator Prasow in 27 LA 40, 48, and Gilden in 6 LA 803, 813, both requiring the employee to specify the job into which he desired to bump. Also see Arbitrator Brandschain in 15 LA 672, 676.

[340] The Thor Corp., 13 LA 319, 323 (Baab, 1949).

tract provision covering this issue, arbitrators have ruled both ways. [341]

Transfer and Promotion of Employees

A commonly recognized distinction between "transfer" and "promotion" is made clear in a statement by Arbitrator George Cheney wherein he pointed out that the term "promotion" generally appears "in a context of collective bargaining agreements connoting an upward movement to a higher occupational classification requiring superior skills or greater effort and to which, for such reasons, a higher minimum wage scale is attached." [342] The term is "never associated with an outward or lateral movement of employees, to the operation of different machines, or the performances of different work drawing identical wage rates." [343] It has also been held that a lateral or downward movement cannot be considered a promotion "even though such a movement may lead to higher pay, a job more to the liking of the worker, and a higher ultimate maximum pay. [344]

In the absence of a contract provision to the contrary, the employer has the sole right to effect promotions; and he is not obligated to consult with the union before selecting the

---

[341] For cases permitting such action, see Arbitrator Witney in 30 LA 938, 947; Prasow in 25 LA 794, 797-799; Ebeling in 24 LA 874, 876-877; Slavney in 22 LA 473, 475; Piper in 18 LA 801, 807; Dash in 18 LA 625, 627. Also see Larson in 29 LA 795, 802-803; Crawford in 23 LA 548, 551. For cases not permitting such action, see Arbitrator Ross in 32 LA 300; Larkin in 25 LA 308, 312; Ryder in 25 LA 83, 84; Donnelly in 24 LA 846, 848; Cole in 24 LA 311, 313; Davey in 24 LA 88, 91-92; Selekman in 14 LA 1031, 1039. Also see Arbitrator Lynch in 32 LA 341; Schedler in 32 LA 244. See this Chapter, topic titled "Scheduling Work."

[342] Bunker Hill & Sullivan Mining & Concentrating Co., 8 LA 1010, 1011 (1947). Also see Arbitrator Kelliher in 30 LA 981, 982; Reid in 26 LA 849, 852, and in 23 LA 159, 162; Selekman in 12 LA 588, 590-591. "Promotion" and "transfer" may be defined in the contract. See Arbitrator Kelliher in 21 LA 707, 708.

[343] Bunker Hill & Sullivan Mining & Concentrating Co., 8 LA 1010, 1011 (1947). Permitting an employee to select his job, machine, or place of work "would in effect be confiding the management of the business, and the direction of the working forces to employees to no small degree." Ibid.

[344] Rochester Telephone Co., 26 LA 231, 238 (Thompson, 1956). Also see Arbitrator Shipman in 30 LA 1017, 1020; Seward in 30 LA 550, 551; Reid in 26 LA 849, 852, and in 23 LA 159, 162; Kelliher in 23 LA 105, 107; Selekman in 12 LA 588, 591. Cf. Arbitrator Klamon in 18 LA 701, 711-712.

employees to be promoted.[345]   The right of management to
promote employees, however, is frequently qualified by the
seniority provisions.   The general problems encountered in the
operation of "seniority" and "fitness and ability" clauses discussed in Chapter 14 apply here.   There are, in addition, some
other considerations which should be noted.

Temporary assignments to better jobs, such as may be
made while incumbents are on vacation, might be held not to
be "promotions" so as to require the application of contract
seniority provisions governing promotions.[346]   To require the
recognition of seniority in such cases would impose a handicap
and serious detriment to management in its direction of the
working force.[347]   Moreover, it has been held that management
has the right to require designated employees to accept temporary promotions against their will.[348]

On the other hand, management has not been permitted
unilaterally to change qualifications customarily required for a
job if the change would impair the right of senior employees to
be promoted in accordance with the contract's promotion
clause.[349]   However, management has been upheld in its refusal to promote a senior employee where the refusal is in the
interest of that employee's health or of the safety of other employees.[350]

Transfers

The general rule regarding the right of management to

---

[345] Parke Davis & Co., 17 LA 568, 569 (Beneduce, 1951).   Also see Arbitrator
Bailer in 20 LA 835, 836.

[346] For cases concerned with the application of "fitness and ability" requirements
of the seniority provisions in temporary promotions, see Arbitrator Emery in 28 LA
733, 734-735; Warren in 21 LA 228, 231.

[347] See Arbitrator Prasow in 24 LA 421, 423, and in 17 LA 644, 646-647; Lohman in 5 LA 695, 696.   Also see Arbitrator Grant in 20 LA 202, 204; D'Andrade in
18 LA 932, 933, and in 12 LA 584, 585. Cf. Arbitrator Copelof in 20 LA 385, 393.

[348] See Arbitrator Justin in 27 LA 877, 879-880; Ryder in 24 LA 132, 135-136.
Also see Arbitrator Kelliher in 23 LA 105, 108-109, involving a permanent promotion.
Cf. Arbitrator McCoy in 20 LA 281, 282.

[349] See Arbitrator Howlett in 26 LA 885, 890-891; Stutz in 26 LA 289, 291;
Frohlich in 14 LA 12, 16.   Also see Arbitrator Gilden in 20 LA 142, 146-147.

[350] See Arbitrator Klamon in 18 LA 392, 399; Prasow in 17 LA 205, 211.   Cf.
Arbitrator L. Smith in 23 LA 289, 294-295.

transfer employees has been stated by Arbitrator David A. Wolff as follows: "Unless restricted by agreement, law, custom, practice, or estoppel, management has the right to effect transfers as a necessary element in the operation of its business." [351] Arbitrator Wolff would find the right to transfer to be included within the right to direct the working force. [352]

Some agreements explicitly recognize management's right to transfer. While such agreements sometimes make the transfer right subject to other terms of the agreement, it appears that arbitrators require any restriction upon the right to be clearly stated. [353]

A transfer may be effected when the employer requires employees to rotate among jobs within their classification, [354] or to move from one shift to another, [355] or to move from one job to another in a different classification in the same job class, [356] or when the employee is moved to a new machine on the same job. [357]

In the absence of a contract provision to the contrary, it has been held that the employer's right to transfer workers is not conditioned upon the willingness of the workers to be transferred, [358] and that the employer has the right to determine whether a transfer is temporary or permanent. [359] Moreover, management has been held to have the right and duty to transfer an employee if his presence in a given occupation creates some undue hazard for himself or others. [360] However, the

---

[351] Chrysler Corp., 6 LA 276, 281 (1947). Also see Arbitrator Sembower in 30 LA 290, 292; Seward in 28 LA 437, 438; Reid in 23 LA 159, 162; Kelliher in 23 LA 105, 107; Feinberg in 14 LA 83, 86; Hepburn in 9 LA 442, 443.

[352] Chrysler Corp., 6 LA 276, 281 (1947). Also see Arbitrator Donnelly in 24 LA 399, 400; Kelliher in 23 LA 105, 107.

[353] See Arbitrator Wettach in 25 LA 629, 634; Singletary in 23 LA 456, 459; Copelof in 23 LA 67, 75; Uible in 11 LA 139, 142-143; Wagner in 8 LA 26, 29.

[354] Simmons Co., 25 LA 194, 198 (Elson, 1955).

[355] Midland Rubber Co., 18 LA 590, 593 (Cheney, 1952).

[356] Bethlehem Steel Co., 28 LA 437 (Seward, 1957).

[357] Gisholt Machine Co., 23 LA 105, 107 (Kelliher, 1954).

[358] See Arbitrator Seward in 28 LA 437, 438; Donnelly in 24 LA 399, 400.

[359] Jones & Laughlin Steel Corp., 23 LA 33, 36 (Cahn, 1954).

[360] International Shoe Co., 14 LA 253, 255 (Wallen, 1950).

right to transfer as a form of discipline appears to be definitely limited. [361]

Demotion of Employees

The collective agreement may specifically recognize the right of demotion as belonging to management. Also the right may be held to be included within a general management rights clause, as, for example, one giving management the right to select, assign, and direct the working force and to promote and transfer employees. [362] Then, too, the right may be held to remain in management, except as restricted by the agreement, as a residual power. [363] This right to demote, however, has been held to be subject to the limitation that it may not be exercised in an arbitrary, or capricious, or discriminatory manner. [364]

The right to demote has sometimes been found to have been contracted away. Such was the case, for instance, under a clause providing that wage rates fixed by the contract should be continued during the term of the contract, since the contractual wage rates were established on the basis of specific individuals. [365] A clause requiring promotions to be made on the basis of ability and seniority was interpreted to require the same for demotions, the arbitrator stating that otherwise the promotion clause would be meaningless as employees could be demoted immediately after promotion. [366] Management was also denied the right to demote under an agreement which was silent with respect to demotion and which provided permanent job status for employees surviving a trial period on the job, the employer

---

[361] See Arbitrator Stutz in 30 LA 505, 506; Montgomery in 26 LA 546, 549; Strashower in 16 LA 922, 926.

[362] Drug Products Co., Inc., 10 LA 804, 805 (Naggi, 1948).

[363] See E. I. DuPont de Nemours & Co., 17 LA 580, 585 (Cornsweet, 1951). Prior to the execution of a collective agreement, management's right to demote is restricted only by the obligation not to violate state and national labor relations acts. WLEU Broadcasting Co., 7 LA 150, 152 (Whiting, 1947).

[364] See Arbitrator Hawley in 26 LA 245, 248; Hale in 24 LA 470, 483; Shister in 19 LA 671, 673.

[365] National Vulcanized Fibre Co., 3 LA 259, 263 (Kaplan, 1946). Also see Arbitrator Aaron in 9 LA 419, 421.

[366] Raytheon Mfg. Co., 15 LA 291, 295 (Healy, 1950). Also see Arbitrator Hale in 24 LA 470, 483. Cf. Shister in 19 LA 671, 673.

being held required to lay off employees in slack periods rather than to demote. [367]

Umpire Harry Shulman stated, in considering an agreement that was silent on the matter of demotion for lack of qualifications, that it may be assumed that, in the interest of achieving optimum performance, management may make periodic or sporadic appraisals of its employees and demote those whose performance falls below standard. Elaborating, he said:

> "We may assume further that the obligation to perform satisfactorily is a continuous condition of the maintenance of the better job and that an employee's performance, though once adequate, may fall below standard and merit demotion, either because his own performance has deteriorated or, though it has not deteriorated, because the standard in his occupation has been raised by the greater ability of those around him. Such a demotion would be an instance of the Company's continuing interest in the satisfactory performance of each of its jobs." [368]

In downgrading for lack of qualifications shortly after an employee begins performing a different job, management may be required to show by substantial proof that the employee is not qualified and cannot qualify for the job within a reasonable time. [369] Where an employee has occupied a job for a long period of time, it has been held that management must show that the employee is no longer able or willing to perform his job duties. [370] However, it has been held that the mere fact that an employee has been retained in a job for a number of years does not necessarily warrant a finding by the arbitrator that he was qualified for it. [371]

A lack of qualifications has been found by the arbitrator,

---

[367] Merrill-Stevens Dry Dock & Repair Co., 10 LA 88, 90 (McCoy, 1948).

[368] Ford Motor Co., Opinions of the Umpire, Opinion A-30 (1943). Also allowing demotion for lack of qualifications: Arbitrator Uible in 9 LA 77, 80; Abernethy in 7 LA 202, 225. Demotion for incompetence has been permitted under an agreement permitting demotion for "cause." Owl Drug Co., 10 LA 498, 508 (Pollard, 1948).

[369] United Aircraft Products, Inc., 10 LA 143, 146 (Wardlaw, 1948).

[370] Dewey & Almy Chemical Co., 25 LA 316, 322 (Somers, 1955). Also see Arbitrator Hale in 24 LA 470, 484; Komaroff in 17 LA 784, 789. For cases dealing with the necessity for warning the employee that his work is poor, see Arbitrator Burris in 25 LA 32, 36; Kelliher in 18 LA 447, 449; Komaroff in 17 LA 784, 789.

[371] E. I. DuPont de Nemours & Co., 17 LA 580, 586-587 (Cornsweet, 1951). Also see Arbitrator Duff in 29 LA 167, 170.

and demotion therefore considered justified, for example, where a truck driver's operator's license was revoked,[372] where the employee was unable to perform the job duties satisfactorily,[373] where the employee was physically unable to perform the job duties,[374] and where a leadman displayed racial prejudice in a plant employing many Negroes.[375] In the latter instance, the arbitrator said that the employee's prejudice "made it clear that he could no longer do an effective job as leadman." One arbitrator, however, refused to permit the company to demote an employee for lack of qualifications where the company was aware of the employee's shortcomings at the time of his promotion but promoted him in spite of them, the promotion was not made on a trial basis, and the employee's work was no worse after the promotion than it had been before.[376]

Some arbitrators have held that management may not use demotion as a form of discipline unless the agreement specifically so provides, since such action would violate the contract seniority rights of the employee.[377] It was held in one case, for instance, that management did not have the right to use temporary demotion as a means of discipline for negligence in job performance (as opposed to lack of ability to perform the job), where such discipline was not provided for specifically by the agreement and where the senior's position was temporarily filled by a junior employee in contravention of the seniority clause. The arbitration board said:

"The company's right to discipline flows from the general managerial prerogative recognized in the management clause. In accordance with established legal construction, the exercise of such general prerogatives is limited by the specific clauses in the labor agreement. Thus, management in exercising its general prerogatives lacks the contractual right to abridge

---

[372] Virginia-Carolina Chemical Corp., 18 LA 892, 895 (Hepburn, 1952).
[373] See Arbitrator Duff in 29 LA 167, 170; S. Wolff in 27 LA 682, 684; Hawley in 26 LA 245, 248; Morris in 24 LA 745, 746; Cornsweet in 17 LA 580, 586-587.
[374] Jersey Central Power & Light Co., 7 LA 560, 563-564 (Copelof, 1947).
[375] North American Aviation, Inc., 20 LA 789, 794 (Komaroff, 1953).
[376] Bethlehem Steel Co., 18 LA 368, 369 (Feinberg, 1951).
[377] See Arbitrator Kelliher in 23 LA 252, 255; Blumer in 6 LA 379, 382. Also see Arbitrator Hawley in 26 LA 245, 247-248; Kelliher in 25 LA 736, 737.

designated contractual privileges of the employees covered by the agreement unless specific provision is made for [such] * * *" [378]

Management has also been denied the right to discipline an employee by demotion where the contract gave the employer the right to discipline employees by various specified means which did not include demotion, on the theory of "expressio unius est exclusio alterius." [379] Management likewise has not been upheld in demoting an employee for occasional carelessness or failure to obey instructions, the arbitrator distinguishing between a lack of ability and temporary poor performance, but recognizing that some form of discipline should be imposed in such a case. [380]

On the other hand, management has been held justified in using demotion as a form of discipline where the employee's refusal to obey a work order was typical of his uncooperative attitude, and the contract did not set out any particular methods of discipline, [381] and where demotion of the employee was deemed necessary as a safety measure. [382]

Discharge and Discipline

The right of management to discipline or discharge employees has been dealt with extensively by arbitrators and is a subject to which a separate chapter is devoted in this book. For discussion of discharge and discipline the reader is directed to Chapter 15.

Merit Increases

Merit rating is concerned not with what an employee does but with how he does it. Thus, it may be immaterial that some employees receive a higher rate than others doing the same

---

[378] American Steel & Wire Co., 6 LA 379, 382 (Blumer, 1946).

[379] See Arbitrator McCoy in 14 LA 882, 883, and in 2 LA 554, 555. Also see Chapter 9, topic titled "To Express One Thing Is to Exclude Another."

[380] Republic Steel Corp., 25 LA 733, 735 (Platt, 1955). Also see Bethlehem Steel Co., 28 LA 330, 332 (recommended decision by Arbitrator Valtin, approved by Impartial Umpire Seward, 1957).

[381] Lewers & Cooke, Ltd., 30 LA 542, 545 (Cobb, 1958). Also see Arbitrator Lehoczky in 8 LA 923, 924.

[382] See Arbitrator Yeager in 29 LA 487, 488; Donnelly & Mottram (Cury dissenting) in 18 LA 457, 458-459. Also see Arbitrator Morgan in 17 LA 328, 329.

work. [383] Furthermore, in determining eligibility for merit increases, there is no presumption of progress or improvement due solely to passage of time. [384]

The collective bargaining agreement may make specific provision for merit increases. In this regard, Arbitrator Dudley E. Whiting has observed: "It is well established that merit increases are an appropriate subject for collective bargaining, and bargaining thereon frequently results in contractual provisions establishing objective standards for merit increases or fixing a regular review period or making such increases subject to review or negotiation by the union, or other types of such provisions." [385]

However, it also appears to be well established that, where the collective agreement contains no provision regarding the granting of merit increases or where it makes provision for merit increases without stating by whom the initial determination is to be made, the determination of when individual employees should be given merit increases still remains the function of management. [386] This right may be held to be included within a general management rights clause; [387] or it may be given specifically to management by the agreement. [388]

Regardless of the source of the right, it appears clear that conclusions of management in regard to merit increases are not generally subject to successful challenge in arbitration unless unfair, arbitrary or discriminatory, [389] or unless the decision is

---

[383] Bethlehem Steel Co., 21 LA 614, 616 (Feinberg, 1953); International Harvester Co., 14 LA 77, 79 (Seward, 1948).

[384] Ralph C. Coxhead Corp., 21 LA 480, 483 (Cahn, 1953).

[385] Sommers & Adams Co., 6 LA 283, 285 (1947).

[386] See Arbitrator Feinberg in 21 LA 614, 616; Beneduce in 17 LA 568, 569; Luskin in 15 LA 180, 181-182; Townsend in 15 LA 4, 12; Updegraff in 10 LA 678, 680; Abernethy in 7 LA 202, 217; Whiting in 6 LA 283, 285; Gorder in 3 LA 1, 3. See also Arbitrator Cahn in 14 LA 96.

[387] McInerney Spring & Wire Co., 9 LA 91 (Platt, 1947).

[388] See Arbitrator Seward in 26 LA 824, 826; Bernstein in 14 LA 139, 142; Updegraff in 4 LA 161.

[389] See Arbitrator Feinberg in 21 LA 614, 616; Cahn in 21 LA 480, 482-483 (who considered criteria used by the employer in evaluating employees' eligibility for merit increases); Bernstein in 14 LA 139, 143; Updegraff in 10 LA 678, 680; Platt in 9 LA 91, 95-96; Abernethy in 7 LA 202, 217.

based upon a misconception of existing facts or insufficient evidence. [390]   In this general connection, Arbitrator I. Robert Feinberg has stated:

> "* * * [M]erit is difficult to prove and the parties themselves, through daily observation of the employee, have usually gained greater knowledge of the employee's abilities and efficiency than the Umpire can ever have. In the absence of detailed proof, a third party is generally not in a position to determine whether an employee has demonstrated increased efficiency or whether the quality of his work has improved. It is recognized that that determination can best be made by the employee's supervisor, who is closest to the employee in these matters. * * *" [391]

Under certain circumstances management may be required to review employees' merit ratings at reasonable intervals. This was the result under an agreement which, in providing for merit increases, gave management the right to make initial determinations but required them to be "fair," [392] and under another agreement which permitted the company to determine merit increases subject only to the restriction that the determination not be arbitrary or capricious. [393]   Of course, as noted above, the contract may specifically provide for periodic review of each employee's rate and record. [394]

Bonuses

Arbitrators have ruled both ways on the question of the right of management, in the absence of contractual limitation, unilaterally to eliminate or alter bonus practices. [395]   In cases where the facts indicated that the bonus had become an integral part of the wage structure, thus constituting a deferred wage payment, arbitrators have held that management may not unilaterally eliminate or alter bonus plans, despite the fact that

---

[390] Bethlehem Steel Co., 21 LA 614, 616 (Feinberg, 1953); Atlas Imperial Diesel Engine Co., 3 LA 1, 4 (Gorder, 1946).

[391] Bethlehem Steel Co., 21 LA 614, 616 (1953). Similar language was used by Arbitrator Cahn in 21 LA 480, 483; Warren in 16 LA 508, 509; Bernstein in 14 LA 139, 143.

[392] International Harvester Co., 13 LA 809, 812 (Seward, 1949).

[393] Bethlehem Steel Co., 26 LA 824, 826 (Seward, 1956).

[394] Pacific Airmotive Corp., 16 LA 508, 509 (Warren, 1951).

[395] For important related materials see Chapter 12, topic titled "Custom and Practice as Part of the Contract."

bonuses were not mentioned in the contract. [396] On the other hand, in cases where the facts indicated that the bonus was a gratuity, given at the discretion of management and not paid as part of wages, management was permitted unilaterally to alter or eliminate the bonus plan in the absence of contractual restriction. [397]

The development of the concept of the compulsory bargaining obligation, treated earlier in this Chapter, has a bearing on what individual arbitrators will do with respect to this type of matter.

Leaves of Absence

It has been held that, except as restricted by the agreement, the granting or denial of leaves of absence is a prerogative of management and the judgment of management will not be disturbed so long as the action taken is not unreasonable or discriminatory. [398] In some cases past practice and custom concerning leaves of absence have determined whether management's action should be upheld. [399]

Compulsory Retirement

Arbitrators have generally held that, in the absence of specific contractual restriction, management has the right uni-

---

[396] See Arbitrator Dash in 22 LA 808, 818-819; Justin in 17 LA 505, 509-510; Prasow in 5 LA 564, 571; Courshon in 2 LA 509, 514; McCoy in 2 LA 483, 490. Also see Arbitrator Stutz in 29 LA 400, 404; Sullivan in 25 LA 165, 170; Lehoczky in 15 LA 618, 622, all involving contract clauses providing for payment of bonuses to employees.

[397] See Arbitrator Klamon in 32 LA 395; Duff in 32 LA 388; Kheel in 26 LA 627, 628-630; Kharas in 25 LA 853, 855-856; Delehanty in 24 LA 500, 506; Cheney in 8 LA 518, 526; Cahn in 6 LA 654. Also see Arbitrator Giardino in 19 LA 421, 422. Under particular contract clauses providing for a bonus, a bonus may nevertheless be considered to be a gratuity. See Arbitrator Cheney in 10 LA 341, 344; Epstein in 3 LA 412, 418.

[398] See I. Lewis Cigar Mfg. Co., 12 LA 661, 662 (Waite, 1949); Union Oil Co., 3 LA 108, 110 (Wardlaw, 1946). Also see Arbitrator Tyree in 19 LA 604, 607; Aaron in 15 LA 928, 933 (both involving medical leave of absence); and Elson in 21 LA 502, 511 (involving maternity leave).

[399] See Arbitrator Levinson in 23 LA 277, 280; McCraw in 19 LA 709; Lesser in 18 LA 528, 531. For related discussion see Chapter 12, topic titled "Custom and Practice as Part of the Contract."

laterally to establish compulsory retirement plans. [400] It has also been held that, up to the point where compulsory retirement becomes a matter of collective bargaining, management may retire any employee because of age so long as the right is exercised in conformance with the employer's established policy and is not arbitrary, discrimnatory, or capricious. [401] These arbitrators and others, however, appear to have emphasized the fact that the retirement plans under consideration in the respective cases were of long standing, established and administered without objection from the union, and that the plans were administered without arbitrariness, discrimination, or caprice. [402] Where the union did not acquiesce, however, but rather objected to the institution of a compulsory retirement plan, the arbitrator found a violation of the contract employment security provisions when management forcibly retired an employee. [403] A similar result was reached where the union understandably believed that the retirement plan was voluntary and did not object until the company forcibly retired an employee. [404]

The development of the compulsory bargaining concept has a bearing on what individual arbitrators will do with respect to matters of this nature. In any event, it has been held that the parties may bargain on the issue of compulsory retirement and, having failed to reach an agreement after bargaining in

---

[400] See Arbitrator Prasow in 27 LA 153, 156; Shister in 25 LA 50, 52-53; Reynolds in 13 LA 326, 328; Gregory in 9 LA 560, 561; Gorsuch in 9 LA 124, 126; Ridge in 7 LA 773, 778; Kirsh in 4 LA 601, 603. Also see Arbitrator Capelof in 13 LA 652, 656-657.

[401] Swift & Co., 9 LA 560, 561 (Gregory, 1946). Also see Arbitrator Reynolds in 13 LA 326, 328.

[402] See Arbitrator Schedler in 29 LA 541, 543-545, and in 27 LA 669, 671; Prasow in 27 LA 153, 156; Shister in 25 LA 50, 52-53; Shipman in 23 LA 214, 216-217; Gilden in 22 LA 732, 734-735, and in 17 LA 81, 85; McConnell in 17 LA 587, 589; Lehoczky in 14 LA 490, 491-492. Also see Arbitrator Grant in 6 LA 590, 592.

[403] S. H. Kress & Co., 25 LA 77, 79-82 (Ross, 1955). Also see Arbitrator Ross in 29 LA 295, 297.

[404] Pullman-Standard Car Mfg. Co., 24 LA 779, 781-783 (Wagner, 1955); Bloomfield Tool Corp. and Kidde Mfg. Co., Inc., 9 LA 921, 925-926 (Justin, 1948).

good faith, the company may then proceed to establish a plan in accordance with its offer at the bargaining table. [405]

Selection and Control of Supervisors

Arbitrators have generally recognized it to be the function and responsibility of management to run the business and to produce profits. It is generally accepted as an incident to management's right to control operations that management must be permitted to select and control supervisory employees without union interference. "It is a fundamental principle of American industry that the selection and retention of foremen or other supervisory personnel is the sole prerogative of management * * *. There is no doubt that the union may not, as a matter of right, demand the dismissal or demotion of a foreman and that such a demand is not a proper subject matter for a grievance." [406]

Thus, Arbitrator Whitley P. McCoy has held that unless the agreement expressly permits, or the employer waives the jurisdiction issue and submits the dispute on the merits, a demand by the union for discipline or discharge of a supervisory employee ordinarily is not arbitrable, and that even where the arbitrator can exercise jurisdiction in such disputes, he should do so sparingly and only on very clear grounds. [407] Under these rulings discipline or discharge of supervisors is left entirely to management.

However, while management may not be required to discipline supervisors, it will be required to compensate employees

---

[405] United States Steel Corporation v. Nichols, 229 F. 2d 396, 399-400, 37 LRRM 2420 (C.A. 6th, 1956), cert. den. 351, U.S. 950. For elated discussion, see this Chapter, subtopic titled "The Duty to Bargain: Right of Unilateral Action."

[406] King Powder Co., 1 LA 215, 216 (Whiting, 1944). This also was the view of the War Labor Board Stanoland Oil & Gas, 20 War Lab. Rep. 211 (1944). Also on the selection of supervisors, see Arbitrator Whiting in 11 LA 1023, 1031 (an "interests" case).

[407] Electro Metallurgical Co., 19 LA 8, 8-10 (1952). Also see Arbitrator J. Williams in 27 LA 432, 436-437; Duff in 26 LA 919, 922; Anrod in 25 LA 452, 455; Emery in 16 LA 48, 50; Klamon in 15 LA 32, 35; Cornsweet in 13 LA 949, 950; Copelof in 10 LA 237, 240; Whiting in 1 LA 215, 216; Y. Smith in 1 LA 75, 78-79; Shulman in 1 ALAA par. 67,011.

injured by their wrongful acts. [408]   Umpire Harry Shulman, for instance, ruled that "to the extent that a foreman or other representative of managerial authority takes action detrimental to an employee and in violation of the parties' contract, the grievance procedure is properly invoked to provide appropriate redress." He added, however, that "what is called for is protection of the employees within their contractual rights as distinguished from mere punishment of the Company's supervisory or other managerial representatives," and that, while punishment of a supervisor may be the only feasible way to stop improper treatment of employees, the Umpire can direct that such improper conduct be stopped, but "how the result is to be achieved is * * * a matter normally left to the Company." [409]

Arbitrator Whitley P. McCoy has recognized management's control over supervisors as a general right but as subject to some limitation. His view is that while a demand for the removal of a foreman ordinarily is not arbitrable, "in very extreme cases, where a foreman's conduct is beyond the limits of lawfulness or decency, making for an intolerable condition which management itself could not with decency condone, it may become arbitrable," or where there is "a menace to the life and health of the employees while at their work" an arbitrable issue may be presented. [410]   In another case, Arbitrator McCoy required an employer to remove from the department a foreman who, on many occasions, had used profanity in the presence of women employees and had addressed obscene remarks to them. In requiring the removal, he said: "* * * managment has, by contract (seniority clauses, etc.), given the employees rights to their jobs under decent working conditions * * *." [411]

---

[408] Profile Cotton Mills, 2 LA 537, 538-539 (McCoy, 1942). Also see Arbitrator Whiting in 1 LA 215, 216; Y. Smith in 1 LA 75, 78; Shulman in 1 ALAA par. 67,011.
[409] Ford Motor Company, 1 ALAA par. 67,011, p. 67,012 (1945).
[410] Goodyear Tire & Rubber Co. of Ala., 5 LA 30, 34 (1946). Also see Arbitrator McCoy in 19 LA 8, 8-10.
[411] Continental Can Co., Inc., 1 LA 65, 68 (1945). Also see Arbitrator Brecht in 27 LA 806, 809-811, where improper and abusive conduct by the foreman was alleged.

Management's right to discipline or discharge supervisors may be limited by contract. For example, where bargaining unit employees acquired rights under the contract and later became supervisors, their discharge has been held to be an arbitrable issue since it involved a dispute or difference between the parties as to the interpretation, meaning or application of the agreement. [412]

Accompanying the right to control supervisors is the function and responsibility of management to inform them fully as to their rights, authorities, and duties. It has been held that management must compensate employees for any loss suffered as a result of its failure to instruct and train its foremen fully.[413]

Awards vary on the question of whether management may, in the absence of a specific contractual provision on the matter, place former bargaining unit employees back into the unit on the basis of seniority accumulated during work in the unit or with accumulated seniority for time spent in supervisory service. For discussion and cases on this issue, see Chapter 14, subtopic titled "Service Outside the Seniority Unit."

---

[412] See Arbitrator Merrill in 29 LA 334, 336; Baab in 28 LA 641, 642-643; Duff in 26 LA 919, 920-921; Emery in 16 LA 48, 50. The question of returning a supervisor to the bargaining unit may also be involved. See Arbitrator Baab in 28 LA 641, 643; J. Williams in 27 LA 432, 436-437; Duff in 26 LA 919, 920-921; Anrod in 25 LA 452, 455; Emery in 16 LA 48, 50.

[413] Standard Oil Co. (Indiana), 11 LA 689, 691 (Updegraff, 1948). Cf. Arbitrator Klamon in 15 LA 32, 35.

CHAPTER 14

SENIORITY

One of the most severe limitations upon the exercise of managerial discretion is the requirement of seniority recognition. In the absence of a definition of the term in the collective agreement, seniority "is commonly understood to mean the length of service with the employer or in some division of the enterprise."[1] Seniority "means that men retain their jobs according to their length of service with their employer and that men are promoted to better jobs on the same basis."[2] "It is generally recognized that the chief purpose of a seniority plan is to provide maximum security to workers with the longest continuous service."[3]

It should be kept in mind that "seniority is a relationship between employees in the same seniority unit, rather than a relationship between jobs."[4] As stated by Arbitrator Paul Prasow:

> "Seniority protects and secures an employee's rights in relation to the rights of other employees in his seniority group; it does not protect him in relation to the existence of the job itself. By use of an objective measure, length of service, the rights of one employee are balanced against other employees' rights."[5]

Because of the interrelationship between employees with respect to seniority rights, one court permitted intervention by employees in an arbitration involving seniority rights of other

---

[1] Curtiss-Wright Corp., 11 LA 139, 142 (Uible, 1948). Also see Industrial Rayon Corp., 24 LA 73, 76 (Dworkin, 1955); Armstrong Cork Co., 23 LA 366, 367 (Williams, 1954).

[2] Lapp, How to Handle Problems of Seniority, 1 (1946). Also see Industrial Rayon Corp., 24 LA 73, 76 (Dworkin, 1955).

[3] Darin & Armstrong, 13 LA 843, 845 (Platt, 1950). Also see Arbitrator Dworkin in 24 LA 73, 76; Williams in 23 LA 366, 367; Reid in 22 LA 379, 381; Cole in 21 LA 231, 232.

[4] Axelson Mfg. Co., 30 LA 444, 448 (Prasow, 1958).

[5] Ibid.

employees in the same seniority unit, the court saying that in such a controversy "for every person whose seniority is advanced, someone will be adversely affected by such advancement." [6]

Seniority issues in arbitration arise out of the attempt by the parties to promote their respective interests. Arbitrator Walter Gellhorn has balanced the interests of management against those of the employees and has analyzed the "costs" of seniority to both management and employees:

> "To be sure, the full utilization of seniors cannot be achieved without costs. When seniors 'get the breaks,' the more ambitious and capable of the junior men may feel frustrated. Moreover, a management that likes to see a clear line of promotability from within the work force does not welcome the inflexibility that sometimes comes from giving preference to older, perhaps less adaptable workers. But these costs were measured when the contract was made. The parties presumably concluded that the price was worth paying. From the standpoint of the men, they must have concluded that the deferment of youthful hope was offset by the assurance of fair opportunity for veteran employees. From the standpoint of management, they must have concluded that an occasional personal rigidity was offset by the enhanced loyalty and stability that are encouraged by an effective seniority clause." [7]

Arbitrator Carl R. Schedler would add the union as an interested party, aside from its representation of the employees:

> "Traditionally, a union considers seniority both as a useful organizing tool and as a basic objective in collective bargaining negotiations. It is, therefore, utilized in invoking what is often considered a latent, if unexpressed, need of workers; and, it is also employed to demonstrate the value of concerted activities as opposed to the results workers can expect from trying to 'go it alone' in dealing with management." [8]

In an arbitration situation involving not only contract interpretation but some "interests" aspects also, Arbitrator Marion Beatty further analyzed the struggle in relation to the application of seniority in the extreme situation. He first considered the objectives of the parties: the union struggling for

---

[6] In re Iroquois Beverage Corp., 28 LA 906, 907 (N.Y. Sup. Ct., 1955). For a discussion of seniority as a property right, see Kramer, "Seniority and Ability," Management Rights and the Arbitration Process, 41, 41-42 (BNA Incorporated, 1956).
[7] Universal Atlas Cement Co., 17 LA 755, 757 (1951).
[8] Schedler, "Arbitration of Seniority Questions," 28 LA 954-960, 954 (1957).

greater security in tenure for certain workmen, and the company trying to avoid a "burdensome seniority system carried to the extreme of shuffling men in the course of one day's work." The objective of both parties, he felt, were proper. Arbitrator Beatty noted that the company was offering the union a job standing list which would provide for promotion, reduction in force and overtime in accordance with strict seniority, but not for such short periods as one day's work. In refusing to award the seniority arrangement requested by the union, he stated:

> "I must agree with the company that carrying seniority to the extreme requested by the union would make for a wasteful, cumbersome and uneconomical method of operation. It has in it an element of 'made work' (the few minutes or hours that would be necessary in making the shifts in personnel). It can hardly be denied anymore that made work is economically unsound. If carried to the extreme it would make for much work and little production. Efficiency of operations is something to be desired in every business, it enures to the benefit of all including the public, and an enterprise that cannot operate as efficiently as its competition will suffer the consequences." [9]

Source of Seniority "Rights"

Even prior to the advent of collective agreements employers generally gave job preference to their older employees, not as any binding obligation but as a matter of equity, so long as they could do the required work. [10] However, seniority benefits exist as "rights" only to the extent made so by contract. [11] As stated by Arbitrator Joseph Brandschain:

> "* * * whatever seniority rights employees have exist only by virtue of the collective bargaining agreement that is in existence between the union and the employer. Such seniority rights depend wholly upon the contract. They arise out of the contract. Before a collective bargaining contract is in existence, there are no seniority rights.

---

[9] Standard Oil Co. (Indiana), 24 LA 424, 426-427 (1954).
[10] Lapp, How to Handle Problems of Seniority, 2-3 (1946).
[11] See Arbitrator Cahn in 30 LA 221, 222; Dworkin in 24 LA 73, 76; Shipman in 21 LA 604, 607. Also see Cournoyer v. American Television Co., 28 LA 483, 495 (Minn. Sup. Ct., 1957); Capra v. Local Lodge No. 273, 102 Colo. 63, 76 P. 2d 738 (1938); Hartley v. Brotherhood of Ry. and S.S. Clerks, 283 Mich. 201, 277 N.W. 885 (1938); Norfolk & Western R.R. Co. v. Harris, 260 Ky. 132, 84 S.W. 2d 69 (1935). Cf. General Cable Corp., 20 LA 406, 408 (Hays, 1953).

"Therefore, until we have a contract, the employer has the right, which he has always exercised, to shift workers around and promote and demote them. The very purpose of collective bargaining was to constrict such rights of management and, reciprocally, to gain for the workers job-security rights based upon seniority and to insure such rights contractually. Thus, we start with the situation, before the existence of a contract, where the employer has all rights in connection with promotions and transfers and need pay no heed to seniority of the workers, and the workers have no rights to promotions or transfers because of length of service.

"How does this situation change when a collective bargaining agreement is in existence? It changes to the extent that these rights are given up by the employer and given to the workers under the terms of the contract. Therefore, whatever the employer has yielded in his absolute time-established rights of hiring, firing, promoting, and demoting and whatever the workers have gained in the way of seniority rights with respect to these matters must be measured entirely by the contract." [12]

Thus an employee who was laid off prior to the effective date of the first contract between the employer and the union was not entitled to any seniority rights or any other rights provided by the contract, which affected only employees of the company who were in its employ on or after the effective date of the contract. [13]

Seniority rights do not necessarily remain static; they may be modified in subsequent agreements, with the current agreement governing. For instance, in ruling that the seniority rights of a returning veteran (who did not have re-employment rights under the Universal Military Training and Service Act) were governed by the contract in effect at the time of his return, rather than the contract in effect at the time he entered the armed forces, Arbitrator Harry Shulman stated:

"Seniority rights under a collective agreement are entirely the products of the Agreement. Their characteristics and their effects are determined solely by the Agreement. In the absence of special provisions to the contrary, the collective Agreement creates rights and bind parties only for the term of the Agreement. Nothing in * * * [any of the parties'] Agreements indicates a purpose to single out seniority rights for individual employees and give them a vested effectiveness beyond the period of the Agreement and beyond the power of the parties to modify by later Agree-

---

[12] Alan Wood Steel Co., 4 LA 52, 54 (1946). Also see Curtiss-Wright Corp., 11 LA 139, 143 (Uible, 1948).
[13] Acme Galvanizing Co., 19 LA 575, 577 (Gooding, 1952).

ments. Modification of prior seniority provisions in subsequent Agreements is a fairly common feature of collective bargaining. And while it is true that such modifications commonly result in the increase of seniority rights of some employees, they also necessarily result in some decrease or change in the seniority rights of other employees." [14]

Collective agreements generally provide for the recognition of seniority in several, and often many, aspects of the employment relationship. Among these are promotions, layoffs, re-hiring, shift preference, transfers, vacations, days off, and over-time work. Indeed, consideration of seniority looms so importantly that it has been said that "one of the principle purposes for entering into a collective bargaining agreement is usually to secure for the employees the prized right of seniority in case of layoff and promotion." [15]

Seniority Units

Seniority rights relate to a specific group or unit. Seniority units are defined by the collective agreement either specifically or by interpretation. Among other possibilities, a seniority unit may be plant-wide, [16] multi-plant, [17] departmental; [18] or based upon the bargaining unit, [19] or upon an occupational group or classification; [20] or upon a combination of the foregoing. [21]

The seniority unit is basic in the computation of length of service and in the assertion and determination of seniority rights. For example, where a contract called for promotions on the basis of departmental seniority, provided the senior employee was qualified, the employer was not required to make promotions on the basis of plant-wide seniority where all bidders for the job were from outside the department in which

---

[14] Ford Motor Co., 23 LA 296, 297 (1954).
[15] Cournoyer v. American Television Co., 28 LA 483, 485 (Minn. Sup. Ct., 1957).
[16] See for example 30 LA 406; 29 LA 83; 29 LA 23; 28 LA 424; 19 LA 159; 13 LA 364; 13 LA 110.
[17] See 11 LA 207. Cf. 25 LA 37.
[18] See 27 LA 685; 25 LA 826; 23 LA 256; 21 LA 524; 14 LA 453; 12 LA 1025.
[19] See 21 LA 604.
[20] See 24 LA 424; 20 LA 300; 14 LA 529; 11 LA 552.
[21] See for example 30 LA 326; 30 LA 267; 27 LA 203; 25 LA 338; 22 LA 379.

the vacancy existed.[22] In another case, where several bargaining units in the plant each had separate agreements with the employer, employees laid off from one unit were not permitted to exercise their seniority to bump employees in another unit; Arbitrator Mitchell M. Shipman stated that since the contracts did not expressly provide otherwise, there was a presumption that lay-offs and promotions "are to be made on an intra-bargaining unit basis, with the employee's seniority or length of service computed on his service within his bargaining unit and applied only among employees therein." [23]

Although seniority often is both acquired and exercised in one unit, the contract may provide (or be so interpreted) that seniority is acquired in one unit and exercised in another. For example, a contract provision stating simply that the employer shall operate "on a departmental and plant wide seniority basis" was construed (in the light of past practice and the history of contract negotiations) to mean that seniority was to be exercised on a departmental basis, but measured by length of service in the plant.[24]

Similarly, seniority rights may be based upon different units with respect to the various aspects of the employment relationship. For instance, a contract may provide that departmental seniority shall govern with respect to lay-off and recall, while providing for plant seniority to be exercised in bumping.[25]

Seniority Standing and Determining Length of Service

Ordinarily, seniority is based upon length of service, although the collective agreement may provide for exceptions such as "super-seniority" for union officers and stewards,[26] loss

---

[22] Charles Bruning Co., Inc., 25 LA 826, 827-829 (Gifford, 1955). Also see Arbitrator Randle in 17 LA 486, 488.

[23] Tide Water Associated Oil Co., 21 LA 604, 607 (1953).

[24] McFeely Brick Co., 22 LA 379, 382 (Reid, 1954). Also see Alside, Inc., 25 LA 338, 340-341 (Kates, 1955).

[25] Harsco Corp., 30 LA 326, 327-328 (Koretz, 1957). Also see International Paper Co., 29 LA 279 (Logan, 1957).

[26] As in 30 LA 803, 804-805.

of seniority in whole or in part under specified circumstances,[27] and the like. Since seniority, length of service, and their concomitant rights are creatures of contract, it is necessary always to look first to the contract in determining length of service and the seniority standing of employees.

Seniority Standing

The seniority standing of an employee is his position on the "preference" or seniority list in relation to other employees in his seniority unit. An employee's seniority standing may be a problem where, among other situations, another employee in the same seniority unit began to work on the same day but at a different hour, or had the same hiring date but began to work on a different day. Arbitrators seem to be reluctant to draw too fine a line in such situations. For example, in interpreting a collective agreement providing that an employee's continuous length of service should be computed from the date he first began to work, Arbitrator Ralph T. Seward held that the seniority standing of two employees who commenced work on the same day, though on different shifts, was the same. He stated that "The legal as well as the popular meaning of the word 'date' imports the day, month and year without reference to the hour." [28] Arbitrator Dudley E. Whiting has further observed that it would be impractical and inconsistent with existing industrial practice to ascertain length of service in units of less than one day.[29]

The contract may be explicit as to the order of seniority. For instance, it may provide not only that seniority is to be computed from the first day worked, but also that new employees are to be registered numerically as they check in on the first day worked with their seniority standing to be in the same order as their names appear on the register. Under such a provision, where two employees were hired on the same day, Arbitrator Ralph R. Williams held that, barring any discrimi-

---

[27] As in 25 LA 479, 480.
[28] Bethlehem Steel Co., 26 LA 567 (1956).
[29] Standard Oil Co. of Ind., 3 LA 758, 759 (1946).

nation in the assignment of shifts, the one who "clocked in" on the first shift had more seniority than the other who commenced work on the same day but on the second shift.[30]

Under another contract defining seniority as continuous length of service, but containing no clause specifying a starting point from which length of service should be computed, it was held that where one employee started to work a day before another, the former had the greater seniority since he had the longer service record, even though both were hired on the same day.[31]

Seniority Lists

In the absence of a contract provision requiring the posting of seniority lists, the employer may be held to be under an implied obligation to make proper and reasonable disclosure, upon demand by an aggrieved employee or his union, of the seniority standing of the aggrieved and that of other employees in his seniority unit. In this regard, Arbitrator Ralph T. Seward stated:

> "An employee—and the union as his representative—clearly has a right to be informed of the seniority date and length of continuous service credited to him on the Company's records. By the same token, since most seniority issues involve a comparison of the relative rights of two or more employees, the employee—and the union as his representative—has a right to know the seniority dates and length of continuous service credited to the other employees in the seniority unit applicable to him at any given time. The only accurate source of such information is obviously the Company. It has the records. It is initiating the various transfers, promotions, demotions, 'bumps', lay-offs, recalls, etc. which are daily causing changes in those records. The information practically obtainable from the employees themselves could never be as accurate, up-to-date or complete as that which the Company can make available. Indeed, some employees might have an interest in concealing information as to their own seniority standing in an effort to protect themselves from being 'bumped.' " [32]

---

[30] Robertshaw-Fulton Controls Co., 22 LA 273, 274 (1954).
[31] National Biscuit Award, 4 ALAA, par. 68,530.1 (Donnelly, 1950).
[32] Bethlehem Steel Co., 24 LA 699, 702 (Seward, 1955). Also see Republic Steel Corp., 18 LA 907, 909 (Platt, 1952).

The collective agreement may specifically provide for the posting of seniority lists.[33] It may also make provision for challenging the seniority list, often with some stated time limit, and failure of an employee to make a timely protest concerning a seniority date may be deemed a waiver of his right to challenge.[34] However, even though an employee does not challenge his posted seniority date for several years, an employer may be estopped from refusing to change an admittedly incorrect date where he has consistently treated the employee in accordance with the accurate date and not the posted one.[35]

Service Outside the Seniority Unit

The length of service credited to an employee and his seniority standing may be affected by service outside the seniority unit. He may lose or retain previously earned seniority or continue to accumulate seniority, depending upon the wording of the collective agreement and how it is interpreted. Special provision may be made that an employee transferred out of the seniority unit to an exempt job continues to accumulate seniority,[36] or retains seniority already earned.[37] In cases where there is no specific contract provision governing the seniority rights of employees transferred out of the seniority unit, awards vary. For example, it has been variously held that in such a situation the employee (1) retained seniority previously earned; [38] (2) could not continue to accumulate seniority while outside the unit; [39] (3) continued to accumulate seniority during tempo-

---

[33] Pickett Cotton Mills, Inc., 17 LA 405 (Soule, 1951).

[34] Jones & Laughlin Steel Corp., 30 LA 432, 433-434 (Cahn, 1958); Republic Steel Corp., 24 LA 286, 287 (Platt, 1955).

[35] Republic Steel Corp., 25 LA 434, 435 (Platt, 1955).

[36] As in 29 LA 220, 27 LA 229, 25 LA 452, 24 LA 60, 23 LA 400, 23 LA 82, 21 LA 746, 15 LA 350, 15 LA 49, 12 LA 795.

[37] As in 30 LA 221, 26 LA 195 (employee could retain his seniority up to one year), 26 LA 67, 24 LA 73, 21 LA 746.

[38] See Arbitrator Baab in 28 LA 641, 645; Howard in 23 LA 440, 446; Ryder in 22 LA 769, 771-773; Myers in 22 LA 704, 705-706; Cahn in 22 LA 492, 495; Healy in 14 LA 916, 918; Lohman in 14 LA 537, 540; Feinberg in 9 LA 962, 964.

[39] See Arbitrator Cahn in 29 LA 828, 830, and in 22 LA 13, 17; Marshall in 17 LA 105, 108; and cases cited in footnote 38.

rary promotion out of the unit; [40] (4) continued to accumulate seniority while working outside the unit for an extended period; [41] and (5) forfeited all his seniority because he had in effect voluntarily quit.[42]

Sale of Company or Merger

When a business is sold, the problem may arise as to whether the employees who continue to work for the successor employer may be credited with length of service acquired during their employment with the predecessor company. In this regard, Arbitrator Sidney L. Cahn has ruled that a contract providing that "continuous service shall be determined by the employee's first employment in any Works of the Corporation" does not entitle employees who were employed by the predecessor company to be credited with service accumulated prior to the change in ownership.[43] Arbitrator L. E. Gooding, however, held that a successor company, which executed a contract providing that "Seniority shall be determined by the length of service and shall commence on date of employment as a regular employee," must credit employees for service with the predecessor company since no change of any kind was made in their employment or in the conditions under which they worked.[44]

Where a successor employer acquired the business at a bankruptcy sale, Arbitrator Albert I. Cornsweet reasoned that since the "very essence of a purchase at bankruptcy sale is legally to buy without incurring *any* obligations which the bankrupt may have had" the successor employer need not compute the employees' seniority from the date of original hire by

---

[40] McLouth Steel Corp., 28 LA 315, 317 (Haughton, 1957). Also see Arbitrator Hotchkiss in 4 LA 21, 24.

[41] See Arbitrator Garrett in 28 LA 740, 743, and in 15 LA 834, 836; Byrnes in 25 LA 595, 596-597; Shipman in 21 LA 682, 685; Fulda in 18 LA 315, 317; Roberts in 14 LA 482, 486; Gregory in 8 LA 51, 52; Reynolds in 3 LA 748, 752. Also see Arbitrator R. Smith in 23 LA 338, 340, citing many cases.

[42] Grand Sheet Metal Products Co., 27 LA 30, 35 (Kotin, 1956); Ford Motor Co., 26 LA 898, 899-901 (Platt, 1956). Also see Arbitrator Marshall in 17 LA 105, 108, where practice influenced the award.

[43] Jones & Laughin Steel Corp., 20 LA 797, 799 (1953). Also see DiGiorgio Wine Co., 28 LA 746, 749-750 (Jones, 1957).

[44] Home Fuel & Supply Co., 25 LA 66, 67-68 (1955).

the previous employer, even though the business was conducted in the same manner and with the same equipment and personnel.[45]

Merger of separate companies or of plants with separate seniority lists may raise the problem of determining how to combine such lists to make a composite list of employees of both operations. This problem has sometimes been resolved by arbitration. Thus, in merging two pilot seniority lists, following the merger of airlines, a board of arbitration took into consideration (1) length of service, and (2) the ratio, in each category, of pilots in one airline to pilots in the other, but with length of service having greater weight.[46] In another case, involving employees who formerly worked in two separate plants of the same employer, each plant having its own seniority list, Arbitrator Harold M. Somers determined that the composite list on merger of the two plants should be established by a method which would give equal weight to (1) overall length of service, and (2) the employees' relative positions on the separate plant lists.[47]

Seniority Provisions

There are two basic types of seniority provisions. The more rigid type requires the recognition of strict seniority— that is, the employer must give preference to the employee with the longest continuous service without regard to any other considerations.[48] The principal thesis underlying this approach is that, as between a junior man of superior qualities and a senior man of lower qualities, the social claim of the latter should override both the needs of the business and the interest of the public in its efficient operation.[49] The more usual provision, however, is written so as to serve the basic aims of seniority, while recognizing other factors, which basically involve the

---

[45] Cliquot Club Bottling Co., 14 LA 260, 261-262 (1950).
[46] Pan American World Airways, Inc., 19 LA 14, 20-22 (Cole, 1952).
[47] Moore Business Forms, Inc., 24 LA 793, 796-802 (1955).
[48] See strict seniority provision in 27 LA 203, 204.
[49] See Clifton, "Management Functions," N.Y.U. First Ann. Conf. on Lab., 89, 97 (1948).

"fitness and ability" of the employee, in determining preference in employment.[50] Such factors may include skill, ability, aptitude, competence, efficiency, training, physical fitness, judgment, experience, initiative, leadership, and the like.

In regard to this "modified seniority," Arbitrator Harry H. Platt has said:

> "Generally speaking, such modified seniority is acceptable to most unions and employers because it acknowledges the fact that wide difference in ability and capacity to perform the work required exists between employees in a plant and that such differences are a logical and legitimate consideration in determining preference in employment, especially in making promotions and demotions as well as in the reduction of forces." [51]

Modified Seniority Clauses

Modified seniority clauses fall into one of three basic categories:

(1) In one category are those clauses which provide in essence that the senior employee shall be given preference if he possesses fitness and ability equal to that of junior employees.[52] This type of clause might be termed a *"relative ability"* clause, since here comparisons between qualifications of employees bidding for the job are necessary and proper,[53] and seniority becomes a determining factor only if the qualifications of the bidders are equal.[54]

The wording of these "relative ability" clauses varies. The contract may provide that seniority shall govern unless there is a marked difference in ability, or unless a junior employee has greater ability. Some clauses provide that seniority shall govern if ability (or other qualifying factor such as physical

---

[50] See Darin & Armstrong, 13 LA 843, 845 (Platt, 1950).

[51] Id. at 845-846. Also see comment of Arbitrator Alexander H. Frey in Atlas Powder Co., 30 LA 674, 676 (1958).

[52] For examples of this type of clause see 30 LA 674, 675; 30 LA 365; 29 LA 262, 265; 28 LA 72, 73; 26 LA 885, 886; 25 LA 480, 481; 23 LA 322, 323; 22 LA 258, 259; 21 LA 565, 566; 20 LA 416, 418; 19 LA 639, 642; 17 LA 898; 16 LA 382, 383; 9 LA 432, 433; 8 LA 278, 280.

[53] Alabama Power Co., 18 LA 24, 25 (McCoy, 1952).

[54] See Arbitrator Frey in 30 LA 674, 677; Brecht in 21 LA 565, 568; McCoy in 18 LA 24, 25.

fitness, competence, etc.) is _relatively equal,_ or _substantially equal,_ or simply _equal._ Even in the latter regard, however, it has been held that the term "equal" does not mean exact quality, but only substantial equality.[55] Nor does "relatively" equal ability mean "exactly" equal ability.[56] Thus, whether the term used is "equal" or "relatively equal" or "substantially equal", it would appear that only an approximate or near equality of competing employees, rather than an exact equality, should be necessary in order to bring the seniority factor into play.[57] Where the junior employee is substantially superior in ability, however, he may be given preference over a senior employee.[58]

(2) The second basic type of modified seniority clause provides in general that the senior employee will be given preference if he possesses sufficient ability to perform the job.[59] Minimum qualifications are enough under these _"sufficient ability"_ clauses.[60] This type of clause may state that preference will be given to the senior qualified bidder, or to the senior employee provided he is qualified or has the "necessary" ability for the job, and the like. Under this type of provision, "it is necessary to determine only whether the employee with greater seniority can in fact do the job."[61] Comparisons between applicants are unnecessary and improper, and "the job must be given to the senior bidder if he is competent, regardless of how much more competent some other bidder may be."[62]. Thus, the senior

---

[55] See Arbitrator Rosenfarb in 23 LA 789, 792; McCoy in 20 LA 416, 419. Cf. 9 LA 432, 435 and comments in 26 LA 885, 889.

[56] See Bethlehem Steel Co., 23 LA 532, 534 (Seward, 1954).

[57] See Republic Steel Corp., 1 LA 244, 247 (Platt, 1945).

[58] See Arbitrator Seward in 29 LA 710, 712; Frey in 19 LA 883, 888; Roberts in 19 LA 270, 278-279.

[59] For examples of this type of clause see 29 LA 29, 31; 27 LA 353, 356; 25 LA 479, 480; 24 LA 517, 518; 23 LA 556, 557; 23 LA 159, 160 and 163; 22 LA 167, 168; 19 LA 257, 258; 19 LA 32, 33; 18 LA 24, 25; 16 LA 790, 791; 16 LA 525, 526; 7 LA 526, 527; 1 LA 59, 59-60.

[60] Central Franklin Process Co., 19 LA 32, 34 (Marshall, 1952).

[61] Republic Steel Corp., 1 LA 244, 247 (Platt, 1945).

[62] Alabama Power Co., 18 LA 24, 25 (McCoy, 1952).

qualified employee will be entitled to preference even though a
junior employee possesses greater skill and ability.[63]

(3) The third basic type of modified seniority provision,
which might be called a *"hybrid"* clause, requires consideration
and comparison in the first instance of *both* seniority and relative ability.[64] The "hybrid" clause ordinarily is worded in such
general terms as "seniority and qualifications shall govern," or
"due consideration shall be given to length of service, aptitude,
and ability," and the like, without indicating the relative
weight to be accorded these factors. Arbitrators, however,
require that fair and reasonable consideration be given to both
seniority and relative ability, although the weight that may be
accorded to each varies from case to case.

It seems clear that under "hybrid" clauses the relative
claims of seniority and of ability must be determined by comparing and weighing against each other the relative difference
in seniority of competing employees and the relative difference
in their abilities. Thus, in comparing two or more qualified
employees, both seniority and ability must be considered, and
where the difference in length of service is relatively insignifi-
cant and there is a relatively significant difference in ability,
then the ability factor should be given greater weight; but
where there is a relatively substantial difference in seniority and
relatively little difference in abilities, then length of service
should be given greater weight. To illustrate, Arbitrator I.
Robert Feinberg, giving effect to both factors under a hybrid
clause, held that a much better qualified junior employee should
be given preference over a senior employee who could perform
the job, since there was relatively little difference in length of
service, thus making relative ability the determinative factor.[65]

---

[63] Central Franklin Process Co., 19 LA 32, 34 (Marshall, 1952). See Blaw Knox
Co., 23 LA 159, 163 (Reid, 1954), where the senior employees were found to have
lacked the necessary ability.

[64] See Arbitrator Davis in 30 LA 862, 870; Cole in 21 LA 183, 185; Cornsweet in
16 LA 280, 283, 285; Frolich in 14 LA 12, 15; Wolff in 11 LA 1190, 1192; Feinberg
in 11 LA 743, 744-745.

[65] Callite Tungsten Corp., 11 LA 743, 744-745 (1948).

Conversely, a senior employee whose qualifications were only slightly less but whose seniority was much greater than that of a junior employee has been given preference over the better qualified junior employee, the seniority factor determining the issue.[66]

Determination of Fitness and Ability

Provisions for modified seniority, designed on the one hand to give recognition to the right and responsibility of management to manage the enterprise and on the other hand to protect senior employees, involve some of the most troublesome questions confronting arbitrators. Unions tend to overemphasize seniority and forget merit and ability, while management tends to overemphasize supervision's personal judgment of merit and ability and forget seniority.[67]

Arbitrators have frequently held that, where the agreement makes "fitness and ability" a factor to be considered along with seniority under one of the modified seniority clauses but is silent as to how and by whom the determination of qualifications is to be made, management is entitled to make the initial determination, subject to challenge by the union on the ground that management's decision was unreasonable under the facts, or capricious, arbitrary, or discriminatory.[68] This right to determine ability may be held by management either as a residual management prerogative or as a necessary adjunct to the right to manage the plant and direct the working forces.[69]

---

[66] See Arbitrator Cole in 21 LA 183, 185; Wolff in 11 LA 1190, 1192.

[67] Ford Motor Co., 2 LA 374, 375 (Shulman, 1945).

[68] See Arbitrator Reid in 29 LA 394, 396; Dworkin in 29 LA 29, 36; Prasow in 27 LA 40, 49; Kelliher in 23 LA 105, 109; Carmody in 23 LA 38; Parke in 22 LA 258, 260; Murphy in 18 LA 757, 758-759; Hawley in 17 LA 516, 518-519; Lockhart in 16 LA 525, 529; Maggs in 12 LA 311, 315; Reynolds in 10 LA 624, 626; Ingle in 9 LA 515, 517; Greene in 7 LA 526, 527; Marshall in 6 LA 838, 841; Platt in 1 LA 244, 247. The various views as to which party has the burden of proof when management's determination has been challenged are discussed in the next topic titled "Review of Management's Determination: Evidence and Burden of Proof."

[69] See Arbitrator Dworkin in 29 LA 29, 36; Williams in 25 LA 748, 751; Reid in 23 LA 322, 326; Parker in 22 LA 258, 260; Baab in 20 LA 137, 141; Hawley in 17 LA 516, 518; Kerr in 14 LA 163, 167; Reynolds in 10 LA 624, 626. Also see Gregory in 9 LA 432, 436.

A collective agreement containing a modified seniority clause may speeifically provide that the employer shall be the judge of the qualifying factors, sometimes also providing for challenge of management's decision by the union through the grievance procedure.[70] However, even where the contract makes the employer the sole judge, arbitrators have held that management's action must not be unreasonable, capricious, arbitrary, or discriminatory.[71]

Review of Management's Determination: Evidence and Burden of Proof

In many cases involving issues of seniority and ability, the arbitrator in reviewing management's determination does not speak in terms of burden of proof, but simply considers all the evidence and arguments of both parties and decides from a consideration thereof whether the company's determination should be upheld.[72] On the other hand, in some cases the arbitrator does speak specifically in terms of burden of proof, placing the onus on one party or the other.[73]

There appear to be several basic approaches as to which party should have the burden of proof in cases involving managerial action taken under "relative ability" clauses.[74] In some cases such clauses have been construed to place a relatively light limitation upon the employer and, in effect, to place the burden

---

[70] See, for example, 30 LA 803, 804; 26 LA 773, 774; 19 LA 402, 403; 19 LA 47, 48; 18 LA 24, 25; 10 LA 423, 424; 6 LA 786, 788.

[71] See Arbitrator Meltzer in 30 LA 803, 807; Disman in 26 LA 773, 778-779; Ralston in 19 LA 402, 405; McCoy in 18 LA 24, 27; Wardlaw in 6 LA 786, 788. Cf., Arbitrator Carmichael in 3 LA 313, 317.

[72] See for instance, Arbitrator Boles in 30 LA 365, 367-374; Ross in 29 LA 262, 265-267; Prasow in 27 LA 40, 49; Howlett in 26 LA 885, 888-892; Disman in 26 LA 773, 779; Reid in 23 LA 322, 326; Parker in 22 LA 258, 260; Platt in 20 LA 460, 462; Marshall in 19 LA 32, 34; Klamon in 19 LA 639, 646; McCoy in 18 LA 24, 27; D. Wolff in 17 LA 898, 903-904; Levinson in 16 LA 790, 792; Ebeling in 14 LA 163, 167; Whiting in 11 LA 495, 497; Reynolds in 10 LA 624, 626. Also see McCoy in 16 LA 1, 3-12.

[73] The contract itself may place the burden of proof on one of the parties. See 29 LA 597, 598; 16 LA 280, 283. Also see 14 LA 316, 317. Cf. 25 LA 618, 623.

[74] See discussion of "relative ability" clauses, supra, topic titled "Modified Seniority Clauses." There are various shadings of opinion within the basic approaches regarding the burden and quantum of proof. In this connection, see Howard, "The Role of the Arbitrator in the Determination of Ability," 12 Arb. J. 14-27 (1957).

of proof on the employee. Under this approach, when the union challenges management's determination it must sustain the burden of proving discrimination, caprice, arbitrariness, or bad faith on the part of the employer or that the employer's evaluation of abilities was clearly wrong.[75]

In some other cases such clauses are construed to place a relatively severe limitation upon the employer and, in effect, to place the burden of proof on him. Under this approach, the employer must be prepared, when by-passing senior employees, to show, by specific and understandable evidence which relates to capacity for the job in question, that the junior man is the abler.[76] In still other "relative ability" cases, an even heavier burden is, in effect, placed on the employer, and he is required when challenged not only to show greater ability in the junior man to whom he has given preference, but also to show the absence of discrimination and arbitrariness and the presence of good faith.[77]

In cases involving "sufficient ability" clauses,[78] arbitrators have placed the burden on the employer to show that the by-passed senior employee is not competent for the job, and the fact that a junior employee is more competent than the senior employee is irrelevant.[79] Apart from this required showing by

---

[75] See Arbitrator Ingle in 9 LA 515, 517; Marshall in 6 LA 838, 841. Also see Arbitrator Doyle in 19 LA 47, 49. In some cases, while the arbitrator did not speak in terms of burden of proof, he noted that there was no evidence that the company had discriminated or acted in an arbitrary or capricious manner or in bad faith. See for example, Arbitrator Disman in 26 LA 773, 779; Jones in 25 LA 600, 604; Brecht in 21 LA 565, 568-569; D. Wolff in 17 LA 898, 903-904; Hawley in 17 LA 516, 519; Prasow in 17 LA 205, 211-212; Marshall in 17 LA 105, 109; Levinson in 16 LA 790, 792; Reynolds in 10 LA 624, 626.

[76] See Arbitrator Garrett in 22 LA 188, 190; Waite in 19 LA 1, 4; Blair in 16 LA 382, 383; Platt in 13 LA 843, 846; Whitton in 13 LA 666, 668; Brandschain in 5 LA 578, 582; Shulman in 2 LA 374, 375-376.

[77] See Arbitrator Frey in 30 LA 674, 677; Klamon in 24 LA 869, 873; Kelliher in 14 LA 1021, 1026. Also see Reid in 29 LA 394, 397.

[78] See discussion on "sufficient ability" clauses supra, topic titled "Modified Seniority Clauses."

[79] Pittsburgh Plate Glass Co., 8 LA 317, 329 (Blair, 1947). Also see Arbitrator Galenson in 25 LA 681, 684; Shister in 25 LA 618, 623; Hale in 25 LA 130, 142; Ross in 23 LA 556, 558; McKelvey in 22 LA 167, 170; Pollard in 16 LA 586, 587. Cf. Arbitrator Cahn in 29 LA 597, 598, where the burden was said to be on the employee by the contract.

the employer under such clauses, if the union specifically alleges discrimination or abuse of discretion, it may be required to prove such allegations by clear evidence.[80]

When a "hybrid" clause is involved,[81] arbitrators appear to place the burden on the employer to show why the ability factor was given greater weight than the seniority factor in by-passing the senior employee.[82]

If "strict" seniority is involved, that is, if the agreement requires the observance of seniority but contains no fitness and ability qualifications, the burden is clearly on the employer to justify a failure to give preference to the senior employee. For example, under a strict seniority clause, an employer passing over a senior but handicapped employee would have the burden of proving that the senior employee is not qualified for the work or that the performance of the work would have injurious effects on him.[83]

Finally, it should be emphasized that the approach taken by any arbitrator as to which party has the burden of proof will depend in great measure upon the terms of the contract and the facts of the case—in one case under one contract in one set of circumstances an arbitrator may decide the issue simply by examining the facts without referring to burden of proof, while in another case under another contract in another set of circumstances the same arbitrator may place the burden of proof on one party or the other.[84] This is by no means a criticism of the arbitrators. Rather, it serves emphatically to bring the problem into focus and to make clear the basic observation

---

[80] See Arbitrator Shister in 24 LA 703, 705; Carmody in 23 LA 38, 39; Greene in 7 LA 526, 527.

[81] See discussion on "hybrid" clauses supra, topic titled "Modified Seniority Clauses."

[82] Southwestern Bell Telephone Co., 30 LA 862, 871 (Davis, 1958). Also see Arbitrator Cole in 21 LA 183, 185, and D. Wolff in 11 LA 1190, 1192, where the employer was held not to have given sufficient weight to the much greater seniority of the senior man. But Arbitrator Feinberg in 11 LA 743, 744, upheld the employer where there was little difference in seniority and much difference in ability.

[83] Chrysler Corp., 5 LA 333, 336 (Wolff, 1946).

[84] See for example, Arbitrator Klamon in 24 LA 869, 873, and 19 LA 639, 646; Platt in 20 LA 460, 462, and 13 LA 843, 846; D. Wolff in 11 LA 1190, 1192, and 5 LA 333, 336.

that, as a practical matter, whether or not the arbitrator speaks in terms of burden of proof, in most cases when management's determination is challenged both parties are expected to produce whatever evidence they can in support of their respective contentions; and they ordinarily do so. The arbitrator in turn considers all the evidence and decides whether management's determination should be upheld as being reasonably supported by the evidence and as not having been influenced by improper elements such as arbitrariness, caprice, or discrimination.

Factors Considered in Determining Fitness and Ability

The determination of ability is by no means susceptible to any set formula applicable to any and all circumstances. The precise factors or criteria applicable in one set of circumstances involving one contract may not be proper or sufficient in another situation under another contract. Nevertheless, reported arbitration awards show that in the absence of contract provision for the method to be used or the factors to be considered in determining ability, management has been permitted or required to use a variety of methods and to consider a number of factors, including, in proper circumstances: use of written, oral, performance or aptitude tests; trial period on the job; reliance upon a merit rating plan or upon the opinion of supervision; consideration of production records, attendance or disciplinary records, education, experience, physical fitness, and the like. It has been held that management is entitled to use any method to determine ability so long as the method used is fair and nondiscriminatory.[85]

Technical qualifications for the job in question or a related job are clearly pertinent to management's consideration of an employee's "fitness and ability" for that job. Some of the factors discussed herein, such as the use of tests, technical training, and experience, point to the technical requirements of the job. However, arbitrators generally have permitted or required

---

[85] See Arbitrator Williams in 25 LA 748, 751; Bailer in 19 LA 257, 260; Blair in 8 LA 278, 280.

management to consider other factors as well in determining employees' qualifications. For example, Arbitrator Jerome A. Levinson has said:

> "To limit consideration to the one factor of technical knowledge of the job, would appear to be unduly restrictive. * * * The Company could properly consider additional factors in deciding who was qualified for the particular job. * * *

> "The criteria used by the Company [education, ability to express himself, alertness, attendance record, flexibility and ability to learn new duties] do not appear unreasonable or arbitrary, as related to the job * * * in this case. They seem to be appropriate and relevant factors for qualification of a man for the duties and responsibilities of this job * * *." [86]

Arbitrator Pearce Davis would go further in that he would impose a duty upon management to consider other matters in addition to technical knowledge. He has stated:

> "In its assessment of comparative abilities, the Company has the right and the duty to prepare, record, and examine *tangible* and *objective* (in so far as possible) evidence concerning such matters as, for example: innate capacity, prior job experience and performance; attendance, health and related factors; tests, if available, such as those to indicate likelihood of successful performance in the new position." [87]

In any event, the factors considered must relate directly to the question of what the job requires and the employee's ability to meet those requirements.[88] Obviously, the factors used must be consistent with the collective agreement. It seems clear that the more objective factors have greater acceptability, and the more of such factors properly considered by management in a given situation, the stronger is the case for the decision reached by it.

The factors most commonly utilized are discussed in detail below. No particular significance is attached to the order in which they are discussed, and note should also be taken of the possiblity that factors other than those considered here may also be pertinent to any given case.

---

[86] John Deere Tractor Co., 16 LA 790, 792 (1951).
[87] Southwestern Bell Telephone Co., 30 LA 862, 871 (1958). Also see Arbitrator Justin in 20 LA 468, 474.
[88] See Arbitrator Brecht in 21 LA 565, 568-569; Baab in 20 LA 137, 141; Cahn in 18 LA 536, 538.

Use of Tests

Even in the absence of specific contract provision, management has been held entitled to give reasonable and appropriate written,[89] oral,[90] performance,[91] and aptitude tests,[92] as an aid in determining the ability of competing employees. Indeed, many arbitrators look with favor upon the use of proper tests in appropriate situations. Arbitrator David L. Cole has declared that use of tests constitutes an "effort to apply some objective measure of qualifications, rather than to leave the determination to the general judgment and subjective reactions of supervision."[93] Arbitrator B. Meredith Reid has stated: "In the absence of proof of bias, prejudice, discrimination or injustice, the reasonable exercise of judgment as to ability is helped rather than hindered by the tests in question"—but he cautioned that this approval of the tests was not "open approval for tests of any kind under any circumstances."[94]

Arbitrators generally hold that tests used in determining ability must be (1) specifically related to the requirements of the job, (2) fair and reasonable, (3) administered in good faith and without discrimination, and (4) properly evaluated. In some awards, the arbitrator may find it necessary to discuss all of the above requirements. In others, he may discuss one or more, the implication being that the rest of the requirements have been met.

(1) With respect to the first requirement, it has been held that the test must be related to the skill and knowledge required on the job. For example, a written test given to ascerain cleri-

---

[89] See, for example, Arbitrator Seward in 29 LA 710, 711; Cahn in 29 LA 597, 599; Howlett in 26 LA 885, 890; Marshall in 25 LA 480, 484; Updegraff in 11 LA 810, 811. Cf. Arbitrator Sembower in 27 LA 353, 357; Barnes in 25 LA 479, 480.

[90] See, for example, Hammarlund Mfg. Co., Inc., 19 LA 653, 655 (Bailer, 1952).

[91] See, for example, Phillips Petroleum Co., 29 LA 246, 249 (Singletary, 1957); Bendix Aviation Corp., 19 LA 257, 260 (Bailer, 1952).

[92] See, for example, Arbitrator Frey in 30 LA 674, 677; Ross in 29 LA 262, 265; Marshall in 25 LA 480, 484-485; Reid in 23 LA 322, 326.

[93] International Harvester Co., 21 LA 183, 184 (1953). Also see Arbitrator Seward in 29 LA 710, 712; Sembower in 27 LA 353, 357; Marshall in 25 LA 480, 484-485; Bailer in 19 LA 257, 260.

[94] Stauffer Chemical Co., 23 LA 322, 326 (1954).

cal and arithmetical ability required on the job is a proper aid in determining ability,[95] as is a test requiring performance of duties identical with those actually performed on the job.[96] It has also been held that the employer may not change the requirements of the job through the test.[97]

(2) A test will probably be considered fair and reasonable if, among other possible characteristics, it covers all relevant factors,[98] the questions are not unduly difficult,[99] and it is given under proper (though not necessarily ideal) conditions.[100] Frequently, the arbitrator will simply state or imply that the test in question has been examined and found to be fair and reasonable.[101]

(3) Where the test is given to all applicants for promotion, it probably will be considered to have been administered in good faith and without discrimination.[102] However, the test may be considered questionable if it is so "critical" that it goes beyond determining the type and amount of ability required by the contract for the job and selects only the exact number of applicants needed to fill the vacancies.[103]

(4) The test must be properly evaluated in the light of the contract provisions relating to seniority and job requirements, and it must not be used in a manner inconsistent with the contract.[104] In this regard, where a contract contains a

---

[95] See Wallingford Steel Co., 29 LA 597, 599 (Cahn, 1957). Also see Hammarlund Mfg. Co., Inc., 19 LA 653, 655 (Bailer, 1952).

[96] See Bendix Aviation Corp., 19 LA 257, 260 (Bailer, 1952).

[97] See Kuhlman Electric Co., 26 LA 885, 890-891 (Howlett, 1956).

[98] See Bendix Aviation Corp., 19 LA 257, 260 (Bailer, 1952).

[99] See Hammarlund Mfg. Co., Inc., 19 LA 653, 655 (Bailer, 1952).

[100] In Hammarlund Mfg. Co., Inc., 19 LA 653, 655 (Bailer, 1952), the fact that conditions under which the test was given were not ideal was not sufficient to make the test unfair or unreasonable.

[101] See Arbitrator Cahn in 29 LA 597, 599; Ross in 29 LA 262, 265; Reid in 23 LA 322, 325; Lehoczky in 18 LA 413, 414.

[102] See Bethlehem Steel Co., 29 LA 710, 711 (Seward, 1957); Bendix Aviation Corp., 19 LA 257, 260 (Bailer, 1952). Also see Arbitrator Cahn in 29 LA 597, 599; Ross in 29 LA 262, 265; Shister in 24 LA 703, 705; Reid in 23 LA 322, 325.

[103] See Ball Brothers Co., Inc., 27 LA 353, 357 (Sembower, 1956).

[104] American Smelting & Refining Co., 29 LA 262, 265 (Ross, 1957).

"sufficient ability" clause a test may not be used to determine "relative" ability.[105]

Finally, it must be kept in mind that arbitrators generally take the view that while the test may be used as an aid in judging ability or as a "verification" of ability, the employer may not base his determination of ability solely upon the results of a test but must consider other factors and other evidence.[106]

Experience

Experience is distinguishable from both seniority and productivity. It is the extent to which an employee has engaged in a particular job, type of work, or occupation. While the term ability does not necessarily imply prior experience on the particular job, experience is ordinarily considered a tangible, objective factor to be taken into consideration in determining fitness and ability.[107] Indeed, management has sometimes been reprimanded by the arbitrator for failing to take into consideration the experience of a senior employee who has been by-passed.[108]

Various views have been expressed concerning the place of experience in determining fitness and ability: Arbitrator Robert G. Howlett has said that "Other things being equal, the man who has had some experience on a job can become a competent employee in the classification faster than the man who has had no such experience." [109] Arbitrator Otto J. Baab has expressed the opinion that it is "reasonable to adopt the criterion of actual experience to determine skill and ability,"[110] but Arbitrator Paul N. Lehoczky has stated that "experience is not the sole criterion in forming a judgment of ability." [111] It has further

---

[105] Ball Brothers Co., Inc., 27 LA 353, 357 (Sembower, 1956).

[106] See Arbitrator Frey in 30 LA 674, 677; Seward in 29 LA 710, 712; Cahn in 29 LA 597, 599; Ross in 29 LA 262, 267; Dworkin in 29 LA 29, 36; Howlett in 26 LA 885, 890-892; Reid in 23 LA 322, 325; Lehoczky in 18 LA 413, 414. Cf. Bendix Aviation Corp., 19 LA 257, 260 (Bailer, 1952).

[107] See Arbitrator Prasow in 24 LA 437, 441; Baab in 14 LA 512, 515.

[108] See International Harvester Co., 21 LA 214, 217-218 (Cole, 1953).

[109] Kuhlman Electric Co., 26 LA 885, 891 (1956).

[110] Thor Corp., 14 LA 512, 515 (1950).

[111] Seagrave Corp., 16 LA 410, 412 (1951).

been asserted that "experience [is not] a factor in determining fitness and ability save and except to the extent that experience may tend to increase one's skill and ability." [112]

In any event, arbitrators generally give some consideration to experience where it is relevant to the job requirements. It may be one of several factors used, or a major factor, or the sole or determining factor. Work experience on the job in question or on a related job could demonstrate an employee's ability to perform the job,[113] with greater weight being accorded to experience on the particular job than on a related job.[114] The weight which the arbitrator gives to experience may depend in large measure upon the emphasis placed on this factor by the parties and upon the evidence, or lack of evidence, concerning other factors relevant in the determination of fitness and ability.[115] In any event the contract language and the fact situation presented to the arbitrator are of prime importance.

Naturally, if experience is not important to the job in question, little or no weight will be attached to this factor.[116] On the other hand, experience in the work may be a basic requirement for the job, thereby justifying management in giving preference to an experienced junior man over a senior who lacks experience.[117] Moreover, the employer may be upheld in giving preference to the junior employee where he has had substantially greater experience than the senior,[118] or where the experience of the junior employee is identical with or is more closely related to the work involved than the experience of the

---

[112] Tin Processing Corp., 17 LA 193, 198 (L. Smith, 1951).

[113] See Arbitrator Griffin in 29 LA 870, 873; Prasow in 24 LA 437, 441.

[114] See Arbitrator Warns in 21 LA 392, 397; Roberts in 19 LA 270, 279; Levinson in 16 LA 790, 792.

[115] For various treatment of experience see Arbitrator Klamon in 30 LA 279, 281-282; Fleming in 30 LA 237, 239-241; Griffin in 29 LA 870, 873; Boles in 28 LA 72, 75-76; Howlett in 26 LA 885, 891; E. Jones in 25 LA 600, 604; Warns in 21 LA 392, 396-397; Levinson in 16 LA 790, 792; Lehoczky in 16 LA 410, 412; Cornsweet in 16 LA 280, 284.

[116] See Temco Aircraft Corp., 28 LA 72, 75-76 (Boles, 1957).

[117] See E. I. Du Pont De Nemours & Co., 18 LA 536, 538 (Cahn, 1952).

[118] See Arbitrator Brecht in 21 LA 565, 568-569; Warns in 21 LA 392, 396-397; Gilden in 15 LA 636, 638; Platt in 12 LA 6, 7.

senior man,[119] or where the job requires intensive training and experience which the junior man has had and the senior man lacks.[120]

Other factors being equal, arbitrators have sometimes held that the senior man should be given a trial period on the basis of his having had some experience,[121] even though the man selected by the company had somewhat more experience.[122] In this connection, it should be noted that some arbitrators have distinguished temporary from permanent promotions in judging fitness and ability, and when temporary, the tendency is to emphasize present fitness and ability and hence to give greater weight to experience.[123]

Trial or Break-in Period on the Job v. Training

Agreements sometimes provide for a trial or break-in period on the job to determine ability, and questions in connection with the interpretation and application of such provisions are frequently arbitrated.[124] In the absence of contractual provision, the question arises as to whether management must give the senior a trial.[125] Obviously, ability to perform the job, or the lack of it, may be demonstrated by a trial or break-in period on the job. As stated by Arbitrator Carl A. Warns, "The best evidence as to whether an employee can do a job is

---

[119] See Arbitrator Fleming in 30 LA 237, 239-241; Brecht in 21 LA 565, 568-569; Warns in 21 LA 392, 397.

[120] See Arbitrator E. Jones in 25 LA 600, 604; Prasow in 24 LA 437, 441-442. Also see Arbitrator Cahn in 18 LA 536, 538-539.

[121] See Arbitrator Klamon in 30 LA 279, 282; Randle in 17 LA 486, 487; McCoy in 12 LA 682, 685. Also see Arbitrator Copelof in 16 LA 359, 365, where the collective agreement provided for a trial period. See topic, "Trial or Break-In Period on the Job," this Chapter.

[122] See Seagrave Corp., 16 LA 410, 412 (Lehoczky, 1951). Also se Arbitrator Rosenfarb in 23 LA 789, 793-794, and L. Smith in 17 LA 193, 198, in both of which the contract contained a provision for a trial period.

[123] See, for instance, Arbitrator Emery in 28 LA 733, 735; Marshall in 23 LA 623, 628; Waren in 21 LA 228, 231.

[124] See 29 LA 29, 31; 28 LA 823, 827-828; 25 LA 661, 662; 24 LA 461, 463: 24 LA 79, 80; 23 LA 779, 780; 21 LA 231, 232; 16 LA 525, 526; 16 LA 359, 361; 9 LA 956, 960; 2 LA 655, 657.

[125] Company policy [as in Columbia Steel Co. 13 LA 666, 670 (Whitton, 1949)] or past practice [as in Nickles Bakery, Inc., 17 LA 486, 487 (Randle, 1951) and Southern California Edison Co., 15 LA 162, 167 (Aaron, 1950)] may be involved.

to give him a fair trial on it." [126] There appears to be a close
relationship between the use of tests or other criteria and a trial
period on the job—some arbitrators have expressed the view
that the employer should grant the senior employee a trial
period on the job, but not training, to demonstrate his ability
if the test results [127] or other criteria used have been inconclusive in determining the ability of the senior bidder.[128]

Thus, arbitrators generally are inclined to the view that
if there is a reasonable doubt as to the ability of the senior
employee and if the trial would cause no serious inconvenience,
it should be granted, but that a trial should not be required in
all cases.[129] There is a similar general agreement that the trial
period should be a short one,[130] but it has also been held that the
trial must be adequate.[131] However, if the senior employee is
obviously unfit or unqualified, as in a situation where the job
in question requires a high degree of skill which can be acquired
only after a long period of training and there is no evidence
that the senior employee has these skills or related skills, then
management is not required to give him a trial period and may
give preference to the junior employee who already possesses
such skills.[132]

While an employer may be required to provide a trial or
break-in period on the job, he ordinarily would be under no

---

[126] Dayton Power & Light Co., 28 LA 624, 626 (1957).

[127] See Linde Air Poducts Co., 25 LA 369, 372 (Shister, 1955). Also see National
Seal Co., 29 LA 29, 37 (Dworkin, 1957), where the arbitrator considered a contract
provision for a trial period as protecting the employer's interests. Some awards appear
to have treated a trial on the job as something in the nature of a performance test.
See Coca-Cola Bottling Co., 18 LA 757, 760 (Murphy, 1952).

[128] See Rome Grader Corp., 22 LA 167, 170 (McKelvey, 1953). The same approach
was taken by Arbitrator Lazarus in 28 LA 823, 828, and Cole in 21 LA 231, 234, both
of which cases involved contract provisions for trial period on the job.

[129] See Arbittrator Reid in 29 LA 743, 746-747; Shister in 25 LA 369, 372; Prasow
in 24 LA 437, 442; McKelvey in 22 LA 167, 170; Shulman in 2 LA 374, 376. But see
Arbitrator Updegraff in 29 LA 50, 52; and Murphy in 18 LA 757, 760. Cf. Arbitrator
McCoy in 23 LA 779, 781.

[130] See Arbittrator Prasow in 24 LA 437, 442; Seward in 23 LA 532, 533-534;
Kerr in 11 LA 567, 568.

[131] See Arbitrator McKelvey in 22 LA 167, 170-171; Copelof in 17 LA 324, 326.

[132] Rome Grader Corp., 22 LA 167, 170-171 (McKelvey, 1953). Also see Arbitrator Shister in 25 LA 369, 372; Prasow in 24 LA 437, 442. The same holds true
even if there is a contract provision for a trial period. See Arbitrator Lazarus in 28
LA 823, 828; Platt in 24 LA 79, 80; Cole in 21 LA 231, 234.

obligation, unless the contract provides otherwise, to provide training for a senior employee in order to enable him to achieve the fitness and ability called for by the contract.[133] If a senior employee would require such extensive training (in order to qualify for a job) as to make it unreasonable under the contract to expect the employer to provide such training, the employer is justified in giving preference to a junior employee who is already fully qualified.[134] The need for training would seem to indicate a lack of skill and ability.[135]

However, where the contract recognizes seniority as a factor, management may not afford training opportunities to junior employees while arbitrarily denying them to senior employees, then promote or retain a junior applicant on the basis of such training.[136] Such action not only may constitute discrimination, but the seniority clause "might be either nullified or circumvented should the Company provide special and preferential training opportunities for low seniority employees."[137]

This is not to say that management may not select employees for training under any circumstances. It has been held that in the absence of a contract provision dealing with training, management should not be denied a reasonable freedom of discretion in selecting employees for training, particularly in connection with new types of activities, but such selection must not be arbitrary or discriminatory or in conflict with the seniority provisions of the contract.[138] Furthermore, where the employer has a policy of providing training for employees desiring to take it, he may not automatically disqualify employees who

[133] See Arbitrator Emery in 28 LA 733, 735; Shister in 25 LA 369, 372; Prasow in 24 LA 437, 442; Seward in 23 LA 532, 533-534; Klamon in 20 ▪A 768, 774; Lehoczky in 16 LA 410, 412; Greene in 7 LA 526, 527.

[134] See Arbitrator Murphy in 30 LA 598, 599; McKelvey in 22 LA 167, 170; Updegraff in 16 LA 909, 911-912.

[135] Poloron Products Co. of Pa., Inc., 23 LA 789, 792 (Rosenfarb, 1955).

[136] See Arbitrator Kerrison in 29 LA 747, 749; Williams in 28 LA 56, 59; Rosenfarb in 23 LA 789, 793; Waite in 19 LA 1, 4; McCoy in 18 LA 834, 835. Also see Arbitrator Reynolds in 25 LA 60, 63. Cf. Arbitrator Emery in 28 LA 733, 736.

[137] Sandvik Steel, Inc., 29 LA 747, 749 (Kerrison, 1957). Also see Poloron Products of Pa., Inc., 23 LA 789, 793 (Rosenfarb, 1955).

[138] See Purolater Products, Inc., 25 LA 60, 63 (Reynolds, 1955).

have not taken such training.[139] That is, the employer may not rely on training so provided as a "conclusive determinant of relative ability" but must affirmatively show that the men selected are actually better qualified.[140]

Opinion of Supervision

While the opinion of supervisors regarding the ability of employees is considered important and is entitled at least to some consideration, such opinion without factual support will not be deemed conclusive.[141] However, when supervisory opinion is substantiated by objective, tangible evidence, it may be the basis for management's determination as to the relative ability of employees.[142] The importance of supervisory opinion has been elaborated by Arbitrator Arthur M. Ross as follows:

> "Considerable weight should be given to bona fide conclusions of supervisors when supported by factual evidence. In the first place, a supervisor is responsible for the efficient performance of his unit and has a legitimate concern that the employees be properly assigned to achieve this objective. In the second place, he has a deeper and more intimate acquaintance with the men under his charge than an arbitrator is able to acquire in a brief hearing." [143]

Arbitrator Harry Shulman has emphasized the necessity for supporting evidence:

> "A supervisor's testimony that he honestly believes one employee to be superior to another with respect to the promotion is certainly a factor to be considered. It is not, however, either conclusive or sufficient. The supervisor must be prepared to state the basis for his belief and to support it, not by repeated assertions but by specific and understandable evidence * * *." [144]

Such objective evidence may include factors discussed elsewhere in this chapter, such as test results, production records, periodic merit ratings, and other documentary material.[145]

---

[139] United States Steel Corp., 22 LA 188, 190 (Garrett, 1953).
[140] Ibid.
[141] See Arbitrator Platt in 20 LA 460, 462; Hays in 12 LA 317, 322.
[142] See Campbell Soup Co., 19 LA 1, 4 (Waite, 1952). Also see Arbitrator Somers in 25 LA 316, 320; Ralston in 19 LA 402, 405; Grant in 11 LA 312, 315.
[143] Pacific Gas & Electric Co., 23 LA 556, 558 (1954). Also see Arbitrator Burris in 25 LA 32, 36; Rosenfarb in 23 LA 789, 793; Cole in 21 LA 214, 218.
[144] Ford Motor Co., 2 LA 374, 376 (1945).
[145] See Campbell Soup Co., 19 LA 1, 4 (Waite, 1952).

Supervisory opinion has been given controlling weight where management's decision to by-pass the senior man was based upon a composite of the opinions of several supervisors who observed or supervised his work, the opinions being formed on the basis of a variety of incidents in the senior's employment record.[146]

Merit Rating Plans

Merit rating plans involve essentially a documentation, usually periodically made, of supervisory opinion concerning various aspects of the "fitness and ability" of the employees. A merit rating plan may include such factors as quantity and quality of work, knowledge of the job, ability to learn, initiative, acceptance of responsibility, ability to direct others, safety habits and accident record, attitude toward fellow employees and management, and personal characteristics such as moral character, physical condition and appearance.[147]

An arbitrator's acceptance or rejection of a merit rating plan as a criterion for measuring ability depends upon whether the factors used and the weights attached to them are consistent with the collective agreement and the requirements of the job in question. Thus, under a contract which provided that seniority should govern where "ability, skill, and efficiency" are substantially equal, Arbitrator Ralph Roger Williams upheld management's use of a plan which did no more than document the opinion of supervisory personnel concerning the ability, skill and efficiency of the employees.[148] However, under a seniority provision which made "ability to do the work available" the standard, Arbitrator Paul N. Lehoczky held that some of the factors in the merit rating plan used by the company had no bearing upon an employee's "ability to do the work" and when

---

[146] See Northwestern Bell Telephone Co., 19 LA 47, 50-51 (Doyle, 1952). Also see Arbitrator Prasow in 17 LA 205, 211.

[147] See Western Automatic Machine Screw Co., 9 LA 606, 608 (Lehoczky, 1948). Many of these factors are discussed as separate criteria elsewhere in this chapter.

[148] See Lockheed Aircraft Corp., 25 LA 748, 750-752 (1956). Merit review sheets were submitted along with other documentary evidence in New Jersey Bell Telephone Co., 11 LA 312, 315 (Grant, 1948).

these were discounted the employees involved were found to have the requisite ability.[149]

Educational Background

Technical training acquired through attendance at trade schools, company or union sponsored training programs, and the like, obviously is highly pertinent to the determination of fitness and ability if such training relates to the requirements of the job in question.

An employee's formal educational background, that is, high school and college education as opposed to technical training, may be a factor in the assessment of fitness and ability if it is pertinent to the job requirements. Where the contract does not specify a formal educational requirement for given jobs, arbitrators appear to have taken several approaches to the question of whether the employer may consider this factor in determining ability. Thus, it has been variously held that (1) management may require high school education where the job is complex and carries with it automatic progressions through several classifications involving additional responsibilities;[150] (2) the formal educational background of the employee may be considered along with other factors;[151] (3) the employer may not automatically disqualify an employee for want of a formal education but may consider formal education in evaluating the employee's training and experience;[152] (4) the employer violated the contract by denying a promotion to senior employees solely on the basis that they lacked high school education or its equivalent.[153]

---

[149] See Western Automatic Machine Screw Co., 9 LA 606, 608-609 (1948). Cf. Merrill Stevens Dry Dock & Repair Co., 17 LA 516, 518-519 (Hawley, 1951)

[150] See Philip Carey Mfg. Co., 30 LA 659, 661 (Warns, 1958). Also see Arbitrator Seibel in 22 LA 446, 449-450. Cf. Arbitrator Copelof in 16 LA 359, 365.

[151] See Arbitrator Frey in 30 LA 674, 677; Howlett in 26 LA 885, 890. Also see Arbitrator Baab in 20 LA 137, 142.

[152] See Union Oil Co., 17 LA 62, 64-65 (Wyckoff, 1951), where the contract provided for promotions based upon seniority, and ability, training and experience.

[153] See Bridgeport Gas Co., 26 LA 289, 291 (Stutz, 1956). Also see Arbitrator Ryder in 20 LA 899, 901-903.

Production Records

An employee's production record is objective evidence of his productivity or output and may be relied upon in whole or in part (depending upon the circumstances) in determining fitness and ability.[154] Arbitrator Herbert L. Spencer has asserted that ability "is most assuredly tied up with productivity" and that productivity must be measured in terms of both quality and quantity of work.[155] Production records may be the sole factor considered where there is a substantial difference in the productivity of the competing employees. Thus, management's determination of relative ability based solely upon productivity was upheld where the grievant's production was "considerably below" that of other workers,[156] and also where there was a 17 percent difference between the senior and junior employee's production earnings.[157] Management's reliance in part upon production records was likewise upheld where an employee consistently failed to make the minimum wage under an incentive system.[158]

However, in situations where there is only a minor difference in productivity, automatic reliance upon productivity alone for the determination of relative ability probably would not be upheld.[159]

Attendance Record

An employee's attendance record has been considered as "tangible and objective" evidence which management may properly consider in its assessment of comparative abilities and qualifications.[160] Thus, under a contract containing a "relative

---

[154] Regarding the type of data necessary in presenting production records as evidence of fitness and ability, see Jonco Aircraft Corp., 22 LA 819, 823 (Merrill, 1954).

[155] Universal Mfg. Co., 13 LA 238, 241 (1949).

[156] Ibid.

[157] Worth Steel Co., 12 LA 931, 934 (Bell, 1949).

[158] See Goodyear Clearwater Mills No. 2, 11 LA 419, 425-426 (McCoy, 1948), where the employee also had a poor attendance record. Also see Arbitrator Abernethy in 23 LA 379, 383; Klamon in 19 LA 639, 646.

[159] United States Steel Corp., 22 LA 80, 81 (Garrett, 1953).

[160] Southwestern Bell Telephone Co., 30 LA 862, 871 (Davis, 1958). But see Central Screw Co., 11 LA 108, 109 (Edes, 1948).

ability" clause, the promotion of a junior over a senior employee
on the basis of comparison of attendance records of the two
employees was upheld, where the records showed a "striking"
difference in favor of the junior and the job required a high
degree of responsibility.[161] In that case, Arbitrator Jacob J.
Blair, in relying largely upon the attendance records of the two
employees, stated:

> "It is well established as a principle that Management has the right to
> expect and require regular attendance on the job. While it is true that
> Management has in this instance been extremely negligent in enforcing
> this right, its negligence does not bar it from applying the right in the case
> of a promotion. * * *
>
> "The action of Management in invoking this right at this time is not
> arbitrary. True, Management could not discipline * * * [grievant] by
> lay-offs or dismissals for an action which they have condoned over a period
> of time without prior notice or warning. But the right to discipline and
> the right of Management to choose between candidates for promotion are
> distinguishable. * * * Management has the right to invoke the attendance
> records of two employees contending for a promotion because to do other-
> wise would condone and even approve a record of irregular attendance at
> work." [162]

It has also been held that the employer may consider the
employee's attendance record in determining whether he is
"qualified," even though his numerous absences were due to
illness.[163]

In cases involving excused absences for the conduct of
union business, it has been held that such absences should not
operate as a bar to giving the senior man preference; but the
arbitrator appears to have based his decision on past practice,[164]
or to have conditioned his award upon the satisfactory performance of the job during a trial period,[165] or upon regular attendance by the employee,[166] reserving explicitly or in effect the

---

[161] Rogers Bros. Corp., 16 LA 382, 383 (Blair, 1951).
[162] Ibid. See topic, "Disciplinary Record," this Chapter. Cf. Cleveland-Cliffs
Iron Co., 24 LA 599, 600 (Kelliher, 1955). Also see Dow Chemical Co., 12 LA
1070, 1071-1072 (Pollard, 1949).
[163] See Arbitrator Levinson in 16 LA 790, 792; McCoy in 11 LA 419, 425-426.
Also see Arbitrator Bailer in 20 LA 835, 836.
[164] See Douglas Aircraft Co., Inc., 23 LA 786, 788 (Warren, 1955).
[165] See Marlin-Rockwell Corp., 17 LA 254, 256 (Shister, 1951).
[166] See Goodyear Decatur Mills, 12 LA 682, 685 (McCoy, 1949).

right of management to take corrective steps should the employee not perform in an acceptable manner.

Disciplinary Record

If an employee's disciplinary record contains offenses which reflect upon his "fitness and ability" for a given job, such record may be given some consideration. For example, it has been held that an employee's disciplinary record could be considered since his offenses demonstrated that he lacked maturity, reliability and a sense of responsibility, and hence the ability, merit and capacity required by the contract.[167] However, if alleged offenses are not made the subject of discipline at the time they are committed, management may not be permitted to rely upon them in assessing employee abilities and qualifications.[168] Furthermore, a single offense for which the worker has been disciplined may not be sufficient to compel the conclusion that he is incompetent.[169]

The collective agreement may provide specifically or in effect that the personnel records of the employees be considered by management in determining ability. Under such an agreement, personnel records showing that four written reprimands were issued to the senior employee in connection with his work were considered by Arbitrator Albert I. Cornsweet to justify management's decision to promote a junior man.[170]

Employee's Physical and Psychological Fitness

Many contracts specifically include phyical fitness as a requirement for job preference.[171] However, even where the contract does not contain the physical ability requirement, it

---

[167] Dewey & Almy Chemical Co., 25 LA 316, 318-319 (Somers, 1955). Also see Arbitrator Klamon in 19 LA 639, 645-647.

[168] See Arbitrator Kelliher in 24 LA 599, 600; Killingsworth in 19 LA 186, 188.

[169] See Copco Steel & Engineering Co., 13 LA 586, 591 (Platt, 1949), where the case seemed to turn on a lack of evidence that the employee had a "careless temperament" and had been negligent on a specific occasion.

[170] Inland Steel Co., 16 LA 280, 284 (1951).

[171] As in 30 LA 237, 238; 23 LA 556, 557; 20 LA 416, 418; 17 LA 486, 487; 16 LA 410, 411; 16 LA 382, 383; 13 LA 238, 241.

has been said that the term "ability" includes physical ability.[172] Health records showing an employee's physical condition have been considered as "tangible and objective" evidence of his fitness and ability.[173]

Moreover, management in some situations has been held entitled to require employees to take physical examinations, as, for instance, before reinstatement of an ailing employee in a job requiring weight lifting activities,[174] or before transfer of an employee to a job demanding greater physical effort, thus giving management "some guide as to the physical ability of the employee" to perform the work.[175] It would seem to be a corollary to this right that it is the duty of the employer to protect the health of his employees despite their willingness to perform heavier duties. In this regard, Arbitrator Joseph M. Klamon has stated:

> "Indeed, the Company might incur a legal liability for failure to exercise due care and reasonable judgment to protect the health of operating employees. The ability to perform a job cannot be disassociated from the health hazards involved to male as well as female employees and action the Company takes in this regard is definitely within the inherent rights of Management to operate the plant safely and efficiently." [176]

When the question of physical fitness for a particular job arises, the primary emphasis may be placed upon the physical disability of the grieving employee to fill the job, another employee's greater physical ability for it being secondary.[177] Thus, it has been held that if certain work contributes to an employee's ill health, he cannot justifiably claim physical fitness for that work under the seniority provisions of the contract.[178] Similarly, a physical defect which impairs an employee's physi-

---

[172] See Doehler-Jarvin Corp., 12 LA 896, 897 (Stashower, 1949).

[173] See Southwestern Bell Telephone Co., 30 LA 862, 871 (Davis, 1958). Also see Arbitrator Howlett in 26 LA 885, 890.

[174] See Fulton Glass Co., 31 LA 824, 826 (Boles, 1958). Also see Arbitrator Bothwell in 27 LA 404, 406, permitting the employer to require physical examinations in recall.

[175] See Doehler-Jarvis Corp., 12 LA 896, 897-898 (Stashower, 1949). Cf. Arbitrator Gilden in 16 LA 446, 453-454.

[176] See Mengel Co., 18 LA 392, 399 (Klamon, 1952).

[177] See Arbitrator Gilden in 16 LA 446, 451; Brandschain in 5 LA 579, 581.

[178] See Universal Mfg. Co., 13 LA 238, 241 (Spencer, 1949). Also see Arbitrator Bailer in 20 LA 835, 836.

cal fitness for a particular job has been held to render him deficient in the requisite physical fitness.[179] However, neither the fact that the senior man weighed less than the junior,[180] nor the fact that the senior man was older,[181] has been considered proof that he was less able to fulfill the physiscal requirements of the job.

In jobs where psychological requirements are important, an employee's fitness in this regard may also be examined. Thus, with respect to a job entailing "psychological strain and stress", Arbitrator Mitchell M. Shipman has stated:

> "And, however intangible these psychological requirements may be, they are not to be minimized. * * * Indeed, just as the Umpire must be convinced that [grievant] does have the requisite experience and ability to do the job, so must he be equally convinced that the psychological requirements thereof can also be fully met by him." [182]

An employee's temperament may be such as to disqualify him for a responsible job, as where an employee's nervousness and excitability in moments of emergency were considered grounds for rejecting his bid.[183] Furthermore, management has been upheld in its refusal to recall an employee in accordance with seniority, where his mental condition was such that he could not perform even the simplest duties without an abnormal amount of supervision.[184]

Personal Characteristics of Employee

Personal characteristics of an employee may be considered only if they relate directly to his ability to meet the job requirements. For example, the filing of suit by an employee against his employer has been held not to affect his qualifications, the word "qualifications" being said to relate to physical fitness and

---

[179] See Bethlehem Steel Co., 5 LA 579, 581 (Brandschain, 1946).
[180] See Seagrave Corp., 16 LA 410, 412 (Lehoczky, 1951).
[181] See Combustion Engineering Co., Inc., 20 LA 416, 419 (McCoy, 1953).
[182] Bethlehem Steel Co., 18 LA 683, 684-685 (1952). Management failed to prove to Arbitrator Shipman's satisfaction that the senior man had exhibited anxiety and fear in connection with his work.
[183] See Pacific Gas & Electric Co., 23 LA 556, 558-559 (Ross, 1954). Cf. Arbitrator Lockhart in 16 LA 525, 528-531.
[184] See White Motor Co., 28 LA 823, 828-829 (Lazarus, 1957).

ability rather than to "moral" qualifications.[185] However, Arbitrator Otto J. Baab has held that management may take into consideration the fact that an employee had been guilty in the past of certain "injudicious conduct and conversation" evincing his interest in the cult of nudism, particularly since the job involved not only technical knowledge but also public relations. Arbitrator Baab stated that:

> "* * * [Grievant's] interest in nudism so expressed itself as to create in management's mind a reasonable doubt as to this employee's discretion and customer-acceptance on the service job for which he bid. It should be made clear that such reaction has no necessary relation to the employee's beliefs or personal ideas. It relates directly to the question of what the job requires and a worker's ability to meet these requirements. A decision as to this is management's right and prerogative." [186]

An employee's attitude may be in issue and may be important, depending upon the nature of the job.[187] However, it has been held that an employee's alleged "surly and uncooperative" attitude could justify denying a promotion only if it were shown that efforts had been made, without success, to correct such attitude, and that his attitude detracted seriously from the employee's ability to perform the job.[188]

Special requirements of the job may call for particular attributes (other than technical knowledge) in the employee filling it, justifying consideration by the employer of the employee's ability to meet those requirements. For example, the job may require a considerable degree of initiative and the capacity to perform responsible work without supervision,[189] or it may involve dealing with a "special class" of customers,[190]

---

[185] See Eagle-Picher Mining & Smelting Co., 8 LA 108, 111 (Potter, 1947).

[186] Gisholt Machine Co., 20 LA 137, 141 (1953). Also see Arbitrator Murphy in 18 LA 757, 760, involving a "special class of client"; and Arbitrator Pollard in 16 LA 586, 587-588, where the company failed to support its allegation of inability to perform the "human relations" part of a job.

[187] See Arbitrator Willcox in 30 LA 740, 743; Howlett in 26 LA 885, 890; Somers in 25 LA 316, 318.

[188] See Bethlehem Steel Co., 19 LA 186, 188 (Killingsworth, 1952). Cf. Bethlehem Steel Co., 5 LA 578, 581 (Brandschain, 1946).

[189] See Dixie Cup Co., 19 LA 639, 647 (Klamon, 1952).

[190] See Coca-Cola Bottling Co., 18 LA 757, 759-760 (Murphy, 1952).

or require that the employee be physically available for emergency work.[191]

Age as a Factor

In the absence of any age limitation in the contract, and in the absence of any showing that the age of the employee (whether young or older) detracts from his ability to perform the job, arbitrators appear reluctant to permit management to rely upon the age factor as justification for passing over a senior in favor of a junior employee, provided the senior meets the job requirements. Thus, reliance upon the age factor in by-passing the senior man was not upheld where the job had been filled in the past, without any age limit, by "older" men,[192] or where the senior man was younger than the junior.[193] Of course, the contract may recognize age as a factor to be considered thereby justifying the imposition of a reasonable age limit.[194]

While the employer ordinarily will not be justified in relying solely upon the age factor, the emphasis may be upon the employees' qualifications which, at an advanced age, may not be sufficient for the job involved. Thus, where a job required close attention continuously and a great deal of visual inspection, the employer's finding that a seventy-three year old man did not have the necessary qualifications was upheld.[195]

---

[191] See Alabama Power Co., 19 LA 393, 396 (Hawley, 1952), where the grievant lived some distance from town and had no telephone.

[192] See Arbitrator Ross in 28 LA 557, 558-559; Gilden in 20 LA 142, 147; Kaplan in 19 LA 508, 513-514.

[193] Central Screw Co., 11 LA 108, 109 (Edes, 1948).

[194] See Sutherland Paper Co., 25 LA 716, 721 (Kallenbach, 1955), involving an apprenticeship program.

[195] See Emmons Looms Harness Co., 11 LA 409, 411 (Myers, 1948).

CHAPTER 15

DISCHARGE AND DISCIPLINE

A significant percentage of cases that reach arbitration involve discharge or disciplinary penalties assessed by management. The present Chapter considers many of the concepts and standards that have been applied by arbitrators in cases of this nature.[1]

Scope of Management Right

In the absence of a collective bargaining agreement it is generally agreed that the only restriction on management's right to discharge and discipline employees is that contained in federal and state labor relations acts or other laws dealing with discrimination.[2] The same result might be reached where a collective agreement exists but contains no express limitation on such right.[3] Where an agreement expressly recognized the right of management to discharge and contained no express

---

[1] For related matter see Chapter 13, topic titled "Plant Rules". For general discussions of discharge and discipline see: Holly, "The Arbitration of Discharge Cases: A Case Study," Critical Issues in Labor Arbitration 1 (BNA Incorporated, 1957); Ross, "The Arbitration of Discharge Cases: What Happens After Reinstatement," Critical Issues in Labor Arbitration 21 (BNA Incorporated, 1957); "Arbitration Awards in Discharge Cases," 28 LA 930 (1957); Myers, "Concepts of Industrial Discipline," Management Rights and the Arbitration Process 59 (BNA Incorporated, 1956); Horton, "Arbitration of Discharge Cases," 9 Southwestern L.J. 332 (1955); "Substantive Aspects of Labor-Management Arbitration," 28 LA 943, 946-947 (1954 statistics); Lazar, Due Process on the Railroads (U. of Calif. Inst. of Ind. Rel., 1953); Skilton, Industrial Discipline and the Arbitration Process (U. of Pa. Press, 1952); Notes on Discharge For Cause, Wash. U.L.Q. 92-196 (Vol. 1949 Fall).

[2] See Arbitrator Potter in 8 LA 634, 637-638; Whiting in 4 LA 399, 403; Babb in 4 LA 56, 64. Also see Wettach in 25 LA 772, 773; Merill in 19 LA 417, 419; Coffey in 17 LA 125, 129; McCoy in 8 LA 66, 67.

[3] See Bohlinger v. National Cash Register Co., 18 LA 595 (N.Y. Sup. Ct., 1952), and cases cited therein.

limitation upon that right an arbitrator was unwilling to read a "just cause" limitation into the agreement.[4]

However, some arbitrators would imply a just cause limitation in any collective agreement. For instance, Arbitrator Walter E. Boles has held that "a 'just cause' basis for consideration of disciplinary action is, absent a clear proviso to the contrary, implied in a modern collective bargaining agreement." [5] The reasoning is: "If the Company can discharge without cause, it can lay off without cause. It can recall, transfer, or promote in violation of the seniority provisions simply by invoking its claimed right to discharge. Thus, to interpret the Agreement in accord with the claim of the Company would reduce to a nullity the fundamental provision of a labor-management agreement—the security of a worker in his job." [6] Moreover, in at least one case it has been held that management does not have an unrestricted right to discharge at its own discretion even where no bargaining relationship exists, since "the fair and generally accepted understanding of employer-employee relations is that there are obligations on the part of both parties" and that an "obligation on the employer is that an employee shall not be dismissed without cause." [7]

Most collective agreements do, in fact, require "cause" or "just cause" for discharge or discipline. The general significance of these terms has been discussed by Arbitrator Joseph D. McGoldrick:

"* * * it is common to include the right to suspend and discharge for 'just cause,' 'justifiable cause,' 'proper cause,' 'obvious cause,' or quite

---

[4] Hillyer Deutsch Edwards, Inc., 19 LA 663, 664 (Emery, 1952). Also see Arbitrator Warren in 24 LA 680, 683-684 (but Cf. Warren in 19 LA 615, 619-621); Krivonos in 22 LA 756, 759-760.

[5] Cameron Iron Works, Inc., 25 LA 295, 300-301 (1955). In general accord, Arbitrator Maggs in 22 LA 761, 763; Donnelly in 13 LA 747, 949. Also see Hebert in 25 LA 439, 440-441; Morvant in 24 LA 453, 455-456. For a case involving a clause providing that no employee could be discharged without union consent, see Crawford Clothes, Inc., 19 LA 475 (Kramer, 1952).

[6] Atwater Mfg. Co., 13 LA 747, 749 (Donnelly, 1949), quoted at length from a similar view expressed by Arbitrator Saul Wallen in another case. Id. at 750-751.

[7] Daily World Publishing Co., 3 LA 815, 817 (Rogers, 1946). During negotiations but prior to adoption of their first agreement, the parties agreed to arbitrate the dispute in question.

commonly simply for 'cause'. There is no significant difference between these various phrases. These exclude discharge for mere whim or caprice. They are, obviously, intended to include those things for which employees have traditionally been fired. They include the traditional causes of discharge in the particular trade or industry, the practices which develop in the day-to-day relations of management and labor and most recently they include the decisions of courts and arbitrators. They represent a growing body of 'common law' that may be regarded either as the latest development of the law of 'master and servant' or, perhaps, more properly as part of a new body of common law of 'Management and labor under collective bargaining agreements.' They constitute the duties owed by employees to management and, in their correlative aspect, are part of the rights of management. They include such duties as honesty, punctuality, sobriety, or, conversely, the right to discharge for theft, repeated absence or lateness, destruction of company property, brawling and the like. Where they are not expressed in posted rules, they may very well be implied, provided they are applied in a uniform, non-discriminatory manner." [8]

Some agreements enumerate the specific grounds for discipline. Arbitrator Clarence M. Updegraff has ruled that the fact that an agreement specifies certain types of misconduct for which employees may be discharged does not mean that causes not expressly stated may not be used where the grounds enumerated are merely illustrative and not exclusive.[9]

Arbitrator Maxwell Copelof has ruled that a contract giving the right to discharge for cause and making no reference to other forms of discipline does not deprive management of the right to impose forms of discipline less severe than discharge.[10] Discharge may be too severe a penalty for the offense under the circumstances of the case.

Asserting that discharge "inevitably casts a shadow on a worker's character and reputation", Arbitrator E. E. Hale would not permit discharge for lack of work where the agree-

---

[8] Worthington Corp., 24 LA 1, 6-7 (1955). For other statements defining "cause" or "just cause" see Arbitrator Parker in 21 LA 671, 672; Barrett in 19 LA 489, 493. Agreeing that there is no significant difference between these terms, Arbitrator Harris in 29 LA 567, 571.

[9] Kraft Foods Co., 9 LA 397, 398 (1947). A similar result was reached in Reynolds Metals Co., 7 LA 752, 755 (Carmichael, 1947). But the listing of some grounds was held to exclude others in Pacific Press, Inc., 26 LA 339, 344 (Hildebrand, 1956). Also see Arbitrator Handsaker in 15 LA 616, 618.

[10] Auto-Lite Battery Corp., 3 LA 122, 125 (1946). Accord, Arbitrator Kleinsorge in 23 LA 711, 713-714; Cornsweet in 17 LA 580, 585. But see Copelof in 18 LA 34, 38; Sugarman in 14 LA 16, 23-24.

ment required just cause for discharge, Arbitrator Hale stating that layoff is the proper action in case of lack of work.[11] Other arbitrators, too, have held that "discharge" is limited to termination due to fault of the employee.[12]

Probationary Employees

It has been held that where, by the agreement, new employees are not to have seniority rights until completion of a probationary period, and where the agreement is otherwise silent as to management rights with respect to new employees, they may be discharged at will,[13] except for the purpose of union discrimination.[14] Under a somewhat more strict limitation placed by an arbitrator upon the right of management to discharge probationary employees, management's action in doing so will "not be set aside unless it was arbitrary, capricious, or discriminatory"; thus, "the question in such a case goes to the good faith of the Company, not to the merits of its conclusion." [15]

Where an agreement was entirely silent as to management rights with respect to new employees, Arbitrator John A. Lapp would not read a probationary period into the agreement but nonetheless would give management wider latitude in determining just cause for discharge of new employees than allowed in case of employees who have served at least for a short period of time.[16]

Discharge v. Resignation

When an employee voluntarily resigns, concepts associated with discharge are not generally applicable. Thus, where the

---

[11] American Republics Corp., 18 LA 248, 253 (1952).

[12] See Arbitrator Howlett in 28 LA 633, 637; Hogan in 23 LA 596, 602; Kelly in 22 LA 266, 268.

[13] Joy Mfg. Co., 6 LA 430, 436 (Healy, 1946). Also see Arbitrator Kerr in 6 LA 98, 102. Cf., Stutz in 28 LA 456, 458.

[14] Flintkote Co., 3 LA 770, 771 (Cole, 1946). Where an agreement permitted discharge of probationary employees for any reason except discrimination, Arbitrator Harry Shulman ruled that they could be discharged for any reason except race, union activity, personal feeling, or sex. Ford Motor Co., 6 LA 853, 854 (1946).

[15] Ex-Cell-O Corp., 21 LA 659, 665 (R. Smith, 1953). To similar effect, Arbitrator Komaroff in 19 LA 565, 569. Also see Cornsweet in 9 LA 625, 630-631.

[16] Park Sherman Co., 2 LA 199, 200 (1946).

employee evidenced clear intent to resign arbitrators have refused to treat the matter as discharge.[17] Moreover, where the
facts and circumstances are such as to lead management reasonably to conclude that intent to resign exists, the matter may
be treated as resignation even though the individual never
actually states any intent to resign.[18]

However, if intent to resign is not adequately evidenced
or if a statement of intent to resign is involuntary or coerced,
an alleged resignation will be treated as discharge for purposes
of arbitral review.[19] Also, Arbitrator Maurice H. Merrill has
observed that: "The overwhelming weight of authority holds
that there is no voluntary quit by reason of an employee's
refusal to perform work to which he is assigned. Unless some
affirmation of an intent to quit the job is manifested by the
employee, the employer's subsequent refusal to let the employee
continue his status constitutes a discharge rather than a resignation." [20]

Conduct Away from Plant

The right of management to discharge an employee for
conduct away from the plant depends upon the effect of that
conduct upon plant operations.[21] In this regard, Arbitrator

---

[17] See Arbitrator Doyle in 29 LA 242, 245; Kelliher in 20 LA 618, 619-621;
Anderson in 20 LA 715, 717-718; Donnelly in 20 LA 47, 49; Stein in 17 LA 256,
257; Cahn in 16 LA 890, 891. Also see Pierson in 24 LA 314, 316. For cases involving efforts by employees to withdraw their resignation see Arbitrator Gray in 22
LA 238, 238-239 (permitting withdrawal); Dworkin in 29 LA 700, 703-704 (not
permitting withdrawal). Also see Slavney in 24 LA 813, 815.

[18] See Arbitrator Kelliher in 30 LA 224, 225; Jaffee in 26 LA 786, 788; Donnelly in 25 LA 608, 610-611; Lewis in 18 LA 808, 809-810; Crawford in 15 LA
282, 290. Cf., Jaffee in 19 LA 189, 191; Kelliher in 15 LA 300, 303-304; Platt in
14 LA 462, 465-466. But see Gilden in 18 LA 576, 580.

[19] See Arbitrator Kesselman in 29 LA 128, 131-132; Miller in 27 LA 11, 15-18;
Klamon in 26 LA 48, 51-52; Browser in 20 LA 868, 870; Killingsworth in 16 LA
683, 684-685; Whiting in 16 LA 170, 172-173; Shipman in 15 LA 698, 702-703; Hand
saker in 15 LA 616, 617; Healy in 6 LA 557, 559-560. Also see In re Sarle, 29 LA
83 (N.Y. Sup. Ct., 1957).

[20] Oklahoma Furniture Mfg Co., 24 LA 522, 523 (1955), citing Arbitrator Rosenfarb in 18 LA 184, 187-188; Lohman in 9 LA 857, 858-859; Cornsweet in 9 LA 625,
626; McCoy in 8 LA 647, 651-652; Wardlaw in 8 LA 248, 249; Gilden in 5 LA
300, 304; McCoy in 2 LA 483, 486; Updegraff in 1 LA 485, 486-487. Also in accord,
Platt in 24 LA 610, 614; Maggs in 23 LA 406, 408-409. For related discussion see
Chapter 5, topic titled "Observance Of Grievance Procedure".

[21] For related material see Chapter 13, topic titled "Plant Rules".

Louis C. Kesselman explained in one case:

> "The Arbitrator finds no basis in the contract or in American industrial practice to justify a discharge for misconduct away from the place of work unless:
>
> "1) behavior harms Company's reputation or product * * *
>
> "2) behavior renders employee unable to perform his duties or appear at work, in which case the discharge would be based upon inefficiency or excessive absenteeism * * *
>
> "3) behavior leads to refusal, reluctance or inability of other employees to work with him * * * [22]

Arbitrator D. Emmett Ferguson also has spoken of the extent to which management may consider conduct away from the plant as the basis for discharge:

> "* * * While it is true that the employer does not [by virtue of the employment relationship] become the guardian of the employee's every personal action and does not exercise parental control, it is equally true that in those areas having to do with the employer's business, the employer has the right to terminate the relationship if the employee's wrongful actions injuriously affect the business.
>
> "The connection between the facts which occur and the extent to which the business is affected must be reasonable and discernible. They must be such as could logically be expected to cause some result in the employer's affairs. Each case must be measured on its own merits." [23]

Employer Action Pending Court Hearing on Conduct of Employee

Where an employee, while on the job, engages in conduct which leads to his arrest, management has been permitted to take action against the employee without waiting for court determination of guilt. In one case the discharge of the employee,

---

[22] W. E. Caldwell Co., 28 LA 434, 436-437 (1957), setting aside the discharge. Discharge for conduct away from the plant was also held improper by Arbitrator Brecht in 29 LA 451, 456-459; Platt in 23 LA 808, 810-812; Marks in 20 LA 175, 177; Abrahams in 15 LA 42, 45. Also see Thompson in 26 LA 575, 578-579; Healy in 10 LA 637, 641,643.

[23] Inland Container Corp., 28 LA 312, 314 (1957), upholding discharge. Discharge for conduct away from the plant was also upheld by Arbitrator Blair in 27 LA 557, 560-562; Kharas in 26 LA 480, 482-483; Holden in 24 LA 810, 812-813; Granoff in 24 LA 603, 605-606; Cole in 21 LA 327, 328-329; McCoy in 8 LA 647, 652-653; Larkin in 6 LA 58, 59-61. Also see Keller in 26 LA 401, 402-414; Simkin in 24 LA 606, 610; Platt in 18 LA 809, 811-812.

effected prior to court trial on the charges, was upheld.[24] In several cases management has been permitted to suspend the employee pending court determination of guilt.[25]

Types of Penalties

The type of penalty assessed for wrongdoing usually is either temporary suspension or discharge.[26] Temporary suspension or "disciplinary layoff", as it is sometimes called,[27] results in loss of pay (and sometimes seniority) for the period of suspension, and mars the employee's record. When an arbitrator reinstates a discharged employee without back pay the end result is not unlike suspension.

Warnings are, in a sense, a lesser type of discipline,[28] and as noted elsewhere in this Chapter they are an important factor in evaluating discipline for subsequent offenses.

The right of management to use types of penalties other than those noted above appears to be definitely limited. This is true, for instance, in regard to use of demotion or downgrading for purposes of discipline.[29] This is likewise true of transfer,[30] withholding monetary benefits (without actual suspension),[31] and forcing public apologies.[32]

Burden and Quantum of Proof

There are two areas of proof in the arbitration of discharge and discipline cases. The first involves proof of wrongdoing; the second, assuming that guilt of wrongdoing is established and that the arbitrator is empowered to modify penalties, con-

---

[24] Continental Paper Co., 16 LA 727, 728-729 (Lewis, 1951). Also see Arbitrator Maggs in 16 LA 829, 833-835.

[25] See Arbitrator Seitz in 29 LA 442, 445-447; Ryder in 26 LA 570, 571-572; Dash in 22 LA 851, 859-860 (but limiting the period of permitted suspension).

[26] Indefinite suspension has been deemed equivalent to discharge. See Arbitrator Brecht in 29 LA 451, 455; Barrett in 27 LA 523, 527.

[27] See Koppers Co., 11 LA 334, 335 (McCoy, 1948).

[28] See Federal Labor Union v. American Can Co., 21 LA 518 (N.J. Super. Ct., 1953). Also see Arbitrator Louisell in 20 LA 826, 831; Sanders in 20 LA 36.

[29] See discussion in Chapter 13, topic titled "Demotion Of Employees".

[30] See Chapter 13, topic titled "Transfer And Promotion Of Employees".

[31] See Arbitrator Ralston in 18 LA 544, 550; Fearing in 9 LA 505, 508.

[32] See Reynolds Metals Co., 22 LA 528, 534 (Klamon, 1954)

cerns the question of whether the punishment assessed by management should be upheld or modified.[33] The latter is treated below in the topic titled "Review of Penalties Imposed by Management". The present topic deals with proof of wrongdoing.

Discharge is recognized to be the extreme industrial penalty since the employee's job, his seniority and other contractual benefits, and his reputation are at stake. Because of the seriousness of this penalty, the burden generally is held to be on the employer to prove guilt of wrongdoing, and probably always so where the agreement requires "just cause" for discharge.[34]

However, the quantum of required proof in this area is unsettled. In some cases proof beyond a reasonable doubt has been required.[35] But in other cases a lesser degree of proof has been required, such as a preponderance of the evidence,[36] or "clear and convincing" evidence,[37] or evidence "sufficient to convince a reasonable mind of guilt." [38]

An arbitrator may require a high degree of proof in one discharge case and at the same time recognize that a lesser degree may be required in others.[39] In this regard, Arbitrator

---

[33] See Arbitrator Levy in 28 LA 65, 67; Reynard in 27 LA 400, 404; Donnelly in 26 LA 913, 913-914; Pollack in 24 LA 401, 405; Howlett in 22 LA 520, 524; Cheit in 21 LA 293, 298; Livengood in 20 LA 451, 455; Stutz in 17 LA 701, 702

[34] Included among the many arbitrators who have held that the burden is upon management to prove wrongdoing are: Arbitrator Bothwell in 29 LA 781, 783-784; Cahn in 29 LA 525, 527; Babb in 29 LA 356, 358; E. Jones in 28 LA 198, 203; Maggs in 27 LA 709, 711; Jaffee in 27 LA 562, 564; Hale in 27 LA 486, 491; Holly in 27 LA 463, 465; R. Smith in 25 LA 906, 908; Kelliher in 25 LA 639, 640; McCoy, Schedler & Alexander in 25 LA 270, 274; Somers in 24 LA 728, 729-730; Pollack in 24 LA 401, 405; Reynard in 24 LA 66, 71; Warns in 24 LA 804, 806; Howlett in 22 LA 520, 524; Murphy in 21 LA 832, 834-835; Parker in 21 LA 410, 413; Cheit in 21 LA 293, 298; Havinghurst in 21 LA 186, 188; Updegraff, Klamon & Raymond in 19 LA 413, 415-416; Platt in 17 LA 423, 424. But the employee has the burden of proving the validity of the defense or excuse which he asserts in justification of his conduct. See Mississippi Lime Co., 29 LA 559, 561 (Updegraff, 1957). Also see Arbitrator Jaffee in 27 LA 562, 564-565.

[35] See Arbitrator Warns in 24 LA 804, 806; Parker in 21 LA 671, 672-673; Wagner in 7 LA 147, 149; Shipman in 2 LA 194, 196. Other instances are cited hereinbelow.

[36] See Arbitrator Levy in 28 LA 65, 67; Hale in 27 LA 486, 491; Pollack in 24 LA 401, 405; Osborne in 21 LA 471, 472; Platt in 1 LA 254, 262-263.

[37] See Arbitrator Dworkin in 27 LA 148, 150; Aaron in 8 LA 261, 268.

[38] Stockham Pipe Fittings Co., 1 ALAA par. 67,460 (1946).

[39] See Arbitrator Babb in 29 LA 272, 277; E. Jones in 28 LA 879, 882-883; Hale in 27 LA 486, 491; Wagner in 7 LA 147, 149-150.

Russell A. Smith has observed that: "In general, arbitrators probably have used the 'preponderance of the evidence' rule or some similar standard in deciding fact issues before them, including issues presented by ordinary discipline and discharge cases." [40] But Arbitrator Smith also noted that a higher degree of proof frequently is required where the alleged misconduct is "of a kind recognized and punished by the criminal law", and he concluded:

> "* * * it seems reasonable and proper to hold that alleged misconduct of a kind which carries the stigma of general social disapproval as well as disapproval under accepted canons of plant discipline should be clearly and convincingly established by the evidence. Reasonable doubts raised by the proofs should be resolved in favor of the accused. This may mean that the employer will at times be required, for want of sufficient proof, to withhold or rescind disciplinary action which in fact is fully deserved, but this kind of result is inherent in any civilized system of justice." [41]

In fact, arbitrators have often recognized that proof beyond a reasonable doubt should be required where the alleged offense involves an element of moral turpitude or criminal intent.[42] Moreover, where the offense is of this type management may be required to prove, by a high degree of proof, both the commission of the act, and the existence of criminal intent.[43] When, however, the alleged offense is not one that is recognized by the criminal law or does not otherwise involve moral turpitude, Arbitrator Benjamin Aaron has urged vigorously that proof beyond a reasonable doubt should not be required by arbitrators.[44]

In many cases the arbitrator may be able to proceed most realistically along the lines followed by Arbitrators Alexander,

---

[40] Kroger Co., 25 LA 906, 908 (1955).
[41] Ibid.
[42] See Arbitrator Bothwell in 29 LA 781, 784; Babb in 29 LA 272, 277; E. Jones in 28 LA 879, 882-883; Holly in 27 LA 463, 465; Somers in 24 LA 728, 729-730; Hale in 24 LA 470, 481-482; Warns in 23 LA 534, 536; Murphy in 21 LA 832, 834-835; Lesser in 11 LA 301, 302-303. Also see Prasow in 27 LA 863, 866, where management had a very high burden of proof after the employee had been acquitted in a court action involving the same incident.
[43] Aladdin Industries, Inc., 27 LA 463, 465 (Holly, 1956); Marlin Rockwell Corp., 24 LA 728, 729-730 (Somers, 1955).
[44] Aaron "Some Procedural Problems in Arbitration," 10 Vanderbilt L. Rev. 733, 740-742 (1957).

McCoy, Schedler and Whiting in reviewing discharges for strike misconduct:

> "The Arbitration Agreement provides that the Arbitrator shall determine whether there was reasonable cause for the discharge. It does not seem to us that in the making of such determination, we should be bound by a doctrine of the criminal law as to proof beyond a reasonable doubt. We think that the issue we have to decide in any particular case is: Is the employee guilty, and if so, is the act that he committed serious enough to justify discharge?" [45]

Review of Penalties Imposed by Management

Several views have been expressed by arbitrators regarding the nature of their function in reviewing disciplinary penalties imposed by management.

The view that the determination of the penalty for misconduct is properly a function of management and that an arbitrator should hesitate to substitute his judgment and discretion for that of management has been elaborated by Arbitrator Whitley P. McCoy:

> "Where an employee has violated a rule or engaged in conduct meriting disciplinary action, it is primarily the function of management to decide upon the proper penalty. If management acts in good faith upon a fair investigation and fixes a penalty not inconsistent with that imposed in other like cases, an arbitrator should not disturb it. The mere fact that management has imposed a somewhat different penalty or a somewhat more severe penalty than the arbitrator would have, if he had had the decision to make originally, is no justification for changing it. The minds of equally reasonable men differ. A consideration which would weigh heavily with one man will seem of less importance to another. A circumstance which highly aggravates an offense in one man's eyes may be only slight aggravation to another. If an arbitrator could substitute his judgment and discretion for the judgment and discretion honestly exercised by management, then the functions of management would have been abdicated, and unions would take every case to arbitration. The result would be as intolerable to employees as to management. The only circumstances under which a penalty imposed by management can be rightfully set aside by an arbitrator are those where discrimination, unfairness, or capricious

---

[45] Southern Bell Telephone & Telegraph Co., 25 LA 85, 87 (1955). Also see Arbitrator Granoff in 17 LA 258, 264.

and arbitrary action are proved—in other words, where there has been abuse of discretion." [46]

Under an agreement requiring just cause, Arbitrator Wilber C. Bothwell held that "the arbitrator should not substitute his judgment for that of management unless he finds that the penalty is excessive, unreasonable, or that management has abused its discretion." [47] In practical effect views such as those quoted above place upon the grievant, once management establishes guilt of wrongdoing, a burden of showing that the penalty assessed by management was too severe and should be modified by the arbitrator.

Arbitrator Harry H. Platt holds the following view concerning the function of the arbitrator in reviewing discipline assessed under agreements requiring cause:

> "It is ordinarily the function of an Arbitrator in interpreting a contract provision which requires 'sufficient cause' as a condition precedent to discharge not only to determine whether the employee involved is guilty of wrong-doing and, if so, to confirm the employer's right to discipline where its exercise is essential to the objective of efficiency, but also to safeguard the interests of the discharged employee by making reasonably sure that the causes for discharge were just and equitable and such as would appeal to reasonable and fair-minded persons as warranting discharge. To be sure, no standards exist to aid an arbitrator in finding a conclusive answer to such a question and, therefore, perhaps the best he can do is to decide what reasonable man, mindful of the habits and customs of industrial life and of the standards of justice and fair dealing prevalent in the community, ought to have done under similar circumstances and in that light to decide whether the conduct of the discharged employee was defensible and the disciplinary penalty just." [48]

---

[46] Stockham Pipe Fittings Co., 1 LA 160, 162 (1945). In this case the submission specifically empowered the arbitrator to determine "what disposition" should be made of the dispute. Arbitrator McCoy repeated portions of this statement in 19 LA 495, 497. Also see similar statements by Arbitrator Stouffer in 26 LA 395, 397; Kadish in 25 LA 568, 571; Gilden in 21 LA 105, 107; Reid in 19 LA 724, 727; Prasow in 13 LA 28, 30.

[47] Franz Food Products, Inc., 28 LA 543, 548 (1957). To similar effect, Arbitrator Meltzer in 28 LA 303, 308; Hale in 27 LA 486, 493; Reynard in 27 LA 400, 404; Stouffer in 26 LA 395, 397; Kadish in 25 LA 568, 571; Dworkin in 23 LA 696, 701; Gilden in 21 LA 105, 107; Anrod in 20 LA 653, 658; Luskin in 19 LA 5, 7; Donaldson in 13 LA 943, 945. Also see Warns in 27 LA 512, 516; Granoff in 24 LA 603, 606; Reid in 19 LA 724, 727.

[48] Riley Stoker Corp., 7 LA 764, 767 (1947). Arbitrator Platt made a similar statement in 23 LA 808, 810. In Indianapolis Chair Co., 20 LA 706, 709 (1953), Arbitrator W Howard Mann stated that in reviewing discharge, "The Arbitrator must accept the responsibility of making an actual determination."

An arbitrator's view of his function in reviewing discipline may vary according to the nature of the offense. For instance, Arbitrator Robert G. Howlett has stated that an arbitrator should be more hesitant to overrule penalties where the offense is directly related to the company's product than where it involves primarily the personal behavior of the employee and is only indirectly related to production.[49] Also, where the safety of the public is a direct factor in a discharge, Arbitrator Whitley P. McCoy would require the union to "show that the decision was arbitrary, made in bad faith, or clearly wrong." [50]

Finally, it should be recognized that while arbitrators do not lightly interfere with management decisions in discharge and discipline matters this by no means suggests that they fail to act firmly when management's decisions are found to be unjust or unreasonable under all the circumstances. In this regard, Arbitrator Charles B. Spaulding replied as follows where an employer cited awards allegedly to the effect that arbitrators should not interfere with discipline assessed by management where the agreement permits it to exercise judgment:

> "Three answers to this line or argument seem appropriate. The first is that arbitrators very frequently do step in and upset the decisions of Management. The second is that, if arbitrators could not do so, arbitration would be of little import, since the judgment of management would in so many cases constitute the final verdict. Finally, the more careful statement of the principle would probably run to the effect that where the contract uses such terms as discharge for 'cause' or for 'good cause' or for 'justifiable cause' an arbitrator will not lightly upset a decision reached by competent careful management which acts in the full light of all the facts, and without any evidence of bias, haste or lack of emotional balance. Even under these conditions, if the decision is such as to shock the sense of justice or ordinary reasonable men, we suspect that arbitrators have a duty to interfere. Since the acts of Management in this case do shock our sense of justice, and since they do seem to have occurred in a situation of emotional tension, in haste, and without a very careful weighing of the facts, we find ourselves inevitably driven to overthrow the decision of this Management." [51]

---

[49] Valley Steel Casting Co., 22 LA 520, 524-525 (1954).
[50] United Air Lines, Inc., 19 LA 585, 587 (1952), wherein the union did make such showing. Also see Arbitrator Lennard in 30 LA 830, 834-835.
[51] Fruehauf Trailer Co, 16 LA 666, 670 (1951)

Authority of Arbitrator to Modify Penalties

Many agreements give the arbitrator express authority to modify penalties found to be improper or too severe.[52] Also the agreement may give him such authority by implication.[53] Some agreements expressly limit the arbitrator's authority to modify penalties. Where the agreement fails to deal with the matter, the right of the arbitrator to change or modify penalties found to be improper or too severe may be deemed to be inherent in his power to decide the sufficiency of cause, as elaborated by Arbitrator Harry H. Platt:

> "In many disciplinary cases, the reasonableness of the penalty imposed on an employee rather than the existence of proper cause for disciplining him is the question an arbitrator must decide. This is not so under contracts or submission agreements which expressly prohibit an arbitrator from modifying or reducing a penalty if he finds that disciplinary action was justified, but most current labor agreements do not contain such limiting clause. In disciplinary cases generally, therefore, most arbitrators exercise the right to change or modify a penalty if it is found to be improper or too severe, under all the circumstances of the situation. This right is deemed to be inherent in the arbitrator's power to discipline and in his authority to finally settle and adjust the dispute before him:" [54]

Leniency

Modification by an arbitrator of a penalty found to be too severe should not be confused with the exercise of leniency (or clemency). The distinction between these actions was

---

[52] The Chrysler Corporation Umpire, for instance, is given this power. Wolff, Crane & Cole, "The Chrysler-UAW Umpire System," The Arbitrator and the Parties 111, 116 (BNA Incorporated, 1958). The parties clothed the arbitrator with this power at the hearing in Dayton Malleable Iron Co., 17 LA 666 (Hampton, 1951).

[53] See McInerney Spring & Wire Co., 21 LA 80, 82 (R. Smith, 1953).

[54] Platt, "The Arbitration Process in the Settlement of Labor Disputes," 31 J. Am. Jud. Soc. 54, 58 (1947). This view was applied by Arbitrator Platt in 9 LA 810, 811, 813. To similar effect as to inherent authority to modify penalties, Arbitrator Levy in 28 LA 65, 69; Wyckoff in 25 LA 634, 637-638; Hebert in 25 LA 439, 442; Dworkin in 19 LA 65, 71-72; Hepburn in 9 LA 345, 348. Also see Gilden in 29 LA 464, 466; Howlett in 21 LA 729, 733; Livengood in 21 LA 456, 460-461; Reid in 21 LA 322, 325; McCoy in 10 LA 260, 261. In Reading Tube Corp. v. Steel Workers Federation, 20 LA 780, 783-784 (Pa. Super. Ct., 1953), power of the arbitrator to modify penalties was deemed necessarily implied in the clause making management's decisions as to discipline subject to arbitration. In general accord, In re Adler, Inc., 20 LA 546 (N.Y. Sup. Ct., 1953); Niles-Bement-Pond Co. v. UAW, 20 LA 520, 522 (Conn. Sup. Ct. of Err., 1953). But see American Brass Co. v. Brass Workers, 22 LA 871, 875 (Conn. Sup. Ct. of Err., 1954).

emphasized by Arbitrator Whitley P. McCoy when he recognized the power of arbitrators to modify penalties found on the basis of mitigating circumstances to be too severe for the offense, but at the same time declared that arbitrators have no authority to grant clemency where the penalty assessed by management is not found too severe.[55]

The fact that an arbitrator considers that he has no power of leniency or clemency, and accordingly that he must sustain management's disciplinary action where just cause is found, does not prevent him from *recommending* leniency when he personally feels that it should be considered by management.[56] Inherent in such recommendations is silent recognition by arbitrators of powers of leniency or clemency in management.[57]

Factors in Evaluating Penalties

Numerous factors may be relevant in the review or evaluation of penalties assessed by management for misconduct of employees. The more prominent of these factors are considered briefly below.

Nature of the Offense: Summary Discharge v. Corrective Discipline

It is said to be "axiomatic that the degree of penalty should be in keeping with the seriousness of the offense."[58] In this regard, too, Arbitrator Whitley P. McCoy has explained:

"Offenses are of two general classes: (1) those extremely serious offenses such as stealing, striking a foreman, persistent refusal to obey a legitimate order, etc., which usually justify summary discharge without the

[55] Chattanooga Box & Lumber Co., 10 LA 260, 261 (1948). Also indicating that arbitrators have no power of leniency or clemency: In re American Safety Razor Corp., 18 LA 594 (N.Y. Sup. Ct., 1952); In re Modernage Furniture Corp., 4 LA 833 (N.Y. Sup. Ct., 1946).
[56] See Arbitrator Rosenfarb in 24 LA 674, 675-676; Dworkin in 23 LA 696, 702; Miller in 22 LA 620, 623; Marshall in 22 LA 573, 576, and in 18 LA 849, 852; Howlett in 22 LA 520, 527; Allen in 21 LA 587, 589; Kelliher in 21 LA 444, 446; Anrod in 20 LA 653, 658; Seward in 17 LA 334, 335. Also see Kaplan in 16 LA 66, 68.
[57] Arbitrators also have expressly recognized this power in management. See Arbitrator McCoy in 12 LA 1190, 1192; Gorder in 9 LA 73, 77. Also see Stowe in 25 LA 13, 16.
[58] Capital Airlines, Inc., 25 LA 13, 16 (Stowe, 1955).

necessity of prior warnings or attempts at corrective discipline; (2) those less serious infractions of plant rules or proper conduct such as tardiness, absence without permission, careless workmanship, insolence, etc., which call not for discharge for the first offense (and usually not even for the second or third offense) but for some milder penalty aimed at correction." [59]

As to the less serious offenses, the concept of corrective or progressive discipline has been noted by arbitrators. Arbitrator M. S. Ryder, for instance, has stated:

"Further, if the employer so chooses, and it is common practice in industry, the employer may adopt a corrective approach toward penalty, by making second and third offenses of the same nature, or of another nature, cumulative in terms of the degree of severity of penalty imposed for each of the subsequent proven offenses so as to dissuade any further commissions." [60]

However, Arbitrator Robert S. Thompson has cautioned:

"In industrial practice discipline is often 'progressive' or 'corrective' in nature. Warning is tried before suspension; suspension before discharge. Penalties are designed to correct if possible. While theories and practices of 'progressive' or 'corrective' discipline may be in wide use, it does not follow that every Company must, in the absence of contract provisions, adopt such views. Every business and industry has its own peculiar conditions. An Arbitrator should be slow to substitute his own judgment as to the appropriateness of penalties on the basis of theories which seem to have wide appeal." [61]

Due Process Considerations

Discharge and disciplinary action by management has been reversed where the action violated basic notions of fairness or due process. This was true, for instance, where the employer gave employees no chance to be heard but discharged them summarily upon learning that they had been convicted of

---

[59] Huntington Chair Corp., 24 LA 490, 491 (1955). Also recognizing the propriety of summary discharge for serious offenses, Arbitrator Jaffee in 27 LA 768, 772-773; McCoy, Schedler & Alexander in 25 LA 270, 276; Stowe in 25 LA 13, 16; Marshall in 22 LA 573, 576; Seward in 19 LA 210, 212; Updegraff in 17 LA 224, 225. In some of these cases the arbitrator expressly stated that summary discharge is permissible even though the employee has long seniority with a good record.

[60] Michigan Seamless Tube Co., 24 LA 132, 133-134 (1955). Also see statement by Arbitrator Platt in 25 LA 733, 735 (applying corrective discipline); McCoy in 24 LA 490, 492; R. Smith in 21 LA 80, 83-84; Allen in 17 LA 217, 221-222. For further discussion see comments by Arbitrator Alexander in Management Rights and the Arbitration Process 76, 79-82 (BNA Incorporated, 1956).

[61] Niagara Frontier Transit System, 24 LA 783, 785 (1955), reducing the penalty on the basis of grievant's long seniority.

larceny by a court.[62] A similar result was reached where management discharged an employee on the basis of a finding by the company physician without giving the employee opportunity to present countervailing medical testimony.[63] Under some agreements management must discuss its complaint against an employee in the grievance procedure before discharging him; a discharge was set aside where management failed to so discuss the complaint.[64]

A discharge was set aside where delay in notifying the employee of his discharge made it difficult for him to obtain witnesses in his own behalf (due to the fact that intoxication was the offense charged).[65]

Post-Discharge Conduct or Charges

Some agreements require that all reasons for discharge action be given to the employee at the time of discharge. Under such provisions it has been held that only evidence bearing on the charges made at the time of discharge should be considered in determining the existence of cause for punishment.[66] Even without such specific contractual provision, arbitrators have held that discharge, to use the words of Arbitrator Paul N. Guthrie, "must stand or fall upon the reason given at the time of discharge"; other reasons may not be added when the case reaches arbitration.[67] Arbitrator James T. Burke reasoned in one of these cases that: "The only relevant evidence are the facts which the person making the discharge was in possession of at the time he acted. A discharge cannot be based upon con-

---

[62] United States Steel Corp., 29 LA 272, 277-278 (Babb, 1957), citing other cases also recognizing the obligation of management to make appropriate inquiry before discharging employees in such situations. Also see Arbitrator Maggs in 16 LA 829, 834. But see Cahn in 19 LA 674, 676.

[63] American Iron & Machine Works Co., 19 LA 417, 419-420 (Merrill, 1952). Also see Arbitrator D. Wolff in 19 LA 471, 474-475.

[64] Oklahoma Furniture Mfg. Co., 24 LA 522, 524-526 (Merrill, 1955). Also see Arbitrator Platt in 17 LA 412, 417-418.

[65] National Carbide Co., 27 LA 128, 130 (Warns, 1956).

[66] See Arbitrator Seward in 29 LA 635, 640-643; Brown in 1 LA 153, 154.

[67] West Virginia Pulp & Paper Co., 10 LA 117, 118 (1947). To similar effect, Arbitrator Brecht in 29 LA 451, 457; Healy in 12 LA 108, 115; Burke in 3 LA 607, 608. Also see Abernethy in 30 LA 1039, 1042-1043.

jecture, surmise, suspicion, or anything but hard, material, and known facts." [68]

However, in some other cases arbitrators have considered post-discharge misconduct or charges based upon evidence not discovered until after the employee was discharged.[69] In one of the latter cases Arbitrator Gabriel N. Alexander stated:

> "Where a Company knows of several reasons in support of discharge or discipline, but only specifies one of them to the employee and the Union, it may well be that it should be precluded from advancing the others to an Arbitrator. But this is not that kind of a situation. Here Management acted promptly to advise the Union of the falsification [discovered after discharge] as soon as it learned of it. I conclude therefore that the falsification is properly part of this case." [70]

In a case where an employee was disciplined for sleeping on duty management failed to prove conclusively that the employee was asleep but Arbitrator Whitley P. McCoy nonetheless upheld the penalty assessed by management since the evidence did establish a related offense:

> "The Association argues that since the Company made no contention that the penalty was imposed for any other reason than being asleep, the Board has no right to justify the penalty unless it finds that he was asleep. I cannot agree with that contention. The penalty was imposed as a result of the facts. * * * Giving a name to those facts is not important. There was a time when the criminal law was so technical that on a given set of facts a conviction of larceny would be set aside on the ground that those facts constituted embezzlement, and vice versa. Arbitration should not be tied up with such technicalities. Cambre did certain things—leaned back in his swivel chair, put his feet on the desk, closed his eyes, relaxed his muscles, leaned his head back against the wall, and assumed the position and appearance of sleeping. Those facts constitute an offense, and I do not think the Board is bound to set a penalty aside merely because the facts fail to prove conclusively that Cambre was asleep." [71]

---

[68] Borden's Farm Products, Inc., 3 LA 607, 608 (1945).

[69] See Arbitrator Simkin in 26 LA 836, 839; McCoy, Schedler & Alexander in 25 LA 270, 274-277; Alexander in 24 LA 353, 355; McCoy in 19 LA 495, 497-498; Updegraff in 17 LA 224, 226-227, and in 14 LA 745, 747. For related matters see Chapter 8, topic titled " 'New' Evidence At Arbitration Hearing"; Chapter 7, topic titled "Extent Of Permissible Deviation From Pre-Arbitral Discussion Of Case".

[70] Lyon, Inc., 24 LA 353, 355 (1955). Discovery of new information can equally well serve the interests of the grievant. See Arbitrator Thompson in 21 LA 58, 58-59.

[71] Esso Standard Oil Co., 19 LA 495, 597-498 (1952).

Double Jeopardy

By application of "double jeopardy" concepts it has been held that once discipline for a given offense has been imposed and accepted it cannot thereafter be increased.[72] In one of these cases an employee who was laid off for five days for fighting could not thereafter be discharged merely because he was formally convicted by a court of assault with a deadly weapon (based upon the fighting incident) ; discharge was said to violate the principle of double jeopardy.[73] The double-jeopardy concept was applied also where management delayed the enforcement of discipline, Arbitrator George S. Bradley declaring:

> "While postponing of the imposition of disciplinary action does not amount to double jeopardy it does have some of the elements thereof. Holding the threat of the penalty over the employee for approximately four months is something of a penalty in itself. Double penalties for the same offense are contrary to our concept of justice and fairness." [74]

On the other hand, where employees were first suspended for participating in an unauthorized work stoppage and later discharged on the basis of subsequently obtained evidence indicating that they had led the stoppage (a dischargeable offense under the contract), Arbitrator W. Willard Wirtz would not honor a plea of double jeopardy. Arbitrator Wirtz stated that the rule of double jeopardy presupposes a full hearing before the first penalty is imposed; since a full hearing of the type assumed by the rule is not customary in industrial disciplinary procedures and was not had in this case when the suspension penalty was imposed, the rule was inapplicable.[75]

Moreover, the fact that an employee has paid a fine or served a jail sentence for acts committed in connection with his employment does not preclude an arbitrator from taking the acts into account in deciding whether the employer had just

---

[72] Durham Hosiery Mills, 24 LA 356, 358 (Livengood, 1955); International Harvester Co., 16 LA 616 (McCoy, 1951). Also see Arbitrator Ryder in 24 LA 132, 134.

[73] Durham Hosiery Mills, 24 LA 356, 358 (Livengood, 1955).

[74] Ashland Oil & Refining Co., 28 LA 874, 878 (1957). Cf., Arbitrator Seward in 12 LA 344, 345.

[75] International Harvester Co., 13 LA 610, 613-614 (1949).

cause for disciplining the employee, despite the claim that this amounts to double jeopardy.[76] Also, arbitrators have rejected the claim that consideration of prior offenses in determining the propriety of the penalty assessed for a later offense constitutes double jeopardy.[77]

Grievant's Past Record

Some consideration generally is given to the past record of any disciplined or discharged employee. An offense may be mitigated by a good past record and it may be aggravated by a poor one. Indeed, the employee's past record often is a major factor in the determination of the proper penalty for his offense.

In many cases arbitrators have reduced penalties in consideration, in part, of the employee's long good past record.[78] On the other hand, an arbitrator's refusal to interfere with a penalty may be based in part upon the employee's poor past record.[79] In one case Arbitrator Morris J. Kaplan held that, although no single incident cited by the employer was sufficient to warrant discharge, the general pattern of the employee's unsatisfactory conduct and performance, as established by a series of incidents over an extended period, was preponderant evidence justifying discharge.[80]

But there are limitations in the consideration of past offenses. For instance, a distinction should be made between rule

---

[76] Westinghouse Electric Corp., 26 LA 836, 846 (Simkin, 1956), where the arbitrator also stated, however, that he could consider the previous punishment in determining the severity of the penalty assessed.

[77] F. J. Kress Box Co., 24 LA 401, 407 (Pollack, 1955); Douglas Aircraft Co., 20 LA 331, 334 (Bernstein, 1953). Prior offenses are often considered in evaluating the propriety of penalties. See this Chapter, subtopic titled "Grievant's Past Record".

[78] E.g., Arbitrator Hebert in 29 LA 604; Dunlop in 28 LA 668; Haughton in 28 LA 394; Thompson in 26 LA 575; Stowe in 25 LA 13; D. Wolff in 24 LA 549; Maggs in 21 LA 676; R. Smith in 21 LA 80; Cole in 21 LA 32; Ralston in 20 LA 465; Sanders in 20 LA 36; Blair in 9 LA 387.

[79] See Arbitrator Sembower in 30 LA 948; Guthrie in 27 LA 358; Simkin in 26 LA 836; Pollack in 24 LA 401; Abersold in 24 LA 145; McCoy in 19 LA 495, 497; Scheiber in 9 LA 765; Bowles in 9 LA 447; Rottschaefer in 6 LA 294; Gilden in 4 LA 434. Also see Bernstein in 20 LA 431, 334.

[80] Electronic Corp. of America, 3 LA 217, 218-220 (1946). To similar effect, National Fireworks Ordnance Corp., 20 LA 274, 275 (Roberts, 1953). Also see Arbitrator Pollack in 24 LA 401, 407; Holly in 24 LA 48, 52. Cf., Dworkin in 29 LA 305, 311; Lehoczky in 9 LA 606, 608-609; Pollard in 8 LA 234, 245.

infractions that have been proved and mere past "charges". Thus, it has been held that while an employer might have the right to post notations alleging rule infractions on employee records, the failure of the employer to notify employees of alleged infractions at the time of occurrence precludes him from using the notations to support disciplinary action at a later date, since employees should not be required to disprove stale charges.[81]   Also, collective agreements sometimes limit consideration of an employee's record to a specified period.[82]

The need for a time limitation in the consideration of past offenses may also be recognized even where the agreement does not expressly impose one.   Thus, Arbitrator John Day Larkin, while emphasizing the need to consider grievant's past record, has observed:

> "In general we should say that in discharge cases the past conduct of the employee in question is of concern to the arbitrator called upon to review Management's disciplinary action. If the employee has an excellent record in the Company's service, the Union is sure to emphasize this. No arbitrator can fail to take note of a good record, the absence of prior warning notice, and other factors which may pertain to the employee's fitness to be continued on his job.

> "By the same token, if an employee's past performance has been one of increasing disregard of his responsibilities to his job and to the employer who is paying him, no arbitrator can rightly sweep this sort of evidence under the rug and confine himself to technical evidence pertaining to a particular incident on a particular day. To do so would not add to the cause of good industrial relations. It might do irreparable harm to the arbitration process.

> "However, this does not mean that we are to consider everything that is introduced as having equal weight and significance. We symphathize with the position often taken by unions that there should be some limitation on how far back in the record one should be permitted to go in the matter of digging up old scores. Such historic incidents should be close

---

[81] Consolidated Vultee Aircraft Corp., 10 LA 907, 909 (Dwyer, 1948). Also see Arbitrator Belkin in 32 LA 86; Scheiber in 24 LA 538, 541. The recording of warnings given to employees of unsatisfactory work has been held to be a form of discipline which may require proper cause. Federal Labor Union v. American Can Co., 21 LA 518 (N.J. Super. Ct., 1953). Also see Arbitrator Louisell in 20 LA 826, 831.
[82] See San Diego Electric Railway Co., 10 LA 119 (Aaron, 1948). Also see Pacific Mills, 3 LA 141 (McCoy, 1946).

enough in their relation to the problem involved in the immediate case to warrant consideration." [83]

Evidence of past acts showing a course of conduct has sometimes been considered relevant in some types of cases as indicating some likelihood that the employee committed the specific act with which he was charged.[84]

Length of Service With Company

Long service with the company, particularly if unblemished, is a definite factor in the employee's favor when his discharge is reviewed through arbitration.[85] Arbitrators have recognized that the loss of seniority may work great hardship on the employee,[86] and that it is not conducive to the improvement of relations between other workers and management.[87]

Knowledge of Rules; Warnings

It has been reported, on the basis of examining over 1000 discharge cases, that one of the two most commonly recognized principles in arbitration of such cases is that there must be reasonable rules or standards, consistently applied and enforced and widely disseminated.[88] Concerning notice of rules, Arbitrator William M. Hepburn has stated: "Just cause requires that employees be informed of a rule, infraction of which may result

---

[83] Borg-Warner Corp., 22 LA 589, 596 (1954). Also regarding "digging up" past matters, see Arbitrator Reynolds in 17 LA 737, 740. Also see Abersold in 24 LA 145, 150.

[84] See Arbitrator Pedrick in 12 LA 262; Gorder in 3 LA 455; D. Wolff in 3 LA 285. But see Sembower in 30 LA 948, 950. For discussion see Wirtz, "Due Process of Arbitration," The Arbitrator and The Parties 1, 20-21 (BNA Incorporated, 1958), where it is noted that caution obviously should be exercised in using evidence of past acts for this purpose.

[85] For instances where this factor was given weight see Arbitrator Gilden in 29 LA 464; Dunlop in 28 LA 668; Marshall in 28 LA 121; Simkin in 24 LA 606; Platt in 23 LA 808; Maggs in 21 LA 676; Cole in 21 LA 32; Young in 20 LA 543; Sanders in 20 LA 36.

[86] Certain-Teed Products Corp., 24 LA 606, 609 (Simkin, 1955); Bethlehem Steel Co., 2 LA 194, 195-196 (Shipman, 1945). Also see Arbitrator Gilden in 29 LA 464.

[87] Argonne Worsted Co., 4 LA 81, 83 (Copelof, 1946).

[88] "Arbitration Awards in Discharge Cases," 28 LA 930, 931-932 (1957).

in suspension or discharge, unless conduct is so clearly wrong that specific reference is not necessary." [89]

In this general regard, too, evidence concerning the giving of warnings of unsatisfactory conduct prior to discharge or discipline is relevant in determining whether the penalty was justified.[90] Where an employee continues prohibited conduct after having been warned, the fact that he was warned stands against him.[91] On the other hand, failure to give prior warnings may be one of the reasons for the refusal by an arbitrator to sustain disciplinary action (particularly discharge).[92] No warning is required where the offense is legally and morally wrong.[93]

Lax Enforcement of Rules

Arbitrators have not hesitated to disturb penalties assessed, without clear and timely warning, where the employer over a period of time has condoned its violation in the past. Lax enforcement of rules may lead employees reasonably to believe that the conduct in question is sanctioned by management.[94]

Unequal or Discriminatory Treatment

It is generally accepted that enforcement of rules and assessment of discipline must be exercised in a consistent manner; all employees who engage in the same type of misconduct must be treated essentially the same unless a reasonable basis

---

[89] Lockheed Aircraft Corp, 28 LA 829, 831 (1957). Also requiring clear notice of rules and of the possible penalties for their violation (particularly where discharge is one of the penalties), Arbitrator Maggs in 21 LA 676; Reid in 21 LA 322; Louisell in 20 LA 826; Prasow in 5 LA 109. For related material see Chapter 13, subtopic titled "Posting Of Rules".

[90] Warnings ordinarily need not be in writing unless required by contract. See Glen L. Martin Co., 6 LA 500 (Brecht, 1947).

[91] See Arbitrator Maggs in 21 LA 676; Scheiber in 9 LA 765; Bowles in 9 LA 447.

[92] See Arbitrator Levy in 28 LA 65; McCoy in 27 LA 160; Wyckoff in 25 LA 634; Marshall in 24 LA 555; Stutz in 23 LA 516; Hazell in 22 LA 649, Granoff in 17 LA 258, 266; Aaron in 7 LA 231; Prasow in 5 LA 109.

[93] Lockheed Aircraft Corp., 28 LA 829, 831 (Hepburn, 1957) Glen L. Martin Co., 27 LA 768, 773 (Jaffee, 1956).

[94] See Arbitrator Levy in 28 LA 65; Howlett in 21 LA 729; Ryder in 20 LA 342; Granoff in 19 LA 125; Davey in 18 LA 27; Kelliher in 8 LA 177; Singer in 6 LA 762; Prasow in 5 LA 109; Brandschain in 3 LA 557; Gilden in 3 LA 423.

exists for variations in the assessment of punishment (such as different degrees of fault or mitigating or aggravating circumstances affecting some but not all of the employees).[95] In this regard, Arbitrator Benjamin Aaron has declared: "Absolute consistency in the handling of rule violations is, of course, an impossibility, but that fact should not excuse random and completely inconsistent disciplinary practices." [96]

Where reasonable basis for variations in penalties does exist, they will be permitted.[97] That variations in penalties assessed do not necessarily mean that management's action has been improper or discriminatory is persuasively elaborated by Arbitrator J. Charles Short:

"* * * The term 'discrimination' connotes a distinction in treatment, especially an unfair distinction. The prohibition against discrimination requires like treatment under like circumstances. In the case of offenses the circumstances include the nature of the offense, the degree of fault and the mitigating and aggravating factors. There is no discrimination, or no departure from the consistent or uniform treatment of employees, merely because of variations in discipline reasonably appropriate to the variations in circumstances. Two employees may refuse a work assignment. For one it is his first offense, there being no prior warning or misconduct standing against his record. The other has been warned and disciplined for the very same offense on numerous occasions. It cannot be seriously contended that discrimination results if identical penalties are not meted out." [98]

---

[95] Arbitrators have frequently refused to uphold variations in punishment where not supported by reasonable basis. See Arbitrator King in 28 LA 775; Dworkin in 27 LA 209; Lehoczky in 27 LA 131; Reynard in 26 LA 934; Duff in 26 LA 915; Stouffer in 26 LA 638; Stowe in 25 LA 13; Somers in 24 LA 728; Kadish in 24 LA 102; Maggs in 21 LA 676; Healy in 12 LA 108; Singer in 6 LA 762. Also see Simkin in 26 LA 836. But see Cahn in 28 LA 355 (permitting unequal punishment as long as there was no discrimination because of union activity). Also see Gorder in 9 LA 73, 77 (recognizing the power of leniency in management). Many arbitrators have recognized that union leaders have a special responsibility to promote use of the gievance procedure in lieu of self-help but arbitrators are by no means agreed as to whether failure to fulfill this responsibility is proper basis for punishment or for variations in punishment. For cases see Chapter 5, subtopic titled "Use of Grievance Procedure vs. Self-Help".

[96] Aaron, "The Uses of the Past in Arbitration," Arbitration Today 1, 10 (BNA Incorporated, 1955). Also see Arbitrator Simkin in 26 LA 836, 844.

[97] See Arbitrator R. Smith in 25 LA 663; Short in 21 LA 843; Undergraff in 19 LA 601; Morrissey in 15 LA 829; Pedrick in 15 LA 308, 313; Wirtz in 13 LA 610; Myers in 11 LA 462. Particularly strong evidence is required to prove discrimination because of union activity. See Arbitrator Carmody in 23 LA 38, 39; Bailer in 20 LA 7, 9; Doyle in 19 LA 111, 122; Scarborough in 2 LA 520, 521; McCoy in 1 LA 447, 448-449.

[98] Alan Wood Steel Co., 21 LA 843, 849 (1954).

Management Also at Fault

Where an employee is guilty of wrongdoing but management (ordinarily the supervisor) is also at fault in some respect in connection with the employee's conduct, the arbitrator may be persuaded to reduce or set aside the penalty assessed by management.[99]

Table of Offenses

Many types of conduct have been the "just cause" basis of industrial discipline—discharge or a lesser penalty. Detailed analysis of each individual type of conduct is beyond the scope of this volume. However, to review the more usual grounds for industrial discipline, and to make numerous cases quickly available to the reader, the following table is offered. Two considerations should be emphasized. First, in some cases the arbitrator considers the misconduct sufficiently serious to justify the employer in discharging for the first offense and even in the face of mitigating circumstances. Second, in the vast majority of cases there is no such "automatic" basis for discharge; in these cases all factors relevant to industrial discipline may be considered by the arbitrator in determining whether the employee deserved discharge, some lesser penalty, or no penalty at all—each case is thus decided largely on the basis of its own facts and circumstances.

Included in the table are the bulk of discharges and discipline cases reported in Volumes 16 to 30 inclusive of The Bureau of National Affairs Labor Arbitration Reports. Most of the cases followed by an asterisk (*) discuss one or more of the following: elements of the offense, proof or evidence required, mitigating or aggravating factors. Some of these emphasized cases are especially thoroughly reasoned and/or cite numerous other cases involving the same type of offense.

---

[99] See Arbitrator Boles in 29 LA 693; Horlacher in 29 LA 528; Hawley in 26 LA 682; Hebert in 25 LA 439; Maggs in 22 LA 570; Warren in 19 LA 615; Granoff in 17 LA 710.

Offense	Discharge Upheld	Lesser Penalty Upheld (as assessed by employer)	Penalty Reduced by Arbitrator	No Penalty Permitted
Absenteeism	30 LA 163	28 LA 524*	30 LA 270	22 LA 649
	29 LA 672*	26 LA 176*	30 LA 231*	19 LA 166
	29 LA 559*	23 LA 683	29 LA 133*	
	25 LA 846*	19 LA 399	29 LA 91*	
	24 LA 401*		27 LA 562	
	23 LA 663*		18 LA 311	
	20 LA 155*			
	19 LA 910			
	18 LA 869*			
	17 LA 745			
	16 LA 474*			
	16 LA 146*			
Absence from Work	29 LA 322*	30 LA 744	29 LA 495*	29 LA 291
	29 LA 146*	19 LA 658	29 LA 286	28 LA 434
	29 LA 77	16 LA 112*	28 LA 65*	28 LA 33
	28 LA 249		27 LA 446*	26 LA 712
	27 LA 812*		27 LA 442*	25 LA 332
	25 LA 846*		27 LA 339*	23 LA 574*
	25 LA 709*		25 LA 614*	22 LA 138*
	24 LA 593*		25 LA 281*	21 LA 151*
	24 LA 52*		21 LA 322*	20 LA 570
	23 LA 542*		20 LA 331	20 LA 451*
	23 LA 418		18 LA 94	19 LA 471*
	21 LA 248*			16 LA 32
	20 LA 527			
Tardiness	30 LA 667			28 LA 761
	23 LA 223			27 LA 99*
				22 LA 649
Assault and Fighting Among Employees	30 LA 948*	26 LA 638	30 LA 68	29 LA 356*
	29 LA 820*		28 LA 775	26 LA 874*
	28 LA 355*		28 LA 198*	26 LA 688*
	28 LA 312*		27 LA 279	21 LA 122*
	28 LA 303*		26 LA 295*	17 LA 258*
	27 LA 557*		24 LA 240	
	24 LA 145		21 LA 32*	
	23 LA 645*		19 LA 609	
	21 LA 186*		16 LA 781	
	19 LA 255			

* See introductory comments.

Offense	Discharge Upheld	Lesser Penalty Upheld (as assessed by employer)	Penalty Reduced by Arbitrator	No Penalty Permitted
Assault of Management Representative	30 LA 253 28 LA 757* 28 LA 51* 27 LA 148* 22 LA 501 22 LA 255* 21 LA 327 19 LA 770		30 LA 763* 28 LA 804 25 LA 404* 21 LA 300 19 LA 177* 17 LA 710*	
Insubordination	30 LA 463 29 LA 728* 28 LA 543* 28 LA 312 27 LA 905* 27 LA 400* 27 LA 148* 26 LA 395* 26 LA 96* 21 LA 587 19 LA 581 18 LA 849* 18 LA 651 18 LA 235* 16 LA 66*	30 LA 860 30 LA 426 29 LA 404* 29 LA 267 28 LA 37* 26 LA 465 26 LA 327 23 LA 311 22 LA 765* 21 LA 53*	30 LA 1039* 30 LA 820 30 LA 430 29 LA 693* 29 LA 414* 27 LA 199 26 LA 713* 26 LA 266 25 LA 439* 23 LA 284* 22 LA 684* 22 LA 528* 20 LA 520* 19 LA 475* 19 LA 455 19 LA 344 18 LA 809* 18 LA 239* 18 LA 94 18 LA 82* 17 LA 737* 17 LA 710* 17 LA 574 17 LA 446 17 LA 142* 17 LA 125 16 LA 939* 16 LA 722 16 LA 132	30 LA 242 30 LA 143 28 LA 83* 28 LA 77 27 LA 892* 24 LA 470* 24 LA 66* 23 LA 785 23 LA 516 22 LA 684* 21 LA 410* 21 LA 335 21 LA 293 20 LA 496 18 LA 772 17 LA 110 16 LA 307*

* See introductory comments.

Offense	Discharge Upheld	Lesser Penalty Upheld (as assessed by employer)	Penalty Reduced by Arbitrator	No Penalty Permitted
Dishonesty (Includes falsifying employment records)	30 LA 41 29 LA 171 28 LA 310 27 LA 337 25 LA 568* 25 LA 435 24 LA 353* 23 LA 534* 20 LA 23 19 LA 854* 19 LA 203 18 LA 833 18 LA 733 17 LA 804* 17 LA 230*	17 LA 544	30 LA 700 29 LA 182* 28 LA 879* 26 LA 913 26 LA 575* 25 LA 13* 24 LA 783* 21 LA 560* 17 LA 412*	27 LA 629 26 LA 934* 24 LA 356* 19 LA 413*
Theft	28 LA 363* 25 LA 270* 22 LA 573 21 LA 444* 17 LA 720* 17 LA 334*		29 LA 781* 29 LA 464* 26 LA 529 26 LA 480* 25 LA 906* 24 LA 728* 24 LA 549 19 LA 615*	29 LA 525* 29 LA 272* 29 LA 137* 27 LA 863* 26 LA 923* 24 LA 470* 21 LA 832*
Disloyalty to Employer	24 LA 674	26 LA 401	20 LA 823 18 LA 490* 17 LA 179*	27 LA 829 24 LA 63* 20 LA 305 19 LA 125*
Disloyalty to Government (Security Risk)	30 LA 642* 27 LA 548 27 LA 265* 26 LA 792* 26 LA 609 24 LA 852* 23 LA 715 21 LA 532* 19 LA 40* 19 LA 39* 16 LA 234	22 LA 709*	28 LA 810* 22 LA 751*	30 LA 636 29 LA 567* 28 LA 668* 24 LA 567* 21 LA 1*

* See introductory comments.

Offense	Discharge Upheld	Lesser Penalty Upheld (as assessed by employer)	Penalty Reduced by Arbitrator	No Penalty Permitted
Loafing		26 LA 61 16 LA 152 16 LA 118	16 LA 563*	28 LA 761 19 LA 699 17 LA 199
Leaving Post (Includes early quitting)	27 LA 780 27 LA 653* 25 LA 544 20 LA 891 17 LA 124*	26 LA 61 25 LA 544 19 LA 446 16 LA 152 16 LA 118	24 LA 555 24 LA 490* 19 LA 607* 19 LA 489* 18 LA 184*	27 LA 831 27 LA 407 21 LA 220*
Sleeping on Job	30 LA 78* 30 LA 121* 29 LA 56 27 LA 512* 26 LA 472 22 LA 498* 20 LA 50*	27 LA 454* 19 LA 495*	29 LA 528* 23 LA 436 21 LA 676* 19 LA 380*	28 LA 874* 27 LA 572*
Incompetence (Including low productivity)	30 LA 638* 28 LA 710* 28 LA 690* 28 LA 456* 26 LA 598* 26 LA 272* 23 LA 652* 23 LA 623* 23 LA 217 22 LA 101 22 LA 23 21 LA 659* 20 LA 891 20 LA 551* 20 LA 353* 18 LA 656* 18 LA 552 18 LA 363*	30 LA 264 28 LA 162* 27 LA 682* 26 LA 245* 20 LA 56 18 LA 457* 18 LA 359 17 LA 580* 17 LA 328*	28 LA 330* 26 LA 682* 22 LA 181 19 LA 677* 19 LA 151* 17 LA 701	30 LA 1048* 29 LA 128 28 LA 505 26 LA 866 25 LA 32* 23 LA 252* 22 LA 819* 22 LA 102 21 LA 293* 20 LA 618 20 LA 483* 19 LA 585* 18 LA 447 17 LA 784* 17 LA 110 16 LA 37

* See introductory comments.

Offense	Discharge Upheld	Lesser Penalty Upheld (as assessed by employer)	Penalty Reduced by Arbitrator	No Penalty Permitted
Negligence	30 LA 212	26 LA 910	30 LA 830*	30 LA 242
	27 LA 846	24 LA 745	29 LA 224	28 LA 761
	25 LA 323	19 LA 529	27 LA 656*	27 LA 576
	25 LA 235	19 LA 89	26 LA 266	25 LA 736
	24 LA 48*	16 LA 421	25 LA 903	25 LA 639
	21 LA 314*		25 LA 733*	22 LA 520*
	21 LA 105*		25 LA 634*	20 LA 622*
	20 LA 706*		25 LA 316*	20 LA 465*
	18 LA 651		24 LA 555*	18 LA 724
	18 LA 282*		24 LA 102*	
	18 LA 198		21 LA 456*	
			19 LA 405	
			18 LA 680	
			16 LA 290	
Refusal to Accept Job Assignment	24 LA 839*	30 LA 633*	30 LA 502	30 LA 648
	20 LA 875*	30 LA 542*	29 LA 538	30 LA 38*
	19 LA 888*	30 LA 347*	29 LA 80*	27 LA 523*
	19 LA 5	30 LA 199*	29 LA 18	23 LA 313*
	18 LA 437	29 LA 412*	28 LA 255*	22 LA 624*
	18 LA 235*	29 LA 267	26 LA 915*	21 LA 335*
	17 LA 280	29 LA 74*	23 LA 406	20 LA 496
		28 LA 486*	22 LA 570	19 LA 767*
		28 LA 394*	20 LA 749*	16 LA 138*
		28 LA 279	19 LA 753*	
		25 LA 802*	19 LA 374	
		22 LA 684	19 LA 65*	
		22 LA 358	18 LA 490*	
		20 LA 653*	18 LA 453	
		20 LA 281	18 LA 320*	
		18 LA 872	18 LA 239*	
			17 LA 666*	
			17 LA 598	
			16 LA 939*	
			16 LA 220*	

* See introductory comments.

Offense	Discharge Upheld	Lesser Penalty Upheld (as assessed by employer)	Penalty Reduced by Arbitrator	No Penalty Permitted
Refusal to Work Overtime	27 LA 486 25 LA 727* 17 LA 217*	30 LA 342* 28 LA 242* 28 LA 37 21 LA 145*	27 LA 614* 20 LA 794* 17 LA 419* 16 LA 421	27 LA 599* 27 LA 458* 24 LA 526* 24 LA 163* 21 LA 513* 20 LA 564* 17 LA 606* 16 LA 311*
Prohibited Strike	30 LA 568 30 LA 72 29 LA 756 29 LA 733* 29 LA 622* 25 LA 663* 22 LA 589* 22 LA 320* 21 LA 843* 21 LA 736* 21 LA 434* 21 LA 421* 21 LA 239* 20 LA 875* 19 LA 763 19 LA 601* 18 LA 565 17 LA 610 17 LA 40 16 LA 664 16 LA 99*	30 LA 295 30 LA 250* 30 LA 181* 30 LA 153 30 LA 109* 28 LA 782* 28 LA 648* 28 LA 369* 27 LA 321	30 LA 513* 30 LA 295 29 LA 681* 28 LA 121 27 LA 131 24 LA 761* 20 LA 15 19 LA 437* 18 LA 379* 17 LA 440* 16 LA 939* 16 LA 664 16 LA 247*	29 LA 644* 29 LA 635* 20 LA 15 17 LA 11

* See introductory comments.

Offense	Discharge Upheld	Lesser Penalty Upheld (as assessed by employer)	Penalty Reduced by Arbitrator	No Penalty Permitted
Misconduct During Strike	26 LA 742* 26 LA 593 26 LA 515 26 LA 250* 26 LA 186* 26 LA 29 25 LA 767* 25 LA 556* 25 LA 474 25 LA 410 25 LA 270* 22 LA 567* 22 LA 320* 17 LA 11		26 LA 836* 26 LA 515 26 LA 29 25 LA 767* 25 LA 410 25 LA 343* 25 LA 270* 19 LA 818* 17 LA 11 16 LA 722*	27 LA 24 26 LA 186* 26 LA 29 25 LA 474 25 LA 470* 22 LA 792 16 LA 829*
Slowdown	18 LA 449* 18 LA 370 17 LA 138	29 LA 769* 29 LA 142* 28 LA 288 27 LA 744 26 LA 279* 26 LA 61 22 LA 77* 18 LA 557* 18 LA 370 17 LA 76	30 LA 430 29 LA 604* 27 LA 614 21 LA 729* 18 LA 882* 17 LA 814	30 LA 857 29 LA 512* 27 LA 420 21 LA 428* 17 LA 423* 16 LA 311*
Union Activities	28 LA 543*		25 LA 124	20 LA 325 17 LA 199 16 LA 666* 16 LA 536 16 LA 208
Damage to or Loss of Machine or Materials	27 LA 463* 21 LA 314* 20 LA 706* 17 LA 138	26 LA 910 21 LA 105*	25 LA 634* 19 LA 650	28 LA 246* 19 LA 665

* See introductory comments.

Offense	Discharge Upheld	Lesser Penalty Upheld (as assessed by employer)	Penalty Reduced by Arbitrator	No Penalty Permitted
Intoxication	30 LA 94* 30 LA 163 30 LA 847 28 LA 226* 25 LA 709* 24 LA 810* 23 LA 418* 21 LA 452 21 LA 367* 20 LA 50* 19 LA 733* 19 LA 57 18 LA 671*	29 LA 362 26 LA 176* 16 LA 317*	29 LA 718 29 LA 305* 28 LA 829* 27 LA 128* 24 LA 720* 21 LA 80* 19 LA 724* 18 LA 400*	18 LA 336*
Use of Profane or Abusive Language	30 LA 463 29 LA 728 21 LA 512 17 LA 224* 17 LA 335*		26 LA 713* 26 LA 390 23 LA 104* 20 LA 543 19 LA 455 19 LA 374 18 LA 82* 17 LA 577 17 LA 710*	27 LA 611 17 LA 110*
Gambling	29 LA 778* 21 LA 788* 17 LA 150* 16 LA 727* 16 LA 461*	29 LA 442*	28 LA 97* 22 LA 851* 22 LA 210*	28 LA 97* 18 LA 938
Attachment or Garnishment of Wages	30 LA 690* 28 LA 421 28 LA 411 28 LA 328 21 LA 709*			30 LA 1058
Physical Inability to Perform Job	20 LA 480		20 LA 784* 19 LA 189* 17 LA 187	24 LA 857* 22 LA 623* 20 LA 266* 18 LA 889*

* See introductory comments.

Chapter 16

STANDARDS IN ARBITRATION OF 'INTERESTS' DISPUTES

Do Standards Exist?

The nature and proper scope of "interests" arbitration, as well as the function of the arbitrator in such arbitration, are discussed in Chapter 3. There it is also noted that one of the important reasons why arbitration of "interests" issues is viewed with suspicion by many persons is the belief that there is an absence of definite criteria or standards to govern the arbitrator. But there are, in fact, a number of standards that can be used and often are used. Many of these standards were used by the National War Labor Board. Not only did the Board give a great impetus to the process of arbitration, but it gave also an impetus to the use of many of these standards.

Not infrequently the parties will specify, in their stipulation for arbitration, the standards to be observed.[1] Even if the parties do not stipulate the standards to be observed, the arbitrator generally will make an award on the basis of one or several of the commonly accepted standards. In such case the selection of the standards used is still determined by the parties, though less directly, since an arbitrator generally will not apply any given standard unless evidence has been introduced to support its application.

---

[1] As in 16 LA 933, 935; 12 LA 608, 609-610; 11 LA 118, 120. For discussion of the pros and cons of this practice see Handsaker, The Submission Agreement in Contract Arbitration (U. of Pa. Press, 1952). It has been emphasized that only the parties, not an arbitrator, should place limitations in the collective agreement as to the standards that may be observed by future "interests" arbitrators. United Traction Co., 27 LA 309, 317-318 (Scheiber, 1956). Also see Arbitrator Cornsweet in 15 LA 263, 273.

The standards used by arbitrators are not pulled out of the air—nor are they artificially created. They are, generally speaking, the very same ones that are used by the parties in their negotiations. But if the arbitrator and the parties all use the same bargaining criteria, how can arbitration successfully resolve disputes where the parties' bargaining has failed? It can do so because the arbitrator is much more likely to be objective and to weigh impersonally the evidence adduced with respect to the various criteria.

Admittedly, most of the criteria are nebulous; but they are equally so whether applied by the parties or by the arbitrator. They are still the same standards regardless of who applies them, and in no case is it possible to determine whether they are being applied in exactly the proper manner. Since a certain amount of risk of misapplication of standards cannot be avoided in any case, it may be contended that it is better for the parties to resort to arbitration when an impasse is reached in negotiations than for them to pay the price of a strike which would be costly to labor, to management, and also to the public.

Without question the most extensively used standard in "interests" arbitration is "prevailing practice". This standard is applied, with varying degrees of emphasis, in most "interests" cases. In a sense the application of this standard results in the indirect adoption by disputants of the results of the successful collective bargaining of other parties similarly situated. The arbitrator is the agent through whom the outside bargain is indirectly adopted by the parties. That the parties may thus indirectly adopt the collective bargain of others is well illustrated by the statement of one arbitration board, which, in applying the "pattern" standards, said through its Chairman, Clark Kerr:

> "Rightly or wrongly, 'patterns' and 'packages' have been established in 'round one' and 'round two' and widely followed in free collective bargaining. There is no magic formula for wage adjudication. Consequently one of the compelling considerations must be what has happened in free and successful collective bargaining. This indicates how experienced bar-

gainers have evaluated the wage influencing factors which have evidenced themselves, and what they consider to be 'just'.

"Arbitration of primary disputes over the terms of a new contract is a substitute for successful bargaining, and the 'pattern' or 'package' indicates what might have evolved from successful bargaining had the parties acted like others similarly situated. Attention to the 'pattern' or 'package,' rather than adherents to any rigid formula, also reduces the risks of parties entering wage arbitration, but also should encourage their own free settlement. It tends to afford equality of treatment for persons in comparable situations. It also provides a precise, objective figure, rather than an artificially contrived rate." [2]

The existence of standards lends a certain amount of predictability to "interests" arbitration, but the arbitrator is anything but a mere automaton. Even with agreed upon points of reference, his discretion is quite broad. He must determine the weight to be given to each of the standards applied in the given case, since very rarely is the number of standards under consideration limited to one. His freedom to weigh the standards, to "mix the porridge", so to speak, means that the results will depend upon the way he applies the standards. [3] It may not often be possible or desirable for the arbitrator to make a strict application of the standards. Rather, they must be applied with the end in view of providing a solution that will be satisfactory enough to both sides to be workable. The circumstances of the parties must always be kept in mind by the arbitrator. His task is to determine what the parties before him, as reasonable men, should have agreed upon by negotiation.

---

[2] Pacific Gas & Electric Co., 7 LA 528, 534 (1947).

[3] A New York court has sustained the right of the arbitrator to decide which standards are to be accorded weight in the given case. In re Hopkins, 13 LA 716 (N.Y. Sup. Ct., 1949), where the arbitrator had based his decision principally on the cost of living factor although the parties had urged other grounds to him. Where the submission agreement limited the arbitrator to consideration of five specified factors and required him to show in his report how each of the factors affected his award, Arbitrator I. Robert Feinberg explained his authority as follows: "As the arbitrator reads the stipulation, he is required to determine whether a wage increase is justified by considering only the factors listed therein. On the other hand, it does not appear that all of the factors must necessarily be considered of the same or equal importance. Rather, their relative importance is for the Arbitrator to determine. He is merely cautioned not to consider any other factors." H. Boker & Co., 12 LA 608, 610 (1949). Where the New Jersey Public Utilities Disputes Act provided that decisions should be based on the five standards set forth in the Act, so far as applicable to the matter in dispute, a decision could not be based on consideration of only one of the five standards. In re New Jersey Bell Telephone Co., 15 LA 238, 244 (N.J. Sup. Ct., 1950).

No single standard is available for universal application in all industries and under all circumstances. Arbitrators generally apply a combination of standards, which varies from case to case. Each party will advance standards believed to support its position in the given case. Standards that may be applicable in times of prosperity or inflation might be of little value during depressions. The number of standards entitled to be given consideration, and possibly some weight, varies from only one in some cases [4] to as many as ten or twelve in other cases.[5]

Sometimes no indication will be given as to the standards considered in arriving at the award. [6] At other times it is difficult to tell from an award the weight given by the arbitrator to any particular standard. Only a few of the standards can be said to be basically objective. The weighing and balancing process is illustrated by the statement of Arbitrator Benjamin S. Kirsh, who, in speaking of the case before him, said:

> "The adjudication of the various factors which are material to this determination have been carefully and conscientiously weighed by the arbitrator. This case involves a just and equitable evaluation of the totality of the considerations herein described and requires that each material factor be given its proper weight, with the final award representing a fair determination of the entire isuse." [7]

Whether this process leads to an award based upon "compromise" is problematical. Often an arbitrator will consciously strive to avoid such a result, and he may deny specifically that the award involves "splitting the difference". [8] In the final analysis, the weight to be accorded a standard in any given case is, or should be, the result of the evidence submitted by the parties in respect to its application. The burden is upon the parties to submit evidence which is both factual and material,

[4] See Arbitrator Kerr in 5 LA 758; Kaplan in 4 LA 794.

[5] See Arbitrator Kerr in 20 LA 30, and in 7 LA 528; Wyckoff in 7 LA 35; Simkin in 6 LA 860.

[6] See Arbitrator Lewis in 6 LA 226; Swacker in 6 LA 127.

[7] Baker & Co., 7 LA 350, 353 (1947). Also see statement by Arbitrator Ross in 29 LA 96, 100; Shipman in 26 LA 651, 659; Kerr in 20 LA 30, 32.

[8] Reliable Optical Co., 7 LA 257, 258 (Rosenfarb, 1947).

for arbitrators can be expected to be "unwilling to enter into the field of speculation."[9]

The remainder of this Chapter is largely devoted to a consideration of each of the standards used with some frequency in "interests" arbitration.[10] Many of the standards to be considered are of greatest value in the arbitration of disputes involving wages or other "financial" issues. In this regard, the reported arbitration awards indicate that a high percentage of "interests" arbitrations involve wage or related matters, although other types of issues have also been submitted to "interests" arbitration.[11]

Arbitrators tend to apply those standards which are sufficiently recognized in practice to warrant acceptance by the parties. The fact that a given standard is advanced in collective bargaining or arbitration does not of itself mean that the standard has been accepted without disagreement or qualification by economists. It is not the arbitrator's function to set forth a systematic theory of wages or working conditions. This does not mean, however, that arbitrators do not at times consider the theoretical economic effects that may result from the application of a standard.

Prevailing Practice—Industry, Area, Industry-Area

In giving effect to the prevailing practice, an arbitrator relies upon precedent, adopting for the parties that which has been adopted by other parties through collective bargaining or, as sometimes is the case, as a result of arbitration awards. An award based upon application of this standard is not likely to be too far from the expectations of the parties, since most persons in the business community have long accepted the idea

---

[9] St. Louis Public Service Co., 8 LA 397, 405 (Holland, Anderson & Hollingsworth, 1947). Also see Arbitrator Feinsinger in 16 LA 501, 504.
[10] For other studies of these standards, see Backman. Economic Data Utilized in Wage Arbitration (U. of Pa. Press, 1952); Kuhn, Arbitration in Transit (U. of Pa. Press, 1952).
[11] For an enumeration of these other issues and for citation of cases in which they were submitted to arbitration, see Chapter 3, topic titled "Purpose and Subjects of 'Interests' Arbitration".

that there should be no basic inequalities among comparable individuals or groups. [12]

If the terms of employment of a given employer are below the standard set by the prevailing practice of comparable employers and if no basis exists for a differential, an arbitrator may conclude that an inequality exists. Many arbitration awards have undertaken to eliminate inequalities, such as inequalities between related industries, [13] inequalities within an industry, [14] inequalities between comparable firms or work within a specific area, [15] and inequalities within the plant itself. [16]

Application of the prevailing-practice standard may involve difficulties. First, what is to be the basis of comparison? For instance, is it to be the entire industry, the particular industry within the area, or industry in general within the area? After it is decided which prevailing practice is to be used, then just what that practice is must be determined. Finally, there remains the problem of applying the practice to the particular company involved in the case. While difficulties may be encountered, they are not insuperable. The application can be made.

Strong reason exists for using the prevailing practice of the same class of employers within the locality or area for the comparison. Employees are sure to compare their lot with that of other employees doing similar work in the area; it is important that no sense of grievance be thereby created. [17] Unions have found, for instance, that the imposition of different wage scales upon the same class of employers in the same locality causes trouble both from employers and union members. [18] Some-

---

[12] See Ross, Trade Union Wage Policy 74 (1948).

[13] See 19 LA 76, 18 LA 599, 7 LA 630, 7 LA 30, 4 LA 251, 3 LA 41.

[14] See 26 LA 651, 25 LA 506, 25 LA 23, 23 LA 429, 23 LA 422, 22 LA 371, 20 LA 75, 5 LA 590, 4 LA 678.

[15] See 13 LA 255, 11 LA 1115, 9 LA 577, 8 LA 961, 4 LA 800.

[16] See 27 LA 343, 26 LA 651, 25 LA 23, 23 LA 733, 10 LA 133, 8 LA 9, 7 LA 673, 6 LA 286, 5 LA 590, 4 LA 689, 3 LA 877.

[17] Condé Nash Publications, Inc., 1 ALAA par. 67,168, p. 67,355 (1942).

[18] Slichter, Basic Criteria Used in Wage Negotiations 28 (1947).

times, however, one party will insist upon industry-wide terms while the other party insists upon an area comparison.

If the parties cannot reach agreement as to the basis of comparison, the responsibility is that of the arbitrator to determine, from the facts and circumstances of the case as indicated by the evidence, the appropriate basis for comparison. In the final analysis it may well be that the prevailing practice which properly should be used for the comparison is that of the employer's competitors, whether within or without the area, or that of other firms or industries so situated that there is a sufficient similarity of interests between them and the employer in question for it to be reasonable to use their practice as the standard; comparison with others similarly situated within the industry or area thus may be the crux of the test.

If the case involves the setting of terms for an entire industry, the comparison may be with a similar industry. In determining whether a significant and close relationship exists between two industries a wide variety of factors might be considered. Such relationship has been found to exist between two industries on the basis of the following factors: "Both are engaged in handling essentially the same products. There is a marked similarity of operations, job titles, job classifications, job duties, and products handled. There is considerable overlapping of union representation * * *. There is competition between the two industries for raw materials as well as for employees. The products of one industry are used almost exclusively by the other." [19] The telephone industry has been determined to be related to the telegraph industry on the basis of the following findings: their products are similar, frequently interdependent, and partially competitive; skills required in key jobs are similar; and requirements in many auxiliary occupations, such as clerical and accounting, are virtually identical. [20]

---

[19] Yakima Cement Products Corp., 3 LA 793, 795 (Prasow, 1946).

[20] Western Union Telegraph Co., 4 LA 251, 259-260 (Wallen, Cahn & Donahue, 1946). For guides developed by the National Wage Stabilization Board (1946) for determining whether industries were related see Policy Statement of that Board at 2 LA XIII.

In any use of area practice, the geographical limits of the appropriate area must be determined. [21]   Also, if the prevailing practice of industry in general within the area is to be used, there is the task of selecting the firms whose practice is to be considered in determining the prevailing area practice. Arbitrators frequently use for the comparison the prevailing practice of the particular industry in question, as opposed to industry in general, within the area. [22]

Where each of various comparisons had some validity, Arbitrator Albert I. Cornsweet ruled that those comparisons which the parties themselves had considered significant in free collective bargaining, especially in the recent past, should be given the greatest weight by the arbitrator.[23]

The selection of the employers whose practices are to determine the standard must, in wage cases, be followed by an analysis of jobs as to comparability. Mere job titles often are not reliable and are by no means conclusive. "The range of duties assigned to a single worker has not been as standardized among plants as is widely assumed. The varying ages and types of equipment, the differing scales of operation between large and small plants, and the different techniques of various managers are factors making for different job contents among firms producing roughly similar goods." [24]   It is incumbent upon the parties to supply reliable job descriptions in order to establish a basis for comparison.

After the prevailing practice has been determined, it must be applied to the particular company involved in the case. This is not difficult where issues involve matters other than wage rates, as for example, where the issue is the number of paid holi-

---

[21] Frequently the metropolitan area or the state is used. The National War Labor Board favored area comparison for the establishment of wage rates. Basic Steel Cos., 19 War Lab. Rep. 568 (1944).

[22] E.g., 29 LA 9, 23 LA 733, 23 LA 429, 22 LA 35, 20 LA 718, 20 LA 610, 18 LA 55, 17 LA 353, 15 LA 847.

[23] Rochester Transit Corp., 15 LA 263, 270 (1950). Also see Arbitrators Sanders, Begley & Gilden in 28 LA 182; Horlacher in 27 LA 295; Donnelly in 22 LA 192; Gilden in 16 LA 539.

[24] Dunlop, "The Economics of Wage-Dispute Settlement," 12 Law & Contemp. Prob. 281, 283 (1947). Also see Arbitrator Hepburn in 26 LA 381, 382-383.

days.   But the application of prevailing wage rates is not so simple.   There may be reasons why the employer in question should
not pay the prevailing rates.   These reasons, which for the sake
of convenience the Authors choose to call the "minor" standards, include such matters as relative general differentials of
skill and training, responsibility, steadiness of employment, hazards of the employment, and fringe benefits, as well as established geographical differentials and wage leadership (these
"minor" standards are discussed below).

Consideration of some of the numerous types of issues
which have been settled on the basis of prevailing practice indicates the very broad application that is given to the standard
by arbitrators, emergency boards, and fact-finding boards.   In
addition to basic wage rates, the following types of issues have
been resolved in some cases largely (and sometimes entirely) on
the basis of the prevailing-practice standard: holidays, [25] vacations, [26] sick leave, [27] hospitalization benefits, [28] pensions and retirement, [29] meal periods, [30] rest periods, [31] union security provisions, [32] length of workday or workweek, [33] shift differentials, [34] work schedules and shifts, [35] overtime provisions, [36]
premium pay for Sundays and holidays, [37] length of contract
term.[38]

Differentials and the "Minor" Standards

There may be, as already stated, reasons why a differential
should exist between the wage terms of an employer and those
of other employers (or between different groups of employees

[25] E.g., 21 LA 494, 17 LA 353, 16 LA 933, 11 LA 1037, 9 LA 540, 4 LA 780.
[26] E.g., 24 LA 835, 18 LA 415, 17 LA 353, 9 LA 666, 6 LA 98, 5 LA 170.
[27] E.g., 21 LA 356, 17 LA 152, 11 LA 450, 7 LA 845, 2 LA 95.
[28] E.g., 21 LA 356, 11 LA 450, 2 LA 624.
[29] E.g., 25 LA 54, 19 LA 538, 13 LA 813, 13 LA 46.
[30] 17 LA 353, 4 LA 548.
[31] 17 LA 353, 7 LA 845, 2 LA 227.
[32] E.g., 18 LA 112, 17 LA 833, 16 LA 611, 6 LA 567, 5 LA 38, 3 LA 41.
[33] E.g., 27 LA 343, 19 LA 358, 18 LA 903, 9 LA 566, 5 LA 504, 2 LA 582.
[34] 9 LA 865, 8 LA 488, 5 LA 71, 4 LA 489.
[35] 9 LA 282, 5 LA 781.
[36] 4 LA 604, 4 LA 548.
[37] 8 LA 700, 6 LA 269, 2 LA 227.
[38] 27 LA 468.

within the same company) with whom a comparison is made in applying the prevailing-practice standard.[39] Sometimes an arbitrator is asked to institute a new differential, and sometimes to prepetuate a differential that has existed in the past. Differentials serve a constructive purpose when supported by sound reasons.

(a) Skill and Training—Arbitrators recognize that wages should be to some degree responsive to the general level of skill and experience required in the plant. For instance, where an employer had a "young shop", composed of workers with relatively less experience and therefore less skill as compared with the average in the industry, the factors of skill and training were given consideration as a proper basis for some differential.[40] The National War Labor Board held that a differential should be reduced but not entirely elmininated where a lesser degree of skill was required to produce a tannery company's product than was required in other tanneries; the quality of leather and the consequent skill required to produce it were found to be superior in the other tanneries to the quality and skill prevailing in the company's plant.[41]

(b) Responsibility—Differentials have been justified, in part at least, on the basis of greater responsibility placed upon one group of employees as compared to that placed upon another.[42]

(c) Steadiness of Employment—Differences in the steadiness of employment may justify differences in wage rates. Wage rates for seasonal workers and workers who otherwise have lim-

---

[39] Economist Sumner H. Slichter would classify wage differentials as follows: "1. Differentials which equalize the attractiveness of jobs in different occupations, industries, and places. 2. Differentials which reflect the efficiency of men in different occupations and of individuals within an occupation." Slichter, Basic Criteria Used in Wage Negotiations 41 (1947).

[40] Reliable Optical Co., 7 LA 257, 259 (Rosenfarb, 1947). Also see Arbitrator McCoy in 20 LA 610; Reynolds in 16 LA 933. Differentials between different groups of employees within the same company often are justified by differences in skill required. See Arbitrator Kagel in 28 LA 600; Townsend in 16 LA 53. Also see W.S.B. in 17 LA 68.

[41] Moench Tanning Co., 8 War Lab. Rep. 54, 60 (1943).

[42] See Arbitrator Dworet in 27 LA 343; Ross in 22 LA 226; Blair in 13 LA 454. Also see Healy in 17 LA 636; Stauffer Chemical Co., 15 War Lab. Rep. 264 (1944).

ited job security frequently are set above those of workers with steady employment. [43] This principle was held to justify a rate differential in favor of construction workers as against utility workers even though both were employed on the same work project, weight being given to the fact that utility workers have much greater continuity of employment. [44]

(d) Hazards and Other Undesirable Conditions of Work—Differentials often justifiably exist in favor of employees who perform hazardous work or who work outside during inclement weather or under other undesirable conditions. [45]

(e) Geographic Differentials—Although the individual worker does not always understand why higher wages should be paid to another worker doing the same work but in a different area, there is believed to be sound reason for geographic differentials, as simply stated by one board of arbitration:

> "* * * everyone knows our country cousins, workmen, professional men, all, on the average, earn less than urbanites; and need less. They get on the whole more comforts, services, and commodities for their dollars." [46]

The existence of past wage uniformity between components of a given industry in adjoining areas and the fact that the two areas may tend to constitute a single labor market for that industry may be held insufficient reason for requiring employers in the industry in one of the areas to grant the same wage adjustment granted in the other area if differences in the economies of the two areas far outweigh the similarities. [47]

Even if the cost of living were the same in all places, geographic differentials could still be justified on the ground that they cause labor and capital to flow into areas where they are most needed. Employment opportunities are diminishing in

---

[43] See Arbitrator Rubin in 23 LA 4; Simkin in 6 LA 860; Taylor in 6 LA 830; Prasow in 3 LA 793.

[44] Consolidated Edison System Cos. of New York, 6 LA 830 (Taylor, 1947).

[45] See Arbitrator Blair in 13 LA 454; Prasow in 3 LA 793; Fly, Black & Harper in 3 LA 165. Also see Hepburn in 26 LA 381, 382.

[46] Chesapeake & Potomac Telephone Co. of Baltimore, 7 LA 630, 641 (Jackson, Healy & Dennis, 1947).

[47] Associated General Contractors et al., 9 LA 201, 221 (Aaron, 1947).

many rural regions and increasing in the cities, and movement of labor from rural to urban areas may be stimulated by relatively high urban wage rates. Capital, on the other hand, often needs to be encouraged to move from a high to a low wage area. [48] Arbitrators give full recognition to the need for geographic differentials and have ordered their institution or continuance in numerous cases. [49]

(f) Fringe Benefits—Basic wages are not the only "money" benefits that employees may receive. Terms of employment include other pecuniary benefits, such as pensions, holidays and vacations with pay, sick leave, shift premiums, social and health insurance, and bonuses. These fringe benefits must be taken into account in making wage comparisons. If the fringe benefits offered by an employer are substantially more favorable to employees than those of the employers whose prevailing practice to being used for comparative purposes and if these favorable provisions are not counterbalanced by other provisions which are less favorable than the prevailing practice, a differential in basic wage rates may be justified in favor of the employer who offers the superior fringe benefits. [50]

(g) Wage Leadership—A differential which has existed in the past by virtue of the employer's position as a wage leader may be the basis of an award of wage rates higher than those paid by prevailing practice. [51] Companies which in the past have set the prevailing wage may be looked to for further leadership when the trend is toward a higher level of wages. It has been emphasized, however, that the lead occasionally passes from one company to another and that wage adjustments need not

---

[48] Slichter, Basic Criteria Used in Wage Negotiations 37 (1947).

[49] E.g., Arbitrator Feinberg in 18 LA 46; Hays, Cole & Stein in 11 LA 276; Leiserson, Bushnell & Wirtz in 9 LA 865; Aaron in 9 LA 201; Hepburn in 8 LA 691; Jacobs, Clothier & Meyer in 8 LA 9. However, geographic differentials have been reduced or eliminated where changed conditions justified such action. See W.S.B. in 18 LA 112; Arbitrators Martin, Lewis & Lesser in 14 LA 574.

[50] See Arbitrator Kliensorge in 23 LA 733; Kerr in 7 LA 528; Simkin in 6 LA 860, 867, 881. Also see Bernstein in 23 LA 457. Cf., Randle in 18 LA 280.

[51] See Arbitrator Donnelly in 26 LA 904; Whiting in 11 LA 1023; Cornsweet in 8 LA 597. But see Kerr in 7 LA 528. A related question arising out of wage leadership is whether the leader's rate should be included in the sample used for determining the prevailing rate.

always wait upon agreement of the parties who usually provide the lead. [52]

(h) *Historical Differentials*—Arbitrators are sometimes reluctant to eliminate historical differentials, [53] or those which initially were established by collective bargaining. [54] This reflects a hesitancy to disturb a stabilized situation except on compelling grounds. [55]

Economist Sumner H. Slichter has pointed out that some may argue that long-established relationships between wages in several occupations, plants, or localities should be maintained because the quality of labor tends to adjust itself to the wage structure, which means that employers who pay wages above the prevailing rate attract a better class of workers, and the retention of customary differentials merely serves to compensate those with superior ability. He has pointed out further, however, that in a rapidly changing world the argument that traditional wage relationships should be preserved has very limited validity. [56]

If There Is No Prevailing Practice

The question sometimes arises as to how arbitrators should treat demands for contract terms sufficiently unprecedented that no "prevailing practice" is available. It might be urged that demands for improved contract terms should not be rejected on the sole ground that they are unprecedented, since the adoption of a contrary principle would seriously impair the usefulness of arbitration as a method of settling labor disputes. It is clear, however, that arbitrators will require a party seeking a novel change to justify it by strong evidence establishing its reasonableness and soundness. Moreover, the absence of prevailing practice may be taken to show that a demand has not yet

---

[52] Tribune Publishing Co., 28 LA 477, 480 (Ross, 1957).
[53] See Arbitrator Ross in 29 LA 96; Pierson in 17 LA 152; Kerr in 14 LA 111 and in 11 LA 458; Dwyer in 5 LA 513; Cahn in 3 LA 729. Also see W.S.B. in 18 LA 676. Cf., Cheney in 5 LA 220; Wasservogel in 4 LA 548.
[54] See Arbitrator Donnelly in 26 LA 904; Cornsweet in 15 LA 263; Horvitz in 3 LA 318. Also see McCoy in 20 LA 610, 613.
[55] Newark Call Printing & Publishing Co., 3 LA 318, 320-321 (Horvitz, 1946).
[56] Slichter, Basic Criteria Used in Wage Negotiations 40 (1947).

been adequately justified by labor within the industry or area.[57] Arbitrators generally agree that demands for unusual types of contract provisions preferably should be negotiated. This view has been elaborated by Arbitrator Whitley P. McCoy, speaking as Chairman of a board of arbitration:

> "We believe that an unusual demand, that is, one that has not found substantial acceptance in other properties, casts upon the union the burden of showing that, because of its minor character or its inherent reasonableness, the negotiators should, as reasonable men, have voluntarily agreed to it. We would not deny such a demand merely because it had not found substantial acceptance, but it would take clear evidence to persuade us that the negotiators were unreasonable in rejecting it. * * *" [58]

New provisions, however, are often included in the recommendations of fact-finding boards. These agencies frequently enter upon policy considerations and considerations of public interest, and they recognize the need for leadership in the introduction of innovations. [59]

Cost of Living

The cost-of-living standard is frequently advanced in collective bargaining and arbitration during periods characterized by pronounced changes in living costs. [60]

The use of this standard has an obvious appearance of fairness, but it is not without criticism. For instance, it is said that a rising cost of living means that the demand for goods at existing prices is outrunning the supply and that increases in wages would simply aggravate the problem except as they reflect increased production through improvements in technique or in employee efficiency. [61] One answer given to this criticism is that the readjustment of wages has been the result rather than the

---

[57] See Fifth Avenue Coach Co., 4 LA 548 (Wasservogel, 1946).
[58] Twin City Rapid Transit Co., 7 LA 845, 848 (1947). Also see Arbitrator Cole in 11 LA 450, 453-454; Hepburn in 3 LA 194, 196.
[59] See, for instance, General Motors Corp., 1 LA 125, 137 (Fact-Finders Garrison, Eisenhower & Stacy, 1946).
[60] During such periods, too, many parties include "escalator" clauses in their agreement, providing for automatic changes in wage rates in response to specified changes in the cost of living. For the matters that should be covered in escalator clauses, see Tile Contractors Assn. of Northern Calif., Inc., 25 LA 9, 11 (Ross, 1955).
[61] Slichter, Basic Criteria Used in Wage Negotiations 15 (1947).

primary cause of increased living costs. Price rises, it is said, are due to many complex causes. [62] A criticism which labor registers against the cost-of-living standard is that its rigid application would result in a stationary real wage rather than a higher standard of living. [63] But in spite of these criticisms, the very frequent use of this standard is strong evidence that it is generally regarded to be of much value, and especially in recent years it has held an important place in the national economy. The case in its favor was strengthened in 1951 by the Wage Stabilization Board's adoption of it as a ground for wage increases without the need of official approval.

In applying the cost-of-living standard arbitrators rely heavily upon the index issued monthly by the Bureau of Labor Statistics of the United States Department of Labor. This index reflects the cost of living as of a date about six weeks prior to its issuance. By use of the index it is possible to measure changes in retail costs of services and commodities and the resulting effect upon the purchasing power of the income of workers in the larger cities. Essentially, the index is the ratio of the current cost of a specified market basket of goods and services to the average cost of the same market basket during some designated past period. The base period for the Bureau of Labor Statistics index is the average for the years 1947-1949.

The Bureau of Labor Statistics does not hold that its index is an exact measurement of changes in the cost of living, but arbitrators can be expected to give it considerable weight. For example, it was held in one instance to be an appropriate measure of the change in living costs although the union claimed that it underestimated the change and the company claimed that it overestimated the change; [64] neither party presented sufficient evidence to support an adjustment of the index figures, which

---

[62] Satter. "Principles of Arbitration in Wage Rate Disputes," 1 Ind. & Lab. Rel. Rev. 363. 367 (1948).

[63] This criticism led one arbitrator to largely disregard the cost-of-living standard, the arbitrator saving that the "uncritical use of the cost-of-living formula often involves the false assumption that all is well when real wages remain constant." 195 Broadway Corp., 7 LA 516, 519 (Meyer, 1947).

[64] R. H. Macy & Co., 9 LA 305 (Shulman, 1947).

the arbitrator said at least carried apparent and official certitude. [65]

The latest index available at the time of the arbitration is ordinarily used in the determination of the cost-of-living adjustment to be paid employees until the next wage review; this is so even though such review is not expected to take place until several months later. Thus, in setting wages for a six-month period, one arbitrator said that "greater emphasis must obviously be placed on known facts than on guesses" as to the index level during the next six months. [66] But a wage increase in excess of that indicated to be justified by the index may be awarded where the amount granted does not exceed "the amount which the Arbitrator finds on the record as a whole is presently justified to offset increases in living costs * * * " [67]

Many arbitration awards have granted wage improvements on the basis, in part at least, of the application of the cost-of-living standard. [68] Often, however, its effect has been modified by the application at the same time of other standards. Many agreements contain reopening clauses providing for the negotiation of new wage terms when the cost of living changes by a certain specified percentage and there appears to be increasing acceptance of this idea. [69] In determining disputes under reopening clauses arbitrators sometimes have limited consideration to the cost-of-living standard only; in these instances there has been a direct relationship between the standard and the new

---

[65] Id. at 308.

[66] Waterfront Employers Assn. of Pacific Coast, 5 LA 758, 761 (Kerr, 1946). To similar effect, Arbitrator Feinberg in 18 LA 55, 58-59. But where an arbitrator awarded a "firm two year contract", the wage increase he granted was based in part upon "anticipated increases in living costs". The New York Times, 15 LA 332, 333 (Dunlop, 1950).

[67] Waterfront Employers Assn. of Pacific Coast, 9 LA 172, 181 (Miller, 1947). Also see Arbitrator Dworet in 27 LA 343.

[68] E.g., 29 LA 96, 29 LA 7, 28 LA 600, 28 LA 477, 23 LA 629, 22 LA 297, 18 LA 686, 18 LA 599, 15 LA 878, 15 LA 496, 13 LA 40, 11 LA 276.

[69] Some clauses provide for reopening when there has been a "substantial" change in cost of living. As to what might be considered "substantial" see Arbitrator Lesser in 17 LA 914; Justin in 17 LA 31; Granoff in 16 LA 944.

terms awarded. [70] Except in such cases, however, arbitrators appear to be reluctant to limit consideration to the cost-of-living standard solely. This is illustrated by the statement of one arbitration board, which, in refusing to guarantee that the employees would be "insulated in toto" against all of the rise in cost of living, said:

> "To rest wage rate raises upon cost of living rises as the sole measuring rod means wages will rise with commodity rises as the thermometer goes up on a hot day. If wages are to be raised solely because commodity prices go up, wages should go down with falling commodity prices, as the mercury goes down to zero in a freeze; unless, like the human elbow joint, the system is created to flex upward, and only upward." [71]

An appropriate base period must be selected in applying the cost-of-living standard. The determination of any adjustment to be made on the basis of a change in the cost of living requires a comparison of the percentage of change in the cost of living with the percentage of change in wages between the base period and the date of the wage adjustment.

The base period that is selected determines the real wage that is to be maintained by the application of the cost-of-living criterion. Generally the date of the last arbitration award or of the parties' last wage negotiations is used as the base date. In "determining the amount of wage increase necessary to offset a rise in living costs the general pratice is to measure only the change in living costs occuring after the parties' last wage negotiation, since there is a presumption that all pertinent factors were considered in the previous bargaining." [72]

That there is strong justification for the presumption in favor of the date of the parties' last negotiations is forcefully stated in a view adopted by Arbitrator Arthur C. Miller:

---

[70] See Arbitrator Lesser in 16 LA 881 (but see Lesser in 17 LA 114); Miller in 9 LA 172; Justin in 8 LA 199; Kerr in 5 LA 758; Kaplan in 4 LA 794. Other factors were also considered in Condé Nash Publications, 1 ALAA par. 67,168 (1942).

[71] Chesapeake & Potomac Telephone Co. of Baltimore, 7 LA 630, 640 (Jackson, Healy & Dennis, 1947). Also see Arbitrator Shulman in 22 LA 297, 298; Dash in 14 LA 662, 669.

[72] Los Angeles Transit Lines, 11 LA 118, 130 (Aaron, 1948). To similar effect, Arbitrator Whitton in 18 LA 174; Lesser in 10 LA 360; Livingston in 9 LA 632; Miller in 9 LA 172; Cole in 7 LA 794.

"'* * * the wage standard agreed to by the parties themselves in their most recent contract negotiations is the proper basic wage standard. * * * The Arbitrator should examine only those wage-determining conditions which have changed since the date of that agreement. * * * The wage standard thus adopted is the result of free collective bargaining by experienced and alert representatives of strong organizations. The assumption that the resulting rate properly reflects the wage determining factors which had evidenced themselves by that time is a valid one. It may be that the validity of this assumption is not enhanced by describing the resultant wage rate in moral terms as 'right' or 'just'; nevertheless the assumption rests solidly upon the realistic fact that a collectively bargained wage rate, among other things, reflects the considered judgment of the parties as to the balance of their relative economic strengths at the time the contract was made. And a wage rate thus fixed by the parties themselves upon the basis of their intimate knowledge of the merits of the claims of each, and the push and pull, compromise and trading which are the characteristic elements of the collective bargaining process, are properly considered the best evidence of the wage standard from which to evalue in an interim wage review any subsequent changes in pertinent wage-determining factors." [73]

But a date other than that of the last negotiations might be selected as the base period. For some years after World War II, for instance, January 1, 1941, was often used by arbitrators. The use of this date was initiated by the National War Labor Board of World War II. [74] But, when the Wage Stablization Board set a base date of January, 1951, for permissible cost-of-living increases, a strong reason was created for use of this date by arbitrators.

In determining whether wages have kept pace with the cost of living, basic wage rates, rather than take-home pay, are generally used for the comparison. [75] The use of take-home pay for the comparison would lead to a distortion of the normal relationship of earnings to hours worked. [76] In making the comparison some changes in wages have been held not to be material. Among these are increases resulting from increased

---

[73] Waterfront Employers Assn. of Pacific Coast, 9 LA 172, 175-176 (1947).

[74] Bethlehem Steel Corp., 1 War Lab. Rep. 325 (1942). But the 1941 date was deemed clearly outmoded in Publishers Assn. of New York City, 22 LA 35, 41-42 (Seward, Slocum & Meany, 1954).

[75] Waterfront Employers Assn. of Pacific Coast, 5 LA 758 (Kerr, 1946); Bee Line, Inc., 1 ALAA par. 67,161 (1946).

[76] Waterfront Employers Assn. of Pacific Coast, 9 LA 172, 177 (Miller, 1947); Waterfront Employers Assn. of Pacific Coast, 5 LA 758, 761 (Kerr, 1946).

skill and effort, [77] increases granted for the sole purpose of eliminating inequities within the industry,[78] and pay raises for length of service or promotions. [79] The following, on the other hand, may be taken into consideration in making the comparison: Increased earnings of incentive workers which result from a simplification of the work or any other increase not the result of increased efforts of the workers; [80] and reclassification adjustments general enough to affect the whole wage structure and thus to be considered general increases instead of merit increases. [81] The use of basic wage rates instead of take-home pay for the comparison eliminates from consideration vacation, holiday, and other fringe benefits granted to employees since the base date. [82]

The cost-of-living standard may be expected to be used much less generally as a basis for wage reductions than as a basis for wage increases. [83] The social and ethical reasons that can be used to suport the application of the standard in times of rising costs are not so readily applicable when costs are on the decline. Rather, these considerations support the constant efforts of labor to attain a higher standard of living. At least, "insofar as a drop in the cost of living is the result of technological progress, it does not furnish a sound reason for wage cuts;" it calls, instead, for a rise in real wages. [84] The Wage Stabilization Board required that escalator clauses negotiated after January 25, 1951, provide for downward as well as upward revision of wage rates. It is interesting to note, too, that a fact-finding board for the basic steel industry, in refusing to recommend a general wage increase, cited, as one of the factors given consideration, the fact that in the prior year the cost of living had de-

---

[77] McGlynn Hays Industries, Inc., 10 LA 360 (Lesser, 1948).
[78] Atlantic & Gulf Coast Shippers, 6 LA 700 (Kleinsorge, 1947).
[79] Trans World Airlines, Inc., 19 LA 308 (Wenke, Boyd & Sharfman, 1952); Fifth Ave. Coach Co., 1 ALAA par. 67,423 (1946). Also see Arbitrator Stutz in 20 LA 178; Lesser in 17 LA 914.
[80] Associated Dress Mfrs. Assn., 6 LA 24 (Copelof, 1946).
[81] Puget Sound Navigation Co., 11 LA 1100 (Haughton, 1948).
[82] See Bee Line, Inc., 1 ALAA par. 67,161 (1946).
[83] See Puget Sound Navigation Co., 13 LA 255 (Kane, 1949).
[84] Slichter, Basic Criteria Used in Wage Negotiations 18 (1947).

clined slightly. [85] Thus, while a decrease in the cost of living may not be strong reason for wage reductions, at least it would seem to be a factor to be considered in determining whether new wage increases are justified.

Living Wage

The living-wage standard is related to, but not the same as, the cost-of-living standard. The living-wage standard is in some respects based upon the ideal that the standard of living of American workers should be raised to the highest level possible,[86] but a more realistic basis for it is the belief that "employees are entitled to wages and salaries sufficient to enable them, through the exercise of thrift and reasonable economy, to maintain themselves and families in decency and comfort and to make reasonable provision for old age." [87] In advancing the living-wage theory, a union may be expected to insist that no privately owned industry should be permitted to insure its solvency or to consider a return upon its investment at the expense of its employees nor to require its employees to subsidize its investment by compelling them to accept wages or working conditions below normal standards of decency. [88]

An important difference exists between the cost-of-living and the living-wage standards. While the cost-of-living standard is used to keep the standard of living of employees in status quo, the living-wage standard (which is not directly tied to changes in the cost of living) is invoked to raise the wages of employees to the point that will allow them a decent standard of living. Application of the living-wage standard may well result in a wage increase greater than that which is indicated by the change in cost of living.

The "budget approach" is sometimes used by parties advancing the living-wage standard. A similar approach underlies

---

[85] Basic Steel Industry, 13 LA 46, 79 (Daugherty, Cole & Rosenman, 1949).
[86] Atlantic & Gulf Coast Shippers, 6 LA 700, 702 (Kleinsorge, 1947).
[87] San Francisco Employers Council, 7 LA 35, 38 (Wyckoff, 1946).
[88] Such a position was taken by the union in St. Louis Public Service Co., 8 LA 397, 402 (1947).

the state and federal minimum wage laws. Generally speaking, budgets have been used in the past primarily as background and supplementary material rather than as a specific criterion in the formulation of wage demands.[89] But in a few cases unions have relied directly upon the budget approach.[90] A board of inquiry for the meatpacking industry, for instance, was asked to give serious consideration to the "City Worker's Family Budget," issued by the Bureau of Labor Statistics in December, 1947.[91] The board stated that a budget approach to wage determination was not invalid or unprecedented and that the union could properly offer it for consideration as a criterion for resolving the dispute.[92] The board concluded, however, that a proper application of the burget approach to that dispute would require more information than the parties had supplied or could supply from their limited study of the subject up to that date, and more than the board could obtain from governmental or other sources.[93]

This illustrates a major disadvantage of the living-wage standard; namely, its indefiniteness. What may be considered a decent standard of living is largely dependent upon time and circumstances. The board also concluded that even with the necessary information, a number of broad policy decisions would have to be made by agreement of the parties. The most important of these decisions were said to be: "(1) whether the size of the family alone * * * or the composition of the family, including size and other characteristics, should be used; (2) whether the necessary income should come only from earnings of the employee or whether income from all sources should be considered; (3) whether income from earnings should be computed on the basis of 2,080 hours (52 x 40 hours) at straight-time, without incentive earnings or 'fringe' benefits,

---

[89] See Meat Packing Industry, 9 LA 978, 998 (Feinsinger, Davis & Schaefer, 1948). Also see Portland Woolen Mills, Inc., 24 LA 38, 43 (Kleinsorge, 1955).
[90] Meat Packing Industry, 9 LA 978, 998 (Feinsinger, Davis & Schaefer, 1948).
[91] Id. at 992.
[92] Id. at 999.
[93] Id. at 998.

* * * or on the basis of earnings from overtime plus incentive earnings and 'fringe' benefits, as well as straight-time earnings; (4) whether the resulting increase should be related only to the job performed or should also vary with number of dependents of individual employees." [94]

It is recognized that budgetary experts are not in agreement as to the composition of an adequate budget. One arbitration board, speaking through its Chairman, Clark Kerr, declared that the particular budget submitted to it had "served the purpose more of a goal to be attained over a period of time than the next step in the improvement of the living standards" of America's wage earners, and that the actual attainment of the budget could be had "through full and efficient production and distributive justice." The Board concluded that the budget could not, at that time, "serve as the sole, or even a significant, basis for wage adjudication." [95] It can be expected that, as long as the living-wage argument is presented only in general terms, giving arbitrators no specific basis of application to the concrete problems before them, the standard will be given very little effect in awards. [96]

Ability to Pay

Although it is a generally recognized principle that large profits do not alone justify demands for wages substantially higher than those which are standard within an industry and that small profits do not justify the payment of substandard wages, the ability-to-pay criterion is of great importance in the determination of wage rates and other contract benefits. [97] This importance lies in the fact that, while an employer's ability to pay is not, in and of itself, a sufficient basis for a change in wages,

---

[94] Id. at 998-999.

[95] Pacific Gas & Electric Co., 7 LA 528, 530 (Kerr, 1947). Also see Portland Woolen Mills, Inc., 24 LA 38, 43 (Kleinsorge, 1955).

[96] See Atlantic & Gulf Coast Shippers, 6 LA 700, 702 (Kleinsorge, 1947). Also see Longshoremen's Union (Hawaii), 12 LA 870, 884 (Coke, 1949).

[97] See Third Avenue Transit Corp., 1 LA 321 (Hays, 1946); General Motors Corp., 1 LA 125 (Garrison, Eisenhower & Stacy, 1946); International Harvester Co., 1 LA 512 (Marshall, Spencer & Holly, 1946).

it is a significant element properly to be taken into account in determining the weight to be attached to other criteria. [98]

The ability-to-pay standard has been advanced more frequently by management than by labor. For this reason, Economist Sumner H. Slichter has stated that perhaps it should be called the "inability-to-pay" standard. [99] Regardless of title, however, the standard has been advanced by management to resist wage demands on the ground of inability to pay, and it has been advanced by labor to support demands for higher wages on the ground of ability to pay. In advancing this criterion, labor may argue that, when the trend is toward higher wage levels, leadership should be taken by employers best able to afford it. [100]

To determine wages exclusively on the basis of ability to pay would lead to wage scales that vary from company to company, and would require a new determination of the wage scale with each rise or fall in profits. The existence of unequal wage levels among different companies would be incompatible with union programs for the equalization of wage rates among companies in the same industry or area. If inability to pay were used as the sole or absolute basis for wage cuts, inefficient producers would receive the benefit of having a lower wage scale than that of efficient ones, regardless of the fact that the value of the services rendered by the employees of each is the same.[101] Indeed, arbitrators have expressed the view that to use the ability-to-pay standard as the sole basis for a wage increase would in effect involve a decision by the arbitrator as to how business revenues should be distributed among stockholders, employees, and the consuming public; arbitrators do not feel themselves

[98] General Motors Corp., 1 LA 125 (Garrison, Eisenhower & Stacy, 1946). Also see statement by Arbitrator Prasow in 27 LA 468, 473.

[99] Slichter, Basic Criteria Used in Wage Negotiations 25 (1947).

[100] A General Motors fact-finding board considered the earning capacity and the good prospects for high profits of the corporation as one basis for its taking leadership in the establishment of a wage pattern for American industry. General Motors Corp., 1 LA 125 (Garrison, Eisenhower & Stacy, 1946).

[101] The employer paying lower scales would, of course, ultimately tend to get less efficient labor.

competent to rule on such a broad issue of social and economic policy. [102]

The National War Labor Board recognized the principle that the mere fact that a company's profits are large presents no basis for a wage increase and that mere inability to pay standard wages does not justify maintenance of a depressed wage scale. [103] But the Board did consider ability to pay in determining retroactivity of its orders. [104] Moreover, it considered ability to pay in certain special cases, such as that where an employer was unable to pay because of inability to get sufficient oil to operate on a profitable basis. [105]

One board of arbitration has indicated three different degrees of weight which may be given to the ability-to-pay factor. [106] That board, speaking through its Chairman, John T. Dunlop, outlined the three situations as follows: (1) "In the case of properties which have been highly profitable over a period of years, the wage rate would normally be increased slightly over the levels indicated by other standards;" (2) "in the case of persistently unprofitable firms, the wage rate would normally be reduced slightly from the levels indicated by other standards;" (3) "in the case of the companies whose financial record over a period of years fails between these extremes, the wage-rate level would be determined largely by other standards." [107]

There have been many instances where the "unfavorable" financial condition of the employer resulted in the granting of smaller increases (or none at all) than otherwise would have been allowed had there been no inability to pay. [108] The same is true where a grant of all of the increase otherwise justified would have put the company in a "distressed" financial condition or

---

[102] International Harvester Co., 1 LA 512, 517 (Marshall, Spencer & Holly, 1946).
[103] See Galveston Model Laundry, 26 War. Lab. Rep. 224 (1943).
[104] James L. Whitaker, 14 War Lab. Rep. 401 (1944).
[105] Consumers Oil & Refining Co., 9 War Lab. Rep. 407 (1943).
[106] Twin City Rapid Transit Co., 10 LA 581 (1948).
[107] Id. at 594.
[108] E.g., Arbitrator E. Jones in 28 LA 40; Scheiber in 27 LA 309; Hogan in 25 LA 247; Abruzzi in 23 LA 334; Stein in 10 LA 813; Albert in 10 LA 18; Taylor in 9 LA 666; Rosenfarb in 7 LA 257; Brissenden in 6 LA 639.

where the company already was in such a condition. [109]   In one instance a reduction in wages was granted because of the employer's precarious financial position, even though there had been a large increase in the cost of living since the last wage increase. [110]   The arbitrator, Maxwell Copelof, in ordering the reduction, said:

> "The Arbitrator is mindful of the fact that the recommendation of a reduction in wage rates at this time, while the general trend is towards the granting of increases, is a very serious and unpopular recommendation. However, the Arbitrator is convinced that, if the property can be saved, it should result in long-range benefits to the employees and that the seniority accumulated by many of the present employees of the Company will be conserved, enabling them to reap the benefits thereof when profitable operations are again resumed." [111]

That decision appears to have been well advised, for a few months later the arbitrator found the Company's financial position to be sufficiently improved to permit a restoration of the prior wage rate. [112]

An arbitrator may give recognition to an employer's weak financial position by ordering that a needed increase be made gradually. [113]   Sometimes an arbitrator will award an increase but will recognize the inability-to-pay factor at least to the extent of ordering a review of the employer's financial situation after a specified period. [114]   Thus appropriate relief can be granted to the employer based on operations under the award during the specified period. [115]   But mere temporary inability to pay generally is not sufficient to cut down an increase warranted on the basis of other criteria.   Moreover, consideration generally

---

[109] Scranton Metal Casket Works, 3 LA 370 (Blair, 1946); River Valley Tissue Mills, Inc., 3 LA 245 (Blair, 1946). Also see Atlanta & St. Andrews Bay Ry. Co., 6 LA 334 (J. Wolfe, Stone & McGown, 1946)

[110] Trailways of New England, Inc., 7 LA 319 (Copelof, 1947). A wage reduction was also ordered on the basis of the employer's precarious position in Tynan Throwing Co., 20 LA 614 (Bailer, 1953).

[111] Trailways of New England, Inc., 7 LA 319, 321 (1947).

[112] Trailways of New England, Inc., 8 LA 363 (Copelof, 1947).

[113] See Arbitrator Brecht in 21 LA 356; Lesser in 17 LA 914; Justin in 9 LA 468. Or the arbitrator might limit the period of retroactivity, as in Felt Companies, 16 LA 881 (Lesser, 1951).

[114] International Braid Co., 6 LA 911 (Brown, 1947).

[115] Associated Food Shops, Inc., 7 LA 870 (Baskind, 1947).

will not be given to short-run variations in profits. [116] Thus, for example, extensive nonrecurring losses charged to current operations were rejected as the basis for a lower wage adjustment. [117] A probable future decline in ability to pay sometimes will be taken into account by arbitrators "as a moderating influence on the amount of the increase recommended." [118]

Inability to pay will be given very slight consideration where the employer's rates are substandard or inequitable in comparison with other rates in the industry or area. [119] While there is a duty to stockholders to make profits, there is also a duty to employees to pay "fair" wages. [120] It has been said that a company "does not expect price concessions from suppliers because of inability to pay, and must recognize its duty to its employees to pay them fair wages." [121] If, however, an increase in wage rates would put the rates above the industry or area standard, the inability to pay factor will be given considerable weight. [122]

Sometimes an increase in wage rates, if granted, would endanger the solvency of the employer. While the basic risk of business belongs to management, not the employees, [123] "high wage rates have no value to employees when layoffs are caused thereby." [124] Arbitrators give consideration to the reason for the absence of profits. If the reason is managerial inefficiency, the employees are not likely to be penalized by the denial of

---

[116] Twin City Rapid Transit Co., 10 LA 581 (Dunlop, 1948).

[117] United States Sugar Co., 5 LA 314 (France, 1946).

[118] Greyhound Bus Co., 1 LA 596, 609 (Simkin, Freidin & Wallen, 1946). To similar effect, American Woolen Co., 11 LA 1132 (Murray, 1949).

[119] See Arbitrator Donnelly in 27 LA 85; Brecht in 21 LA 356; Meyers in 20 LA 258; Cole in 9 LA 577; Frankenthaler in 8 LA 478. Also see Rains in 19 LA 464.

[120] See Arbitrator Donnelly in 27 LA 85; Strong in 7 LA 673; Meyer in 4 LA 604.

[121] Birmingham Electric Co., 7 LA 673, 676 (Strong, 1947). To similar effect, Arbitrator Kleinsorge in 23 LA 733, 740.

[122] Western Union Telegraph Co., 4 LA 251, 263 (Wallen, Cahn & Donahue, 1946).

[123] Capital Transit Co., 9 LA 666 (Taylor, 1947); Atlantic City Transportation Co., 9 LA 577, 580 (Cole, 1948).

[124] Prairie DuChien Woolen Mills Co., 10 LA 73, 75 (Rauch, 1948). To similar effect, Arbitrator Hogan in 25 LA 247, 250-251; Abruzzi in 23 LA 334, 336; Bailer in 20 LA 614, 615; Simkin in 18 LA 631, 645; Brown in 11 LA 984, 990-991.

wage increases to which they are entitled.[125] The theory here is
that if the employer goes out of business new management may
put the company on a paying basis. [126] But, if the reason lies in
causes beyond the control of management or if it is a matter
of strong competition by large firms against small firms, the arbitrator will be less likely to risk the possibility of bankruptcy
of the employer. In making a wage award, one arbitration
board said: "We assume, without deciding, that any wage increase will put the company out of business." Then the board
explained its severe but interesting view as follows:

> "On the record before us, the employer has no better claim to con-
> tinue in business upon the basis of a subnormal payroll than the employees
> have to seek wage increases upon the basis of the size of the employer's
> past profits or the amount of his assets.

> "Never have the wages of the employees of this company been related
> to profit or loss contingencies. The company and its employees have never
> been partners or joint venturers in this enterprise. Over the many years
> when the company made sustained and substantial profits, the employees
> were not offered a share in the benefits. And now, when it is claimed that
> the company faces losses, it is not perceived why the employees should
> be asked to share any of the burden.

> "We therefore conclude that these wages should be fixed without re-
> gard to the financial condition of the company or its ability to continue
> in business." [127]

The National War Labor Board sometimes granted increases despite employer contentions that any increase would
force the company out of business. [128] Some arbitrators, however, take the view that "a clear showing that proposed increases
would destroy a business or cause the discontinuance of a service
would ordinarily be an important and perhaps a controlling factor in an arbitration decision." [129]

Special considerations are involved in the application of the

---

[125] See Western Union Telegraph Co., 4 LA 251, 264 (Wallen, Cahn & Donahue,
1946). Also see Arbitrator Donnelly in 27 LA 85.
[126] See discussion in Centinela Valley Taxicab Co., 28 LA 40, 42-43 (E. Jones,
1957).
[127] California Street Cable Ry. Co., 7 LA 91, 94 (Wyckoff, 1947).
[128] Title Guarantee & Trust Co., 9 War Lab. Rep. 457 (1943).
[129] Georgia Power Co., 8 LA 691, 695 (Hepburn, 1947). To similar effect,
Greater Newark Hotel Assn., 13 LA 384 (Tyree, 1949).

ability-to-pay standard in public utility disputes. It is recognized that, since a public utility produces a basic necessity of life and since the public regulatory body must assure the opportunity for a fair return, capacity to pay generally will exist, potentially at least, and that almost any conceivable level of wages could be paid and a "fair profit" still returned to the stockholders. However, not only "fair wages" and "fair profits" are involved—a "fair price" to the consumer also enters the picture—thus ability to pay should not be made the primary consideration in determining public utility wage rates.[130]

An arbitrator may give some weight to the fact that a company is unable, under the terms of its franchise, to seek an increase in the price of its service to the public. This was done by one arbitrator despite the contention of the union that it should not be made a party to the "straitjacket" in which the company had placed itself.[131] On the other hand, an arbitrator may refuse to grant the request of a public utility that any wage increase awarded should be conditioned on the company's securing a rate increase for its services. Arbitrator John T. Dunlop, speaking as Chairman of a board of arbitration, has explained the view behind such refusal:

> "* * * In public utilities, including the railroads, there appears to be a long tradition of separation of wage and rate setting. This does not mean that rates and prices are irrelevant to wage setting, but rather that wage rates have tended to be fixed with some general reference to financial capacity and then these costs in turn have been taken into account by the rate or fare making body. Such has been the actual relation between collective bargaining or emergency boards determining wage rates and the Inter-State Commerce Commission setting railroad rates and fares. The transit industry has tended to follow an analogous practice.

> "The majority of the Arbitration Board believes it can follow no other precedent in this case. * * * When the Arbitration Board has fixed the wage rates, the appropriate fare making body should then set fares, in accordance with proper standards, including the wage rates set by this Arbitration Board as costs. No other procedure in the fixing of wages and

---

[130] Pacific Gas & Electric Co., 7 LA 528, 531 (Kerr, 1947).
[131] New York City Omnibus Corp., 7 LA 794, 809 (Cole, 1947).

fares, which are necessarily interdependent, by different bodies can be workable." [132]

Employers who have pleaded inability to pay have been held to have the burden of producing sufficient evidence to support the plea. The alleged inability must be more than "speculative",[133] and failure to produce sufficient evidence will result in a rejection of the plea.[134] The paymeent of reasonable dividends to stockholders and of reasonable salaries to top management has been held to render invalid a plea of inability to pay.[135] Management should be prepared to disclose its profit and loss statements in support of a plea of inability to pay. Arbitrators should provide any safeguards needed to protect the confidential nature of such evidence. Failure of management specifically to plead inability to pay might be considered sufficient to establish ability to pay up to the maximum demanded by the union.[136]

Competition

A factor which often must be given consideration in "interests" arbitration is the competitive nature of the employer's business. In some respects this is related to the ability-to-pay standard. In other respects it is related to the prevailing-practice standard. For these reasons it is generally not considered as an independent standard. Where, however, an employer is engaged in a highly competitive business or is faced with special competitive problems, the arbitrator may specifically point out

---

[132] Indianapolis Railways, Inc., 9 LA 319, 330 (1947). In recognition of the problem implied here, it has sometimes been suggested that the whole job should be done by the same agency; i.e., that the rate making body should also have jurisdiction to determine wage rates. It has also sometimes been suggested that wage awards should bind the utility commission. In any event, one arbitrator in effect asked that the regulatory commission grant a rate increase to accommodate the wage increase granted by his award. See Twin City Rapid Transit Co., 16 LA 749, 760 (Platt, 1951).

[133] Restaurant-Hotel Employers' Council of San Diego, 11 LA 469 (Aaron, 1948).

[134] See Arbitrator Justin in 7 LA 241; Feinberg in 6 LA 636; Copelof in 3 LA 437. From the standpoint of the duty to bargain under the National Labor Relations Act, substantiating evidence to support a plea of inability to pay need not always be furnished, but refusal to furnish such evidence on request is one of the factors which may be considered in determining whether the employer has refused to bargain in good faith. Truitt Mfg. Co. v. NLRB, 38 LRRM 2042, 76 S. Ct. 753 (1956).

[135] Employees Transit Lines, Inc., 4 LA 748, 752 (Copelof, 1946).

[136] Oil Industry, 1 LA 168 (Graham, Eliel & Beyer, 1946).

the competitive nature of the employer's business as a factor to be given special consideration in setting contract terms (sometimes even justifying a wage reduction).[137]

Wage "Patterns"

The "pattern" may be defined as a particular kind of solution of collective bargaining issues which has been used on a wide enough scale to be distinctly identified. The pattern standard is obviously closely related to the prevailing-practice standard and could reasonably be considered merely as one of its aspects. However, it is often spoken of as if it were a distinct criterion.

A "pattern" in wage arbitrations is generally stated in terms of a specific number of cents per hour. The pattern standard would recognize that, where companies or industries A, B, and C have granted general wage increases of ten cents per hour, related company or industry D should grant a ten cent increase also. In the application of this standard stress is placed upon the granting of the same amount of increase granted by others, rather than upon the granting of the same total wage that is paid by comparable employers.

A limited number of key wage bargains, or even only one, might set a pattern for a large part of American industry. Recognition of this fact was one of the factors which strongly influenced a fact-finding board for the Basic Steel Industry to refuse to grant a general wage increase; it was felt that any increase granted would probably be urged as a pattern to be followed in other industries, which, considering the best interests of the general economy at that time, would not have been desirable.[138]

---

[137] See Arbitrator Kliensorge in 24 LA 38, 44; Donnelly in 23 LA 843, 844; Hogan in 23 LA 762; Knowlton in 22 LA 653, 654; Bailer in 20 LA 614, 615; Gellhorn in 18 LA 774, 775; Simkin in 18 LA 631, 644-645; Singer in 9 LA 567, 569; S. Wolff in 8 LA 194, 195; Kirsh in 7 LA 350, 353; Whiteacre in 6 LA 749, 750-751.

[138] Basic Steel Industry, 13 LA 46 (Daugherty, Cole & Rosenman, 1949).

Among other possibilities, the pattern observed may be a national pattern for the industry or for related industries,[139] or it might be the pattern for general industry in the area,[140] or for the particular industry in the area.[141] The national pattern may be rejected where a grant of the national figure would upset the trend set by the local area pattern.[142]

Arbitrator Clark Kerr has stated that arbitrators should give great weight to "patterns" or "packages" of wage increases, such as those established during the various rounds of increases after World War II, since "rightly or wrongly" such patterns had been established and widely applied in free collective bargaining.[143] While in many cases the full amount of the pattern figure has been granted, in numerous others the pattern factor has been just one of several considered, with the result that the increase granted was not the exact pattern figure.[144] Then, too, under the circumstances of some cases the "pattern" may be rejected entirely.[145]

"Patterns" do not always call for wage increases. Rather, the "pattern" may be for wage decreases,[146] or, when the economy so justifies, for maintenance of the status quo.

Productivity

The productivity standard is frequently advanced for consideration by arbitrators of wage disputes. Proponents of this standard urge that increases in productivity should be reflected

---

[139] See railroad emergency boards in 28 LA 110, 17 LA 236, 6 LA 334. Also see Arbitrator Reid in 26 LA 14.

[140] Viloco Machine Co., 3 LA 46 (Ziegler, 1946).

[141] See Arbitrator Ross in 29 LA 96; Howard in 23 LA 429; Haughton in 14 LA 655. It might even be a pattern for one company only, as where a pattern resulting from agreements between an employer and several unions was applied to some of his employees represented by still another union. Memphis Publishing Co., 26 LA 381, 382 (Hepburn, 1956). Also see Arbitrator Haughton in 26 LA 124; Klamon in 22 LA 688.

[142] Jamaica Buses, Inc., 4 LA 225 (Cahn, 1946).

[143] Pacific Gas & Electric Co., 7 LA 528, 534 (1947).

[144] See Arbitrator Hogan in 25 LA 247; Healy in 8 LA 124; Pollard in 8 LA 134; Kirsh in 7 LA 350.

[145] See E. Cummings Leather Co., 25 LA 247, 250 (Hogan, 1955).

[146] As in Cheney Brothers, 21 LA 159, 163-165 (Scheiber, 1953). Also see Arbitrator Kleinsorge in 24 LA 38, 44.

by increases in wages. It has been recognized that there is a close relationship between the general level of productivity and the general level of wages,[147] and that both an increase in wage rates and a reduction in hours may be warranted by increased productivity measured in terms of added output per man-hour.[148]

There is a question, however, as to the extent to which increases in productivity in specific industries should be used as the basis of wage increases within those industries. In one case the union advanced figures to show that productivity had been rising over an extended period of time within the plant, and argued that real wages should be increased commensurately. The arbitration board considered productivity to be an "influential but not decisive" factor, and speaking through its Chairman, Clark Kerr, said:

"Normally wages rise somewhat more rapidly in those industries where productivity is rising rapidly and less rapidly where productivity is rising slowly or not at all or even declining. Thus productivity is an influential but not controlling factor. For the whole economy it is of more significance, perhaps than for the individual plant or industry. Real wages can rise significantly in the long run only as physical productivity increases. To tie wages rigidly in each minor segment of the economy to changes in physical productivity in that segment would, however, cause greater distortion as between and among progressive, static and regressive industries than could be sustained." [149]

---

[147] Slichter, Basic Criteria Used in Wage Negotiations, 21 (1947). Time Magazine's review of a 1949 production drive by American industry is of interest in this respect. Time, speaking of the production drive, said:

"Businessmen readily admitted that the drive could not have been so strong except for a remarkable improvement in labor productivity * * *. Much of the improvement was due to better management, a smooth flow of materials unhampered by shortages, and better machinery in the new plants on which management had spent about $18 billion during the year. But there were other reasons. Something like a buyer's market in labor had returned and labor had prudently worked harder. In all, an average of 43 million non-agricultural workers had been employed during the year to turn out almost the same amount of goods that 45 million had turned out the year before—a rough, rule-of-thumb increase in productivity of 4.5%.

"For working harder, labor got more money. The $136 billion in wages and salaries paid out were up $1.5 billion over 1948." Time, p. 76, January 9, 1950.

[148] General Motors Corp., 1 LA 125, 130 (Garrison, Eisenhower & Stacy, 1946).

[149] Pacific Gas & Electric Co., 7 LA 528, 530 (1947). Some weight was also given to productivity by Arbitrator Kagel in 28 LA 600; Hogan in 23 LA 762; Cole in 22 LA 371; Shulman in 22 LA 297; Gilden in 20 LA 219; Guthrie in 20 LA 93; Coke in 12 LA 870; Bushnell in 3 LA 687.

In an important case a fact-finding board for the Basic Steel Industry stated the belief that wage rates in a particular industry should not be tied directly to productivity in that industry but rather should be related to the general industrial rise in productivity; moreover, the board said, that any excesses of productivity in any one industry over the general average should provide primarily the means of reducing the prices of the products of that industry.[150]

Increases in productivity can result in increased wages, decreased prices, increased profits, or some combination of the three. If the increase in output per man-hour is due to greater effort and greater skill there would appear to be no doubt that the gain should accrue to the benefit of the employees. But if the increase is the result of technological progress or better management, several considerations must be taken into account.

It has been pointed out by Economist Sumner H. Slichter that changes in wages affect the attitude of employees toward the productivity of the enterprise in which they work and that they will be more likely to cooperate with management to increase productivity if some of the gains of that increase are passed on to them.[151] On the other hand, Slichter recognized two disadvantages of directly passing such gains to the employees: (1) Increase in wages in such cases would introduce unjustified inequalities into the wage structure of the community; and (2) industry as a whole would be prevented from producing the largest possible product, since the rise of wages in the industries where labor productivity is increasing most rapidly would tend to prevent them from reducing their prices to consumers and thus from expanding output and employment.[152] Slichter concluded, however, that, as between raising wages and lowering prices, both of which are likely to follow technological change, the adjustment of the economy

---

[150] Basic Steel Industry, 13 LA 46, 50 (Daugherty, Cole & Rosenman, 1949). Also see New York Shipping Assn., 20 LA 75, 82-83 (Hays, 1952). Cf., Basic Steel Industry, 18 LA 112, 117 (W.S.B., 1952).

[151] Slichter, Basic Criteria Used in Wage Negotiations 43 (1947).

[152] Id. at 22-23.

to technological progress through higher wages is more favorable to employment and to technological advance than adjustment through falling prices.[153]

While arbitrators may give weight to the productivity factor when increased production is used as the basis of a demand for an increase, it appears that they are not likely to give the factor much consideration when an employer defends against an increase by alleging that his employees have a lower per capita output than is standard. For instance, low productivity has been held not to justify the denial of a pattern increase, for the reasons that employees' efficiency and output are largely within the control of the employer and that the employer should be able, by extending the incentive system, to put the business on a reasonable competitive basis as to production costs.[154]

A board of arbitration has held that an allegedly great reduction in labor efficiency, which the board found to be to some extent true, did not justify the denial of a cost-of-living increase where the inefficiency and high costs in the industry were caused by a variety of factors, including out-of-date technology, high cost of materials, and a shortage of skilled craftsmen.[155] In another case the arbitrator granted a cost-of-living increase without giving weight to the employer's complaint that productivity was low, on the ground that there was a failure to establish a decline in productivity after the execution of the contract.[156]

Numerous reasons exist for the refusal of arbitrators to make productivity a decisive factor in wage determination. The rate of change in productivity varies from firm to firm and even from department to department within a plant. Thus exclusive use of the productivity standard for wage adjust-

---

[153] Id. at 48.
[154] Watson Elevator Co., 8 LA 386, 389 (Copelof, 1947).
[155] Associated General Contractors, 9 LA 201, 226-227 (Aaron, 1947). Also see Dallas, Texas, Newspaper Publishers, 22 LA 88, 93 (Abernethy, 1954).
[156] Waterfront Employers Assn. of Pacific Coast, 9 LA 172 (Miller, 1947).

ments would soon lead to a chaotic wage structure within a single plant or industry.[157] Moreover, the measurement of productivity presents highly difficult problems of economic analysis and statistical measurement.[158] Even after a change in productivity has been measured, the problem still remains of determining whether it was caused by increased skill and effort of employees or by better management or improved technology. The arbitrator also must face the problem of assigning a value to the change in productivity—evidence of changes in productivity is not readily transformed into cents-per-hour wage adjustments.[159]

A powerful factor making for consideration of productivity as an element in determining wage increases came into being with the agreement of General Motors Corporation in 1950 to grant an annual "improvement factor" increase, amounting to four cents per hour. The figure was based on an estimated three percent annual improvement in productivity throughout all industry, a figure which the company stated it expected to surpass.[160]

While granting a wage increase partly on the basis of the "annual improvement factor", Arbitrator Whitley P. McCoy has emphasized that an increase on the basis of this factor is not due automatically in every case, but that this factor is one of the considerations to be taken into account, along with other factors.[161]

Take-Home Pay

Maintenance of take-home pay emerged at the end of

---

[157] Dunlop, "The Economics of Wage-Dispute Settlement," 12 Law & Contemp. Prob. 281, 286-287 (1947).

[158] Id. at 287-288. For an example of the difficulty that may be involved in proving productivity changes, see Waterfront Employers Assn. of Pacific Coast, 9 LA 172, 177-178 (Miller, 1947). Also see Arbitrator Horlacher in 27 LA 295, 299; Fact-Finders Platt, Gemrich & Arsulowicz in 18 LA 686, 690.

[159] Dunlop, id. at 288. Also see New York Shipping Assn., 20 LA 75, 82-83 (Hays, 1952); Arbitrator Aaron in 12 LA 245, 255-256.

[160] Regarding the influence elsewhere of this General Motors step, see Union Railroad Co., 20 LA 219, 224 (Gilden, 1953).

[161] Printing Industries of Indiana, Inc., 29 LA 7, 11 (1957).

World War II as a means of "cushioning the shock" of the transition from an economy of war to one of peace. Sudden and extensive reductions in weekly earnings throughout industry as a result of reduction of hours, especially overtime, became a matter of national concern at the end of the war while living costs were still rising. Labor demanded wage increases to maintain take-home pay as hours of work were reduced. In considering these demands, arbitrators and fact-finding boards were guided by the national wage-price policy laid down in executive orders, regulations under the Wage Stabilization Act, and an address by the President to the nation on October 30, 1945. This national wage-price policy recognized that wage increases were necessary as a means of cushioning the shock of the war-peace conversion but that wage increases which would necessitate price increases would have dangerous inflationary tendencies. On the other hand, the policy recognized that business as a whole was in a very favorable earning position and thus could, and should, make substantial wage increases without seeking price increases.[162]

The maintenance of take-home pay standard has been given consideration in numerous cases. Although it generally has not been the only one considered, it has been responsible for at least a part of the increase granted in those cases.[163] In the application of this standard, potential [164] or probable [165] loss of take-home pay may be considered as well as present loss.

Application of other standards may preclude the maintenance of take-home pay. For instance, lack of ability to pay has been deemed a sufficient reason for permitting the discontinuance of overtime work without at the same time granting a wage increase to maintain take-home pay.[166]

---

[162] General Motors Corp., 1 LA 125, 127-128 (Garrison, Eisenhower & Stacy, 1946).

[163] E.g., 29 LA 7, 21 LA 307, 19 LA 538, 17 LA 682, 15 LA 524, 12 LA 507, 10 LA 581, 6 LA 470, 4 LA 502, 3 LA 566, 3 LA 639, 1 LA 333, 1 LA 125.

[164] F. W. Woolworth Co., 4 LA 502 (Gellhorn, Paley & Miller, 1946).

[165] General Motors Corp., 1 LA 125 (Garrison, Eisenhower & Stacy, 1946).

[166] Roberts Pressure Valve Co., Inc., 8 LA 665 (Singer, 1947). Also see Railroads v. Operating Unions, 14 LA 688 (McDonough, O'Malley & Watkins, 1950).

Several arguments may be advanced against use of this standard. Since a reduction in hours means that less labor is being sold, should not the total amount paid for labor drop accordingly? If the principle of relating total wages to the number of hours worked is sound when hours are increasing, is it not sound when hours are decreasing? Moreover, should not workers be encouraged to leave rather than remain in industries and places where a labor surplus exists? [167]

It has been suggested that the heavy penalty rates required for overtime work by the Fair Labor Standards Act and by most collective agreements will keep such work to minimum in time of peace, hence that the maintenance of take-home pay will not often need to be considered.[168] It may be reasonable to expect, however, that the standard will be given consideration in any instance where, in the absence of a wage increase, a sudden and extensive reduction in earnings within a specific industry or within a large segment of industry generally would result from a reduction of hours.

This, for instance, was the situation where a railroad emergency board was asked to recommend a 40-hour week in lieu of the then existing 48-hour week for approximately one million non-operating railway workers. The board recognized 40 basic hours per week with time and a half for overtime to be the prevailing practice in American industry, a practice which had been put into effect, not only in industries covered by the Fair Labor Standards Act, but to a steadily increasing extent in industries excluded from the Act. The board recommended the adoption of a 40-hour week, and, in connection therewith, it recommended that all basic rates of pay then in effect be increased by 20 per cent to provide the same basic earnings for 40 hours of work as had been received for 48 hours.[169]

A subsequent emergency board recommended a reduction in the workweek of certain operating railroad employees but

---

[167] Slichter, Basic Criteria Used in Wage Negotiations 20-21 (1947).

[168] Id at 19.

[169] Railroads v. Non-operating Unions, 11 LA 752, 761-777 (Leiserson, Cole & Cook, 1948).

did not recommend a requested 20 per cent wage increase to maintain prior take-home pay. The board noted the recommendation of the emergency board for the non-operating employees, but distinguished the cases on the following grounds: (1) the rates of the operating employees were already higher than those of employees in other industries, whereas the non-operating employees' rates had been lower; (2) the requested increase was not justified in view of the railroads' financial condition. The board did, however, believe an increase of 18 cents an hour to be justified.[170]

Past Practice

The past practice of the parties has sometimes, although infrequently, been considered to be a standard for "interests" arbitration. This standard is of special significance when parties are engaged in their initial negotiations. It was stated in one instance by Arbitrator Clark Kerr:

> "The arbitrator considers past practice a primary factor. It is standard form to incorporate past conditions into collective bargaining contracts, whether these contracts are developed by negotiation or arbitration. The fact of unionization creates no basis for the withdrawal of conditions previously in effect. If they were justified before, they remain justified after the event of union affiliation. It is almost axiomatic that the existing conditions be perpetuated. Some contracts even blanket them in through a general 'catch-all' clause." [171]

Arbitrators may require "persuasive reason" for the elimination of a clause which has been in past written agreements.[172] Moreover, they sometimes order the formalization of past practices by ordering that they be incorporated into the written agreement.[173]

In arbitrating the terms of a renewal contract, one arbitrator would consider seriously "what the parties have agreed

---

[170] Railroads v. Operating Unions, 14 LA 688, 707-708 (McDonough, O'Malley & Watkins, 1950).

[171] Luckenbach Steamship Co., 6 LA 98, 101 (1946). Also see St. Paul Department Stores, 2 LA 52 (Johnston, Gydeson & Harmon, 1946).

[172] Minneapolis-Moline Power Implement Co., 2 LA 227 (Van Fossen, Humphrey & Prifrel, 1946).

[173] Sosna Bros., 6 LA 846 (Rosenfarb, 1947); F. W. Woolworth Co., 4 LA 502 (Gellhorn, Paley & Miller, 1946). Also see Railway Express Agency v. Teamsters, 28 LA 182, 196 (Sanders, Begley & Gilden, 1957).

upon in their past collective bargaining, as affected by inter-vening economic events * * *." [174]

Pre-Arbitration Negotiations

It has been said that the award to a wage dispute seldom falls outside the area of "probable expectancy" and that this area is the normal resultant product of the parties' negotiations and bargaining prior to submitting their differences to arbi-tration.[175] In this regard, too, one arbitration board concluded:

> "An examination of the wealth of evidence submitted in this matter in conjunction with the provisions of settlement worked out by the parties indicates that the most satisfactory award which the Board could render would be one in general agreement with those terms on which the parties were able at one time to substantially agree. Obviously, these terms are not what either party wanted. They represent compromise by both parties. However, since the general terms indicate a meeting of the minds, the Board considers that they hold the basis of a just award." [176]

While observing that an "interests" arbitrator usually can make a more useful award if he has knowledge of the bargain-ing positions of the parties prior to the arbitration stage, one group of arbitrators has suggested that if at least one of the parties wishes to exclude consideration of pre-arbitral offers it may be sound policy for the arbitrator to do so lest future bar-gaining be inhibited.[177] However, the members of one board of inquiry declared that type of tribunal to be of such nature that tentative agreements, as well as offers and counter offers, of the parties during the negotiation stage could not be ignored com-

---

[174] United Traction Co., 27 LA 309, 315 (Sheiber, 1956). Also see Arbitrator Abernethy in 22 LA 88.

[175] Justin, "Arbitrating a Wage Dispute Case," 3 Arb. J. (n.s.) 228 (1948). Also see Arbitrator Simkin in 18 LA 631, 643. It is also said that partes sometimes agree upon contract terms but for political reasons want an arbitrator to order them. "Cur-rent Problems of Arbitration, American Unionism," 29 LA 880, 883 (1958).

[176] Durso & Geelan Co., 17 LA 748, 749 (Donnelly, Curry & Clark, 1951). It has been recognized that in "many instances intangible factors such as the indicated bids or offers by the parties in private bargaining * * * will be of considerable im-portance" in the arbitrator's consideration of the case. Backman, Economic Data Util-ized in Wage Arbitration 3 (1952).

[177] Guides for Labor Arbitration 9-10 (1953), by a group of arbitrators in the Philadelphia area.

pletely by the board even though one of the parties protested any consideration of such matters.[178]

Public Interest

The question arises as to how far arbitrators should go in considering the public-interest aspects of "interests" disputes. The public, although not a direct party, has a vital interest in the settlement of some disputes. Fact-finding boards do give strong consideration to the public welfare in making recommendations. For instance, a fact-finding board for General Motors Corporation would recommend only such wage increases as it believed would not have inflationary price consequences.[179] A fact-finding board for the Basic Steel Industry considered the public interest to be one of the two major inquiries which should be made in determining whether a wage increase should be granted. In denying any increase, the board placed strong emphasis on its belief that a wage increase for the steel industry would be used as a pattern for other industries and might well cause price dislocations with adverse effects on the general economy.[180]

It is in respect to public utility disputes that the public-interest criteria are most often invoked. Two considerations are generally involved. The first, and at first glance the most obvious, is that services of public utilities, being constantly consumed necessities of life, should be made available to consumers at a fair price. Since wages paid by a utility will directly affect the cost of its services to the public, the amount of any wage increase granted might be affected by the arbitrator's conclusion as to the probable effect of the increase upon the

---

[178] Rochester Transit Corp., 19 LA 538, 541-542 (Tolley, McKelvey & Turkus, 1952).

[179] General Motors Corp., 1 LA 125, 128 (Garrison, Eisenhower & Stacy, 1946).

[180] Basic Steel Industry, 13 LA 46, 52 (Daugherty, Cole & Rosenman, 1949). In Chesapeake & Potomac Telephone Co. of Baltimore, 7 LA 630 (Jackson, Healy & Dennis, 1947), an increase sufficient to offset the full rise in the cost of living would not be granted where to do so would contribute further to inflation. Cf., Basic Steel Industry, 18 LA 112, 136 (W.S.B., 1952).

price of the service involved. The arbitrator will keep in mind the needs of the consumers.[181]

The second consideration, which has been assuming increasing importance in recent years, recognizes that the public has a paramount interest in continuity of operations of public utilities. The public expects utilities to provide uninterrupted service. Some states have enacted legislation to prevent strikes by public utility employees. Even before the passage of such laws, however, most public-utility labor had come to recognize that its responsibility to the public required uninterrupted services.[182]

Since such employees are under the strongest kind of obligation not to strike, there has been considerable public discussion of the need for a wage policy in public utilities which will assure equitable treatment to their employees, and emphasis usually has been placed upon the desirability of assuring them rates and conditions of work which are as good as or better than those available for comparable work anywhere in the area.[183]

Dr. George W. Taylor, in recognizing these several considerations, has stated that, while a meritorious argument is presented, it is difficult to put them into practice in specific terms.[184] But Arbitrator Clark Kerr believes that it is clear that an effort should be made to assure utility workers "both as high or higher absolute levels and as favorable or more favorable relative changes in wages as other workers generally in the community." [185] Another arbitrator has expressed preference for the view that utility employees should expect to enjoy substantially the same wages, hours, and working conditions—no better and no worse—as those enjoyed by other workers living

---

[181] See Fact-Finders Platt, Gemrich & Arsulowicz in 18 LA 686, 690; Arbitrators Holland, Anderson & Hollingsworth in 8 LA 397, 402; Kerr in 7 LA 528, 530-531; Taylor in 6 LA 830, 836.
[182] Capital Transit Co., 9 LA 666, 679 (Taylor, 1947).
[183] Consolidated Edison System Cos. of New York, 6 LA 830, 834 (Taylor, 1947).
[184] Ibid.
[185] Pacific Gas & Electric Co., 7 LA 528, 531 (Kerr, 1947). To similar effect, Consumers Power Co., 24 LA 581, 584 (R. Smith, Howlett & Sorensen, (1955).

in the area; thus utility employment should be made to conform to local conditions, not to blaze new trails.[186]

As noted in Chapter I, some states have enacted anti-strike laws for their public utilities. Some of these states have also specified standards to be observed in the compulsory arbitration of public utility disputes, such standards being designed to avoid discriminatory conditions of employment for utility employees as compared with other employees in industry. Prevailing practice is the basic test. The objective appears to be to insure that utility employees shall have the same wages, hours, and working conditions as those prevailing for comparable workers in the same or adjoining labor market area.

The statutes generally recognize, however, that wage differentials may properly exist on the basis of differences in skill and ability, continuity and stability of employment, geographical location, fringe benefits, or other justifying factors. The Nebraska provisions, being more or less typical, are of special interest. The Nebraska Act provides for a Court of Industrial Relations, which is empowered to establish or alter the scale of wages, hours of work, or conditions of employment. In respect to the standards to be applied by the Court, the following is provided by the Act:

"* * * In making such findings and orders, the Court of Industrial Relations shall establish rates of pay and conditions of employment which are comparable to the prevailing wage rates paid and conditions of employment maintained for the same or similar work of workers exhibiting like or similar skills under the same or similar working conditions, in the same labor market area and, if none, in adjoining labor market areas within the state and which in addition bear a generally comparable relationship to wage rates paid and conditions of employment maintained by all other employers in the same labor market area. The court shall determine, in each case, what constitutes 'the labor market area' or 'adjoining labor market areas' in the state. If an employer has more than one plant or office and some or all of such plants or offices are found to be located in separate market areas, the court may establish separate wage rates or schedules of wage rates, and separate conditions of employment, for all plants and offices

---

[186] Cleveland Electric Illuminating Co., 8 LA 597, 600, 605 (Cornsweet, 1947). While this view had been advanced earlier by Lee H. Hill, a management spokesman, in the instant case it was approved, but interpreted differently, by both the labor and employer arbitrators.

in each such labor market area. In establishing wage rates the court shall take into consideration the overall compensation presently received by the employees, having regard not only to wages for time actually worked but also to wages for time not worked, including vacations, holidays, and other excused time, and all benefits received, including insurance and pensions, and the continuity and stability of employment enjoyed by the employees. Any order or orders entered may be modified on the court's own motion or on application by any of the parties affected, but only upon a showing of a change in the conditions from those prevailing at the time the original order was entered." [187]

Some of the statutes provide that the specific enumeration of standards shall not be construed as precluding the arbitrators from taking into consideration other factors not confined to the local labor market area which are normally or traditionally taken into consideration in the determination of wages, hours, and working conditions through voluntary collective bargaining or arbitration.[188]

Statutory requirement of the use of the prevailing-practice standard for all types of public utility "interests" disputes is a strong indication of its value and acceptability. The relatively high degree of predictability that its use lends to "interests" arbitration is without serious question one of the strongest assurances of success in such arbitration.

Governmental Wage Stabilization

In times of wage stabilization "interests" arbitrators, emergency boards and fact-finders must take cognizance of governmental stabilization regulations that might apply to the parties. In some cases awards or recommended terms have been made subject to approval by the Wage Stabilization Board.[189] Sometimes arbitrators have ordered one party to join the other in

---

[187] Nebraska Revised Statutes 1943, Sec. 48-818 (Supp.), SLL 37: 235. The Acts of Wisconsin, Pennsylvania, Florida, Indiana, Maryland, and New Jersey also contain standards to be observed, essentially the same as those of the Nebraska Act The Acts of Michigan, Massachusetts, Hawaii, and Missouri do not contain standards since they make no provision for compulsory final settlement, the investigating agency having power to make recommendations only. The Texas Act merely prohibits the disruption of utility services. Virginia and North Dakota provide for seizure and operation of utilities by the government.

[188] See Sec. 111.57, Subchapter III of Chapter 111, Wisconsin Statutes.

[189] See Los Angeles Standard Rubber, Inc., 17 LA 353, 354, 361 (Warren, 1951); Felt Companies, 16 LA 881, 882 (Lesser 1951).

seeking such approval.[190] Then, too, the arbitrator might examine stabilization regulations and reach his own conclusion as to the permissibility of requested increases.[191]

Where the parties in submitting a case to "interests" arbitration specified that the arbitration board should seek Wage Stabilization approval (if necessary) of any increase ordered, the arbitrators stated that the wage stabilization program was just one factor to be considered along with others in determining the amount of any wage adjustment.[192] Another arbitrator declared that while wage stabilization regulations should be taken into account in determining wage adjustments, the influence of wage stabilization on an arbitrator's decision should vary "in direct ratio to the certainty, clarity and stage of its evolution." [193]

---

[190] See Durso & Geelan Co., 17 LA 748, 750-751 (Donnelly, 1951). Also see Arbitrator Hays in 20 LA 75, 76.
[191] See Frederick Loeser & Co., 16 LA 399, 404 (Justin, 1951).
[192] North American Aviation, Inc., 19 LA 76, 77 (Cole, Aaron & Wirtz, 1952).
[193] Merchants Bank of New York, 16 LA 901, 904 (Rosenfarb, 1951). For related discussion see Chapter 10, topic titled "Statutory Law".

CHAPTER 17

ARBITRATION'S PLACE AS AN
INDUSTRIAL INSTITUTION

Arbitration in practice is a distinct institution, the product of a collectively bargained compromise between the alternatives of resort to courts of law, which are not well adapted to the needs of labor-management relations, and resort to work stoppages, which are wasteful and costly to both parties. While arbitration is a distinct institution, however, it would be totally unrealistic to deny the close relationship now existing between it, especially "rights" arbitration, and our formal legal system. Indeed, labor arbitration has drawn heavily from the standards and techniques of that system. In this connection, the authors believe that on the whole sound judgment has been exercised by arbitrators in effectively utilizing established legalisms without paying slavish deference thereto.

Arbitration is an avenue traveled by thousands, indeed millions, of industrial disputants. It is a vital force in establishing confidence and minimizing confusion at all levels of the labor-management relationship and is a major constructive force in the collective bargaining process itself. Arbitration should not, however, be expected or totally relied upon to create either good contracts or cooperative human relationships—it is a supplement to, rather than a substitute for, conscientious grievance processing and genuine collective bargaining. Finally, the authors desire to emphasize their firm conviction that not only is arbitration today an exceedingly useful social and industrial institution but that it will become even more so in the future.

486

INDEX

War Labor Board 35, 315, 330, 459
  arbitration, use of 10
  rulings 465
  tripartite structure 62
  wage adjustments 468
Warns, Carl A. 244, 397
Warren, Edgar L. 321
Whelan, Thomas P. 222
Whiting, Dudley E. 266, 288, 293,
  328, 379
Whitton, Albert K. 220
Wide-open arbitration 297
Willcox, Bertram F. 195
Williams, Ralph Roger 379, 401
Wirtz, W. Willard 174, 179, 197, 236,
  427
Withdrawal from arbitration 66, 148
Witnesses
  absence, effect of 150
  admission to hearing 144
  credibility 185
  examination and cross-examination
    159, 183
  grievant, failure to testify 182
  informers, withholding identity of
    183
  investigators, spotters 183
  oath 155
  outsiders, experts 196
  protection against reprisals 198

Wolff, David A. 196, 236, 259, 336,
  360
Work assignments 360
  outside bargaining unit 348
Work schedules 328
  beginning day of workweek 330
  emergency changes 333
  layoffs, and work scheduling distin-
    guished 331
  reduction of hours 331
Work schedules—Contd.
  temporary changes 334
  vacations 338
Work stoppages (see Strikes)
Working conditions, operation methods
  distinguished 303
Workload
  changes in 307
  hourly-rated employees 308
  incentive wage plans 310
Workweek
  reduction 331
  reduction, maintenance of take-home
    pay 476
Wyckoff, Hubert 281

Y

Yoder, Dale 280